The Interior Dimension

The Interior Dimension

A THEORETICAL APPROACH TO ENCLOSED SPACE

Joy Monice Malnar
Frank Vodvarka

VNR VAN NOSTRAND REINHOLD
New York

Copyright © 1992 by Van Nostrand Reinhold
Library of Congress Catalog Card Number 91-6291
ISBN 0-442-23739-1

Printed in the United States of America.

Van Nostrand Reinhold
115 Fifth Avenue
New York, New York 10003

Chapman and Hall
2-6 Boundary Row
London, SE1 8HN, England

Thomas Nelson Australia
102 Dodds Street
South Melbourne 3205
Victoria, Australia

Nelson Canada
1120 Birchmount Road
Scarborough, Ontario MIK 5G4, Canada

16 15 14 13 12 11 10 9 8 7 6 5 4 3 2 1

Library of Congress Cataloging-in-Publication Data
Malnar, Joy Monice.
   The interior dimension: a theoretical approach to enclosed space / Joy Monice
   Malnar, Frank Vodvarka.
      p. cm.
   Includes bibliographical references and index.
   ISBN 0-442-23739-1
   1. Interior architecture. 2. Space (Architecture) I. Vodvarka, Frank. II.
Title.
   NA2850.M35 1992
   729—dc20
                                                                                          91-6291
                                                                                               CIP

Contents

Preface

Few human enterprises are as *complex in realization,* or *profound in implication,* as the design and raising of a building. Complex, because the construction of a building is a social act, requiring the services of many people with a broad range of technical skills, as well as generous funding. Buildings are meant to serve a diverse audience, enable certain behaviors, and accommodate various functions. Thus buildings are a measure of a culture's economic, political, and technological resources at a particular moment in its development. The enterprise is profound because buildings reflect decisions based on concepts of ethics and morality: how people should live and work and how those buildings should symbolize their beliefs. This profundity takes the form of purposeful arrangement, the organization of tactile, haptic, and visual elements so that a building's message is clear. Elias Cornell provides an operative definition of architecture, ''Architecture is practical reality aesthetically organized.''[1] These two parameters, practicality and aesthetic control, are critical to design expression in its broader cultural context. And they can be united by the formulation and application of design theory.

One of the most fundamental divisions in design is that of interior from exterior, volume from mass. As the interior and exterior are perceptually separate, sustaining coherence between them is a difficult task. It entails a significant divergence in design approach, despite many shared theoretical assumptions and techniques. This divergence accounts for two realities: first, from the eighteenth century to now, the design distinction between interior and exterior has tended to be sharpened; and second, this is partly the result of a radical alteration in the socioeconomic and technical nature of buildings themselves. Le Corbusier states:

> A plan proceeds from within to without. A building is like a soap bubble. This bubble is perfect and harmonious if the breath has been evenly distributed and regulated from the inside. The exterior is the result of an interior.[2]

This statement suggests the primacy of the interior and its generative capacity in spatial design; but design theory has historically emphasized buildings' exterior aspects, not their interiors. And this approach, essentially sculptural, has often had less than a beneficial effect on the buildings' occupants.

This work, however, does address theoretical issues in the design of interior space, the approach to such issues by specific designers past and present, and the influence of ancillary fields on spatial design. We believe that such theory necessarily exists within the history of architecture itself, even if undervalued now. Our goal, therefore, is the review of that part of architectural theory that particularly relates to the interior and includes various information from the fine arts, psychology, philosophy, literature, and the environmental sciences.

The approach is eclectic and attempts to identify those design concerns necessary to proceed ''. . . from within to without.'' The text is divided into three broad and interrelated sections: the elementary design principles themselves; aspects of their historical derivation; and how they manifest themselves culturally and perceptually.

The Character of Interior Space examines the importance of theory and certain attributes of fundamental design elements and their perception. But this text is not intended to describe practical applications of basic techniques already known by the reader. To the contrary, our interest in these fundamental ideas comes from the belief that, however modest, they are rich in association and consequential in their application. Accordingly, the approach is abstract and stresses the generative potential of even the simplest gesture. The metaphysical aspects of elementary visual elements are noted by Kandinsky when he says that ". . . under the visible and comprehensible lies the invisible and incomprehensible."[3] For Kandinsky, a point becomes an ". . . ultimate and most singular union of silence and speech," and a straight line one whose tension represents ". . . the most concise form of the potentiality for endless movement."[4] And we find Emil Nolde's view of colors in vibration—". . . pealing like silver bells and clanging like bronze bells, proclaiming happiness, passion and love, soul, blood, and death"—as persuasive and useful as psychological studies of the effects of colored light on cognitive processes. This is not to negate the critical value of psychological information in design; to the contrary, it is much needed in a field devoted to human spatial requirements. It is rather to affirm the equal design value of such seemingly discrete disciplines as art and science.

The Development of Interior Space examines some of the positions that designers have historically held about design in general, and interior space in particular. This section is arranged chronologically, as designers naturally refer to ideas and principles that precede them. Indeed, sometimes such reference takes the form of tribute. But this text is not a history of architecture in any inclusive sense, and still less in an exhaustive one. Rather, we have chosen individuals who we consider important to spatial design, and have examined those aspects of their ideas and works that deal with interior considerations. In short, these chapters represent a review of particular designers for very specific purposes. This should explain several oddities that the reader will encounter: first, the uneven treatment of historical periods; second, the exclusion of certain well-known works by particular designers in favor of projects that stress some interior aspect; and third, the fairly consistent use of illustrations of the interior. We have also included images taken from other disciplines, as spatial issues are not confined to architectural design.

The Measure of Interior Space addresses a range of concerns that primarily, though not exclusively, affect the interior. These issues are technical, aesthetic, psychological, and ethical. Again, this text is not intended to solve particular design problems; while the examples that we use are tangible, our interest in them is theoretical. Accordingly, we find questions of whether aesthetics can be reconciled with psychology, and proportion with standardization, or whether we can indeed agree that "God is in the details" to be of prime importance. That is, we believe that the underlying questions are the critical ones; they will be of concern long after their particular application has given way to urban renewal. And the semiotic aspects of architectural design may well outlast the pragmatic issues that seem so persuasive at the outset. Put differently, what spaces communicate is often more essential than their simple utility, which should represent only a minimum standard of achievement. Finally, of special concern are those issues dealing with archetypes and ethics, and the qualities that form a place of dwelling. These issues might be individual in nature but can equally include a critique of current housing types or the environmental impact of design decisions. Ultimately, these are the vital matters that affect the future of our world, of which we are only temporary custodians.

Acknowledgments

Acknowledgments, one supposes, are intended as a type of recognition of the contributory efforts of certain people. Such contributions need not have been equal in importance nor necessarily represent anything more than a professional person doing professional work. In the course of constructing a text, the simple things can mean a great deal, and competency reveals its virtues.

We, the authors, should first of all recognize each other's particular abilities and expertise and our constant willingness to reach common accord on what constituted the major issues of spatial design. Our partnership, that of an architect and graphic designer, proved most fortuitous, combining the necessary skills in research, writing, drawing, and photography. It was in every way a successful relationship, personally and professionally, and will be repeated in still other ventures.

But creative enterprises, like men's lives, are touched by many other individuals and institutions, and they deserve notice. We thank Mundelein College, which has long been our academic residence, for its material and moral support. In particular, we thank the chairperson of our department, Patricia Hernes, for her patience and good humor and her willingness to adjust her schedule to our own. And the entire effort was vitally aided by Mundelein's remarkable librarian, Sr. Frances Loretta Berger, BVM, whose interlibrary loan skills are truly astonishing. We thank, too, Loyola University of Chicago, of which Mundelein is now a part, for the enthusiastic welcome they have extended to us as we join their faculty.

We received other help as well, particularly from Mary Woolever, Architecture Archivist at the Burnham Library of The Art Institute of Chicago, and the library staff in general. We thank Gabrielle Hernes for her research assistance (and much-needed translation from the French), and both Carolyn Freeman at the University of Georgia and Michael Gong at Triton College for their critical reading of the text.

Indeed, we much appreciate the critique offered by a host of anonymous reviewers, whose observations are reflected in the final copy, and the occasional sage advice offered by Marilyn Hasbrouck of Prairie Avenue Bookshop. And, of course, we thank the many contemporary designers, on several continents, who have proved so cooperative and supportive of our venture. Finally, we have enjoyed working with Amanda Miller, our editor at Van Nostrand Reinhold; we hope the result is a suitable reward for her patience and advice.

Introduction

There is an old French saying: *Tel le logis, tel le maître*—as is the house, so is the master. Thus is the nature of the bond between the house and its inhabitant. The exterior may be formal and austere, but the interior is a place of individual creation, a refuge. That is how Kenneth Grahame describes Badger's home in *The Wind in the Willows,* a warm place with a well-worn brick floor, wide hearth, and high-backed settles to provide seating for the sociably disposed:

> It seemed a place where heroes could fitly feast after victory, where weary harvesters could line up in scores along the table and keep their Harvest Home with mirth and song, or where two or three friends of simple tastes could sit about as they pleased and eat and smoke and talk in comfort and contentment.[1]

Much later, when Ratty and Mole decide to weather a winter's night in Mole's more modest home, Ratty kindly compliments the accommodations by saying, "What a capital little house this is! So compact! So well planned! Everything here and everything in its place! We'll make a jolly night of it."[2]

Tel le logis, tel le maître—as is the house, so is the master. But if the house is shaped by its owner, the owner is as surely shaped by the house. And so when Mole, away from his home much too long, finally goes to bed that night, he feels a great contentment. Before finally going to sleep he looks around his room at those familiar possessions so long a part of him, which now generously welcome him back:

> He saw clearly how plain and simple—how narrow even—it all was; but clearly, too, how much it all meant to him, and the special value of some such anchorage in one's existence . . . it was good to think he had this to come back to, this place which was all his own. . . .[3]

And so Grahame's most intimate images are entirely interior in nature, a recognition of the compelling power and complexity of the interior dimension.

Part I

The Character of Interior Space

The Role of Theory

1

Interior Spaces

The arrival of humankind was accompanied by a concern for the planning of interior spaces. Indeed, it very likely preceded any concern with the exterior, as human beings occupied interior spaces made by nature long before building their own walls. The very act of moving the hearth from one position in a cave to another, more advantageous one, or choosing a more comfortable stone to sit on is a form of interior alteration (if not design). In *An Essay on Architecture,* a work considered revolutionary in its day (1753), Marc-Antoine Laugier argues that architecture had its beginnings in the fundamental need for shelter; that as humankind first formed structures using "natural instincts," so must architectural principles be based on "simple nature." In his view, architecture grew as an extension of human needs, from the inside out. He states, "Buildings are made to be lived in and only inasmuch as they are convenient can they be habitable."[1] If one sees architecture as a matrix for the resolution of Laugier's "human needs," and beyond that, the place of our desires and dreams, purely poetic views of architecture become completely reasonable. Such is the role given it by the sculptor Alberto Giacometti in his work "The Palace at 4 AM." His description of its creation is both evocative and instructive; in this metaphorical view, divisions between interior and exterior are irrelevant (Fig 1.1). A similarly abstract view has been voiced by Paul Elúard in his *Dignes de vivre:*

> When the peaks of our sky come together
> My house will have a roof.[2]

It is interesting that Elúard's spatial metaphor does not include walls; yet it is the presence of limiting planes that typically characterizes architecture.

It seems clear that the creation of a wall automatically implies the presence of two planar surfaces, usually denoted by the terms interior and exterior. The existence of one defines the other, making them literally inseparable, although one could be differentiated from the other by the scale of the detail, type of surface finish, and character of decoration. Nor is the interior application of these details and finishes procedurally different from exterior applications. The real distinctions, and they are profound, lie in the contradictory character of exterior mass and interior volume, in the treatment of the elements that delineate them, and most significantly, in the way we experience them. Only in the past two centuries have these distinctions become specialized in practice, and only in the past ninety years have they become professionalized.

This specialized division of the architect's functions likely began in the rococo when the interior, of itself, was first considered an appropriate subject for the architect. This distinction was largely the result, not of an aesthetic decision, but of the delicate financial position of the petit aristocracy in prerevolutionary France. In his *Humanistic Inquiries into Architecture,* Elias Cornell postulates three principles of architectural creation: *enclosed outdoor space, interiors,* and *exteriors.*[3] But the experience of enclosure (Cornell's first category), whether in a plaza or a courtyard, is essentially an interior one. It is characterized by the awareness of concave boundary walls, in which only one horizontal plane is needed to physically complete the enclosure (Fig 1.2). Thus two of Cornell's three categories describe interior spatial qualities; and no building type better exemplifies their potential than the *hôtel* of early eighteenth-century Paris. These hôtels, the former townhouses of a landed gentry now turned city dwellers, were usually situated in a continuous street block. The front entrance opened onto a courtyard, which was shielded from the street. The result was to place the entire architectural emphasis on interior effect (Fig 1.3). In works such as his *Livre d'architecture* (1754), Germaine Boffrand professed an aesthetic based on a rich ornamentation and the importance of total composition, an aesthetic he usually applied to the interiors of preexisting structures. That the interior had become so important is clear from his comment, "The interior decoration of apartments at present in Paris makes up a considerable part of architecture."[4]

Before the rococo, the importance accorded the interior or exterior depended on whether one was designing residential or civic architecture. Building forms that function chiefly as dwelling spaces have historically tended to stress interior concerns, while civic structures such as temples, palaces, and courts were exterior in design emphasis, a stance based pri-

1.1

The Palace at 4 a.m. (Construction in wood, glass, wire and string, 25" × 28¹/₄" × 15³/₄"); Alberto Giacometti (1932–3)
"This object took shape little by little in the late summer of 1932; it revealed itself to me slowly, the various parts taking their exact form and their exact place within the whole. It is related without any doubt to a period in my life that had come to an end a year before, when for six whole months hour after hour was passed in the company of a woman who, concentrating all life in herself, magically transformed my every moment. We used to construct a fantastic palace at night—days and nights had the same color, as if everything happened just before daybreak; throughout the whole time I never saw the sun—a very fragile palace of matchsticks. At the slightest false move a whole section of this tiny construction would collapse. We would always begin it over again."[1] (Collection: The Museum of Modern Art, New York. Purchase. Copyright 1991 ARS, N.Y./ ADAGP.)

1.2

Palazzo Massimi—Rome; *Baldassare Peruzzi (1535)*
The façades of the courtyard are usually treated differently from exterior façades, in terms of scale, accessibility, and detail, resulting in an interior experience. (Source: *The Architecture of the Italian Renaissance*, Jacob Burckhardt.)

marily on ideology. It is reasonable that civic buildings have usually claimed the greater historical attention, as they represent the highest ideals of any society, and were built, in technique and materials, to last. It is important, however, that ideals may exist more in belief than in practice and may, in any case, reflect the past. Restated, the artifacts of one generation often represent the beliefs of the previous one. To some degree, this incongruity reflects the sheer time and financial logistics entailed in constructing large civic projects. But perhaps more important is the array of political and ideological factors, since civic buildings inevitably reflect the views of those socially empowered (Fig 1.4). In his *Culture of Cities,* Lewis Mumford observes, ''The more shaky the institution, the more solid the monument.''[5] To some degree, all large cultural statements are suspect, as they usually try to convince us of a certain state of affairs, whether or not it really exists. In this sense domestic architecture, particularly in its interior dimension, is a far more accurate barometer of the current values and beliefs of a particular people (Fig 1.5).

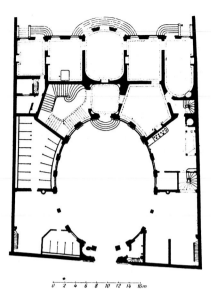

1.3

The Hôtel Amelot de Gournay—Paris;
Gabriel-Germain Boffrand (1712)
The plan indicates a carefully planned town-house laid out around an interior courtyard, accessible from the street through a blind wall. Such walls were essentially flat screens devised to serve as street elevations, granting a civic regularity the hôtels themselves did not have. (Source: *Éléments et Théorie de l'Architecture*, J. Guadet.)

1.4

The Hagia Sophia—Istanbul; *Anthemius of Tralles and Isodorus of Miletus (532–7)*
This church remained the greatest monument of Christendom until the construction of St. Peters in Rome. In plan it is a huge square, topped by a central dome and flanked by two half-domes. The interior is ovoid, with marked concave spatial effects. The height from earth to dome is 184', and the dome is 112' in diameter; the space within is, therefore, vast and airy, an effect that is enhanced by remnants of the translucent tessarae mosaics that covered the surface. At its completion, Emperor Justinian is said to have exclaimed, "O Solomon, I have outdone thee." (Source: *Dynamics of Architectural Form*, Rudolf Arnheim. Permission: The Regents of the University of California and the University of California Press. Copyright 1977.)

References have already been made to the role of *ideology* in the design process; it is, therefore, worthwhile to consider the meaning of the term and how it appears in our buildings. James S. Ackerman has defined ideology ". . . as a largely unconsciously acquired structure, a pattern of thought and action ingrained in the individual by a culture; it is not a particular philosophy or faith that one elects or rejects but rather a state of mind. . . ."[6] The result of this "state of mind" is an inclination in people to accept a particular image of, and role in, their society. As architecture requires the physical, financial, and technical resources of an entire society to come into existence, it is usually regarded as an accurate indicator of that society's beliefs, concerns, and values (both stated and unstated). But just as design elements may be manipulated to produce a certain aesthetic result, so may cultural symbols be controlled to produce certain social and political results.

Ideology is likely responsible for much of our design vocabulary of forms, which are often taken from popular sources and consciously modified by that population's leaders to suggest a historical event or moral position. The tendency to apply ideology to architectural form gives it an imposing ethical quality, clearly represented in the character of its façades—and, frequently, in the planning of its interior spaces as well. In his *Art as Experience*, John Dewey comments on the result of human interaction with design:

> Materials are transformed so as to become media of the purposes of human defense, habitation, and worship. But human life is also made different, and this in ways far beyond the intent or capacity of foresight of those who constructed the buildings.[7]

A

B

1.5

Apartment Anteroom; *Mario Praz*
The interior environment may be regarded as
a collection of memories, associations, and
responses to the larger social milieu; in this
sense it acts as a mirror of a particular culture and the inhabitant's self-selected range
of interests as they develop over time. Thus
this anteroom, as it appeared in c.1936. *(A),*
has been enriched by Praz until it reached its
c.1958 *(B)* incarnation. (*[A]* source: Weiden-
feld & Nicolson Archives, London; *[B]*
source: *The House of Life,* Mario Praz,
Adelphi, Milan.)

Buildings, he says, whether temple or home, influence the future and record
the past, enabling us to live on through the ". . . harmonious mutual adaptation of enduring forces of nature with human need and purpose."[8] And
it is in that effort to reach a "harmonious mutual adaptation" that the ex-
planatory and predictive power of theory is valued.

Theory and Practice

The term theory is complex and has, therefore, tended to mean whatever
people have chosen it to mean. Theory comes from the Greek root *theos,*
to see, implying the ability to look within oneself as well as without. The
term has thus been used in various ways, depending on the user's intention.
It has been used in the critical description of events already past, to project
the likely result of particular actions, and to prescribe methodologies based
on belief patterns. The last definition is what Jon Lang refers to in *Creating
Architectural Theory,* "In architecture, 'design principles,' 'standards,' and
'manifestoes' are examples of such theory. They are based on an ideological
position on what the world, good architecture, landscapes, and urban design
should be."[9] Far from comprising a disinterested speculation about cause
and effect, this position seeks to identify and address *appropriate cause* and
desired effect. In *The Aesthetics of Architecture,* Roger Scruton states:

> Architectural theory consists in the attempt to formulate the maxims, rules,
> and precepts which govern, or ought to govern, the practice of the
> builder. . . . Such precepts assume that we already know what we are
> seeking to achieve: the nature of architectural success is not at issue; the
> question is, rather, how best to achieve it.[10]

To operate from a theoretical base is to be able to make sense of design's
diverse and sometimes difficult problems. Instead of responding with habituated patterns that in the past have been more or less successful, we can
use the predictive power of theory to more creatively select tactics. In his
Intentions in Architecture, Christian Norberg-Schulz notes that ". . . theory
has to be based upon empirical knowledge, but aims at helping the creative
architect to plan and predict, to compare and criticize."[11] In short, theory
can be considered a very practical aspect of design.

Architectural theory has been derived in several different ways: first, through an extraction of design principles based on *historical type;* second, through a commitment to satisfying the *practical needs* (functionalism) of people (usually in disregard of historical precedent); and third, through an *integrative process* that uses a broad spectrum of information from such recent sources as the environmental sciences and semiotics. The first approach dominated the nineteenth century, leading to familiar and predictable designs which, while culturally comforting, increasingly failed to meet the actual needs of the thus-comforted. The failure of these conventional building forms was particularly acute in light of the new industrial functions they so inefficiently clothed. It was largely in reaction to this situation (intensified by World War I), that the ''Functionalist'' approach, which fiercely rejected historical reference, came to dominate the architecture of the interwar years. But while Modernist functionalism produced forms that met the spatial requirements of industry and (to a lesser extent) housing, there are indications that the gains in efficiency and economics were offset by losses in a different area.

More specifically, it may be said of Modernism (at least its later stages) that it defined the term function primarily in terms of formal considerations of structure and materials and the minimum square-footage necessary for specific activities—with little concern for how human beings actually function socially and psychologically. And still less did function refer to the symbolic systems that make up human culture, failing ultimately to ''. . . offer any *new visual order* as a substitute for the 'devaluated' styles of the past.''[12] Norberg-Schulz notes that as time passed, many architects recognized that a functional approach stressing efficiency and economy was too narrow a definition of the building task:

> They understood that it is not *enough* to adopt the most economical solution . . . [and, moreover,] . . . interest has begun to grow in the milieu-creating function of architecture. Environment influences human beings, and this implies that the purpose of architecture transcends the definition given by early functionalism.[13]

He concludes that we should accordingly ask: *''What purpose has architecture as a human product?* The functional-practical, the milieu-creating and the symbolizing aspects constitute three possible answers to the question, all of which have to be investigated more carefully . . .''[14]

The third approach, then, may be seen as the most promising for design. That is, neither historical types nor functionalism, the two ends of a continuum, are enough to serve as a theoretical base if that theory is to account for human beliefs and behavior. Including information from adjunct areas, such as environmental psychology, anthropology, philosophy, the fine arts, and semiotics, seems desirable for many reasons, not the least of which would be to grant design solutions a far greater cultural depth. Moreover, this would allow more latitude in selecting information that design can use. The noted inventor Charles Kettering commented that conventional calculations were based on the past, which was, after all, ''. . . merely the summary of experience, not the limit of possibility.''[15] He felt that the biggest stumbling block to a creative solution is the belief, based on past evidence, that no solution is possible. To Kettering, solutions involved only a change in how one viewed the problem, since the solution itself must be inherent. This approach implies a certain degree of trial and error, something W.R. Lethaby pungently refers to in his *Form in Civilization:* ''Proportion, of course, rests properly on function, material, and size. There may be a perfect proportion, for instance, for a certain class of ships, but that will only be discovered experimentally, and not by measuring Greek galleys.''[16]

This does not suggest, however, that historical analysis is not vital. To the contrary, it is clearly within the scope of architectural history to provide, not the sort of historicism used by the nineteenth century, but a rigorous analysis that can clarify the relationships between problems and their potential solutions. This is possible because theory manifests itself ultimately in the realm of ideas, not things, which must remain imperfect realizations. Malcolm Quantrill refers to this quality in *The Environmental Memory,* when he distinguishes between *model* and *theory:*

> For a theory is just that: it is a metaphor that offers an abstract point of view somewhere between an existing problem and a previously existing model. A theory, therefore, expresses a relationship between a model and a thing or context which that model might represent. In itself a model is neither true nor false; only the theory may be so.[17]

The chief difference between architecture and simple construction is theory, which became universally applied during the Roman Empire. Until then only large civic projects had the benefit of organization, of being built according to a larger design. Domestic buildings usually belonged in the category of vernacular architecture, ''architecture without architects,'' which responds to a personal recitation of client needs, influenced by such models as the client may be familiar with (usually those nearby). Historically, this has resulted in simple regional building types, variable only within certain parameters based on climate, availability of materials, personal finances, and social acceptability. In fact, the term vernacular derives from *vernaculi* (those born within the house), probably referring to the importance of the owner's ideas in the design process. But the situation may be more complex than that, as Alan Colquhoun points out in his *Modernity and the Classical Tradition:*

> . . . both in a certain phase of antiquity itself and in the Renaissance, *classical* signified practices codified in a system of canonic rules which claimed superiority over all other practices. . . . The word *vernacular* is equally derived from social and economic concepts. *Verna* meant slave, and *vernacular* signified a person residing in the house of his master. Hence the later applied meaning . . . of local, indigenous, and lowly forms. Within the context of European history, then, the word *vernacular* can be taken to apply to practices of *making* (linguistic, constructional, etc.) that are either anterior to or untouched by classical theory and practice.[18]

Architecture, in the sense of design that aspires to a higher purpose than simple building, thus necessarily involves theory. In this sense, theory always precedes construction and describes a desired end, usually conceived in terms of symbolic, psychosocial, and practical factors. And while the environmental sciences are useful in the prediction of human behavior, so are technical knowledge and aesthetic intent.

The reference to aesthetic intent is particularly critical, as some might argue that this quality alone separates architecture from the vernacular. In his ''Vernacular Architecture and the Cultural Determinants of Form,'' Amos Rapoport argues for an inclusive definition of architecture, a typology that includes *primitive, vernacular,* and *high-style* environments. The high-style—or grand-design—he argues, can only be understood in the context of a vernacular matrix (perhaps precisely because of ideological content). He points out that built environments have various purposes, from sheltering people and their possessions from the climate, enemies, and the supernatural, to establishing a humanized, socially reinforcing space in a profane and dangerous world. He concludes, ''Socio-cultural factors in the broadest

A

B

C

1.6

(A) **Syrian Qubab Village;** *(B)* **Bungalow,** *Architect's Small House Service Bureau Pattern (1929);* *(C)* **Residence at East Hampton—Long Island, New York;** *Robert Stern (1980)*
Primitive structures *(A)* are responsive only to the basic need for shelter from the environment, although climate, custom, association, and type all influence their final appearance. Vernacular structures *(B)* are standardized to cost and normative cultural factors, as in this suburban "pattern" house designed for a general public known only in the abstract. The high-style design *(C)*, on the other hand, is the aesthetic product of a single designer and client, calculated to specific personal image and physical requirements. (*[A]* permission: Princeton University Press; *[B]* source: *Authentic Small Houses of the Twenties,* edited by Robert T. Jones; *[C]* courtesy: Robert A.M. Stern Architects, New York.)

sense are thus more important than climate, technology, materials, and economics in influencing built form."[19]

Both the primitive and the vernacular perform these cultural tasks with a high degree of congruence and redundancy—the result of the users themselves creating built form through a system of shared assumptions and "rules." For Rapoport, particular cultures design environments that a particular group sees as normative and in keeping with its lifestyle. In this way an order is expressed, ". . . a particular set of cognitive schemata or 'templates' representing some vision of an ideal is given form—however imperfectly . . ."[20] A key difference, then, between the primitive and vernacular, is that the vernacular enjoys a greater degree of latitude in the choice of culturally acceptable solutions, in part because of its familiarity with high-style design. Most important for Rapoport, these solutions reflect a characteristic way of looking at the world and, indeed, of *shaping* the world.[21] Grand-design, implicitly, has less congruence with cultural values and hence is less effective at transmitting what, ultimately, are similar schemata, or information (Fig 1.6).

Rapoport's essentially anthropological approach to design is a fascinating one; of interest here is his inclusive definition of architecture, which holds that all manmade environments are necessarily designed in that they embody human decisions and modify the world in a purposeful way.[22] Supporting this position, he cites virtually every environmental modification that human beings are capable of, from tree cutting to city planning. But one can argue that much human behavior is situationally reactive, based on an obscure tradition or personal habituation; this sort of activity is not genuinely purposeful and may even be counterproductive. This contradicts the definition of design, "to have a plan for; to have as goal or intention." Thus Rapoport's broad and generous view of design tends to render it useless in terms of consciously manipulating materials, symbols, and relationships to specific architectural purposes (a problem in symbolic aesthetics generally).

Since both architecture and vernacular building readily agree on two virtues that come to us from the Roman architect Vitruvius—solid construction and user convenience (even when they are both conspicuous by their absence)—there remains his third dictum, beauty. To identify "architecture," one must transcend simple utilitarian considerations (or spontaneous cultural displays) and turn one's attention to beauty; for it is in beauty that architecture rises above simple construction. Nikolaus Pevsner states it succinctly:

> A bicycle shed is a building; Lincoln Cathedral is a piece of architecture. Nearly everything that encloses space on a scale sufficient for a human being to move in is a building; the term architecture applies only to buildings designed with a view to aesthetic appeal.[23]

The last part of this comment is especially apt; aesthetic intent is necessary to have architecture. This is not to negate the possibility of responding aesthetically to a vernacular building that is unique or attractive (or symbolically reassuring), only that this response is not an experience of art:

> Almost everything can be experienced aesthetically, scenery, an eruption, an engine or tool, as well as a drama, a piece of music, a picture or a building. Aesthetic experience does not emanate exclusively from art. But we must keep in mind that it is only the products of art that are created by the aesthetic purpose of an originator.[24]

In Elias Cornell's view, an aesthetic response may accompany a variety of experiences, but an aesthetic response to art requires a conscious act by someone to induce that response. Traditionally, this has involved an invocation of beauty.

Beauty as an Issue

Any attempt to define beauty is difficult, as it must consider the diverse experiences of humans. Leo Tolstoy devotes an entire chapter of his book *What is Art?* to this problem, beginning with Baumgarten, the progenitor of modern aesthetics, and ending in the late nineteenth century. He concludes that there is no objective definition of beauty and points out that such definitions that do exist note "... that beauty is recognized by the enjoyment it gives. ... "[25] It seems clear, then, that there is at least one identifying aspect of its presence: the ability to move the observer cognitively and/or affectively. Expressed differently, while one may be hard-pressed to pin down the nature of beauty, like electricity, we can know it by its effect.

One of the most persuasive definitions of beauty is George Santayana's in *The Sense of Beauty.* He begins his argument by noting "... a curious but well-known psychological phenomenon, viz., the transformation of an element of sensation into the quality of a thing. If we say that other men should see the beauties we see, it is because we think those beauties *are in the object,* like its colour, proportion, or size."[26] By imbuing the object with our value judgment, we make sense out of the "chaos of impressions" we receive from the world. Thus our varied sensations of that object tend to become simplified into a few primary characteristics and, finally, inherent aspects. In short, we believe our sensations emanate from a source rather than recognizing ourselves as the source. Santayana's definition is, therefore, value positive, intrinsic, and objectified. "Beauty is pleasure regarded as the quality of a thing."[27] It is a value because it is an emotion; and positive because it brings pleasure. Furthermore, this pleasure is intrinsic, in that it does not derive from an object's usefulness, but through its simple perception. And beauty is objectified in that it is seen as innate, rather than as mere sensation.

Not all things, moreover, have the capacity to induce the perception of beauty. Santayana refers to this when he says that "... things are impressive only when they succeed in touching the sensibility of the observer, by finding the avenues to his brain and heart."[28] Tolstoy makes a similar reference when he postulates that the degree to which the artist "infects" others, by allowing them to experience what the artist has experienced, is the measure of the artwork:

> To evoke in oneself a feeling one has once experienced, and having evoked it in oneself, then ... so to transmit that feeling that others may experience the same feeling—this is the activity of art. Art is a human activity consisting in this, that one man consciously. ... hands on to others feelings he has lived through, and that other people are infected by these feelings and also experience them.[29]

One may argue that Tolstoy is speaking of the fine arts, such as painting, literature, and music, and not of design. And this is true. To the degree, however, that architecture is faithful to its historical roots, one might expect a similar evocation to be possible, and even usual. For example, Le Corbusier writes at the beginning of *Towards a New Architecture:*

> The Architect, by his arrangement of forms, realizes an order which is a pure creation of his spirit; by forms and shapes he affects our senses to an acute degree and provokes plastic emotions; by the relationships which he creates he wakes profound echoes in us, he gives us the measure of an order which we feel to be in accordance with that of our world, he determines the various movements of our heart and or our understanding; it is then that we experience the sense of beauty.[30]

These cognitive and emotional aspects of beauty are thus the designer's milieu; effective designers control these aspects so that they influence their client's intellectual and emotional responses. Those elements include proportion, scale, axis, balance, symmetry, and so forth, which in turn become ways of invoking beauty. But as conceptions of beauty are bound by culture and time, so are the mechanisms that allow its experience. Proportion, ornamentation, scale, interior appointments, and the like, are bound by culture, geography, historical experience, religion, mythology, and social structure. While various cultures may agree on a factual description of visual phenomena, their various meanings will differ. This explains why one culture prefers a particular sort of entry system or room arrangement over another and why ornament is considered extraneous in one area of the world and crucial in another. The point is that any definition of beauty, or its constituent parts, is culturally derived. Such derivations inevitably take into account sociological, psychological, ideological, and symbolic concerns. That is, not only are there no fast predictors concerning the nature of aesthetic response generally, but few solid rules about the meaning of particular formal elements of design. This is especially disconcerting in the design of interior space, where the responsibility to the end user is immediate and personal. It is this very responsibility that raises another major question: Whose idea of beauty is it, and who is receiving it?

These sorts of questions raise a crucial issue in the discussion of aesthetic systems generally, that of agreement on a definition of the term and its scope. Santayana identified three separate systems, referring to them as *sensory, formal,* and *symbolic.* The notion of a sensory aesthetic—based on pleasurable sensations—seems, on the surface, to have a certain authenticity. This is especially so when one considers it in light of Santayana's comments about the human capacity to incorporate an element of sensation into the quality of a thing. There has been, however, little concerted effort to pursue this line of inquiry, except as it affects the other two systems. Formal aesthetics, as might be expected, dominates discussions of design issues, as it concerns an appreciation of the shapes and structures of formal order. Jon Lang comments, "In questions of formal aesthetics the question often arises as to whether or not the pleasure we feel in response to certain patterns—proportions and shapes—is biologically based."[31] He concludes that if it is not, but, instead, is based on self-conscious intellectual reasoning, then it indeed belongs to the highest order of human need. If so, formal aesthetics is surely capable of subsuming the sensory concerns, at least ideally.

Symbolic aesthetics is concerned with the associational qualities of the environment that people find meaningful and that, accordingly, give them enjoyment. Lang notes that certain writers (like Rapoport) believe that while designers may place the emphasis on formal aesthetic issues, ". . . most people appreciate the environment mainly in terms of its symbols and its affordances for activities."[32] This is, of course, in keeping with Rapoport's views on the vernacular; that is, that "high-style" environments only represent a particular variant on the broad question of design, and one with a low cultural congruence at that. In this context, it is interesting to note that Gestalt theorists, in their assumption of innate ordering mechanisms, might well agree with the notion that design is manifested generally. Certainly, as symbolic aesthetics is concerned with pleasure derived from the built environment, environmental psychology's contribution will be immense. The real issue, however, is not whether objects have a symbolic existence that gives people pleasure, but whether such qualities, like materials and spatial characteristics, can be controlled to specific design ends. The question, therefore, of whether aesthetics is biologically or culturally based, or whether formal and symbolic aesthetics are simply specialized forms of one another, will likely be answered on the basis of theoretical commitment. As a practical matter, however, little design could take place without all three of these aspects being present. And, in any case, the distinctions may be less clear than it appears. Lang suggests, for example, that the very process of understanding the formal logic of the designed environment provides certain rewards and involves a process of learning (increasing the visual vocabulary of symbols).[33] If so, the question may really be whether a truly universal vocabulary exists (or can be devised).

The definition of good construction practices is fairly clear and is specified by building codes. Also, recent research has begun to comprehend the type of physical and psychological space human beings require. However, little comparable consideration has been given to the aspect of design's expression. In Tolstoy's model, the beauty that was to be transmitted, however socially derived, was ultimately that personal sort owned by a particular artist. According to Tolstoy's view, that artist had to consider the audience's reaction and, therefore, be aware of common cultural symbols; but ultimately the final decisions lay with the artist. And this has probably always been true for the fine arts; design, however, is an applied art. Not only do designers have the artists' considerations, but they must interact with clients who have their own interpretation of the larger milieu and (perhaps) their own view of beauty.

Even the audience is specific to the situation: first, in that the effect the designed space conveys is what the client wishes a given group to receive; and second, in that each individual brings to architecture a personal mix of experiences. This means that the design solution—exterior or interior—consists of an amalgam of aesthetic and cultural information that satisfies client, designer, and audience and considers structure and utility as well. Such a task is difficult; past solutions have often ranged from being indifferent to the client to providing only functional services for mundane settings. One of the essential ingredients of a creative design approach is awareness that the built environment is filled with symbolic meanings that find expression in the spaces people occupy and the things they fill them with. It is also important to be aware of the qualities that especially constitute interior space.

Spatial Character

Throughout history, shifts have occurred in the relative importance of the exterior and the interior. Causes have included the projection of political imagery, disposable wealth, and the fluctuation of power between aristocratic and bourgeois classes. The rising importance of the interior is in large measure a result of the gradual enrichment of a mercantile class whose interest turned increasingly to embellishing aspects of its private life, particularly the residence. This usually entailed the reduction of civic expenditures, which put domestic architecture in direct economic competition with large public projects. The honor accorded the architect has tended to reflect the importance of these civic and commercial commissions—honors not granted to the comparatively exclusive designs of residences. But all commercial projects have budgets, which inevitably brings types of designers into conflict over the finite opportunities thus available; the difference here is not one of domestic versus civic but, rather, interior versus exterior. This fairly recent division involves some consideration of the shifting historical correlation of interior to exterior, shifts that have often been dramatic in their implications for theory. One of the constant factors in this relationship has been, despite occasional reverses, the steady gain in importance accorded the interior.

During the prehistory of humankind, buildings tended to have limited formats, so that a single structural system might be made to serve many purposes. Different areas were, of course, made to function differently, but this was more a socio-religious determination than an architectural one. It is often difficult to determine, based on structure, for example, which room (or building) served as domicile and which as shrine. At best, one can identify important areas by small changes in detail or by the presence of specialized accessories. In fact, it is probably the interior contents and detail of a space, more than any other factors, that grant it a specific character. This is especially true in the absence of any organized concept of structures with individual integrity.

Egypt was one of the earliest civilizations to use a broad range of architectural types. At the mortuary district of Saqqara, there is not only the dramatic step-pyramid of King Zoser but, also, complex and highly derivative temple formats representing both upper and lower Egypt. This complex stands for the most stable and conservative forces in Egyptian society—the pharaoh, aristocracy, and priesthood. It was intended to convey to the populace the mysterious and immutable character of religion; these structures are, therefore, formal and abstract. They use mass and symmetry in such an absolute way as to forever define the appropriate relationship between the gods and humankind, and between classes of people. It is no accident that these structures are studies in exterior character, civic examples of how people should act. We know, however, that there also existed a sophisticated domestic architecture, an architecture that turned its back to the street and, instead, emphasized a lively and colorful interior. These buildings belonged to the vernacular, utilizing traditional models and customary building practices.

The sharp division between exterior civic construction that permitted little or no accessibility, and the domestic interior that chose to close itself from public view, may be Egypt's most notable contribution to architectural tradition. This division, moreover, marked all areas of Egyptian cultural life, including painting, sculpture, and interior decoration. That is, the stiff frontality of aristocratic sculpture and the austere facades of temples contrasted sharply to the warm and accessible art of the mercantile class. Indeed, their walls were often covered with lively and animated images like those at the villa of General Ra'Mose of Amarna (Fig 1.7). In fairness, it should be noted that Amarna was something of an exception to the rule of a highly derivative (vernacular) architecture, growing—over time and without a real blueprint—into larger urban amalgamations. It was a planned city, built at one time with one purpose, and represents one of the few examples of early domestic architecture's taking its cue from civic sources. But a question immediately arises as to the nature of architecture in a society based on a different set of social and political premises from that ruled by landed aristocracy.

Such a society existed on the island of Crete. The Minoan civilization, which flourished between B.C. 2000 and 1200, appears to have enjoyed a commercial economy and, consequently, rule by merchant princes. The Minoans used a distinctive language that has only partially been deciphered; that part, Linear B, has yielded much information about a sophisticated culture based on shipping, trade, and finance. The palace at Knossos is a study in contrast, when compared to the complexes of Egypt. Arnold Hauser comments, ''Crete presents us with a picture of colorful, unrestrained exuberant life. . . . What freedom in artistic life in contrast to the oppressive conventionalism in the rest of the Ancient-Oriental world!''[34] Knossos illustrates the striking differences that sharply altered economic conditions can produce in conjunction with a substantively different role for religion in public life. The palace complex serves as Crete's civic architecture, but it is an architecture that relies on a succession of interior experiences rather than a unified and imposing façade. The highly asymmetrical entries grew out of practical-access considerations, and the maze-like layout of the palace owes more to climatic conditions than to the representation of authority (Fig 1.8).

Of particular interest are the walls—both exterior and interior—that were covered with rich and colorful decoration (Fig 1.9). These walls were obviously not built to express structural integrity, but to colorfully decorate particularized spaces. Knossos might be viewed as an inverted interior, a civic structure domesticated. While the residence continued to gain in architectural importance, it did not again achieve this parity with civic structures until the Renaissance, nor such an equality of economic importance until the rococo. Notably, the Renaissance was also a period of merchant princes, dominated by trade and banking; and the rococo a period of transition from monarchy to an industrial revolution dominated by a wealthy bourgeoisie.

The majority of the conclusions about Crete are speculative. Linear A, thought to be the language of culture, remains a mystery, and few remains of ordinary housing have been unearthed. Such is not the case, however, with Rome. Not only have the ubiquitous monuments of Rome been examined in detail, but so has its residential housing, largely the result of an eighteenth-century fascination with antiquity. So remarkable are these re-

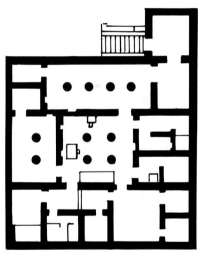

1.7

Villa of General Ra'mose—Amarna, Egypt
(ca. 1360 B.C.)
This interpretive perspective depicts the lively wall surfaces, rich with figuration and color. The columns are painted as if they were alive, and the surfaces are illuminated by the use of clerestory windows. The plan of the house is square, and its symmetry is echoed by the placement of the four columns located in the central main hall. (Drawn by: J. Malnar. Reference: *A History of Egyptian Architecture*, Alexander Badawy.)

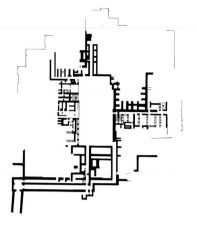

1.8

Palace at Knossos—Crete *(ca. B.C. 1500)*
The palace was a multilevel structure; with
an emphasis on spatial continuity. The passages and rooms are light and airy, with
oddly inverted columns. Spiro Kostof has
noted that, ''The Minoan architect did not
begin with general frames; he did not think
in terms of neat bounding outlines. True
façades, in the main, were ordered toward
the court. Indeed, there is reason to believe
that the layout was planned from inside out,
in units radiating from the central court as
their function required.''[2] (Photo by: Frank
Vodvarka. Drawn by: J. Malnar.)

mains that they require some extended analysis. Indeed, upper-class Roman
housing was, by the third century A.D., extremely sophisticated, enjoying a
long tradition and a rich variety of types and forms to choose from (Fig
1.10). Paul Veyne describes the residence of the wealthy, the domus, as one
of the finest creations of Greek and Roman art. A Roman dwelling, he
notes, was conceived in spatial terms, a series of open spaces including a
covered courtyard, an open courtyard with a portico, and a garden with
central fountains.[35] The visual advantage to such open space was in its
perspective views, which enhanced the illusion of scale and airiness. The
floors, walls, and ceilings of these townhouses were covered with vividly
colored mosaics and paintings of decorative and mythological subjects.
Veyne concludes, ''The essence of this architecture lies in the wedding of
vast, open spaces with small, private rooms without the use of narrow corridors.''[36]

Such a rich and urbane wall decoration suggests that it is the logical
extension of a long tradition. The colorful walls at Amarna and the lush
figuration at Knossos both suggest steps in an ongoing process. The Roman
residence marks the culmination of a long development in the importance
of the private realm of life, as opposed to the public, or civic, aspect. The

1.9

**Interior Reconstruction: Queen's Apart-
ment, Palace of Minos—Knossos, Crete;**
(Sixteenth century B.C.)
This reconstruction drawing of the Queen's
Hall indicates the complexity of the interior
space, which uses multiple entryways and a
hidden stairwell. Room illumination is obtained by the use of two light-wells, on the
east and south, which transmit light to the
interior windows. The walls are highly ornamented with colorful murals of dolphins
and dancing women, as well as intricate ro-
sette designs. (Courtesy: Royal Ontario Museum, Toronto, Canada. Executed by Sylvia
Hahn.)

residence has taken on the opulence formerly the sole domain of civic architecture. Nothing seems capable of preparing us for the absolute extravagance of the imagery. At Pompeii, these images range from mythological scenes to erotica; of special interest are the trompe l'oeil (to fool the eye) architectural settings that may be "seen" through nonexistent windows (Fig 1.11). Actually, the exterior façades of the Roman domus were windowless (save for venting), opening only for entry from the street. Put differently, the domus is inward-turning to the point of opening its facades onto a central court (peristyle) and painting its own exterior architectural views. Here one might recall Cornell's three principles of architectural creation; enclosed outdoor space, interiors, and exteriors, which he maintains were clearly separate categories historically. The Roman domus seems an amalgam of the first two principles, consisting of a series of interior spaces surrounding a central open court, or peristyle. Certainly the external façades, which consisted of multiple street entrances and integrated storefronts, lacked the identifying external consistency of a unified structure.

It would be an error to think of the Roman domus as a residence in our sense of the word. Relationships between upper-class citizens and the multitudes who had business with them were often concluded within the residence. The domus was a large structure comprising areas more or less public; the degree to which this public entered the private areas depended on the nature of the relationship and business. The words that describe these spaces are with us still: the portico, or transition from the street; the vestibule, where a visitor waited for formal entry; the atrium, or formal reception area; and the excedra, a place for private meetings. This view of residence indicates a culture highly attuned to the continuity of relationships and hence to the constantly shifting ratio of public to private concerns. In his essay "Private Life and Domestic Architecture in Roman Africa," Yvon Thébert notes that since private life is a product of social relationships and a defining feature of social formations, it ". . . is subject, from time to time, to radical redefinition . . ."[37]

As the Roman conception of public and private was a social product, so was their architecture. It also partook of considerable theoretical reflection. Thébert notes that during the Roman era architecture freed itself from local limitations and turned its attention to social, aesthetic, and individualistic considerations. This resulted ". . . in a highly elaborate architectural theory, to which both architect and client referred in making proposals and plans,"[38] and was reflected in the planning of cities, in which specification of house plans and lots was provided. The close connection between public and private roles in the Roman residence explains the inclusion of imposing civic motifs within the domus, which likely served the same function as they did in public. It also explains the importance granted the design of domestic structures by the first-century-B.C. architect Vitruvius, who proved so influential in the following centuries. Finally, it provides some rationale

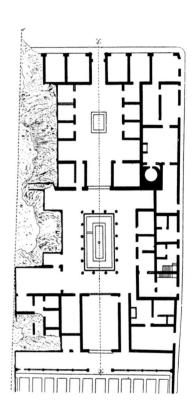

1.10

House of Pansa—Pompeii *(Second century B.C.)*
This is a large mansion, used by the extended family, which occupies an entire insula, or city block. There probably were multiple entries (or porticos) at one time, scaled to indicate their relative importance; these were later modified into separate shops. The single primary entrance that remains opens into an atrium, which serves as formal reception area, containing the shrine of the family gods. The private family areas begin at the peristyle, an open, collanaded court with fountains, sculptures, and plant life. (Source: *Éléments et Théorie de l'Architecture,* J. Guadet.)

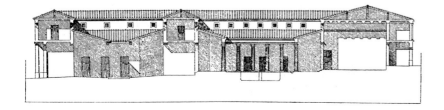

1.11

The Ixion Room—Pompeii *(63–79 A.D.)*
The Ixion Room is in the House of the Vetii and houses extraordinary examples of fully developed Roman illusionistic wall painting. Not only are all the wall surfaces (e.g., marble and wood) painted, so are the paintings, their frames, and the windows. Through these "windows" one can see architectural and natural vistas in a three-dimensional reality broken only by the absence of mathematical perspective. (Source: Alinari/Art Resource.)

1.12

Palazzo Medici-Riccardi—Florence; *Michelozzo (1444)*
This palazzo is an elegant example of design for the wealthy merchant/banking classes of Italy. The structure rises in a clear and definitive statement capped with finality by a distinctive cornice. The first floor contained commercial space, the second floor was reserved for quasi-public family functions, and the third floor contained the private apartments. (Courtesy: Royal Institute of British Architects, London.)

for the ease with which private dwellings encroached on the public domain. We have a picture of residential structures that is as remarkable as it is complex; this picture does not resurface until the Renaissance. Although fifteenth- and sixteenth-century theorists had little real knowledge of the Roman domus, they certainly had access to literary accounts such as Apuleius' *Metamorphoses* and, above all, Vitruvius' *De Architectura.* The social and economic situation of Renaissance merchants somewhat resembled the Roman upperclass, and it is, therefore, not surprising to see this Roman world invoked.

The early Renaissance, or Quattrocento, witnessed, for various reasons, a resurgence of interest in the classical world, particularly Rome. Not only were classical poets again read, so was Vitruvius. Leon Alberti, as evidenced in his *De re aedificatoria* (The Ten Books of Architecture), was greatly influenced by Vitruvius' manuscript, one of the few such to survive from antiquity. And although the two societies were similar, the attention Vitruvius paid to domestic housing was amplified in Alberti's work. The residence once again served as a multipurpose dwelling, with private and public functions. In the design of the Palazzo Medici, for example, Michelozzo has carefully delineated a hierarchy of functions encased in a rusticated stonework that tells us much about the nature of fifteenth-century Florence (Fig 1.12). These palazzi remain distinctly residential, despite using a more imposing façade than was true of the Roman domus. Not until the sixteenth century was there an attempt to visually unite exterior and interior, particularly in the works of Andrea Palladio.

Still, even when working on the structures' interiors, the architect's outlook was exterior; the notion of designing just for the interior remained foreign. It was not until the Rococo that such an approach became acceptable, i.e., when the interior had become financially and symbolically important enough to merit the undivided attention of the designer. Witold Rybczynski captures this distinction in his work *Home:*

Rococo was the first style to be developed exclusively for the *interior,* as opposed to the exterior. This underlined not only that the insides of houses were being thought of as very different from the outside, but also that an important distinction was being made between interior decoration and architecture. This distinction was not as obvious then as it now seems; previously, the architecture of rooms had been the architecture of façades, turned inside out. It was not until the Rococo that architects . . . could specialize in "interior decoration."[39]

It is precisely this distinction that characterizes the work of Germaine Boffrand in his elegant Petit Luxembourg (Fig 1.13). This interior suggests the developing French tradition later espoused by such handbooks as *De la distribution des maisons de plaisance* (1737), by Jacques François Blondel, and C.E. Briseux' *L'Art de bâtir des maisons de campagne,* which became available to designers of that time. And although Robert Adam was far removed in his Neoclassical approach from the forms of the rococo, he too was an architect whose major commissions occurred within existing structures and whose most innovative work involves the interior. One of the most profound legacies of the eighteenth century, then, may be its sharp distinction between the practice of interior architecture and exterior architecture— even when the practitioner is the same person. That is, the terms of design engagement alter when the design conditions change. And no distinction is more critical than interior versus exterior. This is apparent in Blondel's perceptive comment:

> As we have treated the exterior in general, now we are going to put ourselves to the interior, which is that which appears most neglected by most architects. In effect the interior decoration should re-feel the wisdom which one must use on the outside.[40]

There are many warnings against the application of exterior formulae to the interior in the eighteenth century. However, they were certainly not always acknowledged.

1.13

Salon, Petit Luxembourg—Paris; *Gabriel-Germain Boffrand (1710)*
Here one can see the emerging of the new rococo style, with its characteristic lively color, delicate grace, and exuberance. A consistent system of arches has been created over the doors, windows, and mirrors; this in turn creates a kind of scalloped edge that only barely acknowledges the difference between ceiling and walls. Above the molding, the ceiling is coved, further masking the distinction between ceiling and wall planes. (Source: Giraudon/Art Resource, New York.)

Interior Attributes

We can conclude from this brief overview that throughout history there have occurred sharp fluctuations in the definitions of exterior and interior, civic and domestic, public and private. What makes up civic architecture seems clear ordinarily, but we have seen at least one instance in which its characteristics have been inverted. With the development of the open interior courtyard, the distinctions between exterior and interior were blurred. And in certain residential structures the public and private spheres of activity were so intertwined as to be inseparable. This would seem to render absolute definitions inoperative; there are, however, patterns that repeat themselves. It seems clear, for example, that architects have historically understood that the interior is a world apart from the exterior, in terms of materials, light, scale, and time passage, with correspondingly different associations.

For instance, architects in the past have generally been aware that the nature of materials changes with location, so that exterior materials selected to withstand the elements (and to convey that fact) are seldom tactilely or visually appropriate to the interior. Nor do the textures of the exterior translate well when subjected to close scrutiny under vastly different lighting conditions on interior walls. The ancient world, with its delight in rich interior finishes and trompe l'oeil murals, would scarcely understand our habit of repeating rough concrete exterior walls on the interior. As architecture's interior dimension is experienced much more intimately, interior scale becomes smaller than exterior scale, which is seen in a larger view. Consideration of interior finish is important, since the interior is usually seen as a series of events unfolding (save for certain notable examples); and rich color has long been an interior delight in contrast to typical, softer, architectural colors derived from the landscape. Finally, designers have traditionally understood that while the exterior is created in light, the interior is a world of shadows, in which both dramatic effect and physical comfort may be controlled by the inhabitant (Plate 1).

Another way of viewing the situation is to understand that architecture constantly changes in aspect, depending on whether one views its exterior protective aspect or its interior dimension, where it must accommodate complex activities. Thus the exterior is always thought too large for upkeep (though never too large for image), and the interior never large enough for people's tasks (though also too large for upkeep). Therefore, many of the developments in architecture have been the result, not of conscious aesthetic decisions, but of complex psychological and ideological factors. The "rules" of design that have evolved are likely an attempt to visually conceptualize these relationships, themselves a product of time and situation. Taken together, these factors and rules help form a theoretical base, the formulation and utilization of which is critical to design. This involves a consideration of those factors (direct and peripheral) that are thought to appropriately form a base for such theory, the ways in which these factors manifest themselves in design, and the various methodologies utilized by designers (past and present).

Theory systems inevitably involve a concept of order. That is, whatever the human mind wishes to understand must first be arranged in an orderly and, hence, comprehensible manner. In his *Entropy and Art,* Rudolf Arnheim comments:

> Order makes it possible to focus on what is alike and what is different, what belongs together and what is segregated. . . . Man imposes orderliness on his activities because it is so useful, cognitively and technologically, in a society, a household, a discourse, or a machine.[41]

Order is usually apprehended perceptually, through the wide array of incoming sensory data. But, as Arnheim notes, these surface qualities are often simply the outward displays of an underlying functional order.[42] Those basic functions, and our ability to perceive their sensory aspects, are activities of the mind. For this reason, psychological information is essential for the design process. This importance is underscored by David Canter in his *Psychology for Architects;* he says:

> . . . a great deal of the discussion and many of the decisions made in relation to buildings are based upon assumptions about people and their interactions with buildings . . . it is only when these relationships are expressed and understood in the context of scientific psychology that communication amongst decision makers, and the actual decisions made, can develop in an effective and meaningful way.[43]

Canter identifies three categories of psychological information needed by the designer. And he believes this information would be most useful if the designer had a full understanding of its implications:

- Activity Requirements—deal not only with what, when, and how people do things, but how these activities change over time

- Relative Values—the problem of determining design priorities based on finite resources, which involves an examination of fundamental human behavior

- Behavior/Environment Relationships—the study of the interactive relationships of people to their environment, and of the variables that influence specific human behavior

The author points out that while psychological data alone are not enough to serve as the basis of design, there are pertinent data available to the designer that are currently ignored.

Also important, and often overlooked in architectural texts, is theory that has been compiled in fine art—perhaps in the belief that building design is fundamentally different from design generally. Buildings encompass a wide range of aspects, from the utilitarian to the symbolic; it is this quality that gives architecture the power to communicate ideas that ultimately are only peripherally connected to actual functions. The sorts of needs that derive from structural requirements, activities, and real estate values seem so persuasive that it is often assumed that simple, straightforward satisfaction of these needs suffices as good design. It is here that theory derived from the fine arts reminds us that architecture must rise above mere physical service. Herbert Read states that ''architecture, if it is to escape from the primitive, the childish, the archaic, must be inspired by considerations that are intellectual, abstract, spiritual—considerations that modify the strict requirements of utility. It is the eternally reiterated claim of spirit to inform matter, and art ceases to exist when that claim is refused.''[44]

And when we consider the matter, our recollections of past houses will center on the more intangible factors. The philosopher Gaston Bachelard, in his evocative *The Poetics of Space,* says: ''. . . if I were asked to name the chief benefit of the house, I should say: the house shelters daydreaming, the house protects the dreamer, the house allows one to dream in peace. Thought and experience are not the only things that sanction human values. The values that belong to daydreaming mark humanity in its depths.''[45] This is how, Bachelard says, that ''. . . dwelling-places of the past remain in us for all time.''[46] He goes on to name two more benefits; one is the function of the house as the repository of memories, as he says, ''. . . an embodiment of dreams.''[47] As such, it provides us with our visions of existence. Finally, ''A house constitutes a body of images that give mankind proofs or illusions of stability,''[48] a consideration that seems to naturally grow out of the first two ideas and which can surely be applied to architectural situations of many kinds (Fig 1.14). All those who remember the quality of light in a room, rather than its square-footage, and the rich details of the woodwork, instead of the number of closets, will appreciate Bachelard's comments. These aspects, as well as the more prosaic attributes of architecture, are encompassed by the term form, which serves as method in the transformation of materials and utility to expressive structural artifact. Form, then, is the prime concern of the designer, the methodology of manifesting order.

1.14

The Hall of Morpheus; *Jean-Jacques Lequeu (1792)*
This imaginary structure was designed by Jean-Jacques Lequeu; often grouped with such ''visionary architects'' as Ledoux and Boullée, his plans remained responsive only to theory, and to a commonly held knowledge of history and mythology. The full title of this design is ''The Hall of Morpheus, Which Leads to the Cabinet of Sleep''; the decorations include black curtains to keep out the light, and the scent of ''sleep-inducing herbs and odoriferous paneling'' permeates the air. (Source: Bibliothèque Nationale, Paris.)

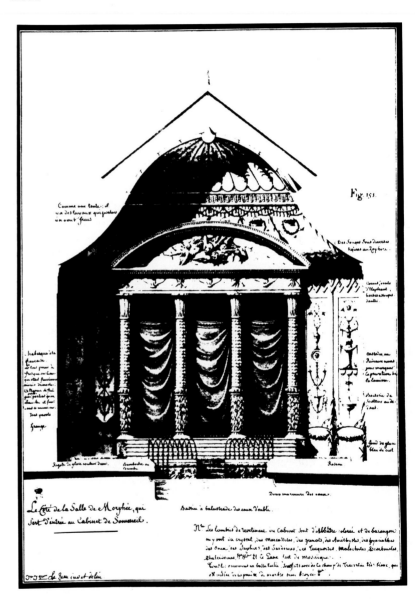

Form and Function 2

Form and Design

Any analysis of the characteristics of ordered space must early on consider principles of form. In general, the artist or designer begins with subject (the visual phenomenon or program) and interprets and arranges that subject through form, resulting in a composition that embodies content, or meaning. Such meaning may closely correlate with the subject, or simply use the subject as a convenient metaphor. In either case, the subject has been consciously manipulated to a more profound purpose than its own existence. The function of the artist or designer, then, is to form: an ability that depends on the presence of programmatic information, personal insight, awareness of cultural symbols, and certain technical skills. The term itself, however, has shades of meaning that need to be understood for optimum effect.

The Oxford American Dictionary offers a remarkable range of definitions of the word form. For the sake of our argument, we have separated them into two categories; form as object or thing, and form as a state of existence. As an object, its definition is clear: a person's body; a customary procedure; a fixed order of words; a manner or style in musical/literary composition; and, most prosaically, a document with blanks for required information. The second definition refers to form-design as noun or verb:

Noun
the shape and structure of something
the basic nature of something
the mode in which something exists
the design or structure of a work of art

Verb
to shape or become shaped
to conceive in the mind
to put in order, to arrange

There is a significant difference in these two definitions: the first refers to a thing; the second to a state of being or, as a verb, a process of becoming. The methods that the designer uses take into account basic visual elements arranged according to complex formulae. The definition suggests that these processes would, however, mean little if they did not serve a significant human purpose.

The first definition corresponds with the common notion of form as a thing that has some sort of function. However, even as a ''thing,'' form is the result of historical experiences that grew from determinable biological, symbolic, and utilitarian functions. In other words, the final appearance of these ''forms'' does not occur accidentally, even though their evolution is not always easy to determine. Artists and designers use ''form'' to describe a *quality of existence,* the way things are. This definition does not simply describe the physical and utilitarian aspects of form, but includes aesthetic, psychological, and semiotic considerations. And from its definition as verb, we see that all these aspects are subject to the conscious manipulation of humans, individually and in groups, in accordance with their own purposes (Fig 2.1). The fundamental difference is that a definition of form as *product* is passive, while the definition of form as *process* is active. It is this latter definition that John Dewey refers to when he says, ''Form may then be defined as the operation of forces that carry the experience of an event, object, scene and situation to its own integral fulfillment.''[1] And it is from this second definition that we derive the notion of design as well:

> to form a plan for
> to have as a goal or intention
> the order or arrangement of the components and details of something
>   in accordance with a plan

The definition of design, then, comes from that of form but is less complex—although convenient. This stems in large part from a compactness that does not immediately suggest the varied aspects of intent, method, and result that are implicit in the word form. That these are implicit, however, is made clear by Josef Albers:

> To design is
> to plan, and to organize,
> to order, to relate and control.
> In short it embraces
> all means opposing disorder and accident.
> Therefore it signifies
> a human need
> and qualifies man's
> thinking and doing.[2]

In short, to form is to mold physical material with a human purpose. In his work *The Origins of Form in Art* Herbert Read states, ''Form in art is the shape imparted to an artifact by human intention and action.''[3] Shape, in this case, represents all the considerations acting upon the subject, in order to produce a coherent work. Put differently, to form is to transform; it is perhaps this view that led to the medieval notion of God as Architect of the Universe (Fig 2.2).

So fundamental is this need to mold, that, as Read suggests, it may be fundamental to the human species—our consciousness having begun with the forms of perception, and human intelligence and spirituality having been marked by the representation of form.[4] The idea of a kind of *will to form* is echoed by Henri Focillon in his remarkable work, *La Vie des Formes:*

> Life is form, and form is the modality of life. . . . The formal relationships within a work of art and among different works of art constitute an order for, and a metaphor of, the entire universe.[5]

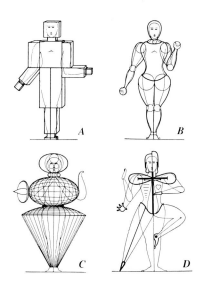

2.1

Man and Artistic Figure; *Oskar Schlemmer (1925)*
These stage costumes, designed by a member of the Bauhaus, illustrate how the human body can be formed according to specific requirements. In *(A),* the cubic shapes are transferred to the human body, resulting in ''Living architecture.'' In *(B),* the costume is based on ''the functional laws of the human body in relation to space . . . result: The jointed manikin.'' The costume in *(C)* is influenced by ''the laws of motion of the human body in space . . . result: A technical organism.'' The last costume *(D)* symbolizes the metaphysical aspect of the human body through the star shape of ''the spread hand, the helix of the crossed arms, the cruciform of the spine and shoulder. . . .''[1] (Source: *The Bauhaus,* Hans M. Wingler. Published by The MIT Press. Copyright 1969 by The Massachusetts Institute of Technology.)

Subject, Form, and Content

Read refers to the subject, form, and content continuum as it occurs in the fine arts. As he makes clear, however, such a conceptual scheme is equally useful when considering architectural design. In this case, the *subject* comprises the program, or utility, and in some measure those materials to be used in the program's realization. *Form* consists of the methodologies and intentions of the designer (which usually involves materials), and *content* is the final statement of structure, i.e., its public existence. And the final statement of any structure depends much more on its symbolic content than on its utilitarian issues. Contemplate the soaring vaults of the Gothic cathedral at Amiens. Here the responds travel energetically upward to the vaulting of the nave, which ". . . would shine with the wonderful and uninterrupted light of most luminous windows, pervading the interior beauty."[6] This poetic description came from Abbot Suger a century before Amiens was built. But it surely applies to this towering structure even more profoundly than to the small abbey church of St. Denis, to which he actually refers. The way in which such buildings have been designed shows that function conceived in purely physical terms is function misunderstood (Fig 2.3).

Read refers to this when he hypothesizes three states all human artifacts pass through: 1) The conception of the artifact as tool, 2) its physical perfecting, and 3) its eventual refinement in a "conception of form-in-itself." He asks, ". . . in what manner, and for what reason, did man quite early in his cultural development, . . . pass from functional form to form-in-itself, that is to say, to aesthetic form?"[7] And, through an interesting deductive process concludes, "In any case, form, having become divorced from function, was free to develop according to new principles or laws—those laws and principles which we now call aesthetic."[8]

In short, form embodies a wide range of *human intentions,* only one of which is utility. Moreover, form has the capacity to eventually become self-contained, to so surpass its primitive utilitarian origins that it stops conforming to any functional expectation. "The problem," says Read, "is to determine at what point elegance ceases to be utilitarian, at what point form is divorced from function."[9] In *The Dynamics of Architectural Form,* Rudolf Arnheim explains that when architects discuss form, they have worried less about the psychological problem of how shape can transmit spiritual meaning than about the question of how form is related to function. He concludes that " . . . it has become evident by now that neither in biology nor the applied arts can form ever be fully determined by function. The reason is . . . that function consists in abstract principles, not in shapes."[10]

Put differently, function—even when viewed narrowly—does not automatically insist on a particular identity. For example, when one wishes to pass from one spatial location to another (as from inside to out, or one room to another), visually or physically, one needs some sort of portal. This may take the form of doorway or window, be wide or narrow, regular or irregular, ornate or plain. The actual function can be satisfied by any of a wide range of shapes and treatments; the final form of the portal will, however, depend on a blend of practical and symbolic issues, and the visual result will vary accordingly (Fig 2.4). And when we later analyze that portal, our comments will likely center on an appearance primarily determined by symbolic factors. That is, the attributes we best remember are seldom the prosaic ones.

Consider the amazing diversity in design approaches granted objects with even simple utility. And as the products of a 1982 design invitational spon-

2.2

Deus Creator Caeli et Terrae, from the Bible Moralisee (Thirteenth century)
This manuscript illumination points to the notion, prevalent throughout the Middle Ages, that the workings of God could be made intelligible through numbers and geometry. Also emphasized, through the use of the dividers, is the historic and theological relationship of geometry to architecture, and therefore the role of God as "Architect of the Universe." (Courtesy: Bodleian Library, University of Oxford, MS. Bodley 270b, fol. 1.)

2.3

Choir Vault—Amiens Cathedral *(begun in 1220)*
The emphasis is on an airy translucency, conveyed by the use of almost continuous clerestory windows topped by a delicate membrane of vaulting 138′ above the ground. Light held special meaning for the thirteenth century mind, "... discussed as the noblest of natural phenomena, the least material, the closest approximation to pure form."[2] These cathedrals represented the concerted national effort of an entire society; indeed, Amiens may be seen as the physical embodiment of the statement by St. Thomas Aquinas, "God enjoyed all things, for each accord with his essence." (Courtesy: National Gallery of Art, Washington, D.C.)

sored by Alessi illustrate, such diversity is usually little concerned with technical improvements (Fig 2.5). These tea and coffee services are fascinating as reflections of design positions; they are equally interesting as responses to program. A reviewer in the January 1984 issue of *Progressive Architecture* notes:

> One concern about these highly artful and impeccably crafted sets, since they are ostensibly utilitarian, is the actual degree of their usefulness. They range from the very *functional* (emphasis ours) designs of Michael Graves, Hans Hollein, and Paolo Portoghesi, whose pot handles are all of heat-resistant material, and whose trays are all easily pick-upable, to that of Charles Jencks, whose tray and columnar vessels are without handles. Ouch when hot![11]

Nor is the dominance of symbolic concerns limited to such objects. To the contrary, this is true of architectural projects as well, accounting for the diverse responses to a single program. A delightful statement of this notion may be seen in the "exquisite corpse" drawing for a hypothetical skyscraper produced by the participants (all of them designers) in a seminar on skyscraper design. This is a drawing that graphically demonstrates variation in response (Fig 2.6).

When Read refers to *form divorced from function* in human artifacts other than architecture, his position is not overly controversial. But he later applies this notion to architecture as well. In his analysis of Greek architecture, he says that the Greek temples were increasingly sophisticated developments of a basic form, so that what began as a utilitarian structure evolved into a symbol for spiritual values we call beauty. But, he points out, these values are essentially formal qualities and can be expressed mathematically; they are commonly referred to as balance, harmony, and symmetry. He thus concludes that "Greek architecture is an attempt to create a plastic image that . . . expresses the idea that *proportion* is one of the highest values in human life . . ."[12] That is, the Greek temple has so established its ideological identity that it has lost any utilitarian function, nor is such a function necessary. This view of architecture may shock those who have regarded Louis Sullivan's dictum "Form ever follows function" in physical terms. But Sullivan believed buildings did indeed relate to the spiritual needs of people; for Sullivan, architecture was linked to the human condition. It is precisely this quality that the brilliant critic and theorist John Ruskin refers to when he says, "All architecture proposes an effect on the human mind, not merely a service to the human frame."[13] And this sentiment was echoed half a century later by one of Ruskin's countrymen, Winston Churchill, when he commented, "We shape our buildings; thereafter they shape us."[14]

What is remarkable about Read's position generally, is not his emphatic attribution of aesthetic qualities to buildings, but his complete lack of concern for any utilitarian aspect. Notably, Read has selected Greek temples for his example, suggesting that in their almost complete devotion to exterior concerns, these forms are essentially sculptural. He believes that, as such, they could not serve any real utilitarian purpose, and he therefore concludes that the other necessary ingredient for true architecture is a concern for interior space.

He reasons that, as architecture is the art of enclosing space, there are two basic elements: space and the enclosing material. Therefore, he says, "For a work of art to emerge from the process it is essential that these two basic elements should produce a unified effect. The art is in the effective synthesis of these two elements."[15] Read believes that it was only with the development of expressive interior space that architecture began to realize its unique aesthetic qualities, an evolution that started less than a millennium ago. It was a development, moreover, that grew out of the unique spatial practices of Christianity. Accordingly, that *expressive interior space* is seen most strikingly in its religious structures.

B

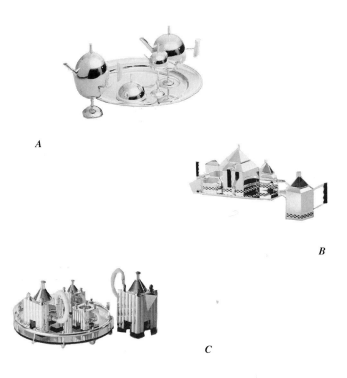

A

A

B

C

2.4

(A) West Portals—Chartres Cathedral (1145) (B) Reception Hall—Fumban Palace *(late nineteenth century)*

The West Portals of Chartres *(A)* were built during the first phase of the cathedral's construction. These portals represent the kings and queens of the Old Testament, suggesting the "divine right of kings." The subject of the motifs used in the statue-columns represents a conscious effort on the part of monarchy and church to mark an association ultimately sociopolitical in nature. King Njoy was Fon of the Bamum, a tribal grouping in the Cameroons of West Africa. In this area, the Fon of such a group serves as political leader, cultural guardian, and living embodiment of the founding of his dynasty. To enter through the portals *(B)* of the palace is to acknowledge the source of his physical and spiritual power by passing support columns that display representations of his retainers. (*[A]* source: Marburg/Art Resource, New York; *[B]* source: Basler Mission, Evangelical Missionary Society, Basel, Switzerland.)

2.5

Program 6; Alessi of Italy *(1982)*

Alessi, a major Italian manufacturing firm, invited twelve architects to submit designs for a service that would include teapot, coffeepot, creamer, and sugar bowl. The designs were shown at the ICSID Congress in Milan in late 1983. Shown here are the services designed by *(A)* Alessandro Mendini, *(B)* Paolo Portoghesi, and *(C)* Michael Graves. (Courtesy: Alessi and The Markuse Corporation, Woburn, Mass.)

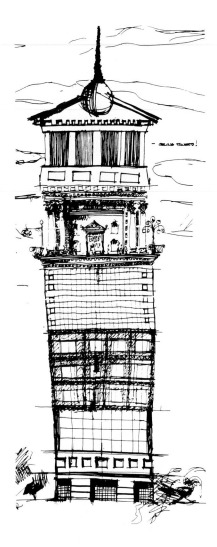

2.6

Exquisite Corpse Drawing *(1983)*
This type of drawing, invented by the sur-
realists in the 1920s, is based on the creative
flow of energy between people and the laws
of chance. A common program was given
seven people, at the close of a Harvard University seminar entitled ''The Skyscraper.''
In each case the person knew only where the
previous design left off, and the extent of the
total project they were responsible for. Only
after every member of the group had contributed a part, was the design in its entirety
revealed. (Courtesy: Frank Vodvarka.)

Form and Function

Christian Norberg-Schulz says that the role of architecture is to control the
environment in order to allow human interaction. He identifies four parameters of the building task:

- Physical control—controlling the inner organization of a building, including mechanical systems

- Functional frame—prescribing the size and quality of interior space and
  access

- Social milieu—noting the wide range of social interactions within and
  without a structure

- Cultural symbolization—embodying common values and symbol-systems[16]

While these are not dramatically new ideas, they are interesting for their
semantic precision and because they primarily cite design parameters that
are sociocultural. The last category may be the most critical:

> As a human product of a pronounced practical character, architecture has
> a particular ability to show how our values, how our cultural traditions
> determine our daily life. Only through cultural symbolization can archi-
> tecture show that the daily life has a meaning which transcends the im-
> mediate situation, that it forms a part of a cultural and historical
> continuity.''[17]

Norberg-Schulz concludes that when architects disagree with their clients
or other architects, it is seldom over practical problems. The disagreement,
rather, centers on symbolical values that are differently experienced, even
when they are perceived as essentially aesthetic problems. Thus design may
begin with a program based on pragmatic spatial requirements—and use
certain materials in its construction—but the final design statement comes
from the application of a complex methodology that comes from a particular
world-view. Honest people may, moreover, disagree about the substance of
that world-view. It is, nonetheless, precisely this final statement that constitutes the *content,* or meaning, of architecture. This content reflects the
cultural and ideological beliefs of a place and time as surely as a manifesto.

The will to form may exist innately, but its realization requires perceptual
techniques that are not easily acquired. In his broad and provocative work
Art as Experience John Dewey comments:

> It belongs to the very character of the creative mind to reach out and seize
> any material that stirs it so that the value of that material may be pressed
> out and become the matter of a new experience . . . every product of art
> is matter and matter only, so that the contrast is not between matter and
> form but between matter relatively unformed and matter adequately
> formed. A work of art elicits and accentuates this quality of being a whole
> and of belonging to the larger, all-inclusive whole, which is the universe
> in which we live.''[18]

One's ability to sense the larger reality is critical to the design process.
Indeed, Dewey suggests that ''it is the context of every experience and it is
the essence of sanity.''[19] Once that reality is sensed, the designer must
convert it to a *perceivable reality.* The designer does this through visual
characteristics and ordered methodologies using the various tools of ''form.''
To develop such a sensitivity to underlying relationships and their visual
manifestations has long been a goal of design education, leading to inventions designed to stimulate the creative mind. The theories behind such

items reached their fruition in the broad range of "educational toys" produced by students of the Bauhaus (Fig 2.7). The goal of all these inventions was to maximize the inherent will to form and to develop an ability to grasp underlying relationships.

But Arnheim tells us that form is not simply function made visible, " . . . rather, it *translates* an object's function into the language of perceptual expression."[20] Thus Arnheim sees form as the particular way in which order is expressed, its visual symbolic manifestation. Form always deals with this dual aspect of order—that of function and its image—therefore, the two must be in concert. Arnheim notes that outer order often represents inner order and must, therefore, not be evaluated on its own. He says also that a lack of correspondence between outer and inner order produces disorder.[21] This disorder may be experienced when the visible order is perceived as fundamentally at odds with known reality, when the chosen elements of form seem inappropriate for the message. Arnheim suggests that such a consonance between function and image results in true order, " . . . a prerequisite of survival."[22] This need may explain the Gestalt position that the human mind always organizes visual perception to specific ends. Experiments have demonstrated consistent perceptual phenomena. Examples include organization based on 1) similarity and balance, 2) size and shape constancies (objects keep one size and shape despite the fluctuating retinal image that results from variation in distance and viewing angle), and 3) persuasive spatial illusions.

These principles form a part of Gestalt psychology, which was developed in Germany after 1912 by Koffka, Köhler, and Wertheimer. Gestalt (loosely interpreted as shape, or form) has as one of its key tenets *pragnanz,* a notion based on "wholeness." This wholeness requires that any visual pattern be perceived in such a way as to make it as legible, clear, and comprehensible as possible. This assumes an innate ability both to recognize figure-ground relationships and organize other forms of visual data. Thus the viewer uses principles like similarity (grouping by like kind), continuity (overall structure), and form-constancy (the complete perception of a suggested shape despite incomplete information) to impose order even when the environment is randomly arranged (Fig 2.8). Two of the most important conclusions reached by Gestalt psychologists are 1) perception is not a response to individual bits of information (sensations) but to a field of interrelated data and 2) human perception actively structures its environment rather than simply reacting to it.[23]

Gestalt is not, however, the only theory of perception in psychology. In his "Visual Perception in Architecture," Julian Hochberg describes what he regards as the three major perceptual theories:

- **Classical theory**—growing out of the works of the philosopher John Stuart Mill and the physicist Hermann von Helmholtz in the ninteenth century

- **Gestalt theory**—growing (as noted) out of the work of Kurt Koffka, Wolfgang Köhler, and Max Werthiemer following World War I

- **Direct theories of perception**(stimulus-response phenomena)—those of J. J. Gibson in particular.

Hochberg favors the classical approach, although never to the exclusion of the other two theories.

The classical approach (sometimes referred to as Empiricism) comes from the belief that perception of shape is complex, formed from much simpler

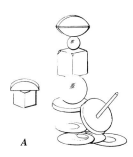

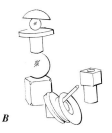

2.7

(A) **Game with Spheres;** *Alma Buscher (1924); (B)* **Colored Peg Top;** *Ludwig Hirschfeld-Mack (1924)*
These toys, designed by members of the Bauhaus, were intended to be stimulating and instructive. Rather than provide a child with a toy that was a scaled-down version of an adult artifact, they provided inspiring material that required the child to be inventive in order to create some type of organization. In the case of Alma Buscher's wood blocks lacquered in color, the educational aim was the "development of the imagination . . . and the feeling for form."[3] (Drawn by: J. Malnar.)

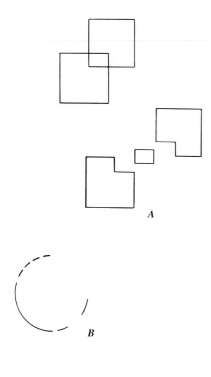

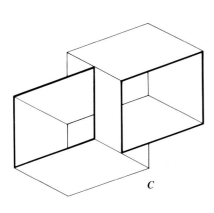

2.8

(A) **Shape-Continuity Diagram;** *(B)* **Form-Constancy Diagram;** *(C)* **Spatial Illusion;** *Josef Albers*
Certain factors in human perception provide that we "see" the two squares *(A)* as two superimposed figures, rather than three discrete (although contiguous) figures. The need to organize patterns so that the simplest structure obtains may also account for our willingness to "complete" suggestive shapes *(B)*, even when that is not a necessary conclusion. Our need to perceive figure-ground relationships is probably responsible for the success of spatial illusions *(C)*. ([A & B] drawn by: J. Malnar; [C] source: *The Bauhaus,* Hans M. Wingler. Published by The MIT Press. Copyright 1969 by The Massachusetts Institute of Technology.

psychological sensations, and that both sensations and their resultant experiences come from learning about how particular physical properties are characteristically related.[24] Thus we form mental constructs of the world that let us generalize, grasp through inference. Hochberg regards three aspects of this theory as especially important: first, as the world has simultaneous structure (characteristic patterns), so do our sensory experiences, and the associations formed in our perceptual memories are also simultaneous; second, living provides successive associations; and third, frequent associations become so persuasive and regular that we can no longer discern single momentary sensations of experience.[25] Therefore, Hochberg states, "Our perception of an object consists of the whole complex of simultaneous associations and of our expectations—our successive associations—as to what sequence of experiences will most likely follow from any act of sensory exploration."[26] And he notes that the current, broader view of any object is that of a structure rather than a simple group of sensations. Therefore, this provides a sequence of sensory stimulation that lets us perceive the arrangement of objects and events that would most frequently produce a particular pattern of stimulation.[27] This habituated way of viewing helps explain such phenomena as shape and size constancies, and, in its emphasis on successive associations, seems appropriate to a continuous visual experience of architectural space.

This emphasis on learning, expectation, and habituation marks a significant difference between the classical theory and Gestalt. But even more important is the classical insistence on fundamental visual sensations as the basis for perception. Gestalt has held that such simple sensations are insufficient to explain either the workings of the nervous system or the actual (often complex) appearance of things. And, in any case, the Gestalt theory of perception also relies on visual organization through spatial inference. Some of the more intriguing—and useful—results of Gestalt theory have included the "law of good continuation" (organization to the fewest lines) and the "law of enclosedness" (enclosed shapes tend to read as figure). The usefulness of such observations (among others) to design is discussed by David Levi in "The Gestalt Psychology of Expression in Architecture." Levi says that both the Gestalt concern with unified wholes in experience, and the qualities of these forms as experienced, lead to the notion of those wholes having expressive qualities.[28] That is, they have enough latitude for the designer to use them for expressive/affective purposes, a latitude that can (in the Gestalt view) be counted on as universal. Both theories acknowledge and seek to explain the various visual phenomena heavily explored by Gestalt psychology, and both theories have implications for spatial design. Hochberg's strong preference for the Classical theory stems from his belief that the basis for Gestalt assumptions is not sustainable and, on a more practical level, that there are perceptual inconsistencies that cast doubt on the entire theory. But he does acknowledge the applicability of Gestalt figure-ground concepts in design theory and later notes that ". . . it is more difficult to achieve solutions that run counter to the Gestalt 'laws.' "[29] Of special interest is the relationship of both theories to the process of *schematization,* described by the child psychologist Jean Piaget. He theorizes that schemata—the stereotypes we have of a thing or event that influence our reactions—are formed during the socialization process and strongly influence perception. Piaget holds that at the simplest levels, such schemata derive from elementary motor activities, while higher-order schemata are based on communication and cultural patterns. Hence Gestalt laws may be seen to correspond to the simple schematizations that are among the first to be acquired, like enclosure, proximity, and the constancies.

But Piaget notes that not all of these schemata are present at the outset, having demonstrated that ". . . as regards size constancy, great differences still persist between an eight-year-old child and an adult."[30] And he notes that the work of others (Brunswik and Cruikshank) has demonstrated its complete absence during the first six months of life.[31] He thus concludes that ". . . the perception of space involves a gradual construction and certainly does not exist ready made at the outset of mental development."[32] This conclusion that all schemata are learned agrees with the classical stance; Piaget nonetheless praises the Gestalt approach to perception, stating:

> They were right to advance the theory of Form, with its notions of field and of totality, in opposition to the atomistic ideal of the proponents of associationistic psychology, who hoped to give an account of perceptual and conceptual totalities in terms of associations between the ultimate elements or "sensations" for which they were searching.[33]

Piaget's only real complaint is that the Gestaltists stopped short of fully exploiting the implications of their discoveries, regarding ". . . the theory as providing an explanation in itself, and not simply a descriptive tool . . . ."[34]

The third theory of perception, the "Direct" approach, assumes that perception is the function of our direct visual response to the sundry relationships between objects and surfaces. Thus perception is a direct response to retinal images, which are formed by light striking the retina—light that is related to the physical attributes of the reflective source. This is an automatic process, so there need not be any concern for "unconscious inference" or prior associations to shape that image (although J.J. Gibson does note that there are certain little-known neural processes at the last stage of perception). Gibson has thus held that distance perception and size constancy would occur without any need for visual processing on the part of the viewer (Fig 2.9). In his *The Perception of the Visual World,* Gibson notes that the visual world is ". . . extended in distance and modelled in depth; it is upright, stable, and without boundaries; it is colored, shadowed, illuminated, and textured; it is composed of surfaces, edges, shapes, and interspaces; finally . . . it is filled with things that have meaning."[35] In short, it comprises concrete properties. But, he says:

> The accepted view of perception is still that the percept is never completely determined by the physical stimulus. Instead, the percept is something essentially subjective in that it depends on some contribution made by the observer himself. Perception goes beyond the stimuli and is superimposed on sensations.[36]

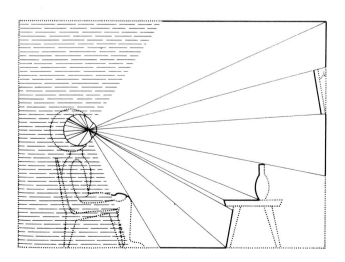

2.9

The Optical Projection of a Room
The important aspect of the optical image is that the reflected light from the various surfaces forms a geometrical projection that reaches the pupil. Interestingly, not all the surfaces can be in focus at the same time, yet there is little blurring. In this sense, the retinal image may be seen as a two-dimensional "pinhole" image. (Source: *The Perception of the Visual World,* James J. Gibson. Copyright 1950 by Houghton Mifflin Company. Used with permission.)

Gibson finds this proposition untenable, as the visual responses of different observers are too much alike for it to be true. And so he states, "If the total stimulation contains all that is needed to account for visual perception, the hypothesis of sensory organization is unnecessary."[37] Gibson offers his own theory, a *psychophysical theory of perception*, based on the assumption that there are exact accompanying variations in the image for the important features of the visual world.[38] His theory is based on a broad and complex stimulus-response model, so it is reasonable to inquire about a stimulus that would provide such variation. Gibson extends the conventional definition of the term stimulus—a variable physical energy falling within a certain range of variation on a receptor or receptors differentially—to mean also a *simultaneous* variation over the set of receptors.[39] He refers to this as the Hypothesis of Ordinal Stimulation, where "ordinal" refers to order or succession. This theory would help explain variables in perception, especially distance cues and texture gradients, and, moreover, has implications for movement. He concludes:

> The correspondence of the visual *field* to the total retinal image is an anatomical point-for-point correspondence which is not hard to understand. The correspondence of the visual *world* to the total retinal image is an ordinal correspondence which is more difficult to analyse and specify. But the latter correspondence *is no less literal and exact,* we may believe, than the former. . . .[40]

This sort of approach obviously appeals to design; it suggests a simple, even elegant, solution to the problem of perception. It even intimates that there may be some constants in perception useful to design, and Gibson points out that perception is not always distorted by needs nor fated to be assimilated to social norms.[41] The problem, according to Hochberg, is that this approach fails to consider either the illusions or Gestalt organizational phenomena (which are no less constant) and, worse, does not adequately address the sorts of visual conditions that occur in architectural spaces.[42]

Although Gestalt theory accounts for only one approach to perceptual psychology, its peculiar contribution to design is immense. Gibson says, "Perhaps the greatest contribution of the Gestalt theorists was that, having taken an unprejudiced look at the visual world they were trying to explain, they formulated problems for space-perception which were genuinely relevant . . . . They were questions about the characteristics of the visual world."[43] And all these theories acknowledge the perceptual Gestalten. But all these approaches, insofar as they have meaning for design, exist to serve an aesthetic end, to allow for prediction and analysis. The designer is an active participant. Arnheim states:

> . . . it is necessary to distinguish between the balancing of forces in the perceptual field itself and the "outside" control exerted by the artist's motives, plans, and preferences. He can be said to impose his structural theme upon the perceptual organization.[44]

The net value of psychological theory may thus be to enrich the notion of form by arming it with certain verifiable principles of human perception, and by providing information that design intention can use as a foundation for reconciling complex spatio-temporal relationships.

No series of relationships is more fundamental and complex than those involved in designing a structure. Arnheim points out that a building is a fact of the human mind, a synthesis of haptic and cognitive experiences.[45] All of this, however, is not to reject the importance of physical construction and utility. Indeed, Arnheim insists that buildings must be seen as beginning with tangible shapes having practical and social functions,[46] and any attempt to ignore such considerations in favor of pure form is abhorrent.

Ideological movements that proclaim the importance of form, the organization itself, as the raison d'etre of architecture have dominated design since World War I. They are grouped under Modernism, and at the outset, were a declaration of freedom from Victorian excesses. And yet no less a Modernist than Mies van der Rohe states:

> We refuse to recognize problems of form, but only problems of building.
> Form is not the aim of our work, but only the result.
> Form, by itself, does not exist.
> Form as an aim is formalism; and that we reject.[47]

Form, then, has little intrinsic value; it exists to transform and make visible a concept into a useful, structural reality, one which embodies the symbols and values of its society. The notions of form as either autonomous aesthetic or programmatic tool are the two ends of a design-continuum. They have often been identified as aestheticism versus practicality, although such a simplistic characterization ignores the reality of their independence. Indeed, the importance accorded form in our century is primarily a determination to treat form as synonymous with function. That is, form is to proceed directly from a mechanical function without any consideration of the complexities of design intention. This interpretation likely proceeds from the public perception of the intent of the aphorism *form ever follows function.*

Louis Sullivan's ideas were mentioned previously, but his dictum has roots that precede him by millennia. Plato expressed such an opinion: "The excellence or beauty or truth of every structure . . . is relative to the use for which nature or the artist has intended them."[48] One of Sullivan's most brilliant contemporaries, John Wellborn Root, postulated that, ". . . the particular thing chosen for the given purpose shall be the best fitted for that purpose—shall in short grow out of it."[49] And Root's comments in turn reflect the earlier ideas of Horatio Greenough, "If there be any principle of structure more plainly inculcated in the works of the Creator than all others, it is the principle of unflinching adaptation of forms to functions."[50] In one way or another, similar sentiments have surfaced regularly over the past two centuries, culminating in the early twentieth-century design movements.

But at least in the case of Sullivan, this is probably a too-literal reading of his aphorism; even a cursory reading of his *Kindergarten Chats,* or his series of architectural essays, would reveal a romantic in the tradition of Thoreau and Whitman. Function, for Sullivan, was connected with a broad range of human concerns, and he regarded social responsibility as the foundation for architectural achievement (Fig 2.10). For that matter, Root, in his essay *Character and Style,* emphatically states that as every building is a thing of "unavoidable prominence," it ought to have ". . . some of the qualities which we find in a gentleman . . . which are Repose, Refinement, Self-Containment, Sympathy, Discretion, Knowledge, Urbanity, Modesty."[51] These are hardly prosaic, utilitarian attributes. A problem may lie in the definition of function itself. It is perhaps an indication of a twentieth-century preoccupation with material needs, that function is so often defined as concerned solely with the structural and utilitarian aspects of space. As Arnheim makes clear, all human needs are matters of the mind:

> Hunger pangs, the chills of winter, the fear of violence, and the disturbance from noise are all facts of human consciousness. It makes little sense to distinguish between them by attributing some to the body and others to the mind. The hunger, the chill, and the fear are on equal footing with the need for peace, privacy, space, harmony, order, or color. To the best of a psychologist's knowledge, the priorities are by no means self-

2.10

Carson, Pirie, Scott—Chicago; *Louis Sullivan (1899–1904)*
The building is notable for many reasons, from its tripartite "Chicago" windows to the skin of terracotta. But of special interest are the magnificent display windows at ground level. Executed by architect George Elmslie and sculptor Kristian Schneider to the designs of Sullivan, they are framed with rich botanical ironwork, and are a tribute to Sullivan's notion that even someone of poor means could feel like royalty while gazing through the glass. (Photo by: Frank Vodvarka.)

evident. Dignity, a sense of pride, congeniality, a feeling of ease—these are primary needs, which must be seriously considered when the welfare of human beings is under discussion.[52]

Since they are requirements of the mind, he points out, they are satisfied not only by good plumbing and heating, but also by light, color, visual order, well-proportioned space, and so forth.[53] Therefore, if a broader definition of function is allowed, one based on physical, symbolic, and psychological factors, Sullivan's comment becomes completely reasonable.

We use the design of a chair to illustrate this idea, as its function seems so obvious (i.e., it is an object to sit on). Of course there are refinements of that function, such as chairs for sitting in an relaxed position or an upright one, but that does not explain all the chairs that have been designed over the centuries. The reason usually given to explain this preoccupation with chair design is that it is to improve the function of sitting. The nineteenth-century architects Percier and Fontaine explain such function:

> Among all the forms of a chair there are some which are dictated by the shape of our body, the needs of convenience . . . what is there Art could add? It should purify the forms dictated by convenience and combine them with the simplest of outlines, giving rise from these natural conditions to ornamental motifs which would be adapted to the essential form without ever disguising its nature. . . .[54]

Looking at the book's illustrations clarifies this changed definition (Fig 2.11). As designed by Percier and Fontaine, the armrest does indeed provide some convenience; but the arm's support serves as a double function. First, it is a support of the armrest, and second, through its overt use of certain imagery, it refers to the Roman Empire. The adherence to its Roman model is surely no accident; such an image suited the architects' patron, Napoleon Bonaparte, who had crowned himself Emperor of France (spiritual inheritor of the Holy Roman Empire) four years earlier. The chair visually affirms that status in the sense that the throne makes the king. Both functions are thus necessary and are accomplished in the designers' minds by "the simplest of outlines," in this case a sphinx. Put differently, these architects realized from the outset that the duality of function was inherent to the design problem.

One may ask, then, whether there is not some shift in the relationship of form to function from Sullivan's time to ours. And Sullivan probably did

B

2.11

(A) **Roman Chair** *(first century* A.D.*)*; *(B)* **Neoclassical Chair;** *Charles Percier and Pierre François Louis Fontaine (1812)*
During the late Roman period furniture became increasingly ostentatious, and one's position in society might be displayed by such objects as this elaborately carved marble chair *(A)*. In this chair the arm supports and armrests have been combined, but in such a way as to function in a symbolic sense only. Early nineteenth-century furniture in France was heavily influenced by Napoleon, whose distaste for the artifacts of his Bourbon predecessors led to the refurnishing of both the Tuileries and Fontainebleau. The admiration for things Roman influenced Napoleon's taste in furniture *(B)*. In the wake of his victories, the Empire style quickly became popular. ([A] source: *Chairs Through the Ages,* edited by Harold H. Hart; [B] copyright 1991 The Art Institute of Chicago. All rights reserved.)

A

conceive a far broader definition of function, one that included social and ideological factors as implicit in every building's program. In such a scheme, form proceeded logically from the program, requiring only that the architect be reasonably sensitive to the task's broader program. There are certain factors that are likely responsible for this wider view: first, "the spirit of the age," one of a laissez-faire egalitarianism that incorporated a sense of social responsibility; second, the idea that every structure should be seen as a complete organism subjected to an array of historical judgments (something of a Darwinian notion); and third, the client's knowledgeable concern that an appropriate identity be transmitted by the building. This was a concern that involved itself in the most minute design details. This liberal conception of the architect whose responsibility transcended simple utility was advanced by Walt Whitman in his *Leaves of Grass:*

> I swear to you that the architects shall appear without fail,
> I swear to you they will understand you and justify you,
> The greatest among them shall be he who best knows you,
> and encloses all and is faithful to all . . .[55]

Exceptions aside, such a view of architecture no longer prevails. Indeed, the client's program is often incredibly minimal, largely concerning square-footage, mechanical systems, and signage. Structures are often conceived with disregard for their impact on the social and physical environment, and fashion may substitute for historical perspective. In such a situation, the designer must enhance this impoverished view of function with a more inclusive definition of form. It is a definition, however, that requires broad knowledge of discrete disciplines and the ability to productively synthesize them. It may also require an altered view of Sullivan's aphorism, one in keeping with the power of form to transform a prosaic utility into poetic vision.

Spatial Organization

As important as an appreciation of cognitive and affective information that form uses, is the knowledge and control of the methods that form uses in its visualization of program. Ultimately, architecture is about the creation of apprehensible mass and space, which is brought into being by the manipulation of an assortment of *elements.* The elements are the basic facts of visual phenomena and include line, value, texture, color, and shape. These elements are often intertwined, as in the ability of *value* to describe *texture,* or *color's* effect on the apprehension of *shape.* Of all these elements, *line* may be the most useful to the design process, as it permits the delineation of spatial characteristics in two dimensions. A line extended creates a plane, and connected planes can define volume. Perversely, line may also account for the greatest confusion in the design process, since it exists only as an abstraction. That is, line does not occur in nature, and a line in a drawing represents only the edge, or meeting, of two planes.

Color can be confusing also, as it has been arranged into various systems, that is, symbolic, aesthetic, psychological, and physiological. The issues surrounding the use of color have become so complex that there are consultants who specialize only in that area. Value, too, is complex, often being regarded as a static quality even though it depends on light sources that alter over time (itself an integral part of the design process). Since value serves also in the delineation of texture, it thus becomes dynamic and useful in the suggestion of spatio-temporal passage (a quality exploited by Frank Lloyd Wright in his Imperial Hotel). Further consideration of these elements follows in the next chapter, but there are two points here: first, these elements have aspects both tangible and abstract; and second, a system of organization is required if they are to be useful to design.

Visual elements by themselves, then, mean little; they are like words without grammar. Structure is provided through *organizational principles* that allow the designer to put things in order, to visually control the type of information transmitted. To order is to make sense of, a very human attribute. Le Corbusier makes this clear:

> One of the highest delights of the human mind is to perceive the order of nature and to measure its own participation in the scheme of things; the work of art seems to us to be a labor of putting into order, a masterpiece of human order.[56]

These organizational methods include balance, arrangement, sequence, scale, and proportion; when used effectively, unity results. Some of these devices are more complex than others, with far-reaching implications for both designer and audience.

Both the visual elements and their organizing principles serve to form a tangible entity from the designer's concept. They are tools, and like most tools, are specialized; this does not, however, mean that they are unrelated. *Balance,* the visual weighing of the composition around axes, depends largely on *arrangement,* and its use of rhythm and repetition. *Sequence* provides hierarchy and the notion of progression through space—an idea inherent in rhythm. *Scale* establishes the size relationships between things, one to another or to the human being. And *proportion* concerns the relationships within the composition as a whole, as well as its message to the audience. All these methods are present all the time, although they are not equally vital at any one time.

Still, no matter how clear the concept, and controlled the use of elements

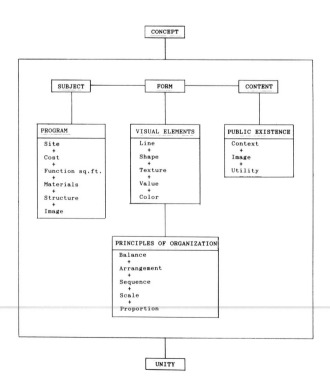

2.12

Concept = Unity *(Developed by: J. Malnar and Frank Vodvarka.)*

and organization, the result cannot be absolutely predicted. That is, the content of the finished design is never entirely clear until the work is finished, until the ideas are translated into a perceivable entity. Arturo Fallico comments that these methods ". . . constitute a vocabulary . . . of elemental felt-images, whose realized presences enter constitutively into the realized presence which is the art-object as a whole."[57] But he also warns that when the elements appear in a work, " . . . their own peculiar kind of interdependent self-discrimination and interrelation also appears."[58] That is, the elements have their own identities, alone and in relationship to others; and they assert themselves in ways that are not altogether predictable (or entirely controllable).

Form uses these organizational principles, then, to order and unify the various visual characteristics, or elements, into a coherent statement of visual perception (Fig 2.12). Elements and principles are analogous to the vocabulary and grammar of written language, allowing the designer to state the design program in visual terms. Important to the concept of form is the knowledge that they are neutral in application. That is, they may be used to communicate information that is profound or banal. Such principles are simply tools in the service of design intention and, while crucial, cannot provide aesthetic sensibility where there is none. Also, they do not discriminate dimensionally; they may be used in two or three dimensions and in the formation of exterior mass or interior space. Finally, the success of organizational principles depends on whether they agree with attributes of human perception, innate or learned. This accounts for the crucial role of psychology in the design process.

Mass and Space

Mass and space are often thought of as inversions of one another. Such definitions are inherent in the notions of space penetration and space enclosure, respectively. An early effort to conceptualize this difference in architectural terms was made by Paul Frankl, who used the terms *mass-forms* (Körperformen) and *space-cells* (Raumzellen) to describe these two phenomena.[59] "This," says Norberg-Schulz, "presupposes a purely quantitative space concept; space is something that can be measured, divided and added."[60] Thus Frankl's view of built form is that it is based on either addition (discrete, well-defined space-cells organized into an articulated mass-form) or division (a highly coherent mass-form subdivided into space-cells).[61] He uses these concepts to differentiate plans of the Renaissance from those of the Baroque, respectively (Fig 2.13). This view of building forms seems to parallel Heinrich Wölfflin's analysis of sculpture and painting (of the same periods), wherein a stylistic distinction was sought in the formal means of development. Frankl's observations about spatial qualities generally are lucid:

> To see architecture means to draw together into a single mental image the series of three-dimensionally interpreted images that are represented to us as we walk through interior spaces and round their exterior shell. When I speak of the *architectural image,* I mean this *one mental image.*"[62]

And so he sees this as the key difference between the experience of Renaissance space and that of the Baroque. Of the Renaissance, he says, "The unconditional demand for completeness, which in the first phase is produced by spatial addition and the radiation of force, means that differences of light and color must permit easy and absolute comprehension of this completeness."[63] And he contrasts this with Baroque spatial phenomena,

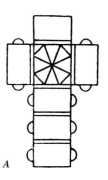

A

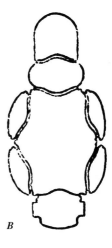

B

2.13

Space-Cell Types; *Paul Frankl (1914)*
The diagram of Sta. Maria del Calcinaio in Cortona (1485) is an excellent example of what Frankl means by additive composition; that is, multiple modules brought together in a larger work *(A).* The plan for Legnidke Pole in Wahlstatt (1727) demonstrates Frankl's ideas about an essentially unified space that has been subdivided into interior cells, "Six spaces are set out radially and all are fused into an undulating unit. . . ." *(B)*[4] (Source: *Principles of Architectural History,* Paul Frankl. Published by The MIT Press. Copyright 1968 by The Massachusetts Institute of Technology.)

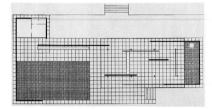

2.14

German Pavilion, International Exposition—Barcelona, Spain *(Floor plan, Final scheme. Made for publication in 1929. Ink and pencil on paper, 22½" × 38½");* Ludwig Mies van der Rohe (1929)*
In the Barcelona Pavilion, the marble wall that slides out beyond the roof prevents the traditional understanding of enclosure as box from occurring. Philip Johnson explains that this approach "... depends upon a new conception of the function of the wall. The unit of design is no longer the cubic room but the free-standing wall, which breaks the traditional box by sliding out from beneath the roof and extending into the landscape. Instead of forming a closed volume, these independent walls, joined only by panes of glass, create a new ambiguous sensation of space. Indoors and outdoors are no longer easily defined; they flow into each other."[5] (Photo—courtesy: Mies van der Rohe Archive, The Museum of Modern Art, New York; Plan—collection: Mies van der Rohe Archive, The Museum of Modern Art, New York. Gift of Ludwig Mies van der Rohe.)

"In the interior . . . that intriguing quality of the unequal images is linked with the principle of spatial division. The great flood of movement that urges us round and through the building does not by any means permit us to look about us with equal comfort in every direction."[64]

Although the distinction between mass and space is usually made to distinguish between exterior and interior, such comparisons are sometimes not convincing. For example, even a cursory examination of Mies van der Rohe's Barcelona Pavilion, in plan or elevation, reveals a startling equivalence of interior and exterior space, only faintly demarcated by the series of vertical planes serving as "walls," and, most tellingly, by the *enclosing* roof (Fig 2.14). Indeed, the designer may use customary expectation as part of a design solution. An extraordinary example of this may be seen in Michelangelo's design of the steps to the Laurentian Library at S. Lorenzo. The steps appear to be in an exterior courtyard, leading upward to the relatively narrow library proper; we assume this because of their demeanor and because the blind "windows" facing onto the space are exterior in nature. Yet the steps, in reality, are in an ordinary room, turned to new use (Fig 2.15). A question arises as to whether the anteroom walls are aspects of mass or space enclosure. Pope Clement VII commissioned the stairway and, in fact, suggested that it should "occupy the whole entrance." But it was the bold way the entire work was organized that led the sixteenth-century architect, artist, and biographer Giorgio Vasari to exclaim, "Thus all artists are under a great and permanent obligation to Michelangelo, seeing that he broke the bonds and chains . . . of common usage."[65]

Despite such intriguing anomalies, architecture's main division is interior versus exterior. Read praises the development of the Christian basilica as a step towards a sensibility for space that expands the interior space to an expressive purpose. He notes the engineering developments that made this possible, such as vault construction. But, he adds that the development would never have occurred without the essentially sculptural feeling for mass being replaced by an architectural feeling for space, ". . . the idea, which the vault made possible, that a building could rise from the ground rather than rest on it."[66] In fairness, Read does note that while this development encouraged architectural unity, unity was not actually achieved, because ". . . the architects of the Christian basilica tended to concentrate on the interior and to neglect the exterior, which often gives the impression of a garment turned outside in."[67] When Read comments about the emphasis on the interior being at the expense of the exterior, he suggest that architecture is essentially sculptural after all.

Read is tacitly acknowledging the compelling power of the object, a fascination that can more easily understand the dominance of the exterior than vice versa. In *The Interior Façade,* Lee Hodgden defines the problem as the perceptual inclination to see objects rather than space, ". . . as space is incorporeal, and architectural space is more a concept than a thing, it can be 'seen' only when it is delineated by suitably disposed defining elements."[68] Since the nature of volumetric space is derived, he notes, we are naturally more apt to see objects than spatial relationships. This leads to the ". . uncomfortable realization that the architecture of the exterior and the architecture of the interior may be totally at variance with one another."[69] One could argue that only rarely, and in the simplest structures, could such literal unity of interior and exterior be attempted, since a visual relationship can be directly perceived only when both parts are in the same image.

Certainly, no spatial problem is more peculiar to architecture than the need to see the relationship between the interior and exterior. Attempts have been made to "see" both aspects at once; some of the more successful have been by sculptors (Fig 2.16). However, while these efforts are interesting, they do not truly replicate an interior experience. It is, after all, very different to look into an interior space—and actually to be inside an enclosed one. One of the most fascinating architectural attempts to resolve this division is seen in Philip Johnson's Glass House, where the walls are transparent (Fig 2.17). This building might well represent how possible such spatial bilocation is. As Arnheim notes, architecture must satisfy the dual function of providing a protective shelter and a congenial internal environment, while also creating a physically functional, visually impressive exterior. And so he concludes, "Perceptually and practically, the worlds of outside and inside are mutually exclusive."[70]

Arnheim could not be more clear; these two aspects of a structure can never be truly continuous. And yet, the two must be coherent. He suggests that the answer lies in treating the interior and exterior like the two different ideas they are, using the formations of biological bodies as model. Arnheim notes the structural differences between the outer and inner structure of the

2.15

Laurentian Library Steps, S. Lorenzo—Florence; *Michelangelo (1524–8)*
The Laurentian Library lies within the complex of S. Lorenzo, designed by Fillipo Brunelleschi in the early fifteenth century. The library is a proportionally awkward room, and quite small relative to the importance of its collection of books and manuscripts belonging to the Medici family. The library steps flow upward from their convex base as though they had to accommodate a multitude of people; two-thirds of the way up, they contract to a single lane of steps, which narrow still further at the door. In a letter to Vasari in 1555, Michelangelo justified the tripartite division of the steps by suggesting that the central path was for the ruler, and the two side paths for retainers. In any case the experience of entering the library after such progressive compression is one of relief. (Perspective, from: *The Architecture of the Italian Renaissance,* Jacob Burckhardt; Section and Plan, source: *Principles of Architectural History,* Paul Frankl. Published by The MIT Press. Copyright 1968 by The Massachusetts Institute of Technology.)

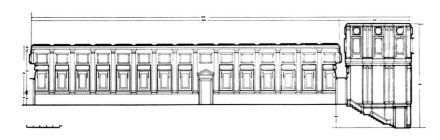

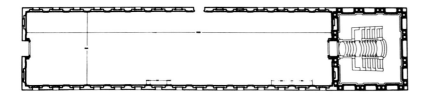

2.16

Working Model for Reclining Figure, Internal-External Forms (bronze); Henry Moore (1951)
Moore's sculptures refer to the bones and joints of the human skeleton, as well as other biological shapes. Here he creates a hollow shell, within which is another mass, more linear in nature. The viewer may move around, and look through, the semi-open outer shell in such way that the inner mass constantly changes in aspect. The interaction of exterior shell and interior mass creates an intriguing, and ultimately mysterious, formal duality. (Reproduced by kind permission of the Henry Moore Foundation, Hertfordshire, England.)

human body and comments, "Only in very simple organisms, notably transparent ones, does one principle of formation govern the body throughout."[71] The interior, then, is a separate entity, existing without a *necessary* relationship to any other aspect of reality. It is, moreover, an entirely knowable world; it relates to the scale of its occupant and is, therefore, more controllable by that occupant. Indeed, in perception and affect, it may be seen as a world apart from the exterior. This does not imply, however, that the interior of a structure cannot reflect the exterior. One of the most persuasive ways to achieve unity is to echo on the interior the basic shapes, rhythms, massing, and detail that represent the exterior. This is what Hodgden refers to when he says that it would be conceptually elegant for the two aspects of architecture to use one composition system for the building's interior and exterior.[72]

In Hodgden's view, it is not possible simply to make an interior over into an exterior, but it is possible to conceive an exterior composed of interior-like elements such as courtyards, porches, balconies, and overhangs. These may be regarded as *transitional* exterior spaces;[73] a similar process could occur in the reverse as well, so that the two aspects merge into one another. Such occurs in the work of Frank Lloyd Wright. This is interesting, as it suggests that in addition to an interior reflecting certain exterior elements (scarcely a new idea), the exterior might express interior character and, in particular, the character of room-like space. This idea is, of course, derived from Wright himself. In 1943 he wrote:

> In integral architecture the **room-space itself must come through**. The room must be seen as architecture, or we have no architecture. We have no longer an outside as outside. We have no longer an outside and an inside as two separate things. Now the outside may come inside, and the inside may and does go outside. They are of each other."[74]

In this process, Wright employed such unifying techniques as the pronounced (and ubiquitous) linear elements that occur both inside and out, and shapes that echo each other's proportion.

Herbert Read refers to the ". . . principle of spatio-plastic unity as the distinctive characteristic of architecture as an art.''[75] But he believes that this unity, however much an ideal, is rarely achieved. Of interest is his tentative attribution of success to Frank Lloyd Wright. He quotes, for example, from Mies van der Rohe's address to the Armour Institute in 1938, where he proclaimed Wright ''a master-builder,'' in whose hands a ''. . . genuine organic architecture flowered.''[76] Read thus suggests that Wright may have realized in his organic architecture, the spatio-plastic unity that Read believes so critical. Wright tried to achieve spatial continuity by using one system of space-defining elements. And in this drive to unify interior with exterior, he granted the interior much distinction. In an interview in 1956, Wright commented on his design approach for Unity Temple:

> I think that was about the first time when the interior space began to come through as the reality of the building. . . . You will notice that features were arranged against that interior space allowing a sense of it to come to the beholder where ever he happened to be. And I have been working on that thesis for a long time because it was dawning on me that when I built that building that the reality of the building did not consist in the walls and the roof, but in the **space within** to be lived in.[77]

Yet, there is little sensory experience of the exterior from within Unity Temple (Fig 2.18). The unity lies in Wright's treatment of shapes, line, and textures as abstract elements occurring both inside and out and, perhaps most significant, in our memory of them. That is, while elements are repeated in each aspect, there is little spatial continuity from interior to exterior except as we thus conceive it. Such close relationships as he refers to developed later in his residential designs, such as Robie House (Fig 9.2). But even in these designs there is a profound sense of protective enclosure; the openings to the exterior tend to be small, and the lure of the hearth primordial.

The point has already been made that the interior and exterior are separate worlds; yet, they must be coherent. They must be more than contiguous but not necessarily continuous—just *coherent*. The second point is that if there is coherence, it is likely the result of *memory*. That is, we remember the exterior of the building and, therefore, see the interior spaces in relation to

2.17

Glass House—New Canaan, Connecticut; *Philip Johnson (1949)*
This striking residence represents an effort to reconcile interior space and exterior massing. Nathan Knobler observes, ''The walls of glass do not act to isolate its exterior from its interior space. The transparent walls give the viewer a hint of the rectangular form of the building as the reflections in the glass delay his perception of the interior. The flat plane of the roof and the supporting columns also work to define the form, but it is the interior volume which dominates the conception of this structure.''[6] (Photo by: Ezra Stoller. Copyright Esto, Mamaroneck, N.Y. All rights reserved.)

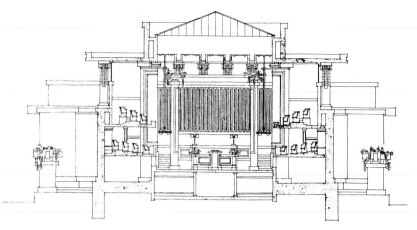

2.18

Unity Temple—Oak Park, Illinois; *Frank Lloyd Wright (1904–6)*
Unity Temple was one of Frank Lloyd Wright's first major commissions. Its modest budget forced him to choose between interior and exterior concerns; that he chose to emphasize the interior was a tribute to his understanding of his client's needs. The interior is an open multilevel place of gathering, with warm woodwork and an overhead lighting system. The exterior, in contrast, is austere and constructed of the situationally unusual medium of concrete. (Courtesy: Ernst Wasmuth Verlag, Tübingen, Germany.)

it, provided the designer has not made that impossible. Indeed, there may be no reason for such space to be continuous, only that it should avoid disconcerting contradiction. Arnheim contends, for example, that there is a certain pleasure in unpredictability. He says, "The frankly informative appearance of buildings whose inside holds few spatial secrets offers little of the teasing richness and sophisticated complexity found in architectural styles that deviate from such elementary parallelism."[78] He goes on to note that such an approach would reflect little of the architect's dramatic struggle in planning from the inside and the outside at the same time.

But does the interior need refer to the exterior at all? That is, could the interior be wholly discrete from the exterior, as long as there exists a *zone of transition*? In the residential building, that zone might be the vestibule, the quasi-public entry to the Roman domus. In the contemporary office block, that function is already served by the lobby and elevator core. The lobby has customarily served to restate the image of the building in the interior (although not on a usual interior scale). The elevator cabs further diminish the scale and add the element of time-passage, easing the transition to the private spaces within. The stipulation of coherency might thus be satisfied by combining transition and memory, provided the movement is spatially and symbolically unified.

The problem is, as suggested above, particularly acute with large office (or apartment) blocks, where size mitigates such coherence. In his *Delirious New York*, Rem Koolhaas states:

> Buildings have both an interior and an exterior. In Western architecture there has been the humanistic assumption that it is desirable to establish a moral relationship between the two, whereby the exterior makes certain revelations about the interior that the interior corroborates. . . . But mathematically, the interior volume of three-dimensional objects increases in cubed leaps and the containing envelope only by squared increments: less and less surface has to represent more and more interior activity. Beyond a certain critical mass the relationship is stressed beyond the breaking point. . . .[79]

And in particularly massive and dense urban areas (such as Manhattan), designers have often dropped the very idea of coherency in favor of a disconnected interior world (Fig 2.19).

Unity can, therefore, never be literal, nor is it necessarily desirable. What is desirable is that the interior and exterior be considered in relation to one another, whether the designer ultimately relates or contrasts them. In this "meeting" of the two aspects, much dynamism occurs; and it is this dy-

2.19

Downtown Athletic Club (seventh floor)— New York; *Starrett & Van Vleck and Barnet Phillips (1930)*
The seventh floor of this building was transformed into a golf course that uses aspects of English landscape, including trees, grass, and a stream. Koolhaas comments that "The interior golf course is at the same time obliteration and preservation: having been extirpated by the Metropolis, nature is now resurrected inside the Skyscraper as merely one of its infinite layers. . . ."[7] (Courtesy: Barnet Phillips, IV.)

namism that strongly suggests that architecture is not limited to what we can apprehend at a single moment. The contemporary designer Robert Venturi states:

> Designing from the outside in, as well as the inside out, creates necessary tensions, which help make architecture. Since the inside is different from the outside, the wall—the point of change—becomes an architectural event. Architecture occurs at the meeting of interior and exterior forces of use and space.[80]

Thus form must make apprehensible to the end user a program that uses mass, space, and materials—to enable a utilitarian function, itself refined in light of a broad range of concerns. In that pursuit, form will have manipulated visual characteristics in accordance with a series of organizational principles to devise a perceptual reality.

The Vocabulary of Design

3

Perceptual Reality

While design principles work in all dimensions, they are frequently used as a two-dimensional language that permits communication—and our own understanding of that communication in the works of others. The better the manipulation of this language, the greater the latitude possible in creative activity. But reality and its representation are not the same thing, so that differentiation between the drawing of the object and its physical actuality becomes crucial.

All designers work with drawn information of one type or another, but the problem is particularly complex for those designing three-dimensionally. This is because line is the element designers most depend on, given its ability to delineate the vital characteristics of the object or space being created. Line, however, exists only as a two-dimensional convenience, a way of conceptualizing a form problem or communicating information, with no actual counterpart in reality. That this is not always clear may be seen from a careful reading of Kandinsky's *Point and Line to Plane,* where he states, ''The use of line in *nature* is an exceedingly frequent one. The line appears in nature in countless phenomena; in the mineral, plant and animal worlds.''[1] He illustrates this point with simple diagrams, using them as examples of line in nature. But the things of nature exist in three dimensions, and all of his examples have mass and volume, albeit small. They are, therefore, not examples of line, but of things *linear.* Indeed, nature abounds with linear, or line-like, objects, sometimes so persuasively linear that it is easy to represent them in a drawing with simple line alone. While such abstraction is common, the reverse—the stipulation in line of objects meant to be built in three-dimensions—presents different problems. Line, after all, is typically used to describe the meeting of two planes or the outermost edge of structural detail, situations that are not linear in fact. Line is filled with risk in the sense that it may represent visual fact in the designer's mind but not convey that fact to anyone else.

Thus if there is one language of visual literacy, that language has *dimensionalized* aspects. While the perceptual nuances of these visual elements differ in dimension, they are alike in kind; they include line, shape, value, texture, color, and the methods used to organize them. These elements and methods depend, in turn, on fundamental attributes of sensory perception, attributes that are operative in all dimensions. In *A Primer of Visual Literacy,* Donis A. Dondis comments:

> Composition is primarily influenced by the diversity of forces implicit in the psychophysiological factors of human perception. They are givens on which the visual communicator can depend. Awareness of visual substance is perceived not only through seeing but through all of the senses, and it provides not isolated individual pieces of information but whole interactive units, totalities which through sight and perception we assimilate directly and with great speed.''[2]

But as became clear in the analysis of perceptual systems, the situation is more complex than that. That is, while human responses to visual data are usually predictable, their dependence on individual, and highly acculturated, personalities suggests that those responses will not be uniform. The presence of line and value may remind one of childhood associations (from sidewalk graffiti to dark corners), shapes may be culturally or personally valued, and color may reflect our socio-economic aspirations. Every designer's audience has a perceptual reality influenced by past experience, socio-cultural training, and particular emotional makeup; it is this diversity that accounts for markedly differing responses to architecture and art generally. This does not mean that there are no predictable aspects of design, only that the situation is more complex than first appears.

Design Elements

While designers usually agree on the character of the visual elements, the relative importance granted any particular element as a design tool depends on the individual designer. In *Point and Line to Plane,* Kandinsky postulates two levels of ''elements,'' basic and secondary. The point, he states, is the primary (basic) fact of the visual world and, as visual lines lead to the center, the ultimate stasis:

> At the beginning of this chapter . . . the point was defined as a concept linked with the idea of silence of shorter or longer duration. The **point,** as such, makes a certain **statement** which is organically bound up with the utmost restraint. **The point is the innermost concise form.** It is turned inwards. Its tension is, even in its last analysis, **concentric.**[3]

Points treated en masse can, of course, be combined into various dynamic compositional relationships, but as an entity, or in regular arrangement, the point has tended to serve as a centralized controlling factor in design. This perceptual control is referred to by the term ''focal point,'' the device that demands and retains our attention (Fig 3.1). Use of a particular point can identify the ideological center of a composition, indicate its spatial parameters, and direct the axis of view and movement. Kandinsky speaks of point-line-plane in two-dimensional terms, making specific reference to their use in painting and the graphic arts. He notes, however, that they are applicable to sculpture and architecture as well, although he does not develop this line of argument.

The point serves also in the delineation of the ''absolute''; that is, it promotes a sense of profound calm and equilibrium that negates the possibility of sudden change. Such attitudes underlie most of our assumptions about our religious, political, and cultural institutions, and it is not surprising to see the point used as both an interior and exterior device to suggest absolute harmony (Fig 3.2). Nor does that harmony have to refer only to public structures and events; the private dining room has long served as

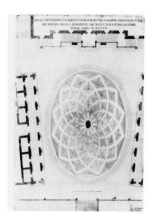

3.1

Campidoglio—Rome; *Michelangelo (1538–39); Plan drawn by Lafreri (1567) and Perspective (1569); after Michelangelo*
Sculpture has often been used to symbolically embody civic virtues, usually in an architectural setting provided for that purpose; such was the role ascribed to the equestrian statue of Marcus Aurelius. The statue's importance required a centralized form, but its orientation and rectangular pedestal were axial. This led Michelangelo to ingeniously select an oval shape, which satisfied both needs. By means of a radiating pavement pattern, the buildings were integrated into a unified composition in which the façades act as containing walls, thus creating an "outdoor room" that revolves around a "point." (Plan—courtesy: Avery Architectural and Fine Arts Library, Columbia University in the City of New York: Perspective—from: *Éléments et Théorie de l'Architecture, J. Guadet.)*

intimate and honored gathering place for the family, a "focal point" of daily life (Fig 3.3).

Kandinsky's view of the point is complex and multifaceted; his notion of line is poetic. He sees line as the energizing of a point so that it bursts forth—hence line is dynamic. Kandinsky describes the process:

> The geometric line is an invisible thing. It is the track made by the moving point; that is, its product. It is created by movement—specifically through the destruction of the intense self-contained repose of the point. Here, the leap out of the static into the dynamic occurs. The line is, therefore, the **greatest antithesis** to the pictorial proto-element—the point.[4]

This is a far cry from the mathematician's static definition of line as the result of a simple extension of a point, or the connecting of two points. Kandinsky goes on to explain that line, dependent on the point, is a secondary element, but this seems a primarily theoretical valuation. For indeed, it is line, the ultimately expressive device, that has been most exploited by designers in both two and three dimensions (Fig 3.4). Line is unique in its ability to express particular information (as in plans and elevations), subjective emotion (through manipulation of time and space), and structural definitions (as in the surface of walls).

Line may be conceived as having four distinct qualities: direction, movement, dimension, and duration (time). *Direction* itself tends to fall into three modes of existence, horizontal, vertical, and diagonal. These, in turn, have been granted psycho-aesthetic attributes, ranging from horizontal "repose" to diagonal "activity." In his *Principles of Art History,* Heinrich Wölfflin seeks to define the aesthetic and cultural character of the Renaissance in part through an examination of its compositional dependence on vertical and horizontal elements in that period's art and architecture. He hypothesizes that this dependence was a direct reflection of the sociopolitical facts of Renaissance life; he contrasted this with the Baroque love of strong diagonals characterizing the Copernican world-view that followed. Wölfflin's system, which also took into account such factors as value-dependence and form closure, has become something of a curiosity, but the underlying assumptions about line-direction and psychosocial factors remain part of our vocabulary.

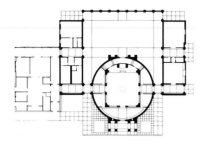

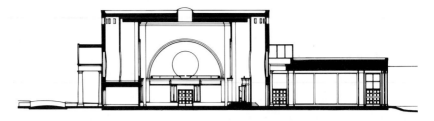

3.2

North Shore Congregation Israel—Glencoe, Illinois; *Hammond, Beeby and Babka (1983)*
The congregation requested a design for a place of worship that would be inward looking and have a sense of intimacy, warmth, and community. The sanctuary, formed of a circle in a square, provides an introverted space with a double emphasis on the center. The center point was marked by the layout of the flooring, and by the Star of David chandelier suspended from the oculus, the traditional aperture providing communication with the heavens. (Courtesy: Hammond Beeby and Babka Incorporated, Chicago.)

Line also possesses *movement,* if only the movement we bring to it culturally. That is, even a nondifferentiated horizontal line tends to be read from left to right due to the language structures in Western culture. And due to a visual legacy from ancient-oriental cultures, we read vertical and diagonal lines from bottom to top. Such habits underlie our notions of cognitive and visual perspective and ensure that even neutral lines serve as spatial indicators. When that line is enhanced, such aspects of movement become persuasive indeed. Together, direction and movement in line grant *dimension* through the definition of multiple planes, either by extension or implication. This dimensionality is particularly convincing when line is combined with the various devices used in optical perspective. There is, finally, the issue of *duration,* or time. Kandinsky believed that time was readily discernible in line, indeed that "length is a concept of time."[5] The time required, however, to follow a curved line is longer than for a straight one (even when identical in length); and the more convoluted the line, the more time it takes. It stands to reason, then, that line can be used to alter one's sense of time passage, and this is as true physically as it is representationally (Fig 3.5). Kandinsky also addresses the issue of plane, the basic unit upon whose surface information—point and line, for example—is placed. His definition is again two-dimensional; this view may be adapted by simply tilting the plane into the horizontal dimension when necessary. The result is manipulatively more complex, but not essentially different from Kandinsky's view of the matter (Fig 3.6). As his argument develops, his concern for plane is replaced by an involvement in shape, and it is shape that ultimately most influences our sense of space.

3.3

Dining-room at Cranbrook—Michigan; *Eliel Saarinen (1928)*
The idea of center, or focal point, is reinforced by the recessed dome and round chandelier. The tabletop is faced with a radial veneer pattern, and its octagonal base rests on a carpet whose pattern is directed towards the compositional center. The shape of the table is used to imply an equality of those gathered, and the total effect of such a setting is to hermetically close off the area without the actual use of physical constraints. (Source: R.M. Kliment & Frances Halsband Architects, New York.)

Shape-types

In addition to placing point and line upon plane, Kandinsky also placed plane upon plane or, more properly, shape upon ground-plane. He concentrated on geometric planes but observed that as such shapes become increasingly complex, they tend to be curved, or wavelike, resulting in the circle. We need not pursue this further, except to note that in this line of reasoning, Kandinsky has suggested the division into geometric (regular) and biomorphic (irregularly curved) shapes. These terms are a convenience only; obviously, curved shapes can be geometric, and straight-edged shapes occur in nature. As a practical matter, however, this distinction between geometry and biology serves to group design intentions according to method and outlook. As with line, specific attributes are given to shape-types, with the geometric granted a higher status. In his discussion of Old Kingdom Egyptian architecture, George Lasser states:

> The Universe, created by the god as a rational and therefore mathematical conception, the highest manifestation of divine wisdom, is imitated, in a mystic way, by the sacred building and its precinct which thus become a reflection of divine order, harmony, and beauty. Geometry, in a specific and circumscribed sense, has to govern the design, and in turn such geometry is holy by virtue of its power to please and attract the godhead.[6]

Nor is such approval of geometric shape limited to the admirers of religious architecture; Le Corbusier comments that, ''Geometry is our greatest creation and we are enthralled by it.''[7]

Biomorphic shape, by contrast, is considered dynamic, unstable, and eccentric (in descending hierarchial order). As such architects seldom use it, although graphic artists and furniture designers do. Even in such seemingly biomorphic structures as Notre Dame du Haut at Ronchamp, Le Corbusier's

A

B

3.4

(A) Exercise in Line Study; *M. Debus (1928);* **(B) Illustration of Line;** *Kandinsky (1926)*
(A) A response to one of the many assignments that Itten gave his students (''line exercises in a square character''). Itten states, ''To create the feeling for the regularity of a form character, I set exercises in which writing and formal representation were developed in the character of the square, the triangle, or the circle.''[1] (B) One of Kandinsky's many studies involving the expressive power of line in its many guises. (Copyright 1991 ARS, N.Y. / ADAGP.)

3.5

The Staatsgalerie New Building—Stuttgart; *Stirling, Wilford, & Associates (1984)*
A relaxed atmosphere is immediately apparent in the entry hall, with its undulating, and highly linear, green-mullioned glass wall. That issues relating to the passage of time were paramount is evidenced in the interior, where Stirling used a parade of rooms, as opposed to free-flowing space. The interior lines (mullions and their shadows, light fixtures, etc.) do lead inward and suggest enclosure. (Photo by: Timothy Hursley, The Arkansas Office, Little Rock, Ark.)

A

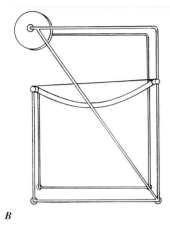

B

3.6

Seconda Armchair; *Mario Botta (1983)*
While this chair is a combination of point, line, and plane, arranged spatially, the situation is complicated by the observer's ability to shift viewing direction. That is, when the chair is viewed obliquely *(A)*, the plane of the seat becomes immediately obvious, while the "point" represented by the backrest ceases to function as such. When viewed in elevation *(B)*, the chair becomes a study in point and line, with the seat appearing in a linear capacity. All the shapes of plane geometry are present: circle, square, rectangle, and triangle. And in their three-dimensional aspect, so are the cylinder and cubic solid. (Drawn by: J. Malnar.)

underlying geometry is clearly evident. That is, the "free curves" of the walls are actually carefully projected geometric shapes (Fig 5.9). Antonio Gaudí represents one of the few exceptions to this pattern; indeed, his Casa Batlló may be regarded as an outstanding example of biomorphic design. Its very structure seems alive, even primal, in its elasticity and total disdain for the constraints of structural limitation. As such, it stands in sharp contrast to mainstream rationalism (Fig 3.7).

Choice of shape-type is, in either case, related to function through the medium of form. And for the designer, shape may seem the most important aspect of the design-process. The relationship of shape to function is, however, fairly open, in the sense that only rarely is a shape-type completely inappropriate to a given function, and form is seldom constrained by the relative availability of shape-types. In *Dimensions,* Charles Moore notes the distinction between shape and form:

> Form, as we have been told, follows function. It delimits an arena in which things can take—that is, be given—shape. Spoons, for instance, are normally devices with a concave surface for holding liquids, with a handle attached to facilitate movement of the liquid and to provide protection for human hands in case the liquid is hot. There are billions of possible shapes a spoon can take . . . . The choice of shapes will be based on various cultural and personal standards.[8]

This is true because, as noted earlier, function exists as a series of abstract needs, and there are many ways to satisfy those needs. Moore goes on to state that there are three *measures of shape,* those commonly shared (the archetypal), those shared intraculturally (the cultural), and those that are a product of our memories (the personal).[9] He suggests that *archetypal* shapes are primordial in nature, arising from the basic human need to understand and order our world; such a desire to seek out these underlying relationships may be found in virtually all societies. The *cultural* preference for particular shapes is peculiar to a specific locale or period—although the design of any period may refer to a previous one, as in the nineteenth-century evocation of the Gothic, or the current reference to the Classical. And finally, there are *personal* preferences, usually based on psychological factors only barely understood by us, who possess them. Taken together, these suggest an overwhelming number of considerations in our perceptions of shapes. As a solution, Moore suggests to the designer that "One useful part of the response is to render unto the mind's eye what is the mind's eye's, but to take care that the images do not interfere with flexibility of human use—to keep, as it were, the myth up off the floor."[10] On a more prosaic level, while shape is a critical aspect of form, it remains only one of the elements that form may use.

Shape has tended to dominate research in human perception, perhaps because it lends itself to the study of simple ordering. It has been observed, for example, that the mind more readily apprehends (and comprehends) regular shapes in the smallest configuration than more numerous complex shapes. And this leads to still another of the more intriguing perceptual principles, that of *form-constancy.* Studies in Gestalt psychology show that the mind suggests closure of shapes (especially geometric ones) even when presented with incomplete data in an irregular formation. The properties granted any configuration include symmetry, regularity, and continuity; and this is true not only within a particular shape, but between shapes. That is, when the shapes are multiple, they tend to be grouped on the basis of *proximity* and *similarity.* There is, therefore, little chance that shapes will be observed randomly, even if that is the designer's intention. A corollary to this is that composition (or arrangement of shapes) would likewise be stipulated by the viewer in the absence of design intention.

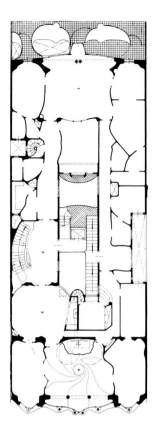

Texture and Value

The elements of texture and value are interdependent, even though distinct in definition. That is because texture cannot be *seen* without value change, and the prime cause of value is texture. There are at least three ways of viewing texture: as *actual texture,* which is tactile, whether real or artificial; as *implied texture,* in which a surface of one sort is made to resemble another—usually as a matter of economy or cleverness; and as an *invention,* using familiar shapes in restated patterns to create a unique appearance. In any case, texture occupies an interesting place among the visual elements due to its ability to elicit viewer response on several levels. It is, first, accessible to the physical sensation of touch, and second, can suggest real data through reproduction of its outward characteristics. Finally, it promotes immediate sensory response through visual appearance alone; consider that certain surfaces are inviting to the touch and others are repulsive. This is texture's psychological dimension, the power of cultural and personal association to grant specific attributes to types of textures. And recent evidence in psychology suggests that the visual sensation of texture may be more important than the tactile one, as Arnheim makes clear in *Art and Visual Perception:*

> . . . there is no doubting the effective interaction of touch and sight at all stages of human development. But the priority of touch or "motor behavior" is another matter. It seems to be a mere assumption, unsupported by evidence. The child psychologist Arnold Gesell asserted years ago that "ocular prehension precedes manual."[11]

Whichever comes first, it is obvious that the senses of sight and touch, when taken together, enable a person to perceive spatial characteristics. The psychologist J.J. Gibson commented on the affinity of vision and touch, and concluded that the flow of sense impressions is reinforced when the subject uses both senses.[12] In his work *The Hidden Dimension* Edward T. Hall notes the significance of active touch, a significance largely lost on designers. That is, textured surfaces both on and in buildings seldom reflect conscious

3.7

Casa Batlló—Barcelona, Spain; *Antoni Gaudí (1905–7)*
The existing structure of what was a typical apartment building, did not restrict Gaudi from applying his theoretical ideas when doing this remodeling job. The indefinite "yielding" quality is brought about by the elimination of the right angle corner and the use of undulating line. The spatial result, evident in the plan, has an enclosing, cavelike quality. In this dining room irregular line and shape are emphasized in the doors and windows; these are both present in the freestanding furniture, where the line creates a tendonlike quality in the legs and arm supports, and the shape surfaces in the material of the back, armrest, and seat. (Photo—courtesy: The Museum of Modern Art, New York; Plan—source: *Gaudí: His Life, His Theories, His Work,* César Martinell. Published by The MIT Press. Copyright 1975 by Editorial Blume, Barcelona.)

3.8

Imperial Hotel—Tokyo; *Frank Lloyd Wright (1922)*
One of Wright's major concerns was the joining of interior and exterior; to create continuity, the exterior building materials of brick and native lava stone were continued into the large public lobby space. As the guests moved to private intimate areas, a substitution was made from these bold rough textures to smooth flat textures. The three-story public lobby had the horizontal line of its balconies articulated with a heavy geometric ornamented banding. In contrast to the coarse, heavy materials, the private guest-rooms are trimmed with a flat, light wood trim. (Lobby—courtesy: Frank Lloyd Wright Archives, Taliesin West; Guest-room—courtesy: Frank Lloyd Wright Home and Studio Foundation, Oak Park, Ill.)

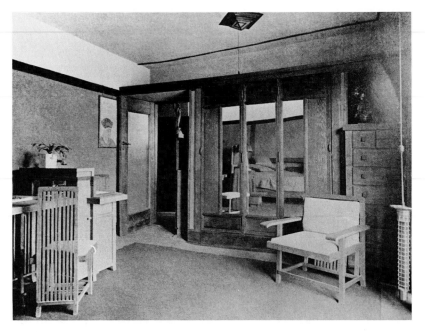

decisions made with psychological or social awareness; thus our urban environment provides few opportunities to ". . . build a kinesthetic repertoire of spatial experiences."[13] Hall suggests that this need is important, as human beings tend to synthesize experience at certain points, that humans learn while they see, and what they learn in turn influences what they see.[14] This, he feels, may account for the high level of spatial sensitivity in certain cultures, particularly in the Orient. And he credits much of Wright's success with the Imperial Hotel to his unusual sensitivity to the textures of interior materials (Fig 3.8).

It is therefore interesting to note that Steen Eiler Rasmussen, in *Experiencing Architecture,* similarly praises Wright for his sensitivity to structural materials in Wright's design for Fallingwater at Bear Run (Fig 10.5)—even though he criticizes him in virtually every other thing. Rasmussen also expresses approval for the program of the Bauhaus, with its experimental methods of architectural education. These methods involved learning through experience:

> By recording their impressions of the various materials they worked with, the students gathered a compendium of valuable information for future use. The tactile sense was trained in experiments with textures systematically arranged according to degree of coarseness. By running their fingers over the materials again and again, the students were finally able to sense a sort of musical scale of textural values.[15]

It should be noted, however, that texture used on the exterior would probably not be perceived in quite the same way as on the interior. The scale of the textured surface would seem larger and, hence, coarser in the limited space of a room. Thus concrete, which appears smooth on exterior mass, would seem rough and confining as a boundary of interior volume, where the effects of kinesthetic feedback are particularly influential.

An especially interesting aspect of texture relates to its dependence on value, the continuum between light and dark, to reveal the surface of a textured surface. As value depends on a light source, the source's angle of incidence is directly responsible for the *perceived intensity* of texture; the smaller the angle, the bolder the effect. It is the photographer's axiom that architectural drama is best achieved either early or late in the day, as surfaces photographed at midday appear flat and characterless. While the exterior of a building relies on sunlight for textural effects, the interior uses controlled lighting. As a rule, a single light source enhances dimensionality, and multiple light sources flatten shapes (Fig 3.9). Rasmussen refers to this perceptual effect in his prescription for light sources:

> A more or less concentrated light—that is, light from one or more sources falling in the same direction—is the best in which to see form and texture. At the same time it emphasizes the closed character of a room. Light alone can create the effect of enclosed space. It follows, therefore, that if you wish to create an effect of openness you cannot employ concentrated light.[16]

While value-change may occur on relatively undetailed surfaces, it is usually associated with masses of dimensional detail. Value may, if the shapes are massive enough, yield highly plastic spatial effects; if relatively flat and detailed, such space tends to the decorative. In either case, value, as seen in interior or exterior façades, has until only recently been used by designers as part of the architectural statement. Value's power as a design tool is immense. In the past it was valued for its dramatic capacity, particularly in civic and religious structures (Fig 3.10). S. Ivo, with its concave and convex interior walls, serves as an extreme example of value-change that enhances the structure's movement and drama. Value was often used when spiritual, mystical, or meditative qualities were sought, particularly those involving time-passage (Fig 3.11). Artificial light, on the other hand, negates the shifting effects that occur throughout the day. A programmatic task orientation has produced scientific information on efficient light levels, but the study of affective value has been largely ignored. (Notably, it is stage designers who seem to understand the importance of value in developing atmosphere.) Rather than developing pools of light and areas of privacy, interiors tend to be flooded with undifferentiated light. The intent was to enhance the sense of openness, improve efficiency and safety, and promote a sense of equality among employees; but the result has been a sameness based on economics.

This obsession to light interiors to the maximum technically possible, is partly a Western one. In his delightful book *In Praise of Shadows,* Jun'ichiro Tanizaki describes the origin of the Japanese house:

B

3.9

(A) **Interior, Little Thakeham;** *Edwin Lutyens (1902); (B)* **Apartment Interior— London;** *John Pawson (1986)*
In the interior by Lutyens *(A)*, all the architectural elements such as door openings, fireplace, and balcony, are framed with projected ornament. The effect is a granting of importance to each of these elements as an "event," and an overall spatial and textural unity based on value change. The south-facing windows are treated to allow a maximum of strong, directed, light to enter the room. In contrast, the minimalist space by Pawson *(B)* treats all surfaces equally, and is correspondingly devoid of ornament. The essentially flat shapes that result offer, therefore, only a minimum of surface to create value gradation. To further the value reduction, louvered blinds are used at each window to allow only a carefully modulated light inside. *([A]* courtesy: *Country Life* (copyright), August 1909; *[(B)]* courtesy: John Pawson, London. Photo by: Ian Dobbie.)

A

3.10

S. Ivo della Sapienza—Rome; *Francesco Borromini (1642)*
The most notable aspect of this church is its central plan, a star-hexagon, which is entirely covered by a dome that reflects the plan's shape. That is, the dome continues the star-hexagon in the vertical dimension with an undulating convex-concave rhythm that finally climaxes in an oculus upon which the lantern stands. The light effects are dramatic, depending as much on the dome's interior surface as on the directionality of the light. (Source: Marburg/Art Resource.)

In making for ourselves a place to live, we first spread a parasol to throw a shadow on the earth, and in the pale light of the shadow we put together a house. . . . The quality that we call beauty . . . must always grow from the realities of life, and our ancestors, forced to live in dark rooms, presently came to discover beauty in shadows, ultimately to guide shadows towards beauty's ends. And so it has come to be that the beauty of a Japanese room depends on a variation of shadows, heavy shadows against light shadows—it has nothing else . . . . This was the genius of our ancestors, that by cutting off the light from this empty space they imparted to the world of shadows that formed there a quality of mystery and depth superior to that of any wall painting or ornament.[17]

Tanizaki rails against the habituated use of electric lighting systems which, in 1933, were new enough to face much conservative opposition. The novelist does not call for complete rejection of the technology, only for an appreciation of its negative effect on most Japanese things, designed, after all, for a world of shadows (Fig 3.12). One can empathize with him when he concludes, ". . . perhaps we may be allowed at least one mansion where we can turn off the electric lights and see what it is like without them."[18]

Color and Light

The study of color is enormously complex and made even more so by its variety of systems. These include aesthetic, psychological, physiological, associative, and symbolic factors, and each has its own method and purpose. Color has an extraordinary power to move us emotionally, leading the painter Emil Nolde to exclaim:

Colors, the materials of the painter; colors in their own lives, weeping and laughing, dream and bliss, hot and sacred, like love songs and the erotic, like songs and glorious chorals! Colors in vibration, pealing like silver bells and clanging like bronze bells, proclaiming happiness, passion and love, soul, blood, and death.[19]

While few designers have spoken so passionately about color, they have long recognized its importance to the design process. This is a small wonder, since few elements affect design as decisively as color. Not only does

3.11

Kimbell Art Museum—Fort Worth, Texas; *Louis I. Kahn (1966–72)*
Noted for his teaching, Kahn's students remember the clarity of such statements as, "The sun never knew how wonderful it was until it shone on the wall of a building," and architecture is ". . . a harmony of spaces in light."[2] In this building, the concrete vault is split at its apex, allowing light to enter and be distributed by a system of stainless steel reflectors. Controlled lighting is obtained by a track-lighting system, but it cannot compete with the primal drawing power of the linear beam of natural light sweeping over the wood floor during the day. In this way the light marks the slow passage of time. (Photo by: Marc Treib, Berkeley.)

it qualitatively alter all other elements, but it may serve as its own subject (i.e., exert influence through its innate qualities). This was not always seen to be so; Leonardo da Vinci believed that light's purpose was to reveal form and that color functioned only locally. Simply put, color served only in a descriptive role, as in the red apple, green grass, etc. This position assumes that an object's color is inherent, which has had implications for the materials used in architectural design. By the Baroque period, this opinion had changed, as seen in its painting, decorative arts, and interior surfaces. Indeed, Rembrandt's conception of color was that it might assume an independent existence revealed by light, a common theme throughout the ninteenth century. In our own century, the sculptor Chryssa said that light, color, and form are essentially contiguous, a sentiment distantly echoed by Emilio Ambasz in *The Architecture of Luis Barragán:*

> The extraordinary emotional effect of Barragán's compositions and the strong sensual qualities of his materials and colors cannot be guessed from his drawings or plans. The architectural richness of Barragán's dramatically sober architecture is based on a few constructive elements bound together by a mystical feeling, an austerity exalted by the glory of his brilliant colors. They pervade all the interstices of space, at once binding and separating artifact and nature. Paint is for him like a garment the wall puts on to relate to its surroundings.[20]

In a manner that seems related as much to the graphic arts as to architecture, Barragán freely applies his color to interior and exterior (Plate 2).

Color has also been widely investigated by psychologists. This has led to discoveries of the psychophysiological attributes of color, as well as an awareness of its socioeconomic dimensions. Such studies have sometimes been misinterpreted, leading to the kinds of assumptions that underlie commercial ventures like cosmetic palettes and "color coordinated" clothing. The psychologist Deborah T. Sharpe, in *The Psychology of Color and Design,* has referred to the writings of "color consultants" as having ". . . for the most part included myth, purloined scientific works . . . and speculation."[21] In short, while many color studies have been conducted by psychologists, few of them could be practically applied as they stand. Indeed, many data on color still need to be gathered and analyzed before a meth-

3.12

Interior of Japanese House
The interior of a typical Japanese house, with a highly directed and singular light source, creates a world of translucency and soft shadows in which pottery glazes and lacquered ware gleam as they reflect the few beams of light. (Source: *Japanese Homes and Their Surroundings,* Edward S. Morse.)

odology can be formulated, although there have been attempts to do so in the past half century. In part this may reflect what Dr. Rikard Küller referred to in 1981 as " . . . a gap between research on one hand and practice on the other, the infamous application gap."[22] But it may equally reflect a lack of color study as it specifically affects design, as well as some uncertainty about the role color should play in design.

Color studies begin with the interaction of light and color, for without light we would observe no color, shape, or space. But our appreciation of light transcends the physical, as Arnheim makes clear; "Even psychologically it remains one of the most fundamental and powerful of human experiences. . . ."[23] Our understanding of light and color was greatly aided by Sir Isaac Newton's discovery that white light contains all visible color. We see colors because wavelengths of light vary; high-energy light (400 on a nanometer scale) appears violet, and low-energy light (approximately 700 nm) appears red. We see all light as white, except when standing in a space lit with colored light, either through colored glass windows or due to particular lighting elements. Most surfaces have the capacity to absorb particular wavelengths; those not absorbed are visible to the onlooker. That is, we believe things have colors because they absorb certain light energies and, being opaque, reflect the energy that is left as color. But what *we* mean by a particular color term may be quite different from what others mean. Sharpe points out that while the eye has the theoretical capacity to discriminate millions of different colors, there are only 150 discernible wavelengths in the spectrum. Also, the average person can, with reliability, name only a dozen or so, and even these change with individual mood and association. In *Colour: Why the World Isn't Grey,* Hazel Rossotti points out:

> But we must recognize . . . that colour is a **sensation,** produced in the brain, by the light which enters the eye; and that while a sensation of a particular colour is usually triggered off by our eye receiving light of a particular composition, many other physiological and psychological factors also contribute.[24]

These psychological and physiological factors, while open to interpretation, may determine our final perception of color. If so, any attempt to "scientifically" define a hue must be suspect. For instance, while the Commission Internationale de l'Eclairage (CIE) has devised a most accurate system based on spectrophotometric measurements of color, such a system cannot predict individual human perception of a given color.

If the transmission of light represents one aspect of color, its reception by the human eye represents the other. As light strikes the retina, the light-receptive area at the back of the eye, it is recorded by rods (brightness receptors) and cones (color receptors). In bright light, the cones are working, but as light dims, our color perception gradually decreases (beginning with low-energy hues) until there is too little light to see color at all. Then the rods take over, allowing a full range "night vision" in value alone. Curiously, we can accurately judge similarity of colors in different light intensities, a phenomenon known as *color constancy.* And, in certain circumstances, color has been "seen" in the absence of light; that is, electrical and mechanical stimulation of the optic nerve can induce color sensation, as can various chemical changes.[25] It is even possible that touch alone can discriminate parts of the electromagnetic spectrum, including color; this is known as dermo-optical perception, a theory based on radiant energy.[26]

Other ways of sensing color via hearing, taste, and smell have also been reported; collectively, these alternative means are known as synaesthetic experiences. Indeed, color sensation can actually be induced with black and white imagery alone (Fig 3.13). Perhaps most problematic for the designer

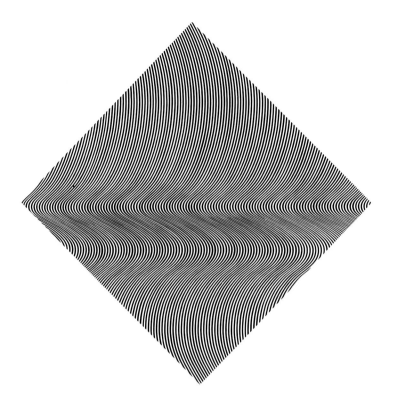

3.13

*Crest (Emulsion on board 65½″ × 65½″);
Bridget Riley (1968)*
Riley is well known for linear paintings that
suggest warps in the surface of the plane. In
addition to such spatial illusions, her work
also has a tendency to induce color sensation
in the viewer. To "see" this color, one has
only to stare at the center of the painting long
enough for the eyes to tire of trying to focus
on the lines; which colors, and the waiting
period, both depend on a series of personal
variables. (Compliments: Mayor Rowan Gallery, London.)

are the afterimages composed of color complementary to the figure's color,
and the variables in expressed preference of color combinations. And the
assessment of particular colors may, in any case, change with our age,
emotional state, and socioeconomic status. Given all this, it is scarcely
surprising that so many classifying systems have arisen, some purely aesthetic and others based on information from the behavioral sciences.

The use of any system assumes some measurable qualities; color is measured in *hue* (character), *value* (brightness), and *intensity* (chromatic
purity). These are commonly measures of reflected color, which is different
from transmitted light. Thus the artist (or designer) speaks of red, blue, and
yellow as primaries, while the physicist (or lighting designer) considers red,
blue, and green as primaries. The addition of all three primaries in pigment
form yields black (or dark grey, due to impurities in the pigment). Such an
addition in light yields, as anyone familiar with a CIE "tongue diagram"
knows, white (Fig 3.14). From the pigment primaries are derived secondaries, orange, violet, and green, and so forth. And from variations in this
color wheel, coupled with alterations in value and intensity, theorists such
as Ostwald and Munsell have derived the systems we now use. But both
Ostwald and Munsell relied heavily on previous theorists; indeed, the roots
of color theory may lie in Book Two of Leon Battista Alberti's *Della Pit-
tura:*

> I should prefer that all types and every sort of colour should be seen in
> painting for the great delight and pleasure of the observer . . . so that the
> clear colours are always near other different darker colours. This contrast
> will be beautiful where the colours are clear and bright. There is a certain
> friendship of colours so that one joined with another gives dignity and
> grace. Dark colours stand among light with dignity and the light colours
> turn about among the dark. Thus, as I have said, the painter will dispose
> his colours.[27]

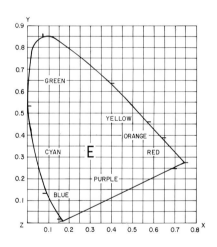

3.14

The CIE Chromaticity Diagram
The wavelengths of the pure spectral hues
are located on the perimeter of the diagram
(with the nonspectral magentas at the bottom). E—the neutral sum of all hues—is located more or less centrally, and represents
pure white light. The area given to certain
hues is disproportionately large; this is because the diagram is based on the spectral
sensitivity of the normal human eye. (Drawn
by: J. Malnar.)

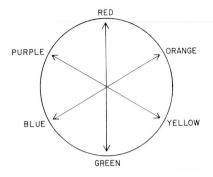

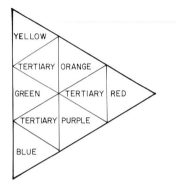

3.15

Color Wheel and Triangle; *Johann Goethe*
Goethe conceived of a simple color wheel
containing the three primaries (red-yellow-
blue) and the three secondaries. All these
colors are treated in equal measure, and lie
equidistant from each other as two triads; in
this illustration, the arrows mark the complementary pairs. He also considered alternatives to this arrangement, such as the color
triangle. In this configuration, the triangles
marked T are the tertiaries, which were made
up of the *three* surrounding hues (unlike the
color wheel, which uses only two). The color
wheel proved the more flexible of the two
systems, and the more enduring. (Drawn by:
J. Malnar.)

Alberti discusses many useful things about the discipline of painting, concluding that all painting '' . . . is made up of these three things: circum-
scription, composition, and the reception of light.''[28] The underlying theme
in his discussion of color is its interrelatedness, a common theme in Johann
Goethe's *Theory of Colours* as well:

> When the eye sees a colour it is immediately excited, and it is its nature,
> spontaneously and of necessity, at once to produce another, which with
> the original colour comprehends the whole chromatic scale. A single col-
> our excites, by a specific sensation, the tendency to universality. In this
> resides the fundamental law of all harmony of colours . . .[29]

Harmony, for Goethe, was something sought by the human organism, ''. . . a
natural phenomenon immediately applicable to aesthetic purposes.''[30]

While Goethe's scientific conclusions have largely been disproved by the
wavelength theory of light, his observations about optical effects and emotional impact remain convincing. The result of his investigations was a
profound, often metaphysical, view of color and the notion of a simple
arrangement of color into the color wheel (Fig 3.15). Critic John Ruskin
echoed this interrelatedness with an often quoted remark that is as accurate
for designers as for artists, ''Every hue throughout your work is altered by
every touch that you add in other places.''[31] The color wheel, in various
configurations, became the standard method of visualizing color relationships; the Bauhaus designer Josef Albers noted that the situation was more
complex, however, than a color wheel might suggest. In his *Interaction of
Color,* he credits Schopenhauer with changing Goethe's six-part color wheel
by differentiating it quantitatively, in order to equalize hues by noting relative brightness. Albers goes on to state ''. . . that certain constellations
within a (color) system provide color harmony.''[32] Ostwald similarly discusses color harmony when he writes in his *Primer of Colors:*

> Experience teaches that certain combinations of different colors are
> pleasing, others displeasing or indifferent. The question arises, what de-
> termines the effect? The answer is: Those colors are pleasing among
> which some regular, i.e. orderly, relationship obtains. Groups of colors
> whose effect is pleasing, we call harmonious. So we can set up the pos-
> tulate, Harmony = Order.[33]

This comment was quoted somewhat critically by Johannes Itten in *The
Elements of Color;* he felt that Ostwald stressed psychological effect over
the sorts of physiological laws cited in works like Goethe's. In this Itten
sought a foundation to aesthetic color theory that would yield more predictable responses. But he did agree with Ostwald on the desirablility of
arranging colors in a system using a color solid, with color defined by both
hue and value. Munsell's theory of harmony was also based on the notion
of common elements arranged by hue, value, and intensity in a spherical
format so that the center of the sphere is the natural balancing point for all
the parameters of color (Fig 3.16). Itten, in an interesting series of comments, provides this rationale for his theories:

> The physiologist investigates the various effects of light and colors on our
> visual apparatus—eye and brain—and their anatomical relationships and
> functions. . . . The psychologist is interested in problems of the influence
> of color radiation on our mind and spirit. . . . Expressive color effects—
> what Goethe called the ethico-aesthetic values of colors—likewise fall
> within the psychologist's province. The artist (or designer), finally, is in-
> terested in color effects from their aesthetic aspect, and needs both phys-
> iological and psychological information.[34]

Itten goes on to discuss the interpretation of subjective color combinations, which, he says, must be based on ". . . the placment of the colors relative to each other, their directions, brilliances, clarity or turbidity, proportions, textures, and rhythmic relationships."[35] And he warns against decorators and designers being guided by their "own subjective color propensities,"[36] as this will simply lead to one subjective judgment conflicting with another. A personal spectrum does not suffice as good design, and he concludes that "Knowledge of objective principles is essential to the correct evaluation and use of colors."[37] It is interesting, in this context, that design firms (Skidmore, Owings and Merrill, for example) have employed artists for color selection.

Itten's insistence on the incorporation of *psychological* and *physiological* factors in the formulation of aesthetic systems is interesting. In fact, a color system for design might be structured in entirely psychophysiological terms, as in the color preferences of particular audiences or the effect a certain color has on affective response. Such uses of color are particularly persuasive when combined with a concern for light sources, especially their reflectivity, brightness, and contrast. One of the first, and highly influential, works in the area of color psychology is by Faber Birren: *Color Psychology and Color Therapy*. This work was published in 1950, with a somewhat revised version appearing in 1961, and another edition in 1982. Birren had, from the early 1940s, been employed by both industry and government to manipulate interior color and light to increase production, improve efficiency, and enhance worker safety and welfare. The first edition consists of a combination of psychological data, general observation, and mysticism, but he clearly was interested in physiology as well.

Thus he notes in the revised edition (1961), ". . . as this book strives to show, the influence of color is by no means limited to the psychological realm; its direct biological and physiological effects are rapidly becoming more evident as new research data accumulate."[38] The ultimate influence of his work may well be his insistence on *functional color,* represented in color schemes that use tangible evidence rather than individual taste for their basis. He notes that the applied science known as *color conditioning,* begun in the 1920s, had long been concerned with the problems of *visibility, acuity,* and *ocular fatigue.*[39] These were, of course, the problems that he was to solve, and that were common to factories, offices, hospitals, schools, and other public buildings, generally affecting people's efficiency and health. In this sense, Birren saw his methods as a systematic extension of extant processes, an extension made critical by the production needs of World War II.

Birren's ideas are referred to by most theories of color application that have followed. Indeed, his work on industrial color specifications, office lighting levels, and comparative brightness ratios has been acknowledged generally, although his ideas concerning therapeutic applications have been less successful. In their *Color and Light in Man-made Environments,* Frank H. Mahnke and Rudolf H. Mahnke note a debt to Birren, and state the premise of their work:

> Color and light are major factors in man-made environments; their impact influences man's psychological reactions and physiological well-being. . . .
> It is no longer valid to assume that the *only* role of light and color is to provide adequate illumination and a pleasant visual environment. . . .[40]

This work not only discusses the effect, psychologically and physiologically, of our artificial environment, but also offers codified, environment-specific advice.

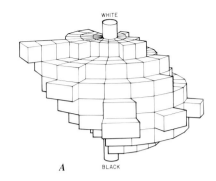

A

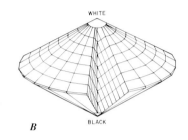

B

3.16

The Color Solids of Munsell and Ostwald
In the Munsell model *(A),* the ten hues that constitute his system are laid out as in the Munsell Color Tree. This system quantifies color in terms of hue, value, and saturation. The tree consists of value gradations along the vertical axis, and an increase in saturation is shown by extending the hue horizontally. As Munsell used the maximum number of steps for each hue, the "branches" of this tree are unequal in length. The advantages of Munsell's system are that all steps are demarcated incrementally (with numerical notation), replacing the nondescriptive nomenclature that had obtained. The Ostwald model *(B)* is quite different in the way it works, despite some similarity in its conceptual model. For one thing, Ostwald's system treats value change as a geometric progression, rather than an arithmetical one; and for another, the solid itself is constructed as a series of twelve double triangular charts composed of precise amounts of black, white, and one of twenty-four hues. (Drawn by: J. Malnar.)

Certain lighting issues do seem more straightforward than others, particularly when they are related to specific task-performance. Thus specifications for brightness ratios, task and ambient lighting types, and general illumination levels have been increasingly codified since 1940. It was in fact one of Birren's tasks to ascertain and specify optimum light levels for various industrial vocations. One of his best-known conclusions concerned brightness levels; if the task-illumination is kept constant while the ambient brightness level is raised, visual acuity improves. He notes, "This improvement will be gradual and constant *and will be at its maximum when the surrounding brightness is slightly lower than, or equal to, the task.*"[41] On the other hand, if the ambient light level exceeds that of the task light level, performance rapidly diminishes. This led Birren to specify a *brightness ratio* of 3:1 as optimal for most tasks, although he thought that it might rise to a level of 10:1 without serious problem.[42]

Unlike many in the lighting profession, Birren did not believe that high light-intensity invariably led to good visibility; to the contrary, he maintained that ocular fatigue was more likely the result of strong brightness contrasts and task difficulty than of low-level ambient lighting. Indeed, he pointed out that levels in excess of 35 footcandles can demonstrate only marginal improvements in acuity, illustrating this in a chart that relates footcandle ranges to brightness differences (Fig 3.17). The conclusions of Mahnke and Mahnke tend to support Birren's position on ocular fatigue, "Glare, constant adjustment to extreme brightness differences, prolonged fixation of the eyes, and constant shifts in accommodation will tire eyes quickly, causing headaches, tension, nausea, and other disturbances."[43] An interesting finding of one illumination study is that under lighting that approximates the spectral quality of natural sunlight there is less perceptual fatigue and improved acuity (Maas, Jayson, & Kleiber, 1974). This raises the issue of *seasonal affective disorder,* the symptoms of which include decreased physical activity and energy level, irritability, and sleep disorders. Norman Rosenthal and associates found, however, that the use of full-spectrum light, in conjunction with time-alertations, tended to alleviate this condition.[44] On the other hand, it has been demonstrated that the use of full-spectrum light decreased hyperactive behavior in school children (Mayron, Ott, Nations, & Mayron, 1974). One thing seems certain; control of light will play a growing role in the physiological considerations of building design.

3.17

Birren's Principle Diagram
This diagram, which establishes relationships between brightness, reflectance, and light levels, demonstrates that high levels of illumination become permissible only when brightness differences in the field of view are minimal. Where this condition does not obtain, light levels should be accordingly reduced. (Permission: Van Nostrand Reinhold.)

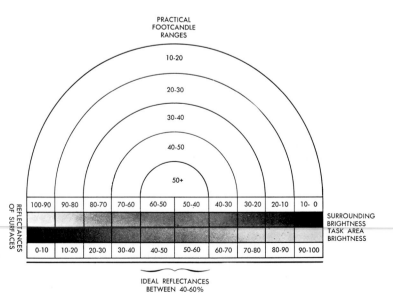

Mahnke and Mahnke document the various studies that have been made to determine color preferences, their cultural associations, and the affective responses particular colors elicit. Using these broad psychophysiological and cultural data, they have assembled color-scheme types for particular kinds of environments. The colors suggested by the authors for a hospital maternity room (dark green floor, pale green ceiling, greyed pink walls, and pale yellow frieze), for example, were chosen for their acceptability by patients and nursing staff and general effect on emotional state. The color scheme Luis Barragán used for his home (Plate 2) illustrates the difference between a palette chosen for clincally beneficial psychological effect and one chosen for its highly expressive (though no less psychological) effect. This difference raises critical questions about design purposes: Should colors thought generally beneficial (if not particularly expressive) be used for all public (nonresidential) projects as a safety measure, or might such color schemes be reserved for nonelective (hospitals and schools) situations alone? And, even more to the point, is color a tool of individual design expression or a part of client health and welfare?

It is certainly true that the sheer quantity of reliable information about the effects of color has increased throughout the past half century. For example, in children and adolescents between the ages of six and seventeen, it has been shown that females prefer warm colors, and males the cool ones.[45] On the other hand, as they grow older, both sexes lose interest in intensity of colors and gain interest in hue.[46] While children reach their peak for color-dominance at age four and a half, they turn to form-dominance by age six (and throughout adulthood);[47] this is accompanied by a lifelong interest in the color blue.[48] The adult preference for blue (increasing with age) may, in part, be physiological. As the fluids in the eye turn yellow with age, the eye absorbs as much as 85 percent of blue light, in contrast to 10 percent in a child's eye; the color preference may, therefore, represent the body's effort to redress the imbalance.[49] An interesting corollary to this is the marked preferences by older adults (over sixty-five) for bright primary, secondary, and tertiary colors over pastel shades; this stands in sharp contrast to popular institutional opinion.[50]

Studies indicate that colors have been identified in conjunction with temperature, weight, smell, sound, and even taste (as in variations of red, which aids in the sensation of sweetness).[51] An early study indicated that time tends to be overestimated in the presence of red light; and that conversely, it is underestimated under blue light.[52] But more recent data (Porter and Mikellides, 1976) contradict this conclusion, instead indicating that blue can extend the sense of time; if true, the use of blue might be a poor choice for children, whose sense of time is already extended. The data on temperature-perception seem more reliable; studies consistently indicate that a blue room is perceived to be three to four degrees cooler than a red one (Porter and Mikellides, 1976), and vice versa (Clark, 1975).[53] A major difficulty in trying to predict how an audience will react to any one of these dimensions is that of cultural relativity. Studies have shown, for example, that while Japanese and Americans may agree on the affective measures of color (e.g., that warm is more exciting), they disagree in their evaluation of such colors.[54] Another complicating factor may lie in our favoring a color in some situations but not in others, or associating a particular color with an experience.

The data on human color preferences are quite consistent, however. Studies (Eysenck, 1941; Guilford and Smith, 1959) have indicated that people prefer colors in the following order: blue, red, green, violet, orange, and yellow. Gender differentiation is minor, with men tending to slightly prefer blue to red, and women yellow to orange—although neither preference is sufficient to offset the above order for the general population. Indeed, this order is consistent even across lines of age and national origin. Such consistency raises intriguing questions about whether such preferences are learned or innate. In fact, J.P. Guilford states that this collective ownership of color preferences ". . . probably rests upon biological factors, since it is hard to see how cultural factors could produce by conditioning the continuity and system that undoubtedly exist."[55]

When the reactions stop being culture-bound or memory-associated, they may be crossing into the physiological realm. Red light has been shown to enhance functions of the autonomic nervous system, evoking more tension, excitement, and hostility than the color blue (Gerard, 1957). For that matter, red light seems to produce anger and anxiety in both infants and the mentally ill, and tests at Yale University have indicated that the color red tends to detrimentally affect such mental activities as problem solving, decision making, and social conversation.[56] Additionally, red light has been shown (in certain subjects) to increase bodily activity and extreme emotion, while blue light is physically calming.[57] The effects of going from the tranquilizing atmosphere of an essentially blue space to one where warm hues dominate may be experienced in Arata Isozaki's Palladium in New York City, although whether it was so intended is not clear (Plate 5). Certainly the notion of passing from the "deep blue sea" to a space of "blinding luminosity" suggests it.

Many of these psychophysiological studies remain speculative and influenced by the difficulty in separating learned versus innate responses. And an everpresent problem is the degree to which limited conclusions obtained in laboratory conditions can be applied to specific aspects of design. It is nonetheless clear that the psychological and physiological aspects of color will become increasingly prominent in design decisions. This will not only raise questions about the potential conflict with color's traditional role as an expressive device, but may also challenge many of our views of color based on association, custom, and symbolism.

Association refers to our giving certain familiar objects particular colors (like Leonardo's red apples). The color may be granted an object, however, by anticipation. E.H. Gombrich refers to this in *Art and Illusion:*

> What we called "mental set" may be precisely that state of readiness to start projecting, to thrust out the tentacles of phantom colors and phantom images which always flicker around our perceptions . . . the world as we see it is a construct, slowly built up by every one of us in years of experimentation. Our eyes merely undergo stimulations on the retina which result in so-called sensations of color. It is our mind that weaves these sensations into perceptions. . . .[58]

If color is manipulated so as to correspond to the viewer's expectation, that color will seem correct. And Rasmussen notes that color can express . . . the character of the building and the spirit it was meant to convey."[59]

Custom is simply the cultural stamp of approval given a particular color or group of colors. While many of these colors appear to be sacrosanct, historical analysis usually reveals a set of socioeconomic realities that were at one time operative. The Swedish use of deep red paint on house exteriors is endemic; the art historian Erik Lundberg believes that it started in imitation of the red brick manor houses of the wealthy. Indeed, paint colors have historically been highly responsive to economic and cultural trends, as in the nineteenth-century use of white paint to indicate personal wealth. Combinations of other colors have been used to indicate aesthetic sensibility and taste, a position articulated clearly, if highly personally, by Edith Wharton in *The Decoration of Houses:*

> Each room should speak with but one voice: it should contain one color, which at once and unmistakably asserts its predominance, in obedience to the rule that where there is a division of parts one part shall visibly prevail over all the others[60]

To strip the walls of a century-old home is to discover the variety enjoyed by customary usage, each layer revealing what was correct during that period.

Symbolism is, in some sense, an outgrowth of association and custom; colors forever associated with a particular phenomenon and sanctified by time and use. They are the colors of our uniforms, social and religious icons, and institutions. They are the colors of our flags, although various studies referred to by Sharpe indicate that even these choices are the ". . . reflection of color preferences within the social-psychological context of traditions and aspirations."[61] They are difficult to use (i.e., transfer meaning from one context to another), but such was attempted in the vaulted golden ceilings of 190 South LaSalle Street in Chicago, designed by Burgee/Johnson. Here the historical trappings of one eminent institution—religion—have been transferred to another—commerce (Plate 3). Manipulation of such symbolism is always risky, as societies tend to invest symbols with vastly grander passion than the more prosaic realities.

The factors that make up a study, and application, of color are many; and they are more complex by their frequent congruence. That is, it is often difficult to know color's role in particular situations. In the first chapter of the book, Sharpe notes that there ". . . is some doubt that science will ever be able to quantify or predict aesthetic values (in color)."[62] And, as previously noted, quantification of data on psychophysiological responses is far from definitive. Not surprisingly, the color system designers most rely on remains the aesthetic. That is, despite more objectified (and reliable) information available to designers from studies in psychology, little finds its way into actual design solutions. This will presumably change as more color research is done directly in the area of environmental psychology. The balance of individual expression with predictive data will undoubtedly prove one of the major problems in design, though by no means an insurmountable one. Of far greater concern, however, are the buildings (particularly in their interior dimension) that use no systematic approach whatever, inflicting what Itten referred to as "a severe stress upon sensitive individuals"[63], the natural result of coloristic anarchy.

The Grammar
of Design

4

Determinants of Space

P rinciples of visual organization, or grammar, simply represent the ways in which design elements can be applied to constructive purposes. Nonetheless, as with the elements of design, these principles have psychosocial dimensions that extend beyond their simple utility. Even the terms have changed meaning over time, in accordance with architectural fashion. These principles include such notions as balance, arrangement, sequence, scale, and proportion—and their various subsets. Each has a relatively specialized use and usually exists in a dynamic relationship with one or more of the others. And as all these principles operate in a spatio-temporal construct, the determinants of space itself become a fundamental consideration in their application.

As noted in the chapter on form, the traditional view of architecture as sculptural mass has tended to prevail before this century, even in those buildings distinguished by their interior space. This is due largely to the derived nature of space, which inclines us to think in terms of objects rather than spatial relationships. And yet it is enclosed volumetric space that is architecture's essential experience, a sentiment that is echoed in the poetic description found in the *Tao Te Ching,* by Lao Tsu:

> Thirty spokes share the wheel's hub;
> It is the center hole that makes it useful.
> Shape clay into a vessel;
> It is the space within that makes it useful.
> Cut doors and windows for a room;
> It is the holes which make it useful.
> Therefore profit comes from what is there;
> Usefulness from what is not there.[1]

This verse is instructive as well as descriptive, as it confirms the value of both the vessel and the void within, the room and its egress. Roger Scruton points out that ". . . the essence of architecture is not space but the enclosure of space, or space as enclosed."[2] That is, our sense of the interior depends, not simply on empty space, but on its interaction with the material that encloses it; it is that material that grants space a specific character, particular shape, and dimensional spatial unity. In support of his thesis, Scruton quotes Bruno Zevi's *Architecture as Space,* ". . . the essence of architecture . . . does not lie in the material limitation placed on spatial

4.1

Development of a Bottle in Space (Silvered bronze [cast 1931] 15″ × 23¾″ × 12⅞″); Umberto Boccioni (1912)
Speed, universal dynamism, and *activism* were all virtues in the futurist movement, which saw a profound beauty in the efficiency of the machine. The futurists also distinguished ''relative'' movement (movement from one point to another) from ''absolute'' movement (potential movement within the object). Their interrelationship was responsible for an ''inner dynamic.'' The result is an appreciation of the bottle from both sides of the glass. (Collection: The Museum of Modern Art, New York. Aristide Maillol Fund.)

freedom, but in the way space is organized into meaningful form through this process of limitation. . . .''[3] He also points out that at least some of the interior detail belonging to, or associated with, that enclosing membrane, is significant quite aside from its space-defining function. And he postulates that ''. . . 'spatial' effect may itself be dependent on significant detail.''[4] Thus the meeting of interior and exterior referred to earlier by Venturi, is made even more complex by the independent characteristics of the defining elements. Various attempts have been made to exploit this meeting place in terms of volume, movement, and mass; once again, many of the successes have been by sculptors (Fig 4.1).

Space can be defined in several ways; the conventional view has been that it simply exists, a great empty void. Such a void may or may not be occupied by things, but it in any case exists. This rather simple observation is important because it implies that space is a preexisting matrix in which the position of every object that does occupy it can be precisely located through a minimal set of three coordinates (measuring height, width, and depth). This Cartesian system has the benefit of being orderly and suggests that some mathematical model underlying nature exists after all. It is an affirmation of the grid's logic, and it is difficult to imagine contemporary structures without this premise. A consequence of postulating such a matrix is that in order to have the dimension necessary to measurement, it must be finite. Space, in this sense, is always a particular space. Cartesian grids are useful for urban planning and, interestingly, for the design of interior space, where the notion of a finite three-dimensional space is entirely familiar. Indeed, the use of such coordinates can bring order to chaos and regulate design relationships through the establishment of a precisely measurable set of modular ratios.

Another way of looking at space involves the relationship that occurs between objects; that is, that space is defined by the presence of objects (or, by extension, fields). This is a physical description; in this conception one object occupies the center of its own space until a second object comes into being, thus creating an axial spatial dialogue between the two. The presence of additional objects further complicates the interactive relationships in this object-space, particularly when certain of the relationships assume greater significance than others, for reasons quite distinct from intrinsic ones. The difference between *absolute-space* and *object-space,* and its significance to design, is profound (Fig 4.2).

There are several interesting aspects to object-space: first, as it assumes no preexisting matrix, it is dynamic in nature; second, the spaces between objects are now active and vital; and third, this physical definition corresponds to the psychophysiological perception of space (i.e., perception of space depends on things occupying it). The human eye measures from itself to the object, or between objects comparatively; and the relative importance granted each object (and its distance) likely depends on personal valuation. There are ramifications for the placement of elements within a defined space (a room, for example), where decisions must be made between formal (Cartesian) relationships based on ideas like symmetry and axis, and relationships based on proxemics (Fig 4.3). Such an approach concerns the necessary distance and direction of objects (animate and inanimate) from each other in the sense that psychological perception is itself bound by culture and spatial necessity. E.T. Hall comments that human perception of space ''. . . is dynamic because it is related to action—what can be done in a given space—rather than what is seen by passive viewing.''[5] And the psychological analysis of behavior shows that human spatial behavior indeed tends to be influenced more by interaction with other people than by the physical enclosure.

A variant of this position is the idea of *body-centered space.* In this view, the range of spatial factors includes haptic experiences as well as visual ones. That is, a space could be constructed that responds to our extended sense of touch alone; such a space might be volumetrically dense, with boundaries demarcated by emptiness (Fig 4.4). The net effect is a space that is aqueous in nature, in sharp contrast to our usual view of enclosure. It is even possible to construct a space that exists in a purely cognitive, or semiotic, mode alone, dependent on cultural memory (Fig 4.5). Charles Jencks comments on the Franklin Court project, ''Here a very appropriate ghost image, in stainless steel, marks the profile of the old, non-existent mansion. . . . Thus the Venturi team has produced here, not a building, but a very amusing garden which combines meanings from the past and present. . . .''[6] ''Buildings'' such as these rely on metaphor and humor for their existence and remind us of our earlier hypothesis that architecture can

B

4.2

(A) City Square (Bronze, 8½" ′ × 25⅜" × 17¼"; Alberto Giacometti (1948); (B) Chicago Park District; John S. Butsch (1975) Giacometti's bronze *(A)* represents a plane, measurable in depth and width, but with a spatial height implied by the dimensions of the figures, whose placement is carefully calculated relative to that plane. These slender, elongated figures are frozen in mid motion in an isolated, essentially abstract space, having no other relationship to each other than mathematical placement. The black and white photograph *(B)* stresses the infinite quality of the boxing ring's edge. The interaction of the figures in the ring—both with each other and the audience—constitutes the dynamic of the scene, which is proxemic in nature. And in contrast to Giacometti's base, the edge is sharp, suggesting that the ring's actual dimension has little meaning beyond a compositional one. ([A] collection: The Museum of Modern Art, New York. Purchase. Copyright 1991 ARS N.Y./ADAGP; [B] courtesy: John S. Butsch, Chicago.)

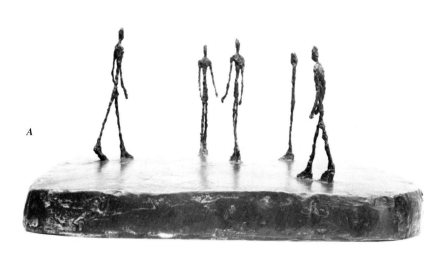

A

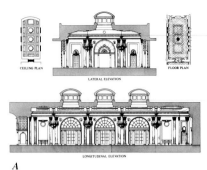

A

B

4.3

(A) Proposed State Department Dining-Room—Washington, D.C.; *Allan Greenberg (1983); (B)* Hole-in-the-Wall Gang Camp—Asford, Connecticut; *Hammond Beeby & Babka, Inc. and Langdon & Woodhouse, Architects (1989)*
The existing dining-room, with its eclectic blend of decor, was 100′ × 50′, with a proportionally low 20′ ceiling. The proposed plans call for increasing the height to 23′ by vaulting the ceiling. The classical wall detail in this new scheme *(A)* strengthens the longitudinal axis and provides three major and two minor cross axes, culminating in the curved end wall. The formal symmetry provides dignity, and the classical references a civic order. In this meeting room *(B)* the walls are uniformly covered with wainscotting and sponge-painted sheetrock. The furniture is mostly lightweight and movable; those few pieces that are not have casters. The area rugs are scattered casually, suggesting that their spatial role is relatively indeterminate; the net effect is one of informality. (*[A]* courtesy: Allan Greenberg, Washington, D.C.; *[B]* photo by: Judith Bromley, Chicago. [All copyrights reserved].)

be a ". . .matrix for the resolution of human needs, desires, and aspirations. . . " Put differently, space is amenable to our varied intentions. Gerald Allen writes:

> If three dimensions can generate what we standardly think of as space, then all the dimensions the mind can conceive are capable of generating *perceptual spaces*. Perceptual spaces, of course, have none of that sense of "whereness" that we associate with three-dimensional space. . . . But it is important to remember, in fact, that the sense of "whereness" may well be no more than a convenient habit. . . .[7]

And Allen notes that perceptual spaces can be multidimensional; their number and kind depend on issues of culture, training, and personal inclination of the beholder.[8] Allen concludes by noting that the standard spatial dimensions are, as one might expect, of particular importance to the designer,

4.4

Penetrable; *Jesús-Rafäel Soto (1975)*
Soto has created vibrating walls of plastic tubing graded in height; by extending, or layering, those walls, the work becomes a three-dimensional installation. When visitors walk through the space, the milk-white tubing becomes opaque and shimmers in the light; both participant and observer become, in each other's eyes, dematerialized and elusive. (Source: Hirshhorn Museum and Sculpture Garden, Smithsonian Institution, Installation Exhibition; Soto: A Retrospective Exhibition, 1975.)

but not necessarily the highest importance. If not the highest, they are nonetheless critical to the depiction of enclosed space and, as noted, it is enclosed space that is the *sine qua non* of architecture. Some of the other considerations are examined later; of interest here are the means, and their implications, at the disposal of the designer in the delineation of these spatial dimensions.

Organizing Principles

Organizing principles are akin to grammar in written language; that is, they permit the efficient and informative ordering of the vocabulary, or design elements. In *The Natural House* (1954), Frank Lloyd Wright comments that every house aspiring to the status of art has a grammar:

> "Grammar," in this sense, means the same thing in any construction—whether it be of words or of stone or wood. It is the shape-relationship between the various elements that enter into the constitution of the thing. The "grammar" of the house is its manifest articulation of all its parts. This will be the "speech" it uses . . . the man who designs the house must, inevitably, speak a consistent thought-language in his design.[9]

Wright considered this grammar crucial in order for each part to relate to the whole, particularly as it affected the underlying structural pattern. In *The Geometry of Environment,* Lionel March and Philip Steadman analyze the plans of three houses by Wright and conclude, "In them he uses a range of 'grammars,' by which he meant, above all, the controlling geometric unit which ordered the plan and pervaded the details."[10] Although the unit differs in each house—an equilateral triangle, a square, and a circle—and each house has a markedly individual appearance, all three are in fact topologically equivalent. That is, their spatial patterns may be mapped onto a common graph (with only minor discrepancies). For Wright, the notion of grammar provided a practical methodological approach to the building task,

4.5

Franklin Court—Philadelphia; *Venturi and Rauch (1972–6)*
Benjamin Franklin's mansion, no longer in existence, was celebrated by Venturi and Rauch for the Bicentennial. The architects elicit interest and amusement by depending on our knowledge of the size and shape of a typical colonial house. It is located on the actual site of Franklin's house, the remains of which may be seen through the viewing devices provided at ground level. (Photo by: Frank Vodvarka.)

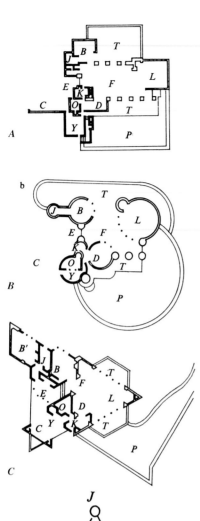

4.6

(A) *Life's "House for a Family of $5000–$6000 Income"; Frank Lloyd Wright (1938);* (B) **Ralph Jester House—Palos Verdes, California;** *Frank Lloyd Wright (1938);* (C) **Vigo Sundt House—Madison, Wisconsin;** *Frank Lloyd Wright (1941);* (D) **Diagram of Room Linkages;** *Lionel March and Philip Steadman (1971)*
Although these three plans are based on diverse shapes, and thus appear dissimilar, they are in fact variations on one spatial program. This becomes clear in an analysis of the room organization, which demonstrates Wright's ideas about appropriate room linkages. (Courtesy: Lionel March, Los Angeles.)

as well as a unifying device (Fig 4.6). Indeed, the most vital principle in design is usually considered to be *unity,* without which it is impossible to grasp the designer's intention. In his *Varieties of Visual Experience,* Edmund Burke Feldman comments:

> Perhaps unity is the only principle of visual organization, and the other principles merely different ways of achieving it. For unity may ultimately represent the desire of the individual viewer to relate the multitude of visual facts and events he witnesses to one person—himself. Therefore, no matter how well or badly an artist organizes the visual elements, *they will be seen as a whole.*[11]

The conclusion is especially interesting, as it postulates a unity independent of intention; if the designer does not imbue the finished work with unity, the audience will. This reflects the psychological need to order perceptual data and negates the possibility of assuming a deliberately noncommittal position. The only question is whether that unity is the designer's or the public's. William Roger Greeley, in *The Essence of Architecture,* confirms the importance of unity as the guiding principle of design, "An architectural mass is a unit if it has a centre of importance, or of attention in a bulk or mass that is single in the sense that it is undivided, or is so divided as to form an easily grasped geometrical pattern or entity."[12] But when the composition is more complex, as with several elements or spatio-plastic relationships, unity calls upon the principles that enable it. That is, unity is the result of the clever adjustment of still other principles that provide precise methodologies. This becomes clear in the definition of unity, which stresses the ". . . arrangement of elements in an artistic work so that each contributes to the main theme" and the "unchanging singleness of purpose or action." One conceptual system in which these elements can be ordered is that of balance, arrangement, sequence, scale, and proportion.

Balance refers to the relationship of two sets of components occupying either side of an axis, such that they appear to be equivalent in weight and force. The axis, or fulcrum, is critical to the notion of balance; if the designer does not overtly use it, it is still postulated by the viewer. The notion of axis does not have to be singular, as components may be arranged on multiple axes. Such components possess *visual weight,* which may be thought of as a combination of the design elements, size, location, and orientation. Obviously, then, the issue of balance is complex, since two (or more) groups of components may be entirely different in appearance and yet be in balance. A further complication is raised by Clark and Pause in their *Precedents in Architecture,* where they define balance as a ". . . state of perceptual or conceptual equilibrium."[13] That is, not only are *perceptual* factors involved (color, shape, size, etc.), but *conceptual* ones as well. This usually involves the particular value that an individual, culture, or historical point places on specific visual data. Thus a certain shape may be given extra weight for reasons unrelated to visual factors.

Visual weight is particularly influenced by orientation, or pattern. As the eye looks upward in space, objects seem to become ever heavier, so that elements meant to be in balance vertically must actually be different in size. And linear elements meant to bisect vertical planes must be somewhat higher than the halfway point on that plane. The situation is difficult in a left/right axial division, as we perceptually tend to grant greater weight to the right side, even though we read the left side first. The tendency to see from left to right is consistent with Western writing, and reinforced by studies that indicate ". . . spontaneous movements of the head are executed more quickly from left to right than in the opposite direction;"[14] this occurs, moreover, in ways only partly related to physical or cultural factors. It would seem that the way to symmetrically view any planar surface (a wall, for example) is asymmetrically. Despite these practical difficulties, balance remains a vital concern in design. Arnheim points out that only by such an effort to stabilize weights and forces can a statement be unambiguous, and furthermore ". . . man strives for equilibrium in all phases of his physical and mental existence. . . ."[15]

Symmetry is a form of balance in which two sets of components mirror one another bilaterally. As noted in the preceding paragraph, perceptual *symmetry* is probably not theoretically possible, yet it remains one of the most constant themes in architectural history. Until well into the eighteenth century, the Vitruvian definition of symmetry prevailed; that is, a coherent arrangement and relationship of all the parts of a design in accordance with a standard. Such a view is, of course, far more complex than can be demonstrated in a simple bilateral distribution of elements. In his *Changing Ideals in Modern Architecture,* Peter Collins contends that this new definition of symmetry was largely the result of Romanticism, with its love of the (asymmetrical) picturesque. He notes that repetition around a central axis characterized symmetry for those who disliked it, and quotes Laugier's principle, ". . . that a 'certain disorder' was the principle merit to be sought."[16] The result of this nonVitruvian view of symmetry has been a simplification such that the question William Blake asks of his Tyger burning bright must seem curious:

> What immortal hand or eye
> Could frame thy fearful symmetry?[17]

The meaning currently given to symmetry has instead taken on a certain morality, or rectitude. We reserve symmetry for our civic structures, and courts, where the axial equality is reassuring, and for situations where its stability, like proportion, suggests a certain level of taste (Plate 4). In *The Decoration of Houses,* Edith Wharton and Ogden Codman, Jr., characteristically state:

> If proportion is the good breeding of architecture, symmetry, or the answering of one part to another, may be defined as the sanity of decoration. The desire for symmetry, for balance, for rhythm in form as well as in sound, is one of the most inveterate of human instincts.[18]

In their characterization of symmetry, there is some remnant of its older meaning, and they later comment that symmetry does not insist on absolute similarity of detail, but simply a correspondence of outline and dimensions.[19] Thus symmetry is far more flexible for interior space than for the exterior, where it is usually predicated on certain structural regularities. When it is used in a nonliteral way, it is generally referred to as *approximate symmetry,* which may be thought of as equivalent components arranged in a nonmirrored manner (Fig 4.7). This approach has the formal advantages of symmetry, but with more dynamic compositional possibilities; furthermore, it lets the viewer become visually involved in the act of order. But even this form of symmetry relies on associations derived from millennia of cultural experience and may not satisfy proponents of modernity.

In *The Modern Language of Architecture,* Bruno Zevi emphatically states:

> Symmetry is one of the invariables of classicism. Therefore asymmetry is an invariable of the modern language. Once you get rid of the fetish of symmetry, you will have taken a giant step on the road to a democratic architecture.[20]

And lest his meaning be mistaken, he further states, "Symmetry = economic waste + intellectual cynicism."[21] What Zevi is reacting to, of course, is the aristocratic content of symmetry, as he makes clear when he says, ". . . what seems rational and logical, because it is regulated and ordered, is humanly and socially foolish; it makes sense only in terms of despotic power."[22] Indeed, much the same objection (minus the conclusion) is raised by environmental psychologists; in a sense it is implicit in the contrast between absolute space and object space. *Asymmetrical* balance is certainly the most dynamic of the methods and, moreover, the most sensitive to valuated weight. Finally, there is *radial symmetry,* in which weighted elements are arranged around a center. Such a methodology might be extroverted, and expansive, using the center as progenitor; or introverted, stressing the exclusivity of the designated center, or focal point. The compositional center of this sort of grouping is thus always filled with tension and energy (Fig 4.8).

Arrangement refers to the planned disposition of the various components that make up the architectural unity. This usually involves a consideration of open form, as opposed to closed form. This contrast simply describes the difference between informal compositions in which components are loosely related, and those formal compositions in which they are interdependent, usually geometrically. In the latter case, the various elements of the composition take on complex roles, usually conceived in an hierarchial way. This distinction is somewhat artificial; while it does describe the difference between spatial thinking as opposed to designing in mass, in fact both aspects are typically employed. And in the repetition of these components (major and minor) lies the vital characteristic of rhythm:

> The word *"rhythm"* is often used in connection with the repetition of similar elements. The simplest case is a uniform succession, but the concept of rhythm is generally introduced when the repetition is combined with certain lawful changes in the relations between the elements. In general the word "rhythm" denotes the *relational* property of succession, while "variations" denotes *element*-properties derived from a common basic source.[23]

Norberg-Schulz's statement is echoed in Dewey's succinct definition of rhythm, "It is ordered variation of changes."[24] And it is this same rhythm that Charles Rennie Mackintosh refers to as ". . . the sustained note of informing purpose—the deep vibration of some unifying undertone now

4.7

Wall with Fireplace in Château-sur-Mer for G.P. Wetmore—Newport; *Ogden Codman Jr.*
Wharton and Codman, Jr. believed that the highest artistic civilizations always displayed a preference for symmetry. Aside from the artistic need, their experience led them to state that the average room became easier to furnish, and more comfortable to live in. In this example, the fireplace decisively occupies the center position, but the walls—to either side, while equally weighted—are only approximately symmetrical.

THE GRAMMAR OF DESIGN 73

rising to accent and emphasis—now sounding faintly. . . ."[25] Thus variation is a part of rhythm. In this sense, variation is not a matter of contrast added to rhythm to prevent monotony, but inherent in our view of rhythm itself (Plate 5).

Sequence may be divided into its constituent parts, hierarchy, progression, and duration. Hierarchy refers to the valuation placed on particular elements in the composition, or arrangement. Such valuation is inherent in the idea of the focal point, the place granted particular importance for functional, visual, and ideological reasons. But hierarchy occurs throughout the arrangement, reflecting a complex series of decisions, which grant the totality its character. Critical to an understanding of hierarchy is the fact that architectural unity itself is experienced sequentially. Arnheim says that a building is ". . . not made to be stared at from a fixed point, but to unfold as one walks around it—a sequential experience."[26] And hierarchy grants the building its key moments of importance.

If that is true of a building in mass, the interior experience is even more a "sequential experience." A given space, by virtue of its enclosed character, is impossible to apprehend in one viewing. Not only is it necessary to turn one's head, but, if the space is large enough, the body as well. This makes it difficult to integrate this series of successive images into one comprehensive image without extensive organization. Both the Gestalt laws and Gibson's Hypothesis of Ordinal Stimulation may be of use in understanding this process, however. And when a building is further composed of a succession of discrete spaces, they are experienced as a progression. How these spaces are seen, and the relative importance granted them, may be thought of as an order of view. In this sense, a progression is never random or arbitrary but is the result of sequencing based on custom, utility, and image (Fig 4.9).

Progression in architectural space occurs both visually and physically; that is, not only do we move through a succession of interior spaces, but our eye is led through a particular space even when we are motionless. The *order of view* is, therefore, complex and crucial to our sense of place—*genius loci*. The notion of a sense of place is complex and depends upon the special interrelationship of things in a particular place at a particular time. These things are thus understood by us, not only as entities, but as parts of an integrated whole that is both cognitive and perceptual. In *The Environmental Memory,* Malcolm Quantrill notes:

> We may *conceive* environmental frameworks that conform to an underlying order of things according to natural or culturally ritualistic principles. However, we will *perceive* those frameworks in terms of certain characteristics of form, material, color, directional emphasis, pattern, texture, and so on, which give a distinctive set of images to a particular building or place.[27]

Arnheim notes that if humans are to interact with a building functionally, there must be visual continuity.[28] The passage through the interior may be thought of as *serial viewing,* although such a progression is conditioned by far more factors than visual phenomena alone. In *The Hidden Dimension,* Edward T. Hall attributes much of Wright's success to his appreciation of the different ways in which people experience space. He notes:

> The old Imperial Hotel in Tokyo [Fig 3.8] provides the Westerner with a constant visual, kinesthetic, and tactile reminder that he is in a different world. The changing levels, the circular, walled-in, intimate stairs to the upper floors, and the small scale are all new experiences. . . . Wright enhances the experience of space by personally involving people with the surfaces of the building."[29]

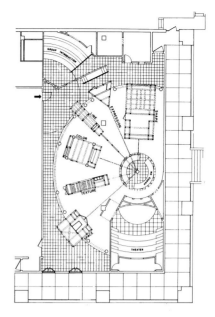

4.8

Impressions Gallery—Jackson, Mississippi; *The Joint Venture Firm of Linda S. Trobaugh/Samuel Mockbee, (1988)*
This children's exhibit, in the Mississippi Museum of Art, encourges interaction with the basic elements of art. The color and shape theories of Johannes Itten were used to form the individual pavilions. To provide equality among the six pavilions within the rectangular space, radial symmetry was employed. The pavilion's axes, which converge at a centerpoint, are marked by overhead colored neon tubes. (Courtesy: Linda S. Trobaugh, N.Y.)

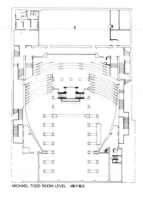

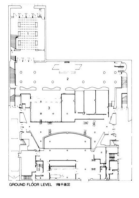

4.9

Palladium—New York City; *Arata Isozaki & Associates (1985)*

The owners requested that the designer provide a place where patrons could make a grand entry, to "see and be seen." Space was developed sequentially, with numerous points of entry; the sense of prolonged passage that ensues leads to the climax of the dance floor. The beige color scheme in the lobby was used to neutralize the chaos of the street, and prepare one to take the "plunge" into the "deep blue sea" foyer. From the foyer guests are drawn up the "stair way to heaven" by its "near-blinding luminosity," and pass through the frescoed "chapel of life's sorrows and joys," where they would finally be presented with a view of the dancers experiencing "heaven on earth." (Courtesy: Arata Isozaki & Associates, Tokyo.)

Hall proceeds to analyze the Japanese treatment of space, concluding that they were ingenious in extending visual space by exaggerating the individual's kinesthetic involvement in it.[30] It seems obvious that in so doing, they have extended one's sense of time-passage as well.

The idea of *duration*, or time-passage, is therefore inherent in both hierarchy and progression, and is a basic attribute of architectural space. Dewey affirms that buildings exist in a mode of "space-occupancy" and further states that "an instantaneous experience is an impossibility, biologically and psychologically. An experience is a product . . . of continuous and cumulative interaction of an organic self with the world."[31]

The designer controls that timeframe, usually through a manipulation of progression and hierarchy. Architecture in its exterior aspect may delight in being timeless, but in its interior dimension it is a study in time-passage. It is common to make judgments about room size, interior appointments, and mode of access based on factors of duration. And duration refers, not only to the present, but to the collective memories of experiences that have indelibly marked particular spaces. In *Body, Memory and Architecture,* Bloomer and Moore comment that:

> The centerplace of the house, like the body, accumulates memories that may have the characteristics of "feelings" rather than data. Rituals over time leave their impression on the walls and forms of the interior and endow the rooms with artifacts which give us access to previous experiences.[32]

Together, the factors that compose sequence help explain the way we view and use particular spaces.

Scale and *Proportion* are critical issues in design and are reexamined in the next chapter; there are, however, certain aspects of each that are of importance here. *Scale* refers to a size comparison between two things; these may be objects, forces, or ideas. But size is absolute (and measurable), and scale is relative. We may view something as large or small, in relation to a standard; thus this thing may be judged relative to its larger composition, against other things of like kind, in light of traditional expectation, or in comparison to humans. The important point is that scale is indeterminate without that standard. Whether small or large, scale has a certain associative content. That is, our perception, visually and affectively, of an object or idea changes as the scale changes. Such manipulation is especially complex in the interior. While windows and doors are quite amenable to assigned roles (in a mansion no one wonders which door is for guests and which for servants), interior furnishings are less flexible in scale change. It is not that there is no hierarchy of desk sizes, only that there is a practical ergonomic limit to this sort of role assignment (Fig 4.10).

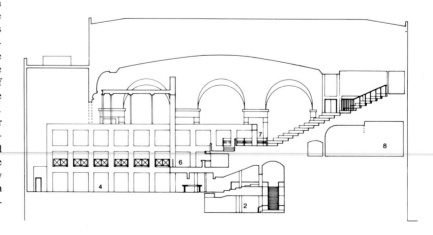

Proportion assumed metaphorical aspects millennia ago, and it is, in some sense, the most complex of the organizational principles. Practically, it simply serves to describe dimensional mathematical ratios such that pleasing qualities of mass and space result; and every society has evolved its own ideal system of proportion. There are several issues about proportion that deserve comment: first, historically, proportion was not invented, but observed and codified; second, rules of proportion are simply intended to make possible replication of results; and third, proportion is always bound to a time and place. Moreover, people do not always agree about proportional relationships, even within a given framework of time and culture. Like scale, proportion is especially complex in the interior dimension, where it becomes practically involved with arrangement and sequence. Interior space is multiple in view, and proportional appropriateness may change from one spatial setting to another. While proportion may unify a structure in its exterior aspect, a similar use may dull it in the interior. This interior aspect is discussed by Wharton and Codman, Jr.:

> Proportion is the good breeding of architecture. It is that something, indefinable to the professional eye, which gives repose and distinction to a room: in its origin a matter of nice mathematical calculation, of scientific adjustment of voids and masses, but in its effects as intangible as that all-pervading essence which the ancients called the soul.[33]

They also comment on the roles of the architect and interior designers, concluding that if two different people are employed to build and decorate, the employer should at least try to ensure that they both were trained in the same school of composition.[34] One clearly senses the broader frame of reference that permeates the authors' concerns; proportion is seen in its wider role.

Concept and Type

All these principles cannot be used equally on all projects; therefore, it is important to choose carefully the principles to be emphasized in a particular project. The choice depends on the *concept.* Concept is the main idea influencing the steps taken and decisions made during a project's design phase. Thus it affects the selection and manipulation of basic design elements and organizational principles to be used in solving a specific design problem. This is in keeping with its formal definition, which is as rich as that of form:

fr. *LL conceptus:* something conceived in the mind;
a general or abstract idea: a universal notion;
a generic mental image abstracted from percepts; and
an idea comprehending the essential attributes of a class.

While the above is scarcely a comprehensive view of the definition, it does isolate several interesting aspects of the term. First, as concept is an abstract mental construct, it should be viewed in terms of cause, not effect; second, there must be some prior basis for a concept's assumptions; and third, a concept ought to be inclusive in its breadth of concerns. In *Drawing Interior Architecture,* Norman Diekman and John Pile note that outstanding works in architecture and interior design are characterized by strong concept, and that a work without concept ". . . may be serviceable, but it is often a jumble that offers no particular satisfaction, is hardly memorable for even an hour, and is certainly not an aesthetic achievement in any sense."[35]

When designers make a concept statement, they are stating their original idea, that which dictated all following decisions. But the concept is rarely

4.10

Main Bedroom in Hill House—Helensburgh; *Charles Rennie Mackintosh (1902–3)* One of the characteristics of furniture is its ability to denote scale; that is, certain pieces of furniture (like chairs) are so familiar that they act as standards. Here Mackintosh has suggested that his chair is very large, thus making the enclosing room also large by implication. Actually, the chair is diminutive, the minimum necessary to its function. (Collection: Royal Commission on Ancient and Historical Monuments, Scotland.)

the first idea one has when approaching a design problem; it more likely occurs out of a process of trial and error as one considers various ways of thinking about (and visualizing) the problem. This stage is usually referred to as preliminary design, the purely creative aspect of design. Once the concept is established, all later decisions are evaluated and judged by their ability to clarify, enhance, relate to, and occasionally contrast with the concept. In that creative process, the designer likely begins with the program (site, function, image, etc.) and the various ways it assumes tangible shape, in light of the designer's own ideas and knowledge about its intended users. Form (visual elements and principles of organization) is used in that realization, adding its own inherent associations and references. As the concept takes final shape, it will look to its intended content for verification. Finally, it is important not to confuse concept and theory; the concept is what we are seeking to achieve, the theory is the explanation of the systems used to obtain it.

The relationship between concept and plan is described by Frank Lloyd Wright in an article printed in *The Architectural Record* of 1928, where he says that buildings ought first to be conceived in the mind before touching paper:

> Let the building, living in imagination, develop gradually, taking more and more definite form before committing it to the drafting board. When the thing sufficiently lives for you then start to plan it with instruments, not before . . . it is best always thus to cultivate the imagination from within.[36]

And Wright cautions the designer that, if the concept fades as the drawing proceeds, not to be afraid to throw out the entire idea and begin over; although he admits that "Few architects have that capacity."[37]

The idea of *type* derives from its original Greek meaning, "impression," in the sense that a coin was "beaten" out. By the late fifteenth century type became a common word associated with the impressions made on a printing press. In architectural design it describes the configurations used historically for particular kinds of buildings. These are not types simply in the sense of basic shapes and flow diagrams; type in this sense means the "correct" way of building for particular purposes, although cultural and regional customs influence the type's appearance. This is what Aldo Rossi refers to when he says, "The typology is a general design that becomes the basis for cultural action which generates a particular architectural form."[38]

In his *Cour d'architecture,* Jacques François Blondel writes that the different sorts of production belonging to architecture, ". . . should carry the *imprint* of the particular intention of each building (and) . . . should possess a character which determines the general form and which declares the building for what it is."[39] Blondel wrote in the eighteenth century; by the nineteenth century a conception of type based on pragmatic need and historicity was emerging, and it became usual to find moral values ascribed to particular types. The distinction between *type* and *model* is important: a type is a general, abstract ordering of spatial elements reflecting broad cultural peculiarities; a model is a concretized image that reflects a particular spatial order. In short, the model is the type made perceptible. Quantrill notes:

> . . . the *typology* gives only an example of the process of spatial ordering. The *model* provides a picture of a particular piece of this process *in operation,* and that model may therefore be copied.[40]

The typology (or type) thus provides a design base that considers socially accepted form and its historical evolution; these are indispensable for the development of a model. Quantrill refers to this when he notes typology's value as a measuring stick for identifying persistent architectural responses to conscious rituals.[41]

There have, therefore, always been two values to type; stability in adherence and standard against which to test ideas. It has been pointed out that to design within a traditional context, in which knowledge of the types being used is shared by designer and audience, is an advantage—in terms of communication and dispensing with inessential decisions.[42] It is far more common in contemporary Western societies, however, to reject the notion of tradition altogether, or to view building types as simple, easily adaptable geometric paradigms. But, as Alan Colquhoun points out:

> . . . we are not free from the forms of the past, and from the availability of these forms as typological models, but that, if we assume we are free, we have lost control over a very active sector of our imagination, and our power to communicate with others. It would seem that we ought to try to establish a value system which takes into account the forms and solutions of the past, if we are to gain control over concepts which will obtrude themselves into the creative process, whether we like it or not.[43]

Use of type is not without its difficulties. For example, new technologies sometimes arise that make possible forms only casually related to function. The marked difference between the theater in the Paris Opera and Chicago's Auditorium Theater may be largely explained by Dankmar Adler's decision to use a cast-iron elliptical arch, resulting in a new stressing of the horizontal; a stress unrelated to the social function of the building. And his decision to use Scott Russell's isacoustic sound curve in the Auditorium changed the design emphasis in that space from sightlines to soundfield. It is also extremely difficult to determine what consideration to give fashion and fad, which might be culturally shortlived. Typology is nonetheless an invaluable tool for the designer and critical to an understanding of culture.

Constructs

To clarify these definitions (vocabulary, grammar, concept, etc.), it helps to analyze two pieces of furniture; a rosewood couch by Mies van der Rohe and a chaise-longue by Le Corbusier and Charlotte Perriand. In each case the concept seems clear, and there is accompanying theory to underpin it. The structure is unambiguous, with a geometric basis, and materials are used with integrity.

The rosewood couch was designed by Mies in 1930, and its concept seems clear: the creation of a chaise-longue that uses modern materials, encourages intimacy, and expresses calm repose through the manipulation of balance and proportion (Fig 4.11). We deduce this; Mies leaves no record (to our knowledge) of his initial concept. He does leave many statements that serve as theoretical base for such designs and that support the assertion of concept. For example, he states, "Technology must create intimacy"[44], and again, "We must learn to work with technology, using the materials of our time."[45]

The structure of the chaise-longue is exposed to view, and the strength of steel is proclaimed in the slender legs. The materials are chrome-plated steel, rosewood (frame), and leather; in each case the character, color, and texture of the material is clearly expressed, their richness replacing the ornamentation of an earlier period. Philip Johnson comments that, "As always, Mies' impeccable craftsmanship plays an important part in his furniture design. Everything is calculated to the last millimeter. . . ."[46] Sensitivity to scale and proportion is evident in the width and spacing of the

4.11

Couch; *Ludwig Mies van der Rohe (1930)*
(Courtesy: Knoll International.)

leather strapping, size of the upholstery buttons, and proportions of the leather rectangles on the cushions. The cushion is not only altered proportionally by being upholstered with a welting process, but gains texture as well. Interest is maintained by a composition that uses a full range of primary elements; point, line, plane, and their volumetric extension. Asymmetry is employed in the placement of the cylindrical cushion, which in turn suggests tension in its seeming ability to move along the plane. Intimacy is encouraged by referring to the human body at rest, and repose by the floating quality of the seating plane, produced by its being cantilevered past the legs. Finally, calm is expressed through proportional relationships and scale alteration in the elements. The result is a piece of furniture with a clear and guiding conceptual base, supported by theory and using the design elements in an organized manner.

Le Corbusier and Perriand designed their chaise-longue in 1928, and the concept seems just as clear: the creation of a chaise-longue that also uses modern materials and methods and proportional ratios. But instead of inducing calm repose, the intent was to provide humans with a "beautiful tool" that would be dynamic and emotionally stimulating (Fig 4.12). This shift in emphasis is supported by such assertions by Le Corbusier as "To search for the human scale, for human function, is to define human needs. . . ."[47] and ". . . art consists in nothing more than significant relationships between expressive elements, provokers of feeling."[48] The structure is clear in this case as well, for he felt strongly that the machine could produce polished steel, ". . . shaped with a theoretical precision and exactitude which can never be seen in nature itself."[49] The materials consist of highly polished tubing and angle steel, rubber-wrapped cylindrical tubes, leather, and hairy skin. As with Mies, the qualities of the materials are forthrightly stated, with an eye to maximizing inherent textures. Renato de Fusco comments that there is in Le Corbusier's work ". . . the use of new techniques, weightlessness combined with solidity, juxtapositioning of different kinds of material, and above all the concept of maximum functionalism."[50]

The designers have employed horizontal, curved, and diagonal lines, which create interest through variety. This dynamic quality is enhanced by the cylinder on the sloped plane of the back; this contrasts with the frame, which is based on the golden section. While the final effect is dynamic, the chaise-longue itself is quite comfortable, and there is an air of ritual attached to it as pronounced as with Mies' chaise. Charles Jencks comments:

> Because the Z-shape is further supported at four points by a sub-structure, the metaphor becomes one of offering up the reclining body for sacrifice or display. It is as if the body is being propped up on fingertips like a precious jewel."[51]

Thus the two chaise-longues, alike in treatment of structure and materials, are quite unalike in final statement (content). A different initial concept has led to a different use of elements and organization. And while both enjoy unity, the end appearance is different perceptually and conceptually.

Design Notation Systems

In their book *Visual Notes for Architects and Designers* the architects Norman Crowe and Paul Laseau describe two skills that make up visual literacy, visual acuity, and visual expression. The former refers to the ability ". . . to *see* information or multiple messages in one's environment with clarity and accuracy." The latter, visual expression, ". . . is the ability to initiate visual messages. While visual acuity is concerned with the messages we receive, visual expression is concerned with the messages we send."[52] The authors go on to cite Donis A. Dondis' contention in *A Primer of Visual Literacy* that, in drawing, there are three types of visual messages: representation, abstraction, and symbolism. Representation is an effort to record—with selective accuracy—what actually appears before us, abstraction is concerned with the careful delineation of particular aspects of a visual reality according to our interests, and symbolism represents a generic view of that reality's type in order to communicate a conceptual message. Each

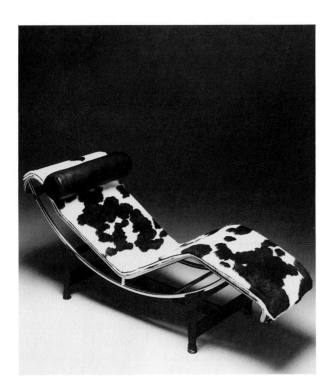

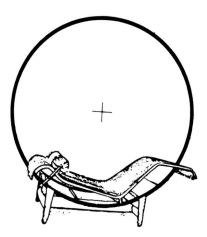

4.12

Chaise-longue a reglage continu; *Le Corbusier and Charlotte Perriand (1928)* (Sketch: Copyright 1991 ARS, N.Y./ SPADEM Chaise-longue: Available through Atelier International, Ltd.)

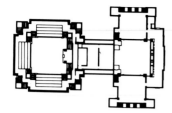

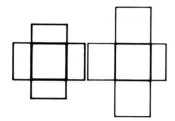

4.13

Parti and Main Floor Plan of Unity Temple
The parti diagram illustrates, in the most simplified way possible, the main concept of Wright's building. It indicates the balance between the place of worship and the place of assembly, and the most important area is shown as a square within a cruciform. This diagram is useful in determining, among other things, where the main entry to the building must occur. (Source: *Precedents in Architecture,* Roger H. Clark and Michael Pause.)

of these communication types has its particular use. But more important, each has its own internal logic or system, which must be consistently applied to be effective. That is, confusion in the use of these drawings usually indicates some confusion about what needs to be communicated.

Dondis' categories are intentionally broad and hence applicable to virtually every area of art and design. Spatial design uses its particular drawing-types, and these design-notation systems may be loosely grouped into three categories: the *formative,* which includes sketches, bubble diagrams, volumetric studies, and program outlines; the *developmental,* which includes plan, elevation, section, axonometric, perspective, and reflected ceiling; and the *informative,* the dimensioned drawings used for specification and construction. This grouping is a convenience; there are other ways drawings can be grouped, and not all of them fit conveniently into categories. The *Parti* diagram, for example, occupies a place between formative and developmental, a drawing-type that Clark and Pause define as ". . . the dominant idea of building which embodies the salient characteristics of that building. It encapsulates the essential minimum of the design. . . ."[53] In other words, it is an abstract guide to a design's development, but the product of a formative process (Fig 4.13).

Pauline Saliga has identified four sorts of architectural drawings: the *preliminary drawings,* which include sketches and notations; the *developmental drawings,* characterized by a certain tentativeness and flexibility; the *presentation drawings,* which are the (usually handsome) elevations, plans, and perspectives prepared for the client which, of course, may still be altered; and the *working drawings,* which are dimensioned for purposes of construction and seldom find their way into any sort of public exhibition. The working drawings represent the final stage before construction, and Saliga notes, "It is at this point that a shift in emphasis occurs from the drawings to the building itself."[54] This shift may also show the degree of congruence between the drawn idea and its physical manifestation.

Usually, the drawing element most relied on is line, which, as already noted, is an essentially abstract device whose inherent qualities change with application. This may be seen in the various meanings line conveys, depending on its weight and direction. A question also arises concerning the persuasive power of representational means. Put differently, to what degree does the designer's use of plan, elevation, and perspective influence the final appearance of the finished work? Line in architectural drawings tends to deny the third dimension. Charles Moore and Gerald Allen allude to this phenomenon in *Dimensions:* "Architects naturally think of the dimensions of space as being of primary importance to what they are doing, though sometimes the practice of designing two-dimensional plans leads them to go repetitively to the third spatial dimension, resulting in ceilings uniformly eight feet high."[55] Deanna Petherbridge also refers to this (more obliquely) when she writes, "But contemporary architects seem to have an almost total reliance on line, and not on mass. . . . And line, it would appear, is limitation: it is outline and definition, it contains rather than activates space."[56] Linear techniques (and air brush), coupled with a disdain for enlarged details, contribute to a flat nondifferentiated view of structures. Such methodologies may partly account for the emphasis on the use of three-dimensional models, which have contributed to new problems connected with their elusive scale, and the artificial viewpoint the onlooker is forced to adopt.

Saliga also notes two more recent drawing-types: the computer-generated rendering and the axonometric drawing. She suggests that the popularity of the latter may be due to architects' use of photographed models, ". . . in which the image of the model is flattened. Like such photographs, the ax-

Plate 1.

13 Lincoln's Inn Fields, London; *John Soane—Drawn by F. Copland (1817)*
Soane observes that the views from his breakfast room into the Monument Court and Museum, in their ". . . variety of outline and general arrangement and the design and decoration of this limited space, present a succession of those fanciful effects which constitute the poetry of architecture."¹ (By Courtesy of the Trustees of Sir John Soane's Museum.)

Plate 3.

190 South LaSalle Street—Chicago; *Burgee/Johnson (1987)*
In this commercial building, the vaulted and gilded lobby ceiling suggests a cathedral. This provides a sense of stability and endurance for its tenants, which include legal, banking, and financial firms. (Photo by: Frank Vodvarka.)

Plate 2.

House for Luis Barragán—Mexico; *Luis Barragán (1947)*
The rich colors of the low interior walls seem intimate compared to the exterior bathed in brilliant light; in fact, the only views to the outside are to the sky and garden. The effect is one of ritual and timelessness. (Photo by: Emilio Ambasz. Courtesy: The Museum of Modern Art, New York.)

Plate 4.

Offices for Vignelli Associates—New York;
Vignelli Associates, Designers (1986)
The reassuring symmetry stands in contrast
to the unorthodox use of materials, which are
bathed in a combination of natural and artificial light. Lella Vignelli notes that, ". . .
we have tried to develop our rational, geometric language as far as possible and create
the ultimate expression of what we are
now."[2] (Photo by: Luca Vignelli, New York.
Copyright 1986.)

Plate 5.

Palladium—New York City; *Arata Isozaki
& Associates (1985)*
The star-like quality of the "stairway to
heaven," leading from the "deep blue sea"
foyer to the Francesco Clemente fresco,
comes from the use of high luminosity glass
circles imbedded in the treads and landings.
The rhythm of the dark wood walls with traditional moldings stands in contrast to that
of the diagonal pipe railing along the steel
and glass stairs. (Photo by: Katsuaki Furu-
date, Tokyo.)

Plate 6.

**Cook-Fort Worth Children's Medical Cen-
ter;** *David M. Schwarz (1989)*
The medical departments are located on the
lower levels of this atrium building, with patient's rooms located in the upper four floors.
The interior facades are made of drywall that
is reflected in mirror glass curtainwall, increasing the apparent size of the atrium.
(Photo by: Jim Hedrich, Hedrich Blessing,
Chicago.)

Plate 7.

State Capitol Rotunda, Hartford, Conn.;
Richard Upjohn (1878)
The Rotunda is actually a series of circles in
perspective, which focus attention on the
lighted cupola in the dome. Thus, the democratic aspect of government is emphasized,
with a suggestion of divine guidance in political deliberations. (Photo by: Frank Vodvarka.)

Plate 8.

Dining Room at Kedleston—Derby; *Robert
Adam (1761)*
Adam unified the entire space through the
use of continuous, ornate plaster-work and a
rich, coordinated color scheme. The niche
has been treated as an apsidal chapel, and in
its ornament and symmetry, provides a focal
point for the room. (Copyright National Trust
Photographic Library 19, London.)

Plate 9.

Bathroom, Villa Karma—Switzerland;
Adolf Loos (1904)
The two sunken bathtubs are surrounded by
richly-veined marble columns, while the adjoining gymnastics room contains a fireplace
illuminated from above. The sink is set into
a niche, which mimics a Roman basilica, or
bath. (Photo by: Roberto Schezen, Milan.)

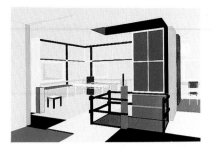

Plate 10.

Schröder House—Utrecht, The Netherlands *(Gouache and pencil on paper, 20½″ × 26″); Gerrit Rietveld (1924)*
Rietveld's color scheme for Schroder House—red, blue, yellow, black, white, and neutral—was derived from both Schoenmaeker's cosmology and from their primary character, thus forming a creative environment. (Collection: The Museum of Modern Art, New York. Interior perspective executed by Hanneke Schroder for The Museum of Modern Art exhibition: *De Stijl*, 1952.)

Plate 11.

Il Palazzo Hotel—Fukuoka, Japan; *Aldo Rossi and Morris Adjmi (1990)*
Rossi and Adjmi designed the building itself, but the program called for separate individuals to independently design the four bars located inside. The El Dorado bar, by Rossi and Adjmi, uses recessed lighting behind the golden facade that is intended to, ". . . make a quote of the (building's) architecture on the inside."[3] (Photo by: Lucy Chen, Cambridge, Mass.)

Plate 12.

Monsoon Restaurant—Sapporo, Japan; *Zaha Hadid Architects (1990)*
Hadid has worked with two trapezoidal floors of the building, contrasting them thematically as "fire" and "ice;" ice being the dining area, and fire the bar area. Of interest is her use of plexiglas models as a way to develop these spaces. Even though this approach is abstract, ". . . the built project is quite similar . . . in form and spirit, with dynamic shapes that suggest movement and infinite space."[4] In this way Hadid uses space itself as a fundamental form-generator. (Model: Dan Chadwick. Model Photo courtesy: Zaha Hadid, London. Interior—Photo by: Paul Warchol, New York.)

onometric is a practical way to indicate in two dimensions the spatial relationships that only a model can convey."[57] The axonometric was developed at the turn of the century by the French architectural historian Auguste Choisy as an instructional device and combines the floorplan, section, and two elevations. This kind of drawing provides a volumetric idea of the space and the relationships between spaces (Fig 4.14). But it is reasonable to inquire about the effect of axonometrics generally. Robert A.M. Stern has commented, "The axonometric is a drawing of the poly-technician and not of the poet, not just because it involves measure (all architectural drawings are 'measured' to some extent), but because it provides the designer and the observer with a conceptual rather than a perceptual view of buildings."[58] Such a drawing may therefore be useful as a dimensioning device, but grants little sense of spatial character.

Inherent in Allen's comments is the notion of an increased emphasis on the creative aspects of design in the formative stage of the process. Michael Graves' list of drawing types is interesting in this regard. His categories are: the *referential sketch,* in which the designer records, on a daily basis, visual architectural fragments that seem interesting; the *preparatory study,* the developmental drawings of ideas in progress; and the *definitive drawing,* which is the informative (and quantifiable) final diagram of the design (Fig 4.15). His way of viewing the drawing process tends to place greater

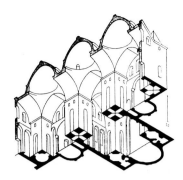

4.14

Saint-Front de Perigueux; *Auguste Choisy (1899)*
Choisy felt the selection of the graphic means of displaying architecture was important because certain techniques could suppress unnecessary information. Choisy used this axonometric to examine and analyze the construction of buildings in his *Histoire de l'architecture.* This is essentially a view of the interior that stresses its volumetric aspect, and alludes to the experience of being within and looking up. (Source: *Histoire de l'Architecture,* Auguste Choisy.)

4.15

Furniture Design Studies; *Michael Graves (1977)*
These studies represent Graves' notion of the "prepatory study," in which an idea is first explored. Graves notes that this type of drawing documents the process of inquiry, examining questions raised by a given intention in a manner that provides a basis for the later, more definitive work—a process involving the reexamination of given questions.[1] (Courtesy: Michael Graves Architect, Princeton, N.J. Photo by: Paschall/Taylor.)

A

B

4.16

(A) **Sketch of Acropolis—Athens;** *Le Corbusier;* *(B)* **Sketch of Acropolis—Athens** *(crayon); Louis Kahn (1951)*
Le Corbusier's sketch *(A)* emphasizes the perception of the Parthenon as a superstructure of a towering platform that rises above the plain below; this may reflect his belief that "profile and contour are the touchstone of the Architect."[2] Kahn, on the other hand, is obviously fascinated with the notions of mass, scale, and the rhythmic movement set up by the shadows of the buttressing *(B)*. Indeed, he seems more fascinated by the massive retaining wall than the vague shapes that rise above it. (*[A]* source: Copyright 1991 ARS, N.Y. /SPADEM; *[B]* courtesy: Sue Ann Kahn, New York.)

emphasis on the importance of formative drawing and the use of the referential sketch to create a comprehensive body of information. Graves comments:

> . . . the drawing does possess a life of its own, an insistence, a meaning, which is fundamental to its existence. Good drawing, by virtue of this intrinsic reciprocity between mind and act, goes beyond simple information. . . . [59]

The reference to the recording of architectural fragments raises another point: the drawing of such plans and details, of buildings past and present, also provides a record of our own design values. We can, through such studies, gain some additional insight to the thinking of other designers. Indeed, a comparison of drawings of the same architectural site by two designers often reveals much about the design aspects that most concern those designers. This in large measure accounts for the importance that has always been attached to designer's travel journals or sketchbooks and the analysis of architectural drawings from the past (Fig 4.16).

Such drawings may serve other purposes, however, beyond the traditional role of physical description. In the concluding pages of her article, Saliga observes that, while the main purpose of architectural drawings is the creation of a building, a certain important group of drawings deals only with concepts—including student works, travel sketches, and polemical drawings.[60] She notes that student sketches may reveal much about prevailing design trends at a particular time, and travel sketches may provide a storehouse of images—a catalog of impressions for later use. The third type, polemical drawings, in which a designer defends or explains a theoretical position, may be the most fascinating for the viewer. For example, in his design of a "Bathroom Addition Project as Homage to Dante's *Inferno*," Stanley Tigerman provides the following rationale, "The bathroom has suffered long enough from the excesses of Victorian privacy and this project intends to herald it as a place of joy."[61] Thus the literary allusion serves as pretense for a penetrating commentary on contemporary notions of domestic life and the associated rituals (Fig 4.17).

The final issue concerns the viability of drawings as architecture or, more to the point, drawings as architectural acts. Gerald Allen refers to this phenomenon when he notes that beautiful drawings are not being made only to illustrate buildings, as they were previously, but also to illustrate more explicitly the ideas that shaped them—and even to illustrate polemical theories about architecture itself. And these are now being bought by collectors, for whom they are works of art as well as architectural talismans.[62] He goes on to state, "It is arguable that the best ideas in architecture today are being found more on paper, and on plastic and photographic film and the other new mediums now being used, than in actual buildings."[63] But Allen's position on the issue of drawings' substituting for architecture is clear when he states:

> Architecture is, quite obviously, a three-dimensional material art. Much less obvious, however, is the fact that the experience of architecture is not simply visual. The rich store of mental images, for instance, possessed by all of us and held in memory is not only useful but indeed critical to informing the three-dimensional reality of architecture with meaning. But also crucial . . . are those perceptual dimensions in addition to the visual ones that are technically known as *haptic*. . . .[64]

Haptic perception, he says, includes a sense of scale, distance, enclosure, etc. And he concludes that it is impossible for drawings to evoke the same perceptions that architecture can, no matter how vividly they may suggest them.[65]

Despite the relegation of drawings to the role of "secondary representation," they nonetheless are vital to the design process. Indeed, Allen points out that when the rich reality of the building conflicts with the limitations of the drawing process, an aspect of the design thought important for a particular reason could be isolated and thus vividly rendered, possibly even more so than in the building itself.[66] Thus were students in the École des Beaux-Arts encouraged to draw with an emphasis on invention and creativity rather than structural comprehensiveness. Put differently, the most useful aspect of the drawing process may be regarded as its ability to visualize concepts and give form to theoretical ideas; and the most useful type of drawing may be the preliminary sketch. Indeed, it is arguable that architectural drawings will, at some future date, be divided into two categories: sketches and freehand developmental drawings, and computer-generated and dimensionalized presentation and working drawings.

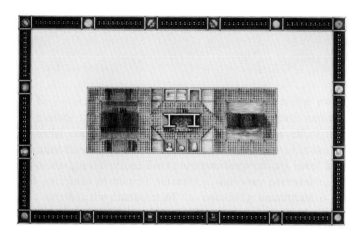

4.17

Bathroom Addition Project as Homage to Dante's Inferno; *Stanley Tigerman, assisted by Deborah Doyle and Patrick Burke (1980)* Tigerman notes that this exercise for the Kohler Company was intended as an independent bathing environment made of glass blocks. He comments, ". . . the metaphor for purgatory is intended as absolution—the internal cleansing of the body. Furthermore water closet, lavatory, bidet, shower and tub reside independently of one another, each in its own altarlike space."[3] The metaphor for hell, he says, is the steambath, while the heavenly metaphor is an elevated chaise longue with trompe l'oeil clouds floating above. (Courtesy: Tigerman McCurry Architects, Chicago.)

in the Greek musical scale. More specifically, what Pythagoras discovered was that the Greek musical consonances could be produced by dividing a string of the lyre in the following ratios: 1:2 (octave); 2:3 (fifth); 3:4 (fourth); and 1:4 (double octave). In "The Changing Concept of Proportion," Rudolf Wittkower comments that this discovery that the musical consonances were arithmetically expressible by the ratios of the first four integers (1:2:3:4) and that there existed a close interrelationship of sound, space (length of string), and numbers ". . . must have left Pythagoras and his associates amazed and fascinated. . . ."[8]

There are ten terms of proportions that have been confirmed by the neo-Pythagorean School; Pythagoras himself recognized three of the most important, those determining the Greek musical scale. They are the *arithmetic* (1,2,3, . . .), the *geometric* (1,2,4, . . .), and the *harmonic* (6,8,12, . . .). But at least one other proportional scale proved influential in shaping design theory, the *Fibonacci* series (3,5,8,13 . . .). When Pythagoras said, "Everything is arranged according to Number,"[9] he had in mind the symbolic qualities of numbers as well as their ability to denote quantity—particularly, the relationship between numbers. Arnheim regards the Pythagorean discovery as critical, noting that this discovery—made more substantial by our present-day knowledge of the simple relations between the wave frequencies of musical sounds—". . . established for all time to come the conviction that harmony depended on spatial measure."[10] These relationships suggested, moreover, that certain proportions were inherently beautiful, in the way Santayana had noted, ". . . the transformation of an element of sensation into the quality of the thing." What we see as beautiful, must be beautiful.

Ratio and proportion are not the same thing. A ratio is the result of quantitatively comparing two like things or groups of things; this can be expressed simply as *a/b*, a comparison on the order of two magnitudes. The definition of proportion comes from Euclid, "Proportion is the equality of two ratios,"[11] implying a necessary minimum of three magnitudes. This is echoed in *Timaeus,* when Plato states that ". . . it is impossible to combine satisfactorily two things without a third one: we must have between them a correlating link."[12] This could take the form of *a/b = c/d* (four magnitudes); or *a/b = b/c* (three magnitudes). In the first instance the geometrical proportion is considered *discontinuous,* and in the second case *continuous.* A continuous proportional series, then, might take the form of *a/b = b/c,* or *b² = ac,* then (*b = √ac*). This last value may be thought of as the proportional mean between *a* and *c*. In *The Geometry of Art and Life,* Matila Ghyka notes that the equation of proportion, discontinuous or continuous, can have any number of terms, but:

> . . . we have always the *permanency* of a *characteristic ratio* (. . . the concept of proportion introduces besides the simple comparison or measurement the idea of a new permanent quality, which is transmitted from one ratio to another; it is this *analogical variant* which besides the measurement brings an ordering principle, a relation between the different magnitudes and their measures).[13]

The simplest asymmetrical section and its corresponding continuous proportion is *The Golden Section.* This relationship can be expressed as follows:

$$a/b = b/c$$

where *c* = *a* + *b*, then *a/b* = *b/a* + *b*, or *b²/a* = *b/a* + 1
If *b/a* = *x*, then *x* = (1 + √5)/2

This last quantity is what is referred to as the Golden Mean (θ).

This may be restated as follows: the Golden Section determines a pro-

Despite the relegation of drawings to the role of "secondary representation," they nonetheless are vital to the design process. Indeed, Allen points out that when the rich reality of the building conflicts with the limitations of the drawing process, an aspect of the design thought important for a particular reason could be isolated and thus vividly rendered, possibly even more so than in the building itself.[66] Thus were students in the École des Beaux-Arts encouraged to draw with an emphasis on invention and creativity rather than structural comprehensiveness. Put differently, the most useful aspect of the drawing process may be regarded as its ability to visualize concepts and give form to theoretical ideas; and the most useful type of drawing may be the preliminary sketch. Indeed, it is arguable that architectural drawings will, at some future date, be divided into two categories: sketches and freehand developmental drawings, and computer-generated and dimensionalized presentation and working drawings.

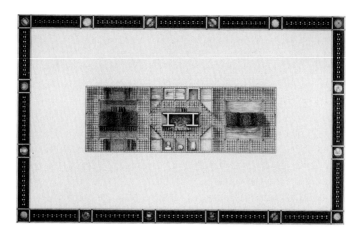

4.17

Bathroom Addition Project as Homage to Dante's *Inferno; Stanley Tigerman, assisted by Deborah Doyle and Patrick Burke (1980)* Tigerman notes that this exercise for the Kohler Company was intended as an independent bathing environment made of glass blocks. He comments, ". . . the metaphor for purgatory is intended as absolution—the internal cleansing of the body. Furthermore water closet, lavatory, bidet, shower and tub reside independently of one another, each in its own altarlike space."[3] The metaphor for hell, he says, is the steambath, while the heavenly metaphor is an elevated chaise longue with trompe l'oeil clouds floating above. (Courtesy: Tigerman McCurry Architects, Chicago.)

Ordering Systems 5

Enclosure

The point was made earlier that architecture is the art of enclosing space. This involves two elements: space and the material enclosing it. If there is to be a unified effect, the two must be in concert, and this *inner order* lies within the control of design intention. There are two implications here: first, the physiological attributes of human perception, however persuasive, can be changed; and second, the character of the enclosing membrane is critical to an awareness of the space it encloses. This seems reasonable, since architectural space is more a concept than a thing, and can be seen only when delineated by containing elements. Enclosure, therefore, consists of limiting surfaces having certain *physical, visual,* and *symbolic* characteristics, and the *finite space* they surround. This view of space is essentially Cartesian; but, as noted, there are other, highly objectified ways of viewing space (Fig 5.1).

In the Preface to his *Enclosing Behavior,* Robert B. Bechtel decisively states that "... there is no such thing as the design of space or spaces. *Behavior,* not space, is enclosed by architecture. No dwelling, building, or city is planned to be empty."[1] And psychology offers evidence that human spatial behavior may be influenced more by interpersonal spacing mechanisms than by reaction to fixed features. This in turn involves the notion of *personal space,* the dynamic outward boundary of human spatial definition. The flexibility of the enclosure and the spatial elasticity of the contained space are eloquently described in the *Mort Lucide,* by Georges Spyridaki:

> My house is diaphanous, but it is not of glass. It is more of the nature of vapor. Its walls contract and expand as I desire. At times, I draw them about me like protective armor . . . at others, I let the walls of my house blossom out in their own space, which is infinitely extensible.[2]

Spyridaki's walls are those that divide interior from exterior; the intimate space within, from the limitless space without. These walls are probably the most profound in their dual aspect, suggesting the most decisive differentiation in visual character. But walls exist that are interior in both aspects; these are the internal walls that subdivide the larger enclosure into smaller, quasi-independent spaces, or rooms. Such spaces must relate to the character of the whole structure, as well as to each other, in a time-dependent order described earlier as sequence. Nor is enclosure necessarily total, if we adhere to the principle that the experience of enclosed outdoor space is essentially an interior one (Plate 6). Finally, the very shape of space—its relative convexity or concavity—affects our apprehension of it. Arnheim refers to this when he observes:

> Although man does not commonly shape his abode by creating a hollow with his own body, a strongly concave interior behaves as though he wielded some such power. The occupant feels elevated and expanded as he reaches out to the confines of the room.[3]

Concave spaces are thus empowered, providing for highly charged, affective experiences; this may account for the relatively special circumstances cultures reserve for them.

Out of the above come four considerations: first, the nature of walls by type and position; second, the hierarchial ranking of walls within the enclosure; third, the type and disposition of elements that characterize the enclosing membrane; and fourth, the way in which the space enables specified behaviors. But these may be difficult issues to reconcile. In the first instance, for example, the definition of exterior wall may depend on certain intricacies of placement; and again, a hierarchial ranking of walls can be difficult when both sides of the wall assert an equal claim to definition. Such definitions have moral overtones; by virtue of their design, walls can affect human relationships, an aspect alluded to in chapter four.

Of interest here, however, are the types, characteristics, and functions of the various elements that design uses to define the *enclosing membrane,* and their inherent moral aspects. In 1914 the poet Paul Scheerbart stated:

> We live for the most part in closed rooms. . . . If we want our culture to rise to a higher level, we are obliged, for better or for worse, to change our architecture. And this only becomes possible if we take away the closed character from the rooms in which we live. We can only do that by introducing glass architecture, which lets in the light of the sun, the moon, and the stars, not merely through a few windows, but through every possible wall, which will be made entirely of glass—of coloured glass.[4]

Scheerbart's ideas are discussed in a later chapter; important here is the moral value he ascribes to his glass walls, an echo of ". . . the humanistic

5.1

Private Places—**Dance Performance;** *Concert Dance, Inc. (1988)*
This photograph is taken from a dance performance choreographed by Venetia Stifler. The photographic note by Frank Vodvarka use architectural interiors as enclosure, but the essential meaning of the performance comes from the ritual interaction of human beings with their spatial setting. (Photo by: Frank Vodvarka.)

assumption that it is desirable to establish a moral relationship . . . whereby the exterior makes certain revelations about the interior that the interior corroborates. . . .''[5] This can be achieved through the treatment of detail, massing of elements, and overt reference, although the demands made by the interior may limit this. That is, it may be necessary for interior walls to reflect behavioral imperatives that the exterior never has to contend with.

Roger Scruton has observed that architectural space relies, in part, on the *significant detail* of the material that surrounds it. He refers to those details such as material-type, carving, and molding-types; but there are also those details that, while not specifically architectural, have a symbolic or narrative character. These elements might include basreliefs, mosaics, and murals that contain subject matter suggesting certain spatial functions and that are framed by the structure. Both the limiting planes and their constituent details are arranged through the use of devices such as proportion, geometry, and scale; these in turn grant space its particular qualities (Fig 5.2). Thus these devices are asked to reconcile the demands of cognition and perception, function and symbol—and do so while accounting for their own inherent properties.

Proportion

Elements of mass and space have dimensions and, therefore, exist in a mathematical relationship to one another. This series of relationships, or ratios, is what the term proportion refers to. Such sequences occur both within entities and between them, thus regulating all we know of reality; it is probably this quality that accounts for the historical importance accorded proportion as a way of grasping both corporeal and metaphysical truths. That importance is reflected in St. Thomas Aquinas' statement that ''. . . each thing will be called beautiful because it has clarity of its kind, whether spiritual or physical, and, correspondingly, because it is constructed in proper proportion.''[6] Certain proportions have been more pleasing than others, and have accordingly been codified into standards. The best known of these, the *Golden Section,* comes from the Greeks, but other societies have derived their own standards. Proportion is, therefore, culturally determined and temporally bound. At any given moment, however, a proportional system may be endowed with spiritual attributes.

Geometry, the measure of the earth, was used in Egypt to redefine farming boundaries after the yearly floods. This involved both social and metaphysical factors, and it is the latter quality that endows geometry with such absolute force in the deliberations of the Greeks, who inherited it. Put differently, geometry was seen from the outset as an approach to the natural order of the universe. And so important was this discipline in the following centuries that it formed one of the Quadrivium (with arithmetic, astronomy, and music) of classical education. In his *Sacred Geometry,* Robert Lawlor points out:

> The laws of simple harmonics were considered to be universals which defined the relationship and interchange between the temporal movements and events of the heavens and the spatial order and development on earth. . . . Thus a seemingly common mathematical activity can become a discipline for intellectual and spiritual insight.[7]

The origins of this tradition are in the ideas of Pythagoras (560–490 B.C.), whose discovery of numerical relationships implied that the structure of the universe could be comprehended through proportion and ratios. And of particular importance were the ratios derived from the harmonic intervals

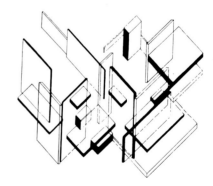

5.2

The Elementary Expressional Means of Architecture; *Theo Van Doesburg and C. Van Eesteren (1924)*
In his *Principles of Neo-Plastic Art,* Theo Van Doesburg used this illustration to explain his statement: "The pure expressional means of architecture is plane, mass (positive) and space (negative). The architect expresses his aesthetic experience through the relationships of planes and masses to internal spaces and to space."[1] (Copyright: Theo Van Doesburg VAGA, New York, 1991.)

in the Greek musical scale. More specifically, what Pythagoras discovered was that the Greek musical consonances could be produced by dividing a string of the lyre in the following ratios: 1:2 (octave); 2:3 (fifth); 3:4 (fourth); and 1:4 (double octave). In "The Changing Concept of Proportion," Rudolf Wittkower comments that this discovery that the musical consonances were arithmetically expressible by the ratios of the first four integers (1:2:3:4) and that there existed a close interrelationship of sound, space (length of string), and numbers ". . . must have left Pythagoras and his associates amazed and fascinated. . . ."[8]

There are ten terms of proportions that have been confirmed by the neo-Pythagorean School; Pythagoras himself recognized three of the most important, those determining the Greek musical scale. They are the *arithmetic* (1,2,3, . . .), the *geometric* (1,2,4, . . .), and the *harmonic* (6,8,12, . . .). But at least one other proportional scale proved influential in shaping design theory, the *Fibonacci* series (3,5,8,13 . . .). When Pythagoras said, "Everything is arranged according to Number,"[9] he had in mind the symbolic qualities of numbers as well as their ability to denote quantity—particularly, the relationship between numbers. Arnheim regards the Pythagorean discovery as critical, noting that this discovery—made more substantial by our present-day knowledge of the simple relations between the wave frequencies of musical sounds—". . . established for all time to come the conviction that harmony depended on spatial measure."[10] These relationships suggested, moreover, that certain proportions were inherently beautiful, in the way Santayana had noted, ". . . the transformation of an element of sensation into the quality of the thing." What we see as beautiful, must be beautiful.

Ratio and proportion are not the same thing. A ratio is the result of quantitatively comparing two like things or groups of things; this can be expressed simply as a/b, a comparison on the order of two magnitudes. The definition of proportion comes from Euclid, "Proportion is the equality of two ratios,"[11] implying a necessary minimum of three magnitudes. This is echoed in *Timaeus*, when Plato states that ". . . it is impossible to combine satisfactorily two things without a third one: we must have between them a correlating link."[12] This could take the form of $a/b = c/d$ (four magnitudes); or $a/b = b/c$ (three magnitudes). In the first instance the geometrical proportion is considered *discontinuous*, and in the second case *continuous*. A continuous proportional series, then, might take the form of $a/b = b/c$, or $b^2 = ac$, then ($b = \sqrt{ac}$). This last value may be thought of as the proportional mean between a and c. In *The Geometry of Art and Life*, Matila Ghyka notes that the equation of proportion, discontinuous or continuous, can have any number of terms, but:

> . . . we have always the *permanency* of a *characteristic ratio* (. . . the concept of proportion introduces besides the simple comparison or measurement the idea of a new permanent quality, which is transmitted from one ratio to another; it is this *analogical variant* which besides the measurement brings an ordering principle, a relation between the different magnitudes and their measures).[13]

The simplest asymmetrical section and its corresponding continuous proportion is *The Golden Section*. This relationship can be expressed as follows:

$$a/b = b/c$$

where $c = a + b$, then $a/b = b/a + b$, or $b^2/a = b/a + 1$
If $b/a = x$, then $x = (1 + \sqrt{5})/2$

This last quantity is what is referred to as the Golden Mean (θ).

This may be restated as follows: the Golden Section determines a proportion between the whole and its two parts, such that the ratio between the smaller part and the larger is the same as that between the larger and the whole. This is usually referred to as a division into mean and extreme ratio. The astronomer and mathematician Johannes Kepler stated, ''Geometry has two great treasures: one is the theorem of Pythagoras, the other the division of a line into mean and extreme ratios, that is θ, the Golden Mean. The first way may be compared to a measure of gold, the second to a precious jewel.''[14] The Golden Section may be geometrically constructed quite easily, using a right angle and compass. Wittkower believes that much of its notoriety derives from a treatise published in 1854 by Adolf Zeising, for whom the Golden Section represented the perfect mean between absolute unity and·absolute variety, between mere repetition and disorder.[15] The rectangle that can be constructed based on these proportions came to be known as the *Golden Rectangle,* and Zeising used it to explain the beauty of the Parthenon.

The Greek use of geometry had certain characteristics that endeared it to theorists, particularly Jay Hambidge, whose *Dynamic Symmetry* was published in 1924. Hambidge's theory was based on the assumption that what the logarithmic spiral means for the structural understanding of growth in nature, the incommensurable root rectangles ($1{:}\sqrt{2}$, $1{:}\sqrt{3}$, $1{:}\sqrt{5}$) meant for the structure of Greek art and architecture.[16] That is, the irrational numbers yielded a *dynamic symmetry* (the Parthenon), as opposed to whole integers, which yielded a *static symmetry* (as in the architecture of the Italian Renaissance). Hambidge believed that dynamic rectangles could produce vital harmonic subdivisions and combinations, in a manner that static rectangles could not. And, like Zeising, he used the Parthenon as an illustration of the root rectangles (Fig 5.3). There is actually little real disagreement in their analyses, since the Golden Rectangle is simply a particular type of root rectangle. Two points are crucial in his theory: first, the power of root rectangles to yield significant subsets; and second, the reference to growth in nature. The root rectangles in fact serve in the construction of logarithmic spirals, which occur commonly in the growth patterns of nature (Fig 5.4). C. Arthur Coan stated, ''Nature uses this as one of her most indispensable measuring rods, absolutely reliable, yet never without variety, producing perfect stability of purpose without the slightest risk of monotony.''[17] And Hambidge characterized dynamic symmetry in nature as ''. . . a symmetry suggestive of life and movement. Its great value to design lies in its power of transition or movement from one form to another in the system. It produces the only perfect modulating process in any of the arts.''[18] But the Golden Section also relates to another course, the Fibonacci series.

This series was discovered by Leonardo of Pisa (1175–1230), called Fibonacci, who published his *Liber Abaci* (Book of the Abacus) in 1202. Aside from this text's value as an introduction of Arabic numerals to Europe, it also contained an interesting entry based on a mathematical progression. Fibonacci (son of Bonaccio, or ''simpleton'') developed a proportional series that was noteworthy for two reasons: first, each number in the series was the product of the previous two, 3,5,8,13,21,34 . . .; and second, any Fibonacci number divided by the next highest yields the figure 0.618034 [although this is not precisely accurate until the 14th point in the series (i.e., 377 and above)]. What makes this so interesting is that 0.618034:1 is the ratio of the Golden Section. It is, in fact, an arithmetical analogue for the geometric section. Ghyka states that this series has ''. . . the remarkable property of producing 'gnomonic growth' (in which the growing surface of volume remains homothetic, similar to itself) by a simple process of accretion of discrete elements, of integer multiples of the unit of accretion; hence the capital role in botany of the Fibonacci series.''[19] And this

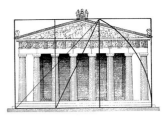

A

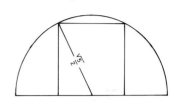

B

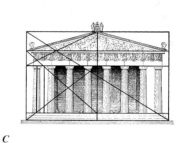

C

5.3

(A) **The Parthenon,** *Harmonic Analysis by Zeising; (B)* **Development of a Root 5 Rectangle;** *(C)* **The Parthenon,** *Harmonic Analysis by Hambidge*
Zeising noted that the rectangular shape of the Parthenon's façade *(A)* was a Golden Rectangle, which is simply an extension of a Golden Section. But in his analysis, Hambidge contended that the façade is based on $\sqrt{5}$ rectangles. The diagram *(B)* confirms that a $\sqrt{5}$ rectangle may be devised by first constructing a Golden Rectangle, and then continuing the arc through the other corner to complete a semicircle. Thus Hambidge's analysis of the façade *(C)* is mathematically related to Zeising's. (Source: Éléments et Théorie, J. Guadet with superimposed grid by J. Malnar.)

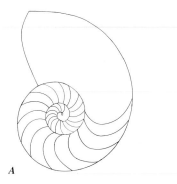

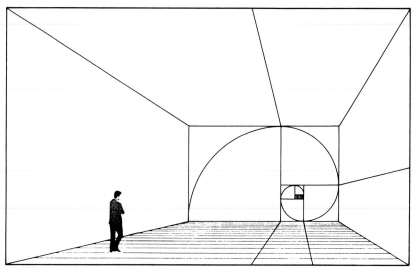

A

B

5.4

(A) **The Golden Spiral;** *(B)* **The Golden Spiral, in a Golden Room**

The diagram *(A)* describes a Golden Spiral which, unlike the $\sqrt{5}$ spiral, may be inscribed inside a Golden Rectangle, and which represents the growth pattern of the famous Nautilus shell. The room *(B)* is in proportion of the Golden Mean, or Θ. ([A] drawn by: J.Malnar; [B] source: *Geometry in Architecture,* William Blackwell, 1984.)

does not include only botany, but growth in snails, shellfish, the horns and claws of animals, pine cones and parrot beaks; the list is not only enormous, but all-encompassing.

Perhaps most important, the series provided an arithmetic approximation for the construction of a geometric shape. For the Renaissance, this was an important issue. Pythagorean-Platonic geometry comprised two different sorts of mathematics: the numerical ratios associated with the harmonic intervals in musical scale, and Plato's view of the universe as represented by perfect geometrical forms. The Platonic solids, and their related geometrical shapes, were favored throughout the Middle Ages and form the basis for much Medieval art and architecture (Fig 5.5). The arithmetic approach, encouraged by Leon Battista Alberti in his admiration for the mathematical relationships of the Greek harmonic scale, came to dominate the Renaissance. In his *De re aedificatoria,* he states that ". . . the same numbers, by means of which the agreement of sounds affects our ears with delight, are the very same which please our eyes and our mind."[20] In a sense, the replacement of geometry by arithmetic serves as a metaphor for the replacement of the metaphysical outlook of the Middle Ages by the empiricism of the Renaissance.

Alberti saw nature ". . . as the greatest artist at all manner of compositions," and so suggests that one should work ". . . to discover the laws upon which she herself acted in the production of her works, in order to transfer them to the business of architecture."[21] In his enquiry into the Beauty of Edifices he observed that *number* was of particular concern, "The first thing they (the ancients) observed, as to number, was that it was of two sorts, even and uneven, and they made use of both, but in different occasions. . . ."[22] For structural support systems, one should always use an even number of columns, ". . . as you shall not find any animal that stands or moves upon an odd number of feet."[23] On the other hand he observed that apertures often used uneven numbers, such as, ". . . the great aperture, the mouth, she has set singly in the middle."[24] Thus the quality of numbers, odd and even, had architectural significance. He notes:

. . . among these numbers, whether even or uneven, there are some which seem to be greater favourites with nature than others, and more celebrated among learned men; which architects have borrowed for the composition of the members of their edifices, upon account of their being imbued with some qualities which make them more valuable than any others.[25]

Alberti's belief in the efficacy of the harmonic scale profoundly affected the architecture of Andrea Palladio, as did Vitruvius and the ideas of Palladio's patron Daniele Barbaro. Barbaro was a Renaissance mathematician, theologian, poet, and Aristotelian scholar, whose views influenced the course of architecture. His position clearly reflects Plato's view, expressed in *The Republic,* that geometers seek to "... get sight of those realities which can be seen only by the mind."[26] Thus, in the 1556 edition of Vitruvius' *De Architectura,* Barbaro comments, "The artist works first in the intellect and conceives in the mind and symbolizes then the exterior matter after the interior image, particularly in architecture."[27] That is, form follows idea; architecture, therefore, represents *le cose alla virtu,* a virtuous thing. Wittkower comments, "It is probable that by associating in the *Quattro libri* virtue with architecture, Palladio like Barbaro regarded as the particular 'virtue' inherent in architecture the possibility of materializing in space the 'certain truth' of mathematics."[28]

In his *Quattro libri dell'architettura* (The Four Books of Architecture), Palladio devotes one of the four sections to his own villas; the highly systematized pattern of the plans is entirely characteristic of his design approach, as is the dependence on proportional ratios based on harmonic scale. Wittkower's analysis of typical plans covering a fifteen-year period indicates that they are variations on a single geometrical formula (Fig 5.6). He comments, "The Villa Thiene at Ciogna, built during the 1550s, shows the pattern most clearly. The rooms together with the porticos are defined by a rectangle divided by two longitudinal and four transverse lines."[29] Indeed, Palladio took great care to employ harmonic ratios both within and between rooms. In his "Systems of Proportion," Wittkower further notes that "The dimensions inscribed by Palladio in the plan of Villa Thiene . . . supply a characteristic example. All the rooms are based on the harmonic series 12-18-36, representing the ratios 1:2, 2:3, and 1:3."[30] Accordingly, Villa Thiene is probably one of Palladio's most rationalized villas although, as we see later, not his most famous (Fig 5.7).

Palladio recommended seven shapes for rooms: circular, square, the diagonal of a square for the length of a room ($\sqrt{2}$:1), a square and one-third (3:4), a square and one-half (2:3), a square and two-thirds (3:5), and two squares (1:2). Only one of these seven ratios is incommensurable, $\sqrt{2}$:1, apparently a legacy of Vitruvius. The heights of the rooms likewise use harmonic proportions: so that a room 6' × 12' would have a ceiling height of 9' (an arithmetic mean); a room 8' × 18' would have a height of 12' (a geometric mean); and one 12' × 24' would have a height of 16' (a harmonic mean). These are the three Pythagorean proportional terms comprising the Greek harmonic scale, leading Wittkower to state that ". . . the three means which determine musical consonances take up a central position in the deliberations on proportion of those architects who absorbed humanist and neo-platonic ideas."[31] This is echoed by James S. Ackerman, who notes, "That numerical equivalents of the terms of musical harmonies could, when applied to spatial relationships in architecture, make visual 'harmonies,' seemed to Palladio and his contemporaries to indicate a universal Design."[32] But Palladio may not have been totally committed to harmonic numbers.

In a fairly exhaustive study, "Harmonic Proportion and Palladio's *Quattro Libri,*" Deborah Howard and Malcolm Longair analyzed Palladio's use of harmonic ratios in the ground plans of his villas. Their quantitative analysis confirms that Palladio did have a definite preference for numbers that can be related in ratios corresponding to the standard musical intervals.[33] About two-thirds of the dimensions Palladio lists in Book II of Quattro Libri use such numbers, but the authors point out that ". . . it is significant that

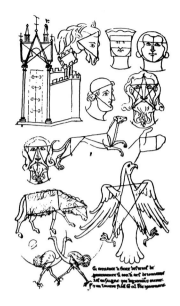

5.5

Notebook of Vuillard d'Honnecourt *(ca. 1235)*
The utter regularity of the five Platonic Solids suggested a divine source, one responsible for the logical construction of the universe. Vuillard d'Honnecourt's drawings thus represent the conviction that such divine intentions must be manifest in all the creatures of earth, whose existence becomes proof of the existence of a deity. (Courtesy: Bibliothèque Nationale, Paris.)

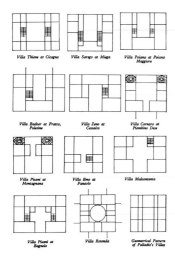

5.6

Schematics of Palladio's Villas
These schematics are remarkable for their regularity and use of precise mathematical ratios. The general pattern, shown in the last diagram, is most closely approximated by the Villa Thiene, shown in the first. (Source: *Architectural Principles in the Age of Humanism,* Rudolf Wittkower, Academy Editions, London.)

all the completely harmonic designs postdate Palladio's collaboration with (Daniele) Barbaro on the Vitruvius edition and the Villa at Maser."[34] They thus conclude that, for Palladio, ". . . common sense and an innate sense of design were more important . . . in determining the proportions of his buildings than any abstract harmonic theory."[35] Moreover, the theoretical leanings of his patrons apparently contributed significantly to the degree of harmony in the schemes they commissioned.[36] This suggests that proportion was an ideological concern for Palladio's clients, but a design methodology for him.

Both proportional systems, the arithmetic and geometric, continue to fascinate designers. The Maison Tonini, designed by Bruno Reichlin and Fabio Reinhardt, uses simple arithmetic harmonies based on the Renaissance tradition (Fig 5.8). The designers quote Alberti, ". . . the 'heart of the house' is the basic part, around it are grouped the subordinate parts as if it were a public square within the building."[37] Accordingly, they have placed the dining room, a place of gathering, where the axes cross. In its proportional relationships and scale, it suggests a compact Villa Capra (Fig 6.10). The geometric system, on the other hand, is useful in that the very characteristics of logarithmic growth can be translated into planar dimensions that suggest some rationale for an exponential increase in data. This suggestion of spiral growth can be put to clever use in design; indeed, such growth may be seen as the essence of the religious experience, as evidenced in Le Corbusier's chapel at Ronchamp, where the altar is adjacent to the windowed spiral-like curve of the structure (Fig 5.9). It is, however, probably significant that current applications of proportion are usually conceived in picturesque terms.

Le Corbusier's *Modulor* may be regarded as a great attempt to construct a proportional system that takes into account geometry (the Golden Section), arithmetic (the Fibonacci series), and anthropomorphic factors (the height of a human as its basis). In *The Modulor,* Le Corbusier describes his device as a measuring tool based on the human body and on mathematics:

5.7

Villa Thiene—Cicogna; *Andrea Palladio (1556)*
Palladio omitted many of the room dimensions in his plans, and all the ceiling heights; this likely reflected his assumption that anyone familiar with proportional systems could easily calculate them with a minimum of information. (Source: *The Four Books of Architecture,* Andrea Palladio.)

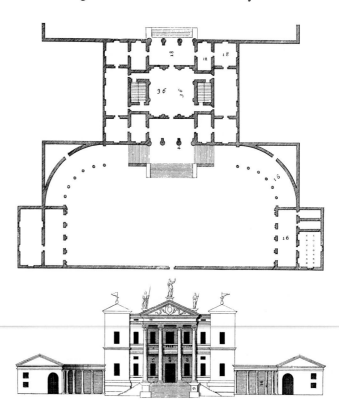

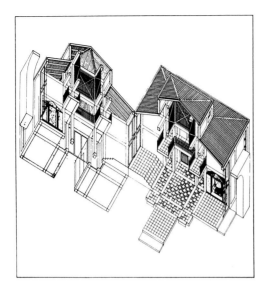

5.8

Maison Tonini—France; *Bruno Reichlin & Fabio Reinhardt (1972–4)*
The shape, symmetry, and proportions refer to Palladio's villas. The center of the house is three stories high; the round dining table is placed in this space, thus emphasizing the importance of the family gathering. (Courtesy: Bruno Reichlin, Geneve, Switzerland.)

A man-with-arm-upraised provides, at the determining points of his occupation of space—foot, solar plexus, head, tips of fingers of the upraised arm—three intervals which give rise to a series of golden sections, called the Fibonacci series. On the other hand, mathematics offers the simplest and also the most powerful variation of a value: the single unit, the double unit and the three golden sections.[38]

The result, however, is a composite system that shares little of the philosophical absolutism of its progenitors (Fig 5.10). Indeed, Wittkower believes that in spite of its ultimate derivation from Pythagorean-Platonic thought, its vacillating quality seems to reflect the spirit of our non-Euclidian age, "What is even more important, by taking man in his environment, instead of universals, as his starting point, Le Corbusier has accepted the shift from absolute to relative standards."[39]

But Le Corbusier's use of "man in his environment" does not necessarily imply a compelling interest in human physiology, and still less a concern about ergonomics. His use of a human height for the system's basis is likely related to Vitruvius' position, "For without symmetry and proportion no temple can have a regular plan; that is, it must have an exact proportion worked out after the fashion of the members of a finely shaped human body."[40] Thus the figure of Vitruvian Man is related to architectural shape on a proportional level, not because it supplied a literal measure for the structure. Arnheim points out that "The architect was expected to create in the image of man, and therefore the relative proportions of the model, not its absolute dimensions, were considered."[41] Indeed, the human figure defies standardization; thus any denotation of height must be somewhat arbitrary. Le Corbusier, at the outset, used a scale based on a 175-centimeter Frenchman, until he was shown that in English detective novels the good-looking men are always six feet tall (182.88 centimeter).[42] Besides, at 175 centimeters, virtually none of the metric values was translatable to feet and inches, a serious drawback in a system meant to serve an international community. The new "Modulor," however, formed an almost perfect match between the two systems. Le Corbusier notes that this improved system "... makes allies ... of the decimal and the foot-and-inch, and liberates the foot-and-inch system, **by a decimal process**, from the necessity for complicated and stultifying juggling with numbers. . . ."[43]

In 1946 Le Corbusier discussed the Modulor with Albert Einstein in New York. He reports that Einstein later wrote to him that "It is a scale of

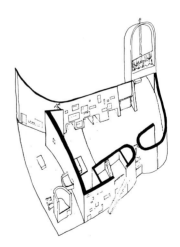

5.9

Notre Dame-du-Haut—Ronchamp; *Le Corbusier (1951–5)*
The symbolic aspect of the spiral is used to evoke the idea of aspiration, and its upward movement stresses the importance of the building's orientation to the East. But the building relies on a highly intellectual and carefully regulated geometric order for its final content, as it uses a rectangular grid proportioned by the Modulor as its basis. (Copyright 1991 ARS, N.Y./SPADEM.)

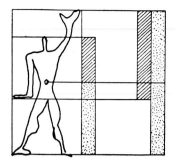

5.10

The Modulor; *Le Corbusier (1943–8)*
Not only does this system represent an attempt to reconcile arithmetic and geometric proportional systems, but also the metric and the English systems of measurement. (Reprinted by permission of the publishers from *Le Modulor: A Harmonious Measure to the Human Scale Universally Applicable to Architecture and Mechanics* by Le Corbusier, Cambridge, Mass.: Harvard University Press. Copyright 1954 by Charles Édouard Jeanneret. Copyright 1991 ARS, N.Y./SPADEM.)

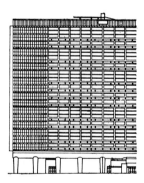

5.11

Unité d'Habitation—Marseilles; *Le Corbusier (1946)*
Far from being an intellectual game, the modulor was intended to be a practical design tool. The first application of the Modular system occurred in the Unité d'Habitation in Marseilles. This apartment building for sixteen hundred inhabitants, used thirteen basic dimensions to regulate elevation, plan, and section. Le Corbusier commented that ". . . such exactitude, such rigour of mathematics and harmony have never before been applied to that simplest accessory of daily life: the dwelling."[2] (Reprinted by permission of the publishers from *Le Modulor: A Harmonious Measure to the Human Scale Universally Applicable to Architecture and Mechanics* by Le Corbusier, Cambridge, Mass.: Harvard University Press. Copyright 1954 by Charles Édouard Jeanneret. Copyright 1991, N.Y./SPADEM.)

proportions which makes the bad difficult and the good easy."[44] Le Corbusier points out, "It maintains the human scale everywhere, leading itself to an infinity of combinations; it ensures unity within diversity, an inestimable boon, the miracle of numbers."[45] As his many "Panel Exercises" make clear, this is no idle claim. Such gridded panels were to play a major role in Le Corbusier's architectural aesthetics, as in his Unité d'Habitation, where it was used for the plan, interior and exterior elevations, and certain of the furniture designs (Fig 5.11). He even used the Modulor for his own "very small office" at 35 rue de Sevres, in an ultimate gesture of commitment (Fig 5.12).

This fascinating system is little used today; few proportional systems are. One argument against proportion, an argument usually directed toward the Modulor, is that it does not lend itself to standardization. And Le Corbusier did regard standardization as critical to the betterment of humanity:

> To standardize, which is to run the **risk** of arbitrary choice, and the reverse of that risk: a wonderful freeing of the methods of economic production. . . . The promise, guaranteed by experience, always to offer harmony, variety, elegance, instead of banality, monotony and lack of grace.[46]

The argument against his system is that its dependence on the Fibonacci series limits the number of proportional relationships available to industry. But even a cursory glance at his "Panel Exercises" would reveal a startling number of possibilities. In 1944 Le Corbusier and his group developed a particular set of panels based on five surfaces used in architecture, obtaining a total of 101 different combinations. He comments, "One hundred and one panels, each supplying a further forty-eight panels: this gives **four thousand eight hundred and forty-eight** combinations, out of which anyone may make his choice, according to taste, circumstance, purpose, and so forth. . . ."[47]

Another, more serious argument centers on whether proportion limits design potential, a view taken by Eliel Saarinen when he asserts, "To lean upon theoretical formulas . . . is a sign of weakness that produces weak art."[48] That proportion is a vital issue was attested to at the 1951 First International Congress on Proportion in the Arts, attended by architects, artists, and musical historians, who agreed that some sort of proportional system was desirable. Notwithstanding, prevailing opinion among designers has tended to agree with Bruno Zevi's assessment in 1957 that no one really

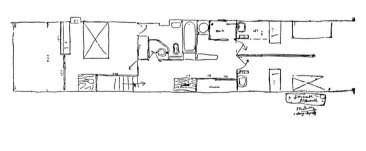

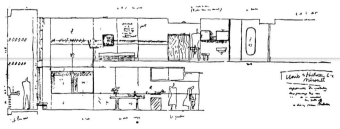

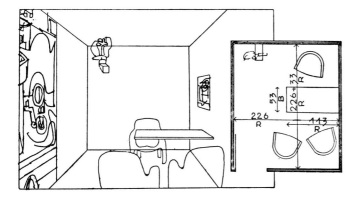

5.12

Design for a Small Office; *Le Corbusier*
The dimensions of this office, as well as the size and location of all its furnishings, were based on the Modulor. Le Corbusier likened his windowless, air-conditioned office to a cell. It was capable of accommodating four visitors, and Le Corbusier attributed their concise speech to the room's design. (Reprinted by permission of the publishers from *Le Modulor: A Harmonious Measure to the Human Scale Universally Applicable to Architecture and Mechanics* by Le Corbusier, Cambridge, Mass.: Harvard University Press. Copyright 1954 by Charles Édouard Jeanneret. Copyright 1991 ARS, N.Y./SPADEM.)

believes any longer in the proportional system.[49] However, proportion is scarcely the simple theoretical formula that Saarinen suggests; to the contrary, Gestalt psychology has demonstrated that humans have innate and complex biological ordering processes that compel "the will to form." And in order to realize its profound value as an ordering mechanism, one need not subscribe to any universal or metaphysical value that proportion may have. Wittkower concludes that when all is said and done, ". . . it must be agreed that the quest for symmetry, balance, and proportional relationships lies deep in human nature."[50] In any case, the use of proportion could hardly be more limiting than the dimensional ratios provided by building-supplies manufacturers or the "proportions" calculated on the basis of square-footage criteria.

Specific Geometry

An extended series of proportional relationships is denoted by the term system, and cultures have routinely arranged information in this manner. Indeed, societies often use more than one system, depending on the symbolic and practical need. Proportion, therefore, is part of a larger cultural dependence on various *geometric-symbolic systems* to communicate that culture's enduring truths. Of all the geometric shapes, the circle has been the most universal in application, having been used for architectural configurations that range from temples to town complexes. In her *Symbolism in the Visual Arts,* Aniela Jaffe comments on the concept of circle (or sphere) as the symbol of self, an expression of the totality of the psyche:

> Whether the symbol of the circle appears in primitive sun worship or modern religion, in myths or dreams, in the mandalas drawn by Tibetan monks, in the ground plans of cities . . . it always points to the single most vital aspect of life—its ultimate wholeness.[51]

It is probably this quality that has ensured a special function for the circle, or sphere, in architectural design. But circles have other notable qualities as well. They have the power, for example, to focus attention equally to a single point from all directions; and circles radiate outward in the same manner (Plate 7). Thus the central character of the circle suggests its role as metaphor for the cosmos. It was this quality that was exploited by the emperor Hadrian when he ordered the Pantheon built in 118 A.D. Significantly, Hadrian combined statues of the gods, set around the perimeter of the temple, with images of Augustus and the deified Caesar. Spiro Kostof comments:

The first theme was of course cosmic. This was a temple to all the gods, and the appropriate symbolism was that of the heavens where they resided. . . . But the building also had a political content. . . . The empire, it was being implied, was an analogy for the cosmos, and the Pantheon—like the empire, a structure of many units but one pervading unity—described this analogy in visual terms.[52]

The interior of the Pantheon is also striking for its towering dome pierced by an oculus that permits a constant play of light on the walls, providing a connection between the heavens and earth (Fig 5.13). The circular plan became synonymous with Rome, and it, as well as plans based on other regular polygons, was used during the Renaissance to evoke the classical.

The importance of the *regular polygons* in large measure derives from the importance of the five Platonic solids. Thus these shapes have a special significance attached to them as primary reflections of universal order. Regular polygons are characterized by being symmetrical, equilateral, and equiangular; they can, moreover, be inscribed within a circle. Polygons may be conceived as existing in a numerical sequence, starting with a straight line representing two sides and ending in a circle—with a range of intermediary shapes having a constantly increasing number of sides. This view of polygonal development is advanced by William Blackwell in his *Geometry in Architecture,* where he states that ". . . the circle and straight line represent the extremes in area enclosure and are perfect complements."[53] The straight line and the circle may, therefore, be viewed as the two ends of a spatial continuum. In conjunction with Kandinsky's elements in *Point and Line to Plane,* a dynamic image of space can thus be constructed with only a few elements (Fig 5.14).

But there are still other ways to view regular polygons. As these polygons serve as units of enclosure, there is a relationship between *area* and the length of *perimeter* required to complete its enclosure. Length and character of perimeter are crucial in design; while it is desirable to maintain as much straight-line perimeter as possible for decoration and standardization reasons, a minimal perimeter is desirable for quantity-of-materials and maintenance reasons. While the shortest distance between two points is the straight line, the shortest distance required to encompass an area is a circle. Thus the circle has the greatest *perimeter efficiency* of the plane shapes, followed fairly closely by the square. Curiously, a rectangle in the ratio of

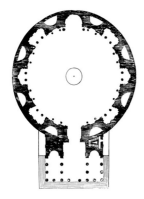

5.13

The Pantheon—Rome; *Emperor Hadrian (118 A.D.)*
The interior of the Pantheon was conceived as an enclosed sphere with its lower half in the form of a cylinder, thus anchoring the entire structure to the earth and lending a sense of permanence. As the analysis reveals, the plan was conceived in strict geometric terms, despite its having been built in sections. (Perspective—source: *The Antichita Romane I,* Giovanni Piranesi, 1756; Courtesy: The British Architectural Library, London. Plan—source: *The Book of Architecture,* Sebastiano Serlio, 1611.)

1:2 is only 5% less efficient than a square, which may help to explain its perennial popularity. And since any subdivision of a shape yields extra perimeter, as in the horizontal subdivisions represented by stories, a two-story building has more outside wall area than a single-story structure with the same square footage. Thus Blackwell comments, "One of the great virtues of the traditional two-story rectangular house is that as many as seven or eight rooms will have at least two different outside exposures."[54] The choice of rectangle depends, however, on the particular function.

Circles and rectangles are not the only regular polygons in common use. For example, the equilateral triangle and, to a lesser degree, the hexagon, have traditionally held interest for a number of societies. The mystical characteristics accorded these shapes depend, in part, on their mathematical properties: ·

> . . . all of the important dimensions of the equilateral triangle—the height, outside radius, area, and inside radius—are functions of the square root of three. . . . There are seemingly endless variations on the rectangle of the equilateral triangle, the equilateral triangle itself, and the hexagon. The common denominator is the square root of three, which, like the key of C minor in a symphony, can be the principal tonality in an architectural composition.[55]

The rectangle that Blackwell refers to is especially interesting, as it is well proportioned, with an unusual diameter. Equally important is its use in the construction of patterns based on the 60° grid, highly prized as a structural tool. A somewhat more familiar grid derives from the square; indeed, such a grid pattern is endemic to architectural design in both plan and elevation, and is the essence of Cartesian space. And when the square is turned at 45°, a familiar checkerboard pattern can be developed. The last of the significant regular polygons examined here is the pentagon, notable for these reasons: first, the side of a pentagon is in relation to its diagonal as $1:(1+\sqrt{5})/2$, or θ (the Golden Section); second, a pentagon can be constructed from a $\sqrt{5}$ rectangle; and third, for the rectangle that derives from the pentagon. The ratio of this rectangle is 1.376:1, producing a pleasing shape that is less pronounced than the Golden Rectangle. The pentagon has held special significance as the symbol of life and served as the basis of many Gothic rose-window mandalas, as well as the measure of Renaissance man.

The final point concerns the *surface efficiency* of geometric solids (i.e., the ratio of volume to surface of enclosure). As a rule, the efficiency of the cube (approximately 80% that of a sphere) increases as its sides are progressively subdivided. That is, the closer the cube (or square) approximates a sphere (or circle), the more efficient it becomes. There are two interesting aspects to this notion: first, the effect of *size* on efficiency; and second, the relationship of efficiency to *proportion*. The first proposition can be simply stated—the larger a geometric solid, the more efficiently it encloses space. Translated into structural terms, this explains the favorable cost:return ratio of large buildings. The second aspect is related to the mathematical relationship between the walls and base of geometric solids; in the cube, for example, the area of the walls must be four times that of the base. But, as Blackwell points out, this relationship between surface areas applies not only to the cube, but to every prismatic solid at its most efficient proportion:

> The shape of the base may be a rectangle of any proportion, a regular or irregular polygon . . . or any other enclosed shape, but *when the area of the walls is four times the area of the base, the total surface required to enclose a volume will be the least possible.* The shape will be at its most efficient proportion in terms of volume enclosure.[56]

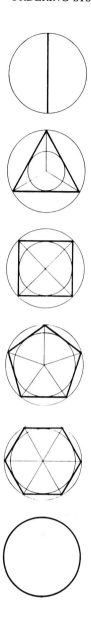

5.14

Six Regular Polygons as a Continuum
This figure demonstrates Blackwell's conceptual view of geometric progression, from a two-sided polygon through a range of multisided figures. (Source: *Geometry in Architecture,* William Blackwell, 1984.)

If, on the other hand, one wished to maximize the wall *and* ceiling areas in relation to walls, the ratio would be 2:1 (walls to floor). Thus the efficiency of geometric solids is largely determined by proportion and scale; this constitutes what Lawlor refers to as ". . . a sort of geometry of perception."[57] Indeed, geometry may be part of a human experience that takes into account biological factors in the human consciousness as well as abstract metric ones.

Scale

In chapter four, scale is described as a size comparison between two things, referring to a standard. In *Dimensions: Space, Shape, & Scale*, Gerald Allen notes that scale is not the same thing as size but is, rather, *relative size*, the size of a thing as it relates to something else.[58] Thus we may judge something as part of a larger composition, against other parts of that composition, in light of usual expectation, or in relation to human dimension. The first two categories are formal in character, having to do with compositional arrangement and perception; the second two involve memory and symbol. These aspects of scale are addressed by Allen when he observes:

> As shape has to do with the meaning of individual things, scale has to do with their importance and their meaning in relation to something else. No matter how unimportant or plain it may be, every part of every building has a size. And so scale, which involves arranging various sizes in some order. . . .[59]

Allen's definition is, in large part, a reflection of Vitruvius' six bases for architecture, two of which are particularly important in regard to scale. These are *order,* a consideration of design elements so that their number and proportion correspond to the proportion of the completed work; and *symmetry,* a quality of overall agreement both between different elements and between elements and the total work in accordance with a standard. It is thus possible to perceive a structure as larger than reality, if only its parts have order and symmetry (Fig 5.15).

In addition to internal consistency and measurement according to a standard, a concern for *contextual* coherence may be added. Thus inconsisten-

A

5.15

The Tempietto, S. Pietro in Montorio—Rome; *Donato Bramante (1504)*
The Tempietto, or little temple *(A)*, commemorates the importance of the site where St. Peter was crucified. While it is actually quite small, it has a monumental scale. This is achieved by the use of a raised stylobate, which supports successive layers of circular elements, culminating in a dome. The colonnade emphasizes the sculptural nature of the building and its powerful use of light and shadow. The original plan *(B)* called for a colonnaded courtyard that would have further exalted the site (actually an exterior room) and provided a strong figure-ground relationship. (Perspective—source: *Édifices de Rome Moderne,* Paul Letarouilly; Plan—source: *The Book of Architecture,* Sebastiano Serlio.)

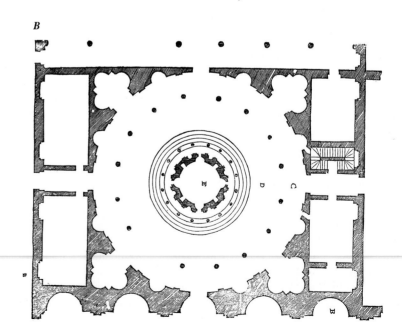

B

A   B

5.16

(A) **Board of Trade, North Lobby—Chicago;** *Holabird & Roche (1930);* *(B)* **Board of Trade, South Lobby—Chicago;** *Helmut Jahn (1980)*
In Holabird & Roche's glittering lobby of glass, polished metal, and rich marble there is a strong emphasis on the vertical dimension. Particularly striking is the upward movement of the marble-clad undulating shape located at the mezzanine level. Jahn repeats this shape in the light fixtures, and at the horizontal second floor line in his new lobby. When this shape is used for the light fixtures, it is small compared with the older shape, and yet large in relation to typical light fixtures. And when the shape is turned on its side at the floor line, it emphasizes the horizontal aspect of the space, altering our sense of spatial dimension through scale and orientation. (Photo by: Frank Vodvarka.)

cies in comparisons of elements with each other, with the whole, and with the milieu (i.e., failures in order and symmetry) are usually perceived as incongruities in scale. Such inconsistencies are most painfully apparent when an older structure—where element size and shape (windows, moldings, etc.) were determined and constructed as functions of scale—is refitted with modern elements responsive only to standardization. In these situations, discrepancies in scale are spatially comparable. But such comparisons can also rely on spatial memory for correlation (the idea of sequence). When the second lobby for the Chicago Board of Trade was designed, there was provision for mnemonic continuity by referring to certain of the art deco shapes of the older lobby in the new one. The effect in the new lobby, however, is very different; this is likely a result of the altered scale relationships (Fig 5.16).

One of the methods developed by Modernism to overcome this problem is a dependency on regularized form, or modules. A *module* is a small unit of measure (from the Latin *modus*) which has the capacity to control the proportions of a structure by virtue of being arranged in a system. Such a series of formal relationships is postulated by Sol LeWitt in his sculpture "A 2 5 8." In addition to the square, he projects its prismatic form (the cube) as well, developing a standard by which the other objects can be measured (Fig 5.17). This particular work is part of a series, which LeWitt described in 1966:

> Serial compositions are multipart pieces with regulated changes. The differences between the parts are the subjects of the composition. . . . The entire work should contain subdivisions which could be autonomous but which comprise(s) the whole.[60]

The advantage of this system in design is that all compositional elements, no matter the size, are dimensionally related to one another. And, as LeWitt makes clear, this relationship can be dynamic when the module is varied with aesthetic intent.

In *Beyond Modern Art,* Carla Gottlieb notes that ''Modular coordination in modern architecture . . . proposes the use of a predetermined standard size in the manufacture of the parts used in the construction of buildings to

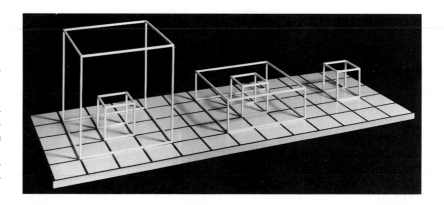

5.17

A 2 5 8 (Baked enamel on steel 19¹/₄″ × 32″ × 81″); Sol LeWitt (1968)
LeWitt's sculpture refers to both the constancy of the universe through its use of precise geometry, and the potential of growth suggested by the use of Fibonacci numbers. (Collection: Krannert Art Museum, University of Illinois, Urbana-Champaign. Copyright 1991 Sol LeWitt/ARS N.Y.)

reduce the costs.''[61] That is, a module is usually established by manufacturers utilizing factors of technology and construction cost. Such a seeming limitation can, nevertheless, be turned to good effect. One of Skidmore, Owings, & Merrill's finest creations is the Inland Steel Building (1957), a design largely based on functional considerations. James W. Hammond, of SOM's Chicago office, writes, ''Exterior, interior partitions, lighting, grid system for flexible attachment of partitions, and air conditioning are all on a 5′-2″ module.''[62] The floor areas of this remarkable building are entirely free of columns, service shafts, and fixed interior walls; interior partitions are, instead, designed to be connected to metal channels in the ceiling grid

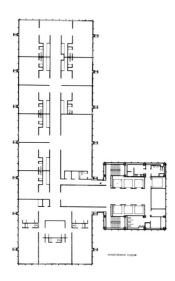

5.18

Inland Steel Building—Chicago; *Skidmore, Owings & Merrill (1957)*
In a 1957 article on modular architecture, the editors of *Progressive Architecture* praised the Inland Steel building for having ''. . . great variety and distinction in design; great imagination in the choice and assembly of component parts.'' When the sunlight falls on this building with its blue-green glass and stainless steel, it has the qualities of a brilliant jewel. (Plan—courtesy: Skidmore, Owings & Merrill, Chicago; Photo by: Hedrich Blessing.)

on the basis of local need (Fig 5.18). But such an approach need not be simple. In his design for House III (1971), Peter Eisenman employs a series of developmental drawings that rely on the opposition developed by two grids set at 45° to one another (Fig 5.19). Thus a very complex modular system can be developed.

The third category of scale may be regarded as a breach of usual expectation; that is, our mental picture (based on prior experience) of an object's proper size is not confirmed. For this to occur, we must be familiar with a typical object of its kind and thus have mnemonic expectations. In such cases, objects (or spaces) are charged with tension and dynamism. Claes Oldenburg, for example, has transformed ordinary objects into imposing monumental objects, whose impact and affect rely on the radical alteration of scale (Fig 5.20). An engaging aspect of his work is that, in its typical urban setting, it creates a scale relationship between both its kind and human size (as gauged against the buildings), thus using two categories of measurement. And if traditional valuation is added (i.e., the degree to which we give a type traditional symbols), scale incongruence can become most complex.

The final category is scale in relation to human dimension, where the human figure serves as the standard against which structure is judged. This might be the most critical, and surely the most obvious, way scale is determined. C. Ray Smith observes that scale is the aesthetic impression conveyed about the physical size of a mass or a space—what we measure size by—and therefore:

> . . . two relative forces are involved in scale: first, a physical aspect—size; and second, a philosophical and psychological aspect—man's image of his own stature. This perception of the size of a space or a building is the product of a gestalt—a ratio between a physical object and the mental impression conveyed to an observer about the size of that object in relation to himself. The affect on the observer, his perception of the object, and his reaction to it are the significant factors.[63]

Smith believes that scale is not a quantitative concept but an affective one, forming a subjective reaction in the viewer. Thus those design elements that are said "to give human scale" are only devices, or tools, to create ". . . the desired impression about the size of the building."[64]

Throughout history scale has been used to make the individual feel small and insignificant in relation to the universe, a deity, and political institutions; or large and significant for many of the same reasons. John Summerson states, "The temple is a building of more-than-human scale, built to house a more-than-human personage—a God. The temple is a building whose scale is deliberately increased beyond the ordinary scale of human needs to express the idea of something greater than humanity."[65] In Summerson's view, therefore, scale is related to a system of values. And so he laments:

> It has always been one of man's greatest and most devastating temptations to borrow the attributes of God. . . . It has been appropriated for the palaces of kings, emperors, dukes and very rich gentlemen; later for the palaces of corporations and institutions; later still for the premises (call them palaces if you must) of large commercial organizations.[66]

He considers the appropriation of monumental scale by "secondary institutions" as fundamentally wrong because it serves the interests of class dominance. It is, in his view, ". . . a form of affirmation; and affirmations are usually made by the few to impress the many."[67] But perception of scale is seldom this absolute, and the meaning of a monumentally scaled structure may escape such simple valuation (Fig 5.21).

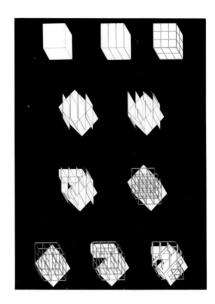

5.19

Schematic Drawing for House III—Connecticut; *Peter Eisenman (1971)*
This sequence of axonometric drawings comment on the highly intellectual design process Eisenman engaged in. The resulting form of the house, although essentially cubic, reveals the complexity of the interior spaces. (Courtesy: Eisenman Architects, New York.)

5.20

Clothespin (Steel, 45' high)—Philadelphia; Claes Oldenburg (1976)
Oldenburg's sculpture gains monumentality both from a comparison with human scale as measured by the building in the background, and by virtue of the unusual point of view the spectator must adopt of a common (and typically diminutive) object. (Courtesy: Philadelphia Convention & Visitors Bureau.)

Perspective

Two developments that occurred during the Renaissance led to the popular understanding of perspective: first, Alberti's theory of perspective as a mathematical discipline; and second, Leonardo da Vinci's theoretical accomplishment of replacing the "imitation of the masters by the study of nature." The former is clearly scientific in conception and method, while the latter is scientific only in the sense that it is accomplished through disciplined observation. Thus they have often been distinguished as architectural technique versus artistic method. But during the Renaissance, little professional distinction was made between artist and architect, one person often assuming both roles. The common ground lay in *mathematics,* as expressed in proportion and perspective. Alberti formulated a logical explanation of the laws of linear perspective, which made possible a type of convincing pictorial representation. Leonardo, on the other hand, supplied an intellectual purpose for clinical observation; that is, to learn from nature, thus encouraging objects' being represented in drawn perspective. Of concern here, however, is perspective in three-dimensions, and its psychophysiological basis.

There are two realities that perspective depends on in our perception of the environment. One is the reality of *what we know* of the actual size and shape of an object by measurement, and the other is the reality of *how we see.* In his *Language of Vision,* Gyorgy Kepes points out, "The experiencing of every image is the result of an interaction between external physical forces and internal forces of the individual as he assimilates, orders, and molds external forces to his own measure."[68] The external force is the world revealed to us by light; the internal force is the dynamic tendency to restore balance and thus keep one's system in relative stability.[69] And every force operates within a field; that is, it only makes sense to us with reference to its milieu. This definition of visual information as existing in a field of relationships is in keeping with Gestalt theory, as confirmed by Köhler, "As so called optical illusions show, we do not see individual fractions of a thing. . . ."[70] When we view three-dimensional space in which the visual field has no boundaries, we typically make spatial judgments based on our own position and spatial orientation.

The eye's limitations usually distort the size, shape, location, and detail of objects. It is this distortion that H.W. Helmholtz refers to in his *Physiological Optics:*

> For the eye has every possible defect that can be found in an optical instrument, and even some that are peculiar to itself; but they are all so counteracted, that the inexactness of the image which results from their presence very little exceeds . . . the limits which are set to the delicacy of sensation set by the dimensions of the retinal cones.[71]

That is, as an image can be focussed on only a small area of the retina, the eye is forced to rotate to gather enough information about an object. And that very movement gives us *kinesthetic* information, spatial clues that let us distinguish the relationship between objects and the information surrounding them. Binocular vision, in fact, depends on two discrete angles of view to distinguish depth, and the size of the retinal image is also a factor. Helmholtz comments, "The same object seen at different distances will be depicted on the retina by images of different sizes and will subtend different visual angles. The further it is away the less its apparent size will be."[72] It is this aspect of vision that is exploited by both the use of linear perspective and its dependence on diminishing size to a vanishing point (or points).

5.21

Gruppo di Scale (**Entitled** *Loco magnifico d'Architectura* **in first edition**); *Giovanni Battista Piranesi (1743)*
Piranesi was one of the most illustrious eighteenth-century engravers, noted for both his realistic representations and his architectural fantasies. He was especially given to the depiction of structures in monumental scale, evoking visions of early Roman grandeur. (Courtesy: National Gallery of Art.)

The physiological facts of viewing are, therefore, very complex. Nonetheless, human beings are remarkably adept at distinguishing characteristics of objects (shape, color, size, etc.), even at great distances and under adverse circumstances. This is referred to as *perceptual constancy,* an example of our knowledge of the world's modifying our perceptions. Canter points out that ". . . perception relies upon a variety of sources other than the retina, not least of which is the experience stored in the brain."[73] The result is that we still see a table as a rectangle, even as the top recedes in perspective; and a round plate remains round, even when seen at an angle. It is, however, this ability that lets us use perspective to change spatial perception. That is, by taking advantage of common expectations and altering the "facts" of what we see the designer can produce a wide range of effects.

In order to manipulate the rules, it is necessary both to understand the characteristics of perspective that the eye reads and to be aware of the different sorts of perspective available to the designer to bring about a particular illusion. The psychologist James Gibson has compiled an interesting list of eleven *Cues for Distance as Stimulation Gradients,* the first eight of which are essentially visual in nature (i.e., what we see). They include: linear perspective; the apparent versus the known size of objects; the apparent motion of objects due to the observer's head movement (motion parallax); the superimposition of one object over another; aerial perspective (involving both color and texture); the upward angular location of objects in the visual field; the relative brightness of objects; and the shading to depth of objects (chiaroscuro). The last three categories are kinesthetic in nature; that is, how we see the following: the disparity of binocular images of the object; the angle of ocular convergence on objects; and the degree of lens accommodation necessary to maximize the definition of the object.[74]

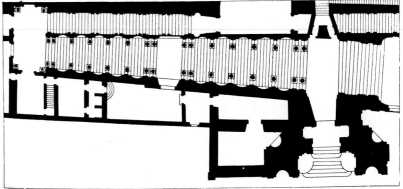

5.22

Scala Regia, the Vatican—Rome; *Gianlorenzo Bernini (1663–6)*
At the bottom of the staircase, Bernini had
enough width to work with and was able to
set the columns out from the wall. As the
staircase ascended it narrowed, so that by
placing the columns closer to the wall, reducing them in height, and placing them
gradually closer together, he made the space
look wider than it was. The accenting of the
light reflective lines in the barrel vault, rather
than the lines of the vault perpendicular
to the observer, helps to reinforce the reading of distance. (Plan and Section—source:
Éléments et Théorie de l'Architecture,
J. Guadet; Perspective—source: *Édifices de
Rome Moderne,* Paul Letarouilly.)

Thus these last three categories, which Gibson considers the most important, are strictly internal; the first eight, then, may be of the most interest
to designers, as they may be manipulated to specific spatial ends.

It is interesting, therefore, to compare this list with the abstraction of
Gibson's data that has been prepared by E.T. Hall for the Appendix of *The
Hidden Dimension.* Hall reorders Gibson's categories in such a way as to
accommodate design use, defining the most important ones as: texture perspective, the gradual increase in density (or smoothness) as a surface recedes; size perspective, the diminution of an object's size as it recedes; and
linear perspective, the joining of parallel lines and shape edges at a vanishing point.[75] Perspective is commonly employed where optical illusions serve
to correct a problem, as in making a room look longer (to emphasize grandeur) or shorter (to seem less overwhelming) than it actually is. It was
Alberti who recommended, "If a wall be too long, adorn it with columns
reaching from top to the bottom, not set too close to each other, which will
be a kind of resting-place to the eyes, and make the excessive length appear
less offensive."[76]

One of the most spectacular products resulting from an understanding of
optical illusion and the manipulation of the characteristics of perspective is
the Scala Regia by Gianlorenzo Bernini. His task was to provide a staircase
that would allow the Pope to descend from the Vatican palace to St. Peter's.
The site was problematic due to an angled wall that caused the space to
vary in width; indeed, the space was actually quite narrow where the walls
converged at the landing. The concept was to make the area more ceremonial. Bernini used the site restrictions by accentuating the perspective of
the converging walls. He placed columns on the sides of the staircase to
support a barrel vault, a device that traditionally adds importance to a processional way by framing the event. By manipulating the distance between
the columns and the wall, he could give a highly irregular staircase the
appearance of regularity. The effect of these adjustments is to make the
space seem wider and thus longer. Standing below, the observer does not

suspect this trickery and reads the optical distortion as normal (Fig 5.22). An extreme example of this sort of manipulation in an essentially linear space is Francesco Borromini's highly illusionist colonnade at the Palazzo Spada in Rome. This colonnade differs in purpose from Bernini's stairway, in that it was not conceived so much as a way to provide depth where there is none but, rather, as a clever spatial dialogue with the educated observer. A recent reference to this highly theatrical work appeared in the winning entry (student category) to the PLACES Competition, sponsored by Columbus Coated Fabrics in 1984. The problem was presented thus:

> Within a volume whose outer limits are 20 × 20 × 15 feet high shall be encompassed
>> A Place of Anticipation
>> A Place of Transition
>> A Place of Gathering
> The volume may be treated as (either) one space or a group of spaces, which may be modulated to provide sequences of movement and repose, access and focus.[77]

This entry was intended to convey the idea of transition from "the mysterious place of anticipation to the clarity and understanding of the open place of gathering."[78] In that process, the designer has enhanced the limited spatial size stipulated by program through perceptual manipulation (Fig 5.23).

Such devices are not limited, however, to ceremonial situations. In a much different vein, Portantina, a retail store in New York City, also converged walls to manipulate the apparent size of the space. By angling one side wall the architects, Machado and Silvetti, created a false perspective which exaggerates the length and size of the space. In this way, a small shop was made to look larger, enabling it to visually compete with the larger stores nearby (Fig 5.24). Illusions are often intended to engage, either emotionally or cognitively, thus drawing people into or through a space. This is typically required of showrooms and retail spaces where the façade's width is slight compared with its depth, or where there is a need for more flexibility.

One of the key issues in perspective is the observer's position. Sometimes it is fixed, but more often a sequential position must be developed that maintains comprehensible spatial relationships. This is aided by space that

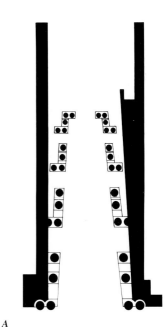

A

5.23

(A) **Plan of the Pavilion of Palazzo Spada—Rome;** *Francesco Borromini (ca. 1635);* **(B) A Place of Worship;** *Shawn Michael Johnson (1984)*

Borromini achieved his startling result by diminishing the size of the columns in diameter and height, as well as decreasing the spacing of groups of columns and the width of the passage. The effect is that of a funnel, although we continue to see it as a long corridor. Johnson has created a similarly extended view (as one exits), but this procedure also has the effect of enhancing the entry and making it loom larger than reality as the altar is approached. *([A] drawn by: J. Malnar; [B] courtesy: Columbus Coated Fabrics, Columbus, Ohio.)*

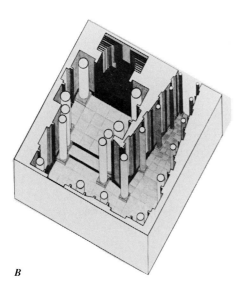

B

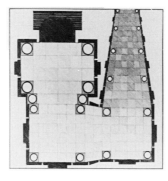

5.24

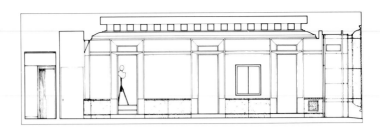

Portantina Store—New York; *Machado & Silvetti (1986)*
The angled wall provides another opportunity to increase the apparent size of the room. The space between the angled wall and the boundary wall contains niches and a few steps. A mirror is carefully placed against the boundary wall, doubling the width of the steps. When standing in the main room, an observer cannot see where the steps lead; but relying on past experiences, assumes that they continue. In fact, they lead nowhere. (Courtesy: Machado and Silvetti Associates, Inc., Boston.)

is linear in nature or that is arranged in a linear format that may be viewed from a single vantage point. Vignelli Associates, in their Dallas Artemide Showroom, direct the observer down the main aisle by organizing a series of bays and establishing symmetry around the main aisle, or axis. The central progression of door openings invites the observer to explore the individual bays, which are not equal as is usually the case. The bays actually get smaller, diminishing from 11 feet and six inches to 10 feet and zero inches to 5 feet and zero inches. It is this exaggerated decrease in size that allows the 2,200-square-foot space to appear larger than it is (Fig 5.25). Lella Vignelli comments that their showroom design ". . . provides a working background for the products. There is a rationale to the space. We never design just for an exercise in creativity. We design for a reason."[79] And perspective is one of the most useful design tools.

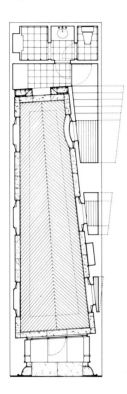

5.25

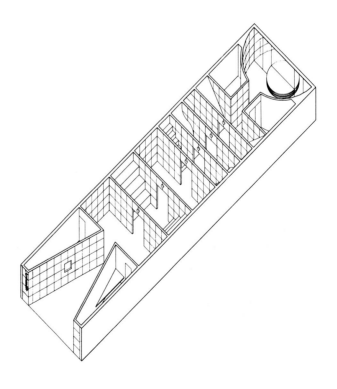

Artemide Showroom—Dallas; *Vignelli Associates (1985)*
To further the illusion, the final room in the sequence is semicircular, with a semicircular table attached to a mirrored end wall. This end wall reflects the room and table, completing the circle and again beginning a progression of door openings, which this time recede into the far distance. The last actual room occurs in the visual middle ground of the sequence. (Courtesy: Vignelli Associates, New York.)

Part II

The Development of Interior Space

Seminal
Viewpoints

6

Vitruvius

Having considered some of Vitruvius' ideas on subject and content, we might now examine his other ideas. And not just Vitruvius but architects like Alberti and Palladio, whose basic views on architecture use his writings as their starting points. Together, their buildings and written theories make an influential body of knowledge, which has been architecture's standard. Of equal importance to the development of interior space, however, is the eighteenth-century designer Adam and the designers Boffrand and Blondel, whose influence extends beyond their works.

One of the earliest authoritative works on the nature of architecture was written by the first-century architect and military engineer Marcus Vitruvius Pollio. His extraordinarily influential work, *De Architectura* (Ten Books on Architecture), was completed during the reign of Emperor Augustus and marked the closing of a long career. In the foreword to his translation of the work, Frank Granger notes that nowhere does Vitruvius mention Octavian by the official name Augustus, which was conferred upon him in 27 B.C.; it is, therefore, likely that the manuscript was completed in the three years before this date.[1] In any case, it is clear that this treatise on architecture had become standard reading by the first century A.D., a distinction enhanced by its many transcriptions and republication in 1486.

For the historian, Vitruvius makes fascinating reading, as he refused to restrict himself to the topic at hand; instead, he digressed so as to cast light on the social life, religious beliefs, law, living habits, and economy of first-century B.C. Rome. To some degree, these digressions may be viewed as part of a desire to inform his patron about every detail of the situation, but, more, they probably stem from his broad definition of architect. Vitruvius conceived the architect's range of abilities and duties to include city planning, the raising of public and private buildings, such medical knowledge sufficient to ensure public hygiene, the design of aqueducts, the construction of fortifications and machines of war, the appropriate use of ornament and orders, healthful and proper room exposures, theater acoustics, and even elementary astrology. Thus his method of city planning carries this admonition concerning the circulatory elements, ''They will be properly laid out if foresight is employed to exclude the winds from the alleys. Cold winds

A

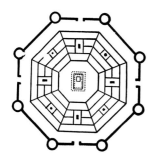

B

6.1

(A) Dial of Winds; (B) Plan of Town
In Book I of *De Architectura*, Vitruvius discusses the importance of the winds in the
laying out of town plans, particularly the
streets and alleys. Figure *(A)* illustrates
the method he uses to discover the true north-
south meridian, and hence the direction of
the eight winds verified by Andronicus of
Athens. Figure *(B)* demonstrates the translation of these wind directions into a town
plan. Note that all these streets (lines leading
from circular towers to the agora) are oblique
to the winds. (Reprinted by permission of the
publishers and The Loeb Classical Library
from Vitruvius, Volume I, *On Architecture*,
Frank Granger translator. Cambridge, Mass.:
Harvard University Press, 1931.)

are disagreeable, hot winds enervating, moist winds unhealthy."[2] In this,
he combines hygiene, astrology, and planning (Fig 6.1).

While he acknowledges that specialists might be more precisely expert
in any one of these areas, architects should be well versed enough in all of
them to fulfill their duties as builders. At the outset of his work, he states:

> Let him (the architect) be educated, skilful with the pencil, instructed in
> geometry, know much history, have followed the philosophers with atten-
> tion, understand music, have some knowledge of medicine, know the
> opinions of the jurists, and be acquainted with astronomy and the theory
> of the heavens.[3]

Such a definition of architect is far broader and more inclusive than the
contemporary one, and it is easy to see why Vitruvius has held such fascination for architectural-theory students over the past two thousand years.
Vitruvius was insistent on the value of history, noting "A wide knowledge
of history is requisite because, among the ornamental parts of an architect's
design for a work, there are many the underlying idea of whose employment
he should be able to explain to his inquirers."[4] That is, to use it effectively,
one must be aware of a device's meaning (Fig 6.2).

Designers' main interest in Vitruvius today lies primarily in his attempt
at a *theoretical approach*. Indeed, he was very insistent that architectural
knowledge is "the child of practice and theory,"[5] although practical concerns tend to dominate the text. He defines *practice* as the manual work
attendant upon the manipulation of materials in accordance with a plan;
theory, ". . . is the ability to demonstrate and explain the productions of
dexterity on the principles of proportion."[6] And no part of architecture
better exemplified the critical nature of proportion than the Orders (Fig 6.3).
In modern terms, practice refers to the production and administration of the
working drawings and specifications; theory refers to the logical and articulated intellectual content of the design. This is important, he suggests,
because in all matters there are two essential points: the thing that is sig-
nified (law or object) and that which grants significance (principle or idea),
which can be ". . . demonstrated on scientific principles."[7] This seems
similar to the more current notion of a subject, form, and content continuum. In his model, Vitruvius does not isolate form but, rather, assumes
that content and form are inseparable. This accounts for his citing certain
types of columns and proportional systems as appropriate for particular
kinds of buildings—for reasons only partially related to structural concerns.
Thus a given space, even when aptly sized and properly appointed, would
not take on the desired character unless properly designed, with regard for
concepts of proportion, scale, balance, and so forth.

From this it is clear that Vitruvius could not conceive an architecture that
existed in structure only; to the contrary, the mechanical aspects of raising
a building formed only part of the architect's labors. To the goal of solid
structure, *Firmitas,* he added that of user convenience, *Utilitas,* and aesthetic pleasure, *Venustas*. Vitruvius believed that the Eustyle temple form
had been developed with a view to these qualities (Fig 6.4). He states: "The
intervals should be made as wide as the thickness of two columns and a
quarter, but the middle intercolumniations, one in front and the other in the
rear, should be of the thickness of three columns. Thus built, the effect of
the design will be beautiful, there will be no obstruction at the entrance,
and the walk around the cella will be dignified."[8] Thus his view is of a
practical building technique serving beauty.

For the two millennia following Vitruvius, these three goals of architecture have been considered so fundamental to its practice that they have often
been raised to the level of canon. Considering the importance given these

goals, we should consider their underlying precepts; these basic principles are order, arrangement, eurythmy, symmetry, propriety, and economy. *Order* may be thought of as attention to elements that are to be used so that their number and proportion correspond to the scale and proportion of the finished work. *Arrangement* refers to how elements, or parts, are adjusted to shape the final work; this involves setting down information using such formats as plan, elevation, and perspective. *Eurythmy* is defined as beauty, but a beauty that springs from harmonious and symmetrical proportion. This idea is placed in a Christian context twelve centuries later in the words of Suger, Abbot of St. Denis, when he says:

> The admirable power of one unique and supreme reason equalizes by proper composition the disparity between things human and Divine; and what seems mutually to conflict by inferiority of origin and contrariety of nature is conjoined by the single, delightful concordance of one superior, well-tempered harmony.[9]

Vitruvius defines *symmetry* as an overall "agreement" among elements and between elements and the total work, in accordance with a standard; thus all the parts of a structure may be seen as multiples of this selected standard, or module. *Propriety* can be thought of as appropriateness for a given situation that may spring from prescription (a determination of what is correct based on social or moral ideas), usage (a consistent approach to interior/exterior, scale, materials, etc.), or nature (an analysis of those factors occurring naturally and affecting siting). Finally, *economy* refers to ". . . the proper management of materials and site, as well as a thrifty balancing of cost and common sense in the construction of works."[10] For Vitruvius, this extends from reasonable choices of materials based on availability and suitability to consideration of the client's social position and the intended use of the structure. Vitruvius' principles might, in newer language, be stated as follows: Internal consistency, effective design, aesthetic sensibility, organic harmony, social and physical correctness, and sensitive cost-factoring. It seems that the architect's task has changed little in two millennia (Fig 6.5).

From these fundamental principles of architecture, Vitruvius derived a working set of structural criteria that remains convincing:

> All . . . must be built with due reference to durability (firmitas), convenience (utilitas), and beauty (venustas). Durability will be assured when

6.2

Caryatides
The caryatids make reference to a city, Caryae, which allied itself with the Persians; when the Greeks later defeated the Persians at Plataea, they destroyed the city and its men, and enslaved the wives. These columns ensured that they would ". . . appear forever after as a type of slavery, burdened with the weight of their shame and so making atonement for their State."[1] (Source: *The Ten Books on Architecture,* Vitruvius, Morris Hicky Morgan translator.)

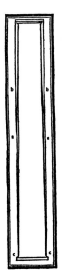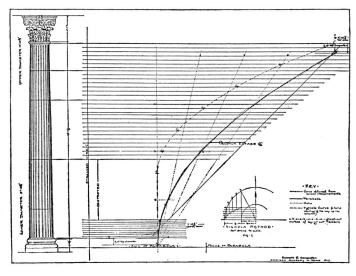

6.3

The Entasis of Columns
Vitruvius explains entasis: "These proportionate enlargements are made in the thickness of columns on account of the different heights to which the eye has to climb. For the eye is always in search of beauty, and if we do not gratify its desire for pleasure by a proportionate enlargement in these measures, and thus make compensation for ocular deception, a clumsy and awkward appearance will be presented to the beholder."[2] (Source: *The Ten Books on Architecture,* Vitruvius, Morris Hicky Morgan translator.)

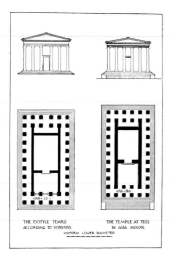

6.4

The Eustyle Temple Form
The Eustyle temple represented for Vitruvius an ideal in terms of proportion and arrangement, serving as a theoretical paradigm. (Source: *The Ten Books on Architecture*, Vitruvius, Morris Hicky Morgan translator.)

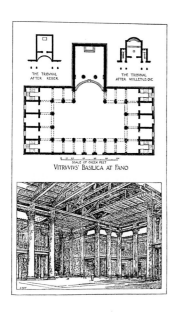

6.5

Vitruvius' Basilica—Fano
Vitruvius designed and superintended the construction of this basilica. In Book I of his work, he presents in detail an explanation of the modular system he used, how it provides for the function, and how it projects the proper "air of sumptuousness and dignity." He does not fail to mention that he also managed to keep the cost down. (Source: *The Ten Books on Architecture*, Vitruvius, Morris Hicky Morgan translator.)

foundations are carried down to the solid ground and materials wisely and liberally selected; convenience, when the arrangement of the apartments is faultless and presents no hindrance to use, and when each class of building is assigned to its suitable and appropriate exposure; and beauty, when its members are in due proportion according to correct principles of symmetry.[11]

De Architectura is a rich source of information and observation on an array of concerns, from the appropriate use of orders and ornament to proper light exposures and, particularly, how abstract concepts like proportion and symmetry manifest themselves visually. Nor does he fail to discuss the spatial and proxemic qualities of rooms, explaining for example, that the length and width of a dining room are determined by the dimensions of ". . . two sets of dining couches, facing each other, with room to pass around them. . . ."[12] In this way one could have proper order and a good view of the garden. The dimensions of the dining rooms might be variable but, in any case, should be twice as long as wide, with their height calculated by adding the length and width and then dividing the result in half.[13] Atria were especially important in terms of public image, and Vitruvius accordingly carefully specifies the three classes of proportional systems as 3:5, 2:3, and 1:1.4, with a height to the girders one-fourth less than the width.[14] The ultimate value of Vitruvius' work, however, may be its impact on the architectural theory that followed, particularly that of Alberti, who acknowledged the debt.

Alberti

Leon Battista Alberti (1404–72) in many ways exemplified the "Renaissance Man," both for his breadth of knowledge and his multiplicity of interests; however, he is best remembered in the areas of classical scholarship and architecture. His great work, *De re aedificatoria* (Ten Books of Architecture), was completed in 1452, although not actually published until 1485, some thirteen years after his death. Alberti's love of antiquity and belief in a theory of harmonic proportion led him to an admiration of Vitruvius' theories. His work is not only closely modeled on the Roman's manuscript, but designed to clarify his ideas for readers in fifteenth-century Italy. In the first chapter of Book VI, Alberti clearly states his concerns:

It grieved me that so many great and noble instructions of ancient authors should be lost by the injury of time, so that scarce any but Vitruvius has escaped this general wreck: A writer indeed of universal knowledge, but so maimed by age, that in many places there are great chasms, and many things imperfect in others. Besides this, his style is absolutely void of all ornaments, and he wrote in such manner . . . (that) he might almost as well have never wrote at all, at least in regard to us, since we cannot understand him.[15]

If Alberti finds Vitruvius' prose style or use of precise terminology lacking, he certainly finds little fault with his ideas. Indeed, Alberti's definition of architect is so close to his predecessor's that it does not require repeating, and his ideas concerning harmony and proportion, while more elaborate, also echo Vitruvius. The close agreement in title and textual format may, however, be somewhat misleading. Alberti's intent is more profound than a simple clarification of Vitruvius and comes from a fundamentally different premise; Françoise Choay makes this clear, "But he has not simply improved on Vitruvius' text: insofar as he uses it at all, he transforms it completely."[16] That is, Alberti has taken the essential elements of Vitruvius' text and devised a new and radical treatise. Thus his translation of Vitruvius' three elements is not only in more subtle form (using *propriety* in place of *utilitas*), but is made dynamic. Choay notes that they now fulfill a structural function, and their role is constructive rather than passive.[17] Moreover, three necessary and dialectically related features are missing in Vitruvius' work, ". . . the intention to formulate a *basic principle;* the hypothesis of the *autonomy* of the act of building; and the concept of *creative time.*"[18] There are several reasons for this (the fact of an intervening 1,500 years, for example), but the effect is a new theoretical stance based entirely on reason.

Choay suggests that the primacy Alberti grants theory in design decisions goes well beyond Vitruvius, then, marking a "second stage" in architecture. To attain proportional perfection, Alberti used techniques from mathematics and musical theory, applying them to forms taken from the monumental architecture of the ancient world—particularly as seen in temple façades and public monuments (Fig 6.6). In his *Architectural Principles in the Age of Humanism,* Rudolf Wittkower notes that the new design elements Alberti introduced in the façade of S. Maria Novella would have remained isolated features save for the unifying sense of harmony, which consists in the relationship of the parts to each other and to the whole. He states ". . . in fact, a single system of proportion permeates the façade, and the place and size of every single part and detail is fixed and defined by it. Proportions recommended by Alberti are the simple relations of one to one, one to two, one to three, two to three, three to four, etc., which are the elements of musical harmony and which Alberti found in classical buildings."[19] These buildings must, therefore, have been Roman, perhaps a reflection of his basic agreement with certain of Vitruvius' premises:

> We consider that an edifice is a kind of body consisting, like all other bodies, of design and of matter; the first is produced by the thought, the other by nature; so that the one is to be provided by the application and contrivance of the mind, and the other by due preparation and choice. And we further reflect, that neither the one nor the other of itself is sufficient, without the hand of an experienced artificer, that knew how to form his materials after a just design.[20]

There are, then, significant differences between the ideas of the two architects—largely the result of the unlike centuries they lived in. Thus the following analysis of architecture probably owes more to issues of morality than to the Greek ethic of moderation *(sophrosyne)*:

> For all building in general, if you consider it well, owes its birth to necessity, was nursed by convenience, and embellished by use; pleasure was the last thing consulted in it, which is never truly attained by things that are immoderate.[21]

Simply, a structure that serves its purpose and proves its aptness through the test of use, is sufficient; excess luxury is unneeded, unwanted, and suspect. Alberti is likewise compelled to address design issues for audiences that were only of minor concern to Vitruvius:

> Now if anything is to be gather'd from all this to our purpose, it is certainly that of the different kinds of building, one sort belongs to the public, another to the principal citizens, and another to the commonality. The chief difference between private houses and palaces is, that there is a particular air suitable to each. . . . [22]

The need to consider what was or was not suitable for the palazzi of the powerful merchant princes of Quattrocento Italy is probably responsible for the extensive discussion of interior spaces. In Books V and IX, especially,

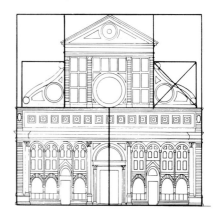

6.6

S. Maria Novella—Florence; *Leon Alberti (1456)*
Among the new design elements introduced by Alberti in the façade of this structure are the scroll-brackets flanking the nave and pediment. The scrolls were a particularly brilliant device since they solved the exterior visual problem of unifying the dual interior requirement (a two-story nave and single-story aisles). The pediment additionally related the building to those of classical antiquity, like the Pantheon. This reflected his belief that consistency between the old and new could be maintained. (Drawn by: J. Malnar.)

he considers how the house of a *principal citizen* ought to be planned, what rooms would be necessary and how they should relate, and considers such items as secret passages, seasonal exposures, entrances, vestibules, and the scale of rooms. These considerations grew urgent as it again became customary that the domicile was also the place of business, either directly or as image. Choay notes that the fact that Alberti addresses such a wide range of problems indicates the importance of psychology and sociology in the constructive dynamics of *De re aedificatoria* and—through these—of imagination and man's requirements.[23]

If these new design concerns were the product of their age, so was the underlying ideology. Out of the class struggles of the fourteenth century that had so devastated Italy came a new economic rationalism based on expedience and calculation. The new class made up of bankers, industrialists, and merchants was devoted to both the acquisition of fortunes and their lavish expenditure. Little remained important that could not be verified empirically, and this became as true for the culture as the economy:

> . . . the rationalism which was a more or less dominant feature of the profit economy from the very outset now became absolute. The capitalistic spirit of the Renaissance consists in the profit motive and the so-called middle-class virtues, acquisitiveness and industry, frugality and respectability. But even this new morality is only another expression of the universal process of rationalism.[24]

This rationalism stood in stark contrast to the metaphysical reality of the immediately preceding centuries, and when members of the mercantile and cultural classes sought models, it is scarcely surprising that they turned to antiquity. This is echoed in the words of Plutarch, when he says, "We must find a way back to the clear splendor of the ancient past."[25]

While Alberti and his clientele enjoyed a new admiration for classical antiquity, they were not unappreciative of the entree to leisure and the good life that economic security allowed, nor the notoriety that accompanied expenditure. Giovanni Rucellai came from a patrician family that had made its fortune in wool, and in his autobiography he writes, "I have now done nothing for fifty years but earn and spend money, and it has become clear to me that spending money gives more pleasure than earning it."[26] Alberti wrote, then, for a sophisticated and wealthy audience, as concerned about order and beauty as it was a structured comfort. Alberti began his study of architecture as part of a study of classical antiquity generally, but at age 40 he became practicing architect as well as educated humanist. In his design for the Palazzo Rucellai, he combines the clear and logical articulation of classical models with the necessary limitations imposed by the functions of an urban residence. The result is a structure that provides for a hierarchy of public and private levels within a clearly articulated and dignified façade. So persuasive was this formula, that its influence may be seen in the commercial structures of the nineteenth century (Fig 6.7).

It is, however, in the extraordinary façade of S. Andrea in Mantua that his formulated concept of *divine proportion* becomes visible. Alberti, while lauding ornament generally, maintains an unusually spare design by the period's standards. Rudolf Wittkower comments that ". . . S. Andrea reflects a change of theory . . . he must have weighed the contemporary demand of a logical wall structure against the authority of classical antiquity and decided to reject the compromise of joining column and wall . . . in favor of a uniform wall architecture."[27] This solution let Alberti use the classical temple facade while maintaining a strong continuity between the scale of exterior and interior (Fig 6.8). He wrote about painting and sculp-

6.7

Palazzo Rucellai—Florence; *Leon Alberti (1446–51)*
In its tripartite horizontal division, this clearly delineated structure expresses a hierarchy of interior functions. The first floor constitutes the public areas, often reserved for mercantile concerns; the second floor contains quasi-public functions such as dining- and reception areas; and the third floor remains entirely private. The horizontality is expressed by the clear division of stories, each with its own cornice and particular order; the verticality is expressed in the clear statement of the pilasters and equal bays. (Source: *The Architecture of the Italian Renaissance*, Jacob Burckhardt.)

6.8

S. Andrea—Mantua; *Leon Alberti (1470)*
This structure represents the superimposition of a triumphal arch over a classical temple façade, thus merging these two systems in a novel way. This is accomplished by the clever use of pilasters, which appear as if they belong to both systems, thus unifying the structure. The vaulted nave rises considerably above the façade and incorporates three side chapels—perhaps imitating Roman basilicas. The most striking feature, however, is the continuity of exterior and interior. The detail of the façade is repeated on the interior wall; and the height of the façade to the entablature is equal to the height of the nave to the point where the vaulting begins. (Source: *Architectural Principles in the Age of Humanism,* Rudolf Wittkower, Academy Editions, London.)

ture as well as architecture, and it is perhaps here that he most clearly articulates the idea of restraint:

> Whoever strives after dignity in his work will limit himself to a small number of figures; for just as princes enhance their majesty by the shortness of their speeches, so a sparing use of figures increases the value of a work of art.[28]

And finally, in his clear and unambiguous formulation of a mathematically based theory of architecture, Alberti provides the methodology for education in the arts. In his discussion of the basis for art, Arnold Hauser comments:

> The scientific conception of art, which forms the basis of instruction in the academies, begins with Leon Battista Alberti; he is the first to express the idea that mathematics is the common ground of art and the sciences, as both the theory of proportions and the theory of perspective are mathematical disciplines. He is also the first to give clear expression to that union of the experimental technician and the observing artist. . . .[29]

Palladio

Both Vitruvius and Alberti were sources for *I Quattro Libri dell' Architettura* (Four Books on Architecture), completed and published by Andrea Palladio (1508–1580) in 1570. Indeed, Palladio states firmly in the preface to his work that Vitruvius was to be his master and guide (*per maestro e guida*), especially as his was the only known architectural work from antiquity. Palladio had illustrated the 1556 edition of Vitruvius for his patron Daniele Barbaro; Barbaro thanked him by noting that he, Palladio, ". . . best understood the true architecture, having not only grasped its beautiful and subtle principles, but also practised it. . . ."[30] But Alberti and Vasari are both praised by Palladio as well, and an interesting tribute is paid to Bramante by the inclusion of his Tempietto in the company of classical buildings. Palladio went much further, however, than either Vitruvius or Alberti in his search for an absolute methodology, a correct way to design, which would unerringly result in beauty. He believed that such a universal grammar of architecture could, and did, exist, and that it was reflected in the buildings of ancient Rome. For Palladio, beauty was a direct result of careful study and application of this grammar. James S. Ackerman comments,

"What differentiates Palladio's proportions from Alberti's is that they are used in integrated systems that bind plan and elevation, interior and exterior, room and room, giving a sense of the pervasiveness of the architect's control."[31]

Palladio was not simply an antiquarian; he was a practicing architect who built churches, town and country houses, public buildings, and bridges. It is, therefore, interesting that to the ideas of *ideal form* and historical correctness, he added a concern for practical building technique. Because of his thorough treatment of these concerns, and because he believed that there were true and universally valid rules in architecture, his name has become synonymous with formal order. Thus, the term Palladian is used to describe any approach to architecture that relies on classical concepts. Much of Palladio's fame rests on the many public and private buildings he designed in Venice and Vicenza, but it was ensured by the publication of *I Quattro Libri dell' Architettura.*

This remarkable work has been reproduced in virtually every European language, and new editions have appeared regularly. Palladio's work, in publication and structure, impressed the English architect Inigo Jones, and, through Jones' enthusiasm, introduced Palladianism to seventeenth-century England. For the next two centuries Palladio's ideas of form and harmony dominated the architecture of England and America, prompting sharp criticism from the eighteenth-century architect Robert Adam:

> The great masters of antiquity were not so rigidly scrupulous, they varied the proportions as the general spirit of the composition required, clearly perceiving that, however necessary these rules may be . . . they often cramp the genius, and circumscribe the ideas of the master.[32]

Adam's comments stem from his conviction that Palladio's dictums reflected Renaissance views of antiquity, not antiquity itself, and that these dictums had evolved into limitations. Palladio was influenced by Alberti to the extent that one of his four books deals entirely with the subject of domestic architecture. This may partly stem from the fact that many of Palladio's commissions were for town and country houses, but also from a growing interest throughout Europe in residential housing. This interest would be spurred on by both the Industrial Revolution—which extended disposable wealth by creating a wealthy bourgeoisie—and an ever-increasing interest in the private sphere.

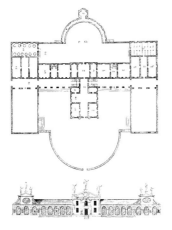

6.9

Villa Barbaro—Maser; *Andrea Palladio (1557)*

The villa at Maser was a working farm, and its long arcades housed the animals and farm implements with which the Barbaros made their income. The Barbaros nonetheless adorned the garden with statuary by Alessandro Vittoria, and the villa's interior was graced by scenes from mythology and contemporary country life by Paolo Veronese. Ackerman notes, "Veronese's world is almost independent of the actual architecture. It removes the walls and carries on in a brilliant space beyond."[3] Perhaps it is this very quality that led Palladio to omit Veronese's name as a collaborator on the project. (Photo—courtesy: Centro Internazionale di Studi di Architettura "Andrea Palladio" di Vicenza; Plan—source: *The Four Books of Architecture,* Andrea Palladio.)

Ackerman comments that during the period from 1530 to 1560, many Venetian landowners moved to their estates on the mainland, creating a need for architects who could design ". . . functional and utilitarian structures for which there was no tradition in earlier architecture, but who would command the classical heritage so as to lend an air of cultivated grandeur to the country estate of gentlemen who still thought like city dwellers, and finally, who would know how to build cheaply as well as grandly."[33] And that, he notes, was certainly Palladio's forte. This new design task has several interesting aspects: first, these villas were not simply residences, but working farms; second, any classical vocabulary would have to be modified to account for the less savory farm elements (e.g., stables.); and third, Palladio usually worked with a limited budget. And, to complicate matters, his clients were well educated and fairly knowledgeable about design. Entirely typical of Palladio's country villas is the Villa Barbaro at Maser, designed in 1557 for his illustrious patron Daniele Barbaro (Fig 6.9). This fascinating building, although set in productive fields, contains magnificent frescos and statuary. Thus the villa ". . . represented the best of two worlds, the farmer's and the gentleman's."[34]

Ultimately, the most interesting aspect of Palladio's *I Quattro Libri dell' Archittetura* may be his division of architecture. He divides it into civic architecture, domestic architecture, public works, and classical temples. The new emphasis he gives residential building exceeds anything contemplated by previous architects; and, in his treatment of these structures, he attempts a continuity between exterior and interior that goes beyond agreement of scale. The design of domestic architecture had always stressed the interior, even as civic architecture had tended to deal with the exterior. In Palladio, one finds them treated as a continuum by the simple expedient of applying classical vocabulary to residential buildings. Thus the Villa Capra combines the regular façades of a Roman temple, geometrically squared, with the function of a luxurious country villa. This is probably his best-known design, although it was an anomaly in that it was situated near a town and had no utility structures. Indeed, it served as a luxurious suburban villa for extravagant galas (Fig 6.10).

Palladio's designs combined ideas from Vitruvius and Alberti, as well as those arising from local conditions. Certain of his solutions (Villa Capra, for example) entailed such absolute and definitive design decisions that Robert Adam might indeed have basis for criticism. Vitruvius never viewed domestic architecture as worthy of such treatment, and Alberti would likely have desired a greater distinction between civic and residential structures. Careful analysis of his buildings, however, would reveal small design variations, since "Palladio thought of strict uniformity as literally unnatural."[35] Nor did he always apply a single proportional system. And, in any case, his designs were far more practical and responsive to clients than popular myth would have it. Thus Palladianism was not so rigid as a casual appraisal of the Villa Capra might lead one to suppose; to the contrary, some of the finest (and varied) creations of Neoclassicism (Thomas Jefferson's striking home at Monticello comes to mind) owe their existence to Palladian models.

In the end, Palladio's view of the nature of architecture was not so very different from that of Vitruvius or Alberti, as is clear from this statement in Book One:

> Beauty will result from the form and correspondence of the whole, with respect to the several parts, of the parts with regard to each other, and of these again to the whole; that the structure may appear an entire and complete body, wherein each member agrees with the other, and all necessary to compose what you intend to form.[36]

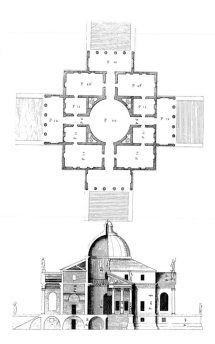

6.10

Villa Capra—Vicenza; *Andrea Palladio (1566)*
The plan of this villa (also called the Villa Rotonda) is based on a Greek cross, with a crossing dome made to look compact and structurally integrated. Palladio uses four similar entry porches, which impart an air of dignity and grant a certain civic virtue to this residential building. It is one of his most symmetrical and uncompromising structures in theory and exterior appearance, yet the interior reflects a lavish and ornate sensibility, which stands in sharp contrast to the exterior, and likely reflected the owner's taste. (Photo—courtesy: Centro Internazionale di Studi di Architettura ''Andrea Palladio'' di Vicenza; Plan—source: *The Four Books of Architecture*, Andrea Palladio.)

What was unique about Palladio was his insistence on absolute values in architecture—obtainable by adherence to classical methodologies and harmonic proportions—and his broad and generous consideration of domestic architecture. He regarded the residence as a structure capable of internal and external nobility, and here he even suggests its primacy:

> . . . I thought it would be very convenient to begin with private houses, because one ought to believe, that those first gave rise to public edifices; it being very probable, that man formerly lived by himself; but afterwards, seeing he required the acceptance of other men, to obtain those things that might make him happy, naturally sought and loved the company of other men: whereupon of several houses, villages were formed, and then of many villages, cities, and in these public places and edifices were made.[37]

The importance accorded residential architecture gave Palladio's theories a vitality that no architect who followed, including Adam, could ignore or not be influenced by. And it is an importance that suggests the new role of the space within as a suitable (and profitable) subject for the designer.

Adam

It may well be that Adam was less distressed with Palladio himself than he was with the rigidly doctrinaire approach that his English admirers adopted. The English Palladian school, led early on by Inigo Jones and later by such figures as Lord Burlington and William Kent, had set the course of English taste at the same time that much of Europe was dominated by the Rococo.

Adam's view was that this approach was stultifyingly predictable and, worse, robbed the ancient world's designs of their vitality. He contended that the essence of the ancient, or antique, approach lay in its purity of forms coupled with flexibility of application. It was not Palladio's admiration of the antique vocabulary or even his insistence on "rules" of form and proportion that Adam objected to; rather, it was the systematic adherence to the idea that a single set of parameters could suffice for every situation.

Robert Adam and his brother James had criticized Palladio's designs as early as 1756, both as they appeared in publication and as the brothers saw them at Vicenza. But, as noted, much of their disapproval must have been directed at the Palladians rather than Palladio himself. In Book 1 of *The Works in Architecture of Robert and James Adam* (1773–1778), Robert Adam states:

> We, by no means, presume to find fault, with the compositions, or to decry the labours of other authors; many of whom have much merit and deserve great praise. Our ambition is to share with others, not to appropriate to ourselves the applause of the public; and, if we have any claim to approbation, we found it on this alone: that we flatter ourselves, we have been able to seize, with some degree of success, the beautiful spirit of antiquity, and to transfuse it, with novelty and variety, through all our numerous works.[38]

He repeats this idea in Book Two and, indeed, in virtually every one of the five books. The result of this was, in Adam's words, to bring about ". . . a kind of revolution in the whole system of this useful and elegant art."[39]

Robert Adam (1728–1792) was the most innovative and theoretical of four brothers, two of whom shared his architectural practice. As in the case of Vitruvius, Alberti, and Palladio, his fame rests both on his written theories and their practical application. As was customary for eighteenth-century English gentlemen, he experienced Europe on the Grand Tour during the years from 1754 to 1758. This tour was critical in his understanding of the monuments of antiquity and directly resulted in the folio entitled *Ruins of the Palace of the Emperor Diocletian at Spalatro in Dalmatia,* published in 1764. This folio immediately established his reputation as historian but, more important, provided Adam with a vocabulary of design motifs, both architectural and decorative. Beyond that, the palace formed the fundamental source for his ideas about domestic architecture and—in particular— interiors. Of equal (or greater) influence on Adam was the 1753 publication of Robert Wood's *Ruins of Palmyra,* which supplied much of the raw information for Adam's practical designs, especially those at Osterley (Fig 6.11).

The forces affecting Adam were many: first, a profound admiration of the Roman world (including Greece), as seen in his constructions and decoration; second, some reference to ideas from the Renaissance and, protestations to the contrary, Palladio; third, an interest in medieval castle architecture (fairly prevalent in eighteenth-century taste); and finally, the Romantic love of the picturesque. This last quality provides the lyrical and exuberant character of Adam's work and reveals his concern for the relationship between architecture and nature. Thus it is in Book One of *The Works in Architecture of Robert and James Adam* that Adam formulates one of his most interesting theories, that of *movement,* which he felt applied to the building in its entirety:

> Movement is meant to express, the rise and fall, the advance and recess, with other diversity of form, in the different parts of the building, so as to add greatly to the picturesque of the composition. For the rising and fall-

6.11

Etruscan Room—Osterley; *Robert Adam (1758)*
The decorations are in what Adam believed to be the style of the Etruscans, although the color scheme of red, green, and black probably comes from late Greek sources. In any case the entire design really represents Adam's ability to abstract classical motifs to his advantage, rather than any actual resemblance to designs of antiquity. The effect is one of charm and airiness. (Courtesy: Victoria & Albert Museum, London.)

6.12

Library—Kenwood; *Robert Adam (1767)*
In this library one can see the "rising and falling" of the barrel vault, and the apsidal ends receding away from the main body of the room. By contrasting these elements with the screen formed by the columns and their cornice, a "swelling sensation" is created. The bright white columns reflect the light from the windows, and so advance dramatically; the columns of the bookcase advance somewhat less, but still appear to hover in front of the stacks of books, which now extend into the distance. (Courtesy: English Heritage, London.)

ing, advancing and receding, with the convexity and concavity, and other forms of the great parts, have the same effect in architecture, that hill and dale, fore-ground and distance, swelling and sinking have in landscape: That is, they serve to produce an agreeable and diversified contour, that groups and contrasts like a picture, and creates a variety of light and shade, which gives great spirit, beauty and effect to the composition.[40]

He cites several structures, including the south façade of his own (incomplete) design at Kedleston, that may exemplify this idea. This notion is essentially artistic rather than architectural and, in its concern for light and shadow, is quite pictorial (Fig 6.12).

Adam did not limit movement to the structure's exterior. The variation in his handling of interior space clearly reflects these exterior concerns, but such movement is most easily found in his use of surface decoration. This decoration, in arrangement and creative conception, provided a rich and lively interior that accounts for his major role in English architecture's revolution:

> Architecture has already become more elegant and more interesting. The parade, the convenience, and social pleasures of life, being better understood, are more strictly attended to in the arrangement and disposition of apartments. Greater variety of form, greater beauty in design, greater gaiety and elegance of ornament, are introduced into interior decoration; while the outside composition is more simple, more grand, more varied in its contour, and imposes on the mind from the superior magnitude and movement of its parts.[41]

This achievement, he notes, is the result of a careful examination, analysis, and adaptation of the decorative forms of the ancient world, resulting in an interior design that reflected that world more accurately in spirit than did the Palladian school:

> . . . on the inside of their edifices the Ancients were extremely careful to proportion both the size and depth of their compartments and panels, to the distance from the eye and the objects with which they were to be compared: and, with regard to the decoration of their private and bathing apartments, they were all delicacy, gaiety, grace, and beauty.[42]

The keys to Adam's success probably include a more precise knowledge of antique design (especially after the discoveries at Herculaneum in 1737 and Pompeii in 1748) and the willingness to adapt to the situation. The willingness to abstract motifs from the classical world and combine them with his vast information about other periods let Adam synthesize a strikingly original vocabulary and grammar. This was a tribute to the individual genius of Adam, who commented that such a methodology "... may do great harm in the hands of rash innovators or mere retailers in the art, who have neither eyes nor judgement."[43] Although Adam considered himself an architect, he is famous for his interiors, which were characterized by a careful and delicate arrangement of all the various elements.

These elements included decoration on walls and ceilings, furniture, lighting, mantles, and the commissioning of works of art. The relationship between stair and hall, and the impression they gave to the visitor, were of special concern to Adam, as was the pattern formed by interior spaces. These concerns partly stemmed from his commissions for London townhouses, such as the Williams Wynn House, where he had to work with irregular and confined spaces (Fig 6.13). Adam notes that "this house . . . is considerably circumscribed with regard to site; notwithstanding which, great care has been taken to make the apartments spacious, and even magnificent."[44] Rather than view it as a limitation, Adam regards the limited size as a challenge, stating: "It is not in a space of forty-six feet that an architect can make a great display of talents. Where variety and grandeur in composition cannot be obtained, we must be satisfied with a justness of proportion and an elegance of style."[45]

The 1778 publication of all five installments of *The Works in Architecture of Robert and James Adam* chronicled the elaborate and elegant interior designs of Adam. Interestingly, when he had the opportunity to design façades, he demonstrated a more Palladian sensibility than he might ever have wished to admit. The south façade at Kedleston, for example, incorporates a reproduction of the Arch of Constantine, in a statement of Roman grandeur that glorifies the act of arrival and confers special status to the occupants and their guests. This is only one way that Adam drew from antiquity. The color scheme and decoration at Osterley, for example, was influenced by Greek vases (which he believed to be Etruscan). After visiting these rooms, Horace Walpole complained that they were ". . . painted all

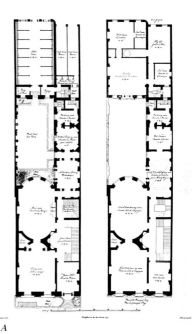

A

6.13

The Williams Wynn House—London; *Robert Adam (1772)*
The plan *(A)* indicates a use of recessed planes, columned screens, and a large paved court, which not only opens up the interior space, but provides light and ventilation for interior rooms that would otherwise have none. The elevation *(B)* suggests that Adam made the most of a comparatively narrow city lot by emphasizing the base and cornice. The large and elegant staircase *(C)* stands inside a space that is both open and articulated, suggesting a far larger dwelling. The balusters are of a delicate foliate design that enhances both the sense of space and grace of movement. (*[A, B]* source: *The Works in Architecture of Robert and James Adam*, Robert and James Adam. *[C]* courtesy: Royal Commission on the Historical Monuments of England, London. Permission: Mewès & Davis Architects, Plymouth, U.K.)

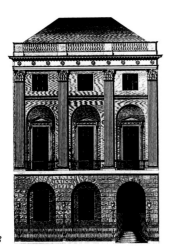

B

C

B

6.14

Sion House—London; *Robert Adam (1762)*
At Sion, Adam had intended to develop a
great rotonda in the central courtyard *(A)*;
this scheme was never carried out, but he did
extensively remodel the Jacobean house. The
mirror *(B)* was designed by Adam as part of
a carefully conceived ensemble for a particular location, adding to the formal qualities
of the space. (Source: *The Works in Architecture of Robert and James Adam,* Robert
and James Adam.)

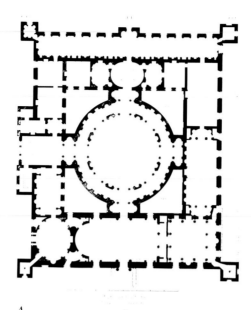

A

over like Wedgwood's ware, with black and yellow small grotesques.''[46] Yet
the delicate colors and graceful ornament from this type of source are developed into bright rooms enriched with white plasterwork (Plate 8).

In his discussion of the interior spaces at Sion, however, he reveals his
real talent, the ability to coordinate the myriad aspects of life within a
structure—from galleries to stairwells to furniture (Fig 6.14). Adam
planned these interiors as sequences of individual rooms, with concave
shapes and engaged and detached columns, to provide highly dimensional
spatial effects. Louise Ade Boger has characterized his furniture designs
as ''. . . praiseworthy for the classic simplicity of their contour, for their
excellent proportions and for the graceful delicacy of their ornament.''[47]
Adam thus concludes:

> We should not have dared to enter so minutely into the description of this
> plan, if we did not imagine that this is one of those branches of our art,
> which has not hitherto been treated of with any accuracy, or studied with
> any care; though of all others the most essential, both to the splendor and
> convenience of life.[48]

Such a view of life might indeed grant credence to Talleyrand's dictum,
''No one who did not live before 1789 knows the sweetness of life.''[49]

Boffrand and Blondel

Gabriel-Germain Boffrand (1667–1754) lived in just such an era as Talleyrand praises; he was both architect and engineer, and author of the influential work *Livres d'architecture.* He had been a pupil of Hardouin-Mansart,
the designer of Les Invalides in Paris, and proponent of the Baroque style.
Boffrand moved away from his teacher in the exaggeration of this style,
often stressing space (voids) over the material aspects (walls) of the structure. While this tended to unify interior and exterior, it also suggested a
conflict between aesthetic concerns and physical practicality. In this he was
reaching back to an earlier Italian Baroque, particularly Bernini. Whatever
difficulties may have existed in applying his ideas to the exterior of build-

ings, the approach worked very well for the interiors of the new *hôtels* being built in Paris. These hôtels, the result of the resituating of the court in Paris and the limited availability of funds, were often the result of a combining and retrofitting of existing structures. The hôtel provided venue for ". . . the development of the non-monumental, anti-architectural mode of interior decoration which produced the Rococo," marked by, ". . . irregular and increasingly sensuous mouldings which actually invaded the field they surrounded, breaking down the distinction between frame and framed."[50]

One of Boffrand's first major commissions was the salon of the Petit Luxembourg in 1710 (Fig 1.13). In this project, he first experimented with the idea of an essentially plastic, nontectonic space. But he is probably best known for his design of the oval salons for the Hôtel de Soubise. This building had been originally designed by Delamair in 1704, out of two existing townhouses. In 1735, Boffrand was employed to enlarge and decorate the building; in this structure he was able to develop to dazzling effect his ideas about space (Fig 6.15). In his *Architecture in the Age of Reason*, Emil Kaufmann comments:

> A parallel to the virtual interpenetration of inner and outer space was the ever increasing use of huge mirrors in the interiors. Boffrand's upper oval salon . . . loses by the mirrors the character of an independent volume unit and becomes virtually a unit in an infinite sequence of rooms. Ascending bands of scrollwork efface the differentiation between the walls and the vaulted ceiling.[51]

The *hôtel interior* became, in the eighteenth century, a leading way for designers to stay employed, and introduced a new approach to architectural design generally. Christian Norberg-Schulz states:

> We may characterize the general trend by the word *individualization*. Instead of forming part of a superior system, the buildings receive a more intimate individuality. . . . Above all, the interior spaces were further differentiated, and a rich playful decoration created a feeling of intimate enchantment. The simple sophisticated exteriors form a meaningful counterpoint and reveal how the focus of life had turned inward.[52]

Much of Boffrand's (and Blondel's) influence rests on written theory. In Boffrand's *Livres*, he says that the building should have a unity of character, in addition to more formal unity; and states, "One should judge the character of the master of the house, for whom it was constructed, by the manner it is arranged, ornamented, and furnished."[53] And, distinguishing between interior and exterior, he says, "One must not use, in the interior, the ornaments which only belong to the exterior."[54] In this work, Boffrand supplied a guide that anticipated Blondel.

Jacques-François Blondel (1705–1774) had a considerable influence on the course of eighteenth-century design, primarily through his many treatises and his effect as a professor of architecture. While he espoused traditional views of architecture, such as the importance of symmetry, proportion, and unity, he also felt that rationality should be the guiding principle. Like Boffrand, he felt that character, simplicity, and atmosphere were crucial to design; he was moreover sensitive to the seemingly conflicting demands of form and function, and gave consideration to the reconciliation of aesthetic principles and practicality. Kaufmann describes this new concept of *unity:*

> Boffrand had remained within the sphere of aesthetic unity when he formed the concept of unity of character. Blondel accepted this concept, but went beyond it in advocating *cette triple unite* of practicality, solidity, and adornment.[55]

6.15

Hôtel de Soubise—Paris; *Gabriel-Germain Boffrand (1735)*
The courtyard façade, in its sense of continuity, successfully masks the complex structure behind it. In 1735 Boffrand was commissioned to remodel the interior; the contrast between the tectonic façade and the curvilinear salon describes the vast difference between the periods in which they were conceived. In the Salon de la Princesse, which remains one of the finest examples of the French rococo, Boffrand has eliminated classical detailing in favor of the curved wall, cove ceiling, and undulating frames. (Source: Giraudon/Art Resource, New York.)

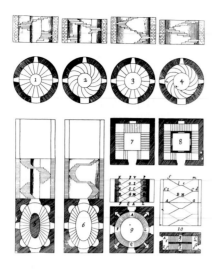

6.16

Pattern Sheet, *Cours d'architecture;*
Jacques-François Blondel (1771)
Blondel describes four types of stairwell systems: rectangular, square, circular, and elliptical. Also included are the possible variations; these include open versus solid core, differential points of tread attachment, and differing tread shape. (Courtesy: The John Work Garrett Library, The Johns Hopkins University.)

Blondel felt that a structure's appearance depended on the degree to which a balance of aesthetics and practicality could be effected and, therefore, postulated a higher value, unity. He states, "Unity in art consists in reconciling in its plan, strength, convenience and order, without any one of these three parts destroying another."[56]

Much of Blondel's *Maison de plaisances* deals with the idea of unity in the interior, where he says, "There is still another part of arranging which pertains to the decoration, the interior more so than the exterior, and the merit of an architect is to render all parts perfectly relative one to the others. . . . I relate these differences to remind of the obstacle the architect often finds, when he must accord proportion of the forms with the symmetry, the arrangement, with the decoration."[57] Blondel reached an interesting conclusion about reconciling interior and exterior; formality might prevail on the exterior and practical function on the interior or, alternatively, such formality might be restricted to civic structures and practicality reserved for private ones. In this, he is observing an old formula indeed. One of his most enduring publications is the *Cours d'architecture* (1771–1776), published in six volumes. Here he lists, as *types,* the sorts of buildings in the architect's vocabulary; these include halls, libraries, factories, baths, prisons—indeed, virtually every form of structure imaginable. And he characterizes not only their appearance, but their programs and character. The *Cours* additionally contained a wide-ranging analysis of ornament, with plates depicting vases, furniture, plasterwork, panelling, and so forth; in this, he supplied a catalogue of types similar to Boffrand's (Fig 6.16).

Boffrand and Blondel were important, then, for two reasons: first, their unambiguous distinction between interior and exterior design, with their particular concerns; and second, the notion that architecture and decoration could be typed and catalogued. This would have important ramifications for the following century, which saw the publication of such encyclopedias of design as the *Encyclopédie Méthodique d'Architecture* by Antoine Quatramère de Quincy and, even more important, J.N.L.Durand's *Recueil et parallèle des édifices en tout genre* (1801). In the latter work, important conclusions would be drawn about the role of form and function in a comparative taxonomy drawn from the methods of natural science. These works would lay the groundwork for the nineteenth-century structural techniques to follow. They would also end the rococo, whose ". . . ornament began, tentatively, to spread from the interior to the exterior of buildings . . . (a) license permissible in private would certainly corrupt if displayed in public. . . ."[58]

Adam's impetus was Neoclassical, while Boffrand's and Blondel's rococo designs were extensions of the Baroque. But the position of these eighteenth-century architects, fundamentally aristocratic, could not satisfy the needs of a vigorous and wealthy merchant class desirous of quickly assuming the appearance of culture; nor could it meet the needs of the burgeoning industrial age. This older outlook was aptly characterized in a recent comment by the contemporary architect and designer Robert McAlpine, who comments that having lived in the South all of his life ". . . has taught me of human frailty and of the importance of grace and accommodation in things and in places and in people. And it has taught me that there is no greater success than to have achieved appropriateness and an understanding of the grace of life."[59]

McAlpine made these comments in a kind of tribute to Thomas Chippendale, who was not only a contemporary of Adam, but in fact constructed some of his furniture designs. McAlpine noted that a Chippendale chair was invented with the remarkable qualities of both responding sympathetically to the sitter and encouraging that sitter to sit gracefully. That is, while in design and construction, the chair was fully prepared to respond to a person's social eccentricities, that same person tended to conform to the view of life the chair represented. It is this quality that McAlpine seeks in his own furniture designs, which are striking for their good humor and grace (Fig 6.17).

The notion that a well-designed piece of furniture might be *morally instructive* finds its counterpart in the interior designs of Adam. It seems clear that in proportion, decoration, historical reference, and arrangement, an Adam interior indicates a propriety that induces the inhabitant to respond in kind. Our first observation, then, is that our current view of designing interiors primarily for comfort would have been unthinkable for designers before 1800. For Adam, the interiors of houses should reflect ". . . appropriateness and an understanding of life." This view is essentially based in a broader conception of society and social obligation than we are accustomed to, and involves a more profound definition of design. The second discernible trend in this succession of architects is the movement from the exterior to the interior; that is, from Vitruvius' emphasis on the construction and façades of structures to the fame accorded the interiors of Boffrand and Adam. Indeed, by 1800, these spatial functions of design have reached a point of specialization that suggests their eventual split into discrete disciplines. In the bourgeois industrial society that follows, the interior, in total expenditure, claims a major share of construction costs and requires advanced technical knowledge.

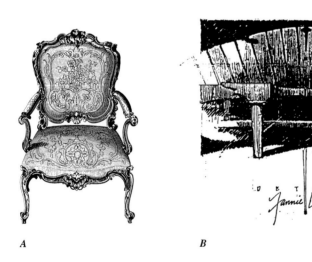

A   B

6.17

(A) **The Chippendale Chair;** *Thomas Chippendale; (B)* **The Rusticated Garden Bench;** *Robert McAlpine (1987)*
After 1760 chair design increasingly reflected the influence of Adam. Chippendale, having constructed some of Adam's designs, was himself affected. He produced an upholstered armchair *(A)* with arm supports and a wide seat, which he termed "French"; his chairs were immediately popular due to their stylishness, fine proportions, and extraordinary comfort. McAlpine notes that a design intended for the garden should have a touch of whimsy; thus a garden bench *(B)* should be overscaled and exaggerated—in short, anything but pretentious.[4] *([A]* source: *The Gentleman & Cabinet-Maker's Director,* Thomas Chippendale, *[B]* courtesy: Robert McAlpine, Montgomery, Ala.)

The
Nineteenth
Century

7

Theoretical Basis

During the nineteenth century, then, all the elements of the industrial revolution came together coherently and efficiently; these included economic theory, techniques of mass production, task-specific machinery, and the new structures to house industry. For Western Europe and the United States, this meant exploiting the properties and techniques of cast-iron. But utilizing cast-iron depended on the identification and standardization of specific structural types, as well as their constituent parts. Put differently, the organized methodology of industrialism required that architectural form be amenable to specification by kind, essentially an abstract, cognitive process. And it is this process that can be seen in the writings of French theorists in the early nineteenth century.

In a sense, the roots of architectural classification by type may be found in the *pattern books* of the eighteenth-century Rococo designers. Blondel, for example, in his definitive *Cours d'architecture* (1771), lists in detail the great variety of building types (and their programs) that architects should be aware of, and concluded that each should attain its ". . . own manner of being, suitable for it alone, or those of its kind.''[1] This kind of system paralleled developments in the natural sciences and suggested that architecture was perhaps a science as well as an art. Antoine Quatremère de Quincy published Volume I of his three-volume *Encyclopédie Méthodique d'Architecture* in 1788 (the last volume was finally completed in 1825), and in it he unambiguously delineates, in dictionary format, all the theoretical considerations of his day. It was intended to be a useful instrument for students and professionals, and reflected ". . . the universality of knowledge comprised by the subject.''[2] In his essay on *Type,* from Volume III, he notes that ". . . each of the principal buildings should find, in its fundamental purpose in the uses to which it is given over, a type which is suitable for it; that the architect should try to conform to this as closely as possible . . .''[3]

Another influential text, *Traité théorique et practique de l'art de batir,* was written by Jean-Baptiste Rondelet in 1802. As the title indicates, the book is concerned with construction techniques, but it seems clear that he intended it to serve as a text for the study and practice of architecture. He writes:

Theory is a science which directs all operations of practice. It is by the means of theory that a clever constructor arrives at the determination of the forms and just dimensions that he must give each part of an edifice, in light of its situation, and the efforts that it might support in order for it to result in perfection, solidity, and economy.[4]

For Rondelet, architecture was a science, not an art; and one that depended on technical skills directed by need and economics.

What were probably the most significant works were compiled by Jean-Nicolas-Louis Durand; the first was entitled *Recueil et parallèle des édifices en tout genre anciens et modernes* (1801). In this work Durand organized a comparative taxonomy of types through the use of illustrations. He was aided in the writing of the text by the architect and historian J.G. Legrand, who thought that the architect should look to works of nature and the mechanisms of the human body for true principles of architecture. These illustrations represented all the known *building types, ".* . . classified according to their kinds, arranged in order of degree of likeness and drawn to the same scale."[5] It is, however, his *Précis des leçons d'architecture données à l'École royale polytéchnique,* published in 1805, that best presents his unique accomplishments. He proposed that the design conditions of architecture were convenience, social need, and economy, stating, "Whether one consults reason, or examines the monuments (of history) themselves, it is evident that to please has never been the object. Utility for the public and for society, such is the goal of architecture."[6]

But Durand was a professor and recognized that there must be some provision for the development of new types, for which the need must already have become obvious. His system was to identify the *basic elements* of architecture—the building blocks—such as walls, columns, doorways, windows, etc. These were to be combined into intermediate forms, such as stairs, rooms, porches, and the like; the whole business would come together in ever larger units to complete the building, the street, the city. In this he employed an unusual method, which was to divide a square into a regular grid drawn to the dimensions of the smallest unit. That is, he started with a plan, which was laid out on "graph paper," and then placed the elements of architecture on the main and subsidiary axes required to link the rooms. At that point he had only to project this grid-plan vertically to establish the three-dimensional reality (Fig 7.1). Thus the manipulation of

7.1

Plates from *Précis des leçons d'architecture;* J.N.L. Durand (1819)
Durand used the underlying grid because it was a quick method to facilitate comparisons and development of building plans and elements in a classroom situation. By working with regular units, functional requirements could be satisfied by the selection of the appropriate elements in related sizes. (Source: *Précis des leçons d'architecture,* J.N.L. Durand.)

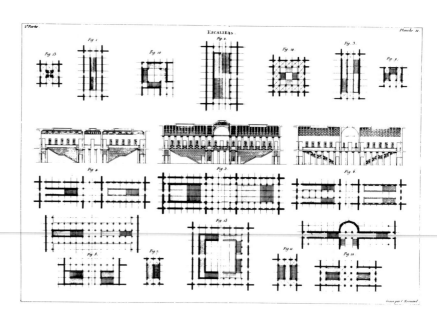

geometry became the *means,* or method, of architecture. The *ends* of architecture rested on the satisfaction of functional needs coupled with economy, a surprisingly modern approach. Anthony Vidler observes that Durand thus substituted for the Vitruvian trinity of commodity, firmness, and delight, the criterion of means and ends judged by their economic union; and he notes, "A former student of Durand recalled in 1810 that his master incessantly repeated the axiom that '. . . the source of beauty in Architecture is Economy joined to Convenience.' "[7]

In Durand's own words, ". . . the arrangement in all cases is the only thing with which the architect should be occupied, it is this arrangement that should be as proper and economic as it can be. . . ."[8] A consequence of this position was the belief that the exterior must reflect the interior function, and nothing more. The exterior façade should be absolutely plain, with a clearly demarcated support system; if decoration is necessary, it might be supplied by ivy or other vines. While absolutist in nature, his methods and ideas were useful to revivalist and rationalist architect alike, especially as they enjoyed the appearance of scientific method. Durand's influence as teacher and theoretician was considerable, and his planning methods pointed to future developments, both technically and through implication; as Vidler notes, "The grid also allowed for the abstraction and standardization critical for the development (and assimilation) of cast iron construction in architecture."[9] Thus out of Durand's system came the forms of the marketplaces, exhibition halls, and railway stations of the nineteenth century.

Cast-Iron Architecture

Durand taught at the École Polytéchnique in Paris from 1795 to 1834; it was one of the premier engineering schools in France, offering alternative (albeit coincidental) study in architecture to that of the École des Beaux-Arts. Indeed, French architecture benefitted greatly from the technical advances made by engineers. Much of Durand's influence was felt through his pedagogical texts; it is here, through his formal and systematic techniques—using a precise, circumscribed set of modular elements—that he suggests the industrial methodology inherent in cast-iron architecture. And his influence does not end there; his theories reappear in such works as Julien Guadet's *Éléments et Théories de l'Architecture,* published in 1902. Gaudet had been a student of Labrouste, and if his structural and functional teachings are evident in this work, so is Durand's method. "Any complete building is not, and cannot be, anything but the result of the assembly and putting together of a greater or lesser number of parts."[10] And as he further elaborates on his theory, it is clear that these parts are the ". . . Elements of Composition, and just as you will realize your conceptions with walls, openings, vaults, roofs—all elements of architecture—you will establish your composition with rooms, vestibules, exits and staircases."[11]

Cast-iron construction is inseparable from the growth of specialized schools of engineering, and most of the advances in cast-iron construction, well into the latter part of the nineteenth century, came from bridge-building methods. This was largely due to the development of precise *engineering tables* to calculate the compressive, tensile, and bending strength of materials; such information was slow, however, to be used by architects, even those regarded as rationalists. In his *Changing Ideals in Modern Architecture,* Peter Collins notes that knowledge of materials' strength was essential to the development of the nineteenth-century structural systems, especially when it involved buildings of immense height or tremendous span. But for most buildings constructed between 1750 and 1900, the rule-of-thumb methods evolved for masonry structures of moderate dimensions were usually still adequate.[12] And, in any case, the engineers as a group were no more interested in interior amenities like heating systems and sound insulation than were the architects. Nor were they interested in any alternative construction materials. The curious situation developed whereby the engineers who developed cast-iron technology were by and large uninterested in its architectural possibilities, while the architects of the Beaux-Arts thought cast-iron construction unsuitable for aesthetic reasons.

Despite its less than total acceptance by architects, and the myriad technical problems involved in its production, cast-iron was increasingly utilized. Through Durand's influence, building construction techniques assumed an important, if not predominant, part of the curriculum of the École Polytéchnique. This curriculum sharply contrasted with that of the École des Beaux-Arts, where virtually no training in construction was given; it, therefore, seems inevitable that building techniques in cast-iron should develop in the engineering schools, and be exploited by a group of architects who remained outside the Beaux-Arts establishment. It seems equally inevitable that form become tied to classical patterns of architecture that readily lend themselves to abstract structural rationalization. *Rationalism,* therefore, consisted in the belief that architecture was defined by structural form, usually arranged formally.

The rationalist position also called for structural forms that were related to the function of the building; the nineteenth century thus saw the development of new architectural types for a rapidly urbanizing population. Mass housing became a pressing need, but so did shopping complexes, marketplaces, railway stations, factories, and comprehensive civic structures. The architects responded with a broad range of essentially new solutions:

> Expansion, interpenetration, and the multiplication of space, both vertically and horizontally, were characteristic of the new forms. Broad, lofty interior spaces were conceived to serve as lobbies or concourses. . . . Light and air perforated the new structures as never before, entering through central skylights and through large façade and court windows, with little obstruction from columns or roof framing."[13]

One of the first major uses of cast-iron in a building was in the Théâtre Français in Paris, where Victor Louis used it to support the roof structure. The roof utilized a framework with a clear span of just over eighty-one feet, based on a truss design, and buttressed by braces attached to thin masonry. By the early nineteenth century, cast-iron was even more popular, enjoying a knowledgeable support from Napoleon. A remarkable competition was held in 1805, for a roof design for the Halle au Blé, a circular grain exchange in Paris. All of the early designs were rejected, and only in 1807 was a design approved by François Belanger; interestingly, the approval was contingent on the dome's iron skeleton's remaining visible—to keep down costs. Of equal interest were Belanger's small adjustments in overall dimensions that he believed would result in an enhanced aesthetic effect on the viewer standing below. His system was technically effective, and its inclusion in nineteenth-century Parisian tour guides attests to public approbation. Certain conclusions may be drawn from these early examples of cast-iron architecture: first, cast-iron was initially valued for its capability to enclose, rather than its ability to project upward; second, the financial imperative of open structural ironwork soon became an aesthetic attribute; and third, iron construction was seen by rationalist architects as useful for its social utility.

As functions in the new, urban bourgeois society became more diverse, forms of buildings responded to the radically *altered programs*. Increasingly, these programs centered on interior aspects of architecture, both because of specific physical needs and because of social need. That is; 1) the new architecture of the train station and marketplace, 2) the extensive open space (the result of fewer columns and reduced beam spans), and 3) pronounced verticality were necessitated as much by concern for the crowds that used them as for the simple mechanical functions. And there were certainly attempts to express the inside's new complexity on the outside.

Such satisfaction of structural and social function is apparent in Paris markethalls, particularly in the design of the Halles Centrales. Designed by Victor Baltard and Felix Callet in 1851, the Halles enjoyed the support of Louis-Napoleon and his remarkable city planner Baron von Haussmann, who reportedly instructed Baltard to use "Iron! Iron! Nothing but iron!"[14] The market proved remarkable from the viewpoint of efficiency and aesthetic appeal, and formed a paradigm for French market structures for the remainder of the century (Fig 7.2). From these markets developed the prototype for the modern department store—actually, the gathering under one ownership of the small specialized shops that previously had been independent. These new entrepreneurs were aware, not only of the methods of mass merchandising, but of the department store's essentially social role as venue for elegant and casual browsing. The models of such department stores may be the Magasin du Printemps and the Bon Marché, designed in 1881 and 1878 respectively; they were conceived as a series of open and spacious light courts which were richly decorated, ". . . Cathedral(s) of modern commerce, solid and light, made for a congregation of clients."[15] This, Émile Zola's allusion to the Bon Marché, reflected contemporary opinion and the place of such institutions in bourgeois society (Fig 7.3). And it is this society, now literate, that accounts for such institutions as Labrouste's Bibliothèque Saint-Geneviève (Fig 8.5), whose program called for gas-lights in the spacious reading room. This was an acknowledgment of the numbers of people who would be using the library, and the time constraints of the working-class day.

Cast-iron was used in England as well, although not with the theoretical base and fervor that it enjoyed in France. On the surface, this is odd, since it was in England that the production of cast-iron was most technically advanced. Indeed, despite incredibly steep tariffs, much French construction proceeded with English iron. There are a number of reasons for this; chief among them was the widespread belief that cast-iron was inherently unsuitable, aesthetically and morally, for buildings. John Ruskin, in *The Seven Lamps of Architecture*, states his opposition to any architectural product that is cast or machine-made. He says, "There are two reasons, both weighty, against this practice; one, that all cast and machine work is bad, as work; the other, that it is dishonest."[16] It should be noted that his disapprobation did not preclude cast-iron's use in English warehouses and cotton mills or, for that matter, in bridge construction. But cast-iron tended to be shunned for civic and cultural works, contrary to the way it was em-

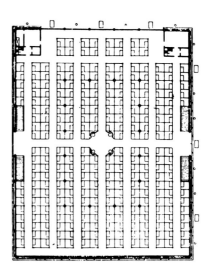

7.2

Les Halles Centrales—Paris; *Victor Baltard (1853–5)*
Baltard's design based on a 19½′ module provided consistency of space throughout this immense building for the numerous merchants who gathered regularly to display their fresh produce. The regular arrangement of columns allowed for clear circulation patterns, and did not use up valuable square-footage necessary for the vendor's booths. (Source: *Éléments et Théorie de l'Architecture,* J. Guadet.)

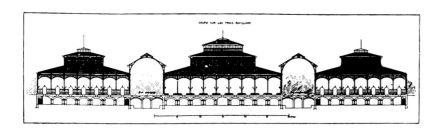

braced in France. And when it was used, it was without enthusiasm and was often disguised.

There were, however, certain architects who used cast-iron's potential, especially the iron column. An early and exotic use of cast-iron columns occurred in the design for the Royal Pavilion, Brighton, in 1818. The Royal Architect, John Nash, made undisguised use of such columns throughout the building, from drawing-room to kitchen. The fantastic columns in the kitchen suggest part of the reason for iron's popularity: it could be cast into any desired shape. The latter part of the nineteenth century was to witness an inundation of hardware—from decoration to sculpture—stolen freely from history and mass merchandized in such a way that Ruskin might have good reason to complain (Fig 7.4).

The most famous English architect of the mid-century was probably Sir Joseph Paxton (1803–1865). Renowned at home and abroad as a landscape and horticultural designer, he was famous for the magnificent conservatory at Chatsworth. As a gardener, he was entirely aware of the potential of framing systems and used such techniques in his best-known work, the Great Exhibition Building of 1851, soon dubbed the Crystal Palace. The structure was immense; its 1,851-foot length contained almost 800,000 square feet of space and employed a system of wooden mullions carried on a cast-iron structure (Fig 7.5). Paxton himself was not convinced that cast-iron should generally be used for such purposes, as wood by itself combined ". . . utility, stability, convenience, and though last but not least, economy."[17] Many thought the structure wanting in other areas, as is clear in a review in the *Ecclesiologist,* ". . . the conviction has grown upon us, that it is not architecture: it is engineering—of the highest merit and excellence—but not architecture. Form is wholly wanting: and the idea of stability or solidity is wanting."[18] In all fairness, the structure was not intended as permanent, and in terms of cost, ease of assembly, and spatial characteristics, it worked very well. The writer of an article in the *Illustrated London News,* 1850, comments:

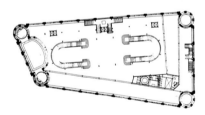

7.3

Magasin du Printemps—Paris; *Paul Sédille (1881–9)*
The Printemps is accented by a central court covered by a glass skylight, based on a structural system that allowed the space to be experienced as an articulated whole. The intriguing variation in shape of the stairs, the openness of the space permitting views of the displayed products, the natural light, and ornamental iron bridges providing easy passage, draw customers through the store. (Source: *Éléments et Théorie de l'Architecture,* J. Guadet.)

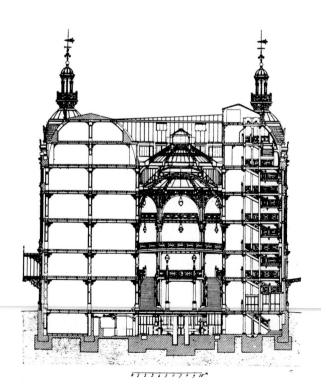

Kitchen, Royal Pavilion—Brighton; *John Nash (1818-21)*
Nash has given full expression to the oriental fantasy in the kitchen; the copper palm leaves on the iron columns are jointed like bamboo, and arranged to form a grove of palm trees. The thin columns allow the bustling kitchen activities to occur with the minimum of interruption. (Courtesy: Royal Pavilion, Art Gallery and Museums, Brighton.)

One great feature in its erection is, that not a vestige of stone, brick or mortar is necessary. All the roofing and upright sashes would be made by machinery, and fitted together and glazed with great rapidity. . . . The whole of the structure is supported on cast iron columns, and the extensive roof is sustained without the necessity of interior walls. . . ."[19]

And in this small excerpt of an admiring article that concluded that such a plan ". . . would be unrivalled in the world"[20], may be seen the key attributes of cast-iron architecture.

Architects in the United States had, almost from the start, fully appreciated these qualities, to which they added ease of prefabrication. Sigfried Giedion suggests that the development of skeleton construction begins with the substitution of iron columns for the masonry of the outer walls, as the floor-supports of a structure.[21] James Bogardus (1800–1874) invented this process, and his cast iron façades typify the stores, warehouses, and office buildings built between 1850 and 1880. A single façade was often attached to the front of a brick shell, but there are abundant examples of iron's having

Crystal Palace—London; *Joseph Paxton (1851)*
A critical alteration to Paxton's initial design was the shift from a 20' to a 24' modular grid system. This resulted from a study of previous exhibition spaces, which indicated that this kind of space best satisfied the needs of exhibitors. The lack of interior walls was seen as a benefit in terms of flexibility and sight lines. (Source: *The Crystal Palace Exhibition: Illustrated Catalogue.*)

7.6

"Moorish style iron building;" *Richard Morris Hunt (1876)*
Hunt's "Moorish" building represents a typical use of the Bogardus facade, which could be obtained in a variety of "styles" and simply bolted to an easily constructed brick box. (Source: *American Architect and Building News,* July 1876.)

been used on more than one façade. There are even a few buildings that stood on their own, like his own factory in New York. The buildings were usually four to six stories tall, but this was a decision based on the practical limit of elevatorless structures (Fig 7.6). The popularity of these façades lay in the conventional building technique of the basic structure and the easy assembly of the prefabricated parts. Also of interest to the public was the great variety of ironwork found in the average builder's catalog; while this was usually exterior in nature, it was sometimes used to cover interior atria.

When Giedion refers to skeletal construction, he is undoubtedly thinking of the occasional iron support structure in some of the larger buildings, and in such free-standing structures as Bogardus' factory. True skeletal construction was first seen in the Menier Chocolate Works at Noisiel-sur-Marne, designed in 1871 by Jules Saulnier, although this work had little effect on American architecture. In any case, the frame of Saulnier's structure served primarily to support masonry. The true exploitation of *skeletal construction* was to take place in the American skyscraper, particularly in Chicago where the architects of the Chicago School used a new type of construction—the iron skeleton. Giedion notes that the importance of the Chicago School for the history of architecture lies in this fact, that ". . . for the first time in the 19th century the schism . . . between the engineer and the architect, was healed."[22] And while his enthusiastic analysis may be overstated, it was with the free adaptation of engineering skills that architects proceeded to rebuild Chicago.

Chicago School

> When I define Beauty as the promise of Function; Action as the presence of Function; Character as the record of Function, I arbitrarily divide that which is essentially one . . . the mechanics of United States have already outstripped the artists, and have, by the results of their bold and unflinching adaptation, entered the true track. . . .[23]

Sculptor Horatio Greenough proclaimed these sentiments in an article entitled "Form and Function"; they were to become the guidelines for three decades of Chicago architecture. Indeed, this approach was to characterize American (original) design, from handtools and machinery to furniture and building types; with few exceptions, these products had no excess ornamentation and were marked by ingenuity. Julius Lessing, first director of the Museum of Industrial Arts in Berlin, stated in a report from Chicago's Columbian Exposition of 1893:

> Here we saw utensils and tools created in the same spirit as railroads, ships, and wagons. Here we saw objects of daily use developed clearly and without any preconception—objects appealing not so much to the calculating intellect as directly to the senses. They convey to the eye the satisfying sensation which only true beauty can give.[24]

And in an essay written in 1913, Walter Gropius comments on the architecture of North America, saying that the buildings

> . . . present an architectural composition of such exactness that to the observer their meaning is forcefully and unequivocally clear. The natural integrity of these buildings resides . . . in their designer's independent and clear visions of these grand, impressive forms.[25]

Many technical innovations that were of seminal importance originated in Chicago, such as George Snow's "Balloon Frame," without which, according to an observer in an 1855 issue of the *New York Tribune,* ". . . Chicago and San Francisco could never have arisen, as they did, from little villages to great cities in a single year."[26] Of course, the balloon frame was aided, in turn, by such inventions as cut nails. But for the typical Chicago and New York skyscrapers to rise, much engineering technology had to be used as well as considerable social innovation. In Chicago, the birthplace of the modern skyscraper, credit for this goes to William Le Baron Jenney (1832–1907). He had trained at the École Polytéchnique and the École Centrale in Paris, and put that technical education to use during the Civil War, building bridges for the Union Army. He thus brought Chicago not only generally excellent credentials in engineering, but real experience in that area most technically advanced—bridgebuilding. The 1871 Chicago Fire had seemingly devastated the city, yet two days after it stopped a *Tribune* editorial titled "Cheer Up" concluded, ". . . the people of this once beautiful city have resolved that CHICAGO SHALL RISE AGAIN."[27] In the post-fire building boom that followed, hard-nosed businessmen were inclined to build structures that were efficient, cost-effective, and fireproof. And these were increasingly tall works using *skeletal construction.*

In an 1880 letter to his agent in Chicago, the Boston developer Peter Brooks writes, "Tall buildings will pay well in Chicago hereafter, and sooner or later a way will be made to erect them."[28] Within a year, Brooks had commissioned Burnham & Root to design the Montauk Block, with its revolutionary "floating raft" foundation. But, by reasonably common agreement, the first true skyscraper was designed by Jenney in 1883, the Home Insurance Building, in which the exterior walls had been reduced to only a skin. Carl Condit comments that this building was ". . . the major step in the conversion of a building from a crustacean with its armor of stone to a vertebrate clothed only in a light skin."[29] The external revelation of the underlying skeleton is often cited as an example of structural honesty, a new aesthetic. But it is likely that Jenney, an engineer, simply intended the structure to be efficient and economical. The architects of the period took a deeper view of commercial buildings; John Wellborn Root commented that ". . . to lavish upon them profusion of delicate ornament is worse than useless. . . . Rather should they by their mass and proportion convey in some large elemental sense an idea of the great, stable, conserving forces of modern civilization."[30] Here Root is addressing a vital notion in Chicago architecture; the correlation of morality and commercial enterprise.

In 1893 the French novelist Paul Bourget wrote that Chicago architecture had impressed him with

> . . . the simple force of need as a principle of beauty. . . . There is so little caprice and fancy in these monuments and these streets that they seem to be the work of some impersonal power, irresistible, unconscious, like a force of nature, in the service of which man has been but a docile instrument. It is this expression of the overpowering immensity of modern commerce which gives to the city something of tragedy, and, to my feeling, a poetry."[31]

In Bourget's citing of the "overpowering immensity of modern commerce," he pinpoints the peculiar features of a new building type, the *office skyscraper.* This fundamentally American structure ultimately reflects a widespread belief in commerce as a great civilizing element. Indeed, an author in the magazine *Industrial Chicago* analyzes Jenney's Second Leiter Building and enthusiastically states that with its construction, ". . . a commercial pile in a style undreamed of when Bounarroti erected the greatest temple of Christianity"[32] had been built. Thus had the 1891 Sears building been

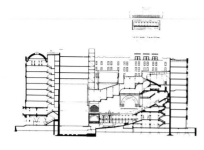

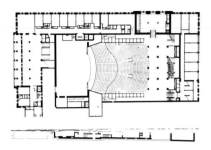

7.7

Auditorium Building—Chicago; *Adler and Sullivan (1886)*
Chicago had numerous cultural institutions in the nineteenth century as well as a fine opera company. When Ferdinand Peck commissioned Adler and Sullivan to design the Auditorium Building, he enjoyed the support of the city, especially for the building's multipurpose aspect. The structure represents, for Adler, a tour-de-force of engineering, from the waterproof foundations and excellent mechanical systems, to the extraordinary precautions to ensure even settling. (Section—courtesy: Roosevelt University, Chicago; Plan—source: *Chicago's Famous Buildings,* Arthur Siegel, editor.)

7.8

Auditorium Theatre—Chicago; *Adler and Sullivan (1886)*
Sullivan used the great elliptical spans, 118′ across, to stunning effect, lighting them with arrays of filament bulbs and organic ornament. The murals at either side of the theatre depicted opposing seasonal views as though through a window, in a manner somewhat reminiscent of LaBrouste's Bibliothèque Nationale. The theater boasted one of the most sophisticated stages in the world, as well as the comforts of heating and air-cooling. (Courtesy: Roosevelt University, Chicago.)

favorably compared with St. Peters. Such a program also explains the extraordinary degree of involvement of developers like Brooks; in an 1881 letter to his agent Owen Aldis, he stipulated the key provisions of the new Montauk Block, concentrating primarily on such interior items as heating systems, plumbing, washroom cabinetry, and electrical conduit. Over the following year, he maintained a correspondence remarkable for its detail and design understanding, including a comment that "the architects are of course indifferent to the future cost of repairs and care, an item worthy of much consideration."[33]

Increasingly, Chicago's commercial architecture became involved with office construction and the development of types based on human function. It was largely the belief that commerce underpinned culture that was responsible for the erection of the Auditorium Theatre. The commission was given to Dankmar Adler and Louis Sullivan in 1886, for the design of a structure that was to house a multipurpose theatre, hotel, shopping arcade, and office tower (Fig 7.7). It was thus hoped that the commercial aspects of the building would pay for a significant portion of its cultural function, so that it would be ". . . self-sustaining and not, like the Metropolitan Opera house, a perpetual financial burden. . . ."[34] The 4,200-seat theatre remains the heart of the building; it is unusual in that its plan was primarily determined by acoustics. To that end, Adler used the Scott Russell isacoustic curve and movable ceiling planes, resulting in superb sound. Nor did the architects neglect such amenities as heating and cooling apparatus, flexible spatial configurations, and easy access for the audience (Fig 7.8).

The notion of function increasingly involved a consideration of human beings; that is, not only what was going on in a space, but how people were doing it. Thus the design of the eighteen-story Fisher Building (1895), by Daniel Burnham, owes much to economic and social factors. The plan indicates two large, highly flexible spaces with access provisions that could be subdivided on demand at both ends of the building. This layout provides for a mix of tenants, with a reduced total reliance on large firms. Burnham noted the desirability of this arrangement, since small tenants, in the aggregate, pay more for their square-footage, make less of an impact when they move, and tend not to overtax the elevators at quitting time. The building is interesting for other reasons as well; the frame is made of steel (utilizing portal framing taken from bridge construction), and the facade is

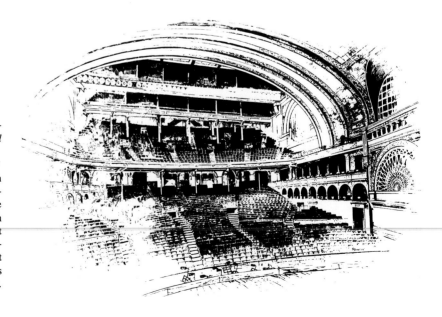

composed of open, airy window bays. But, ultimately, the concern for *occupant-functions* may constitute its real significance (Fig 7.9).

Jenney's importance to the Chicago school was immense. Not only did he bring new techniques derived from engineering, but his office served as atelier for many of the city's young architects, including Burnham and Sullivan. And in the latter part of the century, it was this group of architects who became involved in the larger questions of function, aesthetics, and morality. In *The Chicago School of Architecture,* Carl Condit noted Sullivan's belief that an organic architecture is one that derives naturally from the social and technical factors that form the architect's milieu, and "these factors embrace not only the technical and utilitarian problems of building, but also the aspirations, values, ideals, and spiritual needs of human beings."[35] For Sullivan, this translated into statements of lofty aspiration and the failure ". . . to perceive this simple truth . . . a defamation and denial of man's finest powers."[36]

Arts and Crafts

If morality was the thread that held the Chicago school together, it was the whole cloth for the English Arts and Crafts movement. For such figures as John Ruskin, morality took the form of a complete distrust of the Industrial Revolution and a rejection of its products, especially cast-iron. England had been a leader in the development of modern industry, and while the nation became materially enriched, a terrible price was exacted from the working classes. Gillian Naylor observes that many ". . . saw the destruction of fundamental human values reflected in poverty, overcrowded slums, grim factories, a dying countryside and the apotheosis of the cheap and shoddy."[37] To the degree that the Arts and Crafts movement sought to alleviate this condition, its motivations were essentially moral and social, and its aesthetic was derived from these sources. The socioreligious aesthetic system that underpinned the movement is examined in the next chapter; of interest here is the Arts and Crafts program and contribution to design.

Fundamental to this moral position was the conviction that industrialization was a threat to both the physical and spiritual well-being of people and, as a corollary, the belief that there had been a better time. That better time, for architects and writers like Agustus Pugin, was the Gothic. Pugin, in association with Sir Charles Barry, had designed the Houses of Parliament in 1836; interestingly, his role in this "Gothic" design was almost entirely in its decoration. He postulated two principles of design, *propriety* and *structural fitness,* as basic to design of all kinds. Advocacy of the Gothic was not unique—Viollet-le-Duc was a staunch supporter of the Gothic in France—but Pugin's support was based almost entirely on moralistic grounds. That morality underlies his belief that all ornament should be ". . . appropriate and significant . . . the artist having sought for the most convenient form should then decorate it without concealing the real purpose for which the article has been made."[38] As his admiration for the Gothic was based on faith, he rejected all other stylistic approaches—but especially the Neoclassical, which he felt was derived from "pagan" sources.

Pugin was to have a great influence on John Ruskin, who shared his views on both the Gothic and Neoclassical; although his distaste for the latter was primarily based on his belief that it was essentially mechanical and thus devoid of spiritual content. Ruskin was convinced that Christian (as in the Gothic) architecture was superior to that from the classical world largely because the unique value of the human soul was a tenet of a Christian belief

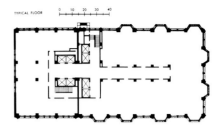

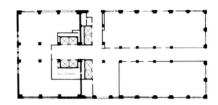

7.9

Fisher Building—Chicago; *D.H. Burnham and Company (1896)*
Despite the death of his partner, Root, Burnham went on to produce well-designed and commercially successful structures like the Fisher Building. Much of Burnham's success lay in understanding the needs of commercial tenants, from spatial requirements to handsome facades and lobby spaces. (Source: *Chicago's Famous Buildings,* Arthur Siegel, editor.)

7.10

Red House—Kent, England; *Philip Webb (1859)*
This vernacular revival house was simply constructed by Webb, whose desire to have his buildings look "commonplace" is achieved by the variation in framing of the openings, such as the Gothic pointed arch of unplastered brick over one door, and the simply joined flatboard framing around the other. The simple furnishings are dominated visually by the wallpaper, with its orderly vine pattern that changes into a more abstract variation at the ceiling. (Exterior—copyright 1991. The Art Institute of Chicago. All rights reserved; Interior—courtesy: Royal Commission on the Historical Monuments of England, London.)

that ". . . not only recognises its value; it confesses its imperfection."[39] And by way of validation, architecture and other human artifacts should display their *handmade* character, even if rough in appearance. The perfection of the machined finish was, in this sense, a rejection of humanity and a questioning of faith. When men are treated like machines, Ruskin says, the labor they perform ". . . is verily a degrading one, and makes them less than men."[40] In his *Seven Lamps of Architecture,* written in 1849, Ruskin states, "Architecture is the art which so disposes and adorns the edifices raised by man, for whatsoever uses, that the sight of them may contribute to his mental health, power, and pleasure."[41] And he insisted that beauty (in all things) was as critical to survival as food and shelter. Ruskin ultimately believed in the redemptive power of art, that by improving the physical and spiritual environment of humankind, one improved humankind.

William Morris (1834–1896) was an Oxford divinity student when he encountered the writings of Ruskin; the result was a radical redirection to architecture and painting. In 1859 he commissioned Philip Webb to design his home, Red House; Webb's approach might be considered a Medieval vernacular. Its simple use of native materials on the exterior, coupled with an elaborate decoration on the interior, seemed to conform with Ruskin's notions (Fig 7.10). And the house certainly met Morris' dictum, ". . . have nothing in your houses which you do not know to be useful or believe to be beautiful."[42] Through the construction of his house, Morris met many artists and craftsmen, and in 1862 he founded the firm of Morris, Marshall, Faulkner and Company. The workshops of this company were intended to serve as alternatives to the factory system; his trained craftsmen created furniture, textiles, carpets, wallpaper, and stained glass. As a group, they supported individuality and truth, a truth derived from nature in the spirit of the Medieval. Morris contributed much theory in the form of essays and lectures, written primarily in the 1870s; one of his more interesting conclusions concerned the intimate link between designer and material, one forged through experience. He states that ". . . it is the pleasure of understanding the capabilities of the special material, and using them for suggesting (not imitating) natural beauty and incident, that gives the raison d'etre for decorative art."[43] Another conclusion, which reached fruition in the following century, was that ". . . a work of utility might also be a work of art, if we cared to make it so."[44]

Morris' firm is well known for furniture designs, which he divided into two categories: the "workaday furniture," which should remain simple and straightforward, and "state-furniture," which would necessarily be far more elaborate and ornate (Fig 7.11). In this duality, Morris was to continue a theme that has dominated design for millennia, but which here seems to suggest a moral contradiction between principle and practice. In his designs for wallpaper and carpets, he insisted on a *truth to nature* that showed itself in logical structure and attention to nature, with a natural unity between form and function. In one of his lectures of 1880, he stated with fervor that those who wait in darkness ". . . will be enlightened by an Art made by the people and for the people, a joy to the maker and the user."[45] But in the end, his works could not be produced in large enough quantity to compete with manufactured goods; while the middle-class bought his products, the poor could not. Morris was compelled to reevaluate the role of the machine, concluding that ". . . it is the allowing of machines to be our masters, and not our servants, that so injures the beauty of life nowadays."[46] The notion of machines in service of design was to resurface over the several decades following Morris, culminating in the ideas of the Bauhaus.

As a practical matter, the Arts and Crafts movement ended in England by 1900 but continued in the United States until World War I. The movement's success in the United States is not surprising; various reform movements had, throughout the mid-nineteenth century, railed against the excesses of the Industrial Revolution, particularly those aspects related to labor. Various individuals helped lay the groundwork for the Arts and Crafts movement, but its dissemination was ensured as much by its insistent work ethic as the issues of social reform. In any case, the design approach, that of functional simplicity, found a ready ear in a population whose native objects of daily use (according to Lessing) had always "been developed clearly and without any preconception."

Various publications helped create a new awareness of the domestic interior. The publication of Charles L. Eastlake's *Hints on Household Taste* in 1868 was especially influential on the course of Anglo-American taste. In this work he addresses virtually every aspect of the domestic house, from

A   B

7.11

(A) **Wardrobe Cabinet;** *Burne-Jones (1858);* *(B)* **Morris Chair;** *Morris, Marshall, Faulkner and Company (ca. 1870)*
The massive cabinet *(A)*, presented to Morris as a wedding present, is not Medieval in ornamental details or motifs but, rather, in its simple construction. The turned columns, set on a sled base, frame a scene from Chaucer's "Prioress's Tale," painted by Sir Edward Burne-Jones. Large flat surfaces were a requirement of this type of furniture since it is the painted surface that makes this piece unique. This "work-a-day" chair *(B)* also is "honestly" constructed; yet its thin turned members are delicate in their arrangement. (*[A]* courtesy: Ashmolean Museum, Oxford; *[B]* drawn by: J. Malnar.)

7.12

Library Bookcase; *Charles L. Eastlake (1868)*
This "rural" piece shown in Charles L. Eastlake's *Hints on Household Taste* also uses simple construction techniques, but in a manner unlike Morris'. Here the side members, rather than being concealed with an elaborate proportional system, honestly express the thinness of the wood boards. The piece is very rectangular and relies on the shaping of the edges of the flatboards and the elongate hinges for ornamental interest. (Source: *Hints on Household Taste,* Charles L. Eastlake.)

7.13

Library Table; *Gustav Stickley (ca. 1908)*
This design was one of many that Stickley provided under the heading "Cabinet Work for Home Workers and Students Who Wish to Learn the Fundamental Principles of Construction." As was all his furniture, this table both looks and is sturdy, and represents the straightforward approach of the American Craftsman style. Stickley's criteria for these furniture designs were that they were fairly easy to construct, and that they should have a use as furnishings. (Source: *Craftsman Homes,* Gustav Stickley.)

entrance vestibules and room character to furniture design and table settings; in all he presents a readable and sensible approach to interior decoration. He was an architect and a designer and illustrated his work with drawings that he hoped would point to the future (Fig 7.12). As a Gothicist, he was much impressed by Pugin and Ruskin but thought their insistence on the religious aspects counterproductive. His own beliefs are in this analysis of decoration, ". . . although it would be undesirable, and indeed impossible, to reject in manufacture the appliances of modern science, we should be cautious of attaching too much importance in decorative art to those qualities of mere elaboration and finish which are independent of thought and manual labour."[47]

In this sentence, Eastlake cautions us against a too-eager embrace of machined products; this book, and the many lectures and exhibitions throughout the last decades of the nineteenth century, formed the basis for the American Arts and Crafts movement, known locally as the *Craftsman movement* after the magazine of that name. The designer Gustav Stickley published *The Craftsman* from 1901 to 1916; through it he disseminated his interpretation of the ideals of the English movement. That is, while he approved of that movement for certain of its works, he also criticized it for its individualism:

> It was a move in the right direction because it meant a return to healthy individual effort. . . . But the Arts and Crafts workers have not succeeded in establishing another permanent style in English furniture for the reason that they have striven for a definite and intentional expression of art that was largely for art's sake and had little to do with satisfying the plain needs of the people.[48]

Thus Stickley's perceptive comments go right to the heart of Morris' dilemma, the difficulty in reconciling an essentially artistic (and elitest) approach with egalitarian goals.

We may also see in Stickley's comments a reflection of American populism; indeed, he points out that a unique type of people was evolving in this country, people with a profound appreciation for the useful. And so he states that to an American, the real thing is something he needs and understands:

> So strong is this national characteristic that it is hardly overstating the case to say that in America any style in architecture or furniture would have to possess the essential qualities of simplicity, durability, comfort and convenience and to be made in such a way that the details of its construction can be readily grasped, before it could hope to become permanent.[49]

Stickley's magazine not only provided a place for discussion of current views on the applied arts in America, but did much to promote the Chicago School as well.[50] And the building designs found in *The Craftsman* touched such a responsive chord in the public that they are to be found almost everywhere (Fig 10.3). Stickley's own furniture designs, made of native oak boards and constructed with simple joinery, were often promoted in this publication. This "honest craftsmanship" and interest in natural materials related to the American tradition, and the simplicity contributed to their popularity with the general public (Fig 7.13). Stickley's furniture enjoyed the active support of Frank Lloyd Wright, who had commissioned Stickley to execute some of his designs and who often urged his clients to buy it for their homes. Wright himself may have been less than committed to this movement and its insistence on handcraftsmanship, as evidenced by his 1901 lecture "The Art and Craft of the Machine," to which we return in chapter nine.

Art Nouveau

The Art Nouveau movement can be traced to a number of developments, primarily in the graphic and decorative arts, that began in the mid-1880s. Arthur Mackmurdo, an English architect and graphic designer, wrote a book in 1883 entitled *Wrens City Churches* in which he designed a title page in a highly energetic, linear, and sinuous style—in short, the hallmarks of the soon-to-emerge Art Nouveau. Mackmurdo was a textile designer, and his patterns were to significantly influence young designers like Heywood Sumner and Aubrey Beardsley; but parallel events in France were equally important. There, the glassblower Emile Gallé produced highly unusual glassware based on botanical motifs and employing rich color; by the early 1890s, the graphic designer and bookbinder Rene Wiener was also producing lush, sensual designs based on nature. Both men were from Nancy, and indeed, Nancy and Paris, along with such other cities as Brussels, Vienna, and Glasgow, were to become centers of Art Nouveau activity until the turn of the century (Fig 7.14).

The actual term Art Nouveau comes from the name of Samuel Bing's shop in Paris (1895), the Galerie de L'Art Nouveau, which featured the work of young avant-garde artisans. Here Bing sought to promote all aspects of the interior space, from fixtures and textiles to furniture and glass. His program was direct: "We must reimmerse ourselves in the ancient French traditions and endeavour to pick up the threads of that tradition, its grace, elegance, purity and sound logic and enrich our heritage with a lively spirit of modernity."[51]

Bing scarcely conceived that Art Nouveau would become as widespread as it did, nor as inclusive. In a letter to *Architectural Record* in 1902, he notes that in most branches of art, no such revival was necessary, "it was only in relation to art as applied to decoration, to furniture, to ornamentation in all its forms, that the need for a new departure was felt."[52] In the pursuit of that departure, he elaborated two fundamental rules, "each article to be strictly adapted to its proper purpose; harmonies to be sought for in lines and colour."[53] Interestingly, Bing had actual experience in the Far East (later opening a shop for Oriental art in Paris) and had visited the United States in 1893, where he was impressed by the decorative work of Louis Sullivan and Louis Comfort Tiffany. In his shop were the influences that shaped the Art Nouveau, which were (in no particular order): the program and motifs of the Arts and Crafts movement; the spirit of Gothicism, or alternatively, anticlassicism; exoticism, exemplified in the avid interest in Chinoisserie and the primitive; and the inherent characteristics of the newly pervasive medium of cast-iron.

Much of the above points to the essentially *decorative* nature of Art Nouveau, which has led to the observation that it never produced a true architecture, only highly decorated structures. It seems clear, however, that in the design of his house at No. 6 rue Paul-Emile Janson in Brussels, Victor Horta (1861–1947) had already, in 1892, brought the ideas of the Art Nouveau to bear on architecture. Excepting the large and ornate central bay (perhaps an early suggestion of the façade of the 1896 Maison du Peuple), the house is fairly simple in its exterior appearance. Indeed, while the exterior was to become more elaborate in Horta's later work, Art Nouveau's real impact on architecture was probably on the interior. This becomes quite apparent in the insistent three-dimensionality of the staircase, and in its clear articulation of space (Fig 7.15). The interior spatial aspect becomes even more obvious in the plan of Hector Guimard's Castel Béranger, begun in 1895 in Paris. Guimard (1867–1942), usually remembered for his Paris

7.14

Blown-Glass Vase w/Brass Stand—Austria *(ca. 1895)*
The whiplash vine so beloved of Art Nouveau finds expression here in the brass stand, which is precisely fitted to the iridescent vase made of Loetz glass. (Collection: Malnar & Vodvarka. Photo by: Frank Vodvarka.)

7.15

No. 6 rue Paul-Emile Janson—Brussels; *Victor Horta (1893)*
The inherent movement associated with the act of ascending a stair, and the upward curve of arches, lent themselves naturally to the energetic motifs of the Art Nouveau style; and when the sinuous lines are applied to the floor they hint at circulation patterns. The motifs are consistently applied to floor, walls, and ironwork, resulting in a consistency of spatial character. (Courtesy: Archives d'Architecture Moderne, Brussels.)

Metro canopies, was offered a commission by Mme. Veuve Fournier to design a thirty-six-unit apartment block. It was to be six to seven stories high, on what was considered a rather small site. This accounts for the long, narrow courtyard, never more than twenty-six feet wide, and often as little as six feet; due to the play of the court façades, the courtyard nonetheless has a grand feeling (Fig 7.16). The building must be considered an unqualified success financially, as Mme. Fournier received a return on her investment double that of the norm. Guimard installed his office in the building; the biographer Claude Frontisi notes that it was by such signs that Guimard intended to imprint his originality and place as inventor of a "contemporary French style."[54]

In the *Architectural Record* of 1902, Guimard states that from his studies he derived three principles of architectural production:

> Logic, which consists in taking into account all the conditions of the case; Harmony, which means putting the constructions into full accord not only with the requirements to be met and the funds available, but also with the surroundings; and Sentiment, which, partaking at the same time of logic and harmony, is the complement of both, and leads by emotion. . . .[55]

And in the decoration generally, and metalwork specifically, is the influence of Viollet-le-Duc's *Entretiens sur l'architecture,* particularly the second volume, published in 1872. Nikolaus Pevsner points out that it is in this volume that ". . . iron trails and leaves appear side by side with iron vaulting-ribs, the one for reasons of the tensile strength of iron, the other for reasons of its ductile nature."[56] Increasingly, French engineers and architects had come to see cast-iron as a medium of decoration as well as structure (Fig 7.17). Since iron could be cast in virtually any configuration, the designer was assured of a rich choice of forms. The task, as Viollet-le-Duc points out, is to ". . . try to find forms suitable to its properties and manufacture; we ought not to disguise it, but seek for those forms until we have found them."[57]

Pevsner notes that it is in Guimard's delight in materials, and the decorative effects that could be obtained in their exploitation, that some insight can be obtained into the works of Antonio Gaudí.[58] Indeed, a real commit-

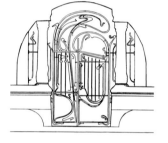

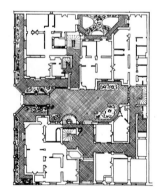

7.16

Castel Béranger—Paris; *Hector Guimard (1894–8)*
The plan abandons traditional axial symmetry, sharply differentiating between the apartments in the front and the less practical plans of those in the rear. In certain cases the interior rooms are open to light and air through small, internal lightshafts. Guimard's principles of architectural production depend on an asymmetrical balance of line, shape, color, and texture. The isolated use of symmetry, combined with unqiue elements, reinforces the individuality of each apartment unit. (Drawn by: J. Malnar.)

ment to the stylistic tendencies of French Art Nouveau can be seen in his post-1905 buildings, such as the Casa Milá and Casa Battló (Fig 3.7) The plans of both structures represent a Castel Béranger unleashed, whose decorative iron "whiplashes" have been transformed into features of the façade. But there were many influences on Gaudí; these included a saturation in the local architecture of the Baroque, itself fantastic, ideas taken from Viollet-le-Duc's tendencies to Gothicism, and an extraordinary (and eccentric) individualism. This last quality was a hallmark of Art Nouveau, one that marks also the character of Charles Rennie Mackintosh.

Art Nouveau is usually divided into two approaches: that which exploited the emotional quality of undulating, curvilinear form; and that dependent on what Pevsner refers to as "chaste straight lines."[59] The movement in general was slow in coming to England, which had been dominated by the Arts and Crafts movement and, throughout the 1890s, the architecture of Charles Voysey. Voysey's country homes were remarkable for their rational, simple design and appropriateness to their setting. And he was joined by other architects like W.R. Lethaby and Edwin Lutyens, who were working in fundamentally refined revival styles. In Glasgow the situation was different. Mackintosh (1868–1928) began work in the 1890s, combining the attention to materials and craft espoused by Morris' group with the radicalism of the French Art Nouveau. An early opportunity came with the commission for the Glasgow School of Art in 1896. The north-facing facade is monolithic in character, with suggestions of Voysey, the Baroque, and Scotland's own Medieval past. This last characteristic is evident in the way that the back of the building rises from the slope of the site. The interior seems an amalgam of a monastery and an Arts and Crafts studio. That is, while Mackintosh has eliminated all historic references in the columns and details, the use of a nave, aisles, and coffered ceiling refers to a meditative church in atmosphere. Of interest is Mackintosh's concern for every aspect of the building, from surfaces and furniture to lighting fixtures and windows (Fig 7.18).

In 1902 Mackintosh was commissioned to design Hill House; his design suggests an abstracted Medieval castle. In the interior dimension, he provides a series of spaces patterned closely on family functions. And in his attention to interior appointments, he provides custom-designed furniture, lighting fixtures, carpeting, and so forth. In construction and purpose, he followed the notions of Arts and Crafts, in much the same relationship as Wright to the Craftsman movement. In his eccentricity and individualism, Mackintosh seems more than a little related to Wright and, before him, Sullivan (Fig 7.19).

Mackintosh enjoyed a great reputation in continental Europe; indeed, he won second prize in the design competition held in Germany in 1901 for his "House of an Art Lover." And, only a year previously, he had shown in a competition in Vienna. It may, in some measure, be due to his influence (and Morris's before him) that the course of the *Vienna Secessionist movement* became increasingly dominated by the use of rectilinear elements in decoration. Certainly this was the case with Josef Hoffmann (1870–1956), who, with Adolf Loos, Otto Wagner, and Joseph Olbrich, formed the nucleus of the Secession. Hoffmann is well known today for his furniture designs, which are enjoying a popular revival, but the Palais Stoclet in Brussels may be his finest creation (Fig 7.20). Like his teacher, Wagner (and Mackintosh), he believed in the complete integration of every aspect of the building, particularly in its interior dimension. Throughout the building, rich and expensive materials abound, from Paonazzo marble and precious metals to Macassar wood and Morocco leather. In a glowing analysis of the building's interior, Eduard F. Sekler says:

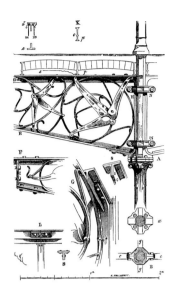

7.17

Detail from *Entretiens; Viollet-le-Duc (1872)*
Viollet-le-Duc comments that "if . . . iron is destined in our modern buildings only to serve as a security for imperfect masonry . . . it would be as well for us to let it alone. . . ."[1] But, he says, if it is *prescribed,* it is incumbent on the designer to find a suitable form. (Source: *Lectures on Architecture,* Eugène-Emmanuel Viollet-le-Duc.)

7.18

Glasgow School of Art—Glasgow; *Charles Rennie Mackintosh (1909)*
Within the 35' square library there are two rows of equally spaced columns defining the central 17' high double-height volume, which is surrounded by an open gallery at the second level. Screens are formed by the exposed section of beams that run out beyond the gallery to support shaped vertical members just before the beam embracing the slender columns. One can view the entirety, yet private spaces are provided by the development of screens. (Courtesy: Glasgow School of Art.)

7.19

Hill House—Helensburgh; *Charles Rennie Mackintosh (1902–4)*
The house is cold white on the exterior, and warm white in its entry way, providing transition. The entry needed to accommodate three different groups of people; business, public (family and friends), and private (individuals). Stairs provide a moment of pause between the divisions, and an overall unity is established by the repeated square motif. Variety is obtained by using the square in a number of ways; punched openings in the doors and furniture, structural grids on the windows, cubic light fixtures, and carpet patterns that define areas. (Perspective—collection: Glasgow School of Art; Photo—courtesy: National Trust for Scotland, Edinburgh.)

These rooms were clearly conceived as a sequence of experiences in space, enhanced by every possible device in the use of light, color and texture in contrapuntal arrangement. The rooms . . . are at the same time in harmony and in contrast with each other and enhance their complementary qualities through highly sophisticated juxtapositions, while at the same time no opportunity is missed to tie together the ensemble by repeating and recalling forms, mouldings, proportions and other elements of composition."[60]

Sekler concludes that "the building was a very personal setting for a way of life based on a profound respect for beauty and the transfiguring power of art. . . ."[61] That the building was very influential in its day is evident from this comment made by Le Corbusier in 1929: "In the history of contemporary architecture, in the steps toward a contemporary aesthetic, Prof. Hoffmann occupies one of the most luminous places."[62]

By the outbreak of World War I, Art Nouveau was no longer a viable force; its demise may be traced to the effects of standardization, lack of cost-effectiveness, and limited public appeal. And perhaps, for all its ostensible modernity, it represented the last best effort of the nineteenth century rather than pointing the way to the twentieth.

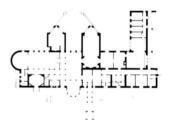

7.20

Palais Stoclet—Brussels; *Josef Hoffmann (1905)*
The Palais Stoclet was designed for a wealthy businessman in Brussels, to serve as a place of entertainment. The stark white facades outlined in metal give the building an abstract planar quality; this technique of outlining continues on the interior walls and floors, uniting interior and exterior. The plan indicates a pronounced axial development that begins in the entryway, and serves to make circulation patterns clear. (Vestibule—courtesy: Princeton University Press/Hoffman Estate [Cat. 104/VII]; Plan—drawn by J. Malnar; Perspective—Reproduced by permission of Academy Editions, London.)

Systematic Applications

8

Aesthetic Systems

Reference was made earlier to Roger Scruton's definition of architectural theory as "the attempt to formulate the maxims, rules, and precepts which govern, or ought to govern, the practice of the builder. . . ." He further states that such precepts assume a prior stance about what is to be achieved. Since architecture occupies the middle ground between pure aesthetics and utilitarian function, it is usual that any design approach refer to a complex matrix of cultural beliefs that are extraneous to the actual mechanics of building. This makes it possible to examine architecture in terms of its engagement with various issues of the day. In this vein John Ruskin insisted that architecture was ". . . the embodiment of the Polity, Life, History, and Religious Faith of nations."[1]

The notion that architecture is a clear representation of the society that produces it is responsible for the following belief—the application of certain principles of vocabulary and grammar to structural form will result in the expression of sociocultural values. This has led George Maybeck to comment that "Architecture is the handwriting of Man."[2] That there is substantial truth to this aphorism is seen in such disparate cultural hallmarks as the Greek temple, the Medieval castle, and the Fascist postoffice, each representing a certain facet of self-image. The problem in using such external benchmarks for the measure of architecture, however, is that one may depart further from the discipline than is strictly necessary. Peter Collins points out that if we examine the most traditional definition of good architecture, which he identifies as the *firmitas, utilitas,* and *venustas* of Vitruvius, it is clear that none of these three components can ever be entirely rejected. Thus revolutionary architecture can only be based on yet another component added to these three, on attaching an unusual emphasis to particular components or on an alteration in the meaning attached to the idea of architectural beauty itself.[3] And, he says, ". . . the only notion added to the Vitruvian trinity was the idea that 'space' is a positive architectural quality, and that it possessed as much, if not more architectural interest than the structure by which it was confined."[4] Collins points out that many late nineteenth- and early twentieth-century currents in architecture, such as an exaggerated emphasis on the structural aspect of buildings (firmitas) or insistence on the preeminence of program (utilitas), can be explained within the tradition of nineteenth-century architecture itself. He concludes that it is with the idea of architectural beauty that revolutionary theorizing occurred.

These definitions of architectural beauty, however, usually had their basis in phenomena only peripherally connected with aesthetics. David Watkin, in his *Morality and Architecture,* describes three of the more "persistent explanations of architecture" as: 1) religion, sociology, or politics; 2) the spirit of the age; and 3) justification on rational or technological grounds.[5] He points out that these impulses are by no means mutually exclusive; to the contrary, a common theme may be found in what he regards as a "collectivist populism," which insists that the architect "is merely the 'expression' of the 'collective unconscious' "[6] of a period. For Watkin, all three of these positions are inadequate (when not actually dangerous). In the first instance, the belief that architecture expresses *religious, moral,* and *social truths* leads inevitably to a notion of what architecture "should be," with a concomitant denigration of whatever is different. It is this belief that "sees architecture as an instrument for the attainment of social policy employed to achieve supposedly 'moral' ends.' "[7]

The second explanation—adherence to the spirit of the age, or *zeitgeist,* is the most disturbing for Watkin. More subtle than the first explanation, in that it does not insist on a particular origin for its spirit, it nonetheless stipulates that every period has an informing essence dictated by measurable socioeconomic, political, and ideological conditions, which, in turn, reflect an inevitable "march of history." The corollary is that those works in keeping with the zeitgeist are of the period, and all others are necessarily retrograde. As it happened, this position became a hallmark of the Modernist movement. Watkin's third explanation, that of *technological justification,* derives from an insistence that practical or technical problems predict their own rational solutions; "the beginning of what we might call the 'programme-worship' of modern architectural theorists who believe that the elaborate specifications which the modern client, often a public body, hands to architects and engineers in the form of a 'programme' will and should dictate their own architectural solution."[8] The effect of Watkin's book is to argue for the uniqueness of individual contribution, although in so doing, he carries his argument to an extreme position.

Actually, the most difficult aspect of such positions is the assumption that not only is homogeneity normal, but all differences are consequently abnormal. This belief in the commonality of human values, goals, and beliefs permeates the nineteenth century, accounting for the ease with which various theorists assume common understandings among their audiences. Louis Sullivan, for example, maintained ". . . that a people can create only in its own *subjective* image . . ." and therefore there is always ". . . *one architecture,* of which the so-called styles were and are variants expressive of differences and changes in civilizations."[9] While Sullivan could easily understand differences in response to a common program geographically and temporally, he did believe that an inviolable architectural truth was established at any one point; that is, he assumed that there was a correct response to a single problem and one "subjective image." Sullivan is assuming a homogeneous society, an ideological melting pot. But people, in fact, typically proceed from widely different starting points and subscribe to diverse ideologies within societies. Hence the "architectural act" is usually the product of widely varied sociopolitical, philosophical, and ideological suppositions and goals, and the degree to which individuals disagree on fundamental truths is startling.

At least two factors are responsible for the universality of architectural assumptions before the nineteenth century: first, history was seen as an unbroken evolutionary thread, with little self-conscious sense of change; and second, architects acted in response to expressed client need reactively rather than proactively. The major change occurred when architecture was first conceived as, at least potentially, prescriptive in nature. Peter Collins (among others) dates the change in architectural outlook from the mid-eighteenth century; and this certainly is borne out by the developments refered to in previous chapters of this work. Nevertheless, he states that the *demand for a new architecture* reached its climax in the mid-nineteenth century and continued for the following fifty years. Collins asserts (perhaps not altogether seriously) that this demand arose primarily because architectural historians were ". . . dominated by one notion, and one notion only; namely that 'a modern building was essentially a collection of potential antiquarian fragments which would one day be rediscovered, and studied by future historians with a view to determining the social history of the Victorian age.'"[10]

Aside from the desire to consciously produce one's own history, there were other reasons for the demand: the pressing need for new building types; the achievements of cast-iron and the rationalization of design; a Victorian penchant for novelty; and the resurgence of morality issues through religious movements. The approaches used in the attainment of a "new architecture" tended, in the absence of any radical technological developments, to derive from various ideological positions. These included: commitment to social responsibility, or morality; emphasis on the structural and programmatic logic of architecture itself; belief in the efficacy of historical models; and faith in the salutary effects of the domestic environment. And the century was thus marked by definitions of architectural beauty filtered through one (or more) of these positions.

Social Responsibility

The first category refers to those aesthetic systems based on social obligation and morality that appeared throughout the nineteenth, and well into the twentieth century. Such systems assume a prior position on the nature of humankind and postulate an aesthetic sensibility based on a response to the human needs that are perceived to derive from that position. Ultimately utopian in nature, such programs view aesthetics as a tool in the self-realization of a people. The roots of these notions can be traced to eighteenth-century thought about the fundamental nature of the human being. Hence, the opening pages of Laugier's treatise, *An Essay on Architecture* (1753), particularly his description of the first "rustic hut," are echoed in Jean-Jacques Rousseau's *Discourse on Inequality* (1754):

> Soon, ceasing to dose under the first tree, or to withdraw into caves, men discovered that various sorts of hard sharp stones could serve as hatchets to cut wood, dig the soil, and make huts of branches, which they learned to cover with clay and mud. This was the epoch of a first revolution. . . .[11]

This sentiment is again echoed in Abbé Batteaux' *Les Beaux-arts réduits a un même principe* of 1776, in which he describes how humans first sought the covering of trees, then intertwined them for increased effectiveness, and finally developed a shelter. He concludes: ·

> Finally, these observations having been multiplied, industry and taste having added something new day by day to these first experiments, either on behalf of embellishment or solidity, there emerged with time that series of precepts we call architecture, which is the art of making dwellings *firm, convenient, and decent.*"[12]

8.1

*"Allegory of Architecture Returning to Its
Natural Model;" Charles Eisen (1755)*
Eisen's engraving, used as a frontispiece for
the second edition of Laugier's *Essai*, illustrates the belief that the original shelter for
human habitation logically developed from
basic natural elements. Here the muse of architecture gestures toward the hut, directing
cupid's attention to the basic arrangement.
The muse is seated on classical ruins, which
are being used to illustrate a "false tradition" in architecture. (Source: *An Essay on
Architecture*, Marc-Antoine Laugier.)

Whether Laugier, Rousseau, and Batteaux equally valued this development
is open to argument, particularly in the case of Rousseau, who maintained
that the advent of shelter was responsible for the first human conflicts. They
did, however, view the physical development of architecture in much the
same way (Fig 8.1). The notion of architectural development is, moreover,
tied to society's growth, social contracts, and morality; this is suggested by
Batteaux' use of "decent" for Vitruvius' *venustas*, usually translated as
beauty, or delight.

Three great currents of eighteenth-century thought that influenced architecture are: first, a broad consideration about the human organism, our
nature and physical requirements; second, science's move to classification;
and third, the historical view that increasingly saw human evolution in terms
of a series of identifiable patterns. It is this last quality, conditioned by the
previous two, that led architects to see the history of architecture as a succession of *styles* based on identifiable factors. For the architects of the late
eighteenth and early nineteenth centuries, this meant that design now depended on making choices. Peter Collins refers to this change in approach
when he notes that one of the most typical features of the theory of modern
architecture has been its concern with morality:

> . . . it is evident that as soon as architects became aware of architectural
> history, and of the architectures of exotic civilizations; as soon as they
> became uncertain as to which of a wide variety of tectonic elements they
> might appropriately use; they were obliged to make basic decisions in-
> volving moral judgments. . . ."[13]

Moral choices need not, of course, involve religion, but in nineteenth-
century Europe they tended to. Thus the two great adversaries in England,
both of whom lauded the Gothic (and were in large measure responsible for
its revival), came from opposing religious camps. Agustus Welby Pugin
(1812–1852), was a convert to Catholicism who saw in the Gothic a representation of the beliefs of the Church; in this case the Church's being that
which was established before the Reformation. Pugin's fame as an architect
sprang from his numerous designs for churches and his work on the Houses
of Parliament, although he sometimes designed domestic structures (Fig
8.2). Pugin's sense of Gothic was almost entirely English, and particularly
fourteenth-century English Decorated, which he regarded as the perfect
form of medieval architecture. His importance to this text, however, is in
his published works, which proclaim his belief that architecture's raison
d'etre was ultimately to be sought in its inherent morality; for Pugin, architecture was revealed doctrine.

Pugin's first major work was published in 1836 and was, significantly,
titled *Contrasts; or, A Parallel between the Noble Edifices of the Fourteenth
and Fifteenth Centuries, and Similar Buildings of the Present Day; Shewing
the Present Decay of Taste; Accompanied by Appropriate Text*. The title is
as self-explanatory as it is lengthy and, with only two minor changes, was
maintained in the extensively expanded version reprinted in 1841. In the
Preface to the second edition, he points out that this decay of taste is due
to ". . . the decayed state of faith . . . which led men to dislike, and ultimately forsake, the principles and architecture which originated in the self-
denying Catholic principle, and admire and adopt the luxurious styles of
ancient Paganism."[14] Thus for Pugin, Protestantism and the Neoclassical
were both the result of lack of faith and doctrinal error, as the contemporary
state of buildings in England seemed to attest. At first glance, Pugin's architectural principles seem familiar:

> It will be readily admitted, that the great test of Architectural beauty is
> the fitness of the design to the purpose for which it is intended, and that

the style of a building should so correspond with its use that the spectator may at once perceive the purpose for which it was erected.[15]

He goes on, however, to state that "the religious ideas and ceremonies of these different peoples had by far the greatest influence in the formation of their various styles of architecture."[16] And, in an argument relating visual form to doctrine, he demonstrates that there is a particular (correct) style that embodies faith and morality, stating, "The three great doctrines, of the redemption of man by the sacrifice of our Lord on the cross; the three equal persons united in one Godhead; and the resurrection of the dead, are the foundation of Christian Architecture."[17] For Pugin, the cross is represented by the plan and form of the church as well as on the spires and furniture; the Trinity is seen in the triangular nature of architectural details; and the resurrection of the dead may be traced through the vertical lines and forms leading upward to great heights. In this way Pugin has formed an architectural aesthetic out of the facts of his religious belief (Fig 8.3).

Nor is his approbation reserved for the shape and detail of buildings alone; he praises also the devoted labor of the builders and masons, whose "whole energies were directed towards attaining excellence." He states that this feeling ". . . may be traced throughout the whole of the numerous edifices of the middle ages, and which . . . still bespeaks the unity of purpose which influenced their builders and artists."[18] This is the crux of Pugin's argument; that certain "correct" forms from the past still command the devotion of builders, and the combination of form and craft in turn expresses its glory to others. And as proof of the degeneracy of the contemporary, he produces contrasting images of functionally equivalent architecture. As one might suppose, the contrast always reveals the shoddy character of the later works, their dishonesty of materials, and the secularization of religious buildings (Fig 8.4). In the rather more carefully constructed and narrowly architectural *Principles of Pointed or Christian Architecture* (1853), he refined his principles:

A

8.2

(A) St. Marie's Grange; *A.W.N. Pugin (1835);* **(B) Library of the House of Lords at the Palace of Westminster;** *Charles Barry & A.W.N. Pugin (1844)*

In Pugin's design for his house *(A)*, Medieval motifs were selected for symbolic reasons; the result, visually, is eccentric. Pugin's best work probably occurred in the Palace of Westminster *(B)*. A report by the Victoria & Albert Museum notes that Pugin was involved in "every aspect of the interior decoration and furnishings" of the Palace. He provided "designs for the entire internal decoration and all the furniture of major importance. It was Pugin's labours and attention to the smallest details of ornament that gave the tremendous sense of unity to the interior of the Palace, and at the same time gave each area its distinctive character and each room its particular status."[1] (*[A]* source: *Recollections of A. N. Welby Pugin, and His Father Augustus Pugin*, Benjamin Ferrey; *[B]* courtesy: Pitkin Pictorials, Andover, U.K.)

B

8.3

Church of St. Augustine—Ramsgate;
A.W.N. Pugin (1842)
Pugin commented that as he was able to be "paymaster, architect, and builder" on this project, he had the opportunity to imbue it with his principles; thus he considered it to be his most satisfactory work. He insisted on the use of local materials, using warm, grey ashlar and dark oak woodwork. His use of ornament was restricted to the richly carved oak screens. The columns are carved and ornamented so as to appear bundled; in this way he could illustrate the point of structural stress through "multiple" supports. (Source: *A History of the Gothic Revival,* Charles L. Eastlake.)

The two great rules for design are these: 1st, that there should be no features about a building which are not necessary for convenience, construction, or propriety; 2nd, that all ornament should consist of enrichment of the essential construction of the building.[19]

His definition of propriety (Vitruvius' *venustas*) is "the external and internal appearance of an edifice (which) should be illustrative of, and in accordance with, the purpose for which it is destined."[20] In this text he makes broad and perceptive observations on the qualities of ornament, craft and historical reference, and "deceptive" cast-iron. His contribution to design theory is summarized by Kenneth Clark:

> Thus Pugin laid the two foundation stones of that strange system which dominates nineteenth-century art criticism and is immortalised in *The Seven Lamps of Architecture*: the value of a building depends on the moral worth of its creator; and a building has a moral value independent of, and more important than, its esthetic value.[21]

Pugin's admiration of the Gothic was shared, though not so exclusively, by John Ruskin, an evangelical Protestant and author of *The Seven Lamps of Architecture*. Ruskin so dominated nineteenth-century thought that most works, from architectural treatises to builders' manuals, refer to him. He is probably best known for his five-volume work *Modern Painters* (1843–1860), but he in fact interrupted that work to write *The Seven Lamps of Architecture* in 1848. In the preface to this work he notes that some may object to his not actually practicing architecture, but states that ". . . in the midst of the opposition and uncertainty of our architectural systems, it seems to me that there is something grateful in any positive opinion, though in many points wrong, as even weeds are useful that grow on a bank of sand."[22] The critique is necessary, he says, because daily the technical aspects of architecture push aside the simplicity and purity of the reflective element, and "this tendency, like every other form of materialism, is increasing with the advance of the age. . . ." And he states:

> . . . there is no action so slight, nor so mean, but it may be done to a great purpose, and ennobled therefore; nor is any purpose so great but that slight actions may help it, and may be so done to help it much, most especially that chief of all purposes, the pleasing of God."[23]

8.4

(A) Chapel Royal Brighton; *Drawn by A.W.N. Pugin (1841);* **(B) St. George's Chapel Winsor;** *Drawn by A.W.N. Pugin (1841)*
Pugin contrasted these two royal chapels to illustrate the deep religious atmosphere evoked in the Chapel Winsor as opposed to the secular theatrical event that occurs at Royal Brighton. Pugin's best-known book, *Contrasts,* is concerned with determining the proper "fitness" between the correct religious and social attitudes and the architecture that would facilitate these attitudes. Under discussion at that time was the major concern as to where the pastor should be located, which would determine the layout of the church. (Source: *Contrasts,* A.W.N. Pugin.)

A

B

In "The Lamp of Truth," Ruskin states that "we may not be able to command good, or beautiful, or inventive architecture; but we can command an honest architecture. . . ."[24] In this he echoes Pugin and other Gothicists. And his text, like Pugin's, reiterates warnings against the shoddy and machine-made, cheap imitations, and the grossly pretentious. He reminds us, in "The Lamp of Memory," that architecture is the repository of our collective history, when he states that "we may live without her, and worship without her, but we cannot remember without her. How cold is all history how lifeless all imagery, compared to that which the living nation writes, and the uncorrupted marble bears!"[25] Ruskin believed that there is sanctity in domestic architecture, stating, "When men do not love their hearths, nor reverence their thresholds, it is a sign that they have dishonored both. . . . Our God is a household God, as well as a heavenly one; He has an altar in every man's dwelling. . . ."[26] For Ruskin, as for Pugin, the primary worth of a building was moral, not aesthetic; accordingly, he states in *The Stones of Venice* that

> . . . we require of any building,
> That it act well, and do the things it was intended to do
> in the best way.
> That it speak well, and say the things it was intended to
> say in the best words.
> That it look well, and please us by its presence,
> whatever it has to do or say.[27]

The lasting influence of both men was perhaps not so much in their efforts at Gothic revivalism, or even their direct influence on the course of architecture generally, but on issues of morality, how people should live. This is most obvious in the plethora of treatises—written in the late nineteenth century by admirers of both men—which dealt primarily with issues of domestic life. One of the nineteenth century's most influential books was Charles Eastlake's *Hints on Household Taste,* discussed in chapter seven; in it Eastlake praises both Pugin and Ruskin and echoes, in simpler, more direct language, their valuations of materials, decoration, and the medieval generally. It is through Eastlake's enthusiasm that Ruskin's ideas gained currency in the United States, particularly in such crucial books as *The Decoration of Houses,* by Edith Wharton and Odgen Codman, Jr.

This book, written in 1897, greatly influenced the decades that followed—due largely to its high level of intellectual content. Indeed, the factors that characterized it were the insistent references to the grammar of form, its treatment of actual spaces rather than just their contents, and a doctrinal respect for architectural theory. It is this last quality particularly that separated it from the vast number of popular journals and magazines that dealt with aspects of the American household. In the introductory notes to the main text, John Barrington Bayley notes that one of the tasks of civilization is to find rituals that grant significance to human existence, concluding, "The rites of daily life are ritualized by *suitable* rooms, *le décor de la vie.*"[28] The authors of this work tried to define those principles—with generous reference to the classical—that would permit this, ". . . in terms of the fundamental architecture of the room, rather than the mere *adding* of ornament to the room."[29] In this spirit they state, "Thus all good architecture and good decoration (which it must never be forgotten, *is only interior architecture*) must be based on rhythm and logic. A house, or room, must be planned as it is because it could not, in reason, be otherwise. . . ."[30] Interestingly, the influence of both Ruskin and Viollet-le-duc is evident, as are references to architectural history. And it is clear that the moral spirit of the century is present as well.

Rationalism

The second great impulse of the nineteenth century was the Rationalist, or structural approach. Peter Collins credits César Daly with the best definition of the term, published in an article in *The Builder* of 1864. Daly describes it as the belief that architectural forms not only required rational justification, but that such justification necessarily came from science.[31] Put differently, those architects who believed that structure is the *sine qua non* of architecture whether that architecture was plain or decorated, classical or Gothic, fell within the definition of rationalism. The latter point is important; the rationalist approach was divided into the two camps of classicism and Gothicism. This division seems spurious however, accounting for the outward forms of buildings, but not their structural logic.

Ultimately, the rationalist approach was based on the idea that architecture should be responsible to its composition and purpose, and only then would what Daly referred to as "the alliance of architecture and sentiment" become possible.[32] This is an important point; Daly never considered the pursuit of abstract tectonic form alone a desirable end, but in an atmosphere dominated by the École des Beaux-Arts, his insistence on the importance of structure and purpose must have seemed revolutionary. This points to the dual aspect of function in rationalist theory; that of *structure,* primarily the province of engineering, and that of *utility,* a concern of architects pressed by rapid socioeconomic change. Henri Labrouste writes, "In architecture, form must always correspond to the function for which it is intended."[33] This is a familiar proposition, but in the rationalist camp, function tended to be defined empirically. Indeed, Viollet-le-Duc stated that throughout history the functional program of building types has altered very little; their form, on the other hand, has changed in accordance with climate, tradition, customs, and taste. He concludes that "ART does not therefore reside in this or that form, but in a principle—a logical method. Consequently no reason can be alleged for maintaining that one particular *form* of art is Art, and that apart from this form all is barbarism. . . ."[34]

The roots of this movement may be traced to the late ideas of Blondel, and especially to the concerns of teachers at the École Polytechnique like Durand and instructors of *stereotomy* (construction mathematics) like Rondelet at the École des Beaux-Arts (whose text on construction, *Traité théorique et practique de l'art de batir,* had become a classic). Durand, in particular, was highly influential—not only for his practical methods in design (discussed in chapter seven), but for his eminently economical sense of form. He remarked that there were only two problems in architecture: ". . . firstly, the problem of private building, which was how to provide the optimum accommodation for the smallest sum of money; secondly, the problem of public building, which was how to provide the maximum accommodation for a given sum."[35] For many architects, the solution to the problem of public construction lay in the use of the new techniques and materials available, particularly cast-iron. Cast-iron's real potential, however, was yet to be exploited. One of the century's genuine innovators was Henri Labrouste (1801–1875), notable for his unhistorical view of history, despite his connection with the École des Beaux-Arts.

Labrouste had studied at the French Academy in Rome, where he and other young students formulated an essentially romantic rationalist architecture. The fourth-year *envoi* (project) he sent back to the Académie des Beaux-Arts, a highly unorthodox reconstruction of the ruins at Paestum, was not well received; but it represented an effort to understand architecture at its very origins, free from assigned historical role. At the opening of his own atelier in 1830, he noted that even if the elements of architecture cannot remain static due to new needs, and the new means made available by industry to satisfy them, they still cannot be handled capriciously. These elements, he says,

> . . . are modified according to the functions they are made to serve and thus demand the selection of materials most appropriate for enabling them to satisfy these functions. The particular qualities of these materials thus exert the most direct influence on the form which it is appropriate to give each element so that decoration is intimately tied to construction.''[36]

Few design opportunities came his way until he received the commission for the Bibliothèque Saint-Geneviève in 1843. This nationalized monastic library was to be built on a small, narrow lot and, moreover, had to be fireproof as it would be gas-lit in the evenings. Because of the need to enclose open, flexible space with fire resistant materials, he chose cast-iron. This construction was light and efficient, and he ensured that the ornamental articulation of this spatial scheme enhance its own qualities instead of filtering them through the conventional columnar dress of neoclassicism.[37] That is, the ornamentation proceeds from the building's purpose and derives from its structure (Fig 8.5). In *The Architecture of the Beaux-Arts,* Neil Levine offers a comprehensive analysis:

> It is clear that Labrouste saw the building as a whole made up of parts necessarily different in character. Yet the exterior and interior intermesh and complement one another . . . the library is Labrouste's solution of the institutional building, which by its form, arrangement, and decoration conveys the manner and meaning of its use.[38]

One way he accomplishes this is by a gradual transition from entranceway to vestibule, then through a darkened hall leading to the "light" of the reading room (a light both figurative and literal) (Fig 8.6). Levine notes that the whole transition is finally read ". . . as a sequence of signs, as intricate and ethereal as the original Byzantine synthesis of spirituality and materiality.''[39] In 1860 he received the commission for the reading room of the Bibliothèque Nationale. Here he exploited cast-iron's possibilities in a design notable for its airiness, translucency, and illusion (Fig 8.7).

Eugène-Emmanuel Viollet-le-Duc (1814–1879) was a leading figure of the century. His theories of architecture highly influenced the course of

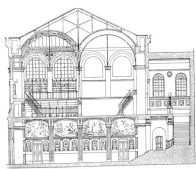

8.5

Bibliothèque Ste. Geneviève—Paris; *Henri Labrouste (1838–50)*
The section illustrates the contrast between the low ceiling of the windowless vestibule filled with columns, and the open double-height space of the reading room. During the day, light flows in through the arched windows; in the evening the space is lit by what was then a new invention, gas light. Stone piers, with images of night and day in high relief, support the slender iron columns that stand in sharp contrast to the outer masonry walls; in some sense, two technologies are combined in this structure. (Section—source: *Éléments et Théorie de l'Architecture,* J. Guadet; Photo—copyright 1991. The Art Institute of Chicago. All rights reserved.)

8.6

Lobby of the Bibliothèque Ste. Geneviève—Paris; *Henri Labrouste (1838–50)*
Labrouste placed the entrance in the center of the longitudinal side of the rectangle. The site is long and narrow, with no allowance for a forecourt. To enhance the act of entering, the visitor was drawn through the complete width of the building, which featured a semidark, ''Egyptian-like'' hypostyle hall. The light at the end of the hall marked the point at which the stairs ascend to the reading room. This iconographic program is relieved by the painting of illusionistic trees and sky, a suggestion of the surrounding park Labrouste thought necessary. (Photo by: Roger-Viollet, Paris.)

8.7

Bibliothèque Nationale—Paris; *Henri Labrouste (1868)*
The regularity of the table arrangement and column placement is visually superceded by the spatial qualities of this room. The billowing domes seem barely tied to the ground by the slender free-standing columns. This extension of space is further developed by the semicircular niche placed beyond the masonry pillars, and the forest scenes painted in the arched openings of the side walls. (Source: *Éléments et Théorie de l'Architecture*, J. Guadet.)

nineteenth-century rationalism, and his series of twenty lectures, the *Entretiens sur l'architecture,* helped form the basis for many of the assumptions that underpin twentieth-century structuralism. Volume I (1863) deals with architecture's fundamental nature and its development through history, concluding with an analysis of his own century's situation. His method throughout relies on a reasoned analysis of form, program, and structure—rather than the simple recitation of accepted architectural truths. This method reflects the position he takes in the preface to Volume I:

> If my lectures should have no further result than to induce in our students a respect for the past, and a habit of founding their judgement not on prepossessions but on careful and thoughtful examination; if moreover, they should foster the spirit of method among artists, I shall have done good service.[40]

He points out that we tend to base our theories on preconception; instead, we should examine practice, for ". . . it is always desirable, when endeavouring to establish theories respecting the origin of particular forms in art, to consult the crafts whose ordinary methods recall primitive modes of proceeding."[41]

Viollet-le-Duc states that while architectural programs vary little in their satisfaction of functional requirements, form varies with time and culture. He says, "Architecture assumes a character, if besides being the faithful interpretation of the programme, it also clothes itself in the form that suits the customs of the period."[42] And he makes clear that the public has a right to such a reflection of their identity when he states that "we cannot require of an architect that he should possess genius; but what we always have a right to demand of him is reason and comprehensible forms."[43] (Here one might recall Ruskin's comment in the "Lamp of Truth"). But, he concludes, such is not the case, and ". . . architecture is dying in the midst of prosperity . . . it is dying of excesses and a debilitating regime."[44]

Volume II (1872) presents a rich series of observations on ornament, construction techniques, domestic architecture, and "The State of Architecture in Europe"—which he finds confined everywhere by conservatism, and France especially, in the hands of the École des Beaux-Arts (Fig 8.8). The three lectures in which he deals with domestic architecture are especially interesting; first, for the subject's having been treated at all; second, for the attention paid to dwellings of modest scale; and third, for the extended discussion of interior refinements. In this vein, he states, "It is high time we thought of giving sober reason, practical common sense, to the requirements of the times, the improvements furnished by manufacturing skill, and economical arrangements and hygienic and sanitary considerations the importance they justly claim."[45] Such "sober reason" was rare, as few architectural treatises examined aspects of practical life within buildings at all; such matters usually fell within the purview of the popular press. It is in this section that Viollet-le-Duc buttresses his arguments for individually owned houses by noting that ". . . a perfect social state would be one in which the great majority of its members were their own landlords, and had an attachment to a home of their own; which would result in warmer family affections, a disposition to work, a more judicious selection of friends, and the abandonment of vain or unwholesome distractions."[46]

Thus rationalism finds its cause, in part, in social responsibility, which in turn finds its form in building types (Fig 8.9). Any design, rationalist or otherwise, is the product of complex forces. As becomes apparent in the next chapter, this complexity of intent had implications for major twentieth-century movements, particularly the Werkbund and Bauhaus, whose programs combined the technical and social.

8.8

Vaulted Hall; *Eugène-Emmanuel Viollet-le-Duc (1864)*
This series of illustrations from *Lectures on Architecture* Vol. II, were developed to show how the geometry of a polyhedron could be used to solve one of the main problems continually facing designers throughout the centuries—how to get the largest space possible with the least amount of material. It is characteristic of his approach that he has used new methods and materials only in those specific areas that affect the task; the rest of the building stays the same to preserve its symbolic meaning. (Source: *Lectures on Architecture,* Eugène-Emmanuel Viollet-le-Duc.)

Academic Instruction

As a term, academic instruction refers to the passed-on wisdom of the academies and universities, such wisdom as is confirmed by practice and approved by custom and tradition. Reyner Banham observes that this tradition owed most of its energy and authority to the *École des Beaux-Arts,* from which there emerged, after the turn of the century, Julien Guadet's compendious summary of his course of professorial lectures.[47] The work that Banham is referring to is Guadet's five-volume *Éléments et Théories de l'Architecture,* published in 1902. This is an interesting work; in spite of its coming from a pillar of the academic tradition, it deals with functional, rational considerations in architecture. But Guadet was not of the Rationalist tradition (like his teacher, Labrouste), however much he dealt with questions of structure; he had taught at the École des Beaux-arts and thus composed from the viewpoint of adapting buildings to defined programs *and* material necessities.[48] In short, he favored composition over structure and believed in need as a motive force; in the adherence to the value of composition, Guadet is eminently of the Beaux-Arts tradition. And if his work tends not to seem interested in the cornerstones of that Beaux-Arts tradition—*historical styles and axial planning*—it may simply reflect his belief that mention of such basic issues was not crucial.

This work of Gaudet includes masses of information on every conceivable aspect of architectural creation; including drafting methods, proportional systems, walls, orders, ceilings, and so forth—in short, all the minutiae of the building art. But interspersed in this information are the bases for his approach; his methods include using history for its principles rather than its shapes, and the idea of assembling all the structural and functional devices required to create a larger entity. The former notion almost certainly comes from Viollet-le-Duc, while the latter depends on Durand. Thus we can hear Durand when Guadet says, "What is it, to compose? It is to put together, weld, unite, the parts of a whole."[49] Whether immersement in historical styles is mentioned in Guadet's text, such interest was fundamental to the Beaux-Arts program of study; and axial planning was the preferred approach to structural development, especially under Guadet's instruction.

Unlike England, where architecture was generally practiced by gifted amateurs until at least the mid-nineteenth century, France had long trained academically. The Académie Royale d'Architecture, one of many academies devoted to the arts and sciences, had been founded in 1671 and was to last until the Revolution. As a reminder of a detested aristocracy, the royal academies were abolished by the National Convention in 1793; the school reopened the same year, but between 1793 and 1802 only thirty-seven students were trained in architecture. In 1803, by a decree of Napoleon, the foundation was laid for the École des Beaux-Arts—however, this school did not include courses in architecture until 1819. In this sense, architecture remained distinctly secondary to art, which dominated the École's interests. It had been thought that the new school, the École Polytéchnique (formed in 1794), might become the center of architectural training, especially given the presence of its distinguished faculty member Durand; but for all practical purposes, the Polytéchnique remained an engineering school. Thus the two institutions that taught architecture did so from opposing views: practical, structural considerations at the Polytéchnique; and composition based on historical precedent at the École des Beaux-Arts.

The emphasis on "correct" historical models led to a five-year training program, in which four of the years were devoted to the study of antiquity.

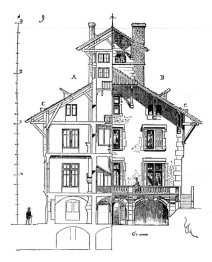

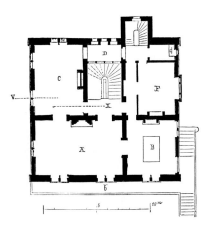

8.9

Country Villa; *Eugène-Emmanuel Viollet-le-Duc (1864)*
Viollet-le-Duc described in detail all that should go into the construction of this building. He concludes: "We may be sure that a country-house thus constructed requires no great amount of repairs, since all parts of the building are sheltered by roofing constructed in the simplest way; that it is perfectly healthy. . . . that the servant's work is facilitated by its arrangements . . . and that the erection of such a house does not require exceptionally expensive appliances. . . ."[2]
(Source: *Lectures on Architecture,* Eugène-Emmanuel Viollet-le-Duc.)

In 1871 Charles Garnier described the essential law of architecture, *consistency:* "A first great principle, a principle of reason and truth. It is the requisite: that the exterior masses, the composition of the outside, indicate the interior plane, the composition of the inside. . . ."[50] Both interior and exterior almost invariably used axial symmetry and a sequential development of space. The external form of these buildings used precise historical references from the student's early years and reflected an intense training in preparing finished drawings in pencil, ink wash, and gouache. This has led the architectural historian David Van Zanten to characterize "Beaux-Arts" in terms of an architectural technique that was entirely willing to compromise logical structure and function for *elegant articulation;* he notes that by the turn of the century composition had become an end in itself and produced an architecture that was superficial—dealing with surface and avoiding substance.[51] The École des Beaux-Arts was nevertheless responsible for buildings notable for their grace.

One of the finest buildings to fall under that label is the Paris Opera, designed by Charles Garnier (1825–1898) in 1861. Completed in 1874, this structure is a good example of Beaux-Arts principles applied to an essentially Neobaroque idea. That is, the building reads in a highly organized axial manner in plan, but the façade and treatment of interior space are decidedly plastic—as much sculpture as architecture, and lavishly ornamented (Fig 8.10). In 1871 Garnier published *Le Théâtre,* which explains his conceptual approach to this building type. The chapter titles are particularly telling; they consider the areas devoted to entering, circulating and socializing, and arriving in the auditorium as being psychological and physical experiences. The plan of the Opera, therefore, reflects the division of the circulation requirement into two types of activities; *processional* and *functional.* An analysis of the total space granted each activity is instructive, the treatment of the Grand Stair suggesting that the real performance may be what occurs before entering the auditorium (Fig 8.11). Garnier remarks that in past periods, no one believed that the view of the crowded staircases might be as much a spectacle of pomp and elegance as the plays being enacted: "But today, luxury is spreading, comfort is demanded everywhere, and there are those who love to see the movement of a varied and elegant crowd. . . ."[52]

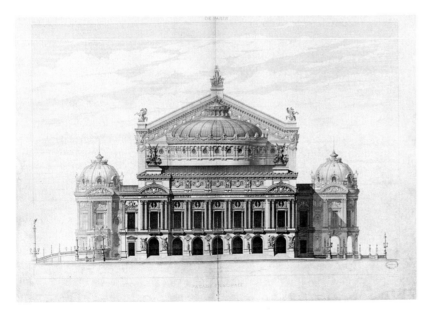

8.10

Paris Opera, Façade; *Charles Garnier (1861–75)*
In the rhythm of the paired columns and windows, the distinctly French use of end pavilions separated from their central tract, and treatment of the piano nobile, strong reference is made to Perrault's east front of the Louvre, begun in 1667. The use of a domed roof system, however, is as Baroque as is the undulating façade which grants the dramatic light effects. The convex shapes illustrate how the interior volumes influenced the exterior massing. (Courtesy: École Nationale Supérieure des Beaux-Arts, Paris.)

8.11

Paris Opera, Grand Stair Hall and Grand Foyer; *Charles Garnier (1861–75)*
The Paris Opera is noted for its grand stairway, which not only provides adequate space for the crowds of people but, more important, provides a stage set for the larger social event. It is significant that Garnier devoted the first four hundred pages of his book *Le Théâtre* to the experience of a graceful and comfortable passage through the theater. (Photo by: Chevojon Frères, Paris.)

During the Opera's construction, Garnier's office produced more than 30,000 working and presentation drawings, so carefully detailed that they were bought in sets by the public. (Indeed, the penchant of the Beaux-Arts architects for highly artistic, polished drawings has occasionally found favor in our own time.) In contrast to Viollet-le-Duc, who believed taste to be unconscious reason, Garnier asserted that reason only follows intuition, the essence of the creative act. He states that the artist has to compose and even execute without worrying too much about these axioms and dogmatic rationalizations. He says, ". . . intuition, in fact, is simply the habit of directing one's thought toward a particular end: it is the outcome of long and persevering study, whose progress is often unseen."[53] In his design, Garnier has, if only intuitively, evoked imagery taken from the past, for the association it grants the project. That is, using one period's historical models in a later period generally assumes that, in addition to the form, one is granted the appearance of the earlier period's values. And the education system at the École des Beaux-Arts ensured that students would be practiced in historicism.

Domestic Environment

The fourth impetus to a new architecture came from the complementary sources of Eclecticism and domestic "self-improvement." It is significant that most of what had been written on architectural theory before 1900 was concerned with public works, religious edifices, and commercial structures. Any consideration given domestic buildings assumed that they were residences for the very wealthy; indeed, in *The Decoration of Houses,* the complete absence of reference to such basic amenities as kitchens assumes the presence of servants. Even Viollet-le-Duc's arguments for a domestic architecture are based more on a concern for society in the aggregate than a regard for the affected people. The arguments between the Gothicists and classicists must have meant comparatively little to the general public, as neither produced building forms that adequately served the public. One movement in architecture that seemed to counter this exclusivity was Eclecticism. This term was originally defined by the French philosopher Victor

Cousins to mean "a composite system of thought made up of views selected from various other systems."[54] Cousins held that since truths recognized neither time nor place, it made little sense to confine oneself to one philosophical system; when combined, seemingly disparate facts might constitute, "a living system."

Such a method in architecture would have several advantages: it would permit the liberal selection of elements from the past, without concern for historical accuracy; it permitted a free reassembly of such elements in response to current problems; and it did not automatically preclude the use of new forms and technologies. Thus each of the other three camps might be placated, if not satisfied. The inherent difficulty of such a system is obvious, and mentioned in *The Builder* of 1845:

> Assuming that the objects and destination of a building are provided for, an original style, characteristic of the age, might be provided by a complete investigation of every style of architecture, and the adaptation of all beautiful features which do not militate with each other and with the actual requirements of the building.[55]

The important thing is to know when to stop and to know when the selected elements have begun to conflict with each other and actually impede the program. The supporters of Eclecticism were well aware of the danger, and constantly reiterated warnings about confusing the *art* of building with the *craft*. But a second development tended to further blur that distinction.

In a lecture given at the 1861 Architectural Exhibition in England, the Reverend J.L. Petit, a once-ardent supporter of the Gothic Revival and author of the two-volume *Remarks on Church Architecture* (1841), suggested that Eclecticism was the right method of proceeding after all. But he went further; in his praise of the buildings erected during the reign of Queen Anne (a period noted for its "spontaneous eclecticism"), he noted that the quality that lent them harmony and expressiveness was their reliance on solutions predicated on time, location, climate, materials, and common usage. In short, the *vernacular* should be the basis for developing a new architecture. In terms of domestic architecture, this made eminently good sense. When the present builder reached for past forms, they would be those forms already used by former builders to solve similar problems. Forms taken from the vernacular were, moreover, more flexible to use than those taken from the monuments associated with "high-style" culture. And finally, there was a familiarity and common sense in their use that appealed to the general public, their enthusiastic acceptance doubtless reflecting what Rapoport refers to as a high cultural congruence. During the last two decades of the nineteenth century in England and the United States, the Queen Anne Style became immensely popular with both designers and the public (Fig 8.12).

In all likelihood, such an embrace of vernacular elements would have occurred anyway, since the builders who began to assemble them into catalogs usually had insufficient historical training to finely discriminate. This is not to say, however, that they were unaware of history. To the contrary, their journals demonstrate a sensibility often rivalling the architects'. The second half of the nineteenth century marked a division between architects and builders, particularly in the domestic housing of the United States. In her *Moralism and the Model Home,* Gwendolyn Wright notes:

> The professional architect's attitudes toward design and social responsibility were radically different from those of the builder. Pattern-book writers made much of the distinction; self-styled crusaders, they presented themselves as being vigorously for the public and against the professional elite.[56]

8.12

William Carbys Zimmerman House—Chicago; *Flanders and Zimmerman (1887)* This fine example of "Queen Anne" style appeared in an 1887 issue of *Inland Architect*. Its compact plan comes from the contiguous character of the rooms, and in its use of the true arch, the entrance dimly echoes the designs of H.H. Richardson. (Source: *Inland Architect*, 1887.)

Increasingly, architects were seen to be remote from the issues of American domestic life. "They were criticized as extravagant and arrogant, concerned only with ideal beauty, or with their own commissions, rather than with the functional issues of daily life and economy."[57] This view was supported by the opinions of even such luminaries as John Wellborn Root, who "contrasted a harmonious environment of anonymous, simple, model cottages for the majority of Americans with a select number of finer, more individualized, expensive dwellings he and his associates would design for powerful and well-to-do clients."[58] (Of course, it can be argued that his view was almost idyllic in light of the actual living conditions of the working class.)

This is the crux of the difference; the architects could not conceive of an inexpensive domestic architecture that would allow them enough latitude, spatially and financially, for a full range of expression. The builders were proposing, in contrast, moderately priced dwellings for Americans that came in a variety of modes, usually with the capacity to be further individualized. Sears, Roebuck and Company was one such provider of instant housing, usually simple shells that could be fitted out with such amenities as plumbing and heating, as the owner's finances permitted. The only real decision for the purchaser, once the choice of style had been made, was the floor-plan, which was specified by numbered code on the order form (Fig 8.13). This sort of house (if limited in options) was very popular, representing for many Americans a chance to own their own home.

Two of the more influential books of the century, *Cottage Residences* (1842) and *The Architecture of Country Houses* (1850), were written by A.J. Downing, who noted:

> It is . . . far more difficult to design a satisfactory cottage than a satisfactory villa. . . . It does not follow, however, that tasteful cottages cannot be designed. There are no buildings, however simple, to which either good forms or something of an agreeable expression may not be given.[59]

And Downing makes clear that the design of a clear, democratic, and reasonable dwelling for Americans is the highest calling of the architect. In the latter book, Downing provides an extensive listing of cottage types, complete with floor-plans, detailing, materials, ornament, and regional pricing. He even provides sections on interior design, furniture, and ventilation systems.

In 1885 George O. Garnsey wrote the first editorial for the *National Builder,* in which he says, ''Architectural journals there are in profusion, but they are too theoretical and aesthetic to meet the needs of practical men actually engaged in the erection of buildings.''[60] But, in fact, both architects and builders subscribed to the notion that meaning in buildings was primarily the result of the various elements used, an idea taken ultimately from Eclecticism and its commitment to mnemonic association. Thus the essence of architecture, its social and moral content, was fairly common to all parties even if seen from different vantage points. Gwendolyn Wright notes that

> . . . professional architects sought an ideal world of harmony, history, and educated response, above the melee of participatory activity favored by the more populist builders. . . . It required a vigorous education to comprehend and be moved by true beauty. Builders, on the other hand, responding to the same sources, delighted in using the principles of associationism to promote personal expression, inventive details, and handicraft skills. Their favorite associations were with more everyday concerns, ranging from sturdy buildings to family stability, rather than with abstract concepts of beauty.[61]

The different groups that vied for attention all used the publishing industry. Wright differentiates three sorts of media: the *professional press,* consisting of architectural journals; the *practical press,* consisting of various builder's journals and pattern books; and the *popular press,* consisting primarily of domestic guides and home magazines for women.[62] This last category was especially aided by the 1879 drop in postage for magazines, making their mass mailing economical. It is probably magazines that most account for the general public's awareness of design issues, if only because of their huge circulation. It is estimated, for example, that in 1861, *Godey's Lady's Book* reached more than 150,000 readers (which in today's figures would be multiplied tenfold).[63]

The architectural journals, such as the *American Architect, Architectural Record,* and *Architectural Review,* were by and large handsomely produced magazines whose circulation remained limited to the field, although at least one journal, *Architectural Forum,* grew out of a practical trade magazine, the *Brickbuilder.*[64] Thus it is difficult to always discern, save in general objectives, the difference between Wright's first two categories, the profes-

U. S. MODEL FARM HOUSE No. 248

8.13

Modern Home No. 248; *Sears, Roebuck and Company (1916)*
This building is an example of the sort of mass-produced basic housing available through mailorder firms; virtually all the utilitarian and ornamental ''parts'' were available for simple assembly. The interior, in its simplicity, is reminiscent of the Arts & Crafts movement, and this simplicity may account for the presence of the furnishings in the perspective drawing. (Courtesy: Sears, Roebuck and Company, Chicago.)

sional and practical press. It is clear, however, that the largest source of information on building plans, interior decorating, furnishings, and landscape design were the magazines of the popular press; by the turn of the century they had names like *House Beautiful* and *House and Garden* and were to be found in homes throughout America.

Model-house plans became increasingly available to the public; over the second half of the century *Godey's Lady's Book* printed the plans for 450 different cottage designs and hundreds of designs for cottage furniture. Its outspoken editor, Sarah Josepha Hale, stated, "We wish to convince our readers that they can . . . with the aid of the patterns we give, combine utility, beauty, and economy."[65] Interestingly, the *firmitas* of Vitruvius' trinity has been replaced with *economy;* this reflects the progress made by the Home Economics Movement and the belief, held even by architects, that detailed knowledge of structures was not necessary for the construction of single-family houses. Indeed, when an architectural licensure act in Chicago was passed in 1897 (the nation's first), such buildings were specifically exempt, at least in part for this reason. The excerpt from Godey's actually has their furniture patterns in mind, but the referenced attributes (utility, beauty, and economy) might serve as the measure of interior design generally (Fig 8.14). One of the largest publishing companies catering to domestic interests was the Curtis Publishing Company, where in 1893, Edward Bok became vice president. By 1895, Curtis' premier publication, *The Ladies Home Journal,* began publishing plans for houses costing from $1,000 to $5,000, for just $5 a set. The well-known architect Stanford White wrote, "I firmly believe that Edward Bok has more completely influenced American domestic architecture for the better than any other man in this generation."[66]

The distinction granted the preceding four categories is a convenience only; social responsibility, Rationalism, and academic instruction are usually intertwined and sometimes congruent in their conclusions. And all three figure in the domestic environment, which in many ways (albeit distantly) reflected their ideological positions. Thus arguments over Ruskin and the Gothic, and the merits of Jeffersonian Neoclassicism, may be found liberally sprinkled throughout the press, whether professional, practical, or popular. The issues raised in the popular press are particularly interesting, for this press dealt with practical, if prosaic, domestic issues. The sources interior design has to draw on are, therefore, extraordinarily rich and not limited to architecture proper.

8.14

Chimney Mantel and Stairway; *fr. Robert W. Shoppell's* Modern Houses, Beautiful Homes (1887)
This illustration depicts the fireplace, ideological heart of the home. Gwendolyn Wright comments, "The symbolic purpose of the prominent fireplace was to declare that the family was the focus here. The living hall might be a pinched and restricted place in a small middle-class home, but with a fireplace it radiated security."[3] Indeed, in its characterizations this illustration points to the essential role the home played in the moral upbringing of children, and its place in domestic life. (Source: *Modern Houses, Beautiful Homes,* Robert W. Shoppell.)

A Bold New Century

9

Frank Lloyd Wright

These four approaches to design—social responsibility, structural or programmatic logic, historicity, and the domestic vernacular—emerged in the nineteenth century and continue to have influence. The first three appear regularly in the writings of architectural historians, and although the last one is included less frequently, its importance was asserted by no less a figure than Frank Lloyd Wright (1867–1959). In his 1910 essay *The Sovereignty of the Individual*, he notes that only by the patient study of Nature in an interior sense can guiding principles ever be established by the Architect; and he concludes that the best way to accomplish this is to study folk-buildings which grew in response to actual needs.[1] To some degree this appreciation of the vernacular derived from his admiration for good workmanship and the ways in which craftsmen found simple, logical solutions to problems in building. In part, this accounts for his early admiration of Japanese structures; while he did not visit Japan until 1905, he was certainly aware of their craft aesthetic from prints and books before then. In his *Modern Architecture since 1900,* William J.R. Curtis comments: "Evidently he admired the refined proportions, the exquisite carpentry, the use of humble materials, and the subtle placement in nature. Moreover, this was an architecture which modulated space and charged it with a spiritual character. . . ."[2] These were often the goals of vernacular builders in America as well, even if not always achieved. But Wright clearly believed it possible to design an *ideal type* of domestic home based on theory derived from machine-based craft, flexible design, and the sorts of sensible needs addressed by the vernacular.

Nor did Wright ignore the possibilities of using the popular press to make his ideas about domestic housing available to the public. In this spirit, he published his plan for "A Home in a Prairie Town" in Bok's *Ladies Home Journal* of 1901 (Fig 9.1). In fact, he published two designs in the *Journal* that year; the second was entitled "A Small House With 'Lots of Room,' " an "economy" version of the first. In both cases, the emphasis was on flexibility and openness. Wright kept the siting in mind as well, conceiving a "Quadruple Block Plan" for multiple unit designs. Henry-Russell Hitchcock comments, "Publication thus made available at once the first fruits of

165

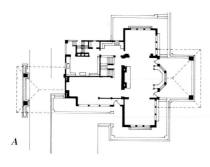

A

B

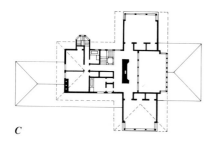

C

9.1

"A Home in a Prairie Town"—Curtis Publishing; *Frank Lloyd Wright (1901)*
The editor of the *Ladies' Home Journal,* Edward Bok, was determined to persuade American women to stop the practice of closing off one room—the parlor—for use on special occasions only: thus this design *(A)* by Wright, in which the library, living-room, and dining-room are arranged on a single axis. The design was intended to be flexible; the second-floor plan *(B)* provides for two extra bedrooms, while an alternating plan *(C)* indicates a raised living-room ceiling as an alternative. The exterior *(D)* is notable for its provision for light, air, and view. (Exterior—courtesy: Frank Lloyd Wright Archives, Taliesin West; Plans—drawn by: J. Malnar.)

Wright's maturity to a wide general public, had they cared to profit from the opportunity."[3]

One may argue that since most of Wright's commissions were residential, his view of design was circumscribed; but this would ignore his long apprenticeship to Sullivan. What Sullivan had done for commercial building, Wright would do for domestic. He believed that it was this dual background that permitted him to formulate an *organic architecture,* one that will consist of native growth in accord with natural feeling and industrial means to artfully serve actual needs.[4] In short, much could be learned from the craft and form of the vernacular, regardless of application. This position has been referred to in the claim that Wright was a strong supporter of the Craftsman movement, but this position may be less than tenable. This becomes clear in an analysis of his address to the Chicago Arts and Crafts Society.

Wright's "Art and the Machine" lecture, given at Hull House in 1901, certainly proved the great respect that he had for Ruskin and Morris, ideological pillars of the Arts and Crafts movement. But early in the address, he stated that with time, ". . . the machine is capable of carrying to fruition high ideals in art—higher than the world has yet seen."[5] He credited Morris with sensing the fundamentally new direction the arts and crafts were taking. And Morris did believe that new art-forms were developing in the last decades of the nineteenth century; if he disparaged the machine as the instrument of transformation, it was only natural. Wright explains that the machine had simply not advanced to the point that its potential was obvious, only its detriments, "Nor was it so grown as to become apparent to William Morris, the grand democrat, that the machine was the great forerunner of democracy."[6] Wright felt that Morris' genius lay in recognizing the value of *simplicity,* even while failing to recognize that this trait was the essence of the machine.

This, then, was the first of Wright's revolutionary ideas, that the machine had the capacity to free humanity from drudgery, ". . . that the margin of leisure and strength by which man's life upon the earth can be made beautiful, may immeasurably widen; its function ultimately to emancipate human expression!"[7] Integral to this vision is the notion of simplicity as the motive force of the machine. In short, the very methodology (or logic) of the machine would guarantee a new architecture in which extraneous ornament, complex shapes, and uneconomical form are to disappear. In the case of wood, Wright says that the machine makes it possible ". . . to wipe out the mass of meaningless torture to which wood has been subjected since the world began. . . . Rightly appreciated, is not this the very process of elimination for which Morris pleaded?"[8] His position on the machine was complex; while he did not value it for its own sake, he did see in it a means of furthering the artistic aims of the craftsman. In this way Wright cast the

D

machine as a seminal force in design and enunciated a formal, but flexible, aesthetic.

The second interesting idea in Wright's address concerned his view of the path that Arts and Crafts ought to take. He asked the audience to imagine an Arts and Crafts Society ". . . that may educate itself to prepare to make some good impression upon the Machine . . . their salvation in disguise." Such a society, he said:

> . . . would be made up of the people who are in the work—that is, the manufacturers—coming into touch with those who assume the practice of the fine arts as profess a fair sense of the obligation to the public such assumption carries with it, and sociological workers whose interests are ever closely allied with art. . . ."[9]

In this way art, machine, and human function might combine in a new sort of design studio, a *suitable experimental station,* where art and science would be united. This notion, of course, was fundamental to the formation of the Bauhaus program of study.

The decade following the Hull House address was one in which Wright perfected his "organic architecture." Reference has already been made to his treatment of space in Unity Temple (Fig 2.18), but particularly interesting is his description of his presentation to the building committee in "A Testament" (1957): "Why not . . . build a temple to man, appropriate to his uses as a meeting place, in which to study man himself for his God's sake? . . . Build a beautiful ROOM proportioned to this purpose. Make it beautiful in this **simple** sense. A **natural** building for natural Man."[10] He states that his main consideration is ". . . to keep a noble ROOM in mind, and let the room shape the whole edifice, let the room inside be the architecture outside."[11] Thus Wright confirms the primacy of the interior space, a sense of that room such that ". . . it may be seen as the soul of the design."[12]

The last of Wright's positions to be examined here is his view that the architectural environment is a totality, consisting of enclosed space and the things that fill it. He maintained that in his organic architecture it was impossible to consider the building as one thing, its furnishings another, and its setting and environment yet a third.[13] And in his desire to control all aspects of the interior, he surpassed even Mackintosh. He believed that the ornamental forms of the built environment should be designed to "wear well," by which he meant that they should make no confusing claim on one's attention through an inflexible composition or arrangement. He states, "Good 'alive' color, soft textures, textural materials, beauty of all materials and methods revealed and utilized in the building scheme itself—these are all means of 'decoration,' so called, although not considered, as such by myself."[14] His list of concerns is far too long to be considered here, but it is notable for its inclusiveness. He especially complains that "the furnishings" are the single feature of design development that has given him the most trouble and the least satisfaction, ". . . because of difficulties inherent in the completeness of conception and execution necessary within the usual building budget and total lack of suitable materials in the market."[15] And he regretfully notes that while he is pleased with the way his chairs fit the building, they do lack something in comfort.

In *An Autobiography,* he lists the nine principles that he employed in the design of a house, the eighth of which is ". . . to incorporate as organic architecture, so far as possible, furnishings, making them all one with the building, designing the equipment in simple terms for machinework. Again straight lines and rectilinear forms. Geometrical."[16] It is in his domestic architecture of the first decade of the twentieth century that these concerns

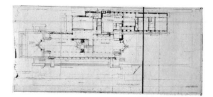

9.2

Robie House—Chicago; *Frank Lloyd Wright (1909)*
The ceiling moldings, grillwork, and furniture make use of "humble" wood and simple craftsmanship, and the rectangular quality develops a strong affinity between the rooms and their furniture. The window-wall on the south elevation is treated as a screen, as are the dining-room chairs; this likely derives from his interest in Japanese design elements. Unlike earlier designs that have a strong axial development, the axis here takes on a more complex character. (Exterior—photo by: Frank Vodvarka; Interior—courtesy: The Domino's Center for Architecture & Design; Plan—copyright The Frank Lloyd Wright Foundation, 1987, Taliesin West.)

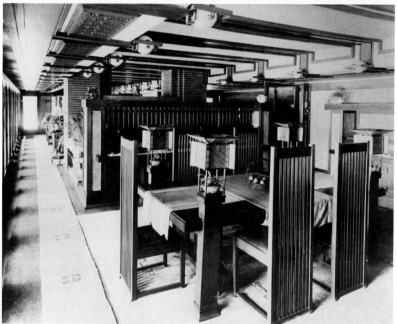

converge, particularly in his remarkable Robie House. In his use of materials and concern for the relationship between the spatial form and its varied contents—furniture, lighting fixtures, glazing, and textural treatments—this structure came to serve as domestic model (Fig 9.2).

The genius of Wright, then, lay is his insistence on forging a unique architecture without reliance on doctrine or previous example; this also tended to limit his commissions. In *A Testament,* he recalls that Professor Kuno Francke, upon seeing his Oak Park buildings in 1909, urged him to come to Germany. Francke counseled Wright that: "My people are groping, only superficially, for what I see you doing organically: your people are not ready for you. Your life here will be wasted. But my people are ready for you."[17] Francke persuaded the German firm of Wasmuth to publish all of Wright's works in Oak Park, and accordingly, Wright spent most of 1910 in Europe overseeing his book, *Ausgefuehrte Bauten und Entwuerfe.* His subsequent influence on the Deutscher Werkbund was considerable.

The Deutscher Werkbund

As an emerging industrial nation, Germany had, from the mid-nineteenth century, been engaged in a process of self-examination. This analysis found German products wanting in direction and quality and not making use of available technology. As early as 1852, the architect and aesthetician Gottfried Semper noted that, "Unremittingly science enriches itself and life with newly discovered useful materials and natural powers that work miracles, with new methods and techniques, with new tools and machines."[18] He said this richness of means posed a danger to the arts and crafts by virtue of their unpreparedness to use them, concluding that the result was a depreciation of both materials and labor. German products tended to remain poor until the 1890s, when industry began to appreciate the value of well-designed, machined products. The British example of craft coupled with economical production led Germany to send Hermann Muthesius (1861–1927) to England in 1896 to study their methods. He stayed for eight years and, on returning to Germany, was given the task of reorganizing education in the applied arts.

By 1907 Muthesius had founded the Deutscher Werkbund, an organization of thirteen designers and ten craft firms; it included Behrens, the Secessionists Hoffmann and Olbrich, and the well-known firm of Wiener Werkstatten. The aim of the organization was to forge an alliance between artist-designers and German industry, the effect of which would be the improvement of the country's products. Curtis notes that the moral tenor of life was to be raised through the influence of good design in the marketplace, the home, and even the workplace—indeed, in the whole environment.[19] Later, in 1911, Muthesius delineated the goals of the Werkbund in an address entitled "Wo stehen wir?":

> To help form to recover its rights must be the fundamental task of our era. . . . The fortunate progress of the arts and crafts movement, which has given new shape to the interior decoration of our rooms, breathed fresh life into handicrafts and imparted fruitful inspiration to architecture, may be regarded as a minor prelude to what must come. . . . Yet even this success is far from completing the Werkbund's task. Far more important than the material aspect is the spiritual; higher than purpose, material, and technique stands form.[20]

This seems direct enough; however what Muthesius had in mind was not individual form, the quasi-mystical *Kunstwollen* (will to form) of Alois Riegl, but form in the service of industry, design for mass production. Reyner Banham comments that this speech, ". . . introduced to the Werkbund the idea that aesthetics could be independent of material quality, it introduced the idea of standardization as a virtue, and of abstract form as the basis of the aesthetics of product design. . . ."[21] In this view, designers should have as their goal *form types,* which by their nature, could become normative. Curtis refers to this as ". . . an ideology in which the artist had to function as a sort of mediator between formal invention and standardization, between personal style and the appropriate form for the *zeitgeist.* . . ."[22] This is the sort of contradiction that Wright had apparently reconciled; the problem later dominated the Werkbund, surfacing especially in the 1914 Deutsche Werkbund Exhibition. Simply put, it was the division of the artistic temperament searching for individual form, from the designer developing ideal types that could serve mass production—the older view of craftsmanship versus the new machine aesthetic.

A founder of the Werkbund, Peter Behrens (1868–1940) was appointed corporate architect-designer to the giant industrial firm of AEG (Allgemeine

9.3

AEG Turbine Factory—Berlin; *Peter Behrens (1909)*
The simple axial plan and open section were requirements predicated on the simple demands of a production facility that used a central gantry crane to move the turbines down the assembly line. Behrens chose to grant this prosaic structure a monumental dignity by using a classical vocabulary and the format of a Greek temple. His use of glass and smooth, curved shapes for the corners combine elegance with strength. (Copyright 1991: The Art Institute of Chicago. All rights reserved.)

Elektricitats Gesellschaft) in 1907. He was to serve as graphic and industrial designer for the firm, giving material form to the destiny of German industry. This included posters for AEG's electrical products, as well as items, like lamps and furniture, for mass production. In 1909 he was asked to design the AEG Turbine Factory and, subsequently, in 1910, the AEG Brunnenstrasse industrial complex. The design for the Turbine Factory far exceeds the requirements for such a structure, indicating Behrens' intention to construct what Kenneth Frampton refers to as "... a conscious work of art, a temple to industrial power."[23] And so it seems in its use of volume and classical symmetry. Nor was he content to design the structure alone; he gave form to virtually all the contents as well (Fig 9.3).

It was through his exposure to the power and potential of industry that Behrens leaned towards Muthesius' position on *normative form types* in the service of function, in which group could also be counted Walter Gropius and Mies van der Rohe. It is significant that Gropius and Mies, as well as Le Corbusier, all received their training in Behrens' office. Indeed, one of the most progressive buildings designed during this period was the Fagus Factory by Walter Gropius and Adolf Meyer, shortly after Gropius left Behrens' employ. His design, particularly the workshop block, echoes Behrens' AEG building, but in its use of glass suggests a new industrial aesthetic with far-reaching implications (Fig 9.4). The emphasis on opening up the interior recalls Muthesius' 1911 address, where he identified the highest architectural achievements as the Greek Temple, the Roman Thermae, the Gothic Cathedral, and the salon of the eighteenth century.[24] Thus, to the classic temple form, he has added three examples primarily important for their exaltation of interior space.

The power of rational industrial forms was lauded by Gropius in the *Deutsche Werkbund Jahrbuch* of 1913, where he highly praised the unsentimental, functional statements of North and South American grain silos and factories. He went on to describe the clearly articulated, logically ordered, unified forms he thought appropriate for "the energy and economics of public life." The ultimate architectural statement of the Werkbund may thus be the Werkbund Model Factory Pavilion in Cologne, designed in 1914 by Gropius and Meyer. This pavilion, whose purpose was to display the products of German industry, was itself intended to express the progress of this industry as a factory prototype. A new vocabulary of transparent glass walls, cantilevered stairs and cornice lines, clear view of internal space,

9.4

Fagus Factory—Alfeld-an-der-Leine; *Walter Gropius and Adolf Meyer (1910–4)*
This structure is important for several reasons: first, for the early use of planar surfaces; second, for the clear statement of interior character on the façade by the use of "glass curtains" stretched between columns; and third, for the manner in which glass is used to dematerialize the structure, most notably in the corners. (Exterior—copyright 1991: The Art Institute of Chicago. All rights reserved; Interior—photograph copyright: Peter Aaron/Esto. All rights reserved.)

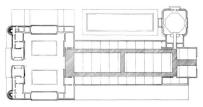

9.5

Werkbund Pavilion—Cologne; *Gropius and Meyer (1914)*
The plan shows a standard module, as it occurs throughout the factory, and a highly integrated circulation system. The plan is based on a grid-system, and uses a strong axis marked by the distinctive office entrance. The overall symmetry is restated in the flanking glass circular stairtowers; the stairs are unusual in that they (as well as their users) are seen hovering in space. The modular factory system has not yet, however, been extended to the office block. (Photo—copyright 1991: The Art Institute of Chicago. All rights reserved; Plan—drawn by: J. Malnar.)

and use of the grid was intended to characterize a new industrial age. The cantilevering, roof line, and internal spatial treatment might echo Wright, but the methods employed in the glazed skin belong to the Werkbund vocabulary (Fig 9.5).

This wing of the Werkbund, therefore, subscribed to the notion of design in the service of a normative type that could serve as a standard for mass production; this sharply contrasted with the other wing of Werkbund, which stood for individual, expressive form. This conflict came to a head at the 1914 Deutsche Werkbund Exhibition, resulting in an exchange between Muthesius and Henry van de Velde. In two of his ten points, Muthesius notes that architecture (indeed, all the Werkbund activities) "... is pressing towards standardization, and only through standardization can it recover that universal significance which was characteristic of it in times of harmonious culture. . . . Standardization . . . will alone make possible the development of a universally valid, unfailing good taste."[25] The remaining eight points concern the German opportunity to market that good taste. Van de Velde responded with quite a different thesis, containing the following protest against a premature move to standardization: "We know that several generations will have to work upon what we have started before the physiognomy of the new style is established. . . . The desire to see a standard type come into being before the establishment of a style is exactly like wanting to see the effect before the cause."[26] He concludes by emphatically stating that the desire to export never produced any good work. There is much value in van de Velde's position; in some ways the "expressive" wing of Werkbund was the more creative. The poet Paul Scheerbart, for example, called for the liberation of enclosed space, stating that ". . . only glass architecture, which will inevitably transform our whole lives and the environment in which we live, is going to help us."[27] His words served as inspiration for the Glass Pavilion in Cologne, designed by Bruno Taut in 1914 (the same year the manifesto was published) in what Taut referred to as the "spirit of a Gothic cathedral." This structure, designed by an architect who was not firmly in either ideological camp, marked an interesting alternative for architecture and an influence on various movements in the 1920s (Fig 9.6).

The Werkbund had its critics; in addition to dissension from within, there were those who stood outside the movement. One such person was Adolf Loos (1870–1933) of Vienna, an architect and writer for the *Neue Freie Presse*. In a 1908 essay that seems to prefigure van de Velde's comments, Loos stated that "The Werkbund people confuse cause and effect. We do not sit like this because the carpenter has made the chair in this or that way,

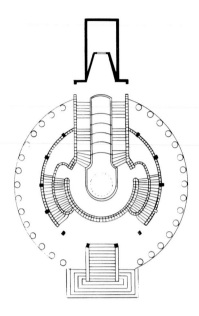

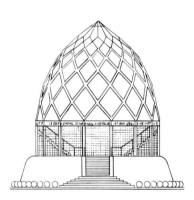

9.6

The Glass House—Cologne; *Bruno Taut (1914)*

In his *Glasarchitektur*, Paul Scheerbart had said such things as "light wants crystal" and, more to the point, "colored glass destroys hatred." The axial, seven-tiered chamber was lit by virtue of sunlight passing through glassblock walls and stained-glass panels. The conical ceiling was made of red and gilded glass tiles, and was pierced by an oculus that illuminated a waterfall cascading over glass pearls. Even the stairs were dematerialized by the use of Luxfer prisms set in steel. (Photo—source: *Bruno Taut*, Kurt Junghanns, Henschelverlag Kunst und Gesellschaft, Berlin; Drawings—drawn by: J. Malnar.)

but, since we want to sit in this way, the carpenter has made the chair like this."[28] In this statement, Loos is referring to a need to understand both tradition and habitation through logical investigation, before theorizing. Indeed, Loos' definition of an architect was a "mason who has studied Latin."[29] Unlike van de Velde, his criticism of the Werkbund was directed against its attempt to combine industry and art at all, for Loos felt that "only a very small part of architecture belongs to art: the tomb and the monument. Everything else, everything that serves a purpose, should be excluded from the realms of art."[30] The effect of this position is to define architecture as a mix of industrial technology and physical function. For Loos, necessity was the motive force; and practical objects must absolutely reflect their purpose, the *sachlichkeit* (reality) imposed by the principle of utility.[31] This exaltation of program was a behavioral argument that was to have impact on the Bauhaus after 1922, and on Modernism generally.

Benedetto Gravagnuolo, in his book *Adolf Loos: Theory and Works,* points out that most of Loos' writings address the more "trivial" everyday or "marginal subjects," concerning habitation and social issues. A glance at the essay titles in *Spoken in the Void* reveals its unique subject matter, which ranges from underwear to good music. Gravagnuolo states that "it should be asked if this might not be the real reason for the significant role his work has played in the history of contemporary architecture."[32] That is, his real contribution to design might be his insistence on using the minutiae of human existence rather than ideal theory to form design principles. The most noted of Loos' essays is his outrageous "Ornament and Crime" published in 1908, and then translated and reprinted by Le Corbusier in his "Esprit Nouveau" of 1920. In this essay he equates decoration with degeneracy; but this moral argument against ornament simply replaced its use with rich (and ornamental) materials (Plate 9). This aspect points to one of the two positions assumed by Bauhaus; the use of rich and luxurious materials, in addition to the dominance of program.

The Staatliche Bauhaus

The Werkbund continued through 1927—but its importance was already superseded by the highly organized Staatliche Bauhaus. The Bauhaus was founded in 1919 in the town of Weimar by combining two institutions: the Academy of Fine Arts and a Kunstgewerbeschule (Arts and Crafts school) founded by van de Velde in 1903. Gropius intended it to be a school open to ideas, a place of intellectual activity and creativity, uniting art, craft, and architecture. This seems a continuation of Werkbund, but the aims of the Bauhaus were far more ambitious:

> The Bauhaus strives to bring together all creative effort into one whole, to reunify all the disciplines of practical art—sculpture, painting, handicrafts, and the crafts—as inseparable components of a new architecture. The ultimate, if distant, aim of the Bauhaus is the unified work of art—the great structure—in which there is no distinction between monumental and decorative art."[33]

Thus the aim of Bauhaus was the *complete architectural entity,* arts and crafts combined under architecture, although this goal was not realized until 1925. Such a vision immediately suggests medieval workshops devoted to the raising of cathedrals, and it is not surprising that the term Bauhaus is derived from *Bauhütte,* a medieval mason's guild. This reference also makes the cover of the Bauhaus Program explicable in form and title (Fig 9.7).

In addition to delineating the aims of Bauhaus, the Program described its methodology:

> Art rises above all methods: in itself it cannot be taught, but the crafts certainly can be. Architects, painters, and sculptors are craftsmen in the true sense of the word; hence a thorough training in the crafts, acquired in workshops and in experimental and practical sites, is required of all students as the indispensable basis for all artistic production.[34]

In this brief description are to be found all the key elements of the Bauhaus system, which are as follows: art belongs to individual inspiration, but craft comes from training; such training should be broad; and academic experience should be augmented by work in industry. Study in more than one craft was enabled by the notion of a separate, identifiable quality called *design,* common to all areas. Not only was the workshop, "real experience," thought superior to the classroom, but the "real workshop," that of industry, was the school's ultimate aim. Indeed, Gropius' vision was that of industry's sending its workers to the Bauhaus for training, ultimately to return to the factories better, more creative workers; this did not, however, quite work out.

The complete curriculum was not actualized until the move to Dessau; it consisted of a six-month *Vorkurs* (preliminary course), which would introduce the student to design fundamentals (the prototype for the Foundation year), followed by three years of study in multiple craft-forms. This study was divided into workshop experience, or *Werklehre,* and classroom training in proportion and scale, rhythm, light, color, and composition, *Formlehre.* Only after the move to Dessau was a final period of study in architecture (building design) possible. The fact that there was no architectural department in the early years was due to the following factors: it was economically infeasible to hire extra instructors; there were few opportunities for students to work in design offices in the war's aftermath; and Gropius had, in any case, an ambivalent view of architecture's direction. Thus his idiosyncratic design for the Sommerfeld House (1921), which stands in sharp contrast to the Fagus Factory or, for that matter, his own offices

9.7

"Bauhaus Manifesto"—*woodcut; Lyonel Feininger (1919)*
Feininger, who taught in the Bauhaus, had titled this work the "Cathedral of Socialism," a reference to both the Bauhütte and the political principles of Bauhaus in the post-war years. In fact, the manifesto referred to a new guild of craftsmen, who would create the building of the future which would, ". . . rise one day toward heaven from the hands of a million workers like the crystal symbol of a new faith." (Source: *The Bauhaus,* Hans M. Wingler. Published by The MIT Press. Copyright 1969 by The Massachusetts Institute of Technology.

at Weimar. Foundation courses in architecture were offered, however, in such areas as spatial design, drafting, and architectural drawing. The deciding factor for inclusion of an architectural program at Bauhaus may well have been Georg Muche's "Experimental House of the Bauhaus," designed in 1923, with the active support of students such as Marcel Breuer. This house was built to showcase the design achievements of the school's first four years, as well as its practical concern for cost-effectiveness (Fig 9.8).

It is perhaps indicative of the early character of Bauhaus that Muche was an instructor of painting and weaving. In fact, virtually all the instructors of design were painters; Gropius felt that painting was the only art-form on "the cutting edge," particularly abstract painting. Thus the early *vorkurs* employed such artists as Wassily Kandinsky, Paul Klee, and Oskar Schlemmer—led by the brilliant form and color theorist Johannes Itten. One of Itten's great legacies may be his belief that there were demonstrable connections between mental states and particular visual formats; this idea is as vital to the idea of form-types as it is reminiscent of Pugin. It was not until 1922, however, that the Bauhaus took its first decisive steps towards the belief in standardized types and importance of program, filtered through a *Gestaltung*, or design (shaping).

The shift occurred for several reasons: first, the Bauhaus students (as well as Gropius) became aware of ideas from De Stijl through the guest lectures of Theo Van Doesburg; second, Gropius seems to have repudiated the "medievalism" of his earlier years; and finally, the opening up of building contracts in German industry offered real opportunities for designers. The impact of Van Doesburg's ideas was particularly important; while there was considerable consonance between De Stijl and Bauhaus ideologies, Van Doesburg had criticized the Bauhaus program of study for ". . . allowing metaphysical speculation and religious sectarianism to side-track or overlay the 'real problems of *Gestaltung*.' "[35] This reference was probably aimed at Itten, but the effect was to imply that the Bauhaus approach was less "modern" than DeStijl's. Thus, while Van Doesburg's direct influence

9.8

Axonometric Drawing, Room for a Woman, Experimental Haus am Horn, Bauhaus Exhibition; *Marcel Breuer (1923)* The living room in this house (designed by Georg Muche) is centrally located within the plan, surrounded by single-function rooms. This allowed for a smaller, more economical structure, which reduced the energy expended on household chores. Breuer designed the "Room for a Woman," making all the items in the Bauhaus workshop (as were all other interior elements in this house). The construction used in the vanity, chair, and bed refer to the craft tradition and show an early De Stijl influence. (Photo—courtesy: The Museum of Modern Art, New York.)

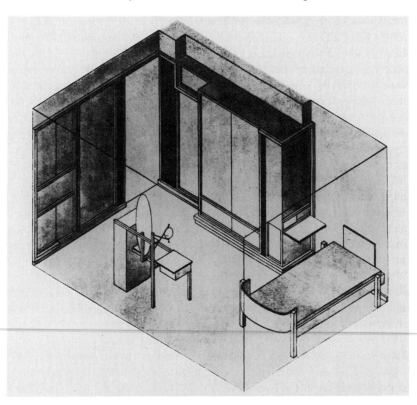

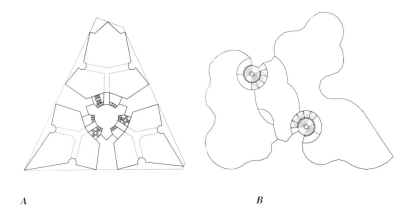

A   B

C

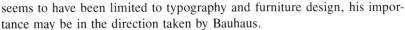

seems to have been limited to typography and furniture design, his importance may be in the direction taken by Bauhaus.

Still another reason for the growth of a more programmatic architecture was the influence of Ludwig Mies van der Rohe (1886–1969). He entered the Friedrichstrasse Skyscraper Competition in 1920 a leading member of the Novembergruppe, which enjoyed close connections with the Arbeitsrat für Kunst (Work Council for Art) and Bruno Taut. Taut's repeated polemics, appearing in pamphlets in 1918 and 1919, may have influenced Mies as much as Taut's 1914 Glass Pavilion. Mies' entry, a glass skyscraper, seems an attempt to give rational form to Taut's highly romantic ideas. In 1921 he modified this design still further (Fig 9.9). He explained: "The curves in the ground plan resulted from three factors: sufficient lighting of the interior, the enormous size of the building, the play of light reflection. The only fixed points of the design are the staircases and lift shafts."[36] The *open plan* employed in this design may be regarded as an early statement of an "office aesthetic," which he elaborates on in this 1923 statement: "The office building is a building for work, organization, lucidity and economy. Light, spacious working rooms, clearly arranged, undivided, only organized according to the pattern of the firm."[37] Nor need such arrangements be used for office blocks alone, as he made clear in a 1927 statement concerning apartment complexes: "If one limits to developing only the kitchen and bathroom as standardized rooms because of their installation, and then also decides to arrange the remaining living area with movable walls, I believe that any justified living requirements can be met."[38] The "new" Bauhaus embraced the machine aesthetic, both for its formal elegance and its willingness to yield to the goals of industry. Thus Schlemmer's statement, "We need living machines instead of cathedrals,"[39] is echoed in Gropius' own assessment that beauty depended on a ". . . restriction to typical basic form and color, intelligible to all."[40] Years later Gropius states: "The creation of standard types for everyday goods is a social necessity. The standard product is by no means an invention of our own era. It is only the methods of producing it that have changed. It still implies the highest level of civilization. . . ."[41] This standardization was critical in obtaining support from industry, in the form of royalty contracts for Bauhaus designs (particularly lucrative in the case of industrial products and textile designs) and practical work situations for Bauhaus students. Gropius did note that a certain similarity was beginning to develop in student projects, but states: ". . . this came about as the result of collaborative work, and also in spite of the co-operation of the most divergent personalities and individualities. It was not

9.9

(A) Friedrichstrasse Office Building Project—Berlin, Germany *(Ink on illustration board 30″ × 40″); Ludwig Mies van der Rohe (1921);* **(B) Glass Skyscraper Project, Typical Floor Plan** *(Redrawn by the Office of Mies van der Rohe, Chicago. Ink on Illustration Board 30″ × 40″); Ludwig Mies van der Rohe (1922);* **(C) Glass Skyscraper Project, Model;** *Ludwig Mies van der Rohe (1922)*

Mies' experiments with glass showed him that what was important was the effect of the reflections—rather than that of light and shadow—on building façades The first prismatic scheme *(A)* evolved into a curvilinear scheme *(B and C).* Although Mies says the plan "fit(s) the needs of the building," there is no indication that they fit the needs of the occupant. *([A, B] collection: Mies van der Rohe Archive, The Museum of Modern Art, New York. Gift of Ludwig Mies van der Rohe; [C] copyright 1991: The Art Institute of Chicago. All rights reserved.)*

based on external stylistic features, but rather on the effort to design things simply and truthfully in accordance with their intrinsic laws.''[42] Perhaps this is so, but it could be argued that such homogeneity was to be expected from a program that was communal in nature, highly structured in pedagogy, and doctrinaire in beliefs and goals.

It was the just-begun move to Dessau in 1925 that was the basis for what is arguably one of the finest designs of the decade, the Bauhaus building by Gropius. Finished in 1926, the building covers more than 113,000 square feet in a clearly articulated plan that states the ideological and practical functions of the various parts. Thus the separation of workshops, classrooms, and private studios is made evident in the treatment of the facades and the differentiation of the spaces. Gropius noted that the interior decoration, design and fabrication of lighting fixtures and furniture—and even the lettering—were designed by Bauhaus masters and students (Fig 9.10).

By 1927 the long-awaited architecture department had been founded under the directorship of Hannes Meyer, who was later named director of Bauhaus when Gropius left in 1928. This was a controversial appointment: Meyer considered himself a scientific Marxist, a stance that invited great hostility from the growing National-Socialist movement. While Meyer did develop the programs, he believed that design was the result of scientific calculation, with aesthetics playing no part. Indeed, the stress on empirical knowledge may account for his sponsoring of lectures at the Bauhaus by practitioners of Gestalt psychology; this was likely the earliest such concern for verifiable principles of perception in design. The appointment of Meyer thus marked the second step in the Bauhaus view of program. In the *Bauhaus* issue of 1928, Meyer describes his beliefs:

> All things in this world are a product of the formula: (function times economics), so none of these things are works of art: all art is composition and hence unsuited to a particular end. . . . Building is a biological process. Building is not an aesthetic process. In its basic design the new dwelling house becomes not only a piece of machinery for living in but also a biological apparatus serving the needs of body and mind. . . . Thinking of buildings in functional and biological terms as giving shape to the living process leads logically to pure construction. . . . Building is only organization: social, technical, economic, psychological organization.[43]

Meyer maintains that these new forms are an expression of a trend in international thought. And he states that the only elements that a designer need consider now are: sex life, sleeping habits, pets, gardening, personal hygiene, protection against weather, hygiene in the home, car maintenance, cooking, heating, insulation, and service.[44] The designer need only calculate all the above, and the resultant form is the correct one; design = program.

Meyer was forced out as director in 1930, and the post taken by the already renowned Mies van der Rohe. Mies had never been a member of Bauhaus but had always empathized with its aims. For a brief time architecture flourished at the school. But by 1932 the National-Socialists were calling for its closing, forcing its move to Berlin; in 1933 the Bauhaus ceased to exist. While director, Mies revised the curriculum, combining the architectural component with the interior design workshop into '' . . . one department called **Bau und Ausbau,** which served to emphasize the unity of space and furnishings, material and colour.''[45] And he added areas like cost-estimating, lighting, and interior planning. His design for the house at Bau-Ausstellung, Berlin (1931) reflects both his Barcelona Pavilion of 1929 (Fig 2.14) and concern for domestic space (Fig 9.11).

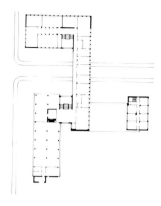

The interior had finally been fully acknowledged in the Bauhaus scheme, as is evident in a 1931 lecture given by Marcel Breuer, entitled ''The House Interior.'' He states:

> The deciding factors for the shaping of the interior, their basis, and their intrinsic possibilities, rest in the house itself—in its interior and total organization, in its floor plan, in its ''architecture'' . . . we see our mission in creating a home that is simpler, lighter, more comfortable in a biological sense, and independent of exterior factors. . . . The necessity for the utmost economy in space demands a machine for living, which must actually be constructed like a machine, with engineering developments and the latest in mechanization. Practically speaking: everything is either built-in or permanent, every object is placed in a specific location . . . everything measured off in the smallest dimensions and interlocking. . . . The house, in other words, should be based on the body.[46]

In this address he makes observations about furniture (which should be modular or built-in), lighting (task and ambient), and color (which must be light but monochromatic); in short, the office prototype. And so, the Bauhaus had developed an aesthetic relating to all areas of *Gestaltung*—architecture; interior, industrial, and graphic design; and crafts—based on program and use of technology. These remain the hallmarks of Modernism.

9.10

The Bauhaus Building—Dessau; *Walter Gropius (1925)*
Gropius resolved the program—which involved organizing many functional requirements and using much donated plate glass—by manipulating mass and volume. The masses were differentiated by color and dimension, and the interior volume was revealed through the use of large expanses of plate glass; the glass additionally provided the proper quality of light for particular functions. (Photo—copyright 1991: The Art Institute of Chicago. All rights reserved; Plan—drawn by: J. Malnar.)

9.11

House, Berlin Building Exposition; *Ludwig Mies van der Rohe (1931)*
This house comprises a series of sliding planes, very like the Barcelona Pavilion, but their closer proximity in this design results in the illusion of partitioned room-areas. Only the kitchen, bathroom, and maid's room are actually walled; the rest of the space is open-plan. The connection of interior and exterior is reinforced by the extension of interior planes into the atrium area, and by the use of glass walls. (Photo—courtesy: Mies van der Rohe Archive, The Museum of Modern Art, New York.)

9.12

Piano and Mandola (Oil on canvas, 36⅛″ × 16⅞″); Georges Braque (1909–10)
In this work, despite the legibility of the subject matter, Braque has represented reality as a continuity of interlocking volumes following only a general outline. In short, he has dissected a familiar idea, and then pointedly reassembled it with only slight regard for its former identity, an essentially abstract approach. (Collection: Solomon R. Guggenheim Museum, New York; copyright 1991 ARS, N.Y./ADAGP. Photo by Robert E. Mates; copyright 1990 The Solomon R. Guggenheim Foundation.)

Modernism

In his *Modern Architecture Since 1900,* William J.R. Curtis notes the striking consistency in European architecture after 1920, finally resulting in the widely shared attributes of an "International Style." He posits the following reasons for this: ". . . the very idea of a modern architecture; Rationalist approaches to history and construction; visual and philosophical concerns with mechanization; attempts at distilling certain essentials of classicism; moral yearnings towards honesty, integrity, and simplicity."[47] But, he concludes, the visual form that Modernism took was highly dependent on the sorts of discoveries about the nature of *space* and *mathematical order* that were being made by various movements in the fine arts, painting in particular.

Cubism, especially in its formative years (1907–1910), had fundamentally changed the way artists viewed the representation of reality on the plane. Not only were multiple views of the subject possible, but more important, the view itself was permitted to unfold in a layered (and time-dependent) way (Fig 9.12). Georges Braque writes: "It was a means of getting closer to objects within the limits that painting would allow. Through fragmentation I was able to establish space and movement in space; and I was unable to introduce objects until after I had created space."[48] But the celebrated "multiple view" so important to art may have been less important to architecture than the interplay of planes that led to a dynamic complexity in spatial definition. In his description of Picasso's 1910 paintings, Roland Penrose comments: "The eye travels over a continuous play of semitransparent recessions and intrusions . . . and in its passage it can continually enjoy moving over surfaces that are convincingly definite and that create a reality of their own. The architecture of the human form reappears as a transparent scaffolding in which the interior and exterior are both apparent."[49]

This description might serve as a statement of Modernist design principles. The movement that Braque refers to may be seen more clearly in the early work of Kasimir Malevich, who referred to his method as "Cubo-Futurist" (i.e., the Cubist view of space combined with a Futurist love of machine movement). Malevich soon evolved his style into the pure abstraction of Suprematism, which renounced all anecdotal reference (Fig 9.13). This was to greatly influence Mondrian and Lissitzky (of De Stijl) and Kandinsky (of the Bauhaus); in fact, Malevich was to later teach at the Bauhaus. Alfred H. Barr, Jr., inventor of the term *International Style,* says that Malevich . . . "stands at the heart of the movement which swept westward from Russia after World War I and, mingling with the eastward moving influence of the Dutch de Stijl group, transformed the architecture, furniture, typography, and commercial art of Germany and much of the rest of Europe."[50] Barr is referring here to the Bauhaus, whose followers admired both Malevich and the Constructivist work emanating from Eastern Europe. Malevich was respected in large part for the inner, spiritual quality of his works, which were intended to transcend referential reality; perhaps equally important was the sense of mathematical order and centrifugal movement so visually evident.

The Bauhaus was not, however, the only nor the most doctrinaire source of Modernist tradition. *De Stijl* (the Style) published its magazine from 1917 to 1932; in it the ideas of Neoplasticism were disseminated. Theo Van Doesburg (1883–1931), in a 1922 "Report of the De Stijl Group," made clear their aim to ". . . find practical solutions to universal problems." He continued: "Building, which means organizing one's means into a unity *(Gestaltung)* is all-important to us. This unity can be achieved only by suppressing arbitrary subjective elements in the expressional means, (instead,) . . . preparing to use objective, universal, formative means."[51] By definition, these were means that should be applied to all forms of creative endeavor, from painting to architecture. Filippo Alison notes that such a purification of expressional means seemed to indicate a new type of ethics, which ". . . by transcending mere artistic creation, would come to pervade all other human activities until it attained a *universal character* which was understood as the 'equilibrium of equivalent relationships.' Daily life would then acquire a new style, controlled in a special way by the order of things (not humans!)."[52] In short, art and architecture serve humankind; the more so because the basis for artistic creation would be an abstract (and morally neutral) series of mathematical links.

Among the founders of the movement were Van Doesburg and the painter Piet Mondrian (1872–1944); within a year they were joined by the cabinet-maker/architect Gerrit Rietveld (1888–1964). In the First Manifesto of 1918 they state, "There is an old and new consciousness of the age. The old one is directed towards the individual. The new one is directed towards the universal. The struggle of the individual against the universal may be seen both in the world war and in modern art."[53] By obtaining an "objective reality," one that can occur only at the level of abstraction, the result would be the elimination of the sort of individualism that had instigated the World War. To provide the theoretical base, De Stijl used the ideas of the mathematician and theosophical theorist M.H. Schoenmaekers, whose work *Het nieu wereldbeeld (The New Image of the World)* had been published in 1915. Not only did the notion of Neoplasticism derive from Schoenmaekers, but also De Stijl's universal cosmology, and even the color schemes that appeared in Mondrian's paintings:

> The three principal colors are essentially yellow, blue and red. They are the only colors existing . . . yellow is the movement of the ray (vertical) . . . blue is the contrasting color to yellow (horizontal firmament) . . . red is the mating of yellow and blue.[54]

Thus Schoenmaekers provided the inspiration for such works as Mondrian's *De Nieuwe Beelding in de Schilderkunst (Neoplasticism in Painting)*, published in *De Stijl* of 1917, and Rietveld's famous "Red/Blue Chair" of the same year. They believed in collaboration between painters, sculptors, and architects on every level; the influence of the experiments in abstract, linear compositions on European architects generally is clear in a comparison of the plan of Mies' Brick Villa of 1922 and a Van Doesburg painting of the same period (Fig 9.14).

The systematic application of De Stijl theory to architecture soon followed. Daniele Baroni, in *The Furniture of Gerrit Thomas Rietveld*, notes that this evolution ". . . occurred when artists turned from the lyrical qualities of pure abstraction to designing for the neo-plastic environment, exchanging, as it were, the picture plane for the three-dimensional constructs of architecture."[55] As early as 1919 Van Doesburg had designed a house that was furnished by Rietveld and published in issue 12 of *De Stijl* (1920); within a year Vilmos Huszar had logically taken the process a step further in theoretical purity (Fig 9.15). Van Doesburg's comment about this design is interesting: "The effect of the colors in their spatial relationship, the unity of furniture, hangings, carpets, have been so harmoniously balanced one with the other in the execution of this design that the result is not only aesthetic, but ethical as well."[56] The last phrase is critical; not only must architecture develop aesthetically, but it must be ethically, or theoretically, pure.

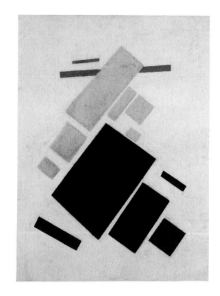

9.13

Suprematist Composition: Airplane Flying (Oil on canvas, 22⅞″ × 19″); Kasimir Malevich (1915; dated 1914)
While the shapes in his earlier works recall cubist principles in their complex faceting, the way they appeared in multiple sequence was part of the futurist vocabulary. But Malevich seems less interested in the aims of these two positions than in the evocation of pure dynamism, expressed in composition alone; indeed, Malevich was probably the first artist to develop a system of pure, non-referential, geometric composition. (Collection: The Musuem of Modern Art, New York. Purchase.)

There followed some intriguing experiments in interior design by Mondrian, in which he manipulated three-dimensional spatial relationships with two-dimensional elements and color. But the definitive De Stijl building was probably Schröder House, designed by Rietveld in 1924. This building represented Rietveld's first opportunity to produce a design for a permanent architectural work that was fully three-dimensional in fact and function (Fig 9.16). Baroni's analysis is succinct: "The house was constructed by germination from within, following the Cartesian axes, and projected through slabs and planes on to the exterior. Rietveld employed the logic of geometry, exploiting its laws to the tiniest fraction and to their farthest consequences. . . ."[57] The house is novel for the following reasons: its highly abstract and flexible sense of spatial unity; the integration of "furniture" into the architectural context; and the ideological use of color on planar surfaces (Plate 10). In 1928 Van Doesburg said, "In modern architecture the surfaces ask to be animated . . . composed with the aid of pure color, the color of space. And even apart from any surface coloring, the appropriate use of modern materials is subject to the same laws as colors in space and time."[58]

He says the result is a tension between colors and between materials, the "equilibrium of equivalent relationships" referred to earlier. One of the most dynamic examples of interior design produced with these principles was Café L'Aubette (1928), which consisted of two large rooms. One was designed by Van Doesburg and dominated by a diagonal relief composition; the other was designed by Hans and Sophie Arp, who were also responsible for the staircase. Thus, the major architectural achievements of De Stijl were interior in nature and relied on two-dimensional effect (Fig 9.17).

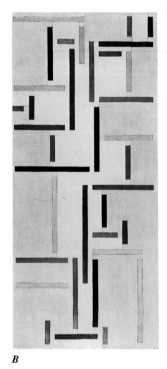

B

9.14

(A) Brick Country House Project; *Ludwig Mies van der Rohe (1924);* (B) Rhythm of a Russian Dancer *(Oil on canvas, 53½″ × 24¼″); Theo van Doesburg (1918)*
Conceptually both plan and painting begin with free-floating, independent linear elements. In both compositions these elements are arranged asymmetrically, denying a dominant axis, and describe interlocking rectangular areas. Where van Doesburg has created an overall balance with vertical and horizontal lines of equal width, Mies has stressed a centrifugal arrangement that causes the villa's interior spaces to extend outward. Here, Mies has changed the wall's function from one of enclosing rooms, to one of defining areas. (*[A]* perspective and plan (no longer exist); Photo—courtesy: Mies van der Rohe Archive, The Museum of Modern Art, New York *[B]* collection: The Museum of Modern Art, New York. Acquired through the Lillie P. Bliss Bequest. Copyright: Theo van Doesburg/VAGA, New York 1991.)

A

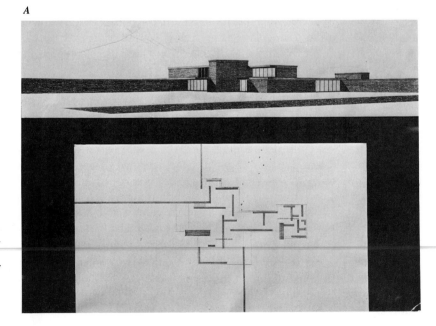

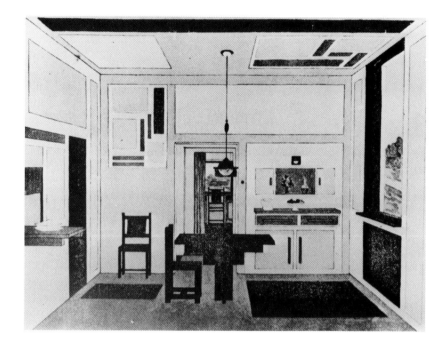

9.15

Form-Color-Composition in a Room; *Vilmos Huszar (1921)*
The De Stijl artists maintained the familiar cubic room-as-box, but treated each surface individually, like a canvas. Rectangular areas of color float on the wall, relating to each other pictorially. Furniture was composed of planar components, and merged so completely with the colors on the wall planes as to lose their individual identity. (Courtesy: Rijksdienst Beeldende Kunst, The Hague.)

Le Corbusier

To the principles of rationalism (as defined by type and program) and social manipulation (or awareness) can be added a commitment to internationalism (the universally applicable)—a natural result of common ideology and experience of the War. The International Style was, in fact, just that. Still, there were marked differences as well; just as the Bauhaus was not as doctrinaire in its beliefs as De Stijl, so this approach could be even more flexible in the hands of an architect like Le Corbusier. Born Charles-Édouard Jeanneret (1887–1965), Le Corbusier began his design career in the office of Auguste Perret, where he likely absorbed the rationalist ideas of Viollet-le-Duc; he later expanded his understanding of technology's potential while working in Peter Behrens' office. It may thus be assumed that his view of

9.16

Schröder House—Utrecht; *Gerrit Rietveld (1924)*
The goal of De Stijl was the improvement of world conditions; nowhere is their ideology more evident than in the contrast between Schröder House and the buildings adjacent to it. The arrangement of the floor plans only barely suggests the force of the internal space that pushes out and becomes the unorthodox exterior. The unique aspect of the second floor is the sliding-wall system, which can be used to divide the floor into isolated rooms, or be removed to allow an open plan. (Drawn by: J. Malnar.)

B

9.17

(A) **Café Aubette, Cinema / Dancehall—Strasbourg;** *Theo van Doesburg (1926–8);*
(B) **Café Aubette, Stairway;** *Hans and Sophie Arp*

Van Doesburg's intent to "animate" the space led him to juxtapose the orthogonal architectural elements of the room (such as the viewing screen, door, window, and gallery) with a pictorial arrangement of colored rectangular planes set at forty-five degrees. Each wall is treated as a separate composition abruptly terminated at the corner junctions, thus preventing continuity between the wall surfaces. In contrast to all this activity, the regularly spaced parallel partitions form an entirely stable base plane. The painted staircase by the Arps is highly planar and geometric, a series of diagonals so conceived as to enhance the act of ascent. ([A] collection: Van Abbemuseum, Eindhoven, The Netherlands; [B] copyright Rijksdienst Beeldende Kunst, The Hague, inv. nr. AB 5116.)

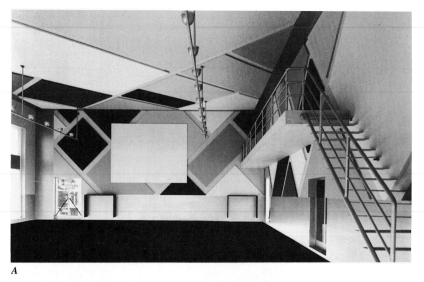

A

rationalism was similar, if not congruent, to Gropius' and Mies'. That he developed in this direction is illustrated by this comment made in 1925, "To search for the human scale, for human function, is to define human needs. These needs are 'type.' " And he goes on to point out that ". . . they are the same for all of us. . . ."[59] Moreover, he freely used such phrases as "purifying technology" and the "mathematical basis of the world." However, he also postulated as conditions for art, "Intelligence and passion; there is no art without emotion, no emotion without passion. Stones are dead things sleeping in the quarries but the apses of St. Peter's are a drama."[60] And, more prosaically, "Architecture supercedes utilitarian necessities."[61]

Le Corbusier's writings express a dual belief: first, the view of the individual artist as a genius, seer, and visionary prophet; and second, a concern for societal issues that inevitably led to utopian socialist sympathies. Le Corbusier's view of architecture was, therefore, complex and imbued with the notion that only through (inspired) form, represented by types that could be mass-produced, could materials reveal their latent power to serve humankind. It was this belief that led him to develop a universal building type. The Maison Dom-ino design of 1914 was Le Corbusier's attempt to combine formwork and steel reinforcement requiring precision skills obtained only with industrial conditions, with unskilled labor at the project site. This house structure was intended to serve as a prototype, as standardized as its namesake; the domino. The title was a pun; the freestanding columns, when drawn in plan, would appear as the domino's dots, and the first three letters suggested the Roman *domus,* or house. It is Frampton's view that Le Corbusier, by developing a scheme that freed the façade from a need to directly respond to interior functional requirements, was trying to ". . . reconcile the private realm of modern convenience with the public façade of architectural order." Thus ". . . the complex interior was held away from the public front."[62] The structure had the capacity, moreover, to join in various combinations as the need arose, an early statement of modular construction. This design approach led to the idea of cellular space, as seen in his 1925 Pavilion; the idea is restated in a later drawing of plug-in living units, using a wine rack analogy (Fig 9.18).

In 1918, he met Amédéé Ozenfant, the brilliant artist and social theorist, who encouraged him to paint; in fact, he and Ozenfant exhibited their work under the title of Purism the following year. The catalog to their exhibition was entitled *Après le Cubisme,* an indication of their sources. But their view

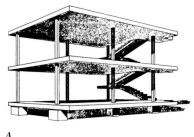

A

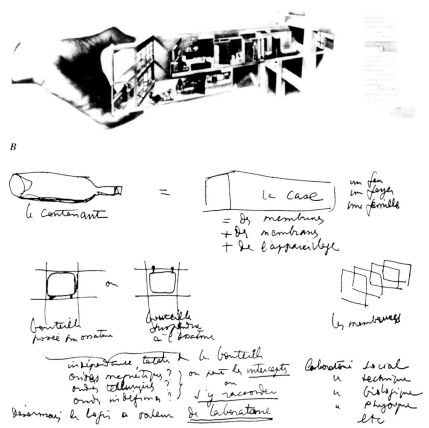

B

9.18

(A) **Dom-ino House;** *Le Corbusier (1914);* *(B)* **Sketches from** *Oeuvre Complete; Le Corbusier (1946–52)*

The original design of Dom-ino was simply an abstract structural type; later Le Corbusier added the staircase, perhaps indicating a commitment to its possible construction. This structure represented the minimum amount of material necessary for a building. In a later sketch Le Corbusier likened the structure to a bottlerack, which while remaining standard, could easily accept different bottles. (Copyright 1991 ARS, N.Y. / SPADEM.)

of cubism was that of layered and fragmented forms organized mathematically, a view that was to later influence Le Corbusier's architectural work. The notion of a complex mathematical type, combined with a love of Greek architecture, led him to the notion of a *classical form,* using *modern types* having an affinity with the *machine.* Thus his characterization of the dwelling as a "machine for living in," appearing in his *Vers une architecture* of 1923, meant something quite different from similar references in the Bauhaus. For Le Corbusier, this meant a building whose functions had been reduced to the necessary minimum; in this formulation can be seen a kind of hygienic asceticism.

Most of his ideas concerning the mass production of highly flexible standardized housing, which could be site-assembled, are to be found in his design of the Maison Citrohan of 1922; however, this structure remained speculative. The first opportunity to concretize these notions came in the design for the Maison La Roche-Jeanneret in 1923; in addition to resolving a difficult program, he projected an interesting series of spaces notable for their diversity (Fig 9.19). Curtis notes that the spaces have been cleverly linked in sequence to grant a gradual exploration of the interior. And he cites Le Corbusier's contention that, unlike typical Beaux-Arts axial plans, a good plan would contain diverse ideas and project volumes into space in a more subtle, ordered hierarchy, leading to the gradual revelation of a building's form and idea.[63]

In 1931 Le Corbusier writes, "We have barely begun. Our works are admissible for the building of a house, but for towns and social life . . . we are only at the stage of stammering our first words."[64] But he had already undertaken to address these issues in just such an environment for the 1925 Exposition des Arts Décoratifs in Paris, about which he later writes: "We

9.19

La Roche-Jeanneret House—Paris; *Le Corbusier (1923)*

Le Corbusier's task was to design this duplex for two very different clients, one who wished intimacy and another who needed much light, open space for displaying his art collection; this necessitated a concern for movement, vistas, viewing areas, and locations for art. The sketch *(A)* illustrates how the back wall was conceived as a thin membrane that could be punctured. It is interesting to compare this interior sketch with the one of Pompeii that similarly shows the door openings as punctures in a back wall *(B)*. The diagonal lines on the façade-elevation *(C)* indicate Le Corbusier's use of a formal proportional system to order exterior elements; this is reflected consistently, if less obviously, on the interior. (Copyright 1991 ARS, N.Y., / SPADEM.)

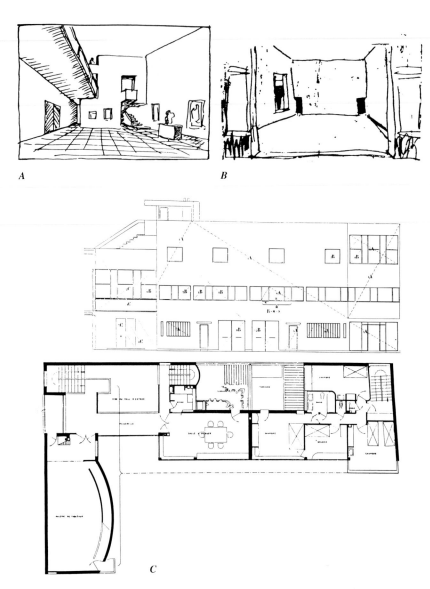

A   *B*

C

dissolubly link the equipment of the home (furniture) to architecture (the space inhabited, the dwelling), and to town-planning (the conditions of life of a society)."[65] The Pavilion de l'Esprit Nouveau (a model apartment for a model city) was designed to be inclusive—incorporating all the details of domestic life, chosen from manufacturers' catalogs (Fig 9.20). Reyner Banham comments that he thus created an entirely homogeneous visual setting, in some ways comparable with interiors designed by such masters as van de Velde or Mackintosh, but with a critical difference: "Only the structure is a work of design by the mind that created the environment, the rest was claimed to be a work of selection almost in the Duchamp manner from standard products, *objets-type,* already on the market."[66]

In this paragraph, Banham is referring to the distinction between Mackintosh's approach of designing both structure and interior artifacts, and Le Corbusier's choice to rely on mass-produced artifacts. Thus Le Corbusier furnished the apartment with objets types, such as a Thonet bentwood chair, oriental rugs, and Leger paintings. This choice of objects was based on an aesthetic standard of judgment that allowed him to select freely from machine-made, folk, and fine art objects. A question naturally arises about the exact nature of that aesthetic standard; Le Corbusier believed that

". . . when a thing responds to a need it is not beautiful," that real art rather consists of ". . . pure art—a concentrated thing free from all utilitarian motives."[67] He, therefore, chose the interior artifacts of the room (as opposed to the paintings on the wall) on the basis of their simple, modest, and utilitarian functionalism. The use of *object-types* would, therefore, permit an unimpeded appreciation of the fine art in the room; this distinction referred to even the furniture of his own design.

One of the purest statements of Le Corbusier's sense of a new Classicism may be his Villa Savoye (1929), at Poissy. This is a country villa with a processional entry, rather like Palladio's Villa Capra. From the exterior, the structure seems geometrically abstract and deceptively simple. In fact, the interior space is multilayered and complex, with a far richer relationship with nature than is first apparent; the use of the interior terrace allows the natural setting to penetrate to the structure's heart. Indeed, Le Corbusier's concern for health explains much of the design for this retreat, where one is to enjoy fresh air, sunlight, and intellectual engagement. In the use of planar elements, *pilotis* (columns) and complex geometry, a remarkable spatial consistency is maintained, as is a devotion to the classical elements of clarity and proportion (Fig 9.21).

Thus Modernism, by the mid-1930s, had spread throughout Western Europe and North America, using a fairly common set of assumptions and vocabulary known as the "International Style." Behind the reliance on glass, steel, and concrete (and their respective technologies), the use of interpenetrating planes and continuous space, and the importance granted machined products lay an abstract utopianism, masked by the term "functionalism."

9.20

Pavilion de l'Esprit Nouveau—Paris; *Le Corbusier (1925)*
Seen from the exterior, this model is clearly based on the ideas contained in his Dom-ino house; that is, a dwelling cell that could be inserted in a larger framework. This self-contained apartment takes advantage, in layout and function, of the lessons learned in the La Roche portion of Maison La Roche-Jeanneret. (Copyright 1991 ARS, N.Y., / SPADEM.)

A

9.21

Villa Savoye—Poissy; *Le Corbusier (1928–9)*
The aerial view *(A)* indicates the interior terrace, which is open to the elements. The window-wall adjoining the terrace allows this sunlight to stream into the living area *(B)*. Curiously, the means of maintaining contact with nature, the interior terrace, is an urban device. In this, Le Corbusier seems motivated by the same classical concerns as Palladio; that is, the ordering of nature by the siting of a geometric "jewel" in its midst. But Le Corbusier has replaced the outwardly expanding dome of Villa Capra with an inverted space—the terrace—which provides the contact with nature set in the program *(C)*. And in the contrast of the stable square building with the dynamic spiral stair and diagonal ramp *(D,)* this structure has replaced the Palladian axial calm with an emotional passage through space. (Copyright 1991 ARS, N.Y., / SPADEM.)

It was probably this polemic that the totalitarian governments of the 1930s reacted against in their insistence on politically "correct" models. For individuals like Hitler and Stalin (and later, Mussolini), this meant rejecting the tenets of Modernism, ostensibly for its spare and machined quality, but actually for its antinationalistic character. In each case, this meant a return to historical model.

B

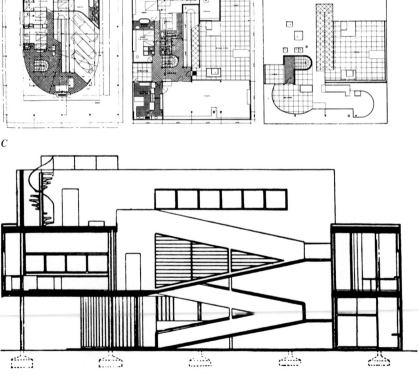

C

D

Emerging Building Types

10

Functionalism

Chapter nine is pointedly attentive to "mainstream" architecture; that is, it represents a fairly conventional view of what are usually considered the critical developments of the twentieth century. But they are certainly not the only developments, nor even the most revolutionary, despite their claim to a historically innovative functionalism. And even the attribution of that quality may be misplaced, especially when applied to the later phases of Modernism. Reyner Banham points out: "Functionalism, as a creed or programme, may have a certain austere nobility, but it is poverty-stricken symbolically. The architecture of the Twenties, though capable of its own austerity and nobility, was heavily, and designedly, loaded with symbolic meanings that were discarded or ignored by its apologists in the Thirties."[1]

He goes on to delineate two reasons for this phenomenon: first, its supporters were increasingly from "outside" the core movement; and second, its unacceptable ideological content meant that it was advisable to advocate this new architecture on the basis of logical and economic concerns rather than for its aesthetic or symbolic character, as that might stir nothing but hostility.[2] Thus Modernism, whatever its origin, came to be characterized by its mechanical aspects, a view that has suited developers of the postwar era for purely economic reasons.

In might, however, be asked whether functionalism, in the sense of a fundamental reexamination of utilitarian assumptions, was ever a hallmark of the International Style. In a piercing series of comments, Buckminster Fuller disputes that estimation:

> The International Style "simplification" . . . was but superficial. It peeled off yesterday's exterior embellishment and put on instead formalised novelties of quasi-simplicity, permitted by the same hidden structural elements of modern alloys that had permitted the discarded *Beaux-Arts* garmentation. . . . In such illusory ways did the "International Style" gain dramatic sensory impingement on society as does a trick man gain the attention of children. . . .[3]

This criticism is not without merit; the structural systems used by Mies van der Rohe and Le Corbusier were those already familiar to architects, and the technology was only the newest version of extant processes. Fuller later makes another point in regard to Modernism's limited agenda when he notes that the designers of the International Style used, for example, standard plumbing fixtures in their buildings. That is, they ventured only to persuade the manufacturers to modify the fixtures' surfaces, without enquiring into the overall problem of sanitary fittings themselves. "In short they only looked at problems of modifications of the surface of end-products, which end-products were inherently sub-functions of a technically obsolete world."[4]

Thus Fuller criticized Modernism for its failure to address the fundamental issues of design, settling instead for cosmetic changes in exterior aspects. In his *Modern Architecture since 1900,* William J.R. Curtis observes that while Fuller's criticisms may have had a point, as architectural criticism, his remarks were beside the point. "They remind one that, for all the rhetoric used in the twenties concerning the honest expression of function, structure, and technology, the game had to go on once removed, as it were, in the field of symbolic forms. . . ."[5] Curtis points out that "functionalist" slogans could not, in any case, be taken as anything more than rhetoric:

> . . . even those few architects of the 1920's who saw themselves as pursuing a purely functional architecture were still stuck with the fact that functions do not, on their own, generate forms. Even the most tightly defined set of requirements may be answered in a variety of ways, and *a priori* images concerning the eventual appearance of the building will enter the design process at some point.[6]

He concludes that function is inevitably translated through style, and the style in this instance contained form-notation that referred to functionalism. Curtis' observations are excellent; on the other hand, there is little evidence that Fuller intended his comments to serve as architectural criticism. Rather, they appear to reflect his conviction that such empty rhetoric was pointless in light of the environmental potential inherent in modern engineering, a potential ignored by Modernism. That the dominant movements of the 1920s had demonstrated little concern for the more prosaic realities of human habitation is reasonably clear, making Fuller's comments fair and cogent; especially as they came from the designer of the Dymaxion House.

Residential Design

The basic design for the 4D house (designated the Dymaxion House in 1929) was completed by Buckminster Fuller in 1928, and he filed a patent application that year regarding its essential features. It was intended to be, literally, "un machine d'habiter," an environment that would minimize daily tasks in addition to providing protection from the elements. Banham succinctly describes this remarkable structure: "As early as 1927, Fuller had advanced, in his Dymaxion House project, a concept of domestic design that might just have been built in the condition of materials technology at the time, and had it been built, would have rendered *Le Heures Claires* (Villa Savoye), for instance, technically obsolete before design had even begun."[7]

The Dymaxion concept represented a radical departure from the more conventional view of a dwelling; it was basically a hexagonal form with walls of variable-gauge plastic, hung by wires from the top of a duralumin mast housing the mechanical services. The structure was highly advanced, using the light-metal technology of aircraft construction, and postulated a fundamental division between *service core* (distributed through the service

10.1

4D Dymaxion House; *R. Buckminster Fuller (1928)*
Fuller referred to this design as the "clean-up model" of two earlier versions, and it demonstrates a far greater commitment to the implications of his idea than does the more conventional drawing submitted for a patent in 1927. The patent does, however, apply to any wire-wheel structure suspended from a central mast. (Copyright 1960, The Estate of Buckminster Fuller. Courtesy: Buckminster Fuller Institute, Los Angeles.)

mast) and *activity area* (a surrounding space of indeterminate size). In *The Dymaxion World of Buckminster Fuller,* Robert Marks describes its basic advantages:

> The central mast, in which basic utilities were factory-installed, came ready for instant use. The windowless walls were of transparent, but swiftly-shutterable, vacuum-pane glass. The house was to be dustless; the air drawn in through vents in the mast was filtered, washed, cooled or heated, then circulated. Laundry was automatically washed, dried, pressed, and conveyed to storage units. Clothes and dish closets, refrigerator and other food compartments contained revolving shelves rigged to move at the interruption of a light beam. The entire house was designed to be relatively independent of piped-in water, thus fully operative wherever it was erected.[8]

Marks continues to describe the advanced attributes of the house, such as atomizer baths that used only a quart of water and pneumatic floors and doors; he concludes that in this house ". . . the occupants were given ample space, and the logical arrangement of the equipment automatically developed the privacy appropriate to psychological grace."[9] The division between service core, which included all mechanical functions, and free-form activity area was revolutionary. For its projected cost to the consumer, once mass-production was under way, the house was revolutionary too. In 1928 Fuller had calculated its retail price to be $1,500; the adjusted 1960 price would have been $4,800, occupant-ready anywhere in the United States.[10] Fuller thereby envisioned, after admittedly high development costs, an incredibly inexpensive solution to the housing crisis—structures that could be marketed via the advanced production and sales methods of the automotive industry (Fig 10.1).

The Dymaxion House, in a much-altered form, did eventually reach realization as the Dymaxion Deployment Unit (D.D.U.) in 1940, and many of these units were used by the military during the war. A more advanced type was designed for production in 1944, designated the Dymaxion Dwelling Machine, but only two prototypes were built (Fig 10.2). Fuller's designs are fascinating for their consideration of virtually all the daily issues of domestic life, and their solution. That these had become important aspects

10.2

Dymaxion Dwelling Machine; *R. Buckminster Fuller (1944)*
The Dwelling Machine's amenities included two bedrooms, two baths, kitchen, living-room, and entry vestibule. The pattern of the mechanical enclosures ensured an absence of "dead corners," and a large living-room area of 28' (measured on the diagonal). The ventilation equipment was located on the roof, and the interior figure of the completed production model, named Wichita House, shows the 37' of plexiglassed panoramic view. (Copyright 1960, The Estate of Buckminster Fuller. Courtesy: Buckminster Fuller Institute, Los Angeles.)

of housing in the twentieth century is clear from this comment in *The Cost of Shelter* (1915):

> The house will become the first lesson in the use of mechanical appliances, in control of the harnessed forces of nature, and of that spirit of cooperation which alone can bring the benefits of modern science to the doors of all.[11]

Ellen H. Richards had been in the vanguard of the Home Economics movement in the last two decades of the nineteenth century, campaigning for "... a more scientific, professionalized approach to the house, its upkeep, and its daily life."[12] Indeed, it was Ellen Richards' group who founded the National Household Economics Association in 1893, thereby aiding in the establishment of homemaking departments in major universities and colleges across the United States. In her *Building the Dream,* Gwendolyn Wright notes that in the first years of this century, a new, highly motivated generation of home economists modernized the old Victorian ideal of the woman who uplifts society, by giving her a new instrument, science. "By treating the home as a laboratory, domestic scientists believed they could promote better health, better families, and more satisfied women."[13]

To this end, a broad spectrum of interests, from domestic scientists to public health officials, endorsed the vision of a domicile that was both simple and standardized, incorporating all available technology, especially in the area of hygiene. By the 1920s, it was believed that science would improve sanitary conditions, increase efficiency, and propose modern standards, using the expertise of sociologists, psychologists, and economists. In this sense, the period following World War I was simply an organized continuation of prewar standardization, during which time the developers extended their social controls:

> The middle-class suburb of the 1920's had covenants with regulations governing their style of architecture, the size of houses, policy toward cars, proximity of business and commerce, and restriction of entry to ethnic and religious minorities.[14]

Such belief in the redeeming virtues of science and engineering (social and technical) should have favored the production of Fuller's designs when they became viable in the late 1920s. But the public's devotion to the symbolic and familiar proved stronger than the simple desire for efficiency.

The buildings that initially met with favor from home economists were those of the Arts & Crafts movement. In his magazine *The Craftsman,*

10.3

Craftsman Fireplace Nook—*The Craftsman,* 1905; *Gustav Stickley*
This room is characterized by the high wainscotting, natural wood (including exposed beams), and recessed window seating. All the furniture is made to appear as though it is part of the planned scheme. (Source: *Craftsman Homes,* Gustav Stickley.)

10.4

Edgar J. Kaufmann House, Fallingwater—Bear Run, Pennsylvania; *Frank Lloyd Wright (1936)*
From the exterior, the concrete slabs seem to hover in space, vaulting over the stream below. This appearance is enhanced by the deeply set strip windows, which open to views on three sides; notably, the house avoids the complete domination of nature. (Perspective—copyright: The Frank Lloyd Wright Foundation, 1962, Talieson West; Section—courtesy: Fallingwater, Mill Run, Pa.)

Gustav Stickley professed an aesthetic that referred, through its rusticity, to an earlier, more "wholesome" (and moral) time. The massive stonework, rough-cut wood, and countrified simplicity proved to be quite popular. His homes were efficient and easily built, with plans available for purchase (Fig 10.3). But ultimately, these designs looked to the past, to a mythical time and place, for their content. In 1901 Edward Bok published the first of a series of *modern* designs by Frank Lloyd Wright, such as his "A Home in a Prairie Town" (Fig 9.1), which placed Craftsman values in a contemporary context. Thus a second great influence on residential housing was Frank Lloyd Wright, whose plans, available at modest cost through the *Ladies Home Journal,* had become popular with the general public. Sets of these plans were sold by the thousands, providing a generic aesthetic that prepared the way for the visual appearance of postwar tract housing.

An analysis of Wright's plan for "A Home" is revealing; an activity area is formed by conjoining the library, living room, and dining room. The kitchen remains separate, perhaps signaling Wright's expectation that servants would continue to be the norm, or frankly acknowledging its distasteful aspects. His commissions did come from wealthy clients, as evidenced by Robie House and the California buildings designed in the 1920s. Here his homes, like the Millard House in Pasadena, are introspective and idiosyncratic, as well as unusual in their use of textured concrete. They seem to suggest the idea of the house as shelter, psychologically separated from nature. In 1931 Wright noted that the sense of interior space in organic architecture coordinates with the enlarged means of modern materials. "The building is now found in this sense of interior space; the enclosure is no longer found in terms of mere roof or walls but as 'screened' space."[15] He later refers to this in *A Testament:*

> As interior space to be lived in becomes the reality of building so shelter thus emphasized becomes more than ever significant in character and important as a feature. . . . *To qualify this common-sense desire for shelter* as most significant feature of architecture is now in organic architecture of greatly increased importance.[16]

One of this century's most remarkable buildings, and a paradigm of shelter in nature, is his Fallingwater. This structure was designed as a vacation home; it consists of cantilevered planes of smooth concrete on a rough ashlar base, boldly projecting from a cliff face over a stream. The marked terrace extensions provide the protected interior with a screened view of the thick woods (Fig 10.4). Wright comments:

In this design for living down in a glen in a deep forest, shelter took on definite masonry form while still preserving protection overhead for extensive glass surface. These deep overhangs provide the interior, as usual, with the softened diffused lighting for which the indweller is invariably grateful, I have found.''[17]

Henry-Russell Hitchcock notes that this house combines two very different, though similarly romantic, views: the grandeur and significance of nature and the power of science. He concludes, ''A house over a waterfall sounds like a poet's dream. A house *cantilevered* over a waterfall is rather the realized dream of an engineer.''[18] The interiors are remarkably luxurious, with furniture crafted from rich walnut and walnut veneers whose graining is presented horizontally to echo the orientation of the house, and to prevent warping. And, as usual, the attention to detail is scrupulous. The plan of the house is unusual, in that it combines the large open space appropriate to a vacation home with private bedroom-balcony suites, so that both privacy and sociability are provided for (Fig 10.5).

Of far greater significance for postwar housing, however, was the design of a moderate-cost house, to be known as the Usonian home. Conceived during the 1930s as a response to the socioeconomic conditions of the period, the house served as an example of Wright's belief in human potential. In *The Living City,* he says, ''Noble life demands a noble architecture for noble uses of noble men. . . . The true center (the only centralization allowable) in Usonian democracy, is the individual in his true Usonian family home.''[19] This house was to be packaged in kit form, using a concrete-slab foundation containing hot-water radiant heating. A ventilation system was contained in the roof slab which, in its horizontal character, was clearly derived from his earlier designs. The walls were designed to take advantage of the new prefabrication methods which, it was thought, would solve America's housing problem. But the real importance of this design may lie in its redefinition of the interior.

In the Usonian house, the traditional dining room was replaced by a small area with a table, a composite of kitchen and living areas. This change may be regarded as a response to the servantless clients who would be likely to purchase such houses, as well as a reflection of the new informality in social

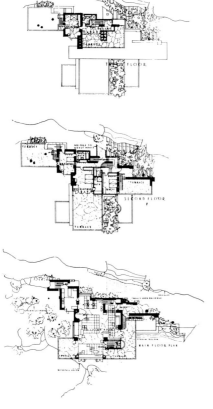

10.5

Edgar J. Kaufmann House, Fallingwater, Interior—Bear Run, Pennsylvania; *Frank Lloyd Wright (1936)*
The plans give some indication of the design's complexity, and Wright's adroit handling of the vertical axis. The living-room reflects his penchant for richly textured surfaces and simple shapes partially derived from the Southwest. (Plans—courtesy: Fallingwater, Mill Run, Pa.; Photo by: Hedrich Blessing, Chicago.)

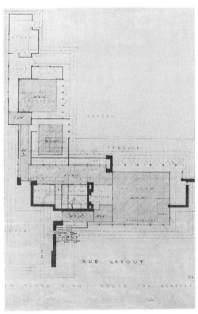

10.6

Herbert Jacobs House—Madison, Wisconsin; *Frank Lloyd Wright (1937)*
This house was one of Wright's first completed Usonian houses. The plan gives some indication of the design's complexity, and its division between the open living-dining-cooking area and the private bedroom wing. The bathroom and kitchen have raised ceilings for ventilation, and the long series of French doors open onto the generous garden. The materials are deceptively simple: board and batten over plywood for interior walls, and crossed 2″ × 4″ supports for the roof. (Copyright 1991: The Art Institute of Chicago. All rights reserved.)

life. Wright had already referred to the kitchen in the Malcolm Willey House (1934) as a *workspace,* one which abutted the living room. In the Herbert Jacobs House in Madison, Wisconsin, the dining area lies just between the spacious living room and the kitchen, now marked *cooking* in the plan (Fig 10.6). In *The Decorative Designs of Frank Lloyd Wright,* David A. Hanks points out that to eliminate unnecessary materials and reduce labor, Wright had to determine the *essential priorities* for the house:

> Radiators were replaced by radiant heating and light fixtures by recessed lighting; plastering, painting, and wallpaper were unnecessary; and basements and interior trim were eliminated. Most furniture was built in as part of the walls and simple enough to be constructed on the job site by millworkers or the owner rather than in a cabinet-making shop.[20]

What Wright considered essential was, however, as important as what was deleted. In *The Architectural Forum* (1938), he noted, "We must have as big a living room with as much garden coming into it as we can afford, with a fireplace in it, and book shelves, dining table, benches, and living room tables built in."[21] He also thought it critical that the architect should supervise the construction and design the furniture and landscaping; and, in the case of multiple development, plan the overall scheme. In his Usonian house, Wright managed to consider and address the key issues in moderate-cost housing, from spatial needs to cultural symbols. Curtis comments that: "It was no accident that Wright's formula should have been adopted so rapidly by building contractors and cheap home catalogues. For its free-plan interiors and exterior patios captured precisely the ethos of an emergent middle-class suburban existence."[22]

He also notes that while these houses were carefully detailed and proportioned, with individual variation at each site in Wright's hands, ". . . the insensitive imitators were all too often clumsy 'ranch-style' shoe-boxes, laid out in jerry-built monotony on the boom tracts of the 1950's."[23] It was the Usonian house, then, that formed the spatial paradigm for postwar American housing. But, ultimately, the model was driven by economic and political considerations, the third great influence on postwar housing.

Postwar Housing

While builders had erected multiple-unit housing with regional characteristics throughout the 1920s and 1930s, the type most favored was the prairie-style bungalow inspired by Wright's early designs. James Casey, in the *National Builder,* wrote, "The new type of home, now so popular, has utility for its fundamental principle. It aims to eliminate all that is superfluous, and to embody all modern improvements."[24] While such popularity played a part in determining housing types, even more important was the influence of housing agencies and government, and the policy-making power of suburban developers. Gwendolyn Wright points out that the developers set standards for construction before actually selling the lots and that these rules might ". . . specify minimum dimensions of lots and houses; placement of outbuildings, such as garages; optimal distance from house to street; even the style of architecture. . . ."[25]

Both the housing agencies and developers agreed that buildings ought to reflect "traditional" imagery; but while traditional imagery was approved by everyone in principle, that did not of itself mean that small, single-family houses had to be built in a predictably regular and dull manner. James Ford, director of the Better Homes in America architectural committee, remarked in 1931 that ". . . the majority of small homes built in America are ugly in design and inconveniently planned."[26] This group of architects had been founded in 1922 by Secretary of Commerce Herbert Hoover, with the aim of improving home design through lectures and design competitions; it is interesting that virtually all of the winners in the 1931–1932 competitions designed homes in regional styles.[27]

In another remarkable civic effort to aid those unable to afford an architect's services, the nonprofit *Architect's Small House Bureau* was founded in 1921. This organization comprised architects nationwide, operating under the loose control of the AIA (American Institute of Architects), and with the approval of the Department of Commerce. Limited to houses of six rooms or fewer, the Bureau supplied perspectives, complete working drawings and technical specifications, and necessary contractual documents; the cost for these ranged from $18.50 for a three-room house to $36.50 for a six-room house. It always counseled that this service did not truly substitute for the services of an architect, especially in the construction phase; although its 1929 publication *Small Homes of Architectural Distinction: A Book of Suggested Plans by the Architects' Small House Bureau, Inc.* contains many fine suggestions. The book is particularly notable for its theoretical outlook (however stated in simple language) and insistence on the predominance of the interior. In that way, follows advice on how to select a design:

> First determine how many rooms you want. Second, study only that group of designs which has the desired number of rooms. Third, eliminate from this group those plans which you do not wish to consider. Fourth, select from the finally retained plans the one which has the exterior you most prefer. To put it another way—read the plans first and choose the exterior afterward. . . . Choose also a home whose well-planned interior gives a practical explanation for every gable or dormer, every sweep of the roof.[28]

To aid in that process, most of the 254 plans in the book came with alternative exterior configurations, as well as choices in detailing (Fig 10.7). Other advice in the book is equally intriguing: the stipulation, for example, that architecture comprises ". . . logic, strength, and beauty";[29] and the noting of ". . . the fine results which may be obtained when the walls are of good proportions. . . ."[30] would be at home in an architectural text-book. There is even a reference to Ruskin. But while the Bureau acknowledged that standardized architecture would be boring, it also warned, "In considering the style of your home, remember that good design is always conservative."[31]

That position was later supported by the powerful *Federal Housing Administration* (FHA) when it was formed in 1934. The FHA's loan guarantees for participating banks made possible low-interest, long-term mortgages; instead of loans covering forty to fifty percent of appraised value, repayable in three to five years at five to nine percent interest, the FHA provided for loans covering eighty percent, repayable in twenty years at five to six percent interest. By 1935 nearly seventy percent of America's commercial banking resources were participants in this program, effectively giving the FHA the power to direct the country's domestic housing (particularly in the postwar years). And it was the severe postwar housing shortage that gave form and impetus to modern development. In 1946 it was estimated that within a decade, almost thirteen million units of housing would be needed;

Construction, 4-A-8: Wood frame, exterior finish wide siding, shingle roof, cement finished base course. Full basement

DESIGN 4-A-8

Construction, 4-A-11: Wood frame, exterior finish wide siding, roof of wood or composition shingles. Space in attic may be finished off. Full basement

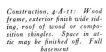

ARCHITECTURE—WHAT IS IT?

Whether in the small home or the mansion its principles are the same

Among many definitions of architecture is this one: "Architecture is putting into building certain qualities —namely, logic, strength, and beauty." Do these seem too high-sounding words when applied to small homes? Not when translated into familiar terms.

Logic means making the house convenient, livable, adaptable to both the family and the site. It means straightforwardness of plan that results in economy.

Strength, of course, means building with good materials. It means honest construction, durability, long life, low depreciation.

Beauty results from naturalness, from simplicity, and from good proportions. It depends upon careful attention to the small details as well as to the larger ones. It is the quality that makes the house a pleasure to see and to know, and to live in through the years.

These three combined make good architecture. Without any one of these a house is a mere building. It is not architecture. The bungalows on these pages show clearly that every important architectural quality that may be possessed by a larger house may also be possessed by the small house. All combine to a satisfactory degree a good plan, a fine exterior, and a sound system of construction.

Both houses on this page include large open porches, which, of course, may be screened or glazed for greater usefulness. In design 4-A-8, at the top of the page, the main roof and cornice have been extended to embrace the porch, thus giving the house an appearance of greater breadth. The entrance porch adds a desirable touch of variety, and the lattice is a delightfully decorative note. The columned porch across the front of the house at the bottom of the page, design 4-A-11, is suggestive of the fine old plantation homes of the South.

DESIGN 4-A-11

10.7

Design 4-A-11; Architects' Small House Service Bureau

(Source: *Authentic Small Houses of the Twenties*, Robert T. Jones, editor.)

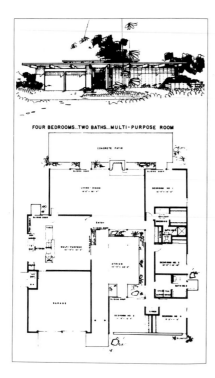

FOUR BEDROOMS...TWO BATHS...MULTI-PURPOSE ROOM

10.8

Tract-Housing Design—California; *Anshen & Allen (ca. 1949)*
This California architectural firm was retained by the builder Joseph Eichler to design this housing prototype. It was rather innovative in plan, with such unusual devices as atria and the popular family-room. It also reflects the strangely American penchant for using the garage as a design element of the façade, and so substituting it for the traditional front door. (Courtesy: Anshen & Allen, San Francisco.)

and prefabrication (and other war-related technologies) was to be the answer. Curiously, the government's faith in the efficacy of technology did not extend to support for Fuller's or Wright's ideas, both of whom had given this problem serious thought. And while professional home economists like Lillian Gilbreth were consulted (Gilbreth served on the planning committee of President Hoover's Conference on Home Building and Home Ownership in 1931), their influence on FHA standards had limited effect on the houses that qualified for government-guaranteed loans.

With support from the FHA and popular press, thousands of more conventional *prefab homes* were built, all conforming to what was becoming the new norm of housing. The power of the FHA in design decision-making was immense (if indirect); by 1957 it had financed over four and one-half million homes, all subject to its approval. With little incentive to individualize units, the developers built uniform structures en masse; the FHA's largest project contained eight thousand such units. The efforts to use architects in the planning process did, however, create new kinds of spaces, often with dramatic implications for interior designers (Fig 10.8). Some of these changes were described in a 1951 symposium held for architects and designers and included: new ways to treat open space, window walls, and strip windows; new types of storage systems; the handling of glass gable ends and skylights; space expansion through the use of mirror walls; and ways of handling eating bars, interior bathrooms, and patio areas. A similar symposium held in 1952 dealt with trends in kitchen design, like the merger of cooking and dining areas, pass-thru's and island counters, and the use of built-in appliances.[32]

In 1954, housing economist Miles Colean advised financial institutions to look more favorably on design progress and technical innovation, commenting that "novelty that produces real advance in comfort, convenience, and eye appeal can diminish risk."[33] But whatever interior technical improvements were approved by lenders, similar efforts on the exterior were discouraged by the FHA:

> . . . FHA evaluators were instructed to lower the rating score of houses with conspicuously modern designs because they were not considered a sound investment. . . . Even noted architects like Frank Lloyd Wright had their work rejected because of a low rating in the "Adjustment for Conformity" category. In November 1955, *House Beautiful* . . . declared that his houses were the quintessence of American life, the legacy of the Declaration of Independence. But Wright's efforts to develop prefabricated "Usonian" houses for a moderate-income community did not win FHA approval.[34]

Indeed, much tract housing (particularly ranch and split-level styles) was spatially derived from a combination of Wright's Usonian house and earlier Prairie School houses, with traditional elements like decorative shutters, generic columns, and porches added on. Developers across the United States appropriated Wright's concepts of radiant slab heating, sliding patio windows, carports, and, above all, the open plan—usually without any acknowledgement. And the "quintessence of American life" turned out to be the houses of Levitt and Sons, notable for their several Levittowns. By 1950 their factories were producing one house every sixteen minutes, with construction costs minimized by mass-produced prefabrication assembled on site. The interior was small, usually not more than seven hundred square feet, and featured Wright's dining alcove. Another parody of a Usonian idea was the built-in features, which included television sets and refrigerators, thus made eligible for inclusion in the mortgage (Fig 10.9).

The role of the social sciences, still modest in the 1920s, became much more authoritative in design decisions, and studies determined the "average American family." One of the better results of these studies was the FHA's *Minimum Property Standards* for one- and two-family homes, issued in 1959. It ". . . simplified, clarified, and raised standards, and included specifications for bigger rooms, better insulation, more storage space, and longer warranties."[35] Psychology was used for "livability studies," which, when coupled with surveys conducted by builders, were used to determine the sorts of activity areas houses should have. These "psychological profiles" had as their stated objective the satisfaction of customer needs, although it can be argued that the studies themselves helped form those needs.

In *The Place of Houses,* Moore, Allen, and Lyndon state that "rooms are *unspecific spaces,* empty stages for human action, where we perform the rituals and improvisations of living. They provide generalized opportunities for things to happen, and they allow us to do and be what we will."[36] But in the tract housing of the 1950s, space was very specific. Virtually every square foot was accounted for, prepared *a priori* for the family whose profile matched the specifications, and reflected specific functions in hierarchial order. Thus the difference between a 650-square-foot house and one fifteen percent larger was the "expendable" dining area; in the larger house it might occupy an alcove, and in the smaller one disappear. The middle ground was satisfied by the use of pass-thru's, possibly made into breakfast bars with tall stools. Other domestic changes reflected the new influence of television receivers which, by 1950, were becoming the focal point of the living room, at least in those houses not large enough to have family rooms. The impact of television can scarcely be calculated in terms of its influence as a medium; perhaps of equal significance is its role in shaping interior space. The furniture groupings that had reflected spatial relationships based on conversation now turned to the television set for their focus; and interpersonal eye contact became secondary to television sight lines, even when the set was nonfunctioning. There is considerable difference between a fireplace, which enjoys rich mnemonic associations even when not lit, and a machine that has meaning only when turned on.

Since normative standardization determined the basic layout of homes within a subdivision, family individuality usually found expression in the furniture, fabrics, and color selection. An interesting aspect of this situation was the development of new types of furniture based on purely economic considerations. The need to maintain affordable home purchase prices, coupled with an increased percentage of that price going into the technological aspects of a home (e.g., appliances and air conditioning), resulted in smaller square-footage than houses enjoyed in the 1920s. This reduction, in turn, meant less area to accommodate furniture and other artifacts of daily life. Much of designer Gilbert Rohde's (1894–1944) success was due to his understanding the public's changing requirements as early as 1930. He stated, "I know how people live and I know how they are going to live. Modern living calls for smaller houses with lower ceilings and this in turn calls for a different kind of furniture."[37]

This led Rohde to develop a new type, the sectional sofa. This seating system comprises modules consisting of armless, single-arm, and corner units. These can be arranged in various configurations, which give the appearance of built-in pieces or can occupy an open plan (Fig 10.10). Rohde's designs formed a paradigm of furniture design for the 1950s; and his ideas were echoed in the statements of such designers as George Nelson, who notes, ". . . the size of the room is not one of the psychological factors determining its comfort. . . ."[38] Nevertheless, it was often such considerations that were responsible for the success of his designs (Fig 10.11). Nor did he design furniture alone; in his Kitchen Work Center (1944), he con-

10.9

Bernard Levey and Family—Levittown, New York (1950)
This model house was published in *Life,* which helped popularize a firm that otherwise relied very little on publicity. The house contained two bedrooms, living-room, kitchen, and dining alcove, with provision for expansion in the attic. Preformed materials were delivered to the site, and assembled piecemeal by nonunion labor to reduce costs. Many of the small annual innovations were to become standard items in the building industry. (Source: Bernard Hoffman, *Life Magazine.* Copyright Time Warner, Inc.)

10.10

Sectional Sofa and Tables—New York Showroom; *Gilbert Rohde (1939)*
The shapes of the sectional sofa, mirror, cocktail table, and even the dropped ceiling are biomorphic in nature; both the furniture designs and shapes, in type and form, reflect a new casualness in American furnishing. Opening his own office in 1929, Rohde continued to supply designs (notably for the Herman Miller Furniture Company) until his death in 1944. These designs were to alter the course of contemporary design. (Courtesy: Herman Miller, Inc., Zeeland, Mich.)

10.11

Comprehensive Storage System (CSS); *George Nelson (1959)*
Nelson appreciated the flexibility needed in a system required to display and store possessions in a small space. This multipurpose furniture system included twenty-two different components, such as drawers, desks, shelves, and vertical dividers for record storage, that could be arranged in various configurations. The components, supported by adjustable aluminum poles, could be added or subtracted to fit varying height and width conditions. After Rohde's death, Nelson helped maintain the considerable reputation of the Herman Miller firm. (Courtesy: Herman Miller, Inc., Zeeland, Mich.; Photo: Rooks.)

sidered the problem of the rationalized food-preparation and dining areas.

One of the most important legacies of postwar housing types has been the altered definition of scale and proportion. Rather than scale's being based on the hierarchial valuation of specific rooms (and their function), it instead had to relate to an open plan with conjoined (and multiple) functions. And, in any case, these buildings lacked the architectural details that usually grant scale. The result has been a view of space as characterless, save for the clues derived from furniture and other artifacts. Proportion likewise has lost much of its prior content, as it became based on fixed measurements and standard manufacturing dimensions. The use of standard two- by four-inch studs, four- by eight-foot sheets of plywood and drywall, and preformed framing elements like windows and doors has resulted in predictable interior elements and relationships. Moreover, the fixed ceiling height has rendered any spatial alterations in the other two dimensions proportionally meaningless. Moore notes that relatively small variations in ceiling height can change spatial perception more than the same variations applied to the width and length of rooms:

> One explanation of this is, of course, the fact that in most rooms the vertical dimension is considerably less than either of the horizontal ones, and so small changes in it are more noticeable than the same changes applied to the plan. But it also seems true that the vertical dimensions of rooms, since they are relatively free from ''functional'' imperatives, are able to carry more than their share of emotional content.[39]

One intriguing aspect of the sacrifice of the expressive aspects of scale and proportion is that historically it has been these very qualities that distinguished the house from the apartment.

High-Rise Living

Apartment complexes, in the sense of two or more rented dwellings under one roof, have been a fact of urban existence for almost two thousand years. Rome, that most urban city, was as much characterized by its *insulae,* complex apartment blocks, as it was its temples and civic buildings. Such housing was then, as now, usually the result of urban land shortage coupled with the lure of economic opportunity in the cities. With the urban expansion that followed the Renaissance, speculative construction became increasingly common in European cities. Across Europe, the rental unit—little changed from Roman times—became the common urban dwelling. Still, this dwelling type, in its various forms, usually remained barely regulated housing for the poor.

During the second half of the nineteenth century, industry's need for concentrated labor supplies encouraged the growth of urban housing, usually taking the form of ghetto tenements. This was particularly true in the factory towns and cities of the eastern United States, where the inhabitants of these ghettos tended to be newly landed immigrants or displaced members of an indigenous rural population. Gwendolyn Wright comments that as middle-class Americans looked back from their suburbs, they noted with horror the poverty, overcrowding, and disease in these ghettos. She also notes that while the term *tenement* had become an Americanism by the mid-nineteenth century, its derivation from medieval English suggested ''. . . an abode for a person or for the soul, in which someone else owned the property.''[40] The *Oxford English Dictionary* actually discerns between ''a building or house to dwell in'' and the secondary, ''an abode; a dwelling place,

10.12

The Stuyvesant—New York City; *Richard Morris Hunt (1869)* These apartments were popularly called "French Flats" because of their suggestion, in layout and demeanor, of rather fashionable Parisian prototypes. They contained two units, each with balcony, per floor. Notably, they also contained individual baths, and provision for servants. (Courtesy: Museum of the City of New York.)

esp. as applied to the body as the abode of the soul." But if Wright has taken some liberty in conflating the two definitions, it was a view shared by tenement-dweller and suburbanite.

The physical conditions of most tenements, coupled with a profound belief in the morality and independence associated with one's own (detached) home, permanently stigmatized all apartment life. The apartment came to be seen as suitable primarily for the indigent, who were characterized by their transience and questionable character. Such value judgments applied even to the apartments of the wealthy, which were seen as useful only for certain approved purposes, such as temporary homes for single professional people or young married couples. This tended to be society's view even while it acknowledged the significant advantages apartment life offered. One of the first apartment buildings to be built in the United States was the Stuyvesant Flats in New York, designed by Richard Morris Hunt in 1869 and consisting of suites of rooms for families and single men. This elegant building had the appearance of a town home, using a mansard roof to disguise its true size and function. Also French was the term for these units—apartments—from *appartement,* which had previously described any series of connected rooms. Hunt's design was successful; within ten years, close to two hundred sets of these "French flats" were constructed in New York (Fig 10.12).

The advantages to apartment living were clear: central steam heat; gas mains for lighting; and fully equipped bathrooms in each unit.[41] Technological improvements that followed included elevators, hot and cold running water, telephones, electric service, and even central vacuum cleaners. Disadvantages were both obvious—cramped rooms and lack of aural privacy—and subtle—the stigma still associated with such rootless life. Indeed, apartment complexes have been the frequent object of zoning restrictions reflecting the bias toward single-family dwellings. Surveys have indicated people's overwhelming preference for living in single-family houses as opposed to apartments; even surveys of apartment dwellers themselves tend to confirm the apartment as temporary expedient. Such preference has never been absolute, as evidenced by the significant movement, with various political motivations, to the semicommunal apartment-hotel. But while this form enjoyed some popularity before 1920, the combination of appliances available for domestic consumption and the spread of single-family homes, reduced that option as a real alternative.

In his essay, *The apartment house in urban America,* John Hancock observes that the most highly esteemed and predominant type of housing in America has always been the detached single-family house, preferably occupant-owned and separated from the neighbors, and yet, ". . . Americans from most social groups have been apartment dwellers at some stage of their lives—and increasingly this is the case."[42] He states that apartment users have always had two things in common; they are renters, and they are considered by society to be in transient social state, at best.[43] It is precisely that image of transience that so concerned the renters of even expensive apartments. When Mrs. E.F. Hutton was persuaded to sell her palatial townhouse in 1924, a condition of sale was that the builder exactly recreate her townhouse on the top three floors of the high-rise that replaced it. The result was a fifty-four-room apartment in the mirror image of her former dwelling. This was not simply the desire to maintain the customary, but a remarkable attempt to grant an apartment all the attributes of a proper house. This desire to associate apartments symbolically with the private home had already led to such oddities as decorative fireplace mantels. Another way of evoking the private house was to vary the single-level plan, which had been attacked for its lack of privacy and "immorality." Thus the Century

Apartments in New York (1931) were characterized by striking corner balconies, multiple penthouses, and more than fifty variations of floor plan, with unit sizes ranging from one to eleven rooms, including three-room duplex configurations.

In *The House as Symbol of the Self,* Clare Cooper comments that most Americans find the apartment complex unsatisfactory as a home because it fails to provide territory on the ground, violates the image of what constitutes a house, and is perceived unconsciously as a threat to one's self-image as a unique personality.[44] She concludes, "The house form in which people are being asked to live is not a symbol-of-self, but the symbol of a stereotyped, anonymous filing-cabinet collection of selves, which people fear they are becoming."[45] It is clear that Cooper is not speaking of such anomalies as the Century, but of the stacked (and anonymous) units that typify most apartment complexes. Indeed, one might argue that the Century has, in its eccentric layout, squandered the very efficiency for which the skyscraper form has been used. But must efficiency take such a structured form? In his *Delirious New York,* Rem Koolhaas reproduces a cartoon published in a 1909 edition of *Life,* dubbing it the 1909 Theorem, an illustration of the ideal skyscraper (Fig 10.13):

> A slender steel structure supports 84 horizontal planes, all the size of the original plot. Each of these artificial levels is treated as a virgin site, *as if the others did not exist* . . . this indeterminacy means that a particular site can no longer be matched with any single predetermined purpose . . . which makes architecture less an act of foresight than before. . . ."[46]

While addressing the ideological drawbacks to apartment life, the solution may leave something to be desired. Rather than *exterior modules* (houses) placed on the structural frame, the answer may lie with *interior modules* placed within a frame. Hence Le Corbusier's Pavilion de l'Esprit Nouveau of 1925, essentially a plug-in module in a concrete frame, surfaces once again. In his *Supermannerism,* C. Ray Smith notes that this notion of "plug-in architecture" is central to the vision of certain contemporary architects and comments, "As elements of plug-in, clip-on systems, 'boxes' raise the tinkertoy construction system idea to an even larger dimension than before, up to a point where a whole living box is a tinkertoy part for a plug-in cage or structural frame."[47] The well-known Habitat, designed by Moshe Safdie for Montreal's Expo '67, is a prime example of this type of assemblage. Habitat consists of 354 prefabricated concrete boxes, which provide apartments ranging in size from one-bedroom, six-hundred-square-foot units, to four bedroom, seventeen-hundred-square-foot units. An inversion of Le Corbusier's idea, the boxes were stacked in a cluster, presenting an image of a hillside village. Thus he has combined the apartment's solution to land-constraint with an articulation suggestive of single-family houses. But the result so lacked traditional symbolism that it initially failed to gain general acceptance (Fig 10.14).

Significantly, in America's major cities apartment construction kept pace with the building of single-family homes through the 1960s; in 1972 apartment construction came to 1,047,000 units, compared with 1,309,000 units of single-family homes.[48] Only after 1976, for a variety of reasons discussed in the next chapter, did single-family housing radically outstrip apartment construction. But this is only part of the picture; while the population of the central city has, overall, decreased in the past forty years, the number of separate households (usually apartments) has continued to increase. Moreover, since 1965, suburban apartments have become increasingly familiar. Urban and suburban apartment units' common denominator is their customer profile, and high rents. Hancock notes that in profile, renters are

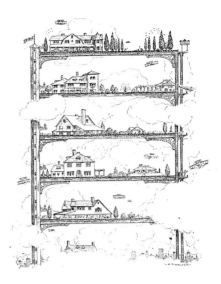

10.13

"1909 Theorem"
Koolhaas notes that as the individual floors are carried with complete neutrality on the structural frame, so "life" inside the building is itself fractured. This may simply be regarded as a poetic representation of urban life—each unit in isolation. (Source: *Life Comic Weekly,* March 4, 1909.)

10.14

Habitat—Montreal, Canada; *Moshe Safdie & Associates (1967)*
The interior consists of 354 standard size boxes arranged asymmetrically to provide 158 apartments, each box conceived as a quasi-independent unit. These "cells" await the installation of kitchen and bath modules; notably, each unit has a private terrace. (Drawn by: J. Malnar.)

10.15

Marina City—Chicago; *Bertrand Goldberg (1959)*
Goldberg's belief that "the box is not the universal package for functions of living in contemporary society" led him to develop a theory of kinetic space as expressed in this building's interiors. Noted for being the first government-sponsored downtown apartment project, its unusual circular shape and non-parallel interior walls were intended to give the illusion of a larger room; other benefits include more direct mechanical distribution, and more usable square-footage. (Courtesy: Bertrand Goldberg, Chicago.)

predominantly young (seventy percent under thirty-four years old), have a low income, and live either alone (fifty-seven percent) or in small households (two to three persons—thirty-six percent). "In effect," he says, "renters are on the lower rungs of what Constance Perin calls 'the ladder of life: from renter to owner'—newcomers in transition to ownership at best, forever doomed outsiders at worst."[49] Moreover, Perin's studies in Houston and Philadelphia suggest that the distinction between owner and renter is read as a primary social sign, used to categorize and evaluate people, in much the same way as race, income, occupation, and education.[50] Ironically, from 1890 to 1970, home ownership rose from thirty-seven percent to sixty-two percent, and housing debt rose from twenty-eight percent to sixty-one percent—effectively creating a nation of home-owning debtors. And not all have made the transition; apartment construction has also grown since 1960, reaching a national high of forty-two percent in 1969. While this growth did not keep pace with that of single-family housing, apartments obviously remain a fact of life.

As the profiles of renters have remained fairly constant, so have standard design parameters. For example, in the 1920s, three- to five-room apartments were the most popular types, and still are, and relatively affluent people still choose apartment buildings for reasons connected with service, views, and address.[51] But as the broader range of renters continue to be either single people or people in transition to ownership, even smaller units are popular as well. Chicago's Marina City, designed in 1964 by Bertrand Goldberg, comprises two sixty-two-story towers. It was conceived as a self-contained complex, with shops, restaurants, theaters, and a skating rink. Of special interest is the layout of the 896 apartments. They are split into pie-shaped wedges, rentable in one-, one-and-one-half-, and two-wedge configurations; these are indicated as efficiency, one-bedroom, and two-bedroom units, each with small kitchen and bath (Fig 10.15). And, typical of high-rise buildings, the larger, more expensive units are on the upper floors. Albert Mehrabian, in his *Public Places and Private Spaces,* relates this phenomenon to human territoriality:

> Apartments located at the upper levels of a building are more in demand because their superior position implies dominance, a feeling of being above it all, or at least of having more people under than above you. These higher apartments are more pleasant because they are farther away from street noise and provide more stimulating views or panoramas.[52]

Thus the height allows the apartment dweller some opportunity to screen out unwelcome intrusion without becoming isolated.

Marina City points to some of the problems in apartment design: limited space, often in difficult configurations; transient clients, which mitigates against built-ins; spatial standardization not always amenable to certain furniture types; standard building features like window covering; and the ever-present problem of individualization. Of all these problems, the last is probably the most difficult to address. Clare Cooper notes that "the fact that the decoration of the house interior often symbolizes the inhabitant's feelings about self is one that has long been recognized."[53] This is echoed by Mario Praz, when he says, "This is the house in its deepest essence: a projection of the ego. And furnishing is nothing but an indirect form of ego-worship."[54] Ironically, while the apartment is less amenable than the single-family home to such attention, it is the high-rise apartment that most requires it.

The Office Environment

During the past 150 years, the economic and logistical realities of industrialization have encouraged a physical separation of businesses' administrative and production sectors. Specifically, there has been a tendency for business to concentrate its managerial, sales, and accounting activities within suites of offices located in relatively small urban areas, isolated from the production aspects. Soaring land value in central cities has meant that office structures, unlike production facilities, have tended to be vertical. As the isolation of the office is a relatively recent phenomenon, the needs of business have effectively evolved a new building type. But as Alan Colquhoun notes, "Both programmatically and morphologically, this building type differs so greatly from any traditional type that when historical forms are applied to it, they operate in a kind of semantic void."[55] That is, the type is so new, that it has yet to evolve its visual character; often resulting in new functions residing in older forms and representing different activities. Colquhoun refers to this as a "lack of connection between the purposes of the building and the historical associations of its artistic form."[56]

While the office structure is not an American invention, its peculiar character was early appreciated (and exploited) here. In an article first published in *Lippincott's* in 1896, Louis Sullivan declared that the architects of this generation were now brought face to face with something brand new, ". . . namely, that evolution and integration of social conditions . . . that results in a demand for the erection of tall office buildings."[57] After stating the conditions calling for the design of such a building type, Sullivan concludes that ". . . in it a new grouping of social conditions has found a habitation and a name."[58] His observation is remarkably close to prescience; but, in fact, he fails to pursue its implications. Indeed, only a few paragraphs later, he describes the mechanics of building such a structure; he notes that above the mezzanine there should occur ". . . an indefinite number of stories of offices piled tier upon tier, one tier just like another tier, one office just like all the other offices—an office being similar to a cell in a honey-comb, merely a compartment, nothing more."[59] In the end, Sullivan looked at the problem purely as an architect, and his concern was with the more familiar problem of finding an aesthetic solution to a new situation. He had much to say about those designers who manifested a "lack of connection" between this building type's "purpose" and the alien "artistic forms" they dressed it in.

Sullivan tacitly assumed that the interior character of such buildings was the responsibility of the particular occupant; if there was a method to such design, he did not acknowledge it. But the interior character of the office does depend on *two earlier models:* first, the private chambers of the Renaissance bankers and merchants whose needs were so carefully noted by Alberti; and second, the familiar model of the factory assembly line. In the first instance, office interiors can draw on the rich history of such spaces as the Studiolo of Francesco I de'Medici, which was located in his residence and demonstrated his role as a patron of the arts in Florence (Fig 10.16). In this model are two of the characteristics found in executive offices: the residential atmosphere's reflection in the furnishings and rich detailing, and the use of art to display gentility as well as corporate support for humanistic values. This institutional power is usually reflected in the noninstitutional character of executive offices and in the prevalence of personal and artistic artifacts usually denied lesser administrators. In his *Office Buildings and Organisational Change,* Francis Duffy notes that buildings betray our values, and offices particularly reveal the values of those who build them and work in them. He says that "it is easy . . . to detect in any plan of an office interior layout which shows furniture as well as room size those managers who have been powerful enough to appropriate spatial as well as organisational influence."[60] But he also warns that while many assumptions about the office are commonly used, there is, in fact, ". . . no full theoretical understanding of the way in which buildings relate to office organisations;"[61] that is, which design elements relate to what.

The second model has evolved from the sorts of efficiency studies originally conducted in factories (e.g., Taylor and Gilbreth) and then transferred to secondary office levels, like secretarial pools and bookkeeping services. Concerned with greater work efficiency, they rely on either rectilinear grid arrangements that use geometric regularity, or irregular, clustered arrangements based on paper flow and communications. Thus the appearance of

10.16

The Studiolo of Francesco de'Medici—Florence; *Giorgio Vasari (1570–2)*
Although this is a small room, a luxurious effect is achieved by the display of the Mannerist painting collection and the few, but finely detailed, pieces of furniture. (Source: Alinari / Art Resource.)

the larger office work area (sometimes referred to as the cabbage patch) may be characterized by rows of orderly desks and work stations, or scattered groups of work stations gathered in common-purpose units (Fig 10.17). The particular choice of layout, however, is largely dependent on corporate style. No matter the layout, a line is drawn between the upper, executive levels of the office hierarchy, and the lower, worker levels; a line made clear by an appearance that usually makes written rules superfluous. Both the office organization and the company's reward and advancement systems depend on this visual code.

Whatever the particular style, the office is driven by certain determining factors; Duffy argues that there are four parameters that need to be defined to determine the nature of the design task:

- Office Technology—those tasks to be performed, the equipment needed to perform them, and the subsequent communication and work patterns that develop

- Office Organization—the network of relationships between people, and the hierarchial systems used

- Building Construction—the materials and methodologies available to the designer

- Real Estate Factors—the prevailing economic conditions that affect the development of a particular property[62]

He says that the first two factors relate to internal concerns, and the latter two are external functions; and concludes that the relationship between the two is critical to the design process.

Of all the design tasks related to the interior, those related to office organization may be the most important. The relationships among the people in an office are numerous, and the smooth operation of these links accounts in large measure for corporate success. The amount of control over employees, their own various interactions, and the business's institutional rewards all directly influence office design—from location and size of offices to personal items allowed on desks. As noted, two managerial styles, very different in scope and execution, have prevailed: first, scientific management principles, in which employees are seen as responsive primarily to financial reward; and second, a recognition that employees have ''. . . innate needs for identity, stimulation, and security,'' which require satisfaction.[63] The first attitude often results in row upon row of identical desks, since this is seen to be physically and economically most expedient (Fig 10.18).

There are several explanations for this: first, the repetition of plan and regular layout permit quantity purchases and speed in assembly; second, such regularity can display corporate solidity and the appearance of equality among the employees; and third, what Duffy refers to as the dominance of external real estate factors. He points out that buildings tend to be seen as negotiable commodities rather than useful places, which is obvious in the impact of land values on the massing of buildings—and in the emphasis on modular construction intended to make subdivision easier.[64] But equally responsible for the standard plan is the long-standing dependence on pyramidal organization in American business, an organization fundamentally based on military analogues. Albert Mehrabian notes:

> In large, older buildings, individual floors often express the dominance aspects implicit in the hierarchy. The corner offices are designed to be occupied by senior executives or heads of departments because they have

A

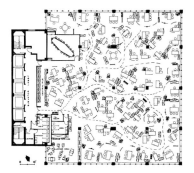

B

10.17

(A) Conventional Layout for du Pont Freon Division—Wilmington, Delaware; *(1967);* **(B) Office-Landscape Plan for du Pont Freon; Wilmington, Delaware;** *Quickborner Team (1967)*

The differences, theoretically and practically, between these two plans for the same square-footage are startling. Edgar Kaufmann, Jr., stated that "clustering is the pattern of human life; regularity is the pattern of theory." Despite the efficiency of the latter plan, business still relies on conventional layouts; this is probably a reflection of corporate distrust of employee integrity and competence, and a systemic need to avoid even the appearance of chaos. (Reprinted with permission from *Progressive Architecture* [May 1968]. Copyright 1968, Reinhold Publishing Corporation.)

10.18

Interior of Administration Building, Larkin Building—Buffalo, New York; *Frank Lloyd Wright (1904)*
Wright's building has been regarded as the prototype of the modern office structure, in its hierarchial organization and application of scientific management principles. The corporate image suggested by regimented rows of employees—sharply divided and under the scrutiny of the supervisor—is reinforced by the use of modern technology and wallmounted slogans. The central atrium further strengthens that corporate identity and organization. (Photo—courtesy: The Museum of Modern Art, New York.)

more windows. . . . One-window offices are occupied by senior middle-management personnel; junior and more subordinate workers occupy an interior set of windowless and usually doorless cubicles or partitioned spaces.[65]

And the general office staff, as noted, occupy the open central areas, as accessible as the executive offices are inaccessible. These formal and informal patterns of status result in the most space (and desirable location) given to the fewest employees, although, as Mehrabian points out, "such floor plans express and maintain more rigidity, formality, and bureaucratic fussiness than sophisticated managers now consider desirable."[66] He points out, however, that the use of cubicles (work stations) to increase employee status through privacy, has tended to constrict office communications.

The second view is more complex, often resulting in individual offices with allowance for personalization. This is in keeping with Abraham Maslow's hierarchial ordering of human needs, which are (in ascending order) the physiological ones, security, love or a sense of belonging, reputation or self-esteem, and (the highest) self-actualization.[67] Using this information, Dr. Douglas McGregor developed his Theory Y, which is in his book, *The Human Side of Enterprise.* This theory postulated a very different approach than that based on scientific management principles. In *The Social Contract,* Robert Ardrey notes that this theory held that, "granted security, the worker was to be trusted, consulted, de-specialized, given every possible control over his own job, encouraged to learn others, allowed identity with the end product of his efforts."[68] But while there have been some attempts to accommodate these ideas in the office (if only loosely), the standard plan continues to be managerially popular.

These alternative ways of viewing office layout gained currency in the mid-1960s, often being referred to as *office landscaping.* Duffy notes that the basic ideas of this method stem from management consultancy and cites three points of origin: first, the sorts of scientific work studies that were developed at the turn of the century; second, the desire to create an egalitarian and relaxed work situation; and third, the idea of an integrated (cybernetic) system.[69] Curiously, two of the three points cited by Duffy that were used to support an "open" office plan are identical to those cited earlier to support more rigid and "orderly" office arrangements. Yet either conclusion can legitimately be inferred. C. Ray Smith comments on the "landscaping" phenomenon: ". . . systematic chaos is accepted, developed to bring out the inclusive vitality of human endeavor. . . . To the designers who espouse chaos, the results of office landscape are exonerated by the fact that actual uses by people are the true and proper determinants of its organized—or disorganized design."[70]

In these alternative plans, the emphasis is on traffic-based furniture arrangement, interpersonal communication, and paper flow. This system was developed in Germany by Eberhard and Wolfgang Schnelle, whose work was characterized by the use of portable furniture and casual desk arrangements. Their intent was to eliminate barriers, and the economic advantages of circulation routes being integrated into the work spaces could be documented by square-footage studies. Notwithstanding, this methodology lost its popularity before 1980 for reasons not altogether clear; however, the development of the work station and the loss of clear territorial demarcation may both have played a role. This lack of clear understanding about how the modern office functions is not surprising; as a type, it is fairly new, and still in the process of evolving. And, we have only lately come to appreciate the importance of the human dimension in design.

Part III

The Measure of Interior Space

The Human Dimension 11

Organizational Factors

The nineteenth century, with its progressive industrialization, witnessed and exploited a remarkable range of technological innovations. The second distinction is an important one; previous centuries had certainly seen a wide range of inventions, from the pneumatic automatons invented by the Greeks of Alexandria, to the various mechanical contraptions envisioned during the Renaissance. The eighteenth century, in particular, witnessed the invention of some clever devices, like Jacques de Vaucanson's mechanical musicians and lifelike duck (1738); such was their fame that Vaucanson was later employed as Inspector of the Silk Manufactures, where in 1740, he invented a mechanical loom for figured silks.[1] The loom, unlike the duck, was not exploited, and it remained for Jacquard to revive those ideas in 1804 and produce a commercially viable machine. Until the nineteenth century, inventiveness was usually the province of well-educated people only secondarily interested in invention's economic potential. In his fascinating study, *Mechanization Takes Command*, Siegfried Giedion contends that a "... collective fervor for invention" and its systematic, rationalized exploitation first occurred in the 1860s; and nowhere more dramatically than in the United States, which, by 1940, was a technological model.

Mechanization occurred in all areas of activity; industrial, agricultural, and domestic. The degree to which it became all-pervasive is extraordinary, and it relied on certain key elements. Giedion identifies these as: *invention* itself, especially applied to the practical elimination of handicraft; *mass production,* as exemplified by the assembly line; and *scientific management,* especially as seen in time-work studies, themselves a logical outcome of a nineteenth-century interest in the mechanics of movement. These elements first appeared in commercial applications, such technology coming only late to the home. Indeed, the time lag between an invention and its domestic dissemination is striking. The reasons for this involve the tedious and costly erection of the necessary infrastructure (like gas and electric service and water mains), the initial expense of adapting industrial appliances for home use, and the fundamental changes in domestic life that their service entailed. Giedion notes that the "rationally planned mechanical core" (service core) was at least partly a reaction to more servantless households and the high cost of mechanical utilities.[2] By 1920 these elements collectively shaped the contemporary American home.

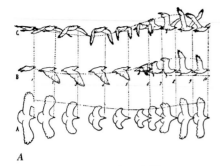

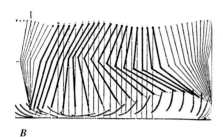

11.1

(A) Gull's Flight Recorded; *E.J. Marey (1890);* **(B) Oscillations of the Leg in Running;** *E.J. Marey (pre-1885)*
Marey graphically represented types of continuous movement as they occurred spatially. To better understand the movement of a seagull, images from three cameras were translated to a two-dimensional drawing. The result is a flight pattern seen from three different positions. The diagram illustrating a running leg was developed from photographs of a model dressed in black, with a metallic strip running down the side of the limbs. (Source: Les Chronophotographies, and Le Vol des Oiseaux, E.J. Marey.)

The scope of Giedion's text is broad, and the three elements identified above do not equally apply in considerations of the household, as he makes clear:

> The factory and the household have only one factor in common, but a crucial one. Both must improve organization and curtail waste labor. . . . The curtailing of household labor is achieved through the mechanization of work processes once performed by hand. . . . Improvements in organization are achieved by closely reviewing old established work processes and ordering them in a more rational way. . . . Curtailed household drudgery and improved organization lead to greater independence. . . .[3]

And as the rational organization of domestic work preceded the new household machines that were to curtail that work, it may be regarded as more critical to the shaping of interior space.

Giedion regards the idea of *movement* as essential to mechanization, whether viewed in the context of the invention's function or in its actual use. Incorporating movement in the machine is fundamental to the concept of the automaton and hence quite old. The scientific study of human movement, however, became practical only with photographic techniques. Thus the discoveries of Etienne Jules Marey, the French physiologist and inventor, were critical to the understanding of movement. His early work centered on the recording of muscular movements on blackened cylinders (the Spygmograph), but he later used photography to record motion in every form of creature, from humans and horses to birds and insects. Of special interest are the studies of human limbs in progressive movement, which explicitly indicated distance and direction (Fig 11.1). Others worked in the same vein; Eadward Muybridge produced many studies of sequential movement, and artist Thomas Eakins photographed single-plate motion studies. In the latter instances, the intent was primarily aesthetic and resulted in such things as animated ''flip-books'' and, still later, motion pictures. But others saw photography as a tool for timework studies, and while there is no clear evidence of Marey's work's being used as a model by the production engineers that were soon to follow, their methods certainly parallel those of Marey and Muybridge.

The two best known of these engineers were Frederick Winslow Taylor (1856–1915) and Frank B. Gilbreth (1868–1924); although Taylor's studies initially had more impact, Gilbreth went on to execute remarkably comprehensive visual studies in the tradition of Marey. Gilbreth's approach was different from Taylor's; where Taylor tended to apply his theories to efficient industrial production, Gilbreth was more interested in the nature of movement itself and applied his ideas freely to all aspects of work, with precise photographic study. That is, while Taylor viewed movement in the task-related aggregate, Gilbreth refined each movement with photographic accuracy ''. . . to eliminate needless, ill-directed, and ineffective motions.''[4] (Notably, he often collaborated with psychologist Lillian M. Gilbreth, who became influential in the Home Economics movement in the 1920s.) Such early studies led Gilbreth to improve the craft of bricklaying, so that individual production was tripled, with decreased possibility of back injury. In his influential *Principles of Scientific Management* (1911), Taylor cites Gilbreth's study approvingly, but characteristically notes that ''it is only through *enforced* standardization of methods, *enforced* adoption of the best implements and working conditions, and *enforced* cooperation that this faster work can be assured. And the duty of enforcing the adoption of standards and of enforcing this cooperation rests with the *management* alone.''[5]

Thus, *Taylorism* could never have had more than a token influence on domestic production. Rather, it was in Gilbreth's time-work studies made after 1912 (using photography) that conclusions were drawn with general application (Fig 11.2).

Both Taylor and Gilbreth initially applied their ideas to the production line, but given that human anatomy is not well adapted to repetitive movement, this may be the least important of their applications. As Gilbreth himself pointed out in "A Fourth Dimension for Measuring Skill" (1924), no series of movements can be precisely continuous.[6] Two of their discoveries, however, have real implications for housework: the *refinement of motion* for a specific task at a certain moment; and the *overall ordering* of a series of tasks, which should be reflected in the arrangement of physical space. These efforts had precedent in Catherine E. Beecher's (1800–1878) influential *Treatise on Domestic Economy*, published in 1841. Giedion points out that while Beecher's book addresses every aspect of production in the home, it omits such prosaic items as recipes and, instead, places household tasks in a broad social context. In 1869 she and Harriet Beecher Stowe wrote a sequel, *The American Woman's Home;* in it they say that "a moderate style of housekeeping, small, compact and simple domestic establishments must necessarily be the order of life in America. . . . This being the case, it should be an object in America to exclude from the labors of the family all that can, with greater advantage, be executed out of it by combined labor."[7]

Significantly, this work assumes only the current state of domestic technology in the layout of the kitchen area (Fig 11.3). In this sense, the book may be regarded as a scientific time-management study rather than a manual for the use of domestic technology. And while she does update that technology in the later edition, it still reflects current availability, rather than the level suggested by patent applications or industrial usage. It is in this managerial mode that Beecher cautions the housewife to prepare ". . . a systematic apportionment of time, and at least aim at accomplishing it; and they can also compare with such a general outline, the time which they actually devote to these different objects, for the purpose of modifying any mistaken proportions."[8] These statements rest on an assumption of servantless households, an idea that is approvingly echoed in Christine Frederick's *Household Engineering: Scientific Management in the Home* (1915),

11.2

Movement Translated into Wire Models; *Frank B. Gilbreth (ca. 1912)*
The models were intended to document the consecutive motions of a specific task, so that they could then be analyzed. Through critique and experimentation, the worker's movements could be refined to save energy and time. By being aware of this, workers could become "motion minded," eventually resulting in increased production. (Source: *Mechanization Takes Command,* Siegfried Giedion.)

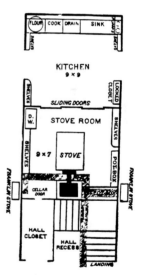

11.3

Continuous Working Surfaces in Kitchen; *Catharine Beecher (1869)*
Of particular concern in the design of a kitchen is the distance between storage and point of use. Beecher and Stowe felt that time and energy were wasted by unnecessary steps in collecting, using, and then returning utensils to storage. Specific instructions were given to guide women in developing their own efficient space. (Source: *The American Woman's Home,* Catharine E. Beecher and Harriet Beecher Stowe.)

11.4

Good and Bad Kitchen Planning; *Christine Frederick (1920)*
Frederick's kitchen plans were the result of time and motion studies that analyzed the component parts of each activity. This resulted in written directions that explained the procedures, equipment, and time required for functions. The dotted lines above illustrate the sequence of tasks involved in preparing (route *A*) and clearing away meals (route *B*). Items that later became standard are the windows above the sink, and broom closets; standardized cabinet and sink depths had not yet been developed. (Drawn by: J. Malnar.)

EFFICIENT GROUPING OF KITCHEN EQUIPMENT   BADLY GROUPED KITCHEN EQUIPMENT

11.5

Kitchen in the Experimental Building, the Haus am Horn—Weimar; *(1923)*
Giedion suggests that this is perhaps the earliest example of the kitchen in which organization is joined to form.[1] The extensive work surfaces separate cabinets into upper and lower sections, and align the depth and height of base cabinets with appliances. These surfaces, coupled with the overhead mounting of cabinets, came to symbolize a modern efficient kitchen. (Photo—courtesy: The Museum of Modern Art, New York.)

notably on the grounds of sound scientific procedures. This book, growing out of a series of articles for the *Ladies Home Journal*, applied time-management studies to the household (Fig 11.4). Frederick notes the time that can be saved by sound management, concluding, "The real object in saving time and effort, is to enable the homemaker to have leisure time to devote to interests which are more important than the mere mechanics of living."[9]

Scientific management applications in the home were intended to provide efficiency in work-completion ". . . to the attainment of the higher ends of personal and family happiness and success."[10] These studies reached a peak in the early 1920s, spurred on by Frederick's book and the studies of the Gilbreths; indeed, it was Frank Gilbreth who observed in 1912 that he hoped the principles of scientific management would be of use to home economics teachers and housekeepers.[11] Such applications did enjoy the general support of the Home Economics movement, which saw housework's professionalization leading to a higher value for its proper execution. These principles, and the development and dissemination of the machines to be managed, were crucial in forming the spatial characteristics of the American single-family home. This is quite different, as Giedion points out, from the European situation. He says, "The Continental trend . . . stemmed neither from industry nor from scientific management. Its mover was the architect. . . . He opened up the house, re-shaped its interior space, created the furniture types, and found his own social awareness."[12]

By way of example, Giedion refers to the Bauhaus structure, Das Haus am Horn (Fig 9.8), whose L-shaped kitchen used standardized cabinetry and contiguous work surfaces (Fig 11.5). This permitted a rationalized relationship between the *storage, cleaning-and-preparation,* and *cooking* areas. Indeed, partial standardization was only to come to the United States with an early effort at continuous work surfaces in 1930. And full standardization occurred only when agreement was reached between gas appliance manufacturers and the cabinet industry in 1945. It was this agreement between thirty-three manufacturers that produced the now familiar dimensions of twenty-five and one-fourth inches for cabinet depth and the thirty-six-inch height of base cabinets, considered standard for women of "average stature."[13] Coupled with statistics that demonstrate other kinds of technology lags (only ten percent of rural homes were electrified in 1938, for example), it is not surprising that most household advances existed more in advertisements than in fact.

Physical Factors

The assumption of such basic domestic technology is quite reasonable in light of the slow mid-nineteenth-century shift from the hearth to cast-iron wood or coal-fired stoves (for cooking and heating), even though highly efficient stoves had been invented by Count von Rumford in the late eighteenth century. Large—and funded by government—their commercial application was limited. His designs were a century ahead of their time, anticipating both the design of gas stoves and kitchen planning (Fig 11.6). Home furnaces were likewise available at the beginning of the nineteenth century but were very expensive. For the majority relying on the cast-iron kitchen stove for heating (with a parlor stove for special occasions), the kitchen was essentially communal, with minimal isolation for the housewife. As heating improved, becoming general, the kitchen became the cook's province, whether that person was servant or housewife.

The kitchen stove was vital; it was the major source of heat, means for cooking, and supplier of hot water for laundry and cleaning. It is, therefore, curious how slowly people came to trust gas for cooking, even though they were using it regularly for room lighting. Nonetheless, between 1880 and 1930, the gas stove came to dominate the home market, aided by its early display at the Great Exhibition of 1851 in London, and because technically advanced gas ranges became available in the 1880s. By 1915 the gas range was equipped with thermostats and flat working surfaces. Throughout the 1920s and 1930s, the gas industry continued to use "demonstration kitchens" to convince the public of their value; one catalog notes that the Compact Table-Top Gas Range (1931) ". . . makes smaller kitchens possible, makes kitchen planning easier."[14]

Electricity was used for cooking only much later; while there was a Model Electric Kitchen at the 1893 Columbian Exposition, operated by the Home Economists, electricity remained associated with lighting. This was prob-

11.6

Standardized Streamlined Mail-Order Kitchen; *Sears Roebuck Co. Catalog (1942)* This kitchen's intent was to save steps, which would save time and labor. The standardized units were designed to allow a person to self-evaluate needs, and then work with Sears personnel, who would help plan a kitchen based on these needs. By purchasing separate units individual family requirements and budgets could be met. (Source: Sears, Roebuck and Company, Chicago.)

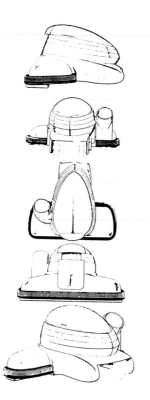

11.7

Streamlined Vacuum Cleaner Casing;
Ralph E. Kruck (1943)
The identifying qualities of a streamlined object are: minimal decoration; curved corners; and smooth, swelling contours. The term comes from hydrodynamics, and refers to the movement of particles; generally indicating a form that has the least resistance to air and water. In appliances, it became a selling point, addressing issues of aesthetics and the appearance of efficiency. (Source: *Official Gazette*, U.S. Patent #135,974, July 13, 1943.)

ably due to minimal line access and lack of standardized operating voltage, as well as appliances's less than dependable performance. Still, the electric appliance industry vigorously promoted its products throughout the 1920s, and the number of home devices that electricity could power multiplied rapidly. During the 1930s, the electric stove became increasingly common, with a form borrowed from its gas counterpart. Other appliances included the washing machine, vacuum cleaner, and dishwasher—patents for which had been registered before 1870. And while few inventions could match the washing machine in importance, the refrigerator and iron were significant additions. There were improvements in nonmechanized tools as well, but the modern service core is distinguished primarily by its powered devices. Thus one of the most critical inventions of the nineteenth century may be Nicola Tesla's one-sixth horsepower alternating current motor, developed for Westinghouse in 1889. It was this motor that made possible a wide range of consumer appliances, most of them adaptations of commercial products. This required a major commitment on the part of industry, as the majority of these devices had to be scaled down, standardized into a product line, and streamlined to suggest their domestic suitability (Fig 11.7). In appearance, these appliances borrowed heavily from the Art Deco movement of the 1920s; this may explain their recent return to popularity.

The other major part of the service core is, of course, the bathroom. Well into the 1930s, the "inside toilet" remained an unattainable luxury for many Americans. Nor were the provisions for bathing much better; an 1895 study indicated that eighty-three percent of urban Americans had no home bath facilities other than basin and sponge.[15] It was not until 1900 that the modern bathroom type evolved; a sink and tub with hot and cold running water, and a watercloset joined to a sewer. The last item was controversial, as fears of sewer gas lingered. Even Beecher had advised the use of the "earth toilet" for just such a reason. After 1920, production of bathroom fixtures expanded, and the bath industry agreed on standard dimensions for the increasingly popular double-wall tubs. The early bathroom tended to be large, often a converted spare room, but by the 1920s the transition to the familiar type was complete (Fig 11.8). Technical problems in *bathroom design* include plumbing connections to either a sewer or septic system, and provision for hot water. But the bathroom's social role in the home may ultimately pose greater problems, raising questions about the public and private spheres of domestic life, and the portion of the budget it should claim. And important to design has been its link to the kitchen, with which it shares certain physical affinities.

The impact of household devices is enormous, especially in their effect on the spatial dimensions of the model American home. Widespread dissemination of home appliances may be seen as the counterpart to the commitment to the single-family house; the appliances allow a high standard of domestic life, and the sales volume resulting from independent households allows low-cost appliances. Appliances have influenced spatial design in at least two ways: they have determined the *actual dimensions* of the spaces that contain them (and optimum operating room for them); and they contribute to a rising percentage of the total *building expenditure* going to the service core (reaching forty percent by the 1950s). This in turn affects the total affordable square-footage possible within a given budget. It was only during the 1930s that the rationalized service core, with standardized work space, was introduced. In 1930 the Brooklyn Gas Company hired Lillian Gilbreth to design a model kitchen based on efficient production; the result, visually chaotic, clearly indicated how far industry had yet to go. The comparison, for example, with the kitchen designed by J.J.P. Oud in 1927 for the Weissenhof Settlement, is striking. Oud, a member of De Stijl, pro-

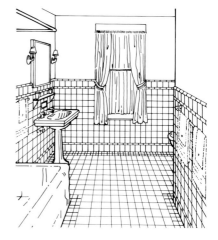

duced a more efficient and compact work space—with an essentially abstract approach—than Gilbreth could obtain as a professional production engineer compelled to work with poorly designed appliances (Fig 11.9). But as Giedion points out, by 1932 the comprehensive integrated work space that Gilbreth postulated had become inevitable, as industry's tremendous resources were made available for this purpose:

> . . . the work process in the kitchen was scientifically investigated down to the last detail of food preparation. Expert staffs of engineers, chemists, architects, nutritionists, and practicing cooks studied everything connected with the kitchen . . . in little time the "streamline kitchen" was complete.[16]

The kitchen that emerged was to ultimately fall into one of two formats, the L-shape or the U-shape—a decision probably based more on time-motion theories than on installation decisions.

Two problems of the service core remained: the high cost of kitchen and bathroom fixtures; and the housewife's relative isolation in structures still dependent, in plan, on the presence of servants. An early solution to service core costs was to make the kitchen and bath areas contiguous, so as to minimize plumbing installation. In a society that usually wants the bathroom and the bedroom joined, this can be difficult; and, in any case, the notion of a single bathroom is alien in even moderate-cost homes. Giedion wrote his *Mechanization Takes Command* in 1947, when the need for housing was acute; it is in that context that he says that the wish to use rooms flexibly, with a total freedom of ground plan, conflicted with a mechanization that sought total concentration of all installations. He thus concludes that "the mechanical core of the house, embracing the kitchen, bath, laundry, heating, wiring, and plumbing, will therefore be factory-made and assembled before being brought to the building site.[17]

In this context he approvingly notes Buckminster Fuller's revolutionary designs for a portable mechanical core and prefabricated bathroom (Fig 11.10). But this approval is of an attempt to solve a difficult problem, rather than the belief that complex ground plans can be served by such configu-

11.8

Typical Bathroom *(ca. 1927)*
This is a typical compact arrangement that sets the watercloset adjacent to the sink and a double-wall tub. The floor and walls are tiled to protect them against water, and for hygienic reasons. Now entirely typical are the full-length, built-in, enameled tub that includes a shower fixture, and the built-in medicine cabinet above the sink. (Drawn by: J. Malnar.)

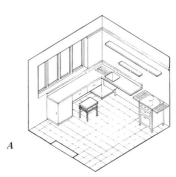

A

11.9

(A) **L-Shaped Kitchen–Weissenhof Settlement, Stuttgart;** *J. J. P. Oud (1927)*
(B) **Experimental Kitchen;** *Lillian Gilbreth (1930)*
Oud's aesthetically designed kitchen for worker's housing featured such items as expansive windows, continuous counters, and a counter-height range; these later became standard features in kitchens. While Gilbreth took into account a logical sequence of tasks, the result lacked visual continuity. The upper section of the range blocks the corner counter and storage area; the central table was required to compensate for this break in the flow of movement. (*[A]* Drawn by: J. Malnar; *[B]* Reprinted from *Architectural Record*, March 1930; Copyright 1930 by McGraw-Hill, Inc. All rights reserved. Reproduced with the permission of the publisher.)

B

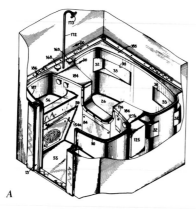

A

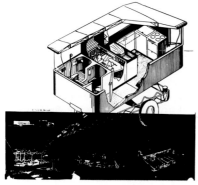

B

11.10

(A) Prefabricated Bathroom; *R. Buckminster Fuller (1938);* **(B) Mechanical Core;** *R. Buckminster Fuller (1943)*

As an indoor space the bathroom had no precedent and thus was perhaps more readily amenable to compartmentalizing and prefabrication than the kitchen. The combining of new equipment, materials, and construction techonology enhanced services and provided additional comfort, but without flexibility. (Copyright 1960, The Estate of Buckminster Fuller; Courtesy: Buckminster Fuller Institute, Los Angeles.)

11.11

H-Shaped House; *Jean Bodman Fletcher and Norman Fletcher (1945)*

This design won first place in a competition "for the average small family house," sponsored by the Pittsburgh Plate Glass Company and the architectural journal *Pencil Points.* The term utility core, used to define the adjacent kitchen and bathroom placed in a central location, indicated an advance in the traditional house. This H-shaped configuration with expanses of glass allows the multipurpose room, dining-, living area, play yard, and social court to be seen from the kitchen. (Courtesy: Norman Fletcher, Cambridge, Mass.)

rations. Nor does Giedion approve of the Dymaxion House (Fig 10.1)—precisely because it is rigidly suspended from its service mast without any possibility of growth or attachment of transitional elements. In short, he believes that a good idea, a central service core, is coupled with a poor one, the inflexible structure. But he does cite another structure, the H-Shaped House by J. and N. Fletcher, as a possible prototype for houses using mechanical cores (Fig 11.11).

There have been various attempts to overcome the second problem, the housewife's isolation in a segregated kitchen. Such efforts characterized the Usonian homes of Frank Lloyd Wright, which combined in various degrees the kitchen, dining, and living areas. This approach is also reflected in Allmon Fordyce's design for a Living-Kitchen with Dining Area and Laundry (1945), one which suggests the older function of the kitchen as a place of gathering (Fig 11.12). And all of these ideas were to play a role in the tract housing of the 1950s, although it is questionable how much the problem could be alleviated in such small spaces. Certainly, giving the kitchen a startling new piece of furniture, the kitchen island (usually fitted with stools), represents an attempt to integrate food preparation with entertaining.

Design approaches using the *open-plan kitchen* have become fairly common today; such a solution can be seen in the addition to a 1940s house by

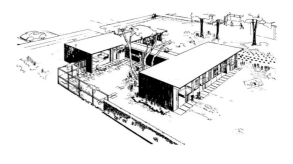

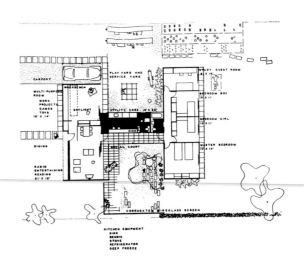

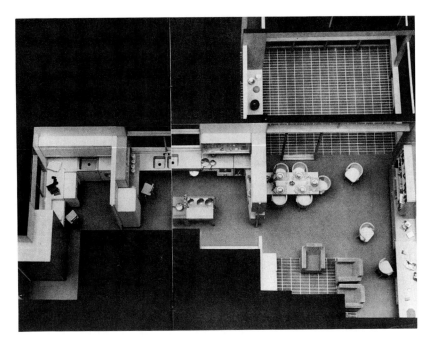

11.12

Living Kitchen; *Allmon Fordyce of Raymond Loewy Associates (1945)*
Fordyce used the term "living kitchen" to stress the importance of combining the activities that occur in the typical kitchen, laundry-, living-, and dining-rooms. The divider between the kitchen and dining area is raised above the floor, dropped below the ceiling, and open between the counter and upper cabinets. The upper cabinets are enclosed with clear glass, and the door between the two areas has been eliminated. (Source: Eric Schaal, *Life Magazine.* Copyright 1945 Time Warner, Inc., N. Y.)

Shelton, Mindel Associates. This 1985 design incorporates kitchen, dining, and informal living areas, characterized by the designers as "an informal house within the house."[18] The cabinetry's layout is L-shaped with a center island (11.13). But while this kitchen type—an updated Great Room—is almost uniformly used, at least one industrial designer believes that the dining room will again be central to family life, changing the role of the kitchen to a high-tech, multiple-use food preparation area that acknowledges the time constraints of dual-income households.[19]

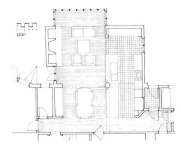

11.13

Kitchen, Dining, and Lounge Addition; *Shelton, Mindel Associates (1985)*
This 700 ft.² addition combining kitchen, dining, and lounge areas won first place in I.C.F.'s first annual kitchen design competition. The 14′ island allows the cook to participate in the two traditional places of gathering; the hearth and dining area. (Courtesy: Shelton, Mindel & Associates, New York; Photo by: Oberto Gill.)

Social Factors

It is easy to assume that the single-family house, comprising service core (with kitchen and laundry facilities) and living areas, has been historically inevitable; but there have been other social movements, based on very different assumptions about domestic life. In her intriguing study, *The Grand Domestic Revolution: A History of Feminist Designs for American Homes, Neighborhoods, and Cities,* Dolores Hayden argues that during the years from 1865 to 1930 there were a number of women (whom she refers to as material feminists) who cited ". . . the economic exploitation of women's domestic labor by men as the most basic cause of women's inequality."[20] And the answer was seen to lie, not only in economic remuneration for that labor, but in a ". . . transformation of the spatial design and material culture of American homes, neighborhoods, and cities."[21] Feminism has historically embraced issues ranging from suffrage to family life, but Hayden is interested in those people concerned with the material conditions of women. She notes that:

> In order to overcome patterns of urban space and domestic space that isolated women and made their domestic work invisible, they developed new forms of neighborhood organizations, including housewives' cooperatives, as well as new building types, including the kitchen-less house, the day care center, the public kitchen, and the community dining club. They also proposed ideal, feminist cities.[22]

Hayden's study of the feminist impact on life's domestic aspects is engrossing, particularly her analysis of the contribution of Charlotte Perkins Gilman (1860–1935), author of the influential *Women and Economics* (1898). In this book Gilman describes a future where women could enjoy both the economic advantages of wage-employment and a rich home life, made possible by day-care facilities and kitchenless living units. Her work reflects an appreciation of the hardships inherent in a domestic setting that, for most women, was appallingly severe; she also had insight into the social ramifications of spatial design for women. In *Building Domestic Liberty,* Polly Wynn Allen comments:

> She analyzed the negative effects of prevailing domestic architecture, with its private systems of food preparation, laundering, child care, and cleaning, on men, women, and children. She characterized the middle-class housewife's familial responsibilities as 'a quiet, unnoticed whirlpool that sucks down youth and beauty and enthusiasm.' She lamented the isolated alienation of many women's lives. . . .[23]

It followed that as long as the single-family home remained the prevailing housing type, women's domestic situation would not improve.

Gilman's critique of the home is worth examining; it rests on four fairly inclusive points. The first is that, as a type, it is *unevolved,* remaining so inefficient that it bears comparison to ". . . a clam in a horse-race."[24] That is, it services often contradictory activities and accommodates certain individual activities, like food preparation and laundry, poorly in any case. She points out that the waste, of both labor and materials, is so appalling that no industry would tolerate it; and that the housewife has, even with scientific management and clever devices, simply been perfecting a medieval system. Not only is labor wasted, but so is money, in the sense that the repetition of physical plant—one household to another—is a disaster for individual family budgets. And in fact, most of the schemes to relieve household work in the nineteenth and early twentieth centuries involved locating cooking and laundry functions outside the home.

Gilman's second point is that the isolated home is fundamentally *unfair* to women, since it reinforces, by its very structure, a division of labor based on sex. Moreover, the work thus assigned to women is remarkably undesirable, constituting a chaotic and unrelenting drudgery, alleviated only by appliances that have replaced servants. Still worse, the arbitrary allotting of domestic labor to women denies them the elementary career choices nominally expected by men, and the satisfaction of self-chosen productive labor. The third point is that the home *injures* all its inhabitants; that through the gross inefficiency, and consequent expense of maintenance, it remains a "workhouse" for women and a "millstone" for men. Men thereby become resentful workers in jobs chosen for mere remuneration, and the inevitable friction caused by a discordant marriage that results can only be harmful to all the family. Her final point is that the home *precludes* the development of ethics, or larger social morality. That is, until the basic nature of the single-family house is changed, no other form of social morality is possible, since the home fosters a narrow view of the world. Allen notes that in Gilman's view, the family was thus guilty ". . . of gross self-indulgence and self-preoccupation, of frantic consumerism, of immoral insularity and aloofness from the world around it."[25]

This is a devastating indictment, and if not completely persuasive, it is cogent. Allen offers an insightful critique of Gilman's position; she notes, for example, that Gilman could have no way of realizing the degree to which industry (and government) would endorse the single-family house with all its waste. And she may, Allen continues, have too emphatically denied the possibility of satisfaction in full-time housework. But there are implications for design worth pursuing: first, the separation of the worst aspects of the service core from the home; second, the assumption that people might subscribe to socialized living arrangements; third, that despite her "modern conveniences," the housewife stays isolated; and fourth, that diverse life-patterns call for diverse designs.

The notions of a separated service core and communal living arrangements are related, but not congruent. The nineteenth century is marked by the efforts of communitarian socialist groups committed to the construction of ideal communities. Their motivations ranged from religious conviction (as with the Shakers) to social ideology (as with the Owenites). Likewise, the living arrangements took various forms, from sexual segregation to conventional family groupings; and the housing varied in building type from individual dwellings to shared apartments. What they had in common was a fundamental conviction that the built environment had to be transformed to reflect a more egalitarian system of production and distribution. Charles Fourier was particularly influential in the 1840s, inspiring the formation of communal associations in France and the United States. Two advantages were seen to accrue in the cooperative: first, household tasks could be unified and rationalized; and second, isolation of individual housewives would be eliminated. The first argument was very persuasive, especially as the efficient machinery devised to lighten workloads had still not been adapted for the household. Fourier's most successful experiment was the Familistère, built in Guise, France, in the 1860s. This was a cooperative industrial community of 350 families, with shared stores, nursery, educational facilities, and restaurants. The services were organized on an industrial model and marked by technical modernity (Fig 11.14).

Whatever the particular ideology, almost all *socialized living* arrangements were kitchenless, with some form of communal cooking/laundry facilities. But far removed from the ideological communities envisioned by the more radical idealists were the urban living arrangements based on simple expediency. So constant was the growth of urban industrial capitalism, that it seemed proper to assume an uninterrupted growth of the city. This assumption is what impelled the development of a new type, the *apartment-hotel,* which afforded an efficiently collective, yet private, lifestyle. Such buildings looked like conventional apartments, except for the common kitchen and laundry, which were operated either cooperatively or professionally (for a set fee). In the latter case they effectively were what their name implied, a hybrid of apartment and hotel. In 1890 John Pickering Putnam (a Bellamy Nationalist), published in *American Architect and Building News* a plan for an apartment-hotel that was ". . . as near an approach to the ideal of a human habitation as has yet been devised."[26] He further asserted, that same year, that "the selfish and narrowing isolation of the separate dwelling will give way to the cooperative apartment-house as surely as the isolated hut of the savage yield to the cities and villages of advancing civilization."[27] And there is much to recommend his design, which is remarkably flexible (Fig 11.15).

These structures had counterparts in New York and Boston, having in common a highly conservative appearance; but in fact, the apartment-hotel did not assume the respectability of even the apartment. This may in part have been the result of the public's fear of their being mass-produced, as well as the hint of immorality inherent in communal existence. Gilman noted that the features of expensive apartment-hotels ". . . can be furnished at much less expense, as soon as far-seeing builders recognize the demand."[28] This argument, appearing in 1907 in an article entitled "Homes without House Keeping: A Present Demand" was likely more a hindrance than a help in persuading a fundamentally conservative society to socialize elements of domestic life.

Another design approach, by Leonard E. Ladd, focused on a centralized service core within a row-house block. In his patent application, Ladd observes that the new dining-room arrangement would have certain advantages: better light and ventilation for both the dining rooms and back rooms of the main buildings; more distance between main buildings; separation from the distasteful aspects of the service structure (containing power generators, heating elements, laundries, and kitchens); and clean, private backyards.[29] It is arguable, however, that in this sort of arrangement the issue of eliminating isolation may have been crucial (Fig 11.16). But the real potential for such types lay in large-scale apartment-hotels; indeed, the

11.14

Familistère Apartment Block—Guise, France; *M. Godin (1859)*
This image of the Familistère, also called the Social Palace, shows the Festival of Labor taking place in the large central atrium. Surrounding this social space are a series of balconies, which provide access to the private apartments, consisting of two- to five-room kitchenless units. (Source: "The Social Palace at Guise." Edward Howland. *Harper's New Monthly Magazine* [December 1871].)

more units serviced by a core, the more efficiently it functions. In this spirit King Camp Gillette designed his Metropolis of the future, a system of twenty-five-story towers (with kitchenless units) so conceived as to house sixty million people (e.g., the population of all North America).[30] The rest of the continent was to remain a vast parkland. This design appeared in his book *The Human Drift* (1894); some of its concerns remain current (Fig 11.17).

Despite all these attempts, socialized living schemes, even simple ones, were rarely successful in the long term and tended to disappear after 1930 with a growth in suburban single-family housing. This growth was actively encouraged by the government with such measures as credit extension in the 1920s, the Conference on Home Building and Home Ownership in 1931, and the creation of the FHA in 1934; by 1970 there were more than fifty million units of single-family housing in the United States. And in the following decade (1970–1980), housing units rose at a growth rate double that of the population.[31] An interesting corollary to this figure is the drop in residents per household from three and one-third in 1964 to two and three-quarters in 1980, a trend toward fewer people occupying more square feet.[32] Aside from the luxury of increased living space, there were (and are) economic advantages to home ownership; house values, for example, doubled between 1970 and 1977, and capital gains from housing averaged three times the size of gains taken by private investors in the stock market.[33] This remarkable rise in home equity provided home owners with the opportunity to purchase larger houses, pay for education and luxury items, and maintain what was seen as an effective defense against inflation. But there are other, more ominous, figures; the economist Alan Greenspan estimated in 1977 that while equity was increasing at $62 billion per year, new mortgages grew at a rate of $60 billion.[34] Put differently, home owners were monetizing their equity gains in the form of new mortgage debt which, while stimulating the economy, assumes ever-increasing valuations.

Available credit and mortgages, improved appliances at lower prices, and the advantages of equity are all responsible for the demise of the various communal schemes; although it is arguable that the interests of industry and government so intertwined as to make that demise inevitable. Hayden contends that in the early 1920s, particularly the "Red Scare" years of 1920 to 1921, most industrialists were convinced that a reliable work force de-

11.15

Apartment Hotel; *John Pickering Putnam (1890)*

Putnam's plans included three types of private dwellings; apartments with kitchens and dining-rooms, apartments with dining-rooms, but no kitchens, and apartments without kitchens or dining-rooms. This provided residents with a choice. This plan shows units with no kitchens or dining-rooms. These residents would have the option of using the main café or the smaller, more intimate—yet public—dining-rooms. (Source: "The Apartment House," *The American Architect and Building News,* [January–March 1890].)

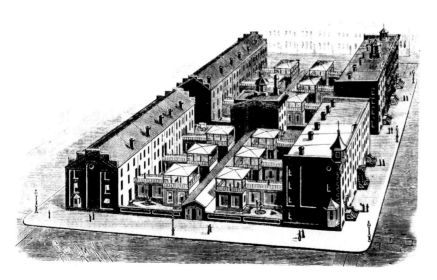

11.16

"Improvement in Dwelling Houses"—Philadelphia; *Leonard E. Ladd (1890)*

In his application, Ladd claimed as new (and patentable) "a series of dwelling-houses and a separate building or station connected by a hallway, said dwelling-houses having a series of dining-rooms communicating directly with said hallway and located at some distance from the dwelling-houses, said station providing a source of supply for food, heat, light, &c, common to all the houses and accessible by the aforesaid hallway. . . ."[2] (Source: "Dwelling-House," Leonard E. Ladd. U.S. Patent #430,480.)

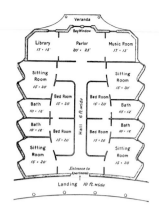

11.17

Metropolis; *King Camp Gillette (1894)*
The private units in this twenty-five-story
high-rise radiate out from a domed central
space that is monumental in size. Each wing
contains four private suites consisting of internal bedrooms and external baths and sitting rooms. The library, parlor, music rooms,
and veranda are shared by the residents of
this wing. Since there are no kitchens in the
wings, all residents would gather in the domed
central dining-room, set within the larger
domed structure. (Source: *The Human Drift,*
King C. Gillette.)

pended on skilled white male workers indebted with mortgages in suburban
homes (Fig 11.18). She quotes literature from the Industrial Housing Associates, a planning firm, that explains to their clients: "Happy workers
invariably mean bigger profits, while unhappy workers are never a good
investment. . . . A wide diffusion of home ownership has long been recognized as fostering a stable and conservative habit."[35] This quote in large
degree echoes that of Viollet-le-Duc fifty years earlier, and gives substance
to Hayden's position.

In her *Never Done,* Susan Strasser contends that the time saved in the
modern suburban home by the advanced systems of appliances has been
devoted, instead, to consumerism. She notes the force of advertising in
fostering the new consumer role: "As large firms combined the methods of
mass production and mass distribution to create and control a national market, they linked the activities of the consumer housewife to their own thorough advertising."[36] One need only consider the remarkable number of
suburban shopping malls and home-specific advertising to see the truth of
this statement (Fig 11.19). But not only is consumerism a dubious virtue in
itself, the isolation of housework (possibly its worst quality) has been reduced only somewhat. Despite the telephone and the second car, the saving
graces of suburban life, the feminist critique remains plausible. It seems
clear that suburban tract-housing represents a waste of energy, and vocational choices for women remain narrow. And, most persuasively, life between 1970 and 1990 has become more socially diverse than ever, calling
for flexible buildings. In her essay "Redesigning the American Dream"
Dolores Hayden notes:

> Americans cannot solve their current housing problems without reexam-
> ining the ideal of the single-family house—its history, and the ideals of
> family, gender, and society it embodies, as well as its design and financ-
> ing, because this is what government has supported most heavily through
> private mortgage deductions and public road building.[37]

But alternative housing types, even simple ones, still tend to be seen as
undesirable (except for specific purposes) by most people; the question must
arise as to the reasons for this adherence to the idea of the single-family
home, aside from current economic advantages. Is this the reflection of a
primordial need or simple ideology; and if the former, how can other building types be made to satisfy that need?

Psychological Factors

In his *Public Places and Private Spaces,* Albert Mehrabian identifies three
dimensions of emotion that subsume all the "feelings" we have terms for;
he states that our confrontation with the environment produces in us ". . . an
emotional reaction that is a distinctive, measurable combination of arousal,
pleasure, and dominance. This emotional reaction in turn causes us to approach or avoid that environment."[38] If that environment is a *high-load* one
(i.e., having a high information level, with much attached uncertainty),
arousal would be high and dominance low.[39] And this is a likely characterization of a dynamic urban lifestyle, an experience people seek to control
when it becomes unpleasurable. He further notes that ". . . Americans tend
to react to the negative effects of high population density by emphasizing
privacy, sometimes to the point of social isolation. Both the car and the
suburb afford a great deal more privacy than public transportation or crowded
urban areas."[40] The suburb, unlike the city, tends to be *low-load*—which
reduces arousal—and fairly high on pleasure; and private ownership of the

home tends to reinforce feelings of dominance. Such privacy can be had in the city, of course, but it is expensive and far more isolating than in the suburb. This is particularly true for the apartment unit, generally located in a building calculated to minimize social interaction:

> How to provide people with apartments that strike an acceptable balance between needed privacy and lowered arousal on the one hand, and needed social interaction and stimulation on the other, is the design problem confronting architects, decorators, and social scientists.[41]

Underlying this seeming contradiction, Mehrabian notes, is the phenomenon of territoriality. This notion served as the basis for two influential books published in 1966; *The Territorial Imperative*, by Robert Ardrey, and *The Hidden Dimension*, by Edward T. Hall. Territoriality is defined by Hall as ". . . behavior by which an organism characteristically lays claim to an area and defends it against members of its own species."[42] Ardrey believes it ". . . to be characteristic of our species as a whole, to be shaped but not determined by environment and experience, and to be a consequence not of human choice but of evolutionary inheritance."[43] Ardrey's point is critical; he believes that territoriality can be influenced by cultural experience but is innate in the species. The argument over heredity versus environment is ongoing and points to the danger of reaching any easy conclusions. In his *Personal Space* (1969), Robert Sommer warns, ". . . it is important that architects guard themselves against *perceptual reductionism*. . . . A person's behavior is affected by how he perceives the world as well as his biological makeup but both are overlaid and shaped through learning."[44]

In fairness, it must be noted that Ardrey's discussion of territoriality as it is directly translated into human behavior, is couched in fairly tentative terms. And he acknowledges the alternative viewpoint, saying, "If we behave as we do in our attachment for property because we have been taught to, because our culture and our social mechanisms demand it of us, then we deal with nothing fundamental. What is learned may be unlearned, and we may assume that man will adjust himself to collective existence or to the lonely crowd."[45] But Ardrey does view this territorial factor as innate and identifies it as one of the three factors (with dominance and security) that shape human behavior, concluding that "the territorial nature of man is genetic and ineradicable."[46] The assumption of territoriality, whether *learned* or *innate*, underlies virtually all psychological theories about space—public and personal.

GOOD HOMES
MAKE
CONTENTED
WORKERS

11.18

Title Page; *Industrial Housing Associates (1919)*
This publication was produced for industrialists and provided ideas for solving their labor problems. To discourage trained workers from leaving or striking, it was recommended that they be encouraged to own their own homes. By tying the worker to a heavily mortgaged home, industry could achieve stability in the labor force. The publication stated that ". . . the man owns his home but in a sense his home owns him, checking his rash impulses. . . ."[3] (Source: *The Grand Domestic Revolution*, Dolores Hayden. Published by The MIT Press. Copyright 1981 by The Massachusetts Institute of Technology.)

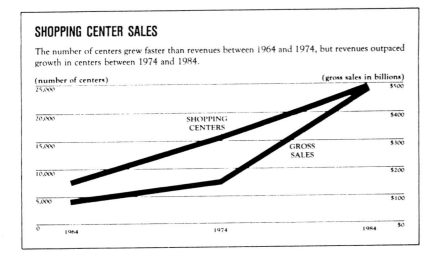

SHOPPING CENTER SALES

The number of centers grew faster than revenues between 1964 and 1974, but revenues outpaced growth in centers between 1974 and 1984.

11.19

Shopping Center Growth and Sales (1964–84)
The growth in suburban shopping centers may be seen as a direct result of massive tract-housing construction, and the consequent need to furnish those homes. That housing boom, however, was itself fueled by a significant expansion of population (the baby boom), a generation that has continued to be major consumers. The result is that shopping centers are now the dominant form of retailing agencies in the United States. (Reprinted with permission, copyright *American Demographics*, November 1985.)

This concept helps explain the habit of apartment dwellers to systematically choose the upper floors of apartment buildings (as reflected in rent structures), demarcate boundary lines (e.g., fences and shrubbery), and consistently choose certain spatial behavior patterns in public places (usually defensive ones). And as the single-family house located within highly definable property lines forms a paradigm for such territorial behavior, it may outlive the single family (Fig 11.20). It is, admittedly, a solution not required by everyone, but the notion of the self-contained unit, as represented by home and hearth, shared food, etc., has certainly proved long-lived. Sommer observes that "even if we do not accept the idea of instinctive territoriality in humans, it is still apparent that people actively defend certain spaces against intruders using the entire repertoire of defensive techniques in the animal kingdom as well as a few new ones."[47] And the problem, he says, is that "Increasing population density makes it obvious that not everyone will have legal title to a land area . . . a man will be spending even more of his life in space he does not own or control. We must understand how he can maintain feelings of privacy and individuality in nonowned space."[48]

11.20

"**The Far Side;**" *Gary Larson (1990)*
(The FAR SIDE cartoon by Gary Larson is reprinted by permission of Chronicle Features, San Francisco.)

"**And now, Randy, by use of song, the male sparrow will stake out his territory . . . an instinct common in the lower animals.**"

Nor is territoriality limited to domestic spaces; it extends to places of employment as well, perhaps with even greater force. This is because, since the relationships are nonintimate, they need even more regulation. Indeed, the modern office, in design and function, is the result and expression of complex social factors more than it is of utilitarian concerns.

At the beginning of *Personal Space,* Sommer comments that "architecture may be beautiful, but it should be more than that; it must enclose space in which certain activities can take place comfortably and efficiently."[49] For this to occur, he asserts that the designer's personal expression must be secondary to the building's intended purpose, and that the designer needs concepts that are relevant to both physical form and human behavior.[50] He is referring, of course, to the historical tendency to view architecture as essentially sculptural, with interior spaces determined by accommodation of square-footage. This tendency has often resulted in minimal estimations of physio-spatial needs. The concept of ergonomics is somewhat of an improvement, in the sense that it expands the ratio of space to task, but the very mechanism of task performance may be less related to physical factors than psychosocial dimensions. Hall, for example, has identified three "hidden zones" in contemporary offices: the actual work surface and chair; the additional areas around the work surface that are within arm's reach; and the extension of space needed to push one's chair back from the work surface. He notes that enclosures that permit movement only in the first instance are considered "cramped," a space sufficient for the second is considered "small," and one that accommodates the third is usually considered adequate and in some cases ample.[51]

Proxemics is Hall's term for ". . . the interrelated observations and theories of man's use of space as a specialized elaboration of culture."[52] And as Hall's theories of spatial organization have had much impact on design, they are worth examining. He divides his model into three parts: the *infracultural,* the basic behavioral patterns—rooted in our biological past—that underlie culture (like territoriality); the *precultural,* physiological basis for perception that relies on culture for structure and meaning; and the *microcultural,* the spatial organization of individual and group activities.[53] Hall points out that it is essential that these three be seen as interrelated, but acknowledges the difficulty in examining a phenomenon occurring on two or more analytic or behavioral levels simultaneously, with equal degrees of precision.[54] Design interest has tended to concentrate on the third area, as it has seemed to be immediately pertinent; but the model should be viewed whole, difficulty notwithstanding.

As a manifestation of microculture, proxemics is divided into three spatial types: fixed-feature, semifixed-feature, and informal. *Fixed-feature space* is probably the most fundamental, and identifiable, way of organizing human activities. Hall notes that it includes both physical manifestations and the hidden, internalized designs that govern human behavior, and he states, "Buildings are one expression of fixed-feature patterns, but buildings are also grouped together in characteristic ways as well as being divided internally according to culturally determined designs."[55] And he points out that Western societies are particularly insistent about such spatial definitions, with specific functions assigned to specific rooms. Definitions of internal spaces have evolved historically, and differ from culture to culture; as do the sorts of activities considered appropriate to a particular space. And how we view space depends on past experience, so that the perception of fixed-feature space is to some degree dependent on the memory of the viewer. Hall acknowledges the consequent difficulty of designing for someone in a foreign culture, but cautions that such incongruity between internalized patterns is not limited to relations between cultures, "as our own technology explodes, air conditioning, fluorescent lighting, and soundproofing make it possible to design houses and offices without regard to traditional patterns of windows and doors.''[56]

Unlike the walls and compartments of fixed-feature space, *semifixed-feature space* is that space regulated by temporary (and adjustable) features like furniture. A study by Robert Sommer showed that furniture arrangements were influential in determining whether people experienced spaces as *sociofugal* (tending to keep people apart) or *sociopetal* (tending to bring them together). The study involved patients in a Canada hospital, where, by rearranging the furniture, opportunities were created to increase verbal interaction. Hall says that certain conclusions may be drawn: first, that there are no universally applicable rules that can be invoked; second, that sociofugal space in one culture may be sociopetal in another; and third, that neither form of space is necessarily good or desirable.[57] He states, ''What is desirable is flexibility and congruence between design and function so that there is a variety of spaces, and people can be involved or not, as the occasion and mood demand.''[58] Semifixed-features can, therefore, significantly affect behavior, but it is an effect that is situation-bound. Moreover, Hall points out that fixed-feature space in one culture may be semifixed in another, and vice versa.

The third spatial type Hall refers to is *informal space*, that space that exists on a barely conscious level between people. Human beings commonly use spacing mechanisms to maintain an appropriate distance between themselves and others, based on activities and relationships. The range of distances is variable, bound by culture and emotion. Hall nonetheless was able to discern four sets of interpersonal distances based on voice level and sensory awareness (skin odor, warmth, focus of vision, etc.), each with a near and far phase. He defines them as follows: *intimate* distance (touching to eighteen inches), from love-making to physical immediacy; *personal* distance (eighteen inches to forty-eight inches), from intimacy to casualness; *social* distance (four feet to twelve feet), from informal business to formal business; and *public* distance (twelve feet to twenty-five feet or more), public speaking to celebrity status.[59] In each case the individual's sensory data and awareness reflect the distance from the other person, an awareness bound by social custom. Hall states that it is human nature to exhibit territoriality, using the senses to discern between spaces or distances. ''The specific distance chosen depends on the transaction; the relationship of the interacting individuals, how they feel, and what they are doing.''[60] Thus an awareness of informal space and its mechanisms is as critical to design as that of fixed-feature and semifixed-feature space. To the contrary, the latter two spatial types must be so formed as to account for varied informal-distance links.

The category Hall refers to as personal distance is often associated with another idea, *personal space,* although they are not precisely congruent. Sommer describes personal space as ''. . . an area surrounding a person's body into which intruders may not come. . . . It has been likened to a snail shell, a soap bubble, an aura, and 'breathing room.' ''[61] He points out that there is a close relationship between *individual distance* (the normal spacing of humans, one to another) and personal space, which may be thought of ''. . . as a *portable territory,* since the individual carries it with him wherever he goes, although it disappears under certain conditions, such as crowding.''[62] The individual distance may vary, in much the way Hall describes informal space; and may fall within or without our personal space. Personal space, therefore, exists absolutely and is the sort of space that W.H. Auden refers to in his ''Prologue: The Birth of Architecture'':

Some thirty inches from my nose
The frontier of my Person goes. . . .[63]

As this poem shows (in part and whole), personal space is usually invoked when it is in imminent danger of being invaded.

In his *Psychology for Architects,* David Canter sounds a warning, much like Sommer's, against simple extrapolations from animal behavior to human behavior, noting that every person has the potential for adapting to his environment through learning.[64] Having said that, he still acknowledges that the ways people use space reveal behavioral influences other than mere functional requirements. He refers, for example, to studies of people in public waiting areas; these people neither distribute themselves evenly in the space, nor necessarily use the most functionally appropriate places.[65] And in studies made in railway stations, it was found that people tended to cluster around the pillars, outside the traffic lanes. Other studies have demonstrated that people in restaurants consistently go to tables on the periphery rather than in the middle of the room (Fig 11.21).

The major problem in interpreting such observations had to do with whether people are reacting to the room's physical objects (e.g., furniture) or other people. Canter comments that these behaviors ". . . could well be re-interpreted in terms of people using the physical environment to enable them to locate themselves in a desired position with respect to the activities of others rather than simply their physical surroundings."[66] This would explain Sommer's finding that if the optimum distance between opposing seating units for casual conversation (three feet six inches) is exceeded, people adopt another seating position; or Canter's finding that variation in furniture and viewing angle can influence student seating patterns in a classroom.[67] While it seems obvious that there is a reciprocal relationship between space and the people who occupy it, that correlation is not always clear; but Canter hypothesizes that ". . . one of the major roles of human spatial behavior is to control the quantities and quality of interaction in which a person will take part."[68] And he points out that by regarding the user as an

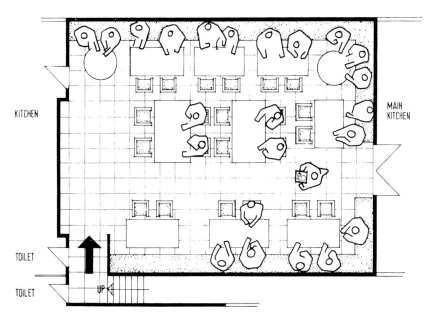

KITCHEN

MAIN KITCHEN

TOILET

TOILET

UP

11.21

Frequency of Location of People in a Restaurant

Employees who depend on tips are probably the best source of information on table sizes, shapes, locations, and arrangements. A two-day observation of a restaurant revealed that people prefer to sit at tables located around the perimeter of the space. Each person in the plan indicates a seat in which ten or more people sat during the study. (Source: *Psychology for Architects,* David Canter.)

active force who is seeking to optimize the balance between received and projected spatial information, it forces the designer to more carefully consider the people who will eventually be using the building.[69]

That the social dimension of space is ultimately more influential than its physical attributes, has been dramatically demonstrated by the *Hawthorne Effect*. This term refers to a famous study conducted between 1929 and 1930 at the Hawthorne Works of the Western Electric Company; in it researchers attempted to ascertain the relationship between production rates and working conditions. Engineers and physiologists varied those conditions through changes in temperature, speed of production line, and lighting conditions (actually reducing the light levels to moonlight conditions); shockingly, the workers' efficiency levels steadily rose—even under adversity. There seemed to be no clear connection between working conditions and production, and the researchers concluded that the work environment was irrelevant. But they overlooked that in order to facilitate the experiments, the workers were not only informed of the manipulations, but had actually participated in certain reorganizations of work situations. In short, they were aware of the experiment, interested in its success, and thought it a positive mark of concern by management. Canter notes that ". . . it changed the direction of industrial psychology away from he study of physical surroundings towards the study of interpersonal relationships and communication networks."[70] But he also cautions that the results did in fact show relationships between environment and behavior; these were not simple causal effects, but ". . . behavioural changes related to the worker's *interpretation* of the environmental modifications."[71] If the workers had perceived these modifications as abusively manipulative on the part of management, the result would likely have been very different.

In his study "Equity and Workplace Status: A Field Experiment," Jerald Greenberg examined employee performance relative to principles of *equity theory*. One hundred ninety-eight employees in a large insurance company were randomly reassigned offices on a temporary basis; these offices were higher, lower, or equal in status to those they normally occupied. Greenberg wished to test the theory that the status change would produce commensurate changes in work performance. He notes that previous research had confirmed that certain indicators of status, such as office size and closeness to windows, are recognized as rewards that symbolize a high standing in an organizational status hierarchy. He thus concludes, "If the characteristics of one's work space are perceived as constituting part of one's work-related rewards, then it follows that receiving work-space-derived rewards greater or less than coworkers of equal status may create conditions of overpayment and underpayment inequity, respectively."[72]

It was further postulated that the more discrepancy in office assignation, the more change in performance. This hypothesis was supported by other research that demonstrated a lower level of dissatisfaction in employees who were underpaid but who worked in environmentally desirable conditions—compared with those who had received no such work-space-related benefits. Greenberg found that it was possible to create conditions of overpayment and underpayment by controlling nonmonetary outcomes, elements of the work environment that are associated with organizational status.[73] And his hypothesis was borne out in terms of changed performance; that is, workers in higher-status offices performed better, in direct proportion to the assigned level, even as the performance dropped for workers in lower-status offices. This study contains some implications that cannot be examined here; but if the perceived status of an office affects job performance, it follows that designers would want to consider what encourages the granting of that status (e.g., size, location, proportion, furniture).

Cultural Factors

Cultural systems rely on abstract concepts like *ritual* (the enacting of a particular social or religious ceremony), *symbol* (a learned device used to represent a particular idea), and *sign* (a token or gesture that serves to indicate a fact or quality) to function. Signs in particular serve in the delineation of built form, as they subsume the notion of symbol, and serve to identify the enactment of ritual. In his book *Simbolo, Communicazione, Consumo,* Gillo Dorfles maintains that architecture could be considered a *sign-system,* pointing out that "the cognitive process lies in our ability to assign a meaning to the things around us, and this is possible because the 'signs' are links between our own consciousness and the phenomenological world. So signs are the first and immediate tools of every communication."[74]

He concludes that architecture must therefore be considered, to some extent, an institutionalized ensemble of signs. Umberto Eco noted that phenomenological analysis of the relationship between ourselves and architectural objects demonstrates that we commonly experience architecture as communication, while recognizing its functionality.[75] In this sense, architecture not only permits events to occur, but suggests the events that are appropriate, and enables them. This has led Eco to certain conclusions critical to the study of semiotics; of interest here, however, is the nature and mechanism of the information being communicated.

Alton J. De Long points out that all systemic aspects of culture may be viewed as having certain levels of integration; the formal, informal, and technical, each operating in a unique but interactive manner.[76] The formal level constitutes the cultural codes that allow us to classify and process our milieu; the informal level is situational, allowing for behavior modification in context; and the technical level allows for a constant supply of newly generated content that society can use.[77] Important here is that this interaction of levels ". . . results in a naturally adaptive process of change and one which all levels of culture are affected by"[78] and that the continual increase in cultural complexity puts perpetual pressure on the formal level of culture. The inevitable result of this pressure is an ever more sophisticated reliance on coding systems that depend on a keen understanding of symbols and rituals. Thus culture not only provides the substance of the message, but supplies its medium of exchange as well. Moreover, it does this through a complex system of codes translated into architectural form.

These codes tie status indicators to performance expectations (as in Greenberg's offices), and—given Eco's position—the offices themselves to status. That is, the role of design in culture is to communicate and enable the psycho-spatial systems active in that place and at that time. And, as noted in chapter two, signs and symbols have the capacity to become independent, so that they remain potent forces even when divorced from immediate function. In his *Interior Decoration,* Mario Praz refers to the ". . . contrast between the surroundings of a man's work, his office, where a flat prosaic atmosphere dominates, and the surroundings of his comfort and his leisure, the home, which must propitiate his dreams and illusions; the world of business is opposed to the world of the heart."[79] This may explain why effort is made to bridge this gap at the highest levels of corporate existence. It may also explain the attachment to particular spaces. For example, John D. Rockefeller, Jr.'s office interior was bought in Spain, reconstructed in Rockefeller's private offices, then dismantled again to be rebuilt on the fifty-sixth floor of the RCA Building.[80] The same mystique of space and artifacts prevailed for Rockefeller as for Francesco de'Medici (Fig 10.16).

In Western culture, that mystique is often seen as a result of a vague, but eminently cultural, quality called *taste*. In an article in *Progressive Architecture,* "Taste in America," Suzanne Stephens defines taste as embracing both preference and judgment, " 'Preference,' that is personal, expressive idiosyncratic choice, we distinguish from 'judgment,' the overview, the distanced perspective from which evaluation is made on impartial and less subjective conditions."[81] Preference is thus short-term and quixotic, while judgment is enduring and informed. The problem, she points out, is that architecture operates on *both* time scales, belonging to fashion and culture, individual expression, and cultural values; and that as architecture is a subculture of a larger milieu, taste in American architecture reflects that fact.[82] The democratization of culture during the 1960s ensured that "instead of total design based on cultural ideals, architects were confronting total design considered only as commodity."[83] Stephens' article concludes with a warning that while shades of taste and their social meanings need to be considered, designers must be concerned with the architectural principles that outlive fashion. Taste clearly has changed its meaning in the past several decades, and no longer suffices as the design arbiter it was earlier (Fig 11.22). However, the principles underlying our spatial coding systems, and their respective symbols and rituals, remain an excellent guide to architectural understanding.

11.22

Just What Is It That Makes Today's Homes So Different, So Appealing? (collage on paper, 9⅞" × 10¼"); Richard Hamilton (1956) The images clipped from popular American magazine advertisements in this collage comment on the values of Western materialism. A stereotypical male and female are shown in an ordinary room filled with comfortable but banal furniture, and the numerous possessions assumed desirable for everyday life in an industrial society. In a catalog of an exhibition at the Tate Gallery (1970), the artist stated his belief that art was simply a reflection of (popular) culture and, as such, ought to reflect its values (e.g., be ". . . popular, transient, expendable, low-cost, mass-produced, young, witty, sexy, gimmicky, glamorous, and big business"). (Copyright: Richard Hamilton/VAGA, New York 1991; Collection: Kunsthalle Tübingen.)

The Space Within

12

Approach and Departure

The *Hobbitt,* J.R.R. Tolkien's great adventure, vividly describes the first steps taken by Bilbo Baggins and his fellow travelers on their quest:

> Long days after they had climbed out of the valley and left the Last Homely House miles behind, they were still going up and up. It was a hard path and a dangerous path, a crooked way and a lonely and a long. Now they could look back over the lands they had left, laid out behind them far below. Far, far away in the West, where things were blue and faint, Bilbo knew there lay his own country of safe and comfortable things. . . . He shivered.[1]

In this short description are the essential elements of approach and departure, ascent and movement, and even the nature of the path. Indeed, Tolkien uses the notion of path as passage through his carefully constructed, albeit literary, world of Middle-earth to dramatize his characters.

While the nature of this journey is epic in a way seldom experienced in our own world, the nature of transition through a structured space is probably familiar in concept. To provide a dramatic structure for human transition has traditionally been one of architecture's primary purposes. Nonetheless, the role of the path, its sequential movement and focal points, seems not to be much appreciated today; indeed, the goal is usually more highly valued than the journey. In *The Environmental Memory,* Malcolm Quantrill notes that the traditional history of architecture is essentially one of spatial ordering and formal expression that relies on constructional ingenuity and proportion for its major themes. Accordingly, the idea of progression and its representative elements, the staircase and corridor, play almost no part. And so he observes that while architectural history, criticism, and theory have centered on such points of arrival as the room, the atrium, and the piazza, ". . . the means of getting there—the street, the alley, the stairs—in some cases the very anatomy of the house or city, is often ignored both in the planning process and in the discussion of spatial and formal order."[2]

Quantrill's point is that these *transitional elements* are not considered very important in architectural theory—even if they are prominent in isolated studies and are acknowledged as functionally necessary. Yet they are

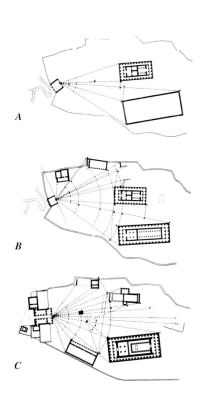

12.1

(A) **Acropolis I,** *ca.* B.C. *530* *(B)* **Acropolis II,** *ca.* B.C. *480* *(C)* **Acropolis III,** *after* B.C. *450*
There are eight principles in Doxiadis' system, some of which are: that the radii from the vantage point were used to determine a three-quarter view of all important structures; that the angles of incidence between radii fell into two internally consistent categories (a ten-part system with thirty-six-degree angles, and a twelve-part system with thirty-degree angles); and that the positions of buildings were also determined by their proportional distance from that vantage point. The shift in systems between Acropolis II and III is apparent in the reorientation of the Propylaea; this structure serves also as the vantage point for the perspective. (Source: *Architectural Space in Ancient Greece,* C. A. Doxiadis. Published by The MIT Press. Copyright 1972 by The Massachusetts Institute of Technology.)

crucial in forming our experience of buildings as sensory objects. In his "Buildings as Percepts," Rudolf Arnheim points out that one's percepts typically concern the autonomous existence of objects as they form in the mind from many individual impressions, particularly as one approaches or passes through a building. And he notes that our end image of an object (or building, as one sort of object) is thus the result of our spontaneous integration of these multiple visual projections into a total perceptual image.[3] Arnheim's theory has three important aspects: first, a comprehensive mental image of a building develops as a purely perceptual process; second, this image must incorporate the sensations generated in the viewer by the building as it is experienced sequentially; and third, a building exists both as a spatial event outside the temporal dimension and as an event unfolding. Thus the first two aspects deal with buildings' visual attributes—attributes that help to form an appropriate *objective percept.* He concludes, "All is well when particular views of aspects display essential structural properties of the design as a whole."[4]

The third point is critical in Arnheim's argument, as it implies several conditions unique to architecture. First, that the viewer's experience of the building is participatory; second, that the appearance of individual components of buildings come from the intended order of view; and third, that the order of view makes sense only in terms of the physical structure of the building, its enduring nature. His conclusion is significant: "Beyond utility, it is aesthetically indispensable that viewers become aware of the interplay between timeless spatial structure and the time-bound avenues through the building."[5] This implies that stationary spaces (like rooms) are timeless in nature, while transitional pathways (like corridors, entries, and stairways) are tied to human participation. This in turn raises questions of how viewers 'see' architectural space or, more precisely, how the designer arranges space to be seen; and whether there are different ways of experiencing spaces that are dependent on their particular type.

Inherent in Arnheim's view of spatial percepts is the *position of the observer.* That is, if the perception of a building is the synthesis of individual projections, the question must arise whether those projections are being viewed from a sequence of relatively *static* positions (as at the entries to rooms), or *actively,* in a haptic continuum (as in corridors). At first, this seems a peculiar distinction, in that the usual assumption is that space is experienced continuously. But it seems that certain architectural configurations (and spaces) are more clearly apprehended from one particular vantage point; and that certain views are more important than others. This has led to at least one approach to architectural analysis based on the notion of dynamic viewing lines that emanate from a static position. Such an approach would help explain certain spatial configurations that seem, at first, not to have an organizing concept in three dimensions.

In his analysis of the Greek acropolis (as a type of square or gathering place), Paul Zucker states that temples and statues were positioned according to prevailing topographical conditions, without benefit of an organized overall plan. That is, he sees no spatial relationship between the individual elements, leading him to conclude that the Greeks ". . . quite obviously . . . did not aim at any kind of spatial unification and integration."[6] The artistic formation of space, he feels, began slowly during the fifth century B.C.; and even then didn't apply to the acropolis. And he similarly notes the lack of desire for spatial integration in the pathway approaching the propylaea (entry) of the acropolis. The seeming disorder in the arrangement of buildings and statuary on various sites led Constantinos A. Doxiadis to postulate a strikingly different system of organization in his *Architectural Space in Ancient Greece.* This system is based on perspective and angles of view from a fixed point. In his investigation of twenty-nine sites, Doxiadis found the layouts sufficiently consistent that the main outlines of a system of design may be discerned, one which depends on the observer. This system becomes quite clear in his analysis of the Athenian Acropolis (Fig 12.1).

Such a system seems contrary to our view of the Greeks as analytical designers. In their *Body, Memory, and Architecture,* Kent C. Bloomer and Charles W. Moore comment, "The curious, unsettling sense of revelation such a radical spatial model contains underscores the extent of our acceptance of and dependence on the rectangular Cartesian grid."[7] Indeed, Doxiadis points out that this system was unknown to the ancient Greeks. "Their layouts were not designed on a drawing board; each was developed on a site in an existing landscape, which was not subject to the laws of axial coordinates. . . . The determining factor in the design was the human viewpoint."[8] And that viewpoint, as the figure shows, was located at the propylaea. Bloomer and Moore conclude that Doxiadis' approach is convincing, ". . . not only because it seems to tally with the facts, but because it seems such an eminently sensible way to lay out a special space that must be entered from a particular point."[9] In much the same vein, Vincent Scully, in *The Earth, The Temple, and the Gods,* praises Doxiadis' theory for two reasons: first, its insistence on a wide arc of vision that rejects ". . . criticism based on the restricted, rectangular window of Renaissance perspective. . . ."; and second, its assertion that the eye is dramatically led toward the landscape beyond.[10]

The second point is critical to the analysis offered by Le Corbusier: "The balance of the parts is in no way a paltry one. It is determined by the famous landscape which stretches from the Piraeus to Mount Pentelicus. The scheme was designed to be seen from a distance: the axes follow the valley and the false right angles are contrived with the skill of a first-rate stage manager."[11] In his description is a suggestion of the reason for changing from the twelve-part system of Acropolis II, which left one angle open to the landscape beyond, to the ten-part system of the classical Acropolis, which contained the view (Fig 12.2). Thus, the last part of Le Corbusier's comments may be the most germane (i.e., that such a fixed visual scheme seems more appropriate to a theatrical stage than a three-dimensional spatial construct that can be entered). Indeed, this point is at the heart of Zucker's rejection of Doxiadis' theory of space, as is apparent when he says that ". . . the continuity of successive visual impressions would certainly not create any simultaneous awareness of volume and still less any feeling of space."[12] And Scully notes that the important experiences of most sites come from walking through them to their centers, the very experiences disavowed by this unusual system. But he notes that this theory ". . . re-

12.2

Sketch of the Athenian Acropolis; *Le Corbusier*
In this pencil sketch the centralized point in plan is shown to be the statue of Athena Promachos. Located on the central axis, it draws the visitor to the proper location for a three-quarter view of the Parthenon and the Erectheum. This view presents the full grandeur of this "outdoor room"; by the slight angle of Athena's placement, the visitor is redirected toward the Parthenon, and Mount Pentelicus beyond. Thus Le Corbusier's view is in close accordance with the system postulated by Doxiadis. (Copyright 1991 ARS N. Y. / SPADEM.)

12.3

Spanish Stairs—Rome; *Francesco De Sanctis and Allesandro Specchi (1721–5)*
There is a certain poetry in the connection of a fountain (whose contained water suggests further depth) at the bottom of the steps, with the obelisk (pointing still higher) at the top; but the real dynamic is the steps themselves, as indicated by the crowds of people who perpetually occupy them. (Source: *Éléments et Théorie de l'Architecture,* J. Guadet.)

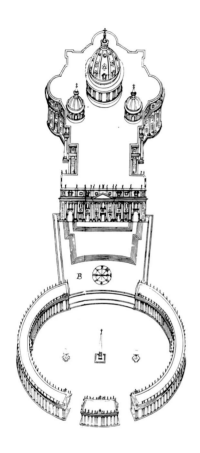

12.4

Piazza of St. Peter's—Rome; *Gianlorenzo Bernini (begun in 1656)*
The repose of the curving colonnade was, for Bernini, expressive of the dignity and majesty of the Church. Wittkower notes that this form contained a specific theme, "Bernini himself compared the colonnades to the motherly arms of the Church 'which embrace Catholics to reinforce their belief, heretics to re-unite them with the Church, and agnostics to enlighten them with the true faith.' "[1] (Source: *Édifices de Rome Moderne,* Paul Letarouilly.)

mains the most challenging one which has yet been advanced''; especially in its implication of a system that is so subtle it appears not to exist at all.[13]

There are other intriguing aspects to Doxiadis' approach, particularly as occur in his analysis of Acropolis III, where the Propylaea has been turned to conform with the axis of the Parthenon. There is in this shift the suggestion of the Acropolis as an outdoor room that must be approached by an ascending path, and viewed from its most intense point, with the formerly open axial view blocked by a view of Mount Pentelicus. Seen this way, the space assumes a more familiar aspect. One could, for example, draw a comparison with Michelangelo's Campidoglio, where the essential experience of the space may be felt at the top of the steps, and where intense spiritual energy is concentrated in the square's center (Fig 3.1). That is not to say that the Campidoglio cannot be transited, only that the vantage point provides an intensified experience of entry that enhances the space. Indeed, the importance of entry and arrival is acute in those spaces intended for ceremony and ritual.

There is, however, a marked difference between an approach to a static point of view (and consequent entry) and one in which the approach itself provides the primary experience. In the latter instance it can be observed that the journey, rather than the destination, represents the point of the design. This becomes clear in an analysis of an alternative to the Campidoglio, the Spanish Steps in front of Sta. Trinità dei Monti, designed by Francesco De Sanctis and Alessandro Specchi in 1721. The historian A.C. Sewter has commented that "their light rising rhythms, punctuated by the oval fountain at the bottom and the obelisk at the top, are a perfect expression of the Rococo delight in spatial flow."[14] The clear reference to the fountain and obelisk show that these steps are an elastic connection between two points, and that it is the act of ascending (or descending) the sensuous, undulating stairs that constitutes their essential experience (Fig 12.3). In his *Modern Architecture*, Vincent Scully comments on the steps:

> They are spacious and swelling and present an open invitation to the drama of movement. At the same time, their spaces, which seem so free, are in fact symmetrically focused by the solid shaft of the obelisk above them. . . . All movement is around fixed points. It is a union of the opposites of order and freedom. . . . It is therefore an architecture that is intended to enclose and shelter human beings in a psychic sense, to order them absolutely so that they can always find a known conclusion at the end of any journey, but finally to let them play at freedom and action all the while.[15]

Some sixty-five years earlier, Gianlorenzo Bernini had been given a commission by Pope Alexander VII that shared some of the spatial characteristics of both the Campidoglio and the Spanish Steps. This project, begun in 1656, was for a design for the Piazza of St. Peter's that would both unify the piazza and meet the ritual needs of the Church. Particularly important was provision for the Papal blessing given from the Benediction Loggia on Easter; this meant designing a piazza to hold large numbers of people—in fact and in symbol (as the blessing is offered *urbi et orbi*)—while maximizing the loggia's legibility. Bernini's solution was to design the piazza in the form of a trapezoid, with a ceremonial colonnade that used a lateral expansion and contraction to dramatize the approach to St. Peters (Fig 12.4). The shape was partly dictated by the need to accommodate the old palace entrance, the Scala Regia, which he substantially redesigned (Fig 5.22). And there is evidence that he had also planned to close the piazza at the now-open end, using the idea of a small "ante-piazza" to grant symmetry.

Of special importance in this regard is Rudolf Wittkower's suggestion that such a space would have allowed the visitor to embrace the entire perimeter of the oval. He says, "Small or large, interior or exterior, a comprehensive and unimpaired view of the whole structure belongs to Bernini's dynamic conception of architecture. . . ."[16] But the effect of the piazza is somewhat different from that of the Spanish Steps in that the manipulation is experienced visually but not kinesthetically; that is, the viewer's movement is not actually guided in the piazza like it is on the steps, nor does actual passage seem so imperative to its experience. This space may thus mark a transitional stage between the Campidoglio and the Spanish Steps in the incorporation of physical movement into spatial design. Finally, a different sort of approach, one exploiting interior effect, is found in the design of the Temple of Khonsu at Karnak. The pronounced compression/expansion is both lateral and vertical, the idea of ascent is exploited, and additionally, there are carefully controlled light effects via the clerestory windows (Fig 12.5).

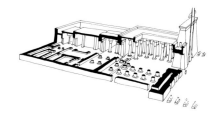

12.5

Temple of Khonsu—Karnak (*B.C. 1198*)
A sense of progression is fostered in this enclosed structure by the telescoping space, massing of columns, and manipulation of light. It is interesting that the Egyptians, in a land of open space and blinding light, chose to represent their ultimate mysteries in a closed space of heavy darkness. (Drawn by: J. Malnar.)

Factors in Spatial Movement

The implication in these various designs is that spaces designed to celebrate movement do not always use the same methodology, nor do they necessarily produce the same result—any more than is the case with spaces seen from a static point of view. This raises the question of which factors are involved in *spatial movement*. In this regard, one might recall Arnheim's description of architecture as a temporal event made up of innumerable individual impressions that are integrated into a total perceptual image. This implies that images are like frames of film, observable both separately and together. In their discussion of theoretical approaches to the development of environmental knowledge, Harry Heft and Joachim F. Wohlwill refer to such momentarily discrete views as "retinal snapshots"; they say that to explain the apparent temporal continuity and spatial extension of our environmental experience, cognitive procedures are required to compile and integrate the incoming data.[17] Thus perception is an indirect and mediated process; this is, of course, the Gestalt view. As noted in a previous chapter, J.J. Gibson offers an alternative view—perception as the result of direct stimulus information (without any cognitive mediation). These stimuli provide information that is both changing (perspective structure) and static (invariant structure); together these provide a temporal flow of information about both movement and the pathway. But Heft and Wohlwill note that these two views are not necessarily mutually exclusive, as various environmental conditions (or *contextual* factors), in addition to personal goals, may ultimately determine whether circumstances require perceptual or cognitive processes:

> In this light, way-finding may be viewed as a form of environmental *perception*, considering perception as involving the pickup of information over time . . . On the other hand, tasks such as constructing maps or models of an environment . . . may draw directly on *conceptual knowledge.*[18]

This is an interesting effort to mediate between the two theoretical approaches. But as Julian Hochberg has noted, Gibson's approach does not consider the Gestalt organizational phenomena, nor the perceptual illusions; he concludes, *"Whether, when, and whence viewers look depends on their perceptual intentions and inquiry,* and . . . these simply cannot be reduced to matters of optics."[19] Therefore, designers must always work within the range presented by—on the one hand—the perceptual constancies (like size and shape) and—on the other—the actual images that form on the retina. If the former was absolutely so, little or no illusion could be generated by the designer; if the latter was so, our spatial world would be one of constant change in which each viewpoint would require design attention. Thus the "film" mentioned above is in constant perceptual adjustment, where the agreement between physical construction and its appearance is subject to individual interpretation. If, however, visual percepts represent an accumulation over time, such discrepancies may not be critical.

There are other aspects of J.J. Gibson's approach to sensory data that have implications for architectural design. He has taken the five senses that have prevailed historically, and redefined them so as to make them far more inclusive, and active rather than passive. This system is likely the result of his view that our sensory apparatus is an information-seeking mechanism with highly integrated aspects, fully capable of discovering information without any necessary cognitive process. Thus, instead of the senses of sight, sound, smell, taste and touch, Gibson lists the senses as the visual system, the auditory system, the taste-smell system, the basic-orienting system, and the haptic system.[20] Gibson's view of visual perception has already been treated; of interest here are the last two systems. The *basic-orienting* system is based on the horizontality of the ground-plane and our contrasting vertical posture. He theorizes that the resultant orientation leads us to seek a symmetrical balance such that we always turn our sensory capacity to that end. This seems related to Gestalt theory, but in Gibson's model it is involuntary and without any inference. The *haptic* system is simply the sense of touch extended to include all possible sensations—temperature, pain, pressure, and kinesthesia (body sensation and muscle movement).[21] It is thus a system in which humans become literally in contact with their environment; indeed, it is very likely a primary way of negotiating the environment. In *Placeways*, E.V. Walter notes, "Haptic perception reminds us that the whole self may grasp reality without seeing, hearing or thinking. It also calls attention to a primitive way of knowing that resembles mythical thought . . . a unified structure of feeling and doing."[22] These two senses in concert would help explain our sense of a place, and our tactile awareness of walls and doors, compression and expansion, ascent and descent—in short, the critical qualities of transition.

The property most exploited in haptic perception is the *kinesthetic* one—the sensation of bodily posture and muscle movements. Its importance is noted in *Town and Square,* by Paul Zucker: "Space is perceived by the visualization of its limits and by kinesthetic experience, i.e., by the sensation of our movements. In the state of 'visual tension,' kinesthetic sensation and visual perception fuse most intensely. . . ."[23] (Such a statement makes his objection to Doxiadis even more clear.) But surely such kinesthetic experience is most acute in transitional areas like corridors, stairways, and doorways. Put differently, a relatively minor dimensional change is quickly apprehended in a doorway, corridors are assessed for their ease of (our) passage, and virtually any alteration of a stair riser creates at least some confusion. Indeed, few dimensions are as codified as the relationship between stair riser and tread, although that code tends to be sightly more liberal on the exterior. The current interior formula—riser + tread = 17 or 17½"—is really a habituated design approach for a habituated audience (albeit with some basis in physiology), one that is altered only at risk. On the other hand, few dimensional alterations are as effective in fundamentally changing the nature of transition. The riser is particularly amenable to this sort of manipulation; high risers tend to exaggerate feelings of exhaustion or exhilaration (depending on the goal), while short risers solemnize situations by causing a slow and deliberate ascent or descent (Fig 12.6).

12.6

Staircase in Palacio de Versalles—Mexico City; *Ricardo Legorreta*
This staircase uses low risers, which in addition to suggesting a slow ascent, make that ascent appear easy. This represents a successful attempt by Legorreta to entice the tenants and visitors away from the elevators, which are expensive to operate. (Photo by: Julius Shulman, Hon. A.I.A. [copyright], Los Angeles [285A, Mexico 11020 D.F.].)

This suggests a generative role for kinesthetic experience in spatial design, particularly where the interaction of body movement and its spatial envelope is intense. Perhaps, therefore, much can be learned from modern dance in this respect, as a dancer's view of space is primarily haptic. Through training, the dancer comes to experience space as tangible, a source of interaction. But the relationship to one's interior space is also essential, an aspect referred to as *centering;* indeed, to feel one's center is considered necessary for movement. Such an awareness of spatial position must have associations: to extend the body and reach upwards, or compress the body into the ground-plane, are movements that immediately become more significant. These metaphorical qualities are what Robert J. Yudell refers to in *Body, Memory and Architecture,* when he notes that the vertical axis is "... closely bound to the concept of transition through the cycles of life."[24] Dancers usually have a far larger repertoire of movement than the general public, whose vertical movements tend to be limited to stairways and elevators. This need not be so; Yudell notes that buildings can serve as a stage for movement, and encourage a dialogue between themselves and the human body.[25]

In a similar vein, John Summerson observes, "Architecture, by virtue of its actual limitations, can exploit our capacity for dramatizing ourselves, for heightening the action of ordinary life; it can increase man's psychological stature to an angel's. . . ."[26] Yudell cites the circulation elements of Le Corbusier's Villa Savoye as an example of dramatic movement, in which the spiral, clockwise stairway and the rectilinear, counter-clockwise ramp together create a complex relationship (Fig 9.21). He notes that in his design, Le Corbusier "... has generated a highly complex periodic pattern of space-time relationships, experienced primarily through body movement. It is most exhilarating when we can sense our movement in relation to a person on the other path. . . ."[27] This sort of interaction was more usual in the past, as seen in the staircase of the Bourbon Royal Palace at Caserta, designed in 1734 by architect Luigi Vanvitelli (Fig 12.7). In his *Architectural Composition,* Rob Krier notes that such staircases perform a social function, acting as a type of hall in baroque palaces, and accounting for their great size and beauty. And he concludes, "The staircase, which formerly was an important area of human communication, has to be given back its appropriate significance in a building."[28]

12.7

Palazzo Reale, Lo Scalone d'Onore—Caserta, Campania; *Luigi Vanvitelli (1734)*
This ceremonial staircase was commissioned by the future Charles III of Spain after he conquered Naples in 1734. Its importance may be gauged by its scale and obvious expense. It leads into a vaulted vestibule, and from there doors open onto the state rooms and chapel. Wittkower observes that "... from the return flights of the staircase the beholder looks through the screen of arches into stage-like scenery beyond. . . ."[2]
(Source: Alinari/Art Resource.)

Path Configurations

The previous reference to dance suggests that spatial design is in some sense analogous to choreography. That is, the designer plans space to be experienced vertically and horizontally, with transitions that are direct or circuitous, and points of entry that are predictable or dramatic (Fig 5.1). Bloomer and Moore point out that ". . . the choreography of arrival at the house (the *path* to it) can send out messages and induce experiences which heighten its importance as a place."[29] But it seems clear that interior paths—corridor, stairway, entry—function in much the same manner. While the destination of the journey (a room, for example) is usually considered the primary point of the design, this is not always so; and, in any case, it is the transitional elements preceding the destination that enhance much of that space's character. And as spaces can be denoted by type (i.e., having a certain form and quality), so can pathways.

In his "Environmental Cognition," Reginald G. Golledge notes that paths consist of an origin and destination. These are connected by groups of procedural rules that are turned into spatial components, which include distance, direction, and orientation.[30] But the precise pathway taken also depends on variables such as efficiency, time, and aesthetics; while the choice may be influenced through design, it cannot be completely controlled. To complicate matters, direct experience and individual memory have a residual influence, as does the clarity of the linked landmarks (or nodes). Golledge concludes that ". . . there is a commonsense reason to expect that a minimal set of primary nodes or landmarks that define the end points of any given path system not only anchor a cognitive configuration but also precede path learning, and that they similarly define a given path segment."[31] On the other hand, Malcolm Quantrill points out that "the path, the way forward and backward, is a basic property of consciousness. A path gives us continuity in space and time. . . ."[32] One may conclude that places (static elements) and paths (transitional elements) together form a coherent system; but this is not to imply that they function similarly or in the same measure.

The term for mnemonic representation of spatial information is *cognitive mapping;* such a "map" may be thought of as all the information we have stored about our various physical and sociocultural environments. The studies made by Kevin Lynch for his work *The Image of the City* are interesting in this regard. Lynch found that environmental images could be divided into three basic components: *identity,* an object recognized as a distinct and separable entity; *structure,* the spatial or pattern relation of the object to both the observer and other objects; and *meaning,* the object's emotional or utilitarian meaning to the observer.[33] "Thus an image useful for making an exit requires the recognition of a door as a distinct entity, of its spatial relation to the observer, and its meaning as a hole for getting out."[34] He has used this system to ascertain what makes cities *imageable,* referring to ". . . that shape, color or arrangement which facilitates the making of vividly identified, powerfully structured, highly useful mental images of the environment."[35] And Jon Lang likewise notes that a highly imageable city, building, or interior is one that is perceived as a well-structured, system of related components.[36]

Lynch's major contribution to cognitive mapping may be his categories of elements that are used to form cognitive images. These are paths, edges, districts, nodes, and landmarks and are defined as follows: *paths* are the channels (like streets and corridors) of our environment; *edges* represent the more or less permeable boundaries (separating areas); *districts* are areas

12.8

Outer Lobby, 1550 No. State Parkway—Chicago; *Marshall and Fox (1911–2)*
Designed by Benjamin Marshall, this is the lobby of one of the elegant apartment buildings that this firm was noted for. The lobby is light, delicate, and easy to transverse. (Courtesy: Chicago Historical Society; Photo by: Kathleen Collins, ICHi-18919.)

with fairly definable characteristics (like waiting areas); *nodes* are strategic focal points (like central stairways); and *landmarks* are easily identified and dominating physical elements. It seems clear that Lynch intended these categories to be used in an urban analysis; they are nonetheless useful for interior application, and have thus appeared in some form in the theories of others. Christian Norberg-Schulz, for example, speaks of places, paths, and domains; and Bloomer and Moore discuss place, path, pattern, and edge.

The suggestion was made earlier that, compared to stationary spaces, transitional pathways are dynamic in nature. But clearly they can be more or less so. Jon Lang uses *functional distance* (between spaces) and *functional centrality* (of commonly used transitional areas) as major predictors of people's patterns of interaction.[37] The functional distance is reduced when pathways (staircases and corridors) lead directly between points, and increased when they are interrupted or provide opportunities for social activities. An efficient functional distance is usually prescribed for certain kinds of pathways, like service corridors and delivery entries, which are not meant to be used by the primary occupant or visitor. This is made apparent by their dedicated character and plain appearance; indeed, such pathways are often hidden from the primary occupants. This is particularly obvious in certain sorts of building types, such as hotels and restaurants, where two separate and distinct circulatory systems coexist. But functional pathways are not limited to service personnel; the nature of the destination or business to be conducted there may be such as to render appropriate a direct, efficient arrival (e.g., into a building's lobby) (Fig 12.8). Indeed, in contemporary societies, efficient arrival is often highly valued.

However, this was not always so, nor does the public always use highly functional transitional zones as intended. The corridors of hospitals, courthouses, and offices are often used for extensive social interaction, both informal and structured (particularly courthouses). In certain situations, however, the functional distance is purposely extended; that is, there are circumstances in which the stairway or corridor—the circulatory elements— have a spatial claim equal to that of the destination. Such an extension proclaims the special character of the space that will eventually be entered and, sometimes, may even conjoin it. Clearly, Charles Garnier's treatment of the foyer and central stairs of the Paris Opera, which he stated were to serve the passage of people through the theater "gracefully and comfortably," is a superb example of circulation elements treated on a grand scale (Fig 8.11). In his approach to architecture, Garnier seems more like a social psychologist determined to calculate and accommodate the behavior of his building's inhabitants than the brilliant engineer-builder that he was. That the external massing of the structure is a reflection of interior spatial necessity has already been commented on; of equal interest is his treatment of the interior façades. Arthur Drexler describes Garnier's approach to these spaces and elements of circulation: "The more commodious the space in which to linger, the more elaborate the detail. Thus the stair hall is like a plaza surrounded by streets, all encased in ornament signaling the appropriate rate of movement. Only when Garnier wants movement to be quick does he eliminate ornament entirely. . . ."[38] And he points out that the ornament is supplemented by other devices that suggest movement, such as the compound curves of the stairway, the curved and projecting balconies, the arches used for the ceilings of the Grand Foyer, and the clever use of integrative color.

Still, Garnier was differentiating between the circulatory elements and the spaces they were meant to serve. It may, however, be desirable to make these elements continuous; this sort of arrangement is entirely usual in exhibition areas like galleries and museums. Thus Frank Lloyd Wright's design for the Morris Gift Shop in San Francisco reflects the essential continuity between the circulation ramp (for display) and the centrally located counters (Fig 12.9). A more recent example of this phenomenon is in the 1985 design of the exhibition space for a show of paintings at the Art Institute of Chicago entitled "A Day in the Country," designed by Paul Florian and Stephen Wierzbowski. This show was unusual in several respects: first, the curators required the paintings be grouped by subject matter for reasons related to context; second, the circulatory system was to be unidirectional, with specific attributes of traffic control; and third, the exhibit was to arbitrate between its inherent architectural elements and the autonomy of the works of art. The designer's solution was a hybrid design that controlled the order of view, but did so in the spatial context suggested by the works of art themselves (Fig 12.10). The object, in both cases, is to gently suggest and facilitate people's movement through space essentially circulatory in nature, which becomes obvious in even a cursory look at the plan.

The plan has often been seen as the design element that is responsible for generating all other aspects of the building. Stanley Abercrombie suggests that "building plans can, indeed, be grouped according to the types of movement they allow, inspire, or demand."[39] He accordingly groups them into four basic types: first, plans that can *direct* linear progressions of movement to a particular goal; second, plans that *free* movement to its own ends; third, plans that *focus* movement to a central locus or activity; and fourth, plans that *organize* movement in predetermined patterns. Each of these goals has a historic archetype, although few contemporary plans adhere rigidly to one particular type (Fig 12.11). He points out that "plans of any type are subject to infinite modifications, being altered by the pressures of internal functional requirements . . . or deformed by the requirements of a predetermined exterior form. . . ."[40] His system is interesting for being based on the possibilities of movement in plan types, rather than the structural development inherent in the notion of plan as axis—a more usual view.

Axes may be defined as particular path types, whose function goes beyond mere circulation; rather, the axis has traditionally been regarded as the essential skeleton of the structure, its informing *raison d'etre*. As such, it is the primary organizing element that may be found in every building,

12.9

Circle Gallery (Formerly the Morris Gift Shop)—San Francisco; *Frank Lloyd Wright (1948)*
The spiral ramp not only connects two display areas, but is itself used as a continuous viewing device (unlike more conventional stairways). Its form, moreover, seems particularly appropriate for connecting areas that are themselves circular. (Courtesy: Mrs. Maynard Parker, Los Angeles. Photo by: Maynard Parker.)

12.10

"A Day in the Country" Exhibit, Art Institute of Chicago; *Paul Florian and Stephen Wierzbowski (1985)*
A one-way circulation system with subordinate areas where crowds could gather was indicated, but the design avoids using a strictly linear sequence. The design approach is tripartite: first, the development of a menu of forms and spatial types that might be employed generally; second, the placement of certain forms to elicit specific movement patterns; and third, the correspondence of spatial forms to attributes of content in the works of art. (Courtesy: Florian Wierzbowski, Chicago.)

12.11

Plan types; *Stanley Abercrombie (1982)*
Abercrombie has identified four basic types of building plan, grouped according to their potential for movement. In more traditional terminology, these same types would be referred to as: *linear* (the highly directed plan seen in sacred buildings and in the circulatory patterns of small shops); *grid* (the open and regular plan typical of exhibition halls); *radial* (the centrally focussed plan typical of the Renaissance); and *multidirectional* (the plan generally used in office planning). (Reproduced with permission from *AIA Journal,* copyright 1982, The American Institute of Architects. All rights reserved.)

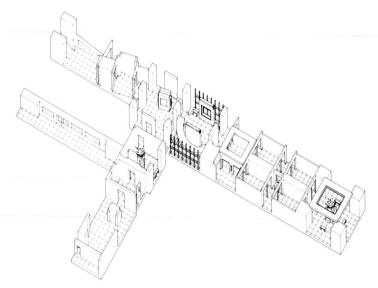

on a more or less formal basis. Since every structure has both major and minor axes, problems can occur when that hierarchy is not clearly defined, or when there exists a conflict in overall intention. The stipulation of a clear axis, arranged in strict, symmetrical formality, has long been regarded as the essence of École des Beaux-Arts' training. David van Zanten comments that the student arranged spaces and volumes symmetrically and pyramidally along axes that intersected at right angles (usually at a major central space).[41] This method, of course, represented one sort of axial planning, a highly ritualized one. That the axis has remained central to twentieth-century design is attested to by Le Corbusier when he says: "Architecture is based on axes. The axes of the schools are an architectural calamity. The axis is a line of direction leading to an end. In architecture, you must have a destination for your axis."[42] Le Corbusier, clearly, is defining axis as a generative pathway, rather than the comparatively static pattern exemplified by the École des Beaux-Arts.

Axial types may thus be arranged according to their path definitions and resultant characteristics. *Linear* axes generally lead in a straight path from origin to destination, with relatively minor interruptions along the route. An excellent example of a highly linear axis is seen at the Temple of Khonsu referred to earlier (Fig 12.5). Paul Zucker notes:

> . . . the aesthetically decisive element is not the individual spatial unit of the courts themselves, but the succession of courts following each other. . . . It is the axis as such which dictates the movement. . . . No deviations into other directions seemed to be allowed, time for a pause did not exist, only the continuous drive and dynamic force of the axis proper, its propellant trend, channeled toward the final goal of the procession.[43]

In this description are the essential characteristics of the linear axis, both spatial and emotional. Moreover, it suggests that features of space may mirror cultural beliefs, particularly in the treatment of pathways. An entirely formal use of axes, as well as traditional detailing, may be seen in the entry of the State Department's elliptical Treaty Room, designed by Allan Greenberg in 1986 (Fig 12.12). This room is the heart of the Diplomatic Reception Rooms, thus serving a symbolic function. In a somewhat different vein, the design for the entranceway to Eleven South LaSalle by Thomas Beeby uses a shift in axis to realign the entry and elevator core. In this case, the approach was born of necessity, to restore through symmetry and use of materials the elegance the lobby had once enjoyed (Fig 12.13).

12.12

The Treaty Room—State Department Building, Washington, D.C.; *Allan Greenberg (1986)*
The Treaty Room uses free-standing Corinthian columns that incorporate the Great Seal of the United States in the capitals and thereby suggest an entirely Roman freedom of modification for symbolic purposes. Visual unity is provided through continuity in detail (the egg and dart pattern, for example, occurs in several places), the floor pattern (which suggests the Campidoglio), and the consistent cornice and base moldings. (Courtesy: Clement E. Conger, Curator, Diplomatic Reception Rooms, U.S. Department of State; Photo by: Richard Cheek.)

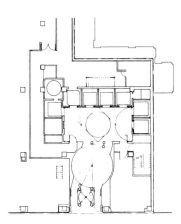

12.13

Lobby, 11 South LaSalle—Chicago; *Hammond Beeby and Babka (1985)*
Both the entry vestibule and elevator bank are tangential to the circular lobby, whose radial character allows entrance at any number of positions on its perimeter. Although the two flanking spaces that abut the lobby are rectangular, symmetry is nonetheless maintained by providing an odd number (three) of columns at both points of entry, to ease transition. The solidity and richness is reinforced by the use of heavily veined marble for the columns and floor. (Plan—courtesy: Hammond, Beeby and Babka, Chicago; Photo by: Karant & Associates, Inc., Chicago. Copyright 1991.)

An entirely different conception may be seen in the use of the *bent axis,* whose configuration is based on an oblique sense of approach. Such a departure from formal symmetry tends to endow pathways with an active and highly directed character. The T.W. Best Newsstand by Eva Madddox Associates occupies a corner location in a commuter railroad terminal; the angled display fixture leads one into the newsstand, past the merchandise to the cashier's stand, and through the adjacent exit to the departure tracks. Thus the axis is used as a form of traffic control, as well as maximizing exposure to the products (Fig 12.14). *Curved* axes are prevalent in the design of stairways, where the sensuality lends richness to residential interiors and a certain dignity to office blocks. An elegant example of this is seen in the interior staircase of the Palazzo Barberini, by Gianlorenzo Bernini (Fig 12.15). Curved axes are also useful in extending time-passage, since a curved line (as Kandinsky pointed out) is sensed as longer than the same length of straight line, a fact which Wright exploited in his Circle Gallery. And in its suggestion of psychological freedom, the curved axis is related to the *random* axis. While truly random axes are a contradiction in terms, pathways may be determined primarily by the need to move the viewer through space in a purposeful manner, as in the Art Institute exhibit previously referred to. But there are certain kinds of exhibitions where traffic flow is sequentially directed, within a space and between spaces. Such was the case with the ''Labyrinth No. 1'' exhibit, put on by the Groupe de Recherche d'Art Visuel in Paris (Fig 12.16). Here the axial movement is related to issues of sequence and focus.

Before proceeding to these issues, however, some discussion of possible *sources for axial types* is crucial to understand planning. Abercrombie noted the effects of internal necessity and external form on the plan; but there are probably sociocultural factors at work as well. In his provocative article ''Figures, Doors and Passages,'' Robin Evans postulates such a connection, noting at the outset that the plan above all describes the nature of human relationships.[44] Through a process of comparing architectural plans and artistic representations of the human figure, he concludes that in the period between the Renaissance and the nineteenth century there had been a complete inversion of the definition of convenience. He states, ''In 16th century Italy a convenient room had many doors: in 19th century England a convenient room had but one.''[45] He points out that this fundamental change

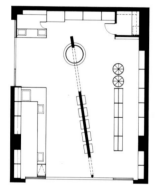

12.14

T.W. Best Newsstand, Northwestern Terminal—Chicago; *Eva Maddox Associates (1987)*
The directional display rack guides the customer, past newspapers on one side and snack foods on the other, directly to the cashier's stand. The central rack also segregates the magazine area, thus allowing browsing in a nontraffic area. The impact of the circulatory pattern is enhanced by the integral use of primary colors (red, yellow, blue) and large product displays in the shape of geometric solids. (Plan—courtesy: Eva Maddox Associates, Inc., Interior Architect, Chicago; Photo by: Jon Miller/Hedrich, Blessing.)

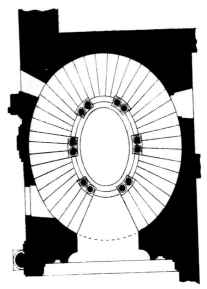

12.15

Central Staircase, Palazzo Barberini—Rome; *Gianlorenzo Bernini (1628-33)*
This remarkable building was begun by Maderno, but after his death in 1629, Bernini completed the structure (with da Cortona working on the theater). It employs an H-shape plan and is set in a large garden, giving it the effect of a country villa. But it is the sensual, curving stair, with its unusually paired columns, that is especially in keeping with the spirit of the baroque. The interior effect of the stair may be further gauged by examining this text's cover photograph. (Source: *Éléments et Théorie de l'Architecture*, J. Guadet.)

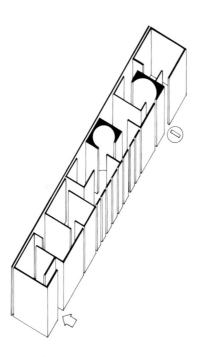

12.16

"Labyrinth No. 1" Exhibit—Paris; *Groupe de Recherche d'Art Visuel (1963)*
This exhibit was shown in the Third Biennial of Paris, as one of a number of collective presentations. It consisted of a series of seven rooms (approximately 70′ long), each room being 10′ wide. Most of these rooms (or niches) follow a series of 90° turns in the corridor; in this way the viewer was prepared for the new art experience in each space by the character of the pathway itself. (Drawn by: J. Malnar.)

A

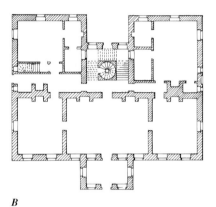

B

12.17

(A) **Palazzo Valmarana—Lisiera;** *Andrea Palladio (1563-4);* *(B)* **Amesbury Abbey— Wiltshire;** *John Webb (ca. 1661)* Both plans are rectangular, compact, and symmetrical. The critical difference in approach is Webb's early use of the central corridor to service the rooms. By the nineteenth century, the desire for privcy made such corridors ubiquitous. *([A] Source: The Four Books of Architecture,* Andrea Palladio; *[B]* Drawn by: J. Malnar.)

not only caused the structure of the house to become rearranged, but thereby altered the human relationships within it (Fig 12.17).

His second point is that, as a corollary, the corridor was developed to minimize the necessary dealings among the various members of the household. Thus in the sixteenth century, circulation patterns are innate in the room layout; by the nineteenth century, the circulatory elements are entirely separate, a system of corridors and passages leading to every portion of the house. And the stately doors between rooms, far from serving the purposes of simple access, are now used to provide generous vistas through the length of the house (and beyond). Evans concludes that ". . . the integration of household space was now for the sake of beauty: its separation was for convenience—an opposition which has since become deeply engraved into theory. . . ."[46] The evolution of the corridor is thus seen as a result of a new emphasis on privacy (among family members) and class awareness (between family and servants). In his analysis of Amesbury Abbey, an early step in this development, John Bold comments: "The disposition of the stairs appears to have been Webb's starting-point in his planning of the house. The neatness of the contrivance, allied with the provision of the corridors, enabled him to make the rear rooms especially usable as self-contained apartments. . . ."[47] There are considerable implications for design in Evans' analysis; they suggest that social factors, rather than compositional issues, were the historic generators of axes.

Sequence and Focus

While it is entirely possible for a pathway to be a clear and easily comprehensible totality, it is more usual for it to be experienced sequentially, marked by distinct focal points. An example of this occurs in the design of a Roman house during the Republic; the visitor would enter through the front door into a corridor (the *fauces*) that led to the *atrium*—and, beyond this space, the *tablinium*—and finally to the open garden. These elements were arranged on a linear axis entirely visible from the street (Fig 12.18). In *The Ancient Roman City,* John E. Stambaugh comments:

> The street-door-fauces-atrium-tablinium-garden sequence is normal in these republican houses, and marks a progression from public to private space. Yet the formal axial arrangement, and the tendency to keep the door open, gave a certain public access deep into the house. What happened in the atrium was visible to the street, and the atrium marked a characteristic intersection of public and private affairs.[48]

Thus one sort of transition, the visual, is contrasted with another, physical movement. That is, while the tablinium was open to view from the street, to actually approach that point meant passage through a series of increasingly private focal points requiring certain sorts of credentials to transit. This long vista was made even more impressive in later designs, by virtue of yet another room added to the tablinium, the Ionic *peristyle.* This space was generally conceived as a formal garden (sometimes with pool), often looking out to still another garden area; such a pronounced axial view occurs in the House of Pansa (Fig 1.10).

The notion of a focussed, sequential pathway is entirely familiar in certain spatial situations, especially those involving merchandising. A contemporary example of this may be seen in Nigel Coates' design for Jasper Conran's Shop in London. The designer's interior concept drawing indicates the importance of both view and movement in converting this small space into an enticing shop. The exterior window frames the view, through which the eye is led horizontally and vertically up to the rear wall. The sensuous steel stair handrail sweeps through the space, and the focal points (the fashions themselves) are seen as a series of momentary stopping places on a circulatory track (Fig 12.19).

An organized and efficient way of viewing sequence has been proposed by the architect Bernard Tschumi. He suggests that all architectural sequences comprise at least three relations: first, the *transformational* sequence, or design methodology; second, the *spatial* sequence, spaces that are aligned along a common axis; and third, the *programmatic* sequence, which involves the social and symbolic considerations that characterize those spaces.[49] For example, Tschumi notes that historically all spatial sequences have emphasized a pathway with fixed focal points linked by continuous movement, but that as architecture is inhabited, programmatic factors are crucial. He states:

> . . . sequences of use, of perception and meaning are always superimposed on those fixed spatial sequences. These are the programmatic sequences that suggest secret maps and impossible fictions, rambling collections of events all strung along a collection of spaces, frame after frame, room after room, episode after episode.[50]

His conclusion is that the spatial sequences are structural, in that they may be viewed independent of assigned meaning, but that the programmatic sequences are inferential (i.e., drawn from the appearance and arrangement of the spaces). This is a dynamic way to view sequence, especially in its suggestion of a continuous resolution of the tension between space and its habitation.

The 1984 PLACES competition, discussed earlier, stressed the generative power of language—the ability of words to suggest spatial types, and groups of related words to suggest configurations. In fact, the words—anticipation, transition, and gathering—composed the project's program. Other interesting aspects of this competition were the equal emphasis given to factors that are variously affective, haptic, and visual, and the stipulation that the design could be situation-specific or abstract in nature. And indeed, the winning entry in the professional category is probably best understood in abstract terms (Fig 12.20).

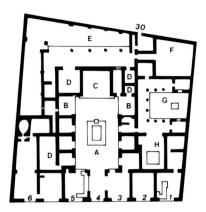

12.18

Plan, House of Sallust—Pompeii *(ca. B.C. 300)*
The plan indicates that this house, characteristic of the republican period, consisted of a central front door flanked by entrances to a series of shops. The entrance corridor led to the Atrium *(A);* beyond the atrium was the tablinium *(C),* which looked out onto the garden *(E).* The sleeping rooms *(B)* also opened onto the atrium, and the dining areas, or triclinia *(D),* were chosen on a seasonal basis. The atrium was particularly important; the family engaged in most of its activities here, and here too could be found the shrine to the household gods. (Source: *The Ancient Roman City,* John E. Stambaugh [Fig. 12, p. 163].)

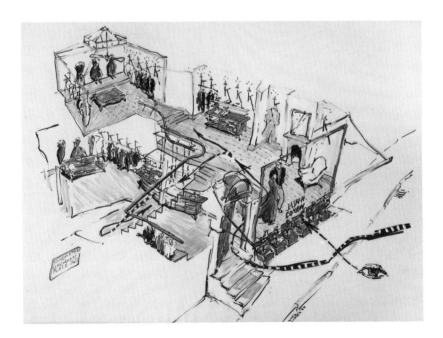

12.19

Jasper Conran Shop—London; *Nigel Coates (1987)*
The sketch clearly indicates Coates' two major concerns, view and circulation. Indeed, the 880-ft.² space is seen as a circulation path with isolated viewing areas determined by particular fashion displays. (Courtesy: Victoria & Albert Museum, London and Branson Coates Architecture, London.)

12.20

A Little Red Riding Hood House; *Livio Dimitriu (1984)*
This was the winning entry in the professional category of the Columbus Coated Fabrics PLACES competition in 1984. Of particular interest is the extreme emphasis given to such transitional elements as entry and staircase. According to Dimitriu, the concept was "to propose the mystery of an abstract volume to be uniquely penetrated by the visitor through a façade cut-out reminiscent of the image of a house." (Courtesy: Columbus Coated Fabrics, Columbus, Ohio; Photo by: The Alderman Company.)

Also clear in this design is the enormous content invested in transitional elements, and their metaphorical qualities. Of all such elements, the door may be the most evocative. It marks the point of passage from the public world to the private, from exterior to interior; it also provides transition from one part of the interior to another, although these doors are seldom experienced in as powerful and moving a way. In *The Door in the Wall,* H.G. Wells describes a particular character's experience of approach to, and entry through, a very special door marking a passage in his life. Although he was hesitant, it was a door that he nevertheless passionately desired to enter:

> Then . . . he had a gust of emotion. He made a run for it, lest hesitation should grip him again, he went plump with outstretched hand through the green door and let it slam behind him. And so, in a trice, he came into the garden that has haunted him all his life. . . . In the instant of coming into it one was exquisitely glad—as only in rare moments and when one is young and joyful one can be glad in this world. And everything was beautiful there. . . .[51]

Doors can inform us about the space within and can set expectations. Which door of a building we are invited to enter, its scale and detail, all tell us much about our relationship with the inhabitant, and prepare us for the space within. Accordingly, few structural elements are as carefully chosen, expensively treated, and symbolically decorated. The door is not the same, however, as the entry, even if they are connected physically. The first experience of a door is visual; entryways, on the other hand, are primarily haptic. That is, the entry is experienced in its three-dimensional aspect through physical penetration. While the door sends out a visual set of expectations that suggest (or promise), the entry fulfills that suggestion. Thus entries are often expanded into porticos; this increases their sensual nature even in such a seemingly pristine setting as the vernacular house (Fig 12.21).

In a provocative article entitled "Japanese Entrances: Cultural Symbols in the Landscape," Marc P. Keane discusses the various sorts of entries the Japanese utilize. The tea garden (the *roji*, or "dewy path") may be regarded as archetypical, as it is an extended entryway through a simple (and undramatic) maze of moss and other woodland plantings. It is meant to suggest the experience of a long journey from the city to a mountain hut, all in a small space marked by a series of critical focal points. Keane notes that the roji consists of a series of landmarks and thresholds, at which the visitor ". . . is encouraged to release the concerns of daily life and progressively enter a 'tea' state of mind."[52] Thus one enters the roofed outer gate, moves through an abstracted and spiritualized middle gate, and, after stopping at various points for spiritual cleansing, arrives at the tea room itself. At the closing of the door, the ceremony begins.

In his *Space and Illusion in the Japanese Garden,* Teiji Itoh traces the development of the tea garden; he distinguishes between the older courtyard garden, the *tsubonouchi,* designed to be seen from the tea room, and the *roji,* which serves as an approach to that room. The tsubonouchi ". . . gave importance to a tranquil scenic or spatial composition to be viewed from a static position, while the roji . . . laid major stress on providing the guests with a series of spatial experiences as they walked through it. To put this even more simply, the tsubonouchi functioned on the premise that the guests would be sitting still, the roji on the premise that they would be in motion."[53] He concludes that the tea garden, ". . . finding support in a new aesthetic philosophy, taught a new concept of design that relied on a sequence of spatial experiences to create its own special effects."[54] This sort of experiential extension, albeit on a smaller scale, also marks the entry to the temple complex. The temple gate resembles a small house with a massive roof, built in such a way as to emphasize heaviness and depth. The essential experience of this gate, however, is in the quality of change in the progressive passage from light to darkness to light again within the wall (Fig 12.22). Keane concludes, "One cannot help but sense that to the Japanese, the entrance and the way of entering are as important as the destination itself."[55]

12.21

Porticoes, *from Small Homes of Architectural Distinction*
This book of pattern plans consistently notes the importance of the doorway; in the case of the open "colonial" portico *(A),* the text states that "it is the hall mark of this type of architecture, varied in form yet always unmistakable in its marked dignity."[3] And in its closed form *(B),* it exudes a certain reserve as well. (Source: *Authentic Small Houses of the Twenties,* Robert T. Jones, editor.)

12.22

Japanese Temple Gate
The temple gate uses a massive roof, composed of hundreds of wooden ribs, to emphasize the act of transition from the active exterior world to the contemplative interior one. In form, the gate reflects certain stylistic features taken from Chinese Buddhist architecture, but translated into an Japanese idiom. (Source: *Material for the Study of Old Japanese Temple Buildings,* Shinpei Masuzama.)

Control of Light

The control of light has aspects that are both *functional* (behavioral and physiological) and *expressive,* the latter considerably predating the former. That is, long before studies were conducted on task-performance, ocular fatigue, and seasonal affective disorder, light served in the manipulation of spatial effect. And, to a large degree, this involved a consideration of its inherent spiritual qualities as well. Thus the expressive virtues of light are made clear in the verses inscribed on the door of St. Denis by Abbot Suger, which include these lines:

> Bright is the noble work; but, being nobly bright, the work
> Should brighten the minds, so that they may travel,
> 　　through the true lights,
> To the True Light where Christ is the true door.[56]

The idea of light as truth and revelation also applies to our view of knowledge, which enabled Henri Labrouste to exploit both its physical and metaphysical qualities in the design of the Bibliothèque Ste. Geneviève in Paris. The long, darkened hall serves to heighten the contrast with the "light of knowledge" at its end, and draws the visitor through to the reading room stairway (Fig 8.6). The appearance of this hall is surely not accidental; its spatial characteristics likely come from structures like the Temple of Khonsu, where the goal was also revelation, albeit a dark and spiritual one.

Brilliant, penetrating light has long been used to good effect in religious structures, where it heightens the sense of drama and mystery. (One might consider Le Corbusier's Notre Dame du Haut at Ronchamp in this regard.) But drama is scarcely limited to churches; secular institutions use it also, particularly those connected with transportation centers—the points of *arrival* and *departure*. Thus both train stations and airline terminals have been treated with intense light effects, although not always to the same ends. Union Terminal in Chicago used natural light; at certain times of day, this light filled the waiting room, transforming the ticket counter into an altar (Fig 12.23). This may represent an older view of travel, one that regarded it as comparatively rare and special. A far more modern treatment of travel

12.23

Waiting Room, Union Station—Chicago; *Graham, Burnham and Co. (1926)* Union Station represented an ambitious effort to consolidate the many rail lines entering Chicago. As such it was the visual symbol of a rich and vibrant center of trade. The natural light changes the interior atmosphere in a slow and deliberate grandeur that suggests the importance of the station. (Courtesy: Chicago Historical Society; Photo by: Frank C. Zak, ca. late 1940s, ICHi-18925.)

can be seen in Helmut Jahn's design of the United Airlines Terminal at O'Hare Airport in Chicago. Here the light, completely artificial, is used to efficiently move travelers from waiting areas to departure gates in what is now, for many, a daily event (Fig 12.24).

But there are other buildings in which the role of dramatic, and usually natural, light seems less clear. In his *Sketches,* Alvar Aalto commends the use of skylights in libraries and museums in order to evenly light the spaces; but he also notes that provisions should be made to ensure that the light remains indirect.[57] That is, while natural (white) light is approved, any evidence of sunlight is not. This forms an interesting contrast to the practice of Louis I. Kahn, whose Kimbell Art Museum uses natural light in a somewhat more dramatic role—as a measure of time (Fig 3.11). Put differently, while both designers rely on both *natural* and *artificial light,* Kahn uses them in distinct roles. Thus Kahn's aphorism, "no space, architecturally, is a space unless it has natural light. . . .," has a definition that includes realizing light's unique properties.[58] For Aalto, natural light's primary value is its intensity; for Kahn, its value is its *temporal* quality; thus he says, ". . . artificial light is a static light . . . where natural light is a light of mood."[59]

Artificial light can, of course, be used very effectively, especially when it is altered by the use of reflective or translucent materials (Plate 11). In this manner, light can be used to obscure as well as reveal, to dissolve detail as well as enhance it. And light can, of course, alter our sense of spatial scale. For example, in Joseph Giovannini's design for a complex of cardiology offices, a subtle perspective is established by progressively narrowing the space between the walls and lowering the ceiling in an area that doubles as a circulation lane and art gallery. In this way, a persuasive illusion of distance is created. The directional aspect is enhanced by the wood floorboards, which are laid lengthwise. At the end is what appears to be an opened door; Giovannini explains that "having tasted the joys of illusionism, I couldn't stop, and sandblasted . . . a plate glass wall to recreate a typical doorway."[60] Quite aside from the novelty, this door also has the effect of bringing natural light into an interior area, albeit a light that is highly diffused (Fig 12.25).

12.24

Concourse, United Airlines Terminal at O'Hare International Airport—Chicago; *Murphy/Jahn (1987)*
In this terminal the light is all artificial, a fact that is exaggerated by the rhythmic pulsations of the neon in the central areas. Thus the light is used to create excitement in a long, underground concourse, and shorten the sense of time-passage. In all of this, it represents a sharp contrast with older views of travel. (Photo by: Timothy Hursley, The Arkansas Office, Little Rock, Ark.)

Issues surrounding the use of artificial light have dominated the literature; indeed, few references to the creative use of natural light (and its corollary, shadow) exist beyond vague mention. This is because, as Ettore Sottsass points out, modern architecture tends to design with electric light after the fact.[61] That is, the vast majority of our offices, supermarkets, banks, department stores, etc., are illuminated by a neutral continuous light that was installed as an afterthought. Even the term illumination may be an unfortunate one; Sottsass notes that ". . . light does not illuminate, it tells a story. *Light gives meanings,* draws metaphors and sets the stage for the comedy of life."[62] He stresses the idea of shade, a shade ". . . that immediately becomes a visible and tangible metaphor for the impenetrable structure of existence."[63] Put differently, the use of natural light immediately involves the consideration of its counterparts, shade and shadow. This is, of course, a far cry from the current practice, prevalent in commercial applications, of lighting for the purpose of ruthlessly eliminating every suggestion of shadow. Finally, Sottsass points out that the conjunction of light and shadow was surely responsible for an architectural "catalog of inventions," from porticoes and cloisters to passages and pergolas.[64] The most fertile ground, then, for advances in spatial lighting may involve the old methodologies rather than the new, and concern the metaphysical rather than the technological.

Indeed, one of the less salutary results of Faber Birren's studies was his approval for the diffused-light ceiling system now used in the world's offices. In his "Psychological Factors in the Use of Light and Lighting in Buildings," D. Geoffrey Hayward points out that large-scale lighting systems commonly assume static lighting requirements; the result of this is that the only option for change is the on-off button.[65] His solution for the design of a lighting scheme would contain the following elements: first, an activity and task analysis; second, a spatial illumination related to factors such as color, form, texture, and direction; third, illumination for (nondisruptive) novelty; and fourth, some provision for individual control of the scheme.[66] This is not an argument to promote the dominance of purely psychophysiological factors in lighting design, but rather for an increased awareness of such concerns in the design of buildings as part of the program. Ettore Sottsass points out that issues surrounding the use of light do not end with simple specifications based on ergonomics; rather, only after this minimum is exhausted do the really sophisticated uses of light begin. After all, ". . . ergonomic systems more subtle that the so-called rational ones have always existed."[67]

12.25.

Cardiology Offices—Washington, D.C.;
Joseph Giovannini (1986)
In her article in *Interior Design,* Monica Geran expands on Giovannini's idea, "In this instance a clear streak down the etched glazing produces the effect of a slightly ajar door, literally providing insight."[4] And she notes that he credits Borromini's Palazzo Spada for the concept of optical distortion that he employs here. (Drawings—courtesy: Joseph Giovannini, New York; Photo by: Walter Smalling, Jr., Washington, D.C.)

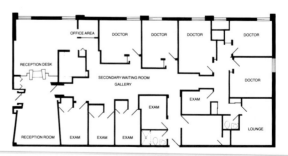

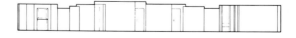

The Enclosure Revealed 13

Inherent Qualities

In a previous chapter, reference is made to Roger Scruton's contention that ". . . the essence of architecture is not space but the enclosure of space, or space as enclosed."[1] But while the formal qualities of enclosure are discussed, little mention is made of the enclosure's substance—the material it is made of. This is, of course, not a small matter. Vitruvius devoted all of Book II of his *De Architectura* to a discussion of materials (specifically, construction materials); and in fact the subject resurfaces in some form throughout the work. Similarly, Alberti relegates all of Book II in his *De re aedificatoria* to the same subject, prefacing this section with the comment, "that no man ought to begin a building hastily but should first take a good deal of time to consider, and resolve in his mind all the qualities and requisites for such a work. . . ."[2]

From Alberti's text, it is obvious that he considers it necessary that such qualities refer to both *strength* and *beauty;* that is, that materials are needed for the actualization of a structure and are, moreover, subject to aesthetic valuation in that process. This duality in the nature of materials is referred to by Henri Focillon in his *La Vie des Formes;* he states, "Unless and until it actually exists in matter, form is little better than a vista of the mind, a mere speculation on a space that has been reduced to geometrical intelligibility."[3] Put differently, even if art wished to repudiate matter, it is in fact dependent upon it for material existence; what is more, matter carries with it its own identifiable characteristics. Focillon thus comments that ". . . form does not behave as some superior principle modeling a passive mass, for it is plainly observable how matter imposes its own form upon form."[4] From this position, Focillon draws two conclusions: first, certain kinds of matter have intrinsic formal vocations, and their inherent qualities can ". . . call forth, limit or develop the life of the forms of art"; and second, these suggestive and individual kinds of matter, ". . . which demand so much from form and which exert so powerful an attraction on the forms of art, are, in their own turn, profoundly modified by these forms."[5]

Thus, for Focillon, a thorough knowledge of materials is critical to design intention, because that intention would always be engaged in a dialogue with the materials it uses. And (following Alberti) that material would invariably possess a dual aspect, that of its *inherent qualities* (physical nature) and that of its *associational qualities* (ascribed nature—Alberti's beauty). *Form,* then, is at the apex of a tripartite scheme in which it is sometimes influenced by the material's inherent qualities, often uses materials for both kinds of qualities, and always transforms inherent qualities into associational ones through its very manipulation. While there have been occasional ideological attempts to keep a congruence among all three attributes, they are nonetheless best understood as separate phenomena. This is especially so in the design of interior spaces, where associational valuation would likely determine the application of a particular material.

There are, of course, various ways in which the inherent qualities of materials can be determined, depending upon the nature of the concern. This could include an examination of their various compressive, tensile, and density characteristics (in the case of structural materials); or alternatively, an examination of the material's perceptual qualities, like texture, color, pattern, and temperature (in the case of surface applications). In these instances, a simple description might suffice to confirm the nature of particular materials. Plastic, for example, can be described as artificial, poured, smooth, nonporous, and poor for detailing; wood is natural, typically planar, easily joined, texturally varied, and a good insulator; and steel is hard, structurally strong, cold, and reflective when polished. And so forth. For the most part, these qualities are well known and codified in various architectural standards.

There is yet another aspect to the inherent qualities of materials (i.e., that those employed by a particular people may simply be those *readily available,* with little opportunity to use any other material. In this situation, inherent and associational qualities might well be congruent, as can be seen in the dwellings of primitive peoples, where the material's intrinsic attributes are always those thought appropriate. In such cases, the form that develops shares some of that congruence in the sense that it is calculated to take advantage of the material's character, although even in these instances choices remain fairly open (Fig 13.1). It seems probable, in light of Rapoport's thesis that primitive (and, to a lesser degree, vernacular) buildings enjoy much cultural congruence, that agreement on form types is due in part to the use of certain culturally approved materials. Certainly the inherent and associational (the prescribed and ascribed) qualities of materials, and the form they take, are seldom so congruent in Western societies, where many different materials are used in structures that tend to take their cues from "high-style" design. These materials, moreover, may be far more responsive to economic factors than aesthetic or symbolic ones, and likely represent a product technology whose processes are relatively autonomous.

Still another way of looking at inherent qualities is to examine their responsiveness to particular needs or *intentions;* that is, how well a material will hold up to our manipulations. In a passage that referred to textile design, but could refer to his entire view of design, William Morris states:

> Never forget the material you are working with, and try always to use it for doing what it can do best: if you feel yourself hampered by the material in which you are working, instead of being helped by it, you have so far not learned your business, any more than a would-be poet has, who complains of the hardship of writing in measure and rhyme. The special limitations of the material should be a pleasure to you, not a hindrance. . . .[6]

And in a manner that seems to reflect the positions of both Focillon and Morris, Mies van der Rohe says: "The expressive value of material is not

13.1

(A) **Ceremonial House—Palimbei Village, Sepik River—Papua New Guinea** *(1978)* *(B)* **Shrine of Nyakang—Fenikang, Nilotic Sudan**
Both structures use materials available locally (wood and grasses), and are designed in such way as to account for changing climatic conditions. The symbolic content of these two structures resides in the particular use of materials, the form that is used, and the specific imagery. It is a content that grows from tradition and extended usage. (*[A]* Courtesy: Royal Institute of British Architects, London. *[B]* Courtesy: Princeton University Press.)

secondary to form. The necessity arises to find the form appropriate to the material or the material appropriate to the form.''[7] (This comment does not, of course, negate the proposition that the ''appropriate material'' might be thought so for inherent or associational reasons.) Thus the real importance of the inherent qualities of materials might be seen as their relative appropriateness to design intention, rather than their innate qualities as such.

The difficulty in all these statements lies in their assumption of an immediate control over the shaping of architectural materials by either the designer or craftsworker. But the sort of hands-on direction that is implied in these statements rarely holds true today. Thus any material intended to assume a specialized form must first be conceived in its final image by the designer, and then translated into the terminology used by specific *product technologies*. These technologies in turn make use of machinery whose productive capacity the craftsworker merely assists. In any case, there would exist economic arguments for simply using the products that are commonly available. In *A Pattern Language*, Alexander, Ishikawa, and Silverstein comment that ''there is a fundamental conflict in the nature of materials for building in industrial society.''[8] They point out that, on one hand, an organic building requires a multitude of small, hand-fabricated, and uniquely shaped pieces; on the other, high labor costs and the comparative efficiency of mass production creates large, identical, standardized materials, which ''. . . tend to destroy the organic quality of natural buildings.''[9]

Their solution is to find materials that are small-scale, easily manipulable, adaptable, readily available, sturdy, and cheap—as well as ecologically sound. They conclude, however, that these *good materials* are quite different from any in common use today.[10] The authors argue for an environmentally sound class of materials, carefully differentiated between structural and interior finish types. Their proposition is interesting, but the eventual acceptance of any new material types for ecological-structural reasons, would likely require a prior acceptance at the aesthetic and symbolic levels. That is, the final worth of materials (whether machined or crafted) would always be measured in traditional terms; for their suitability, and in their assigned valuation through custom and use (their attributed qualities). Thus a clear distinction between inherent and associational qualities needs to be maintained in the design process, if they are to be exploited.

Associational Qualities

This distinction may be easier to say than to see. Noted earlier is Santayana's observation of ". . . a curious but well-known psychological phenomenon, viz., the transformation of an element of sensation into the quality of a thing."[11] That is, we quickly come to see associational qualities as inherent. This point of view permeates architectural writings, accounting for how much materials are adjectivally modified. While everyone seems to agree that marble is "noble," there has been less agreement about iron, which Viollet-le-Duc lauds as "ductile" and Ruskin condemns as crude and "dishonest." In *The Essence of Architecture,* William Roger Greeley comments: "There is a propriety of material arising from association and convention. Some materials are esteemed noble, some are rated as coarse and mean. Psychology enters very deeply into the choice of iron or brass, marble or concrete, oak or ash."[12] Greeley suggests, moreover, that we pay little attention to materials, in any case, until they are altered by design. He concludes that architecture uses many different materials, carefully chosen ". . . both for structural service, and for aesthetic qualities. Be it remembered that the latter includes many elements. It includes the consideration of local tradition and production, of the purpose of the building. . . ."[13]

Materials, in their associational dimension, have often been endowed with *transformational* characteristics; not only are they regarded as repositories of cultural values (as in the case of jade for the Chinese), but they are believed to have the capacity to alter conditions of existence. Thus Paul Scheerbart writes in his *Glasarchitektur* of 1914 that we must hope that ". . . glass architecture will indeed transform the face of our world."[14] Glass, he reasoned, would have this capacity through its innate characteristics, by allowing light to flood the now-open space the glass enclosed. Of course, any material that is used almost exclusively grants a certain character—even content—to the design it is applied to. An enduring example is the aerodynamic and strikingly "modern" Airstream trailer, first constructed in 1937, which continues to utilize a monocoque body made of aluminum. In this sense, it materially represents a certain point of view, or period, in the history of the culture that produced it, both technologically and socially (Fig 13.2).

13.2

Airstream Trailer (1991)
The availability of new light-weight, rigid structural materials like aluminum and plastic re-introduced the notion of a shell-like construction common to the pre-skeletal era. While these materials were often used in rather conventional formats, some designers saw more radical possibilities which seemed to reflect the "modern age." The Airstream trailer has by now become an American legend, embodying certain aspirations and values. (Courtesy: Airstream, Inc., Jackson Center, Ohio.)

Associational valuation may also rationalize the great sums of money spent on materials that, on the surface, seem extraneous to the article's function. Thus was the conflict of valuation between Suger, Abbot of St. Denis, and Bernard of Clairvaux. When Suger renovated the old abbey church of St. Denis in 1139, he recorded the progress in a chronicle on a fairly regular basis. At the project's outset he observes:

> We hasten to adorn the Main Altar of the Blessed Denis where there was only one beautiful and precious frontal panel from Charles the Bald, the third Emperor. . . . We had it all encased, putting up golden panels on either side and adding a fourth, even more precious one; so that the whole altar would appear golden all the way around.[15]

His description continues, noting that this new adornment included a pair of golden candlesticks, as well as pearls, emeralds, and other precious gems, the sum of which shone with ". . . the radiance of delightful allegories."[16]

All of this was little appreciated by the devout Cistercian, Bernard of Clairvaux, who took Suger to task for spending great sums on what, after all, were not necessary to the altar's function and which might instead be spent on the poor. He details all the follies he saw, including the gold, gems, and candelabra, which were ". . . fashioned with marvelous subtlety of art and glistening no less brightly with gems than with the lights they carry."[17] He concludes:

> What, think you, is the purpose of all this? O vanity of vanities, yet no more vain than insane! The church is resplendent in her walls, beggarly in her poor; she clothes her stones in gold, and leaves her sons naked; the rich man's eye is fed at the expense of the indigent.[18]

Both the value of the materials and the craftsmanship that formed them are derided as functionally inessential, and perhaps even worse, profligate (Fig 13.3).

13.4

Boardroom Table for Home Box Office Headquarters—New York; *Rick Wrigley and Kohn Pedersen Fox Conway Associates, Inc. (1984)*
In the aftermath of Patricia Conway's collaboration on the book *Ornamentalism*, KPFC began employing artists who worked with crafts and furniture. The designer responsible for this boardroom table was Rick Wrigley, and the photograph reveals its rich materials (which include precious veneers, verde marble, and mother-of-pearl) and fine craftsmanship. (Courtesy: Rick Wrigley, Gatehouse Furniture Studios, Holyoke, Mass.)

Suger, sophisticated and worldly, was well aware of both the associational qualities of the materials he used and the finely executed form that enhanced those qualities. His defense of both is a classic one:

> . . . out of my delight in the beauty of the house of God, the loveliness of the many-colored gems has called me away from external cares, worthy meditation has induced me to reflect, transferring that which is material to that which is immaterial, on the diversity of the sacred virtues: then it seems to me that I see myself dwelling, as it were, in some strange region of the universe which neither exists entirely in the slime of the earth nor entirely in the purity of Heaven; and that, by the grace of God, I can be transported from this inferior to that higher world in an anagogical manner.[19]

Thus have the rich, beautifully executed appointments permitted (even encouraged) Suger to transcend this earthly life. He values them, not for their economic worth, but for their *allegorical qualities*. This argument provides the rationale, not only for Suger's altar at St. Denis, but for any use of materials chosen primarily for associational qualities.

There is nothing new in this; indeed, it is likely that we have more institutional sympathy for Suger's position than Bernard's. This is demonstrated by our lavish use of materials throughout the built environment primarily for effect (especially in the interior). For example, the boardroom tables of major corporations are seldom constructed of inexpensive materials; rich, finely detailed materials denote a successful company (Fig 13.4). A recent example of a design that combines inherent and associational qualities may be seen in Hans Hollein's Jewelry Shop in Vienna. The hard, uniform marble exaggerates the contradiction inherent in the aperture; and, as Charles Jencks points out, the contrast of ''. . . skin-like marble and the glistening gold lips folding over each other, is explicitly sexual.''[20] Expensive materials and well-crafted detail seem particularly apt in this sort of setting and thus are expected (Fig 13.5). Indeed, the rare utilization of economical (albeit functional) materials, as in the offices of Vignelli Associates, appears unusual—and perhaps, in a role reversal, even striking and exotic (Plate 4). That is, while inherent qualities tend to endure, associational qualities are subject to *fashionable valuation;* accordingly, new materials (or old materials in new situations) may be thought highly avant-garde and progressive despite their low cost.

Two separate, though arguably comparable, groups of designers seem particularly adept at using familiar (and ordinary) materials in novel and exotic ways: stage designers and graphic designers. (A commonality might result from their similar two-dimensional approach to space, and sensitivity to the visual qualities of surface-textures and light effects.) An innovative use of ordinary building materials is seen in Michael Vanderbyl's design for the Esprit Showroom in New York. Noted for graphic and interior design, his approach to the space was to treat it as a ''black box,'' a methodology familiar to stage design. The materials include corrugated steel, rubber institutional matting, and even the shoeboxes themselves; but the success of these elements is based on clever detailing. Put differently, however important fine detailing is in situations of luxurious materials (as in Hollein's shop), it is even more important when the materials are ordinary. According to Stanley Tigerman, ''It is taking materials and using them in unexpected ways, that's part of what we are *all* supposed to be doing for a living; This is brilliant, reductive and inventive.''[21] And so it is (Fig 13.6).

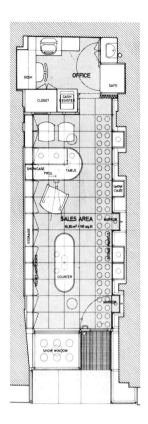

13.5

Jewelry Shop Schullin I—Vienna; *Hans Hollein (1975)*
The luxurious and sensual materials, and clever use of close space, are calculated to entice customers to experience the shop's wares (rather than simply see them.) (Courtesy: Hans Hollein, Architect, Vienna. Photo by: Jerzy Surwillo.)

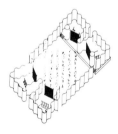

13.6

Esprit Shoe Showroom—New York; *Vanderbyl/Design (1986)*
At the IDEC (Interior Design Educator's Council) conference held in 1990, Vanderbyl jokingly referred to himself as the "King of Cheap." This project, the *Interiors* Showroom and Low Budget Design winner, was a temporary showroom intended to attract buyers over a three-day period. Both the walls and full-scale figures were, therefore, constructed out of readily available and cheap materials that could be assembled and dismantled quickly. (Courtesy: Vanderbyl Designs, San Francisco.)

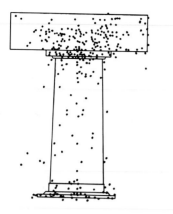

13.7

Records of Eye Fixations; *G.T. Buswell (1935)*
The significance of the transition points, or joints, is demonstrated in this diagram of eye fixations. E.H. Gombrich notes that these "... photographs of eye movements and fixation points show that continuous contours appear to have been less thoroughly inspected than those parts of the design which cannot simply be 'taken as read.' "[1] (Source: *The Sense of Order,* E.H. Gombrich, Phaidon Press Limited, Oxford.)

Detailing

Thus no consideration of materials, either inherent or associational, is sufficient without careful attention to detail. However, the definition of detail is complex, as the term is commonly used to designate phenomena that, while related, are not precisely the same. It can refer to process, drawing, or thing; both structural and ornamental functions; and indicate mass or space. Detail is often thought to refer simply to the joining of two or more building elements. In fact, detailed notations often describe commonplace procedures relating to construction techniques—because either they are not obvious to the craftsworkers, or they must be specified for legal reasons. But these details, hidden in the structure and performing unexciting (if necessary) functions, are seldom the ones that interest designers. To the contrary, it is the revealed, visible detail that designers relish. And because it is visible, it is essentially ornamental; in this sense, it is not the actual joint that constitutes the detail, but what the designer decides will visually and tactilely occur at that joint. Thus the detail aids in either easing or making significant the visual transition from one element to another (Fig 13.7). But the transition (where it occurs and how it appears) is in turn dependent on aesthetic and symbolic factors on the one hand, and economic and technical factors on the other. Accordingly, the definition could be modified to state that ornamental detail is the *meaningful, sensual event that occurs where design elements join.*

Its importance to the design community is underscored by Marco Frascari, in "The Tell-The-Tale Detail," where he notes that possibilities of innovation and invention lie in the details, and that designers may use these to give harmony to a culture's most difficult or disorderly environment.[22] Thus he maintains that "the art of detailing is really the joining of materials, elements, components, and building parts in a functional and aesthetic manner."[23] While the image of elements as material types (alike or otherwise) is usual, the term has also been used to refer to the joining of spatial elements. Indeed, Frascari describes two sorts of details; those dealing with *material joints,* such as a capital (which acts as a connecting device between column shaft and architrave); and *formal joints,* such as a porch, which connect the interior to the exterior.[24] For Frascari, the detail is always a joint, a junction; as the smallest unit of signification in architectural meaning, it is also the expression of the structure and the utility of the building. This view of detail is rather unusual, providing an alternative to the highly object-oriented (and traditional) view represented by the term detail. Such a view seems, on the surface, to correspond to Lee Hodgden's concept of *transitional spatial elements* referred to earlier, spaces that facilitate the transition between interior and exterior. It may recall Wright's notion of "integral architecture" as well.

The second meaning of detail is that of a drawing; more specifically, a highly schematic drawing large enough to permit accurate measurement (Fig 13.8). While the word detail is pervasive it would be more accurate to call this kind of enlarged view a *detail-drawing.* It can be argued that this type, as a necessity, evolved only in the past several hundred years, primarily as a result of a general deterioration of craftsmanship, which itself may be seen as the by-product of industrial culture. In preindustrial societies, buildings were viewed as the repositories of a common culture, and architects worked with craftsworkers who were knowledgeable about structural and decorative details. Thus detail-drawings were largely unnecessary, as long as there was a shared design intent. Frascari notes that as buildings became economic investments, workers no longer inferred detail construc-

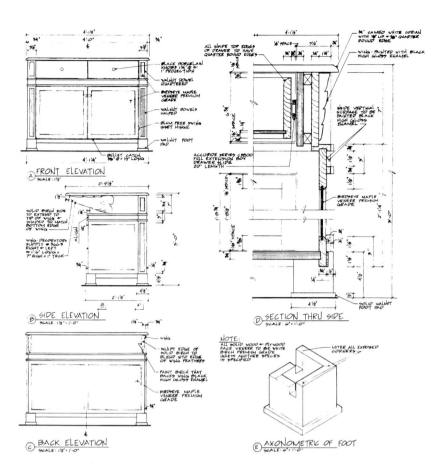

13.8

Furniture Detail, Greystone Kitchen—Chicago; *Joy Monice Malnar (1989)*
This kitchen island is intended to conform to a style of cabinetry common in late Victorian homes, even though it did not yet exist as a furniture type. Thus expensive materials (birdseye maple and walnut) from an older tradition have been combined with a corian top; the design is ultimately dependent, however, on a clear articulation of structural and decorative elements. As the use of cantilevering is an essentially modern concept, the seating overhang is braced by "wings," and pilasters are used to suggest support. Such detail-drawings are useful to the cabinetmaker, in this case R. Wolf Loebach of Chicago. (Courtesy: Joy Monice Malnar; Photo by: Frank Vodvarka.)

tions from design drawings but, instead, relied on intricate detail-drawings worked out on the board. The result, he says, was that "draftsmanship was substituted for workmanship, and the development of 'real details' was replaced by 'virtual' procedures."[25] A second result, he continues, can be seen in the use of such drawings to match workers with tasks—a new role of vocational assignment.

There are ramifications in all this. The loss of input from the craftsworkers resulted in lower construction standards and a loss of content. Put differently, worker input had ensured that a certain element of vernacular meaning always found its way into formal design; even more important, those formal elements infiltrated the vernacular. This may help explain the reasonably consistent view of architectural design that prevailed across socioeconomic and educational lines before the nineteenth century. The result of this situation has been the production of evermore precise, comprehensive, and specific detail-drawings, although there have been other approaches. In his "Detailing," Frank Gehry notes the lack of pride construction workers have in their work, and the consistent trend to shoddiness. He says that since he could not change the workers, he ". . . decided to accept their craft, or lack of it, as a virtue and use it like one uses the tools available."[26] He, therefore, exploits processes and materials that reflect the current state of craft and technique, and notes that the workers (particularly the carpenters and sheet-metal workers) often become involved with his projects because he incorporates them (Fig 13.9). He concludes that the details of a building grow out of the culture, the politics, the collaborators, the craft, the context, and the moment of truth.[27]

13.9

Frank O. Gehry House—Santa Monica, California; *Frank Gehry (1979)*
This axonometric illustrates the new addition that wraps around the older portion of the house. The materials are corrugated siding, wire-mesh fence, plywood, asphalt, and gypsum board. All materials are either viewed from the interior or actually brought inside. Especially interesting are the old exterior façades, which have now become interior walls. (Courtesy: Frank O. Gehry & Associates, Inc., Santa Monica, Calif.)

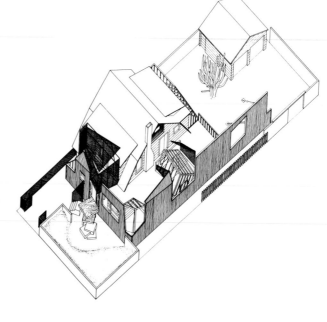

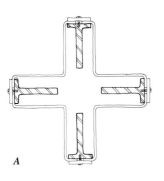

A

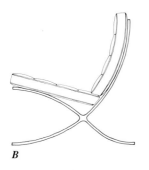

B

13.10

(A) Column Detail, Barcelona Pavilion; *Mies van der Rohe (1929);* **(B) Furniture Detail, Barcelona Pavilion;** *Mies van der Rohe (1929)*
The column, cruciform-shaped, is nonetheless based on a grid pattern, as is every other element in the Pavilion. While the use of the grid is rigid in the column, the cross members on the chair yield to accept the chair's occupant. While the chair appears to use the latest industrial technology, its pristine refinement relies on the steel's being hand sanded and polished and the grid on the leather cushion hand-sewed. (Drawn by: J. Malnar.)

Finally, detail refers to a *tangible presence* in the structure, detail in its physical sense. Of course, designers do not build details, they build structures with details. Details have always tended to measure design excellence, to such a degree that a mystique has grown around their use. And as detail has become less obviously ornamental in recent history, individual manifestations of detail have had to carry proportionately larger shares of the content. In this event, Mies van der Rohe's famous aphorism "God is in the details" becomes explicable, especially since it comes from the son of a mason who spent his early years designing stucco ornament. An extraordinary use of rich materials, finely detailed to convey content, occurs in his 1929 Barcelona Pavilion (Fig 2.14). The materials consist of richly patterned stone (marble and onyx) matched vertically and horizontally; glass screens and windows, whose mullions are carefully aligned with the paving joints; and elegant, cruciform columns clad in chromium-plated sheet metal (Fig 13.10).

Indeed, every part of this structure demonstrates a pronounced spatial sensitivity and attention to detail, both of which use the grid as an organizational structure. Thomas Beeby notes that this process is identical to that of ornament making, and that ". . . what is usually referred to as architectural detailing is actually a process of decoration in the hands of Mies."[28] That is, he has conceived of the materials and their method of development in ornamental terms, except that here it is the constructive elements that supply the visual effect rather than an applied ornament. The notion that the Miesian aesthetic relies on an ornamental framework is not so strange; Mies' entire basis for architecture grew out of a classical tradition that understood the perceptual and cognitive capacities of ornamental detail.

This explains, for example, Alberti's treatment of the façade of the Palazzo Rucellai, which depends on the orderly pattern of the stone veneer for its visual unity (Fig 6.7). The façade actually is composed of irregular stonework whose surface was carved to produce these regular grooves after the construction had been completed. This attention to detail is essentially decorative, much like the chromium-plated columns in the Barcelona Pavilion. Alternatively, in a clever display of cognitive effect, the sixteenth-century architect Giulio Romano took advantage of an educated public's knowledge to produce an air of whimsy in the design of the Palazzo del Tè. Here Romano developed various architectural elements in an irregular and decorative manner, thus calling attention to their unique role (Fig 13.11).

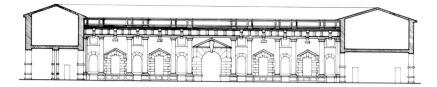

This is similar to the process Mies employs in his semantic separation of wall and column in the Pavilion or in his emphasizing the bolt that connects the chrome plate to the I-member.

Such examples bring into question the relationship between *detail* and *ornament*. Detail, although three-dimensional, often looks two-dimensional. And the structural qualities that detail alludes to are often little more than pretense. The definition of ornament, on the other hand, is far-ranging— including much that is detail, and much that is not. The separation currently maintained usually tries to identify ornament as flat, applied, and "non-functional," although there is ornament that exists in the round. Thus the distinctions in the description of the Illinois Housing Development Authority offices, designed by Booth/Hansen & Associates, are based on a current valuation, one that refers to the ". . . *detailed* glass wall panels" and the silkscreen stencil pattern as ". . . a colorful but inexpensive *decorative* element."[29] To the author of this review, there exists a marked distinction having something to do with structure, dimension, and cost. It is arguable, however, that this view does not reflect any visual reality, and that the above simply represents two particular kinds of ornament (Fig 13.12).

13.11

Palazzo del Tè—Mantua; *Giulio Romano (1526–34)*
Romano was known as an architect whose designs revealed a subtle sense of humor. Thus the keystones in the arches have been moved either higher or lower than their normal position, and the tryglyphs have been strangely lowered. The visual puns even extend to the treatment of materials used in the surfaces, particularly the exaggerated rustication in the window frames. (Drawn by: J. Malnar.)

13.12

Illinois Housing Development Authority—Chicago; *Booth/Hansen & Associates (1988)*
The stencil pattern stands in sharp contrast to the severely angular window mullions; and they are very different in materials and treatment. (Photo by: Wayne Cable, copyright Cable Studios, Inc., Chicago.)

Ornament

The dispute between Abbot Suger and Bernard of Clairvaux has been deemed important for several reasons: first, it examines the degree to which the associational qualities of materials are crucial to the content of their form; second, it questions whether craftsmanship in the pursuit of ornamental embellishment is craft well applied; and third, it points to a divergence in assessment of the fundamental role of the Church (a debate we make no attempt to address at all). Thus the historical question of ornament, particular materials aside, assumed an ecclesiastical dimension during the Medieval period. But, by the Renaissance, ornament was seen in a far more secular light, as something that gave (or at least enhanced) enjoyment. And with the increased emphasis on private life and the consequent enrichment of the residence, enjoyment of material things became an acceptable end in itself. Alberti addresses all of these:

> It is generally allowed, that the pleasure and delight which we feel on the view of any building, arise from nothing else but beauty and ornament, since there is hardly any man so melancholy or stupid, so rough or unpolished, but what is very much pleased with what is beautiful, and pursues those things which are most adorned, and rejects the unadorned and neglected. . . . When we lift up our eyes to heaven, and view the wonderful works of God, we admire him more for the beauties we see, than for the conveniences which we feel and derive from them.[30]

He says that this is so in all areas of life, but especially in the case of architecture. But how then does Alberti define *beauty,* and what is the role of *ornament?* He addresses these questions in Book VI, in what has become one of his best-known statements:

> In order therefore to be as brief as possible, I shall define beauty to be a harmony of all the parts, in whatsoever subject it appears, fitted together with such proportion and connection, that nothing could be added, diminished, or altered, but for the worse . . . and we may define ornament to be a kind of an auxiliary brightness and improvement to beauty.[31]

It is in the last part of this definition, that of ornament, that the question occurs. If nothing could be added, subtracted, or altered without being for the worse, how can the addition of ornament be an improvement? How can best be made better? It seems likely that Alberti conceived ornament to be a deferred application of planned detail to a structure built on principles of proportion and harmony, as in the case of the stonework of the Palazzo Rucellai; this is, of course, the antithesis of ornament as an added enhancement or afterthought. But a view of ornament as something essentially extraneous to form, an embellishment that serves no necessary function (or still worse, as absolution for poor work), still holds true.

In his article "What is Ornament and What is Not" John Summerson contends that the discussion of ornament as a problem arose only with the Victorian age. He points to a fairly typical assessment of ornament, in this case in *The Art of Decorative Design* (1862) by Christopher Dresser, "Ornament is that which, superadded to utility, renders the object more acceptable through bestowing upon it an amount of beauty which it would not otherwise possess."[32] As Summerson observes, it is the phrase *superadded to utility* that is really the problem, ". . . the sort of juxtaposition which made the Modern Movement inevitable."[33] Summerson's position is interesting; starting from the proposition that "all ornament is wilfully uneconomic," he asks, "Is whatever is uneconomic ornament?" He points out that a certain amount of "ornament"—detail that is not structurally critical—may be necessary to make a thing what it is, that needed to make a thing "... a grammatical form of communication. ... "[34] And he concludes that it is, therefore, necessary to distinguish between uneconomical elements that are linguistic and those that are ornamental.[35]

This distinction is helpful. Summerson is saying that if the so-called ornament is critical to an object's message *qua* object—as in the case of a particular capital and base denoting a particular sort of column—then it is not merely ornament but an essential part of architecture. If, on the other hand, no necessary communication occurs, it may be "ornament" in some simple, excessive sense. But what is "excessive"? In his *Figures of Speech or Figures of Thought,* Ananda K. Coomaraswamy notes that the modern use of the words ornament and decoration imply something luxurious "... added to utilities but not essential to their efficacy."[36] He observes that in traditional philosophy, the artwork is a reminder:

> ... the summons of its beauty is to a thesis, as to something to be understood, rather than merely enjoyed. Unwilling as we may be to accept such a proposition today, in a world increasingly emptied of meaning, it is even harder for us to believe that "ornament" and "decoration" are, properly speaking, integral factors of the beauty of the work of art. ...[37]

In any case, ornament (in the sense of adornment) has historically had metaphysical (even magical) properties. Coomaraswamy notes that these issues remain current: "... if, for example, the judge is only a judge in act when wearing his robes, if the mayor is empowered by his chain, and the king by his crown, if the pope is only infallible and verily pontiff when he speaks *ex cathedra,* 'from the throne,' none of these things are mere ornaments. ..."[38] He says ornament's being defined as necessity is suggested by its Latin source, *ornare,* "to fit out, furnish, provide with necessaries."[39] And, as is pointed out *In a Pattern Language,* "all people have the instinct to decorate their surroundings."[40] Here the authors contend that ornament, properly used, can unite the various parts of design into a larger whole. They contend, for example, that such objects as Oriental carpets have this capacity to serve both as figure and boundary at various levels. And they thus conclude that *"the main purpose of ornament in the environment—in buildings, rooms, and public spaces—is to make the world more whole by knitting it together. ..."[41]*

Such a favorable assessment raises the question of how ornament came to be so devalued during the Victorian period. It had certainly enjoyed a good reputation during the eighteenth century; this was especially true in England where Adam used highly ornamental patterns to unify his designs, notably in the case of surfaces (Fig 13.13). Siegfried Giedion sees the devaluation of ornament as having its roots in at least two critical phenomena dating from the beginning of the nineteenth century: first, the inception of the Empire Style by Napoleon's court designers, Charles Percier and Pierre François Louis Fontaine (what Giedion refers to as the beginning of a *ruling taste*); and second, the cheap *industrial production* of adornment generally (and ornament in particular). A third phenomenon might be added, the remarkable absence of a unified world-view that could produce a coherent system of design such as had prevailed in the previous century. The lack of such a system in large measure contributed to the atmosphere of exoticism.

Giedion points out that for all of Napoleon's remarkable achievements, he nonetheless failed to use the opportunities offered by the Revolution to create a new social form. Giedion says that, ultimately, he looked to the devices and mechanisms of the past for confirmation of his imperial stature.[42] Indeed, Giedion believes this to be the fate of the entire century, accounting for the fervor with which symbols were appropriated and multiplied in every area of endeavor. Thus to confirm his status, Percier and

13.13

Sion House, Hall Ceiling—London; *Robert Adam (1762)*
This ceiling demonstrates Adam's tight control of detailed surfaces. In appearance, it evokes the flat-field ornament of the Near East. (Source: *The Works in Architecture of Robert & James Adam,* Robert & James Adam.)

13.14

Flower Stand; *Charles Percier and Pierre François Louis Fontaine (1801)*
Designed for a Swedish count, this stand was to be placed in the middle of a salon. It is a tripartite construction, its sections accommodating a goldfish bowl, the flower arrangement, and a birdcage. Flowers may also be seen rising from the heads of the sphinxes. Mario Praz notes that the book containing these plates became the standard for the Empire Style. (Copyright 1991. The Art Institute of Chicago. All rights reserved.)

Fontaine lavishly used *symbol-systems* particularly dear to Napoleon—those of imperial Rome. Such was their influence, however, that in the period from 1794 to 1812, they set the course of taste (by definition, a ruling taste) for Europe. This resulted, Giedion notes, in an extraordinary devaluation of symbols by their exaggeration and inappropriate application, a decay of spatial cohesiveness due to the new dominance of individual pieces of furniture (furniture as architecture), and a corresponding growth of influence for the upholsterer.[43] In an atmosphere of "more is more," the visual result could be startling (Fig 13.14).

The industrial production of furniture, utensils, and ornamental detail likewise had repercussions. Giedion notes that "the machines began to pour forth statuary, pictures, vases, flower bowls, and carpets in mass"; and the less it cost to produce, the more it flourished.[44] These were, after all, the very objects that had once been handcrafted, and had been correspondingly costly. Now they were within everyone's reach. The differences were profound. Not only were the machined products inferior to the handcrafted ones (as Ruskin liked to point out), but the cheapest were naturally the most popular. And it is likely that there had never before been such a penchant for stuffing rooms with replicas of artifacts and handicrafts—freely stolen from history and cheaply reproduced in ersatz materials. This even included the electroplating of plaster to produce the appearance of bronze (Fig 13.15).

The first reactions to this strange abuse of industrial processes came, not with the Werkbund and other design movements of the twentieth century, but as early as the mid-nineteenth century. The *Journal of Design,* published by Henry Cole between 1849 and 1852, represented an early voice for an aesthetic based on cooperation between designer/artist and manufacturer. Thus Cole's goal was different from that of William Morris, who favored a return to handicraft; and Cole agreed still less with Ruskin. Some of his collaborations with industry for *art manufactures* were notable, including designs for the Coalbrookdale Iron Works and Wedgewood Potteries.[45] But the most dramatic result obtained by Cole and his group—The Society for the Encouragement of Arts, Manufactures and Commerce—was the organizing of the Great Exhibition of 1851. Cole served on the Exhibition's executive committee, which offered the commission for the building—a Crystal Palace—to Joseph Paxton, whose design was in many ways a tribute to the industrial age (Fig 7.5). The exhibition was a revelation; everywhere the crafts of various nonindustrialized countries shone with quality and an honesty of design. The products of India were particularly fine in their two-dimensional integrity, affirming ". . . that the degree of industrialization is

13.15

Victorian Interior—Germany; *H. Kirch-mayr (1890)*
This drawing gives some idea of a plush Victorian interior, which typically reflected both extreme eclecticism and an ingrained *horror vacuii* (fear of empty spaces). (Courtesy: Angelo Hornak, London.)

no measure of culture or of our ability to shape life.''[46] Nor were machined products neglected; particular tribute was paid to the inventions of the United States, which were refreshing in their originality and complete clarity of purpose.

Thus, Giedion comments, ''The instinct that led Cole to grasp these two poles simultaneously, primitive expression on one hand and products of high mechanization on the other, the two wellsprings of modern art, shows him far ahead of his own time.''[47] Still, Cole's influence remained limited. This in part reflected industry's reluctance to change. But it also resulted in large measure from the phenomenon noted earlier (i.e., the inability of the period to produce a *coherent system* of design). A member of Cole's group, Owen Jones, openly stated, ''We have no guiding principles.''[48] That failure may be seen most persuasively in Jones' own great work, the *Grammar of Ornament,* published in 1856. This is not to fault the work itself; it likely represents one of the finest collections of ornament, taken from a variety of cultures, ever published. Its plates are detailed, rich, and comprehensive within their chosen areas; and the text is informative (Fig 13.16). In the preface, Jones comments that his aim:

> . . . has been to select a few of the most prominent types in certain styles closely connected with each other, and in which certain general laws appeared to reign independently of the individual peculiarities of each. I have ventured to hope that . . . I might aid in arresting that unfortunate tendency of our time to be content with copying . . . the forms peculiar to any bygone age, without attempting to ascertain, generally completely ignoring, the peculiar circumstances which rendered an ornament beautiful. . . .[49]

Again, in Proposition 36 of his General Principles, he states, ''The principles discoverable in the works of the past belong to us; not so the results. It is taking the end for the means.''[50]

Jones' intent is clear; by a close examination of the styles contained in his text, one might discern the characteristics of shape and pattern that repeat themselves in any particular style, and the relationship of these characteristics to the forms of nature. In the article referred to earlier, Summerson notes that this approach was intended to provide a basis for the formulation of new design systems. That is, even as previous cultures had formed systems appropriate to their peculiar circumstances and temperament, so might contemporary cultures. But, says Summerson, while the theory was attractive, it never worked. ''Designers were constantly swayed by the organic wholeness of this or that historic style—*one* style.''[51] And those historic styles were applied systematically to structures, whether appropriate or not. Nor is this unreasonable; not only is a style enjoying organic consistency difficult to separate into its constituent parts, so is the clear identification of such parts in styles that are physically and temporally removed from personal experience. Thus, while Jones' intention was laudable, he may not have been realistic in forwarding it; and while the Victorians exploited his work, they probably did not understand it. In *The Grammar of Ornament/Ornament as Grammar,* Thomas Beeby observes, ''Instead of instigating a new synthesis, as he had hoped, Owen Jones unintentionally contributed to the contextual disassociation of ornament from structure.''[52]

Not everyone during the Victorian period was engaged in this odd pursuit. In an article entitled ''Architectural Ornament: On, In, And Through The Wall,'' David van Zanten contends that the current view of architectural ornament tends to stress its value as a system of conventional signs identifying building functions, but that its meaning was more complex during the

13.16

Pompeian No. 3 Plate, from the *Grammar of Ornament; Owen Jones (1856)*
This mosaic pavement, entirely common in Roman homes, illustrates the flat- and shallow-relief patterns so admired by Jones. He does note, however, that it represents a lessening of refinement compared with its Greek predecessors. (The original plate is in color, and handsomely reproduced.) (Source: *The Grammar of Ornament,* Owen Jones.)

nineteenth century. He notes, for example, that Gottfried Semper, in *Die Vier Elemente der Baukunst,* argued that the roof, walls, foundation, and hearth constitute the primordial elements of building. Moreover, each aspect is associated with a particular craft: carpentry, weaving, masonry, and ceramics (to repeat the preceding order)—a craft whose memory is reflected in the ornamentation of the structure (even when different materials are used). Thus van Zanten concludes, "Ornament was, for Semper, the means of denying the actual, physical reality to reveal a transcendental reality by reminding people of the original, primordial elements of structure."[53] And John Ruskin referred to architecture's rich mnemonic function in "The Lamp of Memory" when he stated that "we may live without her, and worship without her, but we cannot remember without her."[54] Van Zanten comments that both men felt ornament rendered a building monumental through the *embodiment of memory,* embracing the devices of both pure illusion and technology in the process.[55] But such people were the exception; in the main, the nineteenth century was satisfied with superficial allusions in its evocation of historical styles.

Indeed, so entrenched was revivalism, that any attempt to rationalize ornament may be seen as remarkable and very likely misunderstood in its own time. Thus John Wellborn Root's comment that to lavish a "profusion of delicate ornament" upon commercial structures is "worse than useless" must have seemed as strange a notion as it was, given Root's buildings, a contradiction. One can only assume that Root's definition of ornament, as was the case with Louis Sullivan, assumed that it was strong, vigorous, and (most important) developed out of the building forms themselves. In this sense it might be seen to meet Summerson's criterion (i.e., that it serve a linguistic purpose, a specific grammatical construction). Sullivan contended that any building that was a work of art was, in its nature and being, an expression of emotion, and therefore possessed a life. He believed that it necessarily followed from this *living principle,* that an ornamented structure should be indelibly characterized by this quality: ". . . that the same emotional impulse shall flow throughout harmoniously into its varied forms of expression—of which, while the mass-composition is the more profound, the decorative ornamentation is the more intense."[56]

He clarifies this point by asserting that while an excellent and beautiful building can be designed without any ornament at all, it is equally true that ". . . a decorated structure, harmoniously conceived, well considered, cannot be stripped of its system of ornament without destroying its individuality."[57] For this to occur, two factors must be uppermost in the designer's mind: first, that the presence of ornament (or lack thereof) be a design consideration from the outset; and second, that the ornament should seem to "grow" from the surface it enhances, fundamentally constituting an organic system. Thus did Sullivan believe it possible to transform through manipulation the "blank" block into enhanced form through a series of systematic organic changes he designated as *morphology.* Indeed, the systems of ornament conceived by Sullivan not only are contained by the structural form, but seem—in their dependence on botanic shapes and growth principles—to have come from the same sources used by such contemporary movements in Europe as Arts & Crafts and Art Nouveau (Fig 13.17). These exceptions aside, it waited for the early twentieth-century movements (like the Werkbund and the Staatliche Bauhaus) to attempt a break with the ornamental tradition. A prominent denunciation against ornament was delivered by Adolf Loos in 1908, in an article entitled "Ornament and Crime." The background of this treatise is discussed in an earlier chapter; of interest here is its content. It is in the form of a manifesto, in which he states that both the primitive and the child are amoral, and thus not accountable for their acts; significantly, both primitives and children delight in ornamentation. In contrast, the adult in an advanced society is socially responsible and abhors ornament: ''. . . the man of our day who, in response to an inner urge, smears the walls with erotic symbols is a criminal or a degenerate.''[58] What is natural at one level of ''development,'' is retrograde at another: *''The evolution of culture is synonymous with the removal of ornament from utilitarian objects.''*[59] In this view, the willful perpetuation of ornament is an impediment to such evolution and a crime against the economy in its waste of human labor, money, and material.

This manifesto was republished in *L'Esprit Nouveau* in 1913, and thus took on a widespread notoriety. Certainly few theorists had ever equated the production of ornament with criminality; although he does acknowledge that he is only preaching to the ''aristocrat'' who should know better, not the common worker. But what exactly is the nature of Loos' critique? He makes several points that, once freed from their abusive tone, are quite arguable: first, since ornament is no longer a natural attribute of our society, its production is necessarily retrograde and thus poorly rewarded; second, ornament is obviously a waste of material and labor, in that it contributes nothing to the utility of the object while raising its cost of manufacture; and third, beyond the economic argument, ornament represents a reactionary nostalgia that hinders social progress.

This approach argues that insofar as the production of ornament serves

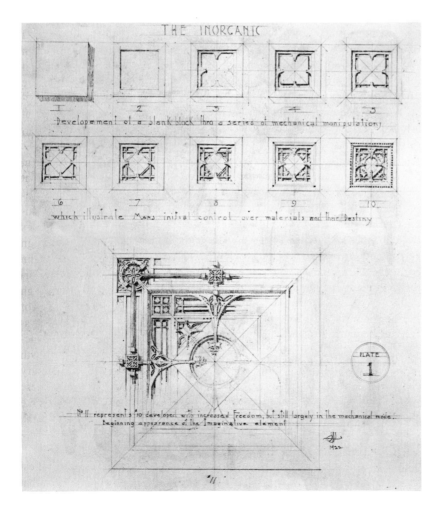

13.17

Plate from *A System of Architectural Ornament; Louis Sullivan (1924)*

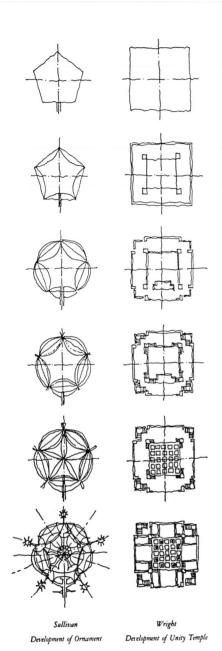

Sullivan
Development of Ornament

Wright
Development of Unity Temple

13.18

Developmental Diagrams; *Thomas H. Beeby (1977)*
Beeby's illustration demonstrates certain commonalities in approach between Sullivan's development of ornament and Wright's approach to spatial design. As Wright considered Sullivan his mentor (lieber meister), such a relationship is entirely plausible. (Courtesy: Thomas H. Beeby, Chicago.)

an adverse economic and social function, it can be neither beautiful nor moral. But is he really opposed to ornament, or just the form it takes? Benedetto Gravagnuolo asks, "Is not proposing the elimination of the ornamental option from architecture equivalent to abolishing—at least in intent—the symbolic and representational content that is superimposed on pure and simple construction?"[60] That is, architecture without ornament assumes a self-sufficiency of material substance itself; indeed the only task that Loos would leave to the architect is the organization of form and material, with aspects of communication belonging to the latter. But has the material, with its inherent and associational qualities, and the detailing that gives it expression, not thereby taken on the attributes of ornament? This would help explain his own approach to design, one which relied on a highly sensitive (and often lavish) use of materials (Plate 9). In taking this position, Loos may have contributed what soon became the standard Modernist approach to the use of expensive and ornate materials, practiced even while its proponents continued to deride the use of "ornament."

But ornament may be viewed, beyond its surface enrichment, as a particular way of "seeing," inevitably leading to a certain *organizational methodology.* Put differently, how ornament is spatially organized may be similar in approach to how space is organized generally. Thomas Beeby makes this point when he notes that the design processes in Wright's Unity Temple (Fig 2.18) and in the development of ornament by Sullivan (Plate 4 of *A System of Architectural Ornament*) are analogous.[61] Sullivan begins with a pentagon, and Wright with a square; and in both cases all further manipulations follow logically from that starting point. Wright applies his ornament—the strips of wood that connect column, wall and ceiling—much as Sullivan developed his foliate lines, creating in both instances a complex rhythm that freely interacts with the geometric structure (Fig 13.18). Beeby notes that Wright's strips are ". . . in direct contrast to the structure since they flow freely throughout the space, independent of the logic of the structure."[62] The result is a continuity of interior space and surfaces that, while based on a solid geometric structure, is spatially rich and dynamic, ". . . an astounding performance by Wright, yet quite predictable."[63]

The point has already been made that during this century detailed materials have become an expression of ornament (at times, the sole ornament); but it is also true that the structure itself has become ornamental. Structural elements have always enjoyed that potential, as in the ornamental vaulting of the Gothic cathedral. And recently that task has been amplified. There are certain advantages in exploiting the ornamental possibilities of the structural form, especially the clarity of communication that ensues (the essential agreement between subject and content). The Formica Showroom, designed by Stanley Tigerman, is an excellent example of both an *ornamental structure* and clarity of message. Tigerman states:

> The purpose of the project is simply to demonstrate that this product does not require things extrinsic to itself in order to verify, indeed to justify, its existence. Therefore, what is presented is nothing more than the product. . . ."[64]

The plan consists of a pair of interlocking grids, set at forty-five degrees to each other, providing a pathway through the product. It is even complete with a cabinet for the Formica literature, which the designer refers to as "the object of desire" (Fig 13.19).

Symbolic Content

The use of ornament is endemic; it appears in the visual *richness of materials, elegance of detail,* and *complexity of structure.* Only when traditional *symbolic ornament* is used, does the situation look problematic. Put another way, as long as ornament belongs to one or more of the above categories, it is noncontroversial, but comparatively limited in vocabulary—yet the basic vocabulary of symbolism available to current designers is one belonging to another time. Indeed, most attempts to develop a contemporary ornament have centered on clever references to the older tradition, as in Robert Venturi's use of the single "Ionic" column in his addition to the Allen Memorial Art Museum (Fig 13.20). In this, Venturi is depending on a knowledgeable audience with an understanding of the Orders. Thus he appreciatively notes James Ackerman's observation that Michelangelo ". . . invariably retained essential features from ancient models in order to force the observer to recollect the source while enjoying the innovations."[65] And as Venturi himself points out, ". . . old cliches in new settings achieve rich meanings. . . ."[66]

Venturi's translation of the Ionic column has precedent; the manipulation of ornament, even ornament as profound as the Orders, has occurred before. The more ingrained in our memory is the sign, the more significant is any departure from its normal appearance. In *The Sense of Order,* E.H. Gombrich notes the power and pervasiveness of habit, which itself derives from the sense of order. Habit, according to Gombrich, establishes the ". . . frame of reference against which we can plot the variety of experience."[67] He believes that although *art and artifice* have grown from the

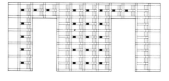

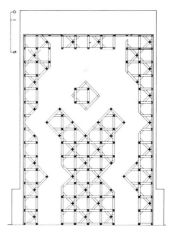

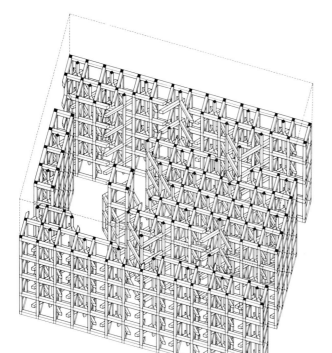

13.19

Formica Showroom—Chicago; *Tigerman, Fugman, McCurry, Architects (1986)*
Two interlocking grids comprise the structure, one black and one white. Where the pedestrian path cuts the grid, the members are capped with formica in various colors. This intriguing system thus creates a space with the material being exhibited. (Courtesy: Tigerman McCurry Architects, Chicago).

13.20.

**Allen Memorial Art Museum addition—
Oberlin, Ohio;** *Venturi & Rauch (1977)*
Venturi has diagonally cut off the corner of
the new gallery and sheathed the steel support column with wooden slats and a capital
with two-dimensional volutes. The window
that is set across the diagonal cut reveals this
fanciful gesture to visitors inside. (Courtesy:
Venturi, Scott Brown and Associates, Inc.,
Philadelphia.)

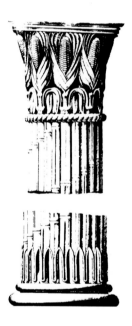

13.21

**Corn Column, des. for Capitol, Washing-
ton;** *Benjamin H. Latrobe (1809)*
Latrobe used both corn and tobacco plants
in place of the traditional acanthus leaves, in
an effort to adjust the Orders (with their inherent symbolic content) to their setting in a
new country. Thus he has maintained the
form for its meaning, while adjusting the
specific iconograhy for its geographic location. (Source: *History of the United States
Capitol,* Glenn Brown.)

same psychological roots, "it is artifice first of all which is called upon in
human culture to resist change and to perpetuate the present." [68] And so we
believe art to be radical, and artifice (ornament and decoration) conservative—an evocation of the past. This implies that ornament carries with it
the symbolic content of the age in which it was first produced, which gives
it special significance. There have been many efforts (particularly in the late
eighteenth century) to draw on that content—combined with deliberate
changes—to create a substantially new symbolic content (Fig 13.21).

Another contemporary application of ornament is in Chestnut Place, by
Weese Hicky Weese. The artist Richard Haas, a *trompe l'oeil* specialist,
was employed to create the appearance of the Medieval church of San Min-
iato in Florence within the lobby of the building. The emphasis is on the
term appearance, as this is essentially an illusion constructed in order to
make a contemporary reference to an older tradition, much like Venturi's
column (Fig 13.22). This return of symbolic, illusionistic ornament to design is refreshing in many respects but, as van Zanten concludes, "To carry
conviction, the principle of ornamenting must be thought out in relation to
contemporaneous techniques and images. . . ." [69] This is not easy, but understanding how ornament is formed would greatly help. One of the largest
problems in this may be the casual assumption made in the previous paragraph (i.e., all ornament is necessarily symbolic). Gombrich warns that,

"from the observation that decorative motifs can have a symbolic meaning, it was only too tempting a step to conclude that all motifs were originally conceived as symbols—though their meaning had been lost in the course of history."[70] This conclusion might be justified in language (the cult of etymology), whose purpose is communication, but is less so in visual data, whose purpose might be expressive.

Therefore, van Zanten's cautionary comment seems appropriate; the formation of new ornament (or use of the old) necessarily involves an understanding of current "techniques and images," as well as a consideration of its potential for symbolic content (willed or not). The last part of this prescription is likely the most difficult. Gombrich notes that with the rise of semiotics (the language of signs) came an interest in symbolic content at least equal to that of form and style, which has resulted in the blurring of familiar distinctions. "One of these is the distinction between designs and signs, between the merely decorative and the symbolic. Where it is proposed to treat everything as a sign, it becomes doubly important to reinterpret the old commonsense terminology. . . ."[71] The relationship between these two elements, *design* and *symbol,* becomes clear in the ensuing text, when Gombrich says, "It is the function of signs to attract attention, to be conspicuous and clear, and it is the business of the designer to enhance this effect by creating the proper setting."[72] That is, after a partial separation of design from symbol in the post-Loos era, an attention to these considerations is emerging again (Plate 12).

13.22

Chestnut Place—Chicago; *Weese Hickey Weese with murals by Richard Haas (1982)* The ornament is not only decorative, but unifies the space in a statement of grandeur that obscures the lobby's true size. The symmetry of the scheme is reinforced by the floor pattern, and the ambient lighting system, which is inside the central element. (Photo by: Paul Zakoian, Chicago.)

Archetypes and Ethics

14

Spatial Archetypes

Earlier, typology is described as generalized design elements that, in light of particular cultural circumstances, generate a certain architectural form. What is not discussed, and may be of critical importance, is the genesis of typology. The idea of type depends on abstract constructs that are special, shapes that declare themselves to be, and are so considered, functionally and ideologically correct. Accordingly, Aldo Rossi states, "The type developed according to both needs and aspirations to beauty; a particular type was associated with a form and a way of life, although its specific shape varied widely from society to society. The concept of type thus became the basis of architecture. . . ."[1] The reason for the wide variance in appearance has already been noted (i.e., the *type* is the general and informing framework of spatial ordering that assumes a variety of shapes while the *model* is the highly refined and specific architectural form that is derived from the type). With this in mind, however, one may still inquire as to the basis for a type's becoming so.

Types, of course, provide us with historical continuity, usually being so long-established that their origins have become obscure. But they are themselves a product of an initial impetus, the primitive *archetype,* the original set of human circumstances that impelled an architectural type in the first place. For an archetype to be transformed into a spatial type with specific (if situationally variable) characteristics, it likely has attributes that are fundamental in nature. Malcolm Quantrill notes that architectural form ". . . is capable of connecting us to the deep well of human consciousness, keeping open the channels of historical continuity by the myths, ideas, rituals, and events which it represents."[2] Indeed, type derives its authenticity and persuasiveness from its capacity to spiritually embody these aspects, and its usefulness for its ability to inspire coherent models. In short, the type stands midway between the abstract archetype and the concrete model; in this scheme the archetype may be seen as the type's generator.

One of the many contributions of Carl Jung was to forward such concepts as the *collective unconscious,* the *archetype,* and the *symbol.* Jung contrasted the notions of personal unconscious, which had been postulated by

275

Sigmund Freud, with the collective unconscious, a deeper layer that does not derive from personal experience. He notes that this phenomenon is, therefore, universal in character: ". . . in contrast to the personal psyche, it has contents and modes of behavior that are more or less the same everywhere and in all individuals. It is, in other words, identical in all men and thus constitutes a common psychic substrate of a suprapersonal nature which is present in every one of us."[3]

Jung theorized that this collective unconscious connected human beings with their primordial past through its contents; these he designated archetypes—universal images that have existed since the remotest times. Thus the term archetype

> . . . designates only those psychic contents which have not yet been submitted to conscious elaboration and are therefore an immediate datum of psychic experience. . . . The archetype is essentially an unconscious content that is altered by becoming conscious and by being perceived, and it takes its color from the individual consciousness in which it happens to appear.[4]

Hence the archetype, upon entering the conscious mind, assumes an evocative image commonly referred to as a symbol. If architectural form is "capable of keeping open the channels of historical continuity," it is reasonable to suppose that spatial types are invested with a symbolic character that proceeds from unconscious human experience. And in no type are these properties more potently expressed than in the house, which may be viewed as a repository of archetypal experience. Such a concept would go far toward explaining our affection for, and fascination with, our houses. It would also account for the emphasis accorded certain aspects of the house, like entries and hearths, which are primordial in nature, and often sacred.

In his autobiography, Jung explains a dream in which he finds himself exploring the interior of a two-story house. He begins his journey on the upper floor, and descends through the ground floor to the cellar, finally ending in a cave below the cellar. Each layer reaches further back in time:

> It was plain to me that the house represented a kind of image of the psyche—that is to say, of my then state of consciousness, with hitherto unconscious additions. . . . The deeper I went, the more alien and the darker the scene became. In the cave, I discovered remains of a primitive culture, that is the world of the primitive man within myself. . . .[5]

14.1

Cross-Section of the Cosmopolitan's House; *Antoine-Laurent-Thomas Vaudoyer (1785)*
Vaudoyer wished to create a house appropriate to the character of his patron, M. Debracq, a self-styled "cosmopolitan." This sphere was richly decorated, with functions specific to each room. In 1802 this engraving appeared in the magazine *Annales de Musée,* which was owned by painter C. Landon. Landon noted that "this may not be great architecture; but if it were a poem, it would be a madrigal."[1] (Courtesy: Bibliothèque Nationale, Paris.)

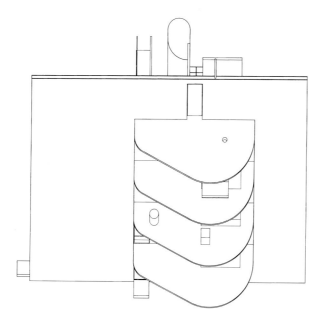

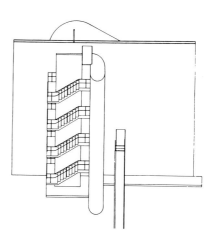

14.2

Wall House 1; *John Hejduk (1968–74)*
This house is best seen in its symbolic form, although it was conceived in physical terms as well. Each function was given a different floor level: level 1 served as entry and dining area; level 2 for living and study; and level 3 the bath and sleeping area. Central to Hejduk's vision is the placing of only one opening in the wall, thus emphasizing ". . . the 'idea' of the present, the celebration of the two dimensional. . . .'" (Courtesy: John Hejduk, New York.)

He realized that his dream pointed to a cultural history consisting of successive layers of consciousness, thus suggesting an impersonal nature of instinct, or archetypes.[6] Whether one subscribes to the Jungian concept of the collective unconscious, there exist powerful (and seemingly universal) aspects to spatial types that, while not fully understood, nonetheless require design consideration.

A profound importance has been granted the house by philosopher Gaston Bachelard: ". . . our house is our corner of the world . . . it is our first universe, a real cosmos in every sense of the word."[7] As such, ". . . the house is one of the greatest powers of integration for the thoughts, memories and dreams of mankind."[8] Not only does the house shelter and protect the daydreamer, but it also provides a site for memory. And if it is a complex house, with an attic and cellar, and niches and corridors, memories are more clearly delineated than if they were to inhabit a featureless space (Fig 14.1). So vital are spatial memories, that Bachelard suggests a name for their study, *topoanalysis,* ". . . the systematic psychological study of the sites of our intimate lives."[9] Spatial memories are particularly evocative, because they exist outside the normal flow of measured time. Bachelard notes, "In its countless alveoli space contains compressed time. That is what space is for."[10]

The profound dichotomy of up and down within the house has also been noted by Bachelard; in this sense, the tower and the cellar may represent the vertical polarities of the conscious (rationality) and the unconscious (irrationality), which Jung referred to in the account of his dream. Jung emphasized the revelatory aspect of his descent to the cellar, where he made discoveries within himself that he said could scarcely be illuminated by consciousness.[11] Thus the house is not only a psychic metaphor, but an instrument through which we can come to realize ourselves. Such a view is expressed by John Hejduk in his *Mask of Medusa,* where he describes his Wall House 1 (Fig 14.2):

> On one side of the wall (the past), the circulatory elements—ramp, stair, elevator—were placed. They were volumetric, opaque, monochromatic, in perspective with the structure grounded. . . . Once the single inhabitant passed through the wall he was in a space overlooking a landscape (trees?

water? earth? sky?) which was basically private, contemplative and reflective. . . . The new space was that space which was the quickest, the most fleeting, the most compressed, the shortest distance, the present. It was meant to heighten the fact that we are continuously going in and out of the past and future, cyclical.[12]

Two of Bachelard's ideas are especially important here. "A house that has been experienced is not an inert box. Inhabited space transcends geometrical space."[13] This statement, in conjunction with an earlier comment, ". . . all really inhabited space bears the essence of the notion of home,"[14] suggests the generative role that may be ascribed to the habitation. The second comment clearly suggests that the critical quality of house is its suitability as home, a place of dwelling. It is precisely this idea of dwelling that Martin Heidegger refers to in his *Poetry, Language, Thought:* "Man's relation to locations, and through locations to spaces, inheres in his dwelling. The relationship between man and space is none other than dwelling, strictly thought and spoken."[15]

This may require explanation. Heidegger says that we attain to dwelling by means of building; that is, building's goal is dwelling. The domain of dwelling, he points out, extends even over those buildings that do not serve to shelter us. Of itself, however, this is no guarantee that dwelling takes place: ". . . residential buildings do indeed provide shelter; today's houses may even be well-planned, easy to keep, attractively cheap, open to air, light, and sun, but—do the houses in themselves hold any guarantee that *dwelling* occurs in them?"[16] Yet the very root of the word building, the Old English and High German word *buan,* means to dwell, and hence all buildings are semantically invested with the notion of dwelling. The essential nature of dwelling in turn rests on the notion of being at peace with nature, a position that he again deduces semantically. How, then, does building belong to dwelling? The building, as a thing, grants importance to its location; it gathers to itself, as it were, what Heidegger refers to as earth and sky, divinities and mortals—*the fourfold,* an essential unity with the world. It thus becomes a *location,* and he says that only things that are locations in this sense allow for spaces. To summarize Heidegger's position; the desire/need to dwell produces a built form, which becomes a location expressed in spaces. *"Accordingly, spaces receive their being from locations and not from 'space.' "*[17]

The spaces that we daily occupy, then, are informed by their sense of location, which takes meaning through human dwelling. This seminal connection between location and space is made clear by Heidegger: "To say that mortals *are* is to say that *in dwelling* they persist through spaces by virtue of their stay among things and locations."[18] And it is this lack of "groundedness" that spells out the "real plight of dwelling" which, he points out, does not lie in a lack of houses. Rather, the plight is that ". . . mortals ever search anew for the nature of dwelling, that they *must ever learn to dwell.*"[19] Heidegger's approach to buildings as profound locations helps explain the failure of housing projects designed in the complete absence of any sense of place. In his *Placeways,* E.V. Walter observes that the moral and emotional qualities of a place grant it its familiar characteristics. He thus concludes that for a person living in a place with bad experiences, "the elegance of the 'space' or its rational appeal will hardly determine whether a person stays there or moves away. The action in the place . . . and the sense of how good or bad it is will probably be decisive."[20]

This may also explain the deep attachment people have for what seem, on the surface, rather unremarkable buildings. Indeed, such intense reaction to attributes of buildings, and the desire for spatial permanence, together may account for the public's affection for older houses in established neighborhoods, and hostility toward typical housing developments. For the most part, these developments replace a living record of human dwelling with a pure form unrelated to experience. Martin Pawley notes that neither the notion of consumer housing nor demolition recognizes ". . . the importance of place or known objects, and neither comprehends the significance of the kind of behavioural history that accompanies and stabilizes successive generational occupations of the same dwelling."[21] The power of place, a location, to act as a storehouse of memory is attested to by Thomas Wolfe in his *You Can't Go Home Again:*

> He loved this old house on Twelfth Street, its red brick walls, its rooms of noble height and spaciousness, its old dark woods and floors that creaked; and in the magic of the moment it seemed to be enriched and given a profound and lonely dignity by all the human beings it had sheltered in its ninety years. The house became like a living presence. Every object seemed to have an animate vitality of its own—walls, rooms, chairs, tables, even a half-wet bath towel hanging from the shower ring above the tub. . . .[22]

This points to another aspect of place; that is, that the location-spaces that result from dwelling still require concrete form to be perceived. Quantrill describes the sensory aspects of our environment as the *genius loci,* or sense of place, noting, "The very concept, spirit of place, depends upon the particular relationship of things to each other in a particular place."[23] He says we may *conceive* environmental frameworks that conform to an underlying order of things, but we *perceive* those frameworks in terms of particular characteristics of form, material, color, directional emphasis, etc., that provide a distinctive set of images to a building or place. He further notes that an ongoing familiarity with places and spaces (and their constituent details) increases their mnemonic potency so that time becomes compressed into memorable spatial images ". . . generating an architecture of spatial consciousness."[24] And, as previously noted, he discusses the remarkable ability of built form to provide continuity with the past by representation of its myths and rituals.

This often takes the form of ascribing a spiritual persona to particular aspects of a building. E.V. Walter comments: "The *genius loci* . . . stood for the independent reality of a place. Above all, it symbolized the place's generative energy, and it pictured a specific, personal, spiritual presence who animated and protected a place."[25] Indeed, it was the Roman custom to place various features of the house under the stewardship of particular spirits. Hence certain points in the house had more weight than others; it is both expected and instructive that they still do. Walter notes that a place is a location of experience: "It evokes and organizes memories, images, sentiments, meanings, and the work of imagination. The feelings of a place are indeed the mental projections of individuals, but they come from collective experience and they do not happen anywhere else."[26]

It is reasonable to ask whether there have been conceptual frameworks advanced that do not rely on a collective unconscious, primordial archetypes, sense of place, and so forth, for their content. Such an exhausting and imprecise range of concerns must be dismaying to the designer, prompting the thought that it would be more convenient if an abstract system, not dependent on memory and universally applicable, could be discovered. Such a theoretical system was proposed by the De Stijl group during the early 1920s. Central to the De Stijl vision was the proposition that in the art of the past, relationships were veiled and confused because they were subordinated to the depiction of natural form. And so Mondrian states, "The more neutral are the plastic means, the more possible is it to determine the immutable expression of reality. We can consider as relatively neutral those forms which show no relationship with the natural appearance of things or with some kind of 'idea.' "[27] Thus would neutral forms encourage the expression of a new, universal iconographic language that would be impersonal and immediately understood by everyone. Such a language would not only reject any reliance on natural forms, but all mnemonic functions as well.

The De Stijl program, when applied to architectural form, is startling, especially as it was defined by Mondrian:

> As long as man is dominated by individualism, and neglects to cultivate his universal essence, he does not seek nor can he find his own person. The house too becomes the place where this fleeting individuality is cultivated, and its plastic expression reflects this trivial preoccupation. **The exteriorization of this self-centeredness has been fatal to the whole period.**[28]

And in order to promote a new, more "healthy" beauty, it was necessary for our environment to cease being an "outflow of our wretched personality."[29] The opposite of the thus condemned "lyrical expression" was to be a highly improved "plastic expression," permitting art to attain the universal (Fig 14.3):

> . . . the house will no longer be enclosed, shut in, detached. . . . The idea of a house—house dear house, home sweet home—must disappear. . . . And man? Being nothing in himself, he will be merely a part of the whole, and then, having lost the vanity of his small and trivial individuality, he will be happy in this Eden which he himself has **created!**[30]

After such passionate invective, it is instructive to examine the major architectural achievement of De Stijl, the conceptually elegant and intriguing Schröder House by Gerritt Rietveld. Its interior is particularly demanding in terms of visual ideology; one does wonder, however, where to place the family pictures (Plate 10).

14.3

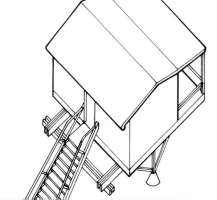

Week-end Huis; *Gerrit Rietveld with T. Schröder (1938)*
This small (7.4 m in diameter) house was easily erected, and contained the minimum amenities necessary for its purpose. It is curious that Rietveld was an ardent supporter of prefabrication, yet also believed that "functional architecture" should go beyond supplying only the basic "necessities of life." (Drawn by: J. Malnar.)

Sign and Ritual

Quantrill notes that architectural frameworks can offer the possibility of furthering the experience of interior space and opening up vistas of an exterior world within our interior perspective. They do this by formulating, and adhering to, certain conventions that are significant if they either profoundly alter the ordering of space and form, or advance a new and distinctive hypothesis of how space and form might be understood.[31] Quantrill says Renaissance classicism exemplified the former, and De Stijl the latter. The notion of an aesthetic based on a common human experience seems to agree with Jung's principles in his view of the collective unconscious, except in the absolute quality demanded by De Stijl. But a more serious problem may lie in the translation of this idea to the language of perception. So Quantrill observes that while the abstract *structure* of modernist concepts may have had intellectual appeal, their *representation* as perceived forms has enjoyed a less universal appeal than with any previous historical style.[32] This is, of course, precisely what Reyner Banham meant when he referred to functionalism as "poverty-stricken symbolically." If this is so, it is probably because such an abstract approach does not agree with our sense of place, and fails to draw on our deep well of unconscious associations.

The two ends of the continuum—abstract functionalism and archetypal symbol—may be seen in two very different concepts of building, the *existenzminimum* unit and Jung's home at Bollingen. In 1928 delegates from various countries gathered in La Sarraz, Switzerland, and founded the group CIAM (Congrès Internationaux d'Architecture Moderne), which remained influential for the next three decades. The La Sarraz Declaration states these architect's aims clearly and forcefully: that "building" is an elementary activity linked with the development of human life; and that there was a need for an entirely new conception of architecture that could satisfy the spiritual, intellectual, and material demands of contemporary life.[33] The congress held the following year in Frankfurt saw the first real applications of their position, which centered around the *existenzminimum,* the problem of housing the poorest sector of society. The requirements of such housing were set out by Gropius, who noted that this ". . . is the question of the basic minimum of space, air, light, and heat which is necessary to man . . . (who) . . . from a biological standpoint needs improved conditions of ventilation and lighting and only a small quantity of living space, especially if this is organized in a technically correct manner."[34] Of interest here is not so much the program or the resultant plan (which lives up to its name), but the emphasis on the phrase "technically correct manner." While such plans agreed with the stated program of functionalism, they were less successful in accounting for the psychological needs of humans, and the symbols that manifest them (Fig 14.4).

Jung's house at Bollingen, on the shore of Zurich's upper lake, represents the other end of this continuum, a structure built largely of archetypal form that expanded by accretion. Jung notes the reason for such a building, "I had to achieve a kind of representation in stone of my innermost thoughts and of the knowledge I had acquired. . . . I had to make a confession of faith in stone."[35] The structure began (in 1922) as a primitive dwelling centered around a hearth; but Jung almost immediately changed it in the vertical dimension, effectively producing a low tower. "The feeling of repose and renewal I had in this tower was intense from the start. It represented for me the maternal hearth."[36] But still he was not satisfied and consequently added a towerlike annex in 1931 that contained a "retiring room." In 1935 he added a courtyard and loggia by the lake. His final alteration came (on the occasion of his wife's death) in 1955, when he added an upper story to the structure. And so the building represents the work of almost thirty-five years (Fig 14.5). When Jung speaks of this building, it is with profound introspection:

> From the beginning I felt the Tower as in some way a place of maturation—a maternal womb or a maternal figure in which I could become what I was, what I am and will be. . . . There is nothing in the Tower that has not grown into its own form over the decades, nothing with which I am not linked. Here everything has its history, and mine; here is space for the spaceless kingdom of the world's and the psyche's hinterland.[37]

He notes the absence of electricity and running water, preferring to tend his own lamps and cut firewood in a kind of harmony with nature. The point here is not to attempt a direct comparison of the existenzminimum design to Bollingen—their impulse and purpose are too dichotomous for that—but to compare their sharply different attitudes about what constitutes the essential content of architectural form, and methods of design.

Walter points out that the criteria used in the formation of rational space are sometimes used to condemn mythic space, while to the mythic formation of consciousness, rational space is intangible and devoid of meaning. "Modern 'space' is universal and abstract, whereas a 'place' is concrete and particular. People do not experience abstract space; they experience places."[38] Walter refers to the subjective dimension of located experience as an *expressive reality;* that is, it refers to what people feel and think and imagine, in the same way that there are physical, perceptual, and cognitive realities. Thus he notes, "A place is a concrete milieu and an expressive universe within specific social and physical boundaries. . . . 'Expressive' means laden with emotional and symbolic features of experience."[39] The form this expression takes is familiar to every city dweller, ranging from culturally approved decoration to the graffiti that (more or less eloquently) signifies disapprobation—and it is these forms that Walter is primarily concerned with. But this might also include the expressive details of the interior, which mark the character of place and time as well. Thus the interior of the Rome apartment of Mario Praz reflects the character of its owner, and his twenty years of ownership, in a highly specific and expressive space (Fig 1.5).

14.4

Existenzminimum Model; *Proposal to CIAM (Congrès Internationaux d'Architecture Moderne) (1929)*
The plan indicates a highly efficient apartment module located on two floors (with an internal stair). Such a unit type lends itself to multiplication in both the vertical and horizontal dimensions, thereby permitting the standardization that would lower costs. (Drawn by: J. Malnar.)

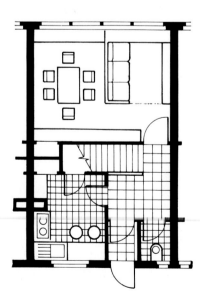 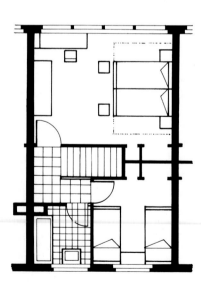

14.5

The House of Carl Jung—Bollingen; Switzerland (1922–55)
Despite having been built by a process of accretion, for reasons related to the symbolic rather than the physical, the house maintains an entirely coherent appearance. The interior image is of the kitchen. Jung notes, "In practical matters, especially in the kitchen where one really should have an open fire, there are to be found mysterious ecstasies of which the purely functionally-minded never dream."³ (Courtesy: Frau Niedick-Linder, Zurich.)

Sigmund Freud's study in London, now a museum, offers another remarkable view of an interior devoted to objects. Not only are there paintings and photographs, and walls of well-used books, but also an incredible range of archaeological artifacts. These range from Roman glass and Sumerian seals, to statuettes and Chinese jades—some twenty-three hundred pieces in all. They were, of course, objects of aesthetic interest, but they also gave Freud insights into the human condition. And their acquisition served still another function, that of emotional gratification. In her article for *Smithsonian* (August 1990), Helen Dudar comments that "Freud bought steadily the way collectors often buy: for the joy of buying, for the pleasure and for the childlike, almost primitive sense of power that ownership of valuables evokes."⁴⁰ And the fact that he wished all of his objects to be arranged in his new study in London precisely as they had been in Vienna, attests to their role as an integral part of his persona (Fig 14.6).

It would seem that few people have the mania for collecting that Freud did; yet most of us have vastly more artifacts than we might suppose. (Thus moving day is usually a revelation.) And, like Freud, we use those artifacts for pleasure and communication of persona. When Gilbert Rohde designed his sectional sofa in the 1930s, it was usually accompanied by a cocktail/coffeetable to facilitate the physical aspects of social gatherings (Fig 10.10). But the table's real role may have been to provide a central place for collections of artifacts. In their *Place of Houses,* Moore, Allen, and Lyndon point out that these can provide a clue to the owner's sensibilities:

> We require that the clues to our host's concerns be combined and multiplied and personalized. A coffee table laden with the objects its owner derives pleasure from and which reflect his current concerns serves a useful role, enhancing verbal intercourse instead of killing it as the television does.⁴¹

The efforts to individualize quasi-personal areas, such as desks and work stations, may thus be related to our desire to confirm our identity, as well as communicate that information to others. In this sense, objects and the space they occupy have a communicative function that operates through a shared system of rituals and symbols.

In earlier chapters reference is made to culture's reliance on concepts like *ritual, sign,* and *symbol. Semiotics* is the study of culturally recognized sign-systems. It developed from two sources: first, Ferdinand de Saussure's work on conceptual structures growing out of his *Course in General Linguistics* (1966); and second, the work of philosopher Charles Sanders Peirce in sign-theory. Saussure gave this study the title semiology (i.e., what constitutes signs and what laws control their behavior). Pierce gave this study the name semiotics, referring to it (in 1940) as "... a quasi-necessary or formal doctrine of signs."[42] In the sense that all cultural phenomena are sign-systems (including design), architecture may thus be seen as communication as well as having spatial functions. In "Function and Sign: The Semiotics of Architecture," Umberto Eco speculates whether this notion might be "... applicable to *any type of design producing three-dimensional constructions destined to permit the fulfillment of some function connected with life in society.* "[43] His definition would embrace the design of clothing and food, but exclude objects designed to be aesthetically contemplated. This would certainly help explain our attachment for the ordinary objects with which we fill our spaces, objects of daily use and mnemonic function; but it would also explain Freud's passion for collecting objects that satisfied certain professional purposes. Eco concludes that, in any case, it is clear that we do experience architecture as communication, while still recognizing its functional aspect.[44] That is, architecture permits events to occur, suggests the events that are appropriate, and assists in their formation.

Thus Eco has restated the *form follows function* principle: "... *the form of the object must, besides making the function possible, denote that function clearly enough to make it practicable as well as desirable.* ..."[45] This denotation should be so clear that it inclines one to successfully fulfill it. He concludes, therefore, that the tie between form and function needs to be explicitly communicated, and that the function is denoted on the basis of established habits and expectations, that is, a system of codes.[46] There are two rather interesting inferences that may be drawn from this claim: first, design, no matter how avant-garde, always draws on past codes if it is to have any meaning at all; and second, the meaning of *function* must be extended to include all possible uses (including the symbolic) of design.

14.6

Sigmund Freud's Study—London *(1938)*
This photograph depicts a portion of Freud's three-thousand-volume library, as well as a small part of his vast collection of artifacts. Thus Freud's study is a repository of the world's culture—its collective wisdom—over recorded time. (Courtesy: Freud Museum, London.)

Eco postulates three possible approaches to design: complete acquiescence to popular codes; an avant-garde approach that denies all existing codes; and an architecture that acknowledges the existing codes while anticipating future user-need and cultural developments. The benefits of the last category are probably obvious. But aside from the aesthetic advantage, there is something persuasive about the consequent necessity of incorporating information from a variety of adjunct fields, and a need for criticism outside architecture proper.

The usefulness of the semiotic approach to design is clear. In his "Semiology and Architecture," Charles Jencks contends that as every act, object, and statement perceived by humans is meaningful, ". . . we are in a literal sense condemned to meaning, and thus we can either become aware of how meaning works in a technical sense (semiology), or we can remain content with our intuition."[47] That is, once the "intuitive" is raised to the conscious level, the opportunity for responsible choice is increased. By way of making the parameters of the architectural act clear, he uses a model developed by Ogden and Richards *(The Meaning of Meaning,* 1938), by expanding its number of terms (Fig 14.7). At first glance, it looks remarkably similar to the continuum that derives from the fine arts: subject (referent) = form (symbol) = content (thought). Indeed, two of the terms are identical in Jenck's version; however, the relationship between terms is somewhat different. And so he says that ". . . the main point of the semiological triangle is that there are simply *relations* between language, thought, and reality."[48] That is, one area does not determine another. When he later refers to the triangle as encompassing ". . . form, content and percept," it becomes clear that the subject (thing) is not at issue, but its perception (with all that implies).

The importance that has been granted the role of ritual and symbol in the semiotic approach not only smacks of authenticity, but allows a rich possibility of conceptual approaches. In his essay "The Time House: or Argument for an Existential Dwelling," Martin Pawley argues for a definition of design that takes into account the intimate identification of individual with object. ". . . *design is the arrangement and metamorphosis of objects to correspond to the ambiguous demands of human consciousness.*"[49] By way of example, he depicts an elderly pensioner sitting in the midst of his years of furniture, bric-a-brac, photographs, and so forth, which together represent the "object-evidence" of his life. Pawley suggests that it is these mementos that sustain him against a cold and hostile world, offering evidence of a former time.[50] This is a persuasive image, one that argues for the power of objectified space, and against the notion of an essentially abstract, functional plan devoid of memory and detail. The problem, says Pawley, is that ". . . it is impossible to functionally define the *act of dwelling,* which is a continuously evolving drama, not a pattern established once and retained forever."[51] However, people fill their dwellings with objects and information with both iconic (symbolic) and functional value, and one would be hard put to precisely appraise their subjective worth—because objects express values as well as ideas and images.

The dwelling is, therefore, special, and Pawley has devised a most peculiar dwelling, the *Time House,* based on five interrelated axioms. Two of these are especially interesting: first, through dwelling people authenticate their environment (the individual dwelling); and second, a continuous record of object relations would enable the individual to cope with environmental change as a necessary condition of existence in a technological society.[52] And so the Time House is designed to absorb the "object-evidence of experience," to be a "neutral memory" that will serve to externalize

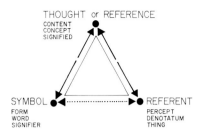

14.7

The Semiological Triangle; *Charles Jencks (1969)*
The semantic triangle was developed by C.K. Ogden and I.A. Richards. Jencks adapts their system to form his semiological triangle, which he uses for design purposes by expanding the nomenclature and affirming the equality of the relationships (i.e., that one does not determine another). (Drawn by: J. Malnar.)

the person/object interface, and having the capacity to replay the recorded experience. This process, argues Pawley, would give the occupants access to continuous information that can grant new perspectives about the way they live, and open up self-perception and the chance to relive experience. We could, in this sense, make our own behavior intelligible (Fig 14.8).

This is an interesting proposition, more fantastic than serious, but with great significance for the course of design in the future. That is, it combines the two areas that seem the most promising for developments in spatial design: semiotics and environmental psychology. In the introduction to *Signs, Symbols and Architecture,* Geoffrey Broadbent notes these two approaches to architectural meaning: ''. . . it seems to me that neither, alone, throws sufficient light on the subject but the two together offer some of the most exciting developments in the whole of architectural research.''[53] If these two approaches seem too abstract to be of use, he says, they represent a vast improvement over the built abstractions that surround us, which ''. . . convey blank alienation and contempt for humanity.''[54] While this is a forcefully stated position, it is hardly unfair.

Experiential Space

A quite different analysis is made by Bill Hillier and Julienne Hanson in *The Social Logic of Space:* ''Insofar as they are purposeful, buildings are not just objects, but transformations of space through objects.''[55] The authors say that space thus creates a special relation between function and social meaning, and that the ordering of space in buildings is really concerned with the ordering of relations among people.[56] The proposed theory is interesting, being based neither on the proxemic assumptions derived

14.8

The Time House; *Martin Pawley (1968)*
Pawley's Time House is conceived as a concrete bunker, built for introspection and defense. It is filled with cameras, sensors, and other recording devices that continuously record all behavior of the occupant along with other environmental data—all of which awaits recall in the replay room. Pawley notes that this method would yield a truly complete picture of ourselves, without the distortion inherent in the fragmented mirror image we receive from others. (Courtesy: Martin Pawley, Devon, U.K.)

from territoriality, nor on semiotic models (which are faulted for tending to treat architecture as just another type of artifact). The basis of this theory is that the designed physical world "... is already a social behaviour. It constitutes (not merely represents) a form of order in itself; one which is created for social purposes, whether by design or accumulatively, and through which society is both constrained and recognisable."[57] In displaying the variety of spatial forms that result from this pervasive system of generators, the authors are using a structuralist method; that is, spatial form is seen as the result of a system of abstract (and involuntary) rules of behavior.

This theory has interesting aspects. The authors say that in contrast to exterior space, building interiors characteristically have more categoric differences between spaces and well-defined differences in the relations of spaces, as well as a greater definition of what and where things can happen. "Interior space organization might, in short, have a rather well-defined relation to social categories and roles."[58] They conclude that the differences between interior and exterior are, fundamentally, differences in the way societies generate and control encounters, noting that "... interiors tend to define more of an ideological space, in the sense of a fixed system of categories and relations that is continually reaffirmed by use, whereas exteriors define a transactional or even a political space. ..."[59] This duality is, therefore, "... a *function of different forms of social solidarity.*"[60] The characteristics of interior and exterior can be viewed, moreover, as a continuum; that is, either can serve as a spatio-organizational model for the other.

There is also an issue of spatial division. The relational continuum between the interior and exterior suggests that the essential difference between the two is simply one of scale, but, say the authors, this is misleading.

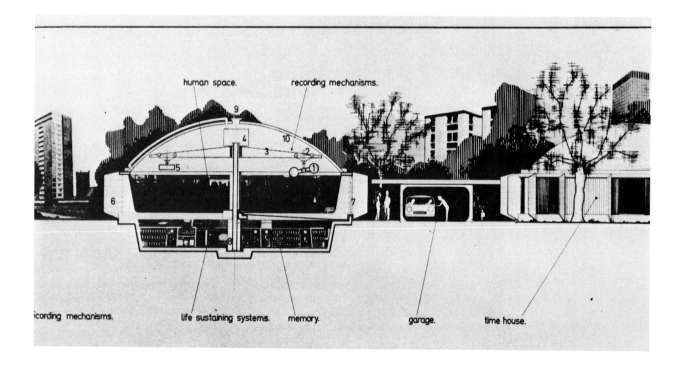

human space.   recording mechanisms.

recording mechanisms.   life sustaining systems.   memory.   garage.   time house.

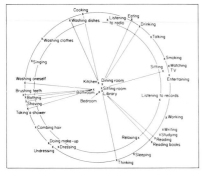

A

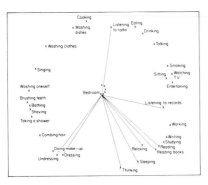

B

14.9

(A) **Room-Activity joint space;** *(B)* **Room-Activity space—"Bedroom"**
Students were asked to indicate the sorts of activities that they identified with particular rooms; thus thirty activities were related to six types of rooms *(A)*. The lines connect the rooms to their appropriate activities, the inner circle indicating activities suitable to multiple venues. The second chart *(B)* indicated student responses for a single room. Note the broad range of activities thought appropriate for a room that adults would likely define more narrowly. (Courtesy: David Fulton Publishers, London.)

Rather, the interiors are divided by boundaries, and "the spaces inside the boundaries . . . are a series of—potentially at least—separate events, not a continuous system."[61] They conclude that, "The relations between interiors are experienced as conceptual rather than as spatial entities. . . ."[62] The authors refer to *boundaries* that separate interior from exterior, and one interior from another. But the question of boundary also invokes the notion of internal wall, that wall that divides the interior cell into subportions. It seems clear, for example, that walls that divide the domain of a person (or related group of people) are different in kind (and, therefore, treatment) from walls separating unrelated people. In her provocative "The Party Wall as the Architecture of Sharing," Jill Stoner says that the party wall is different from other walls in that it participates in the enclosure on both sides. "While other walls separate domains that can be defined as interior or exterior independently of one's own position, the space on either side of the party wall is either 'interior' or 'exterior' relative to one's own position." She concludes that the geometry of the party wall and its dual program is, therefore, symmetrical.[63] The definitions of *wall types* within enclosures are complex, the more so when they separate unrelated parties with equal claim, as in apartment blocks. Stoner notes, however, that the party wall can also act as a mediator between adjacent units, thus encouraging us ". . . to focus on the potential for social relationships to act as generators of dwelling form."[64]

All the above clearly points to the multiple aspects of buildings, and the attendant difficulty in obtaining common agreement about the meaning of those aspects. David Canter and Stephen Tagg say a starting point for an architectural classification system might be the implications that various manipulations of form have for the architect, and the possibly parallel implications for the building's user.[65] "If we are to classify buildings (and thus inevitably their parts) from a semiological viewpoint that has its roots in recordable human responses then it is of value, initially, to consider the different ways in which buildings can act as signs or symbols."[66] They divide these aspects into three (overlapping) areas: first, the *physical* attributes of buildings; second, the (affective) *evaluations* we may make of them; and third, the type of *activities* we expect to occur within them (Fig 14.9). Canter and Tagg conducted a series of studies using, for example, connections between the physical characteristics of rooms and people's evaluations of them based on adjective-pairs. Specifically, these attributes have included window size, ceiling shape, and furniture layout, which were systematically varied and evaluated by the test subjects.

The following are two of their more interesting discoveries: the building type has a direct effect on the way people classify aspects of that building (for both the building generally and the room); and furniture types relate to both room scale and activities, with certain furniture treated generically. The second conclusion is interesting considering data that show furniture to be the most important determinant of room friendliness.[67] Their study is significant here for at least two reasons: first, their subject's concept of place and its relation to function seemed to be well structured and clear (suggesting that this sort of study would yield accurate information and a common vocabulary for client and designer); and second, two of the three architectural categories are concerned with the human aspects of the building rather than its structure.

An interesting approach to reconciling human factors with physical aspects of space occurs in Gordon Cullen's *The Scanner* (1966). Essentially, Cullen projects a dual system: an Integration Chain based on human activities; and a Space Chain of physical spaces. The two chains describe an urban environment where people both establish their being in space and

THE SCANNER: Have I considered .... ?   HUMAN FACTORS

	Health		Wealth		Worth	Security	
TENURE	*Physical* Use of body in exercise Population drift in old age Preventive medicine in planning	*Mental* Effects of high density Loneliness symptoms going to (a) doctor (b) pub (c) church	*Personal* Money buys the best sites 2-house, 2-car families Wealth sets trend for mass imitation	*Regional* Population drift to favoured areas Balanced use of wealth for amenities	Personal character contributions, as a 'card,' etc Leadership in marginal skills, spare-time activity and sport	*Physical* Railings Segregation of motor-car etc Security of person and property	*Mental* Assurance Leasehold Rights of ownership CPO's

	Work found in leisure	Leisure Scale			Leisure found in work
WORK/LEISURE	Employment for the old " for housewives " for the financially independent " for doers of good works " during vacations	*Day* Lunch clubs Tea breaks TV Pub Entertaining Homework Extra-mural studies	*Weekend* Spectator activity Sport Theatre, gardening Shopping Gatherings social church political	*Holidays* First holiday travelling tourism caravans coastline Second holiday at home park, communal facilities such as workshops, halls, arena	Vocation Dedication Religious orders

	Primary		Secondary			Religion
ASSOCIATION	*Childless couple* Place of one's own Town centre Entertainments Near work Minimum maintenance	*Married with children* Life-cycle housing Mechanization in home Flexibility of plan Garden Quiet Hygiene	*Entertainment* Pubs and clubs Societies Parade and loitering Town centre Library Home entertainment	*Place of work* Working groups Leadership Social clubs Sports	*Education* Schools as community centers Youth Club Walking distance to school Car rota	Place of worship Place to preach Needs of various religions (e.g education, lay activities, rites, calendar events)

	Integration Chain			Between Incomes	Between Ages
INTEGRATION	*Individual* *opting out opting in* The key Living room Solitude Play area Retreat Communal garage Withdrawal Pets	MAZE FACTOR → *Family* *opting out opting in* House boundary Schools Integrity of Church family Shopping Sunday lunch Tenant groups	MAZE FACTOR → *Community* *opting out opting in* Identity of place New blood Close, alley, Development courtyard Transport links Village, town	Mixed housing Common ground through marginal skills, spare-time activity and sport	Graduated retirement Tidal flow to common ground between age groups Life-cycle housing

	Conforming			Non-conforming		
ZESTS	*Out there* Adventure playgrounds Speed, danger, climbing, sailing, walking, pot-holing	*Group or team* Dancing, choir, music, games	*The senses* Sex Food and drink Arts Human spirit Search for meaning	*Out there* Rebellion Nomads and tramps Hooligans	*Group or team* Gangs Vandals	*The senses* Perversion Drunkenness Pep-pills Car-idolatry

THE SCANNER: Have I considered .... ?   PHYSICAL FACTORS

	Size	Composition	Location	Region	Growth
COMMUNITY	Choice of climacteric sizes based on Time cycle (e.g weekly sufficiency) Growth of amenities Transport capacity	Balance or imbalance of Ages Occupation Wealth	The art of siting Catchment area Dominant or dependent Economic viability Communications	Regional characteristics Seasonal fluctuations	Projected growth Change of composition Self-limiting community

	Density			Transport		Given Patterns		
PATTERN	*Low* Peace, tranquility, space, health, low land-use, random pattern, poor public transport, difficult for industrialized building, cash sale of houses, limited traffic segregation	*Medium* Degree of privacy and space, medium land-use, possibility of corporate visual groups, viable for public transport, viable for industrialized building, mortgage, horizontal segregation (Radburn etc)	*High* Maximum need for amenity space, optimum land use, greater possibility of visual cohesion, public transport, optimum industrialized building, council rent, vertical traffic segregation	*Traffic to people* Transport flow motor-way, clearway, amenity of traffic Problem of proximity noise, smell, sight, nodal points, parking	*People to traffic* Exercise Peace of mind Environment Commuting Ease of contact or segregation	*By-laws* Daylighting Road widths Sight angles Fire access	*Trends* Snob designs and colours Pop-art Layouts and gimmicks	*Industrialized building* Crane swing Unit weight Factory siting Production flow

	Categories			Climate	Nature	Agriculture & industry
LANDSCAPE	Wild nature National park Uplands Coastline, estuary	Arable land Industrial land Parkland Green Belt	Rough Green Belt Twilight land Suburb City	Prevailing wind Local climate Artificial climate Population drift	Wild life Nature reserves Ecology Air pollution Industrial waste	New patterns of farming Factory farming Clean industry Automation Power/service grids

	Space Chain			Light	Perspective	Serial Vision
OPTICS	*Internal* A room Sequence of rooms Flow of spaces Connection stairs ramps	MAZE FACTOR → *External (built)* Courtyard Street Square Formal garden	MAZE FACTOR → *External (natural)* Avenue Park and lake Hills and sea Horizon and sky Panorama	Cubism Geometry Silhouette Texture Colour Artificial light Exploratory power of light	Effects of foreshortening Division and organization of space Intrusion and excision by height The visual globe	Seeing in movement Development Joining and separating Growth of apparent size

	Site sympathy			Combination	
IDENTITY OF PLACE	*Ambience* City Market town Suburb Quartier Village Genius foci	*Objects* Character of building Historical appraisal Vitality Significant position	*Nature* Levels Sky Water Trees and plants	Homogeneity Conformity Manners Hierarchy Enclosure	Foils Scale Style Surprise Follies

14.10

The Scanner; *Gordon Cullen, Alcan Industries Ltd. (1966)*
(Courtesy: David Fulton Publishers, London.)

experience a continuum of spaces that affect that being. Such circumstances would allow a broad range of social interaction for the individual, the complexity of which Cullen indicates with his use of a Maze Factor (Fig 14.10). In ''A Semiotic Programme of Architectural Psychology,'' Geoffrey Broadbent approvingly notes Cullen's interlinking of these chains as ''. . . a great improvement on the architect's tendency to consider the Spatial-optic Chain on its own and the psychologists' to consider the Integration Chain.''[68] The types of studies referred to above indicate the rising importance given environmental issues in design, as well as their still unbridged connection with the formal and semiotic aspects of buildings. Thus while the environmental sciences loom as critical in any discussion of design issues, they have yet to meaningfully find their way into the preliminary design phase.

The Spatial Environment

The aforementioned approaches nevertheless suggest the emerging importance of the environmental sciences (especially psychology and sociology) in the past three decades. This is especially clear if one considers the ever-growing number of conferences, publications, and organizations like EDRA (Environmental Design Research Association) devoted to the area. The primary problem in this area may be the difficulty in obtaining systematic, reliable data on human behavior generally, and especially as they relate to design issues. Broadbent has commented on this problem, suggesting a range of research techniques that are largely outside the purview of this text. Pertinent here, however, are his conclusions about the likely sources for a comprehensive theory of environment. For example, he notes that most existing theories draw on multiple sources (as in the suggestion by Ittelson, et al. [1978], that three major theories, Freudian psychoanalysis, Watsonian behaviourism, and Köhlerian Gestalt, provide a triangle within which all other psychological theories can be plotted) and cites their conclusion that this array of theoretical viewpoints nonetheless ". . . falls short of providing definitive directions."[69]

Much of the problem is the complexity of the human subject; that is, the human organism is always in a state of learning about the environment, and altering consequent interaction accordingly. Moreover, much of human life exists, not in space alone, but on a symbolic level, so that any space that is conceived as only physical would likely fail at the semiotic level. It has been pointed out that human beings are not simply historical, social, and goal-directed organisms, but also organisms driven ". . . by a 'rage for order.' Man seeks to make sense out of his surroundings and to define and locate himself with respect to these surroundings."[70] To this end, humans are directed toward organizing their environment, giving it significance, and assessing their position in the altered structure that ensues. This involves a constant interpretation of events and objects with respect to internal schema.[71] Thus how do designed spaces relate to the people destined to occupy them? A designed space, by definition, is meant to encourage and facilitate certain kinds of behavior within it, and communicates that fact through the use of codes. But clearly spaces may undergo a change of significance when used by persons who no longer accept those codes, especially spaces that have failed their users. In any case, spaces are subject to individual interpretation, itself a product of expectation.

In terms of the environmental sciences, it may be productive to ask how the building actually functions, aside from design intention. Hillier has proposed a model based on four interrelated functions: first, how enclosed space (e.g., rooms and corridors) facilitates or inhibits *activities;* second, how buildings provide comfortable *internal conditions* to live in; third, how the building serves as *cultural symbol;* and fourth, the *economic implications* of the structure.[72] These categories seem useful, and again, the emphasis is on the behavioral aspects of the building. Still, no amount of behavioral analysis ever caused a building to be constructed, nor would a building responsive only to activity factors be satisfying in the long term. Yet the environmental sciences need to be joined to architectural design, especially if the more spectacular failures—for example, the Pruitt-Igoes—are to be avoided. Unfortunately, the environmental sciences (sometimes referred to as the human sciences) have had an uneasy relationship with design. Several factors are responsible; the most basic is that their fundamental methodologies are at variance—a difference clearly expressed in a comparison of the scientific method using an abstraction of data with the dynamic and particular act of design.

In an article in the *Journal of Architectural Education* (1968), Robert Gutman notes that students and teachers of design turn to sociology looking for answers to ethical and evaluative issues that arise in studio work, especially those involving a decision about the relative significance of individual and public requirements for buildings.[73] This sort of situation-specific and narrow (in the social scientist's view) answer is precisely what the human sciences are not capable of giving, nor should design believe it desirable. Max F. Millikan has said that while social science cannot usually predict, ". . . it may make very important contributions to effective prediction. Social Science cannot replace intuition and experience, but it can greatly enrich them, clarify them, and make them more general."[74] The real question may thus center on the particular point at which such information affects the design process.

In her *With Man in Mind*, Constance Perin suggests that the appropriate place for such information is at the *inception process*, leading to the formulation of the program, as opposed to *the conception process*, the design phase. She believes that the search for theory belongs in the conception of new environments, which takes place at the drawing boards of designers. The process might include the history of people's contentment with their environment, standards for the strength and appropriateness of materials, aesthetic criteria, and architectural history. The process makes use also of the personal characteristics of the individual designer, such as training and skill in form creation, and the ability to empathize with people outside immediate experience.[75] However, she says that ". . . a cluster of equally essential components not so well known relates less to the conception of a new environment and more to its *inception:* the original impetus for a new environment—that is, why it is needed and what it will do for the people who will inhabit it."[76] Perin sees the *design program* as the mediator between inception and conception, the supplier of the essential information the designer needs to effectively design. She notes that the program might include the activities of people, their functional relationships to one another, limitations imposed by climate or locale, performance standards for physical qualities, and even ". . . objectives and priorities relating to the health, welfare, happiness, and efficiency of the new inhabitants."[77] She concludes, "The 'new strategy' I propose . . . is the redefinition of the design program as the instrument of collaboration, to involve the human sciences as they have not yet been involved in creating a more humane environment."[78]

Ethics and Ideology

Perin points out that at least one way that the success of the built environment can be measured is how productively people interact with that environment. But her approach to the subject is somewhat unorthodox; instead of assuming that people simply respond to their environment, she postulates that the effect of environment on behavior ". . . is actually *the extent to which the environment responds to the stimulus of human demands,* so that the adaptations people make are the measure of the appropriateness of a physical response."[79] Put differently, the more people must adapt to their environment to meet their needs, the less successful the environment. In turn, human purposes have certain characteristics that evoke responses from the environment. "Thus the two ends of the environmental continuum are *structured, directive,* and *authoritarian,* on the one hand, and *minimal, open,* and *flexible,* on the other."[80] The point is that environments of the first sort exact a high adaptive cost, which people willingly pay only when the rewards are considerable. Perin makes this point clear when she says,

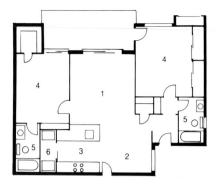

14.11

Tierra Vista—Serrano Highlands, California

The mingles type is designed for two people who need to share housing costs but want to maintain privacy, independence, and equality. It is these factors that influence the plan, which contains two bedrooms with private bathrooms that spatially display that equality. In order to enhance privacy the bedrooms are placed at opposite ends of the unit, with the kitchen and living-room serving as common areas. (Courtesy: Karen A. Franck.)

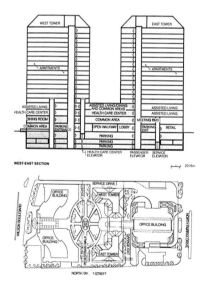

14.12

The Marriott Jefferson—Arlington, Virginia; *Cochran, Stephenson & Donkervoet (1989)*

This project includes 325 one- and two-bedroom apartments, placed above 57 assisted-living and 31 skilled-care units. This type of project has increased fire-safety concerns, and issues of whether the elevators should bypass nursing floors to maintain the residential character and avoid psychological distress. (Courtesy: Cochran, Stephenson & Donkervoet, Inc., Baltimore.)

"Contemporary alienation from and frustration with the physical environment stem, in these terms, from authoritarian environments imposed on human purposes that really require a diversity of spaces and places in order to be carried out without unwanted adaptive cost."[81]

In his "Environmental Determinants of Human Life," Rene Dubos observes that as more persons have the opportunity to express their biological endowment under diversified conditions, society would become richer; but if the surroundings are highly stereotyped, the only components of human nature that would flourish are those that have adapted to the narrow range of prevailing conditions.

> Hence the dangers of many housing developments, which, although sanitary, are inimical to the development of human potentialities and are designed as if their only function was to provide disposable cubicles for dispensable people. . . .[82]

Nor should such comments be seen as relevant for large housing developments only. In *The Place of Houses*, Moore, Allen, and Lyndon offer excellent advice about setting out the program for a residence, noting that ". . . our experience as architects leads us to believe that houses can and should be more suited to the lives of their inhabitants. . . ."[83] Thus a good house is created from many parts that are economically and meaningfully assembled:

> It speaks not just of the materials from which it is made, but of the intangible rhythms, spirits, and dreams of people's lives. . . . In its parts it accommodates important human activities, yet in sum it expresses an attitude toward life.[84]

Future spatial paradigms will almost certainly acknowledge environmental aspects of work and residence that are now granted only secondary importance, such as flexible boundaries and alternative living arrangements. This should lead, not to the dominance of a mechanical series of psychophysiological factors, but to their inclusion in the fundamental program that precedes the design phase, along with the more familiar issues of square-footage and physical amenities. And as alternative ways of viewing buildings will likely expand in the future, so will the categories of building types that are considered "customary."

In *New Households New Housing*, Sherry Ahrentzen points out that the 1950s image of the traditional American family (i.e., wage-earner husband, homemaker wife, and their young children—as in "Ozzie and Harriet") is no longer valid. She cites figures indicating that nearly seventy-nine percent of the households created after 1980 are "atypical" by those standards; by 1985 the greatest growth had been in single-person households (to twenty-four percent), and the number of single-parent households had risen as well (to twelve percent). This reduced the percentage of married-couple households to approximately fifty-six percent of the total; and if situations in which wives are wage-earners are excluded, the percentage drops to only ten percent. What makes these demographics so surprising is that the myth of the "typical" family has remained so prevalent, despite all evidence to the contrary. No less surprising is the adherence to the ideal of the single-family house in a period when real income has diminished, and the cost of housing has escalated out of common reach. Ahrentzen notes that the 1950s archetype has dominated our landscape, but cautions that "while the single-family house effectively answered a number of needs for many Americans—space, sanitation, security, status, and privacy—today's demographics and household economics call into question the relevance of these cultural values, and in particular the means of achieving them, for *all* households."[85]

The argument here is for a commitment at the design level to search for new housing types that reflect a remarkably diverse population. In Ahrentzen's text, three broad categories of housing are identified as alternative types: *collective* housing; housing for *single-parent households;* and *single room occupancy* housing. Within the first category, Karen A. Franck discerns between *shared housing* and *collective housing,* a separation recognized in the nineteenth century. In shared housing certain spaces, which might include living/dining rooms, kitchens, and even bathrooms, are shared by all. Collective housing, on the other hand, usually comprises discrete, self-contained units with supplemental common space used for group purposes. An important characteristic of all these groups is that they have agreed to some form of affiliation based on social and economic factors, need for specialized amenities, and practical advantage. Shared housing, the more common in America, is usually reserved for the young (as in student dormitories), the elderly (as in nursing homes), and groups with specialized needs (like the handicapped); but it could also refer to long-term living arrangements between roommates, where separate bedrooms, baths, and entries become a consideration (Fig 14.11).

Collective housing is seen in the various *retirement communities,* with households that are usually self-contained, but where the participants have access to common-area functions. In an article in *Progressive Architecture,* entitled "Aging in Place in the 1990s," Daralice D. Boles identified six different configurations such communities assume, including the "campus," high-rise, and hotel formats (Fig 14.12). It is usual to find three types of living arrangements in these complexes: self-contained units for the active; assisted-living situations for those needing moderate help; and facilities for full nursing care. Boles notes that the largest (and newest) of the providers of such private housing are the Marriott and Hyatt Corporations, which have altered the nature of the buildings. "The shift in emphasis from health care to hospitality is having an impact not only on the services offered but on the architectural envelope in which they are provided."[86] One effect is the residential look of the buildings, especially the interior spaces (Fig 14.13). And this may be the fastest-growing area in design; the Census

14.13

St. Catherine's—Madison County, Mississippi; *Cook Douglass Farr and Mockbee Coker Howorth (ca. 1986)*
"Included in this project is independent living for active senior citizens; assisted living for those with temporary disabilities or in need of moderate help; and full nursing care. . . . the senior resident can remain at St. Catherine's indefinitely by purchasing a life care package, which for an initial fee and monthly charges includes whatever care the resident may require throughout his or her lifetime."[4] Together the red-tiled roofs, towers, steeples, and stucco walls provide an image obtained from Siena, Italy—where St. Catherine, patron of the Roman Catholic Dominican order, was born. (Courtesy: Cooke Douglass Farr/Ltd., Jackson, Miss., Photo by: John O'Hagan, Birmingham, Al. copyright.)

Bureau has calculated that the over-sixty-five population in the United States will more than double by 2030, to sixty-five million.[87] Sadly, only two percent of the elderly can afford such communities, despite their beneficial effect on longevity. As Sandra C. Powell notes in her essay ''Elderly Housing: Warping the Design Process,'' HUD regulations affecting subsidized housing for the elderly virtually guarantee an injurious public housing image and atmosphere in the future.[88]

Collective housing may well enjoy a wider base than is suggested by such specific applications. Communal forms of family living, while rare in the United States, have been established in Europe. Elena Marcheso Morena discusses such living arrangements in Denmark, in an article entitled ''Cohousing Comes to the U.S.'' She describes cohousing cooperative communities as those in which individual dwelling units (usually townhouses) are clustered around a common hall, with shared dining-, child-care-, and laundry facilities. She notes that ''although residents take turns shopping and cooking for the whole community and may eat in the common building as often as they wish, each house has its own kitchen and dining area and is self-sufficient.''[89] There are certain advantages: a shared environment, collective child care, and group decision-making about one's neighborhood. Economics usually play only a small part in the equation, as the group facilities are essentially an extra cost not compensated for by the smaller size of the personal spaces (Fig 14.14). Nor are design services for such enterprises inexpensive; given the chance to participate in the design decision-making, few residents choose the standardization that makes them economically feasible. And the problems for a designer with multiple clients are considerable. Moreover, housing types that completely commit to an ideological principle run the risk of being unsalable later, an important concern in what is essentially single-family housing.

For these reasons, *dedicated multi-unit* housing, such as housing for single parents, may be easier to manage. Such housing may serve as temporary shelter (with social services) or as long-term habitation. This kind of housing is very difficult to design; single parents typically have limited resources yet require features that are expensive (e.g., child-care facilities, specialized space, and high security). And, due to their time constraints, single parents

1. Kitchen
2. Dining room
3. Television room
4. Bathroom
5. Guest room
6. Children's room
7. Library
8. Laundry
9. Workshop
10. Store
11. Freezer
12. Photography darkroom
13. Storage
14. Teen room
15. Furnace

14.14

Trudeslund—Copenhagen, Denmark; *Vandkunsten Architects (1981)*
This community consists of thirty-three split-level and two-story residences, each privately owned; such ownership also includes a percentage of the common areas. Dinner is available in the common house every night except for two Saturdays a month, when the space is available for private parties. The dinner is prepared by the residents, who rotate the duties. The kitchen is well located in that the residents ''walk by but not through'' it, thus avoiding isolation of people performing kitchen tasks. (Source: Courtesy Kathryn M. McCamant and Charles R. Durrett.)

require spaces that are easy to use and maintain on a daily basis. One of the most interesting complexes was designed by Sylvester Bone in 1972. Located in London, Fiona House consists of twelve self-contained units with communal playroom and linked intercom system; a separate child-care center for thirty-one children is located across the adjacent green space (Fig 14.15).

Diverse housing types are becoming more common as designers respond to a new set of social realities. In this context the program for the *New American House* competition (1984), inspired by architect Harvey Sherman, and sponsored by the Minneapolis College of Art and Design and the National Endowment for the Arts, is significant. It stated that "the intent of this competition is to generate and disseminate innovative concepts for the design of urban housing units which will accurately reflect the needs of nontraditional, professional households."[90] The *Architectural Record* notes that this included single-parent families, unrelated roommates, adults without children at home, and active retired people. Additionally, there was to be some provision for the growing number of people who use their residence as a professional workplace.[91] The final designs all consisted of a series of six units, each incorporating one thousand square feet of living and work areas in flexible plans that allow for collective child care; the entries praised most were those that addressed ". . . the tension between the workplace and home, and looked for an esthetic that comes from that tension."[92] The winning entry, by Troy West and Jacqueline Leavitt, features an integral garden area in a modified row-house configuration; all three designs were notable for their consideration of the various, and often incongruent, human needs expressed in the program (Fig 14.16).

Thus the range of work and residential types is slowly expanding in response to what are perhaps the most significant changes in human spatial needs in history. A common theme in environmental literature, and inherent in the types discussed above, is the need to understand buildings as expressions of our private dreams and aspirations, which are nonetheless linked in a highly interrelated way to those of others. Moore, Allen, and Lyndon feel that we need an environment that we can comprehend in the same way we comprehend houses, ". . . as places that have been made by and for

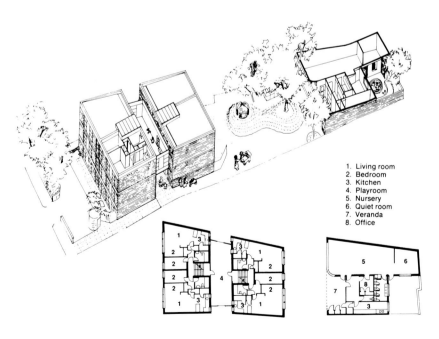

1. Living room
2. Bedroom
3. Kitchen
4. Playroom
5. Nursery
6. Quiet room
7. Veranda
8. Office

14.15

Fiona House—London; *Sylvester Bone (1972)*
The enlarged interior corridor connecting the four apartments per floor was designed to act as a playroom for the children. The area is carpeted, and each apartment unit has windows in the kitchen, allowing supervision. There is also an intercom system connecting the playroom to each apartment, permitting parents to communicate with their children and other parents in the building. The developer, Nina West, believes that the on-site daycare building is critical in enabling parents to work outside the home. (Drawn by: David Jaeckels. Courtesy: Sherry Ahrentzen.)

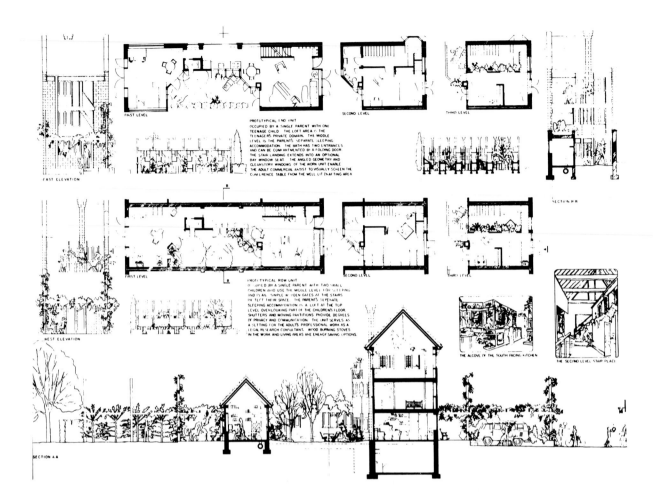

14.16

New American House Competition (1984)
Harvey Sherman, an architect (and single parent) led the development of the program. The winning design, by Troy West and Jacqueline Leavitt, provided flexibility and a concern for enabling the inhabitants to individualize their units to meet their needs and personalities. Of note is the unusual inclusion of people in the drawings. (Courtesy: Harvey Sherman, project director.)

people, where the processes of systematic ordering and exchange that underlie our civilization are included within our grasp, bent to clear human purpose."[93] To this end, they recommend that the spaces that are communally used be as various and as richly invested with personal care as our private places (Fig 14.17). This assumes that our private places, the intimate spaces that contain our collective persona, do in fact reflect such qualities in their design. In his introduction to *The Decoration of Houses* by Edith Wharton and Ogden Codman, Jr., William Coles notes that their book is really about the art of civilized living, "The Decoration of Houses could just as appropriately be entitled *The Graces of Life,* for its real subject is not just houses but the quality of life in them, the classical question of *how to live.*"[94]

We, the authors, believe that such houses—indeed, virtually all buildings—will necessarily grow from the inside out, that the design program will increasingly be shaped by the concerns of human habitation. In this view, the aesthetic, psychological, symbolic, and environmental aspects of enclosed space should be the predictors of external form, rather than mediators of form developed sculpturally. To this end, the designer might profit from the expertise of many people in diverse fields, in what is perhaps the most remarkable act humans are capable of, the design and construction of

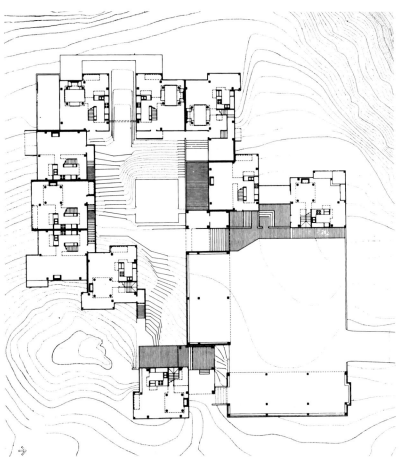

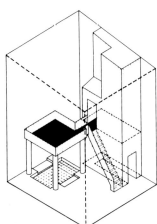

Typical condominium unit

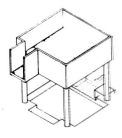

Typical condominium four-poster

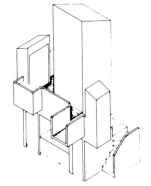

Typical condominium kitchen and bath

14.17

Sea Ranch Condominium—California;
Moore, Lyndon, Turnbull, Whitaker (1965)
The developer's approach was unusual in that from the outset landscape architects were employed to make studies of the local ecology and conditions associated with wind, weather, and site. The architect's own approach was notable as well, concerning itself with human-activity patterns, spatial imaging, and inherent problems of territoriality. In their desire to create a "sense of place," they used successive degrees of enclosure, starting with a place in the landscape and moving to progressively more protected (and private) interior spaces—from solariums to glass porches to sheltered rooms within. This is a perfect foil for the limitless Pacific coast. (Courtesy: Charles Moore and William Turnbull.)

a human environment. Critical to this purpose, however, is to understand that environment as human needs expressed spatially, a situation in which the interior dimension is likely the most vital one. Equally important, is the realization that what first appear as intangibles—beauty, memory, desire—are ultimately what design is about (Fig 14.18).

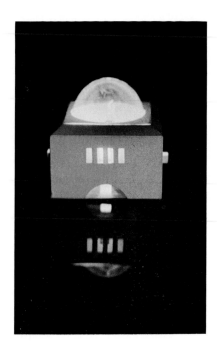

14.18

House for a Hero; *Joy Monice Malnar (1981)* The program was George Ranalli's inspiration, and required the development of a structure that conveyed the characteristics of a contemporary hero. This particular structure, designed for journalist Oriana Fallaci, is concerned with the course (or pathway) traversed during the interviewing process. That is, the journalist's role may be seen to be that of penetrating the external façade in order to uncover the interior personality and motives. Thus the stark façade, with pronounced balconies for public declarations, is seldom as rich as the inner world of the spirit. (Courtesy: Joy Monice Malnar; Photo by: Frank Vodvarka.)

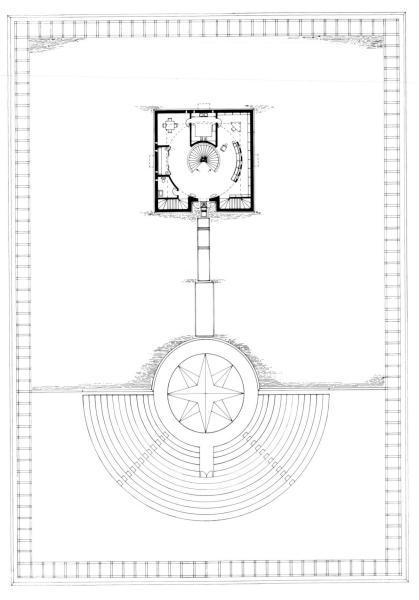

Notes

Preface

1. Elias Cornell, *Humanistic Inquiries into Architecture* (Goteborg, Sweden: Elanders Boktryckeri Aktiebolag, 1959), 19.
2. Le Corbusier, *Towards a New Architecture,* trans. Frederick Etchells (New York: Holt, Rinehart and Winston, 1960), 167.
3. Wassily Kandinsky, *Point and Line to Plane* (New York: Dover Publications, Inc., 1979), 134.
4. Ibid., 25, 57.

Introduction

1. Kenneth Grahame, *The Wind in the Willows* (New York: Bantam Books, 1982), 51.
2. Ibid., 77.
3. Ibid., 85.

Chapter 1. The Role of Theory

1. Marc-Antoine Laugier, *An Essay on Architecture,* trans. Wolfgang and Anni Herrmann (1753; Los Angeles: Hennessey & Ingalls, Inc., 1977), 81.
2. Paul Elúard, *Dignes de vivre* quoted in Gaston Bachelard, *The Poetics of Space* (Boston: Beacon Press, 1969): 38.
3. Elias Cornell, *Humanistic Inquiries into Architecture* (Goteborg, Sweden: Elanders Boktryckeri Aktiebolag, 1959), 54.
4. Gabriel-Germain Boffrand, "Les décorations intérieures des appartements font à present à Paris une partie considérable de l'architecture." *Livres d'architecture* (1754): 41.
5. Lewis Mumford, *Culture of Cities* (1938; New York: Harcourt Brace Jovanovich, Publishers, 1970), 434.
6. James S. Ackerman, "The History of Design and the Design of History," *VIA: Culture and the Social Vision,* eds. Mark A. Hewitt et al., 4 (Cambridge: The Graduate School of Fine Arts University of Pennsylvania and The MIT Press, 1980), 15.
7. John Dewey, *Art as Experience* (1934; New York: Capricorn Books, G. P. Putnam's Sons, 1958), 231.
8. Ibid.
9. Jon Lang, *Creating Architectural Theory* (New York: Van Nostrand Reinhold Company, 1987), 13.
10. Roger Scruton, *The Aesthetics of Architecture* (Princeton, N.J.: Princeton University Press, 1979), 4.
11. Christian Norberg-Schulz, *Intentions in Architecture* (1965; Cambridge: The MIT Press, 1985), 87.

12. Ibid., 21.

13. Ibid., 17.

14. Ibid., 22.

15. Mark Bernstein, "Charles Kettering: Automative Genius," *Smithsonian* (July 1988): 126.

16. W.R. Lethaby, *Form in Civilization* (1922; New York: Oxford University Press, 1957), 14.

17. Malcolm Quantrill, *The Environmental Memory* (New York: Schocken Books, 1987), 31.

18. Alan Colquhoun, "Vernacular Classicism," *Modernity and the Classical Tradition: Architectural Essays 1980–1987* (Cambridge: The MIT Press, 1989), 22.

19. Amos Rapoport, "Vernacular Architecture and the Cultural Determinants of Form," *Buildings and Society,* ed. Anthony D. King (London: Routledge & Kegan Paul, 1980), 285.

20. Ibid., 287.

21. Ibid., 287.

22. Ibid., 291.

23. Nikolaus Pevsner, *An Outline of European Architecture* (1943; New York: Penguin Books, 1974), 15.

24. Cornell, *Humanistic Inquiries into Architecture*——9.

25. Leo Tolstoy, *What is Art?* trans. Almyer Maude (1896; Indianapolis, Ind.: Bobbs-Merrill Educational Publishing, 1982), 47.

26. George Santayana, *The Sense of Beauty: Being the Outline of Aesthetic Theory* (1896; New York: Dover Publications, Inc., 1955), 29.

27. Ibid., 31.

28. Ibid., 65.

29. Tolstoy, *What is Art?*——51.

30. Le Corbusier, *Towards a New Architecture,* trans. Frederick Etchells (1927; New York: Holt, Rinehart and Winston, 1960), 7.

31. Lang, *Creating Architectural Theory,*——180.

32. Ibid., 180.

33. Ibid., 197.

34. Arnold Hauser, *The Social History of Art* (1951; New York: Vintage Books, 1960), Vol. I, 51.

35. Paul Veyne, "The Roman Home," foreword to "Private Life and Domestic Architecture in Roman Africa," by Yvon Thébert in *A History of Private Life,* ed. Paul Veyne, trans. Arthur Goldhammer (1985; Cambridge: The Belknap Press of Harvard University Press, 1987), 316.

36. Ibid., 316.

37. Thébert, "Private Life and Domestic Architecture,"——320.

38. Ibid., 327.

39. Witold Rybczynski, *Home: A Short History of an Idea* (1986; New York: Penguin Books, 1987), 89.

40. Jacques-François Blondel, "Comme nous avons traité l'extérieur en général, nous allons nous attacher à l'intérieur qui est celui qui parait la plus negligé par quelques architectes . . . En effet la décoration intérieure doit se resentir dê la sagesse dont il faut user dans les dehors."

De la Distribution de Maisons de Plaisance, (1737), 66 and 94.

41. Rudolf Arnheim, *Entropy and Art* (1971; Berkeley: University of California Press, 1974), 1, 34.

42. Ibid., 2.

43. David Canter, *Psychology for Architects* (New York: John Wiley & Sons, 1974), 4.

44. Herbert Read, *The Origins of Form in Art* (1964; New York: Horizon Press, 1965), 99.

45. Gaston Bachelard, *The Poetics of Space,* trans. Maria Jolas (Boston: Beacon Press, 1969), 6.

46. Ibid., 6.

47. Ibid., 15.

48. Ibid., 17.

Chapter 2. Form and Function

1. John Dewey, *Art as Experience* (1934; New York: Capricorn Books, 1958), 137.

2. Attributed to Josef Albers.

3. Herbert Read, *The Origins of Form in Art* (New York: Horizon Press, 1965), 66.

4. Ibid., 86.

5. Henri Focillon, *The Life of Forms in Art,* trans. Charles Beecher Hogan and George Kubler (1934; New York: Zone Books, 1989), 33.

6. Abbot Suger, *Abbot Suger on the Abbey Church of St.-Denis and its Art Treasures,* ed. and trans. Erwin Panofsky, 1946, 2d ed. Gerda Panofsky-Soergel (Princeton, N. J.: Princeton University Press, 1979), 101.

7. Read, *The Origins of Form in Art,*——69.

8. Ibid., 71.

9. Ibid., 71.

10. Rudolf Arnheim, *The Dynamics of Architectural Form* (Berkeley: University of California Press, 1977), 255.

11. David A. Morton, ''Architectural Argent,'' *Progressive Architecture* (January 1984): 23.

12. Read, *The Origins of Form in Art,*——100.

13. John Ruskin, *The Seven Lamps of Architecture* (1849; New York: Farrar, Straus and Giroux, 1979).

14. ''Schools of Tomorrow,'' *Time* (September 12, 1960), 74.

15. Read, *The Origins of Form in Art,*——104.

16. Christian Norberg-Schulz, *Intentions in Architecture* (1965; Cambridge: The MIT. Press Paperback Edition, 1985), 112, 127.

17. Ibid., 126.

18. Dewey, *Art as Experience,*——189.

19. Ibid., 194.

20. Arnheim, *The Dynamics of Architectural Form,*——263.

21. Rudolf Arnheim, *Entropy and Art* (1971; Berkeley: University of California Press, 1974), 2.

22. Ibid., 3.

23. David Canter, *Psychology for Architects* (New York: John Wiley & Sons, Inc., 1974), 34.

24. Julian Hochberg, "Visual Perception in Architecture," *Via: Architecture and Visual Perception,* 6 (The Graduate School of Fine Arts University of Pennsylvania and The MIT Press, 1983), 37.

25. Ibid.

26. Ibid., 38.

27. Ibid., 38.

28. David Levi, "The Gestalt Psychology of Expression in Architecture," *Designing for Human Behavior,* eds. Jon Lang, Charles Burnette, Walter Moleski, and David Vachon (Stroudsburg, Pa.: Dowden, Hutchinson & Ross, Inc., 1974), 112.

29. Hochberg, "Visual Perception in Architecture,"———43.

30. Jean Piaget and Barbel Inhelder, *The Child's Conception of Space,* trans. F.J. Langdon and J.L. Lunzer (1984; London: Routledge & Kegan Paul, 1956), 5.

31. Piaget and Inhelder, *The Child's Conception of Space,*———5.

32. Ibid., 33.

33. Jean Piaget, *The Mechanisms of Perception,* trans. G.N. Seagrim, (1961; New York: Basic Books, Inc., Publishers, 1969), xxv.

34. Ibid., xxvi.

35. James J. Gibson, *The Perception of the Visual World* (Boston: Houghton Mifflin Company, 1950), 3.

36. Ibid., 13.

37. Ibid., 25.

38. Ibid., 61.

39. Ibid., 63.

40. Ibid., 76.

41. Ibid., 211.

42. Hochberg, "Visual Perception in Architecture,"———40.

43. Gibson, *The Perception of the Visual World,*———23.

44. Arnheim, *Entropy and Art,*———34.

45. Arnheim, *The Dynamics of Architectural Form,*———4.

46. Ibid., 2.

47. Philip C. Johnson, *Mies van der Rohe* (1947; New York: The Museum of Modern Art, 1978), 189.

48. Plato, *Timaeus and Critias,* trans. H. D. P. Lee (Baltimore: Penguin Books, 1971).

49. John Wellborn Root, "The Equipment of the Architect," in *Roots of Contemporary American Architecture,* ed. Lewis Mumford (1952; New York: Dover Publications, 1972), 272.

50. Horatio Greenough, "Form and Function," in *Roots of Contemporary American Architecture,* ed. Lewis Mumford (1952; New York: Dover Publications, 1972), 51.

51. John Wellborn Root, "Character and Style," in *Roots of Contemporary American Architecture,* ed. Lewis Mumford (1952; New York: Dover Publications, 1972), 278.

52. Arnheim, *The Dynamics of Architectural Form,*———3.

53. Ibid., 3.

54. E.H. Gombrich, *The Sense of Order* (Ithaca, N.Y.: Cornell University Press, 1979), 32.

55. Walt Whitman, "A Song of the Rolling Earth" in *Leaves of Grass* (1891-2; New York: Random House, Inc.), 184.

56. Attributed to Le Corbusier.

57. Arturo B. Fallico, *Art and Existentialism* (Englewood Cliffs, N.J.: Prentice-Hall, Inc., 1962), 43.

58. Fallico, *Art and Existentialism,*——47.

59. Norberg-Schulz, *Intentions in Architecture,*——97.

60. Ibid., 97.

61. Ibid., 97.

62. Paul Frankl, *Principles of Architectural History: The Four Phases of Architectural Style, 1420-1900,* trans. and ed. James F. O'Gorman (1914; Cambridge: The MIT Press, 1968), 142.

63. Ibid., 142.

64. Ibid., 148.

65. Giorgio Vasari, *Lives of the Artists,* trans. George Bull (1550; New York: Viking Penguin, Inc., 1985), 366.

66. Read, *The Origins of Form in Art,*——105.

67. Ibid., 105.

68. Lee Hodgden, "The Interior Facade," *The Cornell Journal of Architecture: The Vertical Surface* 3 (The Cornell Journal of Architecture and Rizzoli International Publications, Inc., Fall 1987), 32.

69. Ibid., 32.

70. Arnheim, *The Dynamics of Architectural Form,*——92.

71. Ibid., 93.

72. Hodgden, "The Interior Facade,"——32.

73. Ibid., 33.

74. Frank Lloyd Wright, *An Autobiography* (New York: Duell, Sloan & Pearce, 1943).

75. Read, *The Origins of Form in Art,*——106.

76. Ibid., 108.

77. "Interview with Frank Lloyd Wright," Caedmon Record TC 1064 (Spring 1956).

78. Arnheim, *The Dynamics of Architectural Form,*——102.

79. Rem Koolhaas, *Delirious New York* (New York: Oxford University Press, 1978), 82.

80. Robert Venturi, *Complexity and Contradiction in Architecture* (1966; New York: The Museum of Modern Art, 1977), 86.

Chapter 3. The Vocabulary of Design

1. Wassily Kandinsky, *Point and Line to Plane,* trans. Howard Dearstyne and Hilla Rebay (New York: Dover Publications, Inc., 1979), 103.

2. Donis A. Dondis, *A Primer of Visual Literacy* (Cambridge: The MIT Press, 1973), 183.

3. Kandinsky, *Point and Line to Plane*,——32.

4. Ibid., 57.

5. Ibid., 98.

6. George Lesser, *Gothic Cathedrals and Sacred Geometry* (London: Alec Tiranti, 1957), 2.

7. Le Corbusier, *The Decorative Art of Today*, trans. James Dunnett (1925; Cambridge: The MIT Press, 1987), 111.

8. Charles Moore and Gerald Allen, *Dimensions: Space, Shape & Scale in Architecture* (New York: Architectural Record Books, 1976), 12.

9. Ibid., 12.

10. Ibid., 15.

11. Rudolf Arnheim, *Art and Visual Perception* (Berkeley: University of California Press, 1974), 165.

12. Edward T. Hall, *The Hidden Dimension* (Garden City, N.Y.: Anchor Books, 1969), 60.

13. Ibid., 62.

14. Ibid., 66.

15. Steen Eiler Rasmussen, *Experiencing Architecture* (Cambridge: The MIT Press, 1962), 177.

16. Ibid.

17. Jun'ichiro Tanizaki, *In Praise of Shadows* (New Haven: Leete's Island Books, Inc. 1977), 17, 18, 20.

18. Ibid., 42.

19. Attributed to Emil Nolde.

20. Emilio Ambasz, *The Architecture of Luis Barragan* (New York: The Museum of Modern Art, 1980), 107.

21. Deborah T. Sharpe, *The Psychology of Color and Design* (Totowa, N.J.: Littlefield, Adams & Co., 1981), 55.

22. Rikard Küller, *Non-Visual Effects of Light and Colour*, Annotated Bibliography. Document D15:81 (Stockholm: Swedish Council for Building Research, 1981), 238.

23. Arnheim, *Art and Visual Perception*,——303.

24. Hazel Rossotti, *Colour: Why the World Isn't Grey* (Princeton, N.J.: Princeton University Press, 1983), 16.

25. Ibid., 142.

26. Richard P. Youtz, "Letters" in regard to paper read at the Psychonomic Society Meeting, 1963, 1964. *Scientific American* (June 1965): 10.

27. Leon Battista Alberti, *On Painting*, trans. John R. Spencer (1435–6; Haven: Yale University Press, 1966), 84.

28. Ibid., 85.

29. Johann Wolfgang von Goethe, *Theory of Colours (1810)*, trans. Charles Lock Eastlake (1840; Cambridge: The MIT Press, 1982), 317.

30. Ibid., 320.

31. Rossotti, *Colour: Why the World Isn't Grey*,   105.

32. Josef Albers, *Interaction of Color* (New Haven: Yale University Press, 1976), 39.

33. Johannes Itten, *The Elements of Color,* ed. Faber Birren (New York: Van Nostrand Reinhold Company, 1970), 21.

34. Ibid., 12.

35. Ibid., 26.

36. Ibid., 26.

37. Ibid., 27.

38. Faber Birren, *Color Psychology and Color Therapy: A Factual Study of the Influence of Color on Human Life* (New Hyde Park, N.Y.: University Books, Inc., 1961), vii.

39. Ibid.

40. Frank H. Mahnke and Rudolf H. Mahnke, *Color and Light in Man-made Environments* (New York: Van Nostrand Reinhold Company, 1987), x.

41. Faber Birren, *New Horizons in Color* (New York: Reinhold Publishing Corporation, 1955), 4.

42. Ibid., 5.

43. Mahnke and Mahnke, *Color and Light in Man-made Environments,* ——40.

44. Ibid., 53.

45. Sharpe, *The Psychology of Color and Design,* ——18.

46. Ibid., 19.

47. Ibid., 9.

48. Birren, *Color Psychology and Color Therapy,* ——176.

49. Ibid., 180.

50. Sharpe, *The Psychology of Color and Design,* ——136.

51. Ibid., 131.

52. Birren, *Color Psychology and Color Therapy,* ——146.

53. Mahnke and Mahnke, *Color and Light in Man-made Environments,* ——18.

54. Sharpe, *The Psychology of Color and Design,* ——41.

55. Ibid., 149.

56. Ibid., 86.

57. Rossotti, *Colour: Why the World Isn't Grey,* ——209.

58. E.H. Gombrich, *Art and Illusion: A Study in the Psychology of Pictorial Representation* (Princeton, N.J.: Princeton University Press, 1969), 227.

59. Rasmussen, *Experiencing Architecture,* ——218.

60. Edith Wharton and Ogden Codman, Jr., *The Decoration of Houses* (New York: W.W. Norton & Company, Inc., 1978), 28.

61. Sharpe, *The Psychology of Color and Design,* ——33.

62. Ibid., 5.

63. Itten, *The Elements of Color,* ——27.

Chapter 4. The Grammar of Design

1. Lao Tsu, "Eleven," in *Tao Te Ching,* trans. Gia-Fu Feng and Jane English (6th century B.C.; New York: Vintage Books, 1972), 22. Translation copyright © Gia-Fu-Feng. Reprinted by permission of Alfred A. Knopf.

2. Roger Scruton, *The Aesthetics of Architecture* (Princeton, N.J.: Princeton University Press, 1979), 43.

3. Ibid., 43.

4. Ibid., 47.

5. Edward T. Hall, *The Hidden Dimension* (1966; Garden City, N.Y.: Anchor books, 1969), 115.

6. Charles Jencks, *The Language of Post-Modern Architecture* (New York: Rizzoli International Publications, Inc., 1977), 88.

7. Charles Moore and Gerald Allen, *Dimensions: Space, Shape & Scale in Architecture* (New York: Architectural Record Books, 1976), 4.

8. Ibid., 4.

9. Frank Lloyd Wright, *The Natural House* (New York: Horizon Press, 1954), 181–183.

10. Lionel March, and Philip Steadman, *The Geometry of Environment: An Introduction to Spatial Organization in Design* (1971; Cambridge: The M.I.T. Press, 1974), 28.

11. Edmund Burke Feldman, *Varieties of Visual Experience* (New York: Harry N. Abrams, Inc., 1972), 327.

12. William Roger Greeley, *The Essence of Architecture* (New York: D. Van Nostrand Co., Inc., 1927), 46.

13. Roger H. Clark and Michael Pause, *Precedents in Architecture* (New York: Van Nostrand Reinhold Company, 1985), 6.

14. Rudolf Arnheim, *Art and Visual Perception* (Berkeley: University of California Press, 1974), 35.

15. Ibid., 36.

16. Peter Collins, *Changing Ideals in Modern Architecture* (Kingston: McGill-Queen's University Press, 1965), 54.

17. William Blake, "The Tyger," from *Songs of Experience* (1794) in *Blake Complete Writings with Variant Readings,* ed. Geoffrey Keynes (1957; New York: Oxford University Press, 1966), 214.

18. Edith Wharton and Ogden Codman, Jr., *The Decoration of Houses* (New York: W.W. Norton & Company, Inc., 1978), 33.

19. Ibid.

20. Bruno Zevi, *The Modern Language of Architecture* (New York: Van Nostrand Reinhold Company, 1981), 15.

21. Ibid., 15.

22. Ibid., 12.

23. Christian Norberg-Schulz, *Intentions in Architecture* (Cambridge, The MIT Press, 1985), 153.

24. John Dewey, *Art as Experience* (New York: Capricorn Books, 1958), 154.

25. Robert MacLeod, *Charles Rennie Mackintosh: Architect and Artist* (New York: E.P. Dutton, Inc., 1983), 131.

26. Rudolf Arnheim, *The Dynamics of Architectural Form* (Berkeley: Uni-

versity of California Press, 1977), 129.

27. Malcolm Quantrill, *The Environmental Memory* (New York: Schocken Books, 1987), 46.

28. Arnheim, *The Dynamics of Architectural Form,*——133.

29. Hall, *Hidden Dimensions,*——51.

30. Ibid., 51.

31. Dewey, *Art as Experience,*——220.

32. Kent C. Bloomer and Charles W. Moore, *Body, Memory, and Architecture* (New Haven: Yale University Press, 1978), 49.

33. Wharton and Codman, Jr., *The Decoration of Houses,*——31.

34. Ibid., 24.

35. Norman Diekman and John Pile, *Drawing Interior Architecture* (New York: Whitney Library of Design, 1983), 39.

36. Frank Lloyd Wright, "The Concept and the Plan," *The Architectural Record* (January, February, 1928) in *Frank Lloyd Wright: Writings and Buildings,* eds. Edgar Kaufmann and Ben Raeburn (Cleveland: Meridian Books, 1964), 221.

37. Ibid.

38. Quantrill, *The Environmental Memory*——47.

39. Jacques Francois Blondel, *Cours d'architecture,* vol. 2 (Paris: 1771–1777), 229, found in Anthony Vidler "The Idea of Type: The Transformation of the Academic Ideal, 1750–1830," 99.

40. Quantrill, *The Environmental Memory,*——81.

41. Ibid., 95.

42. Hassan Fathy, *Architecture for the Poor* (Chicago: University of Chicago Press, 1973), 24, found in Kathleen Dugas Arceneaux "Value Based Opportunities in Architectural Education," in *Debate & Dialogue: Architectural Design & Pedagogy.* Proceeding of the 77th Annual Meeting of the Association of Collegiate Schools of Architecture, 13.

43. Alan Colquhoun, "Typology & Design Method," in *Meaning in Architecture,* ed. Charles Jencks and George Baird (New York: George Braziller, 1969), 275.

44. Werner Blaser, *Mies van der Rohe Furniture and Interiors* (Woodbury, N.Y.: Barron's Educational Series, Inc., 1982), 7.

45. Ibid.

46. Philip C. Johnson, *Mies van der Rohe* (1947; New York: The Museum of Modern Art, 1978), 49.

47. Le Corbusier, *The Decorative Art of Today,* trans. James I. Dunnett (Cambridge, The MIT Press, 1987), 72.

48. Ibid., 126.

49. Ibid., 112.

50. Renato De Fusco, *Le Corbusier, Designer: Furniture, 1929* (Woodbury, N.Y.: Barron's, 1977), 36.

51. Charles Jencks, *Le Corbusier and the Tragic View of Architecture* (Cambridge, Harvard University Press, 1976), 82.

52. Norman Crowe and Paul Laseau, *Visual Notes for Architects and Designers* (New York: Van Nostrand Reinhold Company, 1984), 7.

53. Clark and Pause, *Precedents in Architecture,*——3.

54. Pauline Saliga, "The Types and Styles of Architectural Drawings," in *Chicago Architects Design,* eds. John Zukowsky and Pauline Saliga (Chicago: The Art Institute of Chicago and Rizzoli International Publications, Inc., 1982), 25.

55. Moore and Allen, *Dimensions: Space, Shape & Scale in Architecture,*——3.

56. Deanna Petherbridge, "At the Other End of the Line," *The Architectural Review,"* Vol. CLXX, No. 1014 (August 1981), 77.

57. Saliga, "The Types and Styles of Architectural Drawings,"——24.

58. Robert A.M. Stern, "Drawing Towards a More Modern Architecture," *Architectural Design* (June 1977): 383.

59. Michael Graves, "The Necessity for Drawing: Tangible Speculation," *Architectural Design,* (June 1977), 384.

60. Saliga, "The Types and Styles of Architectural Drawings,"——28.

61. Stanley Tigerman, *Versus: An American Architect's Alternatives* (New York: Rizzoli, 1982), 132.

62. Gerald Allen and Richard Oliver, *Architectural Drawing: The Art and the Process* (New York: Whitney Library of Design, 1981), 10.

63. Ibid., 10.

64. Ibid., 12.

65. Ibid., 13.

66. Ibid., 14.

Chapter 5. Ordering Systems

1. Robert B. Bechtel, *Enclosing Behavior* (Stroudsburg, Penn.: Dowden, Hutchinson & Ross, Inc., 1977), vii.

2. Gaston Bachelard, *The Poetics of Space,* trans. Maria Jolas (1958; Boston: Beacon Press 1969), 51.

3. Rudolf Arnheim, *The Dynamics of Architectural Form* (Berkeley: University of California Press, 1977), 97.

4. Paul Scheerbart, *Glass Architecture,* ed. Dennis Sharp, trans. James Palmes (1914 New York: Praeger Publishers, Inc., 1972), 41.

5. Rem Koolhaas, *Delirious New York* (New York: Oxford University Press, 1978), 82.

6. Paul Frankl, *The Gothic* (Princeton, N. J.: Princeton University Press, 1960), 105.

7. Robert Lawlor, *Sacred Geometry: Philosophy and Practice* (London: Thames and Hudson Ltd., 1982), 6.

8. Rudolf Wittkower, "The Changing Concept of Proportion," *The Visual Arts Today* in *Daedalus: Journal of the American Academy of Arts & Science* (Winter 1960): 199.

9. Matila Ghyka, *The Geometry of Art and Life* (1946; New York: Dover Publications, Inc., 1977), xi.

10. Rudolf Arnheim, "A Review of Proportion," in *Journal of Aesthetics and Art Criticism* 14 (Sept. 1955): 46.

11. Ghyka, *The Geometry of Art and Life,*——2.

12. Ibid., 3.

13. Ibid., 2.

14. Lawlor, *Sacred Geometry,*——53.

15. Wittkower, "The Changing Concept of Proportion,"——205.

16. Jay Hambidge, *The Elements of Dynamic Symmetry* (1919; New York: Dover Publications, Inc., 1967), 206.

17. William Hoffer, "A Magic Ratio Recurs Throughout Art and Nature," *Smithsonian* 6 (December 1975): 117.

18. Hambidge, *The Elements of Dynamic Symmetry,*——xv.

19. Ghyka, *The Geometry of Art and Life,*——13.

20. Leon Battista Alberti, *The Ten Books of Architecture* (1485), trans. Giacomo James Leoni (1755; New York: Dover Publications, Inc., 1986),.197.

21. Ibid., 195.

22. Ibid.

23. Ibid.

24. Ibid., 196.

25. Ibid.

26. Lawlor, *Sacred Geometry,*——9.

27. Rudolf Wittkower, *Architectural Principles in the Age of Humanism* (1949; New York: W. W. Norton & Company, 1971), 67.

28. Ibid., 68.

29. Ibid., 71.

30. Rudolf Wittkower, "Systems of Proportion," in *Architect's Year Book* 5 (London: Elek Books Limited, 1953), 11.

31. Wittkower, *Architectural Principles in the Age of Humanism,*——113.

32. James S. Ackerman, *Palladio* (1966; New York: Penguin Books, 1979), 162.

33. Deborah Howard and Malcolm Longair, "Harmonic Proportion and Palladio's *Quattro Libri,*" in *Journal of the Society of Architectural Historians* 41:2 (May 1982), 116.

34. Ibid., 116.

35. Ibid., 118.

36. Ibid., 127.

37. Charles A. Jencks, *The Language of Post-Modern Architecture* (New York: Rizzoli International Publications, Inc., 1977), 130.

38. Le Corbusier, *The Modulor* (Cambridge: Harvard University Press, 1954), 55.

39. Wittkower, "The Changing Concept of Proportion,"——212.

40. Marcus V. Pollio Vitruvius, *Vitruvius on Architecture,* ed. and trans. Frank Granger (Cambridge: Harvard University Press, 1931), 159.

41. Arnheim, "A Review of Proportion,"——49.

42. Le Corbusier, *The Modulor,*——56.

43. Ibid., 57.

44. Ibid., 58.

45. Ibid., 90.

46. Ibid., 107.

47. Ibid., 100.

48. Wittkower, "The Changing Concept of Proportion,"——211.

49. Ibid., 210.

50. Ibid., 213.

51. Aniela Jaffe, "Symbolism in the Visual Arts," in *Man and His Symbols,* eds. Carl G. Jung and J.-L. von Franz (1964; Garden City, N. Y.: Doubleday & Company Inc., 1971), 240.

52. Spiro Kostof, *A History of Architecture* (New York: Oxford University Press, 1985), 218.

53. William Blackwell, *Geometry in Architecture* (New York: John Wiley & Sons, 1984), 13.

54. Ibid., 18.

55. Ibid., 23.

56. Ibid., 129.

57. Lawlor, *Sacred Geometry,*——5.

58. Charles Moore and Gerald Allen, *Dimensions* (New York: Architectural Record Books, 1976), 18.

59. Ibid., 17.

60. Carla Gottlieb, *Beyond Modern Art* (New York: E. P. Dutton & Co., Inc., 1976), 191.

61. Ibid., 190.

62. "Modular Architecture," *Progressive Architecture* (November 1957): 158.

63. C. Ray Smith, *Supermannerism* (New York: E. P. Dutton, 1977), 226.

64. Ibid.

65. John Summerson, *Heavenly Mansions* (New York: W. W. Norton & Company, 1963), 203.

66. Ibid.

67. Ibid., 205.

68. Gyorgy Kepes, *Language of Vision* (1944; Chicago: Paul Theobald and Company, 1967), 16.

69. Ibid.

70. Ibid., 17.

71. Ibid., 34.

72. Ibid., 86.

73. David Canter, *Psychology for Architects* (New York: John Wiley & Sons, 1974), 40.

74. James J. Gibson, *The Perception of the Visual World* (Boston: Houghton Mifflin Company, 1950), 71.

75. Edward T. Hall, *The Hidden Dimension* (1966; Garden City, N.Y.: Anchor Books, 1969), 191.

76. Leon Battista Alberti, *The Ten Books of Architecture (1485),* 1435–6, trans. John R. Spencer (1755; New York: Dover Publications, Inc., 1986).

77. "Places: Columbus Coated Fabrics Design Competition," Problem devised by Peter Chermayeff, Charles Gwathmey, Robert A. M. Stern, and Stanley Tigerman (Columbus, Ohio: 1983), ?

78. "Places: Columbus Coated Fabrics Design Competition," Press Release.

79. Edie Lee Cohen, "Dallas Lights: The Artemide Showroom by Vignelli Associates," *Interior Design* (June 1985): 222.

Chapter 6. Seminal Viewpoints

1. Marcus Vitruvius, *De Architectura* (1st century B.C.), trans. Frank Granger (1931; Cambridge: Harvard University Press, 1934), xiv.

2. Marcus Vitruvius, *The Ten Books on Architecture* (1st century B.C.), trans. Morris Hicky Morgan (1914; New York: Dover Publications, Inc., 1960), 24.

3. Ibid., 5.

4. Ibid., 6.

5. Ibid., 5.

6. Ibid.

7. Ibid.

8. Ibid., 80.

9. Abbot Suger, *Abbot Suger on the Abbey Church of St.-Denis and its Art Treasures,* ed. and trans. Erwin Panofsky, 1946, 2d ed. Gerda Panofsky-Soergel (Princeton, N. J.: Princeton University Press, 1979), 83.

10. Vitruvius, *The Ten Books on Architecture,*——16.

11. Ibid., 17.

12. Ibid., 180.

13. Ibid., 179.

14. Ibid., 177.

15. Ibid., 111.

16. Francoise Choay, "Alberti and Vitruvius," ed. Joseph Rykwert, *Architectural Design: Leonis Baptiste Alberti* 49, no. 5-6 (1979), 26.

17. Ibid., 27.

18. Ibid., 29.

19. Rudolf Wittkower, *Architectural Principles in the Age of Humanism,* (1949; New York: W. W. Norton & Company, 1971), 45.

20. Leon Battista Alberti, *The Ten Books of Architecture* (1485), trans. Giacomo James Leoni, (1755; New York: Dover Publications, Inc., 1986), viii.

21. Ibid., 13.

22. Ibid., 84.

23. Choay, "Alberti and Vitruvius,"——30.

24. Arnold Hauser, *The Social History of Art,* vol. 2, trans. Stanley Godman and Arnold Hauser (1951; New York: Vintage Books, 1960), 23, 25.

25. Attributed to Plutarch.

26. Hauser, *The Social History of Art,* vol. 2,——40.

27. Wittkower, *Architectural Principles in the Age of Humanism,*——47.

28. Hauser, *The Social History of Art,* vol. 2,——91.

29. Ibid., 64.

30. Wittkower, *Architectural Principles in the Age of Humanism,*——65.

31. James S. Ackerman, *Palladio* (1966; New York: Penguin Books, 1979), 167.

32. Robert Adam and James Adam, *The Works in Architecture of Robert and James Adam,* ed. Robert Oresko (1773–1822; New York: St. Mar-

tin's Press, 1975), 46.

33. Ackerman, *Palladio,*——53.

34. Ibid., 40.

35. Ibid., 164.

36. Andrea Palladio, *The Four Books of Architecture* (1570), trans. Isaac Ware, (1738; New York: Dover Publications, Inc., 1965), 1.

37. Ibid., xxi.

38. Adam, *The Works in Architecture of Robert and James Adam,*——46.

39. Ibid., 45.

40. Ibid., 46.

41. Ibid., 56.

42. Ibid., 47.

43. Ibid., 23.

44. Ibid., 60.

45. Ibid.

46. Marian Page, *Furniture Designed by Architects* (1980; New York: Whitney Library of Design, 1983), 21.

47. Louise Ade Boger, *The Complete Guide to Furniture Styles* (1959; New York: Charles Scribner's Sons, 1969), 301.

48. Adam, *The Works in Architecture of Robert and James Adam,*——49.

49. Hauser, *The Social History of Art,* vol. 3,——49.

50. Anthony Blunt, Alastair Laing, Christopher Tadgell, and Kerry Downes, *Baroque & Rococo: Architecture & Decoration,* ed. Anthony Blunt (New York: Harper & Row, Publishers, 1978), 134.

51. Emil Kaufmann, *Architecture in the Age of Reason* (1955; New York: Dover Publications, Inc., 1968), 130.

52. Christian Norberg-Schulz, *Late Baroque and Rococo Architecture* (1972; New York: Rizzoli International Publication, 1985), 126.

53. Gabriel-Germain Boffrand, "Si le maître . . . en forte que l'on peut juger du caractère du maître de la maison, qui l'a fait contruire pour lui, par la manière dont elle est disposée, ornée et meublée." *Livres d'architecture* (Paris: 1754), 11.

54. Ibid., "Il ne faut pas employer dans l'intérieur d'une maison les ornemens qui ne doivent être que dans l'extérieur." 22.

55. Kaufmann, *Architecture in the Age of Reason,*——132.

56. Jacques François Blondel, "L'unité consiste dans l'art de concilier dans son projet la solidité, la commodité, l'ordonnance, sans qu'aucune de ces trois parties se détruisent." *De la distribution des Maisons de plaisance* (1737–8) as cited by Emil Kaufmann, *Architecture in the Age of Reason,* 132.

57. Ibid.

58. Blunt, *Baroque & Rococo,*——136.

59. Robert Frank McAlpine, "The Southern Vernacular: A Regional Experience," *Journal of Interior Design Education and Research* 13, no. 1 (Spring 1987), 3

Chapter 7. The 19th Century

1. Jacques François Blondel, *Cours d'architecture* (Paris, 1771–1777) in "The Idea of Type: The Transformation of the Academic Ideal, 1750–1830," Anthony Vidler, *Oppositions* 8 (Spring 1977), 101.

2. Quatremère de Quincy, *Encyclopédie Méthodique* 1 (1788), in "Type: Quatremere de Quincy," Anthony Vidler, *Oppositions,* 8 (Spring 1977) 147.

3. Quatremère de Quincy, *Essay from the Encyclopédie Méthodique, Architecture,* vol 3, p. II (Paris 1825) in "Type," Anthony Vidler, 150.

4. Jean-Baptiste Rondelet, "La théorie est une science qui dirige toutes les opérations de la pratique. C'est par le moyen de la théorie qu'un habile constructeur parvient à déterminer les formes et les justes dimensions qu'il faut donner à chaque partie d'un édifice en raison de sa situation et des efforts qu'elle peut avoir à soutenir, pour qu'il resulte perfection, solidité et économie." *Traité théorique et practique de l'art de batir* (1802) vol. 1, p. V, in *Neoclassical and 19th Century Architecture,* Robin Middleton and David Watkin (1977; New York: Harry N. Abrams, Inc., 1980) 20.

5. Jean-Nicolas-Louis Durand, *Recueil de parallèle des édifices de tout genre anciens et modernes* (1801), in "The Idea of Type," Vidler, 107.

6. Jean-Nicolas-Louis Durand, "Soit que l'on consulte la raison soit que l'on examine les monuments, il est évident que plaire n'a jamais pu être son objet. L'utilité publique et de la société, tel est le but de l'architecture." *Précis des leçons d'architecture données à l'École royale polytéchnique* (1802–1805) vol. I, p. 18 in *Neoclassical and 19th Century Architecture,* Middleton and Watkin, 20.

7. Vidler, "The Idea of Type,"——108.

8. Durand, "Que la disposition est dans toutes les cas la seule chose dont doive s'occuper l'architecte, si cette disposition aussi convenable et économique qu'elle peut l'être, . . ."*Précis des leçons d'architecture données à l'École royale polytéchnique* (1805) vol. 2, 7.

9. Vidler, "The Idea of Type,"——108.

10. Reyner Banham, *Theory and Design in the First Machine Age,* 2d ed. (Cambridge: The MIT Press, 1960), 16.

11. Banham, *Theory and Design in the First Machine Age,*——20.

12. Peter Collins, *Changing Ideals in Modern Architecture* (1965; Kingston: McGill-Queen's University Press, 1984), 188.

13. Frances H. Steiner, *French Iron Architecture* (Ann Arbor, Michigan: UMI Research Press, 1984), 5.

14. Sigfried Giedion, "Du fer! Du fer! Rien que du fer!" *Space, Time and Architecture* (1941; Cambridge: The Harvard University Press, 1949), 165.

15. Emile Zola, *Au Bonheur des Dames* in *Les Rougon-Macquart,* vol. III (Paris: Bibliothèque de la Pleiade, 1964), 611–12 in *French Iron Architecture,* Steiner, 60.

16. John Ruskin, *The Seven Lamps of Architecture* (1849; New York: Farrar, Straus and Giroux, 1979), 55.

17. George F. Chadwick, *The Works of Sir Joseph Paxton 1803–1865* (London: The Architectural Press London, 1961), 74.

18. Ibid., 122.

19. Ibid., 108.

20. Ibid., 109.

21. Giedion, *Space, Time and Architecture,*——129.

22. Ibid., 316.

23. Horatio Greenough, ''Form and Function,'' ed. Lewis Mumford, *Roots of Contemporary American Architecture* (1952; New York: Dover Publications, Inc., 1972), 41, 56.

24. Giedion, *Space, Time, and Architecture,*——276.

25. Walter Gropius, ''Die Kunst in Industrie und Handel,'' *Jahrbuch des Deutschen Werkbundes* (Jena, 1913), 21–22, in *Space, Time, and Architecture,* Giedion,——278.

26. Ibid., 285.

27. Ibid.

28. Harold M. Mayer and Richad C. Wade, *Chicago: Growth of a Metropolis* (Chicago: The University of Chicago Press, 1969), 128.

29. Ibid., 129.

30. Giedion, *Space, Time, and Architecture,*——316.

31. Ibid., 315.

32. Ibid., 319.

33. Condit, *The Chicago School of Architecture.*

34. Dankmar Adler, ''The Chicago Auditorium'' *Architectural Record* 1 (April–June 1982), in ''Adler on the Auditorium,'' *Louis Sullivan and the Architecture of Free Enterprise,* ed. Edgar Kaufmann, Jr. (Chicago: The Art Institute of Chicago, 1956), 24.

35. Condit, *The Chicago School of Architecture.*

36. Sullivan, ''The Chicago Period in Retrospect,'' in Roots of Contemporary American Architecture,——314.

37. Gillian Naylor, *The Arts and Crafts Movement* (1971; Cambridge: The MIT Press, 1980), 8.

38. A.W.N. Pugin, *The True Principles of Pointed or Christian Architecture,* 1841, in *The Arts and Crafts Movement,* Naylor, 14.

39. Naylor, *The Arts and Crafts Movement,*——27.

40. Ibid., 28.

41. Ruskin, *The Seven Lamps of Architecture,*——15.

42. William Morris, *The Beauty of Life, 1880* as cited in *The Complete Guide to Furniture Styles,* Louise Ade Boger (1959; New York: Charles Scribner's Sons, 1969), 397.

43. William Morris, *Arts and Crafts Essays* (Longmans Green & Co., 1899; reprinted 1903), 38, in *The Arts and Crafts Movement,* Naylor, 104.

44. William Morris, ''Printing,'' *Arts and Crafts Essay* (1893), 133, in *The Arts and Crafts Movement,* Naylor, 110.

45. William Morris, ''The Beauty of Life,'' *William Morris: Selected Writings,* ed. G.D.H. Cole (Nonesuch Press, Centenary Edition, 1948) 564, in *The Arts and Crafts Movement,* Naylor, 108.

46. William Morris, ''How we live and how we might live,'' *William Morris: Selected Writings,* ed. G.D.H. Cole, in *The Arts and Crafts Movement,* Naylor, 110.

47. Charles L. Eastlake, *Hints on Household Taste* (1868; New York: Dover Publications, Inc. 1986), 106.

48. Gustav Stickley, *Craftsman Homes: Architecture and Furnishings of the American Arts and Crafts Movement* (1909; New York: Dover Publications, Inc., 1979), 154.

49. Ibid., 157.

50. Naylor, *The Arts and Crafts Movement,*——174.

51. Laurence Buffet-Challie, *The Art Nouveau Style,* trans. Geoffrey Williams (New York: Rizzoli International Publications, Inc., 1982), 38.

52. Samuel Bing, ''L'Art Nouveau,'' *Architectural Record* (vol xii, 1902) in *New Free Style,* ed. Ian Latham (London: Architectural Design and Academy Editions, 1980), 7.

53. Ibid.

54. Claude Frontisi, ''Hector Guimard: Castel Beranger 1895–7,'' in *New Free Style,* Latham,——33.

55. Hector Guimard, ''An Architect's Opinion of L'Art Nouveau,'' in *New Free Style,* Latham, 6.

56. Nikolaus Pevsner, *Pioneers of Modern Design,* (1936; New York: Penguin Books, Inc., 1986), 104.

57. Eugène-Emmanuel Viollet-le-Duc, *Lectures on Architecture,* vol. 2, trans. Benjamin Bucknall (1872; New York: Dover Publications, 1987), 120.

58. Nikolaus Pevsner, *The Sources of Modern Architecture and Design* (1968; New York: Oxford University Press, 1979), 103.

59. Ibid., 114.

60. Eduard F. Sekler, ''The Stoclet House by Josef Hoffmann,'' in *Essays in the History of Architecture Presented to Rudolf Wittkower,* eds. Douglas Fraser, Howard Hibbard, and Milton J. Lewine (New York: Phaidon Publishers Inc., 1967), 235.

61. Ibid., 236.

62. Ibid., ''Dans l'histoire de l'architecture contemporaine, dans la marche vers une esthétique contemporaine, le Prof. Hoffmann, occupe l'une des places les plus lumineuses.'' 228.

Chapter 8. Systematic Applications

1. Gwendolyn Wright, *Moralism and the Model Home* (Chicago: The University of Chicago Press, 1980), 13.

2. Attributed to George Maybeck.

3. Peter Collins, *Changing Ideals in Modern Architecture* (1965; Kingston: McGill-Queen's University Press, 1984), 22.

4. Ibid.

5. David Watkin, *Morality and Architecture* (1977; Chicago: The University of Chicago Press, 1984), 3.

6. Ibid.

7. Ibid., 4.

8. Ibid., 8.

9. Louis Henri Sullivan, ''Towards the Organic,'' in *Roots of Contempo-*

rary American Architecture, ed. Lewis Mumford (New York: Dover Publications, 1972), 78–79.

10. Collins, *Changing Ideals in Modern Architecture,*——131.

11. Jean-Jacques Rousseau, *Discourse on Inequality,* trans. Maurice Cranston (1754; New York: Viking Penguin Inc., 1984), 112.

12. Anthony Vidler, *The Writing of the Walls* (New York: Princeton Architectural Press, 1987), 7.

13. Collins, *Changing Ideals in Modern Architecture,*——40.

14. Augustus Welby Northmore Pugin, *Contrasts; or, a Parallel between the Noble Edifices of the Fourteenth and Fifteenth Centuries, and Similar Buildings of the Present Day; Shewing the Present Decay of Taste; Accompanied by Appropriate Text,* (1836; New York: Humanities Press, 1969), iii.

15. Ibid., 1.

16. Ibid., 2.

17. Ibid., 3.

18. Ibid., 6.

19. Augustus Welby Northmore Pugin, *The True Principles of Pointed or Christian Architecture; set forth in Two Lectures Delivered at St. Marie's, Oscott* (1841; Oxford: St. Barnabas Press, 1969), 1.

20. Ibid., 35.

21. Kenneth Clark, *The Gothic Revival: An Essay in the History of Taste* (1928; New York: Harper & Row, Publishers, 1974), 149.

22. John Ruskin, *The Seven Lamps of Architecture* (1849; New York: Farrar, Straus and Giroux, 1979), 6.

23. Ibid., 23.

24. Ibid., 39.

25. Ibid., 169.

26. Ibid., 171.

27. John Ruskin, *The Stones of Venice* (New York: International Book Company, 1851), 49.

28. John Barrington Bayley, ''The Decoration of Houses as a Practical Handbook,'' in *The Decoration of Houses,* Edith Wharton and Ogden Codman, Jr. (1897; New York: W. W. Norton & Company, Inc., 1978), ix.

29. William A. Coles, ''The Genesis of a Classic,'' in *The Decoration of Houses,* Wharton and Codman, Jr.,——xxxvi.

30. Wharton and Codman, Jr. *The Decoration of Houses,*——10.

31. Collins, *Changing Ideals in Modern Architecture,*——198.

32. Ibid., 199.

33. Frances H. Steiner, *French Iron Architecture* (Ann Arbor, Mich.: UMI Research Press, 1984), 33.

34. Eugène-Emmanuel Viollet-le-Duc, *Lectures on Architecture,* vol. 1, trans. Benjamin Bucknall (1872; New York: Dover Publications, Inc., 1987), 56.

35. Collins, *Changing Ideals In Modern Architecture,* 25.

36. Leon Labrouste, *Esthétique monumentale* (Paris: Schmid, 1902), 214 in ''Henri Labrouste,'' David T. Van Zanten, *Macmillan Encyclopedia*

of Architects, ed. Adolf K. Placzek (New York: The Free Press, 1982), 593.

37. Van Zanten, *Macmillan Encyclopedia of Architects,*——594.

38. Neil Levine, ''The Romantic Idea of Architectural Legibility: Henri Labrouste and the Neo-Grec,'' in *The Architecture of The Ecole Des Beaux-Arts,* ed. Arthur Drexler (New York: The Museum of Modern Art, 1977), 344.

39. Ibid., 355.

40. Viollet-le-Duc, *Lectures on Architecture,* vol. 1,——6.

41. Ibid., 38.

42. Ibid., 328.

43. Ibid., 335.

44. Ibid., 447.

45. Ibid., 291.

46. Ibid., 294.

47. Reyner Banham, *Theory and Design in the First Machine Age,* 2d ed. (Cambridge, Mass.: The MIT Press, 1960), 14.

48. Ibid., 20.

49. Ibid.

50. David Van Zanten, ''Architectural Composition at the École Des Beaux-Arts from Charles Percier to Charles Garnier,'' in *The Architecture of the Ecole Des Beaux-Arts,* ed. Arthur Drexler——118.

51. Ibid., 115.

52. Ibid., 268.

53. Ibid., 286.

54. Collins, *Changing Ideals in Modern Architecture,*——118.

55. Ibid., 119.

56. Wright, *Moralism and the Model Home,*——46.

57. Ibid., 47.

58. Ibid., 2.

59. A.J. Downing, *The Architecture of Country Houses,* (1850; New York: Dover Publications, Inc., 1969), 70.

60. Wright, *Moralism and the Model Home,*——14.

61. Ibid., 55.

62. Ibid., 4.

63. Ruth E. Finley, *The Lady of Godey's: Sarah Josepha Hale* (Philadelphia: J.B. Lippincott Company, 1931), 177.

64. Frank Luther Mott, *A History of American Magazines: 1885–1905,* vol. 4 (Cambridge: Harvard University Press, 1957), 323.

65. Finley, *The Lady of Godey's,*——144.

66. Mott, *A History of American Magazines: 1885–1905,* vol. 4,——545.

Chapter 9. A Bold New Century

1. Frank Lloyd Wright, *The Sovereignty of the Individual: In the Cause of Architecture* (Berlin: Wasmuth, 1910). Reprinted as introduction to exhibition Palazzo Strozzi, Florence, Italy, 1951, 4.

2. William J. R. Curtis, *Modern Architecture Since 1900* (1982; Englewood Cliffs, N. J.: Prentice-Hall, Inc., 1983), 78.

3. Henry-Russell Hitchcock, *In the Nature of Materials* (1942; New York: Da Capo Press, Inc., 1975), 31.

4. Wright, *The Sovereignty of the Individual,*——5.

5. Wright, "The Art and Craft of the Machine," (1901) in *Frank Lloyd Wright: Writings and Buildings,* eds. Ben Kaufmann and Edgar Raeburn (Cleveland: Meridan Books, 1964), 55.

6. Ibid., 56.

7. Ibid., 59.

8. Ibid., 66.

9. Ibid., 68.

10. Frank Lloyd Wright, *An Autobiography* (New York: Longsmans, Green and Company, 1932), 154.

11. Ibid.

12. Ibid., 161.

13. Wright, *The Sovereignty of the Individual,*——15.

14. Ibid.

15. Ibid.

16. Wright, *An Autobiography,*——143.

17. Frank Lloyd Wright, *A Testament* (New York: Horizon Press, 1957), 132.

18. Kenneth Frampton, *Modern Architecture: A Critical History* (New York: Oxford University Press, 1980), 109.

19. Curtis, *Modern Architecture Since 1900,*——61.

20. "Hermann Muthesius: Aims of the Werkbund" (1911), trans. Michael Bullock (1970) in *Programs and Manifestoes on 20th-Century Architecture,* ed. Ulrich Conrads (Cambridge: The MIT Press, 1975), 26.

21. Reyner Banham, *Theory and Design in the First Machine Age,* 2d ed. (Cambridge: The MIT Press, 1960), 72.

22. Curtis, *Modern Architecture Since 1900,*——60.

23. Frampton, *Modern Architecture,*——111.

24. Banham, *Theory and Design in the First Machine Age,*——73.

25. "Muthesius/Van de Velde: Werkbund Theses and Antitheses," (1914) in *Programs and Manifestoes on 20th-Century Architecture,* ed. Ulrich Conrads, 28.

26. Ibid., 29.

27. Paul Scheerbart, *Glass Architecture* (1914), ed. Dennis Sharp, trans. James Palmes (New York: Praeger Publishers, Inc., 1972), 71.

28. Benedetto Gravagnuolo, *Adolf Loos: Theory and Works,* trans. C. H. Evans (1982; New York: Rizzoli International Publications, 1988), 20.

29. Ibid., 18.

30. Frampton, *Modern Architecture,*——92.

31. Gravagnuolo, *Adolf Loos,*——19.

32. Ibid., 18.

33. Hans M. Wingler, *The Bauhaus,* ed. Joseph Stein, trans. Wolfgang Jabs and Basil Gilbert (1962; Cambridge: MIT Press, 1969), 32.

34. Wingler, *The Bauhaus,*——32.

35. H. M. Wingler, "The Bauhaus and De Stijl," introd. in *Principles of Neo-Plastic Art,* Theo Van Doesburg, trans. Janet Seligman (New York: New York Graphic Society Ltd., 1966), ix.

36. Ludwig Mies van der Rohe, *Frühlicht* (1922) in *Bauhaus: 50 Years German Exhibition.* Preparation Committee Herbert Bayer, Ludwig Grote, Dieter Honisch, and Hans M. Wingler, (Chicago: Illinois Institute of Technology, 1969), 163.

37. Ludwig Mies van der Rohe, *"G"* (issue 1, 1923) in *Bauhaus: 50 Years,* Bayer et al., ——, 164.

38. Ludwig Mies van der Rohe, *Zu Meinem Block in Bau und Wohnung,* ed. Deutscher Werkbund (Stuttgart, 1927) in *Bauhaus: 50 Years,* Bayer et al.,——165.

39. Oskar Schlemmer, *Briefe und Tagebücher* (Munich, 1958), 132 in *Bauhaus: 50 Years,* Bayer et al.,——20.

40. Walter Gropius, "Neue Arbeiten der Bauhaus Werkstätten," *Bauhaus Books* (Munich, 1925, no. 7, p. 4–7) in *Bauhaus: 50 Years,* Bayer et al.,——20.

41. Walter Gropius, *Scope of Total Architecture* (1943; New York: Collier Books, 1962), 26.

42. Gropius, *Scope of Total Architecture,*——27.

43. Hannes Meyer, *Bauhaus* (issue 4, 1928), pages 12–13 in *Bauhaus: 50 Years,* Bayer et al.,——162.

44. Meyer, *Bauhaus,* in *Bauhaus: 50 Years,* Bayer et al.,——162.

45. Ludwig Grote "Architecture as a Field of Study," (1969) in *Bauhaus: 50 Years,* Bayer et al.,——77.

46. Marcel Breuer, "The House Interior," (Lecture given at the Technical University, Delft, 1931) in *Marcel Breuer: Furniture and Interiors,* Christopher Wilk (New York: The Museum of Modern Art, 1981), 184.

47. Curtis, *Modern Architecture Since 1900,*——91.

48. Georges Braque, 20th Century Art?

49. William S. Lieberman, ed., *Modern Masters: Manet to Matisse* (New York: The Museum of Modern Art, 1975), 142.

50. Ibid., 72.

51. Theo van Doesburg, *Principles of Neo-Plastic Art,* trans. Janet Seligman (1925; New York Graphic Society Ltd., 1966), 2.

52. Filippo Alison, foreword to *The Furniture of Gerrit Thomas Rietveld,* Daniele Baroni (Woodbury, N. Y.: Barron's, 1978), 7.

53. Theo van Doesburg et al., " *'De Stijl': Manifesto I''* (November 1918) in *Programs and Manifestoes on 20th Century Architecture,* ed. Conrads,——39.

54. Frampton, *Modern Architecture,*——143.

55. Baroni, *The Furniture of Gerrit Thomas Rietveld,*——24.

56. Ibid., 83.

57. Ibid., 85.

58. Ibid., 89.

59. Le Corbusier, *The Decorative Art of Today,* trans. James I. Dunnett (1925; Cambridge: The MIT Press, 1987), 72.

60. Le Corbusier, *Towards a New Architecture,* trans. Frederick Etchells (1927; New York: Holt, Rinehart and Winston, 1960), 152.

61. Baroni, *The Furniture of Gerrit Thomas Rietveld,*——105.

62. Frampton, *Modern Architecture,*——158.

63. Curtis, *Modern Architecture Since 1900,*——110.

64. Baroni, *The Furniture of Gerrit Thomas Rietveld,*——103.

65. Le Corbusier, *The Decorative Art of Today,*——xiv.

66. Banham, *Theory and Design in the First Machine Age,*——247.

67. Peter Collins, *Changing Ideals in Modern Architecture* (1965; Kingston: McGill-Queen's University Press, 1984), 165.

Chapter 10. Emerging Building Types

1. Reyner Banham, *Theory and Design in the First Machine Age,* 2d ed. (Cambridge: The MIT Press, 1960), 320.

2. Ibid., 321.

3. Ibid., 326.

4. Ibid.

5. William J. R. Curtis, *Modern Architecture Since 1900* (1982; Englewood Cliffs, N.J.: Prentice-Hall, Inc., 1983), 181.

6. Ibid., 182.

7. Banham, *Theory and Design in the First Machine Age,*——326.

8. Robert Marks and R. Buckminster Fuller, *The Dymaxion World of Buckminster Fuller* (1960; Garden City, N.Y.: Anchor Press Edition, 1973), 18.

9. Ibid., 19.

10. Ibid., 20.

11. Gwendolyn Wright, *Building the Dream: A Social History of Housing in America* (New York: Pantheon Books, 1981), 158.

12. Ibid.

13. Ibid., 159.

14. Ibid., 157.

15. Frank Lloyd Wright, ''Young Architecture'' (1931) in *Programs and Manifestoes on 20th-Century Architecture,* ed. Ulrich Conrads (Cambridge: The MIT Press, 1975), 125.

16. Frank Lloyd Wright, *A Testament* (New York: Horizon Press, 1957), 227.

17. Frank Lloyd Wright, '' 'Fallingwater': Kaufmann House,'' *The Architectural Forum,* 68 (January 1938), 36.

18. Henry-Russell Hitchcock, *In the Nature of Materials* (1942; New York: Da Capo Press Inc., 1975), 90.

19. Frank Lloyd Wright, *The Living City* (New York: Bramhall House, 1958).

20. David A. Hanks, *The Decorative Designs of Frank Lloyd Wright* (New York: E. P. Dutton, 1979), 47.

21. Ibid.

22. Curtis, *Modern Architecture Since 1900,*——203.

23. Ibid.

24. Wright, *Building the Dream,*——168.

25. Ibid., 200.

26. Joseph B. Mason, *History of Housing in the U.S. 1930–1980* (Houston, Tex.: Gulf Publishing Company, 1982), 14.

27. Ibid., 15.

28. Robert T. Jones, ed., *Authentic Small Houses of the Twenties,* Reprint of *Small Homes of Architectural Distinction: A Book of Suggested Plans Designed by The Architects' Small House Service Bureau, Inc.* (1929; New York: Dover Publications, Inc., 1987), 271.

29. Ibid., 7.

30. Ibid., 263.

31. Ibid., 271.

32. Mason, *History of Housing in the U.S. 1930–1980,*——71.

33. Ibid., 70.

34. Wright, *Building the Dream,*——251.

35. Mason, *History of Housing in the U.S. 1930–1980,*——65.

36. Charles Moore, Gerald Allen, and Donlyn Lyndon, *The Place of Houses* (New York: Holt, Rinehart and Winston, 1974), 82.

37. Ralph Caplan, *The Design of Herman Miller* (New York: Whitney Library of Design, 1976), 24.

38. George Nelson, *Problems of Design* (New York: Whitney Publications Inc., 1957), 182.

39. Moore, Allen, and Lyndon, *The Place of Houses,*——91.

40. Wright, *Building the Dream,*——117.

41. Ibid., 138.

42. John Hancock, ''The Apartment House in Urban America,'' in *Buildings and Society,* ed. Anthony D. King (London: Routledge & Kegan Paul, 1980), 151.

43. Ibid., 152.

44. Clare Cooper, ''The House as Symbol of the Self,'' in *Designing for Human Behavior,* eds. Jon Lang, Charles Burnette, Walter Moleski, and David Vachon (Stroudsburg, Penn.: Dowden, Hutchinson & Ross, Inc., 1974), 134.

45. Ibid.

46. Rem Koolhaas, *Delirious New York* (New York: Oxford University Press, 1978), 69.

47. C. Ray Smith, *Supermannerism* (New York: E. P. Dutton, 1977), 40.

48. Mason, *History of Housing in the U.S. 1930–1980,*——155.

49. Hancock, ''The Apartment House in Urban America,''——157.

50. Ibid., 158.

51. Ibid., 167.

52. Albert Mehrabian, *Public Places and Private Space* (New York: Basic Books Inc., 1976), 109.

53. Cooper, "The House as Symbol of Self,"———134.

54. Mario Praz, *An Illustrated History of Interior Decoration*, trans. William Weaver (1944–1963; New York: Thames and Hudson, Inc., 1982), 21.

55. Alan Colquhoun, *Modernity and the Classical Tradition* (Cambridge: The MIT Press, 1989), 252.

56. Ibid.

57. Louis H. Sullivan, "The Tall Office Building Artistically Considered," in *Kindergarten Chats and Other Writings* (1918; New York: Dover Publications, Inc., 1979), 202.

58. Ibid.

59. Ibid., 203.

60. Francis Duffy, "Office Buildings and Organisational Change," in *Buildings and Society,* ed. Anthony D. King (London: Routledge & Kegan Paul, 1980), 255.

61. Ibid.

62. Ibid., 258.

63. Robert Ardrey, *The Social Contract,* (New York: Atheneum, 1970), 331.

64. Duffy, *Office Buildings and Organisational Change,*———279.

65. Mehrabian, *Public Places and Private Spaces,*———141.

66. Ibid.

67. Abraham Maslow, *Motivation and Personality,* 2d ed. (New York: Harper & Row, 1970).

68. Ardrey, *The Social Contract,*———160.

69. Duffy, "Office Buildings and Organisational Change,"———274.

70. Smith, *Supermannerism,*———124.

Chapter 11. The Human Dimension

1. Siegfried Giedion, *Mechanization Takes Command* (1948; New York: W. W. Norton & Company, 1969), 35.

2. Ibid., 9.

3. Ibid., 512.

4. Ibid., 30.

5. Frederick Winslow Taylor, *The Principles of Scientific Management* (New York: Harper & Brothers Publishers, 1911), 83.

6. Giedion, *Mechanization Takes Command,*———47.

7. Catharine E. Beecher and Harriet Beecher Stowe, *The American Woman's Home* (1869; Watkins Glen, N. Y.: Library of Victorian Culture American Life Foundation, 1979), 333–334.

8. Ibid., 225.

9. Susan Strasser, *Never Done* (New York: Pantheon Books, 1982), 218.

10. Ibid.

11. Giedion, *Mechanization Takes Command,*———522.

12. Ibid.

13. Ibid., 616.

14. Ibid., 541.

15. Ibid., 659.

16. Ibid., 616.

17. Ibid., 625.

18. Edie Lee Cohen, ''ICF's Kitchen Design Competition,'' *Interior Design* 56 (April 1985), 197.

19. Virginia T. Habeeb, ''Kitchens '85: New Attitudes and New Technology,'' *Interior Design* 56 (April 1985): 202.

20. Dolores Hayden, *The Grand Domestic Revolution* (Cambridge: The MIT Press, 1981), 1.

21. Ibid.

22. Ibid.

23. Polly Wynn Allen, *Building Domestic Liberty* (Amherst: The University of Massachusetts Press, 1988), 5.

24. Ibid., 63.

25. Ibid., 76.

26. Hayden, *The Grand Domestic Revolution,*——192.

27. Ibid., 189.

28. Allen, *Building Domestic Liberty,*——106.

29. Leonard E. Ladd, *Specification forming part of Letters Patent No. 430, 480, dated June 17, 1890.* United States Patent Office.

30. Hayden, *The Grand Domestic Revolution,*——138.

31. Joseph B. Mason, *History of Housing in the U.S. 1930–1980* (Houston, Tex.: Gulf Publishing Company, 1982), 140.

32. Ibid.

33. Ibid., 141.

34. Ibid.

35. Hayden, *The Grand Domestic Revolution,*——283.

36. Strasser, *Never Done,*——251.

37. Dolores Hayden, ''Redesigning the American Dream,'' *Progressive Architecture* 65 (July 1984): 85.

38. Albert Mehrabian, *Public Places and Private Spaces* (New York: Basic Books, Inc., 1976), 21.

39. Ibid., 12.

40. Ibid., 312.

41. Ibid., 107.

42. Edward T. Hall, *The Hidden Dimension* (1966; Garden City, N.Y.: Anchor Books: 1969), 7.

43. Robert Ardrey, *The Territorial Imperative* (New York: Dell Publishing Co., 1966), vii.

44. Robert Sommer, *Personal Space* (Englewood Cliffs, N.J.: Prentice-Hall, Inc., 1969), 170.

45. Ardrey, *The Territorial Imperative,*——103.

46. Ibid., 116.

47. Sommer, *Personal Space,*——43.

48. Ibid.

49. Ibid., 5.

50. Ibid., 160.

51. Hall, *The Hidden Dimension,*——53.

52. Ibid., 1.

53. Ibid., 101.

54. Ibid., 102.

55. Ibid., 103.

56. Ibid., 107.

57. Ibid., 110.

58. Ibid.

59. Ibid., 116.

60. Ibid., 127.

61. Sommer, *Personal Space,*——26.

62. Ibid., 27.

63. W. H. Auden, "Prologue: The Birth of Architecture," *About the House* (New York: Random House, 1959), 4.

64. David Canter, *Psychology for Architects* (New York: Halsted Press, a division of John Wiley & Sons, Inc., 1974), 109.

65. Ibid., 110.

66. Ibid., 113.

67. Ibid., 115.

68. Ibid., 122.

69. Ibid., 123.

70. Ibid., 125.

71. Ibid.

72. Jerald Greenberg, "Equity and Workplace Status," *Journal of Applied Psychology,* 73 (No. 4, 1988), 606.

73. Ibid., 611.

74. Gillo Dorfles, "Structuralism & Semiology in Architecture," in *Meaning in Architecture,* eds. Charles Jencks and George Baird (New York: George Braziller, 1970), 39.

75. Umberto Eco, "Function and Sign: The Semiotics of Architecture," in *Sign, Symbols, and Architectue,* eds. Geoffrey Broadbent, Richard Bunt, and Charles Jencks (New York: John Wiley & Sons, 1980), 12.

76. A. J. De Long, "Coding Behavior and Levels of Cultural Integration: Synchronic and Diachronic Adaptive Mechanisms in Human Behaviour," in *Meaning and Behaviour in the Built Environment,* eds. Geoffrey Broadbent, Richard Bunt, and Tomas Llorens (New York: John Wiley & Sons, 1980), 265.

77. Ibid., 267.

78. Ibid.

79. Mario Praz, *An Illustrated History of Interior Decoration,* trans. William Weaver (1944–1963; New York: Thames and Hudson, Inc., 1982), 25.

80. Rem Koolhaas, *Delirious New York* (New York: Oxford University Press, 1978), 153.

81. Suzanne Stephens, ''Taste in America,'' *Progressive Architecture* (June 1978): 50.

82. Ibid.

83. Ibid.

Chapter 12. The Space Within

1. J. R. R. Tolkien, *The Hobbit: or There and Back Again* (New York: Ballantine, 1966), 64.

2. Malcolm Quantrill, *The Environmental Memory* (New York: Schocken Books, 1987), 177.

3. Rudolf Arnheim, ''Buildings as Percepts,'' *Via: Architecture and Visual Perception* 6 (The Graduate School of Fine Arts and University of Pennsylvania and The MIT Press, 1983), 13.

4. Ibid., 14.

5. Ibid., 17.

6. Paul Zucker, *Town and Square* (1959; Cambridge: The MIT Press, 1970), 28.

7. Kent C. Bloomer and Charles W. Moore, *Body, Memory, and Architecture* (New Haven: Yale University Press, 1977), 98.

8. C. A. Doxiadis, *Architectural Space in Ancient Greece,* ed. and trans. Jaqueline Tyrwhitt (1937; Cambridge: The MIT Press, 1972), 4.

9. Bloomer and Moore, *Body, Memory, and Architecture,*——110.

10. Vincent Scully, *The Earth, The Temple, and The Gods* (1962; New Haven: Yale University Press, 1979), 5.

11. Le Corbusier, *Towards a New Architecture,* trans. Frederick Etchells (1927; New York: Holt, Rinehart and Winston, 1969), 50.

12. Zucker, *Town and Square,*——29.

13. Scully, *The Earth, The Temple, and The Gods,*——5.

14. A. C. Sewter, *Baroque and Rococo* (Harcourt Brace Jovanovich, Inc., 1972), 202.

15. Vincent Scully, Jr., *Modern Architecture* (1961; New York: George Braziller, 1974), 11.

16. Rudolf Wittkower, *Art and Architecture in Italy 1600–1750* (1958; New York: Penguin Books, 1980), 195.

17. Harry Heft and Joachim F. Wohlwill, ''Environmental Cognition in Children,'' *Handbook of Environmental Psychology,* vol. 1, eds. Daniel Stokols and Irwin Altman (New York: John Wiley & Sons, 1987), 179.

18. Ibid.

19. Julian Hochberg, ''Visual Perception in Architecture,'' *Via: Architecture and Visual Perception* 6 (The Graduate School of Fine Arts University of Pennsylvania and The MIT Press, 1983), 35.

20. James J. Gibson, *The Senses Considered as Perceptual Systems* (Boston: Houghton Mifflin Company, 1966), 53.

21. Ibid.

22. Eugene V. Walter, *Placeways* (Chapel Hill: The University of North Carolina Press, 1988), 135.

23. Zucker, *Town and Square,*——6.

24. Robert J. Yudell, "Body Movement," *Body, Memory, and Architecture,* Bloomer and Moore, 1977, 59.

25. Ibid.

26. John Summerson, *Heavenly Mansions* (New York: W. W. Norton & Company, 1963), 112.

27. Yudell, "Body Movement,"——68.

28. Rob Krier, *Architectural Composition* (New York: Rizzoli International Publications, Inc., 1988), 113.

29. Bloomer and Moore, *Body, Memory, and Architecture,*——78.

30. Reginald G. Golledge, "Environmental Cognition," *Handbook of Environmental Psychology,* eds. Daniel Stokols and Irwin Altman (New York: John Wiley & Sons, 1987), 140.

31. Ibid., 142.

32. Quantrill, *The Environmental Memory,*——50.

33. Kevin Lynch, *The Image of the City* (Cambridge: The Technology Press & Harvard University Press, 1960), 8.

34. Ibid.

35. Ibid., 9.

36. Jon Lang, *Creating Architectural Theory* (New York: Van Nostrand Reinhold, 1987), 137.

37. Ibid., 157.

38. Arthur Drexler, "Engineer's Architecture: Truth and Its Consequences," *The Architecture of the Ecole Des Beaux-Arts,* ed. Arthur Drexler (New York: The Museum of Modern Art, 1977), 38.

39. Stanley Abercrombie, "The Plan as Determinant of Movement," *AIA Journal* (October 1982), 72.

40. Ibid., 74.

41. David Van Zanten, "Architectural Composition at the Ecole des Beaux-Arts from Charles Percier to Charles Garnier," *The Architecture of the Ecole des Beaux-Arts* (New York: The Museum of Modern Art, 1977), 118.

42. Le Corbusier, *Towards a New Architecture,* trans. Frederick Etchells (1927; New York: Holt, Rinehart and Winston, 1960), 173.

43. Zucker, *Town and Square,*——25.

44. Robin Evans, "Figures, Doors and Passages," *Architectural Design,* 48, no. 4 (1978), 267.

45. Ibid., 270.

46. Ibid., 272.

47. John Bold, *John Webb: Architectural Theory and Practice in the Seventeenth Century* (Oxford: Clarendon Press, 1989), 95.

48. John E. Stambaugh, *The Ancient Roman City* (Baltimore: The Johns Hopkins University Press, 1988), 16.

49. Bernard Tschumi, "Sequences," (New York: Committee for the Visual Arts, Inc., 1981), 1.

50. Tschumi, "Sequences,"——2.

51. H. G. Wells, "The Door in the Wall," in *The Door in the Wall and Other Stories* (1911; Boston: David R. Godine, 1980), 9.

52. Marc P. Keane, "Japanese Entrances: Cultural Symbols in the Landscape," *Landscape Architecture* 78 (September/October 1988): 120.

53. Teiji Itoh, *Space & Illusion: In the Japanese Garden* (1965; New York: John Weatherhill, Inc., and Kyoto: Tankosha, 1973), 69.

54. Ibid.

55. Keane, "Japanese Entrances,"———125.

56. Abbot Suger, *Abbot Suger on the Abbey Church of St.-Denis and its Art Treasures,* ed. and trans. Erwin Panofsky, 1946, 2d ed. Gerda Panofsky-Soergel (Princeton, N. J.: Princeton University Press, 1979), 47.

57. Alvar Aalto, *Sketches,* ed. Goran Schildt, trans. Stuart Wrede (Cambridge: The MIT Press, 1978), 78.

58. Louis Kahn, *Light is the Theme,* ed. Nell E. Johnson (1975; Fort Worth, Texas: Kimbell Art Foundation, 1978), 15.

59. Ibid., 17.

60. Monica Geran, "Perceived Perspectives," *Interior Design* (June 1986): 300.

61. Ettore Sottsass, "Travel Notes," *Terrazzo* (Spring 1989): 38.

62. Ibid.

63. Ibid., 32.

64. Ibid.

65. D. Geoffrey Hayward, "Psychological Factors in the Use of Light and Lighting in Buildings," in *Designing for Human Behavior: Architecture and the Behavioral Sciences,* eds. Jon Lang, Charles Burnette, Walter Moleski, David Vachon (Stroudsburg, Pa.: Dowden, Hutchinson & Ross, Inc. 1974), 126.

66. Hayward, "Psychological Factors in the Use of Light and Lighting in Buildings,"———128.

67. Sottsass, "Travel Notes,"———36.

Chapter 13. The Enclosure Revealed

1. Roger Scruton, *The Aesthetics of Architecture* (Princeton, N.J.: Princeton University Press, 1979), 43.

2. Leon Battista Alberti, *The Ten Books of Architecture,* trans. Giacomo James Leoni, 1755 (1485; New York: Dover Publications, Inc., 1986), 21.

3. Henri Focillon, *The Life of Forms in Art,* trans. Charles Beecher Hogan and George Kubler (1934; New York: Zone Books, 1989), 95.

4. Ibid., 96.

5. Ibid., 97.

6. Gillian Naylor, *The Arts and Crafts Movement* (1971; Cambridge: The MIT Press, 1980), 104.

7. Werner Blaser, *Mies van der Rohe Furniture and Interiors* (Woodbury, N.Y.: Barren's Educational Series, Inc., 1982), 7.

8. Christopher Alexander, Sara Ishikawa, Murray Silverstein, with Max Jacobson, Ingrid Fiksdahl-King, and Shlomo Angel, *A Pattern Language* (New York: Oxford University Press, 1977), 956.

9. Ibid.

10. Ibid., 957.

11. George Santayana, *The Sense of Beauty: Being the Outline of Aesthetic Theory* (1896; New York: Dover Publications, Inc., 1955), 29.

12. William Roger Greeley, *The Essence of Architecture: Being a Brief Essay upon the Principles of Composition* (New York: D. Van Nostrand Company, Inc., 1927), 31.

13. Ibid., 34.

14. Paul Scheerbart, *Glass Architecture,* 1914, trans. James Palmes and Bruno Taut, *Alpine Architecture,* 1919, trans. Shirley Palmer, ed. Dennis Sharp (New York: Praeger Publishers, 1972), 71.

15. Abbot Suger, *Abbot Suger on the Abbey Church of St.-Denis and Its Art Treasures,* ed., trans., and annotated Erwin Panofsky, 1946, 2d ed. Gerda Panofsky-Soergel (Princeton, N.J.: Princeton University Press, 1979), 61.

16. Ibid., 63.

17. Attributed to Bernard of Clairvaux.

18. Ibid.

19. Suger, *Abbot Suger on the Abbey Church of St.-Denis and Its Art Treasures,*——63.

20. Charles A. Jencks, *The Language of Post-Modern Architecture* (New York: Rizzoli International Publications, Inc., 1977), 32.

21. Beverly Russell, "Showroom and Low Budget Design Winner," *Interiors,* 146, no. 6 (January 1987): 172.

22. Marco Frascari, "The Tell-The-Tale Detail," *Via: The Building of Architecture,* eds. Paula Behrens and Anthony Fisher, 7 (The Graduate School of Fine Arts University of Pennsylvania and The MIT Press, 1984), 23.

23. Ibid.

24. Ibid., 24.

25. Ibid., 26.

26. Frank Gehry, "Detailing," *Terrazzo* (Spring 1989), 60.

27. Gehry, "Detailing,"——62.

28. Thomas H. Beeby, "The Grammar of Ornament/Ornament as Grammar," *Via: Ornament,* ed. Stephen Kieran, 3 (The Graduate School of Fine Arts University of Pennsylvania and The MIT Press, 1977), 24.

29. Chicago Chapter American Institute of Architects, *Architecture Chicago: The Divine Detail,* 6 (Chicago: Chicago Chapter AIA, 1988), 173.

30. Alberti, *The Ten Books of Architecture,*——112.

31. Ibid., 113.

32. Christopher Dresser, *The Art of Decorative Design,* 1 in "What Is Ornament and What Is Not," Sir John Summerson, *Via: Ornament,*——5.

33. Ibid., 5.

34. Ibid., 7.

35. Ibid.

36. Ananda K. Coomaraswamy, *Figures of Speech or Figures of Thought: Collected Essays on the Traditional or "Normal" View of Art* (London: Luzac & Co., 1946), 86.

37. Ibid., 85.

38. Ibid., 89.

39. Ibid., 94.

40. Alexander, Ishikawa, Silverstein, et al., *A Pattern Language,*——1147.

41. Ibid., 1149.

42. Siegfried Giedion, *Mechanization Takes Command: A Contribution to Anonymous History* (1948; New York: W.W. Norton & Company, 1969), 331.

43. Ibid., 338–42.

44. Ibid., 344.

45. Ibid., 348.

46. Ibid., 351.

47. Ibid., 352.

48. Ibid., 353.

49. Owen Jones, *The Grammar of Ornament* (1856; New York: Van Nostrand Reinhold, 1982), 1.

50. Jones, *The Grammar of Ornament,*——8.

51. Summerson, "What Is Ornament and What Is Not,"——6.

52. Beeby, "The Grammar of Ornament/Ornament As Grammar,"——11.

53. David Van Zanten, "Architectural Ornament: On, In, And Through The Wall," *Via: Ornament,*——49.

54. John Ruskin, *The Seven Lamps of Architecture* (1849; New York: Farrar, Strauss and Giroux, 1979), 169.

55. Van Zanten, "Architectural Ornament: On, In, And Through The Wall,"——50.

56. Louis H. Sullivan, "Ornament in Architecture," orig. publ. in *The Engineering Magazine,* 1892, *Kindergarten Chats* (New York: Dover Publications, Inc., 1979), 188.

57. Ibid.

58. Adolf Loos, "Ornament and Crime," (1908) in *Programs and Manifestoes on 20th-Century Architecture,* ed. Ulrich Conrads, trans. Michael Bullock (Cambridge: The MIT Press, 1975), 19.

59. Ibid., 20.

60. Benedetto Gravagnuolo, *Adolf Loos: Theory and Works,* trans. C.H. Evans (1982; New York: Rizzoli International Publication, Inc., 1988), 70.

61. Beeby, "The Grammar of Ornament/Ornament As Grammar,"——20.

62. Ibid., 21.

63. Ibid.

64. Grace Anderson, "Object of Desire," *Record Interiors 1986,* 174, no. 11 (Mid-September, 1986): 100.

65. Robert Venturi, *Complexity and Contradiction in Architecture* (1966; New York: The Museum of Modern Art, 1977), 44.

66. Ibid.

67. E. H. Gombrich, *The Sense of Order: A Study in the Psychology of Decorative Art* (Ithaca, N.Y.: Cornell University Press, 1979), 171.

68. Ibid., 173.

69. Van Zanten, ''Architectural Ornament: On, In, And Through The Wall,''———54.

70. Gombrich, *The Sense of Order,*———218.

71. Ibid., 217.

72. Ibid., 234.

Chapter 14. Archetypes and Ethics

1. Aldo Rossi, *The Architecture of the City,* trans. Diane Ghirardo and Joan Ockman (Cambridge: The MIT Press, 1982), 40.

2. Malcolm Quantrill, *The Environmental Memory* (New York: Schocken Books, 1987), 48.

3. Carl G. Jung, *The Basic Writings of C. G. Jung,* ed. Violet Staub De Laszlo, 1938 (New York: Random House, 1959), 287.

4. Ibid., 288.

5. Carl G. Jung, *Memories, Dreams, Reflections,* recorded and edited by Aniela Jaffe, trans. Richard and Clara Winston (1961; New York: Vintage Books div. of Random House, 1973), 160.

6. Ibid., 161.

7. Gaston Bachelard, *The Poetics of Space,* trans. Maria Jolas (1958; Boston: Beacon Press, 1969), 4.

8. Ibid., 6.

9. Ibid., 8.

10. Ibid.

11. Jung, *Memories, Dreams, Reflections,*———160.

12. John Hejduk, *Mask of Medusa* (New York: Rizzoli International, 1983), 59.

13. Bachelard, *The Poetics of Space,*———47.

14. Ibid., 5.

15. Martin Heidegger, *Poetry, Language, Thought,* trans. Albert Hofstadter (New York: Harper & Row, Publishers, 1971), 157.

16. Ibid., 146.

17. Ibid., 154.

18. Ibid., 157.

19. Ibid., 161.

20. E. V. Walter, *Placeways: A Theory of the Human Environment* (Chapel Hill: The University of North Carolina Press, 1988), 145.

21. Martin Pawley, ''The Time House,'' in *Meaning in Architecture,* eds. Charles Jencks and George Baird (New York: George Braziller, 1970), 135.

22. Thomas Wolfe, *You Can't Go Home Again,* (1934; New York: Harper & Row, 1973), 10.

23. Quantrill, *The Environmental Memory,*———46.

24. Ibid., 47.

25. Walter, *Placeways,*———15.

26. Ibid., 21.

27. Daniele Baroni, *The Furniture of Gerrit Thomas Rietveld* (Woodbury, N.Y.: Barron's, 1978), 19.

28. Baroni, *The Furniture of Gerrit Thomas Rietveld,*——24.

29. Ibid.

30. Ibid., 26.

31. Quantrill, *The Environmental Memory,*——65.

32. Ibid., 64.

33. CIAM, "La Sarraz Declaration," (1928), trans. Michael Bullock (1970), in *Programs and Manifestoes on 20th-Century Architecture,* ed. Ulrich Conrads, 1964 (Cambridge: The MIT Press, 1975), 109.

34. Baroni, *The Furniture of Gerrit Thomas Rietveld,*——106.

35. Jung, *Memories, Dreams, Reflections,*——223.

36. Ibid., 224.

37. Ibid., 226.

38. Walter, *Placeways,*——142.

39. Ibid., 143.

40. Helen Dudar, "The Artful Addiction of Sigmund Freud," *Smithsonian* 21 (August 1990): 104.

41. Charles Moore, Gerald Allen, and Donlyn Lyndon, *The Place of Houses* (New York: Holt, Rinehart and Winston, 1974), 99.

42. Geoffrey Broadbent, "A Semiotic Programme for Architectural Psychology," in *Meaning and Behaviour in the Built Environment,* eds. Geoffrey Broadbent, Richard Bunt, and Tomas Llorens (New York: John Wiley & Sons, 1980), 338.

43. Umberto Eco, "Function and Sign: The Semiotics of Architecture," in *Sign, Symbols, and Architecture,* eds. Geoffrey Broadbent, Richard Bunt, and Charles Jencks, ed. (New York: John Wiley & Sons, 1980), 11.

44. Ibid., 12.

45. Ibid., 22.

46. Ibid.

47. Charles Jencks, "Semiology & Architecture," in *Meaning in Architecture, eds.*——13.

48. Ibid., 16.

49. Pawley, "The Time House,"——123.

50. Ibid., 126.

51. Ibid., 129.

52. Ibid., 143.

53. Geoffrey Broadbent, "General Introduction," in *Signs, Symbols, and Architecture, eds.*——3.

54. Ibid., 4.

55. Bill Hillier, and Julienne Hanson, *The Social Logic of Space* (1984; New York: Cambridge University Press, 1988), 1.

56. Ibid., 2.

57. Ibid., 9.

58. Ibid., 19.

59. Ibid., 20.

60. Ibid.

61. Ibid., 144.

62. Ibid.

63. Jill Stoner, "The Party Wall as the Architecture of Sharing," in *New Households New Housing,* eds. Karen A. Franck, Sherry Ahrentzen (New York: Van Nostrand Reinhold, 1989), 127.

64. Stoner, "The Party Wall as the Architecture of Sharing,"———127.

65. David Canter and Stephen Tagg, "The Empirical Classification of Building Aspects and Their Attributes," in *Meaning and Behaviour in the Built Environment,*———1.

66. Ibid., 2.

67. Ibid., 16.

68. Broadbent, "A Semiotic Programme for Architectural Psychology,"———320.

69. Ibid., 323.

70. S. Wapner, B. Kaplan, and S. B. Cohen, "An Organismic-Developmental Perspective for Understanding Transactions of Men and Environments," in *Meaning and Behaviour in the Built Environment,*———225.

71. Ibid.

72. Broadbent, "A Semiotic Programme for Architectural Psychology,"———336.

73. Robert Gutman, "What Schools of Architecture Expect From Sociology," *Journal of Architectural Education* (March 1968): 69.

74. Constance Perin, *With Man in Mind: An Interdisciplinary Prospectus for Environmental Design* (Cambridge: The MIT Press, 1970), 13.

75. Ibid., 59.

76. Ibid.

77. Ibid., 60.

78. Ibid., 67.

79. Ibid., 42.

80. Ibid.

81. Ibid., 44.

82. Rene Dubos, "Environmental Determinants of Human Life," in *Environmental Influences,* ed. David C. Glass (New York: Rockfeller University Press and Russell Sage Foundation, 1968), 153.

83. Charles Moore, Gerald Allen, and Donlyn Lyndon, *The Place of Houses* (New York: Holt, Rinehart and Winston, 1974), viii.

84. Moore, Allen, and Lyndon, *The Place of Houses,*———49.

85. Karen A. Franck and Sherry Ahrentzen, ed., *New Households New Housing* (New York: Van Nostrand Reinhold, 1989), xii.

86. Daralice D. Boles, "P/A Inquiry: Aging in Place in the 1990's," *Progressive Architecture* (November 1989): 86.

87. Ibid., 84.

88. Sandra C. Howell, "Elderly Housing: Warping the Design Process," *Progessive Architecture* (July 1984): 86.

89. Elena Marcheso Moreno, ''Cohousing Comes to the U.S.,'' *Architecture* (July 1989): 64.

90. Jacqueline Leavitt, ''Two Prototypical Designs for Single Parents,'' in *New Households New Housing,* eds. Franck and Ahrentzen, 1989, 170.

91. ''Design Awards/Competitions: A New American House,'' *Architectural Record* (August 1984): 64.

92. Ibid.

93. Moore, Allen, and Lyndon, *The Place of Houses,*——274.

94. William A. Coles, ''The Genesis of a Classic,'' (1978), in *The Decoration of Houses,* Wharton and Codman, Jr., xix.

Caption Notes

Chapter 1. The Role of Theory

1. Peter Selz, *Alberto Giacometti* (New York: The Museum of Modern Art, 1965), 44. Copyright 1991 ARS, N.Y./ADAGP.
2. Spiro Kostof, *A History of Architecture Settings and Rituals* (New York: Oxford University Press, 1985), 108.

Chapter 2. Form and Function

1. Hans M. Wingler, *The Bauhaus* (Cambridge: The MIT Press, 1969), 119.
2. Spiro Kostof, *A History of Architecture* (New York: Oxford University Press, 1985), 330.
3. Wingler, *The Bauhaus,*——312.
4. Paul Frankl, *Principles of Architectural History: The Four Phases of Architectural Style, 1420–1900,* trans. and ed. James F. O'Gorman (1914; Cambridge: The MIT Press, 1968), 65.
5. Philip Johnson, *Mies van der Rohe* (New York: The Museum of Modern Art, 1978), 30.
6. Nathan Knobler, *The Visual Dialogue* (New York: Holt, Rinehart and Winston, Inc., 1971), 340.
7. Rem Koolhass, *Delirious New York* (New York: Oxford University Press, 1978), 130.

Chapter 3. The Vocabulary of Design

1. Johannes Itten, *Design and Form* (New York: Van Nostrand Reinhold Company, 1975), 68.
2. Spiro Kostof, *History of Architecture Settings and Rituals* (New York: Oxford University Press, 1985), 742.

Chapter 4. The Grammar of Design

1. Michael Graves, ''The Necessity for Drawing: Tangible Speculation'' in *Architectural Design* (June 1977): 384.
2. Le Corbusier, *Towards a New Architecture,* trans. Frederick Etchells, (1927; New York: Holt, Rinehart and Winston, 1960), 186.
3. Stanley Tigerman, *Versus: An American Architect's Alternatives* (New York: Rizzoli, 1982), 132.

Chapter 5. Ordering Systems

1. Theo Van Doesburg, *Principles of Neo-Plastic Art* (1925; New York: New York Graphic Society Ltd., 1968), 15.

2. Le Corbusier, *The Modulor: A Harmonious Measure to the Human Scale Universally Applicable to Architecture and Mechanics* (Cambridge: Harvard University Press, 1954).

Chapter 6. Seminal Viewpoints

1. Marcus Vitruvius, *The Ten Books on Architecture* (1st century B.C.), trans. Morris Hicky Morgan (1914; New York: Dover Publications, Inc., 1960), 6.

2. Ibid., 86.

3. James S. Ackerman, *Palladio* (New York: Penguin Books, 1966), 40.

4. Robert Frank McAlpine, ''The Southern Vernacular: A Regional Experience,'' *Journal of Interior Design Education and Research*, 13, no. 1 (Spring 1987): 5.

Chapter 7. The 19th Century

1. Eugène-Emmanuel Viollet-le-Duc, *Lectures on Architecture*, vol. 2, trans. Benjamin Bucknall. (1872; New York: Dover Publications, 1987), 120.

Chapter 8. Systematic Applications

1. Sir Francis Watson, *The History of Furniture* (New York: Crescent Books, 1982), 239.

2. Eugène-Emmanuel Viollet-le-Duc, *Lectures on Architecture*, vol. 2, trans. Benjamin Bucknall (1872; New York: Dover Publications, Inc., 1987), 359.

3. Gwendolyn Wright, *Moralism and the Model Home* (Chicago: The University of Chicago Press, 1980), 32.

Chapter 11. The Human Dimension

1. Siegfried Giedion, *Mechanization Takes Command: A Contribution to Anonymous History* (New York: W.W. Norton & Company, 1969), 523.

2. Leonard E. Ladd, *Specification forming part of Letters Patent No. 430, 480, dated June 17, 1890;* United States Patent Office.

3. Dolores Hayden, *The Grand Domestic Revolution: A History of Feminist Designs for American Homes, Neighborhoods, and Cities* (Cambridge: The MIT Press, 1981), 284.

Chapter 12. The Space Within

1. Rudolf Wittkower, *Art and Architecture in Italy, 1600–1750,* (1958; New York: Penguin Books, 1980), 193.

2. Ibid., 398.

3. Robert T. Jones, ed., *Authentic Small Houses of the Twenties* (1929; New York: Dover Publications, 1987), 255.

4. Monica Geran, "Perceived Perspectives," *Interior Design* (June 1986), 300.

Chapter 13. The Enclosure Revealed

1. E.H. Gombrich, *The Sense of Order: A Study in the Psychology of Decorative Art* (Ithaca, N.Y.: Cornell University Press, 1979), 122.

Chapter 14. Archetypes and Ethics

1. Dominique de Menil, foreword, J.-C. Lemagny, introduction, *Visionary Architects: Boulle, Ledoux, Lequeu* (Houston: University of St. Thomas, 1968), 227.

2. John Hejduk, *Mask of Medusa* (New York: Rizzoli International, 1985), 59.

3. Carl Jung, 26 July 1934 letter. In *C. G. Jung Word and Image*, ed. Aniela Jaffe (Princeton, N.J.: Princeton University Press, 1979), 196.

4. Robert A. Ivy Jr., " 'A City Set Apart' for the Elderly," *Architecture*, 78 (July 1989): 61.

Color Plates Notes

1. David Dunster, ed., *John Soane* (New York: St. Martin's Press, 1983), 34.

2. Paul M. Sachner, "The Lords of Discipline," in *Architectural Record Interiors 1986*, vol. 174, no. 11 (Mid-September 1986), 122.

3. Edie Lee Cohen, "Multiple Talents," *Interior Design*, 61 (May 1990), 209.

4. Hiroshi Watanabe, "Fire and Ice," *Progressive Architecture* (February 1991), 66.

Selected
Readings

Aalto, Alvar. *Sketches*. Edited by Goran Schildt. Translated by Stuart Wrede. Cambridge: The MIT Press, 1978.

Abercrombie, Stanley. *A Philosophy of Interior Design*. New York: Harper & Row Publishers, 1990.

———. "The Plan as Determinant of Movement." *AIA Journal*. (October 1982): 72–77.

Ackerman, James S. *The Architecture of Michelangelo*. 1961. 2d ed. Chicago: The University of Chicago Press, 1986.

———. *Palladio*. 1966. Reprint. New York: Penguin Books, 1979.

———. "The History of Design and the Design of History." *Culture and the Social Vision*. Vol. 4 of *Via*. Edited by Mark A. Hewitt, Benjamin Kracauer, John Massengale, and Michael McDonough. Cambridge: The Graduate School of Fine Arts University of Pennsylvania and The MIT Press (1980): 12–18.

Adam, Robert, and James Adam. *The Works in Architecture of Robert and James Adam*. 1773–1822. Edited by Robert Oresko. New York: St. Martin's Press, 1975.

Albers, Josef. *Interaction of Color*. 1963. Revised edition. New Haven: Yale University Press, 1975.

Alberti, Leon Battista. *On Painting*. 1435–6. Translated by John R. Spencer. 1956. Revised. New Haven: Yale University Press, 1966.

———. *The Ten Books of Architecture*. 1485. Translated by Giacomo James Leoni. 1755. New York: Dover Publications, Inc., 1986.

Alexander, Christopher, Sara Ishikawa, Murray Silverstein, with Max Jacobson, Ingrid Fiksdahl-King, Shlomo Angel. *A Pattern Language: Towns, Buildings, Construction*. New York: Oxford University Press, 1977.

Allen, Gerald, and Richard Oliver. *Architectural Drawing: The Art and the Process*. New York: Whitney Library of Design, 1981.

Allen, Polly Wynn. *Building Domestic Liberty: Charlotte Perkins Gilman's Architectural Feminism*. Amherst: The University of Massachusetts Press, 1988.

Altman, Irwin, and Carol M. Werner, eds. *Home Environments*. Vol 8 of *Human Behavior and Environment: Advances in Theory and Research*. New York: Plenum Press, 1985.

Ambasz, Emilio. *The Architecture of Luis Barragán*. New York: The Museum of Modern Art, 1976.

Anderson, Grace. "Object of Desire." *Record Interiors 1986.* 174 (Mid-September, 1986): 100–3.

"The Apartment-House." *The American Architect and Building News.* 27 (January-March 1890): 3–5.

Ardrey, Robert. *The Social Contract: A Personal Inquiry into the Evolutionary Sources of Order and Disorder.* New York: Atheneum, 1970.

——. *The Territorial Imperative: A Personal Inquiry into the Animal Origins of Property and Nations.* New York: Dell Publishing Co., Inc., 1966.

Arnell, Peter, and Ted Bickford, eds. *James Stirling Buildings and Projects.* New York: Rizzoli International Publications, Inc., 1985.

Arnheim, Rudolf. *Art and Visual Perception: A Psychology of the Creative Eye.* 1954. Expanded and revised edition. Berkeley: University of California Press, 1974.

——. *The Dynamics of Architectural Form.* Berkeley: University of California Press, 1977.

——. *Entropy and Art: An Essay on Disorder and Order.* Berkeley: University of California Press, 1971. Paperback edition 1974.

——. "Buildings as Percepts." *Architecture and Visual Perception.* Vol. 6 of *Via.* Edited by Alice Gray Read, Peter C. Doo with Joseph Burton. Cambridge: The Graduate School of Fine Arts University of Pennsylvania and The MIT Press (1983): 13–9.

——. "A Review of Proportion." *Journal of Aesthetics and Art Criticism.* 14 (September 1955): 44–57.

Auden, W. H. *About the House.* New York: Random House, 1959.

Bachelard, Gaston. *The Poetics of Space.* 1958. Translated by Maria Jolas. The Orion Press, Inc. 1964. Foreword by Etienne Gilson. Boston: Beacon Press by arrangement with Grossman Publishers, Inc., 1969.

Banham, Reyner. *Theory and Design in the First Machine Age.* 2d ed. Cambridge: The MIT Press, 1960.

Baroni, Daniele. *The Furniture of Gerrit Thomas Rietveld.* Foreword by Filippo Alison. Woodbury, N.Y.: Barron's, 1978.

Bayer, Herbert, Ludwig Grote, Dieter Honisch, and Hans M. Wingler, Preparation Committee. Wulf Herzogenrath, Preparation of Catalog. *Bauhaus: 50 Years German Exhibition.* Chicago: Illinois Institute of Technology, 1969.

Bechtel, Robert B. *Enclosing Behavior.* Stroudsburg, Penn.: Dowden, Hutchinson & Ross, Inc., 1977.

Beeby, Thomas H. "The Grammar of Ornament/Ornament as Grammar." *Ornament.* Vol. 3 of *Via.* Edited by Stephen Kieran. Cambridge: The Graduate School of Fine Arts University of Pennsylvania and The MIT Press (1977): 10–29.

Beecher, Catharine E., and Harriet Beecher Stowe. *The American Women's Home, or, Principles of Domestic Science; Being a Guide to the Formation and Maintenance of Economical, Healthful Beautiful and Christian Homes.* 1869. Introduction by Joseph Van Why. Watkins Glen, N.Y.: Library of Victorian Culture American Life Foundation, 1979.

Belluschi, Pietro, Ralph Flewelling, J. Byers Hays, Robert M. Little, Louis Skidmore, Philip Will, Jr., and Hugh A. Stubbins, Jr., Chairman. "Report of the Jury: Pencil Points—Pittsburgh Architectural Competition." *Pencil Points.* 26 (May 1945): 54+.

Bernstein, Mark. "Charles Kettering: Automative Genius." *Smithsonian.* 19 (July 1988): 125–135.

Birren, Faber. *Color Psychology and Color Therapy: A Factual Study of the Influence of Color on Human Life.* 1950. New Hyde Park, N. Y.: University Books, Inc., 1961.

Blackwell, William. *Geometry in Architecture.* New York: John Wiley & Sons, 1984.

Blake, William. "The Tyger," *Blake Complete Writings with Variant Readings.* Edited by Geoffrey Keynes. 1957. New York: Oxford University Press, 1966.

Blondel, Jacques François. *Cours d'architecture.* Paris: 1771–7.

———. *De la distribution des Maisons de plaisance.* 1737–8.

Bloomer, Kent C., and Charles W. Moore with a contribution by Robert J. Yudell. *Body, Memory, and Architecture.* New Haven: Yale University Press, 1977.

Blunt, Anthony, Alastair Laing, Christopher Tadgell, and Kerry Downes. *Baroque & Rococo: Architecture & Decoration.* Edited by Anthony Blunt. 1978. New York: Harper & Row, Publishers, 1982.

Boffrand, Gabriel-Germain. *Livre d'architecture.* Paris: 1754.

Boger, Louise Ade. *The Complete Guide to Furniture Styles.* 1959. Enlarged Edition. New York: Charles Scribner's Sons, 1969.

Bold, John. *John Webb: Architectural Theory and Practice in the Seventeenth Century.* Oxford: Clarendon Press, 1989.

Broadbent, Geoffrey, Richard Bunt, and Charles Jencks, eds. *Sign, Symbols, and Architecture.* New York: John Wiley & Sons, 1980.

Broadbent, Geoffrey, Richard Bunt, and Tomas Llorens, eds. *Meaning and Behaviour in the Built Environment.* New York: John Wiley & Sons, 1980.

Buffet-Challié, Laurence. *The Art Nouveau Style.* Translated by Geoffrey Williams. New York: Rizzoli International Publications, Inc., 1982.

Canter, David. *Psychology for Architects.* New York: Halsted Press a division of John Wiley & Sons, Inc., 1974.

Canter, D., and S. Tagg. "The Empirical Classification of Building Aspects and Their Attributes." In *Meaning and Behaviour in the Built Environment.* Edited by Geoffrey Broadbent, Richard Bunt, and Tomas Llorens, 1–19. New York: John Wiley & Sons, 1980.

Caplan, Ralph. *The Design of Herman Miller.* New York: Whitney Library of Design, 1976.

Chadwick, George F. *The Works of Sir Joseph Paxton 1803–1865.* London: The Architectural Press London, 1961.

Chang, Amos Ih Tiao. *The Tao of Architecture.* Princeton, N.J.: Princeton University Press, 1956.

Chicago Chapter American Institute of Architects. *The Divine Detail.* Vol. 6 of *Architecture Chicago.* Chicago: Chicago Chapter AIA, 1988.

Clark, Kenneth. *The Gothic Revival: An Essay in the History of Taste.* 1928. New York: Harper & Row, Publishers, 1974.

Clark, Roger H., and Michael Pause. *Precedents in Architecture.* New York: Van Nostrand Reinhold Company, 1985.

Charlish, Anne, ed. *The History of Furniture.* Introduction by Sir Francis Watson. 1976. Revised. New York: Crescent Books, 1982.

Cohen, Edie Lee. "ICF's Kitchen Design Competition." *Interior Design.* 56 (April 1985): 196–201.

———. "Multiple Talents." *Interior Design.* 61 (May 1990): 202–9.

Collins, Peter. *Changing Ideals in Modern Architecture: 1750–1950.* 1965. Reprint. Kingston: McGill-Queen's University Press, 1984.

Colquhoun, Alan. *Modernity and the Classical Tradition: Architectural Essays 1980–1987.* Cambridge: The MIT Press, 1989.

———. "Typology & Design Method." In *Meaning in Architecture.* Edited by Charles Jencks and George Baird, 267–77. 1969. New York: George Braziller, 1970.

Conrads, Ulrich, ed. *Programs and Manifestoes on 20th-Century Architecture.* 1964. Translated by Michael Bullock. 1970. Cambridge: The MIT Press, 1975.

Coomaraswamy, Ananda K. *Figures of Speech or Figures of Thought: Collected Essays on the Traditional or "Normal" View of Art.* Second Series. London: Luzac & Co., 1946.

Cooper, Clare. "The House as Symbol of the Self." In *Designing for Human Behavior: Architecture and the Behavioral Sciences.* Edited by Jon Lang, Charles Burnette, Walter Moleski, and David Vachon, 130–46. Stroudsburg, Penn.: Dowden, Hutchinson & Ross, Inc., 1974.

Cornell, Elias. *Humanistic Inquiries into Architecture.* Part I–III. Transactions of Chalmers University of Technology, Nr. 219. Goteborg, Sweden: Elanders Boktryckeri Aktiebolag, 1959.

Crowe, Norman, and Paul Laseau. *Visual Notes: for Architects and Designers.* New York: Van Nostrand Reinhold Company, 1984.

Curtis, William J. R. *Modern Architecture Since 1900.* 1982. Englewood Cliffs, N.J.: Prentice Hall, Inc., 1983.

De Fusco, Renato. *Le Corbusier, Designer Furniture, 1929.* Woodbury, N. Y.: Barron's, 1977.

"Design Awards/Competitions: A New American House." *Architectural Record.* (August 1984): 64–5.

Dewey, John. *Art as Experience.* 1934. New York: Capricorn Books, G. P. Putnam's Sons, 1958.

Diekman, Norman, and John Pile. *Drawing Interior Architecture.* New York: Whitney Library of Design, 1983.

Dondis, Donis A. *A Primer of Visual Literacy.* Cambridge: The MIT Press, 1973.

Downing, A.J. *The Architecture of Country Houses; including, Designs for Cottages, and Farm-Houses, and Villas, with Remarks on Interiors, Furniture, and the best Modes of Warming and Ventilating.* 1850. New York: Dover Publications, Inc., 1969.

Doxiadis, C. A. *Architectural Space in Ancient Greece.* 1937. Translated and edited by Jacqueline Tyrwhitt. Cambridge: The Massachusetts Institute of Technology, 1972.

Durand, Jean-Nicolas-Louis. *Précis des leçons d'architecture données à l'École royale polytéchnique.* 1802–5. Paris: 1809.

————. *Recueil et parallèle des édifices de tout genre, anciens et modernes, remarquables par leur beauté, par leur grandeur ou par leur singularité, et dessinér sur une même échelle.* 2 vols. Paris: 1800.

Drexler, Arthur, ed. *The Architecture of the École des Beaux-Arts.* New York: The Museum of Modern Art, 1977.

Eastlake, Charles L. *Hints on Household Taste: The Classic Handbook of Victorian Interior Decoration.* 1868. 4th ed. 1878. Reprint. Introduction by John Gloag. New York: Dover Publications, Inc., 1986.

Eco, Umberto. "Function and Sign: The Semiotics of Architecture." In *Signs, Symbols, and Architecture.* Edited by Geoffrey Broadbent, Richard Bunt, and Charles Jencks, 11–69. New York: John Wiley & Sons, 1980.

"Efficiency Methods Applied to Kitchen Design." *The Architectural Record.* 67, no. 3 (March 1930): 291–294.

Evans, Robin. "Figures, Doors and Passages." *Architectural Design.* 48, no. 4 (1978): 267–78.

Fallico, Arturo B. *Art and Existentialism.* Englewood Cliffs, N.J.: Prentice Hall, Inc., 1962.

Fathy, Hassan. *Architecture for the Poor: An Experiment in Rural Egypt.* Chicago: University of Chicago Press, 1973.

Fehrman, Cherie, and Kenneth Fehrman. *Postwar Interior Design: 1945–1960.* New York: Van Nostrand Reinhold Company, 1987.

Feldman, Edmund Burke. *Varieties of Visual Experience: Art as Image and Idea.* 2d ed. Revised and Enlarged. New York: Harry N. Abrams, Inc., 1972.

Finley, Ruth E. *The Lady of Godey's: Sarah Josepha Hale.* Philadelphia: J. B. Lippincott Company, 1931.

Frampton, Kenneth. *Modern Architecture: A Critical History.* New York: Oxford University Press, 1980.

Franck, Karen A., and Sherry Ahrentzen, eds. *New Households New Housing.* New York: Van Nostrand Reinhold, 1989.

Frank Paul. The Gothic: Literary Sources and Interpretations through Eight Centuries. Princeton, N.J.: Princeton University Press, 1960.

————. *Principles of Architectural History: The Four Phases of Architectural Style, 1420–1900.* 1914. Translated and edited by James F. O'Gorman. Foreword by James S. Ackerman. Cambridge: The Massachusetts Institute of Technology, 1968.

Frascari, Marco. "The Tell-The-Tale Detail." *The Building of Architecture.* Vol. 7 of *Via.* Edited by Paula Behrens and Anthony Fisher. Cambridge:

The Graduate School of Fine Arts University of Pennsylvania and The MIT Press (1984): 23–37.

Gandee, Charles K. "Tradition Rekindled." *Architectural Record.* (June 1983): 104–13.

Gehry, Frank. "Detailing." *Terrazzo.* (Spring 1989): 60–2.

Geran, Monica. "Perceived Perspectives." *Interior Design.* (June 1986): 296–301.

Ghyka, Matila. *The Geometry of Art and Life.* 1946. Slightly Corrected Republication. New York: Dover Publications, Inc., 1977.

Gibson, James J. *The Perception of the Visual World.* Boston: Houghton Mifflin Company and Cambridge: Riverside Press, 1950.

———. *The Senses Considered as Perceptual Systems.* Boston: Houghton Mifflin Company, 1966.

Giedion, Siegfried. *Mechanization Takes Command: A Contribution to Anonymous History.* 1948. New York: W. W. Norton & Company by arrangement with Oxford University Press, Inc., 1969.

———. *Space, Time and Architecture: The Growth of a New Tradition.* 1941. 8th Enlarged Printing. Cambridge: The Harvard University Press, 1949.

Gillette, King Camp. *The Human Drift.* 1894. Introduction by Kenneth M. Roemer. Delmar, N.Y.: Scholar's Facsimiles & Reprints, 1976.

Goethe, Johann Wolfgang von. *Theory of Colours.* 1810. Translated by Charles Lock Eastlake. 1840. Cambridge: The MIT Press, 1970.

Golledge, Reginald G. "Environmental Cognition." In *Handbook of Environmental Psychology.* Vol. 1. Edited by Daniel Stokols and Irwin Altman, 131–174. New York: John Wiley & Sons, 1987.

Gombrich, E. H. *Art and Illusion: A Study in the Psychology of Pictorial Representation.* Princeton, N. J.: Princeton University Press, 1969.

———. *The Sense of Order: A Study in the Psychology of Decorative Art.* Ithaca, N.Y.: Cornell University Press, 1979.

Gottlieb, Carla. *Beyond Modern Art.* New York: E. P. Dutton & Co., Inc., 1976.

Gravagnuolo, Benedetto. *Adolf Loos: Theory and Works.* 1982. Preface by Aldo Rossi. Translated by C. H. Evans. New York: Rizzoli International Publications, Inc., 1988.

Graves, Michael. "The Necessity for Drawing: Tangible Speculation." *Architectural Design.* 47 (June 1977): 384–94.

Greeley, William Roger. *The Essence of Architecture Being a Brief Essay upon the Principles of Composition.* New York: D. Van Nostrand Company Inc., 1927.

Greenberg, Jerald. "Equity and Workplace Status: A Field Experiment." *Journal of Applied Psychology.* 73 no. 4 (1988): 606–13.

Gropius, Walter. *Scope of Total Architecture.* 1943. New York: Collier Books, 1962.

Guadet, Julien. *Éléments et Théorie de l'Architecture.* 4 vols. Paris: Librairie de la Construction Moderne, 1909.

Gutman, Robert. "What Schools of Architecture Expect from Sociology." *Journal of Architectural Education.* (March 1968).

Habeeb, Virginia T. "Kitchens '85: New Attitudes and New Technology." *Interior Design.* 56 (April 1985): 202–9.

Hall, Edward T. *The Hidden Dimension.* 1966. Garden City, N.Y.: Anchor Books, 1969.

Halpin, JoBeth, and Theresa Luthman Angelini, eds. *Detail.* Vol. 3 of *Threshold: Journal of the School of Architecture, The University of Illinois at Chicago.* New York: Rizzoli International Publication, Inc., 1985.

Hambidge, Jay. *The Elements of Dynamic Symmetry.* 1919. Reprint of 1926 work. New York: Dover Publications, Inc., 1967.

Hanks, David A. *The Decorative Designs of Frank Lloyd Wright.* New York: E. P. Dutton, 1979.

Hauser, Arnold. *The Social History of Art.* 1951. 4 vols. Translated by Stanley Godman in collaboration with Arnold Hauser. New York: Vintage Books, 1960.

Hayden, Dolores. *The Grand Domestic Revolution: A History of Feminist Designs for American Homes, Neighborhoods, and Cities.* Cambridge: The MIT Press, 1981.

———. "Redesigning the American Dream." *Progressive Architecture.* 65 (July 1984): 85.

Hayward, D. Geoffrey. "Psychological Factors in the Use of Light and Lighting in Building." In *Designing for Human Behavior: Architecture and the Behavioral Sciences.* Edited by Jon Lang, Charles Burnette, Walter Moleski, and David Vachon, 120–9. Stroudsburg, Penn.: Dowden, Hutchinson & Ross, Inc., 1974.

Heft, Harry, and Joachim F. Wohlwill. "Environmental Cognition in Children." In *Handbook of Environmental Psychology,* Vol. 1. Edited by Daniel Stokols and Irwin Altman, 175–204. New York: John Wiley & Sons, 1987.

Heidegger, Martin. *Poetry, Language, Thought.* Translated, complied and introduced by Albert Hofstadter. New York: Harper & Row, 1971.

Hejduk, John. *Mask of Medusa.* New York: Rizzoli International, 1983.

Hillier, Bill, and Julienne Hanson. *The Social Logic of Space.* Cambridge: Cambridge University Press, 1984.

Hitchcock, Henry-Russell. *In the Nature of Materials: The Buildings of Frank Lloyd Wright 1887–1941.* 1942. New York: Da Capo Press, Inc., 1975.

Hochberg, Julian. "Visual Perception in Architecture." *Architecture and Visual Perception.* Vol. 6 of *Via.* Edited by Alice Gray Read, Peter C. Doo with Joseph Burton. Cambridge: The Graduate School of Fine Arts University of Pennsylvania and The MIT Press (1983): 27–45.

Hodgden, Lee. "The Interior Facade." *The Vertical Surface.* Vol. 3 of *The Cornell Journal of Architecture.* New York: The Cornell Journal of Architecture and Rizzoli International Publications, Inc. (Fall 1987): 30–43.

Hoffer, William. "A Magic Ratio Recurs Throughout Art and Nature." *Smithsonian* 6 (December 1975): 110–12+.

Howard, Deborah, and Malcolm Longair. "Harmonic Proportion and Palladio's *Quattro Libri." Journal of the Society of Architectural Historians.* 41:2 (May 1982): 116–42.

Howland, Edward. "The Social Palace at Guise." *Harper's New Monthly Magazine.* 44 no. 259 (December 1871): 701–16.

Itoh, Teiji. *Space & Illusion: In the Japanese Garden.* 1965. New York: John Weatherhill, Inc. and Kyoto: Tankosha, 1973.

Itten, Johannes. *Design and Form: The Basic Course at the Bauhaus and Later.* 1963. Revised. New York: Van Nostrand Reinhold Company, 1975.

———. *The Elements of Color: A Treatise on the Color System of Johannes Itten Based on His Book The Art of Color.* 1961. Edited by Faber Birren. Translated by Ernst Van Hagen. New York: Van Nostrand Reinhold Company, 1970.

Jencks, Charles. *Le Corbusier and the Tragic View of Architecture.* Cambridge: Harvard University Press, 1973.

———. *The Language of Post-Modern Architecture.* Revised. New York: Rizzoli International Publications, Inc., 1977.

———. "Semiology & Architecture." In *Meaning in Architecture.* Edited by Charles Jencks and George Baird. 1969. New York: George Braziller, 1970.

Johnson, Philip C. *Mies van der Rohe.* 1947. 3rd ed. revised. New York: The Museum of Modern Art, 1978.

Jones, Owen. *The Grammar of Ornament.* 1856. New York: Van Nostrand Reinhold Company, 1982.

Jones, Robert T., ed. *Authentic Small Houses of the Twenties.* Reprint of *Small Homes of Architectural Distinction: A Book of Suggested Plans Designed by the Architects' Small House Service Bureau, Inc.* 1929. New York: Dover Publications, Inc., 1987.

Jung, Carl G. *The Basic Writings of C. G. Jung.* 1938. Edited by Violet S. De Laszlo. New York: The Modern Library, 1959.

———. *Memories, Dreams, Reflections.* Recorded and edited by Aniela Jaffe. 1961. Translated by Richard and Clara Winston. Revised edition. New York: Vintage Books, 1973.

Jung, Carl G., and J.-L. von Franz, eds. *Man and His Symbols.* 1964. Reprint. Garden City, N.Y.: Doubleday & Company Inc., 1971.

Kahn, Louis. *Light is the Theme.* Compiled by Nell E. Johnson. 1975. Fort Worth, Tex.: Kimbell Art Foundation, 1978.

Kandinsky, Wassily. *Point and Line to Plane.* 1926. Translated by Howard Dearstyne and Hilla Rebay. Edited and prefaced by Hilla Rebay. 1947. New York: Dover Publication, Inc., 1979.

Kaufmann Jr., Edgar, ed. *Louis Sullivan and the Architecture of Free Enterprise.* Chicago: The Art Institute of Chicago, 1956.

Kaufmann, Emil. *Architecture in the Age of Reason: Baroque and Post-Baroque in England, Italy, and France.* 1955. Reprint. New York: Dover Publications, Inc., 1968.

Keane, Marc P. "Japanese Entrances: Cultural Symbols in the Landscape." *Landscape Architecture.* 78 (September/October 1988): 120–5.

Kepes, Gyorgy. *Language of Vision.* Introductions by S. Giedion, and S. I. Hayakawa. 1944. Chicago: Paul Theobald and Company, 1967.

King, Anthony D., ed. *Buildings and Society: Essays on the Social Development of the Built Environment.* London: Routledge & Kegan Paul, 1980.

Knobler, Nathan. *The Visual Dialogue: An Introduction to the Appreciation of Art.* 2d ed. New York: Holt, Rinehart and Winston, Inc., 1971.

Koolhaas, Rem. *Delirious New York: A Retroactive Manifesto for Manhattan.* New York: Oxford University Press, 1978.

Kostof, Spiro. *A History of Architecture: Settings and Rituals.* New York: Oxford University Press, 1985.

Küller, Rikard, *Non-Visual Effects of Light and Colour.* Annotated Bibliography. Document D15:81. Stockholm: Swedish Council for Building Research, 1981.

Krier, Rob. *Architectural Composition.* New York: Rizzoli International Publication, Inc., 1988.

Labrouste, Henri Leon. *Esthétique monumentale.* Paris: Schmid, 1902.

Ladd, Leonard E. *Specification forming part of Letters Patent No. 430, 480.* United States Patent Office. June 17, 1890.

Lang, Jon. *Creating Architectural Theory: The Role of the Behavioral Sciences in Environmental Design.* New York: Van Nostrand Reinhold Company, 1987.

Lang, Jon, Charles Burnette, Walter Moleski, and David Vachon, eds. *Designing for Human Behavior: Architecture and the Behavioral Sciences.* Stroudsburg, Penn.: Dowden, Hutchinson & Ross, Inc., 1974.

Latham, Ian, ed. *New Free Style: Arts and Crafts, Art Nouveau, Secession.* London: Architectural Design and Academy Editions, 1980.

Laugier, Marc-Antoine. *An Essay on Architecture.* 1753. Translated by Wolfgang and Anni Herrmann. Los Angeles: Hennessey & Ingalls, Inc., 1977.

Lawlor, Robert. *Sacred Geometry: Philosophy and Practice.* London: Thames and Hudson Ltd., 1982.

Lawrence, Roderick J. *Housing, Dwelling and Homes: Design Theory, Research and Practice.* Foreword by David Stea. New York: John Wiley & Sons, 1987.

Le Corbusier. *The Decorative Art of Today.* 1925. Translated and introduced by James Dunnett. Cambridge: The MIT Press, 1987.

———. *Towards a New Architecture.* 1927. Translated by Frederick Etchells. New York: Holt, Rinehart and Winston, 1960.

———. *The Modulor: A Harmonious Measure to the Human Scale Universally Applicable to Architecture and Mechanics.* Cambridge: Harvard University Press, 1954.

Lesser, George. *Gothic Cathedrals and Sacred Geometry.* Vol. 1. London: Alec Tiranti, 1957.

Lieberman, William S., ed. *Modern Masters: Manet to Matisse.* New York: The Museum of Modern Art, 1975.

"Life Presents . . . A Portfolio of Ideas for Home Planning." *Life,* 18, no.

22 (May 28, 1945): 49+.

Lynch, Kevin. *The Image of the City.* Cambridge: The Technology Press & Harvard University Press, 1960.

Macleod, Robert. *Charles Rennie Mackintosh: Architect and Artist.* E. P. Dutton, Inc., 1983.

Mahnke, Frank H., and Rudolf H. Mahnke. *Color and Light in Manmade Environments.* New York: Van Nostrand Reinhold Company, 1987.

March, Lionel, and Philip Steadman. *The Geometry of Environment: An Introduction to Spatial Organization.* 1971. Cambridge: The MIT Press, 1974.

Marks, Robert, and R. Buckminster Fuller. *The Dymaxion World of Buckminster Fuller.* 1960. Revised. Garden City, N.Y.: Anchor Press Edition, 1973.

Maslow, Abraham. *Motivation and Personality.* 2d ed. New York: Harper & Row, 1970.

Mason, Joseph B. *History of Housing in the U. S. 1930–1980.* Houston, Tex.: Gulf Publishing Company, 1982.

Mayer, Harold M., and Richard C. Wade with the assistance of Glen E. Holt. *Chicago: Growth of a Metropolis.* Chicago: The University of Chicago Press, 1969.

McAlpine, Robert Frank. "The Southern Vernacular: A Regional Experience." *Journal of Interior Design Education and Research.* 13, no. 1 (Spring 1987): 3–8.

Mehrabian, Albert. *Public Places and Private Spaces: The Psychology of Work, Play, and Living Environments.* New York: Basic Books, Inc., 1976.

Middleton, Robin, and David Watkin. *Neoclassical and 19th Century Architecture.* 1977. New York: Harry N. Abrams, Inc., 1980.

Moore, Charles, and Gerald Allen. *Dimensions: Space, Shape & Scale in Architecture.* New York: Architectural Record Books, 1976.

Moore, Charles, Gerald Allen, and Donlyn Lyndon. *The Place of Houses: Three Architects Suggest Ways to Build and Inhabit Houses.* New York: Holt, Rinehart and Winston, 1974.

Mott, Frank Luther. *A History of American Magazines: 1885–1905.* Vol. 4. Cambridge: Harvard University Press, 1957.

Mumford, Lewis. *The Culture of Cities.* 1938. Harcourt Brace Jovanovich, Inc., 1970.

Mumford, Lewis, ed. *Roots of Contemporary American Architecture: 37 Essays from the Mid-Nineteenth Century to the Present.* 1952. Revised 1959. New York: Dover Publications, Inc., 1972.

Naylor, Gillian. *The Arts and Crafts Movement: A Study of its Sources, Ideals, and Influence on Design Theory.* 1971. Cambridge: The MIT Press, 1980.

Nelson, George. *Problems of Design.* New York: Whitney Publications Inc., 1957.

Norberg-Schulz, Christian. *Intentions in Architecture.* The Massachusetts Institute of Technology, 1965. Cambridge: The MIT Press Paperback Edition, 1968.

————. *Late Baroque and Rococo Architecture.* 1972. New York: Rizzoli International Publications, Inc., 1985.

Page, Marian. *Furniture Designed by Architects.* 1980. New York: Whitney Library of Design, 1983.

Palladio, Andrea. *The Four Books of Architecture.* 1570. Republication of the work. Translated by Isaac Ware in 1738. Introduction by Adolf K. Placzek. New York: Dover Publications, Inc., 1965.

Pawley, Martin. *Theory and Design in the Second Machine Age.* Cambridge: Basil Blackwell Ltd., 1990.

————. "The Time House: Or Argument for an Existential Dwelling." In *Meaning in Architecture.* Edited by Charles Jencks and George Baird. 1969. New York: George Braziller, 1970.

Perin, Constance. *With Man in Mind: An Interdisciplinary Prospectus for Environmental Design.* Cambridge: The MIT Press, 1970.

Petherbridge, Deanna. "At the Other End of the Line." *The Architectural Review.* 170, no. 1014 (August 1981): 77–80.

Pevsner, Nikolaus. *An Outline of European Architecture.* 1943. Reprint with new format and revised bibliography. New York: Pelican Books, 1974.

————. *Pioneers of Modern Design: From William Morris to Walter Gropius.* 1936. Revised. New York: Penguin Books, Inc., 1986.

————. *The Sources of Modern Architecture and Design.* 1968. New York: Oxford University Press, 1979.

Piaget, Jean. *The Mechanisms of Perception.* 1961. Translated by G. N. Seagrim. New York: Basic Books, Inc., 1969.

Piaget, Jean, and Barbel Inhelder. *The Child's Conception of Space.* 1948. Translated by F. J. Langdon, and J. L. Lunzer. London: Routledge & Kegan Paul, 1956.

Placzek, Adolf K., ed. *Macmillan Encyclopedia of Architects.* New York: The Free Press, 1982.

Praz, Mario. *An Illustrated History of Interior Decoration: From Pompeii to Art Nouveau.* 1944–63. Translated by William Weaver. New York: Thames and Hudson, Inc., 1982.

Pugin, Augustus Welby Northmore. *Contrasts; or, a Parallel between the Noble Edifices of the Fourteenth and Fifteenth Centuries, and Similar Buildings of the Present Day; Shewing the Present Decay of Taste.* 1836. Reprint of 1841, 2d ed. Introduction by H. R. Hitchcock. Leicester University Press, 1969.

————. *The True Principles of Pointed or Christian Architecture; set Forth in Two Lectures Delivered at St. Marie's, Oscott.* 1841. Reprint of 1853 Impression. Oxford: St. Barnabas Press, 1969.

Quantrill, Malcolm. *The Environmental Memory: Man and Architecture in the Landscape of Ideas.* New York: Schocken Books, 1987.

Rasmussen, Steen Eiler. *Experiencing Architecture.* 2d ed. Cambridge: The MIT Press, 1959.

Read, Herbert. *The Origins of Form in Art.* New York: Horizon Press, 1965.

Rossi, Aldo. *The Architecture of the City.* 1966. Introduction by Peter Eisenman. Translated by Diane Ghirardo and Joan Ockman. Revised for the American Edition by Aldo Rossi and Peter Eisenman. Cambridge: The MIT Press, 1984.

Rossotti, Hazel. *Colour: Why the World Isn't Grey.* 1983. Princeton, N.J.: Princeton University Press, 1985.

Rousseau, Jean-Jacques. *A Discourse on Inequality.* 1754. Translated by Maurice Cranston. New York: Penguin Books, 1984.

Ruskin, John. *The Seven Lamps of Architecture.* 1849. New York: Farrar, Straus and Giroux, 1979.

––––––. *The Stones of Venice.* New York: International Book Company, 1851.

Rybczynski, Witold. *Home: A Short History of an Idea.* New York: Viking Penguin, Inc., 1986. New York: Penguin Books, 1987.

Rykwert, Joseph, guest ed., and Haig Beck, ed. "Leonis Baptiste Alberti." *Architectural Design.* 49, no. 5-6, (1979).

Saliga, Pauline. "The Types and Styles of Architectural Drawings." *Chicago Architects Design: A Century of Architectural Drawing from The Art Institute of Chicago.* Edited by John Zukowsky and Pauline Saliga, 20-30. Chicago: The Art Institute of Chicago and Rizzoli International Publications, Inc., 1982.

Santayana, George. *The Sense of Beauty: Being the Outline of Aesthetic Theory.* 1896. Reprint. New York: Dover Publications, Inc., 1955.

Scheerbart, Paul. *Glass Architecture.* 1914. Edited by Dennis Sharp. Translated by James Palmes. New York: Praeger Publishers, 1972.

Scruton, Roger. *The Aesthetics of Architecture.* Princeton, N.J.: Princeton University Press, 1979.

Scully Jr., Vincent. *The Earth, The Temple, and The Gods.* 1962. New Haven: Yale University Press, 1979.

––––––. *Modern Architecture: The Architecture of Democracy.* 1961. New York: George Braziller, 1974.

Sekler, Eduard F. "The Stoclet House by Josef Hoffmann." In *Essays in the History of Architecture Presented to Rudolf Wittkower.* Edited by Douglas Fraser, Howard Hibbard, and Milton J. Lewine. New York: Phaidon Publishers, Inc., 1967.

Selz, Peter. *Alberto Giacometti.* New York: The Museum of Modern Art, 1965.

Sewter, A. C. *Baroque and Rococo.* London: Thames and Hudson, Ltd., 1972.

Sharpe, Deborah T. *The Psychology of Color and Design.* 1974. Totowa, N.J.: Littlefield, Adams & Co., 1981.

Smith, C. Ray. *Supermannerism: New Attitudes in Post-Modern Architecture.* New York: E. P. Dutton, 1977.

––––––. "Burolandschaft U.S.A." *Progressive Architecture* (May 1968): 174-7.

Sommer, Robert. *Personal Space: The Behavioral Basis of Design.* Englewood Cliffs, N.J.: Prentice Hall, Inc., 1969.

Sottsass, Ettore. "Travel Notes." *Terrazzo* (Spring 1989): 23-38.

Stambaugh, John E. *The Ancient Roman City*. Baltimore: The Johns Hopkins University Press, 1988.

Steiner, Frances H. *French Iron Architecture*. Ann Arbor, Mich.: UMI Research Press, 1984.

Stephens, Suzanne. "Taste in America." *Progressive Architecture* (June 1978): 49–51.

Stern, Robert A.M. "Drawing Towards a More Modern Architecture." *Architectural Design*. 47, no. 6 (1977): 382–3.

Stoner, Jill. "The Party Wall as the Architecture of Sharing." In *New Households New Housing*. Edited by Karen A. Franck and Sherry Ahrentzen, 127–40. New York: Van Nostrand Reinhold, 1989.

Strasser, Susan. *Never Done: A History of American Housework*. New York: Pantheon Books, 1982.

Suger, Abbot. *Abbot Suger on the Abbey Church of St.-Denis and Its Art Treasures*. 1140–1. Edited, translated and annotated by Erwin Panofsky. 1946. 2d by Gerda Panofsky-Soergel. Princeton, N.J.: Princeton University Press, 1979.

Sullivan, Louis H. *Kindergarten Chats: And Other Writings*. 1918. Revised. New York: Dover Publications, Inc., 1979.

———. *A System of Architectural Ornament: According with a Philosophy of Man's Powers*. New York: Press of the American Institute of Architects, Inc., 1924.

Summerson, John. *Heavenly Mansions: And Other Essays on Architecture*. New York: W. W. Norton & Company, 1963.

———. "What is Ornament and What is Not." *Ornament*. Vol. 3 of *Via*. Edited by Stephen Kieran. Cambridge: The Graduate School of Fine Arts University of Pennsylvania and the MIT Press (1977): 4-9.

Tanizaki, Jun'ichiro. *In Praise of Shadows*. 1933. Translated by Thomas J. Harper and Edward G. Seidensticker. Foreword by Charles Moore. Afterword by Thomas J. Harper. New Haven, Conn.: Leete's Island Books, Inc., 1977.

Taylor, Frederick Winslow. *The Principles of Scientific Management*. New York: Harper & Brothers Publishers, 1911.

Thébert, Yvon. "Private Life and Domestic Architecture in Roman Africa." Foreword by Paul Veyne. In *From Pagan Rome to Byzantium*. Vol. 1 of *A History of Private Life*. Edited by Paul Veyne, 313–409. 1985. Translated by Arthur Goldhammer. Cambridge: The Belknap Press of Harvard University Press, 1987.

Tigerman, Stanley. *Versus: An American Architect's Alternatives*. New York: Rizzoli, 1982.

Tolkien, J. R. R. *The Hobbit: or There and Back Again*. 1937. Revised. New York: Ballantine Books, 1966.

Tolstoy, Leo N. *What is Art?* 1896. Translated by Almyer Maude. Introduction by Vincent Tomas. Indianapolis, Ind.: The Bobbs-Merrill Educational Publishing, 1960.

Troy, Nancy J. *The De Stijl Environment*. Cambridge: The MIT Press, 1983.

Tschumi, Bernard. "Sequences." *Architecture Sequences.* Organized by Bernard Tschumi. New York: Artists Space, January 17–February 28, 1981.

Tsu, Lao. *Eleven.* In *Tao Te Ching.* 6th Century B.C. Translated by Gia-Fu Feng and Jane English. New York: Vintage Books, 1972.

Van Doesburg, Theo. *Principles of Neo-Plastic Art.* 1925. Translated by Janet Seligman. Introduction by H. M. Wingler. Postscript by H. L. C. Jaffe. New York: New York Graphic Society Ltd. 1966.

Van Zanten, David. "Architectural Ornament: On, In, and Through the Wall." *Ornament.* Vol. 3 of *Via.* Edited by Stephen Kieran. Cambridge: The Graduate School of Fine Arts University of Pennsylvania and The MIT Press (1977): 49–54.

Vasari, Giorgio. *Lives of the Artists.* 1550. Translated by George Bull. Reprinted with minor revisions. New York: Viking Penguin, Inc., 1971.

Venturi, Robert. *Complexity and Contradiction in Architecture.* Introduction by Vincent Scully. 1966. 2d ed. The Museum of Modern Art, 1977.

Vidler, Anthony. *The Writing of the Walls: Architectural Theory in the Late Enlightenment.* New York: Princeton Architectural Press, 1987.

———. "Type: Quatremère de Quincy" *Oppositions: A Journal for Ideas and Criticism in Architecture.* No. 8. Cambridge: The MIT Press (Spring 1977): 147–50.

———. "The Idea of Type: The Transformation of the Academic Ideal, 1750–1830." *Oppositions: A Journal for Ideas and Criticism in Architecture.* No. 8. Cambridge: The MIT Press (Spring 1977): 95–115.

Viollet-le-Duc, Eugène-Emmanuel. *Lectures on Architecture.* 1872. Translated by Benjamin Bucknall. 2 vols. Revised. New York: Dover Publications, Inc., 1987.

Vitruvius, Marcus. *The Ten Books on Architecture.* 1st century B.C. Translated by Morris Hicky Morgan. 1914. New York: Dover Publications, Inc., 1960.

———. *De Architectura.* 1st century B.C. Translated by Frank Granger. 2 vols. Cambridge: Harvard University Press, 1934.

Walter, Eugene Victor. *Placeways: A Theory of the Human Environment.* Chapel Hill: The University of North Carolina Press, 1988.

Wapner, S., B. Kaplan, and S. B. Cohen. "An Organismic-Developmental Perspective for Understanding Transactions of Men and Environments." In *Meaning and Behaviour in the Built Environment.* Edited by Geoffrey Broadbent, Richard Bunt, and Tomas Llorens, 223–52. New York: John Wiley & Sons, 1980.

Watkin, David. *Morality and Architecture: The Development of a Theme in Architectural History and Theory from the Gothic Revival to the Modern Movement.* 1977. Chicago: The University of Chicago Press, 1984.

Wells, H. G. "The Door in the Wall." In *The Door in the Wall and Other Stories.* 1911. Boston: David R. Godine, 1980.

Wharton, Edith, and Ogden Codman Jr. *The Decoration of Houses.* 1897.

Introductions by John Barrington Bayley and William A. Coles. New York: W. W. Norton & Company, Inc., 1978.

Whitman, Walt. *A Song of the Rolling Earth.* In *Leaves of Grass.* Book XVI. 1891–2. New York: Random House, Inc., n.d.

Wiebenson, Dora, ed. *Architectural Theory and Practice from Alberti to Ledoux.* 2d ed. rev. Architectural Publications, Inc. 1982. Chicago: University of Chicago Press, 1983.

Wilk, Christopher. *Marcel Breuer: Furniture and Interiors.* Introduction by J. Stewart Johnson. New York: The Museum of Modern Art, 1981.

Wingler, Hans M. *The Bauhaus: Weimar Dessau Berlin Chicago.* 1962. Edited by Joseph Stein. Translated by Wolfgang Jabs and Basil Gilbert. English Adaption. Cambridge: The MIT Press, 1969.

Wittkower, Rudolf. *Architectural Principles in the Age of Humanism.* 1949. Revised ed. New York: W. W. Norton & Company, 1971.

———. *Art and Architecture in Italy 1600–1750.* 1958. New York: Penguin Books, 1980.

———. "The Changing Concept of Proportion." *The Visual Arts Today* in *Daedalus: Journal of the American Academy of Arts & Science* (Winter 1960): 199–215.

———. "Systems of Proportion." *Architect's Year Book* 5. London: Elek Books Limited (1953): 9–18.

Wright, Frank Lloyd. *The Architectural Forum.* 68 (January 1938).

———. *An Autobiography.* New York: Duell, Sloan and Pearce, 1943.

———. *Frank Lloyd Wright: Writings and Buildings.* Edited by Edgar Kaufmann and Ben Raeburn. New York: The World Publishing Company, 1960.

———. *The Living City.* New York: Bramhall House, 1958.

———. *A Testament.* New York: Horizon Press, 1957.

"Interview with Frank Lloyd Wright." Caedmon Record. TC 1064 (Spring 1956).

Wright, Gwendolyn. *Building the Dream: A Social History of Housing in America.* New York: Pantheon Books, 1981.

———. *Moralism and the Model Home: Domestic Architecture and Cultural Conflict in Chicago 1873–1913.* Chicago: The University of Chicago Press, 1980.

Youtz, Philip N. *Sounding Stones of Architecture.* New York: W. W. Norton & Company, Inc., 1929.

Youtz, Richard P. "Letters." In regard to report to Psychonomic Society, 1963, 1964. *Scientific American.* 212 (June 1965): 9–10.

Zevi, Bruno. *The Modern Language of Architecture.* Part I, "A Guide to the Anticlassical Code" Translated by Ronald Strom. 1973. Part II, "Architecture versus Architectural History." Translated by William A. Packer. 1974. New York: Van Nostrand Reinhold Company, 1981.

Zucker, Paul. *Town and Square.* 1959. Cambridge: The MIT Press, 1970.

Index

Le Corbusier, 11, 36, 49–50, 77, 78–
  79, 92–94, 170, 181–186, 233
Le Théâtre, 159
Legrand, J.G., 128
Leonardo of Pisa, 89
*Les Beaux-arts réduits a un même
  principe,* 149
Lessing, Julius, 134
Lethaby, W.R., 8, 143
Levi, David, 30
Levine, Neil, 155
Levittown (New York), 196–197
LeWitt, Sol, 99
Liber Abaci, 89
Light, 54–63
  artificial, 251
  control of, 250–252
  source, 53, 59
Line, 35, 45, 46, 47–48, 80
Linear A, 15
Linear B, 14
The Living City, 192
Livre d'architecture, 4, 122
Logarithmic spirals, 89
Longair, Malcolm, 91–92
Loos, Adolf, 143, 171–172, 268–269,
  270
Louis, Victor, 130
Lundberg, Erik, 62
Lutyens, Edwin, 143
Lynch, Kevin, 239–240
Lyndon, Donlyn, 197, 283, 292

Machines, 166–167
Mackintosh, Charles Rennie, 72–73,
  143, 184
Mackmurdo, Arthur, 141
Magasins du Printemps (Paris), 132
Mahnke, Frank H., 59–61
Mahnke, Rudolf H., 59–61
Maison La Roche-Jeanneret (Paris),
  183, 184
Maison Tonini (France), 92, 93
Maisons de plaisances, 124
Malevich, Kasimir, 178
Man and Artistic Figure, 24
Marble, 256
March, Lionel, 69
Marey, Etienne Jules, 210
Marina City (Chicago), 202, 203
Marks, Robert, 189
Mask of Medusa, 277–278
Mass, 37–43, 75
Mass-forms, 37
Mass production, 209
Materials, 254–256
Maybeck, George, 147
McAlpine, Robert, 124
McGregor, Douglas, 206
Mechanization Takes Command, 209, 215

Media, 163–164
Mehrabian, Albert, 202, 205–206,
  222–223
Men, 219
Menier Chocolate Works (Noisiel-sur-
  Marne), 134
Meyer, Adolf, 170
Meyer, Hannes, 176
Michelangelo, 38
Michelozzo, 18
Mies van der Rohe, Ludwig, 33, 77–
  78, 170, 175, 176, 254–255, 262
Mill, John Stuart, 29
Millikan, Max F., 291
Minoan civilization, 14
Mnemonic expectations, 101
Model, 9, 76
Model-house plans, 164
Modern Architecture, 235
Modern Architecture Since 1900, 165,
  178, 188
Modernism, 8, 33, 99, 148, 178–180,
  185–186, 187–188
Modernity and the Classical Tradition, 9
The Modern Language of Architecture,
  71–72
Modern Painters, 152
The Modulor, 92–94
Modules, 99–100, 201
Mondrian, Piet, 179, 180, 280
Montauk Block (Chicago), 135, 136
Moore, Charles W., 50, 74, 80, 197,
  199, 233, 239, 283, 292
Moral choices, 150
Moralism and the Modern Home, 161
Morality and Architecture, 148
Moral values, 86, 137, 149
Morena, Elena Marcheso, 294
Morphology, 268
Morris, William, 138–139, 254
Morris Gift Shop (San Francisco), 241
Mortgages, 221
Mort Lucide, 85
Motion parallax, 103
Movement
  Adam's theory of, 119–120
  human, 210
  linear, 48
  spatial, 236–238
Muche, Georg, 174
Mumford, Lewis, 5
Munsell, Albert Henry, 57, 58
Muthesius, Hermann, 169, 171
Muybridge, Eadward, 210

Nash, John, 132
National Household Economics
  Association, 190
The Natural House, 69
Naylor, Gillian, 137